MW01193406

Single-Sideband Systems and Circuits

William E. Sabin

Edgar O. Schoenike

Editors

Advanced Technology and Engineering Department,
Collins Defense Communications,
Rockwell International Corporation,
Cedar Rapids, Iowa

Written by members of the Engineering Staff,
Collins Divisions, Rockwell International Corporation

McGraw-Hill Book Company

New York   St. Louis   San Francisco   Auckland   Bogotá
Hamburg   London   Madrid   Mexico   Milan
Montreal   New Delhi   Panama
Paris   São Paulo   Singapore
Sydney   Tokyo   Toronto

Library of Congress Cataloging-in-Publication Data
Expansion and revision of Single-sideband principles
and circuits by E. W. Pappenfus, W. B. Bruene, and
E. O. Schoenike. 1964.
Dedicated to the employees of the Collins divisions
of the Rockwell International Corporation on the
fiftieth anniversary of the founding of the Collins
Radio Company.

Single-sideband systems and circuits.
Includes index.
1. Radio, Single-sideband. I. Sabin, William E.
II. Schoenike, Edgar O. III. Pappenfus, E. W.
Single sideband principles and circuits. IV. Collins
Defense Communications. Advanced Technology and
Engineering Dept. V. Collins Radio Company.

TK6562.S54S56 1987   621.3841'53   86–27717
ISBN 0–07–054407–7

234567890 DOC/DOC 89321098

ISBN 0-07-054407-7

*The editors for this book were Daniel Gonneau and Lester Strong,
the designer was Naomi Auerbach, and the production supervisor
was Annette Mayeski. It was set in Century Schoolbook by University Graphics, Inc.*

Printed and bound by R. R. Donnelley & Sons Company.

Contents

Contributors

David H. Bliss Ph.D. (EE), Iowa State University, 1971. Member of and subsequently manager of HF Technology Group, Advanced Technology and Engineering Dept., Rockwell-Collins Defense Communications, since 1975; member of technical staff, Bell Labs, 1971–1975, where he developed digital communication systems. Widely experienced in radio propagation and connectivity analysis, ECCM system and equipment design. Contributor to *Handbook of Electronic System Design,* 1980 (McGraw-Hill).

Roderick K. Blocksome MSEE, Kansas State University, 1973. Manager of HF Power Amplifier Group, Rockwell-Collins Defense Communications, since 1981; Air Force officer, 1969–1972, communications system design. Designs HF power amplifiers and systems integration. An expert on PA protection and spurious emission reduction. Holds one U.S. patent.

Warren B. Bruene BSEE, Iowa State University, 1938. Staff Engineer, Electrospace Co., since 1984; Senior Engineer with Rockwell-Collins, 1939–1984. Registered P.E., Texas; Fellow of the IEEE, 1961 "for Advancing SSB Radio Communication"; IEEE Section Chairman, 1962; Rockwell DaVinci Medal, 1982, for engineering excellence; Engineer of the Year, Texas Professional Engineers Society, 1975; listed in *Who's Who in Engineering* and *Leaders in Electronics;* awarded 22 U.S. patents.

David H. Church   BSEE, Iowa State University, 1974. Project Design Engineer, HF Products Dept., Rockwell-Collins Defense Communications; joined Rockwell-Collins in 1974. Registered P.E., Iowa. Involved with design, development, and support of HF receivers, exciters, and receiver/exciters.

Neil R. Coonrod   BSEE, University of Missouri at Rolla, 1978; MSEE, University of Iowa, 1986. Design Engineer, LOS Design Dept., Rockwell-Collins, since 1985; Design Engineer for power supply equipment, Advanced Technology Dept., Rockwell-Collins Defense Communications, 1978–1985. Member Tau Beta Pi and Eta Kappa Nu.

Robert L. Craiglow   BSEE, Ohio State University, 1947. Systems analyst and consultant in the area of radio communications techniques since 1947. Widely experienced and recognized in the design and analysis of data communications, modulation, signal processing, and speech processing; awarded 11 U.S. patents. Previous experience in oscillator and vocoder design; has performed pioneering work in digital signal processing analysis and design.

Sylvan L. Dawson   BSEE, Kansas State University, 1954; MSEE, Kansas State University, 1960. Project Engineer in the HF Engineering Dept., Rockwell-Collins Defense Communications; joined Collins Radio Co. in 1956; Radio Officer, U.S. Army, 1954–1956. Has been in charge of design of HF preselectors, receivers, and transceivers; awarded four U.S. patents.

 **Richard C. Edwards**   BSEE, University of Iowa, 1965; MSEE, Iowa State University, 1985. Senior Design Engineer in the LOS Equipment Design Dept., Rockwell-Collins Defense Communications, since 1965. A specialist in the design of passive networks and filters for multicouplers and broadband matching networks; awarded one U.S. patent.

 **Marvin E. Frerking**   BSEE, University of Missouri, 1958; MSEE, University of Iowa, 1964. Group Manager, Advanced Technology Dept., Rockwell-Collins Defense Communications. Supervises the application of new technology to the design of communications equipment; author of *Crystal Oscillator Design and Temperature Compensation*, 1978, and coauthor of *Precision Frequency Control*, 1985; member of Frequency Control Symposium Program Committee for 8 years; member of four honorary technical societies; awarded 12 U.S. patents.

 **Richard A. Groshong**   BSEE, University of Minnesota, 1976. Design Engineer, Advanced Technology Dept., Rockwell-Collins Defense Communications, since 1977. Involved in the design of HF SSB receivers and exciters and digital signal processing for a variety of applications in digital radio equipment.

 **David B. Hallock**   MSEE, Worcester Polytechnic Institute, 1954. Technical Staff Member, Advanced Technology Dept., Rockwell-Collins Defense Communications, since 1954. Responsible for analysis and design of receivers over the frequency range 2 to 400 MHz; received Rockwell DaVinci Medal, 1984, for engineering excellence; awarded four U.S. patents. Has served as a consultant on a large number of difficult company projects.

Stephen J. Harmening Attended University of Iowa and Iowa State University, 1965–1982. Designer of microprocessor and digital control software and hardware for digitally controlled radio equipment since 1965.

James V. Harmon BSEE, University of Missouri at Rolla, 1966. Program Manager for SELSCAN equipment at Rockwell-Collins Defense Communications. Awarded three U.S. patents.

Bill D. Hart BSEE, Iowa State University, 1972; MSEE, Iowa State University, 1982. Design Engineer in the Advanced Technology Dept., Rockwell-Collins Defense Communications, since 1972, participating in equipment design. Registered P.E., Iowa; holds commercial and amateur FCC licenses; member IEEE.

Wayne A. Kalinsky BSEE, Iowa State University, 1966. Design Engineer and project leader in power supply technology in the HF Equipment Design Dept., Rockwell-Collins Defense Communications, 1966–1971 and since 1973. Awarded two U.S. patents.

Donald E. Phillips MA, University of Wisconsin, 1949. Synthesizer Design Engineer in the Advanced Technology and Engineering Dept., Rockwell-Collins Defense Communications, since 1973. Awarded five U.S. patents. Has developed numerous contributions in the areas of direct digital synthesis (DDS), phase discriminators, and computer-aided analysis.

Edward G. Silagi   BSEE, University of Illinois, 1978. Technical Staff Member in the HF Product Design Dept., Rockwell-Collins Defense Communications, since 1980. Responsible for the design of solid-state linear amplifiers; awarded three U.S. patents. Highly experienced in the design of ultra-low distortion power amplifiers.

Glenn R. Snider   BSEE, Michigan Technological University, 1966. Design Engineer in the HF Antenna Coupler Group, HF Product Dept., Rockwell-Collins Defense Communications, since 1966. Concerned with antenna coupler design, network theory, and control system theory, and design. Awarded two U.S. patents.

Joseph A. Vanous   BSEE, University of Iowa, 1949. Joined the Collins Radio Research and Development Division in 1949. Technical Staff Member in the HF Products Design Dept., Rockwell-Collins Defense Communications; U.S. Army, 1943–1946. Participated in the design and development of early SSB radio equipment. Awarded four U.S. patents.

William R. Weaverling   BS in Physics (with distinction), Indiana University, 1963. Synthesizer and RF Design Engineer with the Advanced Technology Dept., Rockwell-Collins Defense Communications, since 1965. Involved in low noise, fast tuning synthesizer design and research for HF, VHF, and UHF equipment.

About the Editors

William E. Sabin is a Design Engineer in the Advanced Technology Department, Collins Division, Rockwell International, Cedar Rapids, Iowa, where he has been working since 1964. He received the MSEE degree from the University of Iowa and is widely experienced in HF receiver and exciter design, synthesizer design, power supplies, spread spectrum techniques, and digital design.

Edgar O. Schoenike is Senior Technical Staff Member in the Advanced Technology Department at Rockwell and holds five U.S. patents. He received the MSEE degree from Iowa State University, and has completed all course work for the Ph.D. (EE) degree. He was a coauthor of SINGLE SIDEBAND PRINCIPLES AND CIRCUITS, McGraw-Hill, 1964.

Preface

It was 23 years ago that McGraw-Hill published *Single Sideband Principles and Circuits,* by E. W. Pappenfus, W. B. Bruene, and E. O. Schoenike. Since then many changes have occurred in the components, circuits, and systems analysis used in SSB technology. In 1964 transistors were just beginning to become dominant in low-power amplifiers and oscillators, while vacuum tubes still reigned supreme for medium- and high-power amplifiers. Integrated circuits were just beginning to be used in SSB equipment, and microprocessors were unknown. The development of these new electronic components has led to new circuits, greater flexibility in design, and more sophisticated equipment control.

One aim of this book is to incorporate an explanation of the developments that have taken place in the design of SSB equipment while retaining explanations of those techniques which have withstood the test of time. Thus, solid-state power amplifiers and power supplies are discussed in detail, but advances in high-power vacuum tube amplifiers are not overlooked. Similarly, balanced diode mixers and modulators, instead of being superseded, are used today perhaps more widely than ever before, and so are also fully covered.

This book was written at the level of the practicing engineer, although it will be appreciated by the engineering student and advanced amateur as well. Most explanations are intended to be practical in nature, but the theoretical basis of SSB is treated in some detail, design principles are not overlooked, and, when relevant, performance tradeoffs are discussed. However, only amplitude modulation SSB is discussed. Angle-modulated single sideband is beyond the scope of the book.

Special emphasis is placed on the system analysis and system design of the SSB communications link. The cost and complexity of modern communications equipment and systems are such that accurate estimates of performance, prior to commitment of resources, are essential.

Greater sophistication in design has led to specialization, and it is therefore appropriate that a large number of experts in specialized areas should contribute to this book. It is almost impossible for one person to completely master all of the disciplines involved; therefore the editors have gathered together some of the leading equipment designers and analysts from the Collins Division of the Rockwell Corporation to contribute chapters in their fields of specialization.

Besides the chapter authors, the editors give special thanks to our engineering colleagues for their ideas and contributions to this book, and to Rockwell International for its permission to publish.

We also owe a special debt to the many secretaries who contributed their spare time to the word processor typing chores.

In chapters where multiple authors appear, names are listed in alphabetical order.

One final note: Recognizing as we do the important and growing role of women in the sciences, every effort has been made to use gender-neutral language in the writing of this book. In the single instance of "specsmanship," however, no generally recognized gender-neutral equivalent exists; thus the term should be taken in a purely generic sense, intended to apply to both women and men.

WILLIAM E. SABIN
EDGAR O. SCHOENIKE

This book is the result of a difficult and comprehensive team effort by many members of the Engineering Staff of the Collins Divisions of Rockwell International. It is dedicated to them and to all the employees, past and present, of the Collins Divisions of the Rockwell International Corporation on the occasion of the fiftieth anniversary of the founding of the Collins Radio Company.

Overview of Single Sideband

William E. Sabin

1.1 The Radio Link

The principal task which confronts a radio communications link between two or many mutually distant points is to provide, within the framework of a limited available transmitter power, reliable, high-quality communication. Very often, real-time voice contact is desired. Opposing this goal are the inimical characteristics of the radio frequency (RF) spectrum. Among these are noise from the ionosphere and the galaxy, artificially produced electrical noise, severe variations in the received signal strength (fading) which are observed over time spans from milliseconds to hours or days, propagation disturbances, interference from other users of the spectrum, and multiple arrivals of the signal along different paths. Interference caused to other users is aggravated by technical limitations in transmitter spectral purity and directional antenna design. Interference experienced from other users is increased by deficiencies in receiver design and receiving antennas. One especially difficult mode of interference is between transmitters and receivers which are in close proximity (colocated). Also involved here is the creation of false signals (intermodulation or IM) due to nonlinearities within the colocated environment.

The approach to reliable communication used by radio engineers is to obtain from a given amount of available transmitter power the maximum amount of intelligibility of a speech signal or the minimum error rate of a digital signal (at the distant receiver) under the conditions described above. Two important constraints in this design are the conservation of bandwidth and time. That is, the spectrum in use very often requires a small ratio of RF bandwidth to baseband message bandwidth in order to accommodate a large number of users. Also, the time used to transmit a message is very often required to be nearly the same as the duration of the original message; in this situation the amounts of redundancy and encoding available must be small. An equivalent statement is that the ideal communication channel, in the sense described by Shannon [1], is, in most near-real-time situations, not approached. In practice, voice or digital messages usually contain inherently high levels of redundancy or predictability, except for key elements which may be repeated several times by a good operator.

One of the principal system design approaches used is to select a method of modulation which is optimal within the environment and the constraints described above. For real-time speech communication, from 10 kHz to 250 Mhz, and in recent times up to as high as 10 GHz, the use of single-sideband (SSB) suppressed-carrier (or quite often reduced-carrier) modulation has provided a very satisfactory answer. A long period (65 years) of analytical and experimental investigation has proven the efficacy of this method, especially in the high-frequency (HF) band, which is a difficult arena.

A further consideration in situations where the volume and weight of the transmitter are critical is that SSB is competitive with narrow band frequency modulation (FM), in terms of communications effectiveness for a given weight and size. The results of recent studies will be considered in later sections. SSB also is a decisive improvement, in nearly all respects, over high-level double-sideband amplitude modulation (AM).

One of the costs involved in SSB, as compared with AM, is the additional complexity of the receiver vs. the conventional low-cost AM broadcast receiver. Various responses to this will be considered in this book. In the transmitter, the need for large amounts of linear amplification of the RF signal is a technical and economic burden.

The development of phase-locked loop (PLL) techniques has opened up many uses of reduced-carrier SSB, where the reduced pilot carrier provides frequency-locked and phase-locked reception and serves other functions. The improvements in frequency synthesizer design and low-cost, portable frequency standards have made SSB practical at much higher frequencies than were possible a few years ago.

A further enhancement of SSB has been the development of speech processors which utilize the peak power capabilities of the transmitter more effectively by compressing the dynamic range of human speech, thereby increasing the average power. The Lincompex system and other companders have the ability to restore the original dynamic range at the receiver, providing a telephone-grade signal. Vocoder and other techniques which help to reduce bandwidth with no appreciable loss of intelligibility have been undergoing a continuous development.

In long-distance HF (2- to 30-MHz) communication, a major problem is to locate a favorable frequency very quickly and automatically tune to it (automatic connectivity). The extensive application of microprocessor technology has produced highly programmable, remotely controllable radios which combine with the recently perfected SELSCAN™ technique to pro-duce orders of magnitude of improvement in HF link reliability. Link quality analysis (LQA) quickly determines the ability of the selected channel to support message transfer.

In very recent years the revolution in digital signal processing technologies has been applied to SSB receivers and transmitters, to produce levels of performance and flexibility (programmability) which are setting new standards in radio design. Also, developments in high-power solid-state transistors and circuit design have revolutionized linear power amplifier (LPA) design. The development of ultralinear power amplifiers using feedforward techniques promises to reduce transmitter distortion products by two or three orders of magnitude. Improvements in high-power, fast-tuning vacuum tube amplifiers will be described in this book. Advanced measurement techniques for high-performance receivers and transmitters have been developed. The design of antenna couplers used in SSB transmitters has been elevated to a high level of sophistication which will be described. To complete the discussion, recent developments in intermediate-frequency (IF) filters, tunable bandpass filters, and power supplies for SSB equipment are covered.

1.2   Overview of Single-Sideband Equipment

The transmitter

Figure 1.1c shows a complete SSB transmitter block diagram which uses the filter method of generating the desired wave. A baseband signal $f(t)$ has a spectrum $F(\omega)$ which is shown in Fig. 1.1a. For the purpose of this discussion, it is often preferred, but not essential, to use the concept of a "two-sided" spectrum shown in Fig. 1.1b, where the physical signal is decomposed mathematically into two coherent, complex conjugate segments, one of which is at a fictitious "negative frequency."

This $f(t)$ is multiplied in a balanced mixer by the local oscillator (LO) wave $\cos(2\pi f_0 t)$. The spectrum at the mixer output, Fig. 1.1d, is therefore the convolution of $F(\omega)$, the spectrum of $f(t)$, and the spectrum of the LO, shown at Fig. 1.1e. Observe that, although the balanced mixer output contains very little carrier, the phase noise impurities in the LO are transferred to the output signal in the form of amplitude sidebands, as shown. These often tend to establish the maximum in-band signal-to-noise (S/N) ratio of the desired transmitter signal.

The narrowband filter passes accurately one of the sidebands and sharply attenuates the other sideband, the carrier frequency, high and low speech frequencies, wideband LO noise and other noise, and spurious emissions from the low-level stages of the transmitter. Therefore this filter is a critical item in the design. Alternative approaches which attempt to eliminate this filter will be considered in Chap. 2.

Following the filter, amplification, frequency translation, speech processing (to increase the average power), and power amplification occur. During these processes, LO contamination, amplifier noise, out-of-band and in-band

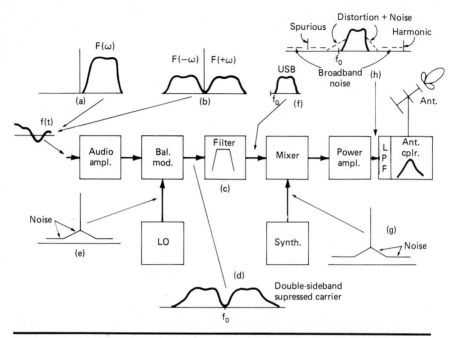

Figure 1.1 Block diagram of an SSB transmitter. Parts (*a*) and (*b*) show the baseband signal as one-sided or two-sided spectra; (*d*) is the double-sideband suppressed-carrier signal; (*f*) is the filtered SSB signal which is amplified, contaminated, and filtered as it moves to the antenna; (*h*) is the output of the PA; (*e*) and (*g*) show the contaminated local oscillator signals.

distortion products, discrete spurious frequencies, and harmonics are added to the desired signal. These spurious emissions either degrade the desired signal or are a source of interference to other users, especially those who are colocated or on closely adjacent or certain other frequencies. At the output of the transmitter, the impedance of the antenna is transformed to the desired power amplifier (PA) load impedance, and band filtering is also performed. Adjacent transmitters must be electrically isolated from each other to prevent interactions between their outputs. The antenna tries to focus the energy on the desired destination.

The design challenge for the transmitter can thus be defined: to provide accurately the required power output with levels of fidelity, frequency stability, and undesired emissions which are acceptable to the user, and to provide as much communications effectiveness as possible. The desired usage may require that a carrier signal be wholly or partially inserted if needed.

Other aspects of the design are weight and size restrictions, temperature rise, reliability, and duty cycle. Furthermore, the equipment may have to perform Morse code and data transmission functions in addition to voice. In some cases the desired output may be two or four independent adjacent channels with low levels of cross-channel interference. The radio may require some kind of remote control, automatic tuning, or unattended operation. Finally, there are always cost constraints imposed by the marketplace. The design process, then, consists of finding a set of technical and economic compromises which satisfy the user in all these respects.

SSB power relationships

As an aid to understanding later discussions, consider Fig. 1.2. The RF signal voltage, with carrier absent, varies in amplitude in accordance with the modulation. The line joining the tips of the RF cycles is the envelope. At the highest point of the envelope the instantaneous voltage reaches its highest value. The peak instantaneous power (or simply peak power) is determined at this point. Calculated over one cycle of the RF voltage at this highest point, the resulting average power is called the peak envelope power (PEP). Over a period of time which is much longer than the modulating waveforms, the average power is determined from the average value of the square of the rms voltage, as shown.

The receiver

Figure 1.3 is a block diagram which exemplifies the design problems for an SSB receiver. The desired signal frequency is translated to the passband of a narrowband filter. The circuitry to the left of the second mixer, called the "front end," or translator, is vulnerable to undesired signals which produce intermodulation distortion (IMD), desensitization, reciprocal mixing (noise modulation) which is caused by synthesizer phase noise, spurious responses due to undesired mixer products and synthesizer contamination, and damage due to nearby transmitters. The antenna lead also can conduct undesired

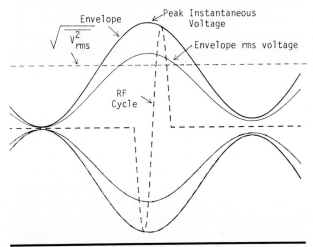

Figure 1.2 The RF output voltage of the transmitter for a modulated SSB signal is used to determine the peak power, the peak envelope power, and the average power.

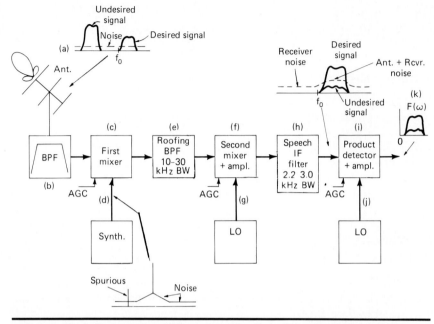

Figure 1.3 Block diagram of an SSB receiver. The desired signal at (a) is accompanied by noise and undesired signals. Local oscillator noise and spurious responses at (d) further contaminate the desired signal. The narrow filter at (h) rejects out-of-band interference and noise. The desired output at (i) is degraded by noise and spurious responses.

receiver emissions, which are radiated and produce local interference. The reception of weak signals may be restricted by in-band noise generated by the receiver, but at lower frequencies noise picked up by the antenna usually sets the limit of sensitivity unless the receiving antenna is very inefficient. A design goal is to make internal noise negligible in comparison, but this goal conflicts with the need for immunity to undesired signals. A directional antenna augments the intended signal-to-interference ratios.

The block diagram in Fig. 1.3 shows also that selectivity may precede the receiver input. Increased immunity to interference is then possible, but at considerably greater cost. A goal is to minimize this selectivity cost. This desire has led to the development of receiver front ends having very high dynamic range. In many systems multiple receivers must operate effectively, using diplexing networks, from the same antenna. "Active" receiving antenna arrays having electronically steerable directivity are coming into use in some systems.

A high order of frequency stability and precise frequency control are needed in an SSB receiver. Frequency synthesis, controlled by a stable frequency standard, is ubiquitous in high-quality SSB equipment. Following the roofing filter, more amplification and conversion take place. Further narrowband filtering at a lower IF frequency, closely conforming to the desired single-sideband frequency band, is needed. The circuits between these two filters are subject to overload by strong signals on closely adjacent frequencies which are within the passband of the wider filter. These stages and also those after the narrow filter are sources of noise and distortion added to the desired signal. After the final filter a product detector having very desirable weak-signal properties translates to baseband. The output level is accurately regulated by an automatic gain control (AGC) which is operated by the speech sideband energy. The AGC also protects the IF and RF stages from overload by the desired signal and must have excellent transient response, since it is driven by the rapidly fluctuating speech signal and by undesired impulses. An optional noise blanker removes these impulses.

The receiver may also utilize a reduced pilot carrier for frequency/phase-locked reception and for AGC and squelch purposes. Coherent phase-locked AM reception is also optional. The same receiver is also usually used for continuous wave (CW), radio teletype (RTTY), and conventional AM modes. Additional features are voice-actuated squelch, computer control of frequency and other functions, speech companding, and telephone line and IF outputs.

1.3 Attributes of SSB

There are two principal advantages to SSB: its narrow bandwidth, both in transmission and reception (these enhance each other), and its efficient usage of the transmitter's primary power source. This latter point translates also into weight and volumetric efficiencies which are crucial in many situations. It used to be that a 100-W transmitter stood in a 5-ft rack and weighed hundreds of pounds. Now a vastly superior transmitter (plus a receiver) can be hand-carried in a small luggage case. The absence of a carrier means that the entire peak power capability is devoted to the information-bearing content of the signal. There is, however, an anomaly inherent in the SSB wave which Chap. 2 evaluates. Under certain conditions the baseband waveform can produce excessive peaks in the RF wave which result in distortion in the power amplifiers. A comparable overload effect can occur in the receiver and has limited the use of SSB in certain data applications.

The narrow bandwidth is achieved only when spurious emissions are tightly controlled; therefore SSB logically demands an extremely high signal purity. This reduces somewhat the efficiencies mentioned above, since the design must be more conservative than would otherwise be needed. Despite this, and because of technical developments, the choice between double-sideband suppressed carrier (DSBSC) and SSB has, for nearly all systems, been resolved in favor of the reduced spectral usage of a clean SSB signal. Also, a possible signal-to-noise ratio improvement of 3 dB exists for SSB, relative to DSBSC, when compared on the basis of equal peak envelope power.

At the receiver, the product detection and narrow bandwidth imply that the signal-to-noise ratio (for a perfect receiver) remains constant along the signal path. The quieting effect associated with FM, for example, is normally absent in SSB. However, an equivalent effect can be synthesized, as discussed in Chap. 3. The use of product detection also means that the severe distortion caused by carrier dropout, which is so well known in conventional AM, is eliminated. This kind of detection, when applied to AM receivers, is called "exalted-carrier" reception.

Frequency differences between signal and receiver are detrimental to SSB and reduce the intelligibility and musical quality considerably. This is discussed in Chap. 2, and it turns out that for speech some offset is tolerable, which makes SSB for speech much easier to implement since the pilot carrier is often (but not always) unnecessary.

In an SSB receiver without pilot carrier the AGC is derived from the speech content. During a pause the noise level increase can sometimes be annoying in a commercial or military link (amateurs and some others do not seem to care as much). Therefore SSB AGC and squelch designs are needed which circumvent this natural problem: or, as mentioned before, the pilot carrier can be used. In SSB the use of voice-actuated transmit/receive (T/R) switching has been widely adopted, perhaps coincidentally. This practice has led to more efficient channel usage and better communication practice.

1.4   Historical Development

At one time it was believed by many that modulation was a linear process, the simple summation of a carrier signal and an audio signal. This process does not produce any new frequencies which can be detected by a wave meter [2]. However, in 1914 Carl Englund [3] described a nonlinear process similar to that described in Sec. 1.2, above, in which sidebands showed up. This was later backed up by experiments and analysis performed by R. A. Heising in the same year. In 1915, H. D. Arnold tuned a very-low-frequency antenna to the upper sideband and implemented reduced-carrier and reduced-lower-sideband transmission. In that year, B. W. Kendall patented the homodyne (product) detector, which enhanced the detection process. Based partly on these results, in 1915 J. R. Carson developed [and later (1923) patented] the concept of single-sideband, suppressed-carrier communication. In 1918 SSB was first used in a wire telephone frequency multiplex system. In 1922 a trans-Atlantic station designed by L. Espenscheid operated at 57 kHz using upper sideband at 150 kW. Shortwave SSB did not appear until 1936 [4], pending advances in frequency stability and receiver/transmitter design. The radios which AT&T built used crystal filters, multiple conversion, and pilot carriers for automatic frequency control (AFC) and AGC. During the next 10 years shortwave SSB proliferated in long-haul telephone links. In 1948 and subsequently for several years, amateur radio articles by O. G. Villard of Stanford University, D. E. Norgaard and S. G. Reque of General Electric, F. M. Berry, A. H. Nichols, C. E. Weaver, J. N. Brown, and Byron Goodman (at ARRL), and many other hams pioneered the amateur usage of SSB using home-built gear. In 1954 to 1956 ham gear manufacturers like Collins Radio and a few others introduced manufactured ham equipment designed especially for SSB.

Also during those years, interest rapidly increased among commercial and military users, and a long and active process of evolution began in receiver, transmitter, and transceiver design, first vacuum tube and then solid state. SSB eventually became the standard mode at HF frequencies in just about every environment.

The original application of SSB for telephone work has reappeared at microwave frequencies [5] in order to triple the number of available channels. Space diversity is used to reduce multipath fading. SSB has recently emerged as a competitor to narrow-bandwidth FM (NBFM) in vehicular radio [6]. In both applications its narrower bandwidth has greatly increased the number of speech channels. Numerous design improvements, which will be discussed later in this book, have contributed to the viability of these new applications.

REFERENCES

1. C. E. Shannon, "Communications in the Presence of Noise," *Proc. IRE,* vol. 37, January 1949, pp. 10–21.
2. August Hund, *High Frequency Measurements,* McGraw-Hill, New York, 1933, pp. 22–26.
3. A. A. Oswald, "Early History of Single Side Band," *Proc. IRE,* vol. 44, December 1956, pp. 1676–1679.
4. F. A. Polkinghorn and N. F. Schlaak, "A Single Sideband Short Wave System for Transatlantic Telephony," *Proc. IRE,* vol. 23, July 1935, pp. 701–716.
5. R. E. Markle, "Single Sideband Triples Microwave Radio Route Capacity," *Bell Labs Rec.,* vol. 56, April 1978, pp. 105–110.
6. Barry Manz, "SSB Technology Fights Its Way into Land-Mobile Market," *Microwaves & RF,* vol. 22, August 1983, pp. 72–80.

Chapter

2

System Design Considerations

Dr. David H. Bliss *(Section 2.4)*
Robert L. Craiglow *(Section 2.1)*
James V. Harmon *(Section 2.5)*
Edgar O. Schoenike *(Sections 2.2, 2.3)*

As pointed out in Chap. 1, the basic building blocks of an SSB communication system include the transmitter, the receiver, and an antenna. For many purposes, these are adequate for satisfactory communication. For more complex systems, additional specialized equipment supplement these basic components. Following this chapter, we cover specialized topics in transmitter and receiver design, such as transceivers, exciters, power amplifiers, filters, speech processing, frequency standards, and power supplies, as well as other system elements such as preselectors, postselectors, and antenna couplers. When other than analog speech is to be transmitted, a modulator/demodulator (modem) is required as well, but this subject has become quite specialized and is beyond the scope of this book.

Preselectors and postselectors, discussed in Chap. 8, are often required in a system when simultaneous operation (SIMOP) is required of a cosited transmitter and receiver. A preselector may also be necessary if receiver operation is required in close proximity to an unrelated nearby transmitter operating in the same frequency range. When the antenna impedance varies widely over the operating band, a transmitting antenna coupler is required to present a more constant load impedance to the power amplifier.

The purpose of this chapter is not to discuss the system elements, but to describe important topics in system design and analysis. Section 2.1 starts with the basic voice signal that is to be transmitted. The nature of speech and hearing is reviewed, and speech intelligibility and the articulation index (AI) are given precise definitions. The effect of speech clipping on these characteristics is discussed. Next, Sec. 2.1 continues with an exposition of signal representations and Hilbert transforms, leading into the various forms of amplitude modulation, including SSB. For completeness, and to form a basis of comparison with SSB, angle modulation is also discussed. Finally a comparison is made between the various forms of AM and FM.

Section 2.2 covers colocated system designs. The various factors that cause problems in simultaneous operation of receiver and transmitter are discussed. These include transmitter out-of-band noise and distortion, receiver distortion and reciprocal mixing, and transmitter back-intermodulation distortion.

One of the reasons for a resurgence of interest in HF radio transmission by the military services is its use as a backup to satellite communications. To meet modern needs for communication in a potential jamming environment, such equipment must be designed to incorporate electronic counter-counter-measures (ECCM). Those elements of ECCM design that affect the SSB receiver and transmitter are discussed in Sec. 2.3.

Communications link design is the subject of Sec. 2.4. After a review of system design tradeoff considerations, an overview is given of propagation performance prediction using the IONCAP prediction program, followed by a design example showing how a radio link may be designed.

The communications link example of Sec. 2.4 demonstrates the need for frequency management techniques, of which one of the most desirable features is automatic connectivity. The latter subject is covered in Sec. 2.5, which gives general design principles and an example of a highly developed system in current use for global HF communications.

2.1 Analog Voice Modulation

In this section we introduce the tools necessary for the evaluation and comparison of the various analog voice modulation systems. In order to better understand the factors affecting speech intelligibility, we briefly review the processes of speech and hearing and present a method for the calculation of the articulation index, an empirical measure of intelligibility. The effects of speech processing techniques are evaluated and the common voice modulation systems analyzed and compared.

Speech intelligibility

Speech sounds are controlled by the position of lips, teeth, tongue, and velum, which establish a set of acoustic resonant frequencies that characterize the vocal tract. These resonances are excited by harmonic-rich, quasiperiodic pulses of air from the vocal chords for voiced sounds or by the hiss of turbulent air passing through a constriction in the vocal tract for unvoiced sounds. The resultant speech spectrum shows these characteristic resonances or formant frequencies.

The ear performs a short-term spectral analysis of the speech sounds over an interval of some ⅛ s with a frequency resolution of 50 to 500 Hz, thus determining the characteristic resonant or formant frequencies of the vocal tract which determine the speech sound.

Intelligibility

Intelligibility can be measured either experimentally in terms of syllable, word, or sentence test scores or in terms of a calculable empirical measure known as the *articulation index*. Test scores can be obtained only after the communication system has been built or simulated in detail. The AI, on the other hand, can be readily calculated from the known characteristics of a proposed system and has been shown to be a reliable indicator of intelligibility for a wide range of system characteristics and test procedures [1]. AI is therefore used here as the measure of intelligibility for the evaluation and comparison of speech processing and voice modulation systems. The articulation index varies from 0 for a completely unintelligible system to 1 for a system giving the maximum possible intelligibility. Typical relationships between syllable, word, and sentence test scores and AI are shown in Fig. 2.1 [2].

There is a critical level of intelligibility for every task, below which satis-

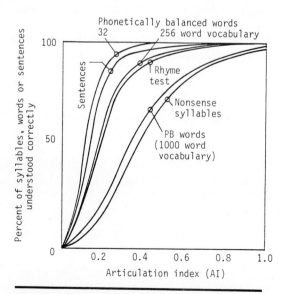

Figure 2.1   Relation between AI and various measures of speech intelligibility.

factory performance can no longer be achieved. It occurs near an AI of 0.3 for a wide variety of applications, although trained communicators using a limited vocabulary and appropriate protocol can communicate with AIs as low as 0.2 [3, 4]. The threshold will be taken here as 0.3.

While an AI of 0.3 provides a usable communications link, fatigue is high and user acceptance low. For day-to-day operations, therefore, the AI should be 0.5 or higher.

The articulation index

A speech sound or phoneme can be characterized by its short-term power spectral density. Low-frequency resonances in the vocal tract have narrower bandwidths than high-frequency resonances. Similarly, the resolution bandwidth of the ear is narrower at lower frequencies. One might suspect, therefore, that the lower speech frequencies would contribute more to intelligibility per hertz of bandwidth than higher frequencies. Indeed, this has been verified experimentally [5, 6]. A frequency weighting function $W(f)$ is used to give different weightings or importance to various portions of the spectrum. The short-term spectral density of speech, $S(f,t)$, at any given frequency f varies with time t over a range of some 30 dB and contributes to intelligibility in noise only when it is greater than the noise power spectral density $N(f)$ at the same frequency. The speech spectrum $S(f,t)$ at frequency f contributes to intelligibility in direct proportion to the percentage of the time that it is greater than $N(f)$, and in direct proportion to $W(f)$ for that frequency. These observations form the basis for calculating the AI.

Several methods for the calculation of AI have been developed by different investigators [1–3, 5–7]. The details of these methods differ, but the principles and results are essentially the same. The integral form of the articulation index will be presented here.

Frequencies in the range of 200 to 6100 Hz contribute to intelligibility in direct proportion to the frequency weighting function given by:

$$W(f) = 5.0 \times 10^{-4} \exp\left[-4.2 \times 10^{-4}f\right] \qquad 200 \le f \le 6100 \text{ Hz} \qquad (2.1)$$

In the absence of noise the AI for speech which is bandwidth-limited between f_a and f_b is given by:

$$\text{AI} = \int_{f_a}^{f_b} W(f)\, df \qquad (2.2)$$

Let $P(f)$ be the portion of the time or probability that $S(f,t)/N(f)$ is greater than 1. The articulation index in noise is thus given by:

$$\text{AI} = \int_{f_a}^{f_b} W(f)P(f)\, df \qquad (2.3)$$

The short term power spectral density $S(f,t)$ is distributed uniformly in dB over a range from 18 dB below the long-term spectral density $S(f)$ to 12 dB above $S(f)$. Therefore, if $S(f)/N(f)$ is 18 dB or greater, $P(f)$ is 1, and if it is -12 dB or lower, $P(f)$ is 0. Within the range of -12 dB $< S(f)/N(f) < 18$ dB the probability $P(f)$ is directly proportional to $S(f)/N(f)$ in dB or:

$$P(f) = \frac{12 + 10 \log_{10} [S(f)/N(f)]}{30} \qquad \begin{array}{c} -12 \text{ dB} \leq \dfrac{S(f)}{N(f)} \leq +18 \text{ dB} \\[4pt] 0 \leq P(f) \leq 1 \end{array} \qquad (2.4)$$

In order to calculate the articulation index, we must know the long-term speech spectral density $S(f)$ and the noise spectral density $N(f)$. The long-term voice spectrum for an adult male voice drops off at 6 to 12 dB/octave above 500 Hz with an average spectrum approximated by:

$$V(f) = \frac{1 + (f/4000)^4}{[1 + (200/f)^4][1 + (f/500)^{3.7}][1 + (f/8000)^4]} \qquad (2.5)$$

If $H(f)$ is the voltage-frequency response of the overall speech communications system, then the filtered speech spectral density is given by:

$$S(f) = V(f)|H(f)|^2 \qquad (2.6)$$

The noise-power spectral density is determined by the nature of the system. On radio links, the background noise is generally white over the band of interest, and this will be assumed here.

Figure 2.2 shows the articulation index as a function of the long-term average audio signal-to-noise ratio $\overline{S}/\overline{N}$ for normal, bandwidth-limited speech in

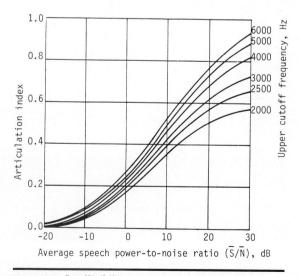

Figure 2.2 Intelligibility of normal speech in white noise with 200-Hz lower cutoff frequency vs. signal-to-noise ratio.

white, bandwidth-limited noise where the average speech power $\overline{S}$ is given by

$$\overline{S} = \int_{f_a}^{f_b} S(f)\, df \tag{2.7}$$

and the average noise power $\overline{N}$ is given by:

$$\overline{N} = \int_{f_a}^{f_b} N(f)\, df \tag{2.8}$$

In this figure the lower cutoff frequency f_a is 200 Hz and the upper cutoff frequency f_b is between 2000 and 6000 Hz.

For white noise it is generally more useful to give the AI as a function of the ratio of the average signal power $\overline{S}$ to the noise density N_0, or $\overline{S}/N_0$, as shown in Fig. 2.3. The curves of Figs. 2.2 and 2.3 are for ideal bandpass filters.

Preemphasis

Since the higher-frequency components of normal speech are very weak, they are readily lost in noise. Therefore these components are often boosted or preemphasized. The preemphasis which maximizes AI when the average speech power $\overline{S}$ and the noise-power spectral density $N(f)$ are fixed can be found using variational calculus.

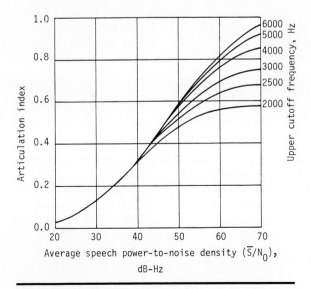

Figure 2.3 Intelligibility of normal speech in white noise with 200-Hz lower cutoff frequency vs. signal-to-noise-density ratio.

Assume that $\overline{S}$, given by Eq. (2.7), and $N(f)$ are fixed and that we wish to maximize the articulation index given by Eq. (2.3). In the region in which $S(f)/N(f)$ is between -12 and $+18$ dB, $P(f)$ is given by

$$P(f) = \frac{12 + 10 \log_{10} [S(f)/N(f)]}{30} = K_1 + K_2 \ln [S(f)/N(f)] \tag{2.9}$$

where K_1 and K_2 are constants. The integral to be maximized therefore becomes

$$AI = \int_{f_a}^{f_b} W(f)K_2 \ln [S(f)/N(f)] \, df + K_3 \tag{2.10}$$

The details of the derivation are omitted, but the optimum spectrum is of the form:

$$S_0(f) = K_4 W(f) \tag{2.11}$$

where K_4 is a constant. Surprisingly, this optimum speech spectrum is independent of $N(f)$ within the range of $S(f)/N(f)$ from -12 to $+18$ dB.

If $S(f)/N(f)$ is above $+18$ dB at some frequency, the useless excess speech power should be redistributed throughout the rest of the frequency range according to Eq. (2.11). Similarly if $S(f)/N(f)$ is below -12 dB at some frequency, then this wasted power should be completely removed and redistributed throughout the remaining frequency range according to Eq. (2.11). If the initial bandwidth is 200 to 6100 Hz, the resulting speech spectrum will have both the optimum preemphasis and bandwidth.

In a typical communications system $\overline{S}/N(f)$ at the receiver is not known a priori and the design must be optimized for some assumed value. In most practical situations the speech spectral density given by Eq. (2.11) is nearly optimum without power redistribution. The corresponding preemphasis is thus

$$|H(f)|^2 = \frac{W(f)}{V(f)} \tag{2.12}$$

where $V(f)$ is given by Eq. (2.5) and $W(f)$ is given by Eq. (2.1). The exact preemphasis is not critical, and an adequate approximation to the optimum is a preemphasis of 6 dB/octave above 500 Hz.

Figure 2.4 shows the AI vs. the average signal-to-noise ratio $\overline{S}/N$ for speech with optimum preemphasis in white noise, while Fig. 2.5 shows the AI vs. $\overline{S}/N_0$. It will be noted that an AI or 0.3 is obtained with a 2- to 5-dB lower signal-to-noise ratio than for unpreemphasized speech.

Intelligibility in nonwhite noise

In the case of frequency modulation systems operating above the FM improvement threshold, the audio output noise-power spectral density is not

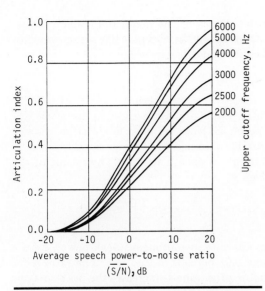

Figure 2.4 Intelligibility of preemphasized speech in white noise with 200-Hz lower cutoff frequency vs. signal-to-noise ratio.

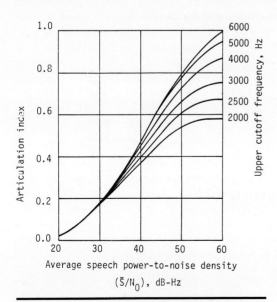

Figure 2.5 Intelligibility of preemphasized speech in white noise with 200-Hz lower cutoff frequency vs. signal-to-noise-density ratio.

white but rather increases as the square of the audio frequency (f^2-type noise). Articulation index curves for speech in f^2-type noise are shown with and without preemphasis in Figs. 2.6 and 2.7.

Peak speech power

Up to this point we have related intelligibility to the long-term average speech power for continuous speech, $\overline{S}$. However most modulation systems are peak-power-limited. The results obtained for average speech power $\overline{S}$ can be extended to peak instantaneous speech power S_p by means of the peak-to-average-power ratio given by

$$R = \frac{S_p}{\overline{S}} \tag{2.13}$$

Since it is difficult to define an absolute instantaneous peak power, we use the value which is exceeded only 0.01 percent of the time. The ratio R for normal speech is 14.5 dB. Optimum preemphasis increases the peak-to-average power ratio by 4.5 dB, thus generally offsetting the 2- to 5-dB reduction in the required average power. Preemphasis alone therefore does not generally improve communications efficiency for peak-power-limited systems.

Peak clipping

The peak-to-average power ratio of speech can be reduced by symmetrical clipping of the positive and negative voltage peaks. In the limit of infinite

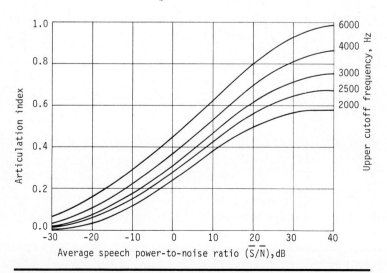

Figure 2.6 Intelligibility of normal speech in f^2 noise with 200-Hz lower cutoff frequency vs. signal-to-noise ratio.

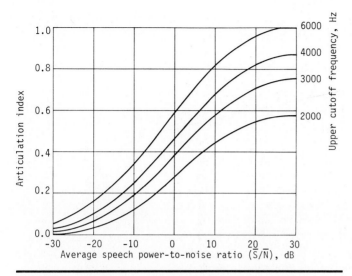

Figure 2.7 Intelligibility of preemphasized speech in f^2 noise with 200-Hz lower cutoff frequency vs. signal-to-noise ratio.

clipping, speech is reduced to square waves with a peak-to-average power ratio of 1 (0 dB). Clipping causes an increase in signal bandwidth because of the generation of distortion products. It is generally necessary, therefore, to refilter speech back to its original bandwidth. This increases R somewhat but there is still a significant overall reduction. Typical reductions in R with clipping and refiltering are shown in Fig. 2.8. The amount of clipping is taken as the ratio of the power peaks before clipping to the instantaneous power level at which peak clipping commences. The amount of repeaking which occurs depends on the filter bandwidth, cutoff rate, and delay distortion, and the results will therefore depend heavily on the filter used.

Surprisingly, the distortion introduced by clipping has little effect on intelligibility [8], and although it reduces the power level fluctuation with time, it has little effect on the shape of the short-term power spectrum or the location of the formant frequencies. It is generally assumed that peak clipping does not affect the intelligibility vs. signal-to-noise ratio curves (Figs. 2.2 through 2.7) for a range of preemphasis of from 0 to 12 dB/octave [8]. Beyond these limits the attenuated high- or low-frequency portions of the spectrum will be masked by clipper distortion products, and the intelligibility is therefore degraded. This masking effect is minimized by preemphasis of between 6 and 12 dB/octave above 500 Hz. This means that the optimum preemphasis to minimize distortion after clipping is approximately the same as that for average-power-limited sytems without clipping.

Peak clipping degrades the *subjective* quality of speech, primarily because of the increase in background noise between syllables and words. While infinite clipping greatly increases communications power efficiency for peak-power-limited systems, the intersyllable noise is annoying and fatiguing. In

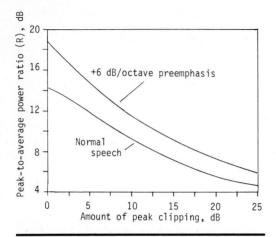

Figure 2.8 Peak-to-average-power ratio for speech vs. the amount of symmetrical audio peak clipping, with postclipping refiltering to bandwidth of 50 Hz to 12 kHz.

general clipping levels significantly above 24 dB result in unacceptable levels of intersyllable noise for day-to-day operation. Extreme clipping is acceptable only for emergency communications where peak power efficiency is the only criterion. For most applications, optimum preemphasis followed by a modest amount of some 12 to 24 dB of symmetrical peak clipping will provide a good compromise between high communications efficiency and fair subjective quality for peak-power-limited systems.

For peak-power-limited systems, optimum preemphasis followed by 21 dB of audio peak clipping will reduce the power required to achieve an AI of 0.3 by 9 to 12 dB. By contrast, for average-power-limited systems, optimum preemphasis will reduce the power required to obtain an AI of 0.3 by only 2 to 5 dB, but peak clipping will have no beneficial effects.

Representations of signals

It is useful to analyze analog modulation systems in both the time and frequency domain. Each representation has its own strengths and weaknesses, and together they provide a more complete understanding of modulation systems. In the frequency domain, phasor notation is often used. This notation will be briefly reviewed and expanded to include the closely related concept of two-dimensional time signals composed of in-phase and quadrature or real and imaginary components and referred to as "analytic signals." These concepts are useful not only in the analysis of modulation systems but also as models for the efficient implementation of a wide variety of modulation and signal processing functions.

A sine wave signal can be represented by a rotating vector, as shown in

Fig. 2.9, where the time waveform is the projection of the vector on the horizontal real or in-phase axis or

$$i(t) = \rho \cos (\omega t + \theta) \tag{2.14}$$

where ρ is the peak amplitude, ω is the radian frequency, t is time, and θ is the initial phase.

The rotating vector also has a vertical, imaginary, or quadrature component given by

$$q(t) = \rho \sin (\omega t + \theta) \tag{2.15}$$

The complex rotating vector is given by

$$
\begin{aligned}
x(t) &= i(t) + jq(t) \\
&= \rho[\cos (\omega t + \theta) + j \sin (\omega t + \theta)] \\
&= \rho e^{j(\omega t + \theta)}
\end{aligned}
\tag{2.16}
$$

This vector is rotating in a counter-clockwise direction, representing a positive frequency. The corresponding negative-frequency rotating vector is given by

$$y(t) = \rho e^{-j(\omega t + \theta)} \tag{2.17}$$

A purely real sine wave is obtained by adding the two counter-rotating vectors or

$$
\begin{aligned}
z(t) &= x(t) + y(t) \\
&= \rho(e^{j(\omega t + \theta)} + e^{-j(\omega t + \theta)}) \\
&= 2\rho \cos (\omega t + \theta)
\end{aligned}
\tag{2.18}
$$

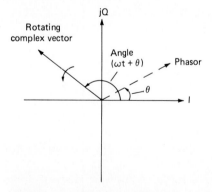

Figure 2.9 Rotating complex vector representation of a sinewave.

Thus a real-time signal is composed of complementary, counter-rotating vectors as shown in Fig. 2.10, where the imaginary components of the counter-rotating vectors cancel. In phasor representation it has become customary to represent only the phasor associated with positive frequencies, the complementary, negative-frequency phasor being implied. A general time function can be decomposed into a sum of the different frequency components.

In the foregoing discussion, the imaginary or quadrature (Q) signal component was added as a mathematical convenience with no physical significance. It is, however, possible and useful to design signal processing systems in which both the in-phase, or I, component and the quadrature, or Q, component have physical significance. Here, two ports or lines are required, one representing the in-phase and the other the quadrature component. There is no need to associate imaginary numbers with the Q component but it provides a mathematical convenience in some calculations and a label to identify the Q port in the physical implementation. This association will therefore be made freely here.

If the frequency of rotation ω is positive, then the quadrature component lags the in-phase component by 90° while if ω is negative, the quadrature component leads. Thus, for a quadrature signal representation, positive- and negative-frequency components are independent and separable.

The Hilbert Transform

The Hilbert Transform, a mathematical transform which generates a broadband 90° phase-lagged signal $q(t)$ from a real input signal $i(t)$, is defined by:

$$q(t) = \frac{1}{\pi} \int_{-\infty}^{\infty} \frac{i(t-\tau)}{\tau} \, d\tau = \lim_{\epsilon \to 0} \left[\frac{1}{\pi} \int_{-\infty}^{-\epsilon} \frac{i(t-\tau)}{\tau} \, d\tau + \frac{1}{\pi} \int_{+\epsilon}^{\infty} \frac{i(t-\tau)}{\tau} \, d\tau \right] \qquad (2.19)$$

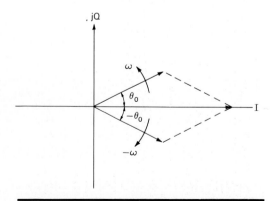

Figure 2.10 A purely in-phase signal generated by equal counterrotating complex vectors.

where the Cauchy principal value is taken because the integrand is unde-fined at $\tau = 0$. Physically, this operation is performed by passing the signal $i(t)$ through a filter with an impulsive response $1/t$.

A complex signal of the form $i(t) + jq(t)$, which is synthesized from a real signal $i(t)$ by taking the Hilbert Transform, has only positive frequency com-ponents and is known as an "analytic signal." This type of signal is often used to simplify analysis and to implement physically mixers, filters, mod-ulators, and demodulators. Frequency translation and filtering are two basic processing algorithms which will be considered briefly now.

Frequency translation

Mixing, or frequency translation, is equivalent to the complex multiplication of the complex signal $x(t)$ and the complex injection $y(t)$, or

$$\begin{aligned}
z(t) = x(t)y(t) &= [i_x(t) + jq_x(t)][i_y(t) + jq_y(t)] \\
&= [\cos(\omega_x t) + j\sin(\omega_x t)][\cos(\omega_y t) + j\sin(\omega_y t)] \\
&= \cos(\omega_x + \omega_y)t + j\sin(\omega_x + \omega_y)t \\
&= e^{j\omega_x t}e^{j\omega_y t} = e^{j(\omega_x + \omega_y)t}
\end{aligned}$$
(2.20)

Note that this complex mix produces only the sum frequency. It is imple-mented electrically as shown in Fig. 2.11, where a full, complex multiplica-tion is implemented by the four multipliers.

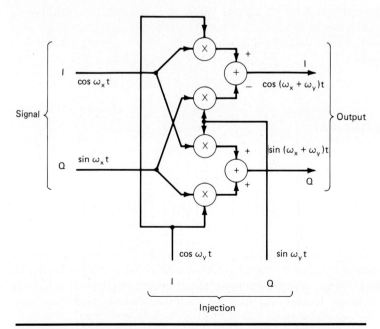

Figure 2.11 Implementation of a full complex mixer or frequency translator.

Single-sideband filters

A purely real or in-phase signal with no imaginary or quadrature component has equal positive- and negative-frequency components. This can be changed to a signal having only positive-frequency components by synthesizing a quadrature signal component from the in-phase component, by shifting all in-phase input frequency components by $-90°$.

This is a special case of a general complex filter which passes only positive-frequency components which can be implemented as shown in Fig. 2.12. This can be readily verified by inputting a positive-frequency signal, $\cos(\omega t) + j \sin(\omega t)$, and a negative-frequency signal, $\cos(\omega t) - j \sin(\omega t)$, and carrying out the indicated trigonometric operations. For the positive input frequency the output is $2[\cos(\omega t) + j \sin(\omega t)]$, while for a negative input frequency the output is zero. Alternatively the filter can be designed to pass only negative frequencies by changing the signs into the adders as shown in the figure.

The amplitude modulation family

The amplitude modulation family includes full-carrier amplitude modulation, double-sideband suppressed-carrier modulation, single-sideband modulation, and amplitude equivalent modulation (AME). We will discuss each of these forms of modulation and demodulation.

Amplitude modulation. In amplitude modulation the amplitude of an RF sine wave carrier is made to vary in direct proportion to the modulating function, as shown in Fig. 2.13. AM may be produced by multiplying a sine wave carrier, $A \cos(2\pi f_c t)$, by a modulating function $m(t)$ plus a direct current (dc) offset:

$$x(t) = \left[1 + \frac{m(t)}{e_p} \right] A \cos(2\pi f_c t)$$

$$\text{Modulation}$$
$$\text{envelope}$$

$$= A \cos(\omega_c t) + A \frac{m(t)}{e_p} \cos(\omega_c t)$$

$$\text{Carrier} \qquad\qquad \text{Sidebands}$$

(2.21)

where A is the peak amplitude of the sine wave carrier, $m(t)$ is the modulating function, e_p is its peak value, f_c is the carrier frequency, and ω_c is the radian carrier frequency. Generally, AM is demodulated by a rectifier or envelope detector. Since the output of such a demodulator depends only on the absolute voltage of the modulated signal, severe output distortion will result if the modulating voltage into the multiplier goes negative. It is therefore necessary to add a dc component to the modulating signal.

Multiplication of the modulating waveform by a sine wave carrier is equivalent to frequency translation of the modulating frequency by an amount f_c.

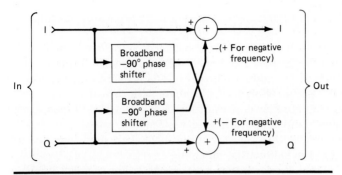

Figure 2.12 Filter which passes only positive-frequency components.

If the modulating waveform is represented by the Fourier series

$$\sum_{i=1}^{N} a_i \cos (\omega_i t + \theta_i)$$

the modulated waveform is

$$x(t) = A \left(1 + \sum_{i=1}^{N} a_i \cos (\omega_i t + \theta_i) \right) \cos (\omega_c t) \qquad (2.22)$$

Multiplying out the terms and using trigonometric identities gives:

$$x(t) = \underbrace{A \cos (\omega_c t)}_{\text{Carrier}} + \underbrace{\tfrac{1}{2} A \sum_{i=1}^{N} a_i \cos [(\omega_c - \omega_i)t - \theta_i]}_{\text{Lower sidebands}}$$

$$+ \underbrace{\tfrac{1}{2} A \sum_{i=1}^{N} a_i \cos [(\omega_c + \omega_i)t + \theta_i]}_{\text{Upper sidebands}} \qquad (2.23)$$

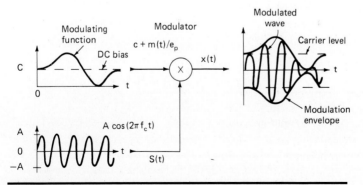

Figure 2.13 AM modulator block diagram.

Spectra of typical modulating and modulated waveforms are shown in Fig. 2.14.

A corresponding rotating vector representation of a single tone-modulated waveform is shown in Fig. 2.15. The upper and lower sideband rotating vectors combine vectorially to add or subtract in phase with the carrier vector so that the overall resultant is a vector in phase with the carrier vector but having a sine wave fluctuation in amplitude. For more general modulating functions, the upper and lower sideband vectors still combine to form a resultant vector in phase with the carrier and having an amplitude fluctuation proportional to the modulating function.

From Eq. (2.21), the carrier power is $P_c = A^2/2$. The average sideband power P_{sb} is

$$P_{sb} = \frac{A^2}{2} \frac{E[m^2(t)]}{e_p^2} = \frac{A^2}{2} \frac{1}{R_m} = \frac{P_c}{R_m} \tag{2.24}$$

where $E\,[\,]$ is the average or expected value operator and R_m is the peak-to-average-power ratio of the modulating function. The total average power P_{avg} is:

$$P_{avg} = P_c + P_{sb} = P_c\left(1 + \frac{1}{R_m}\right) = \frac{P_c(1 + R_m)}{R_m} \tag{2.25}$$

For 100 percent modulation where the peak value of $m(t)$ equals e_p, the peak voltage is $2A$ and the peak instantaneous output power P_p is

$$P_p = 4A^2 = 8P_c \tag{2.26}$$

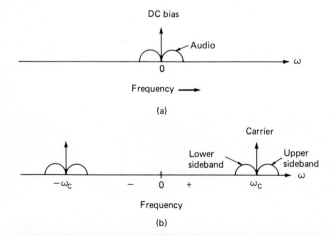

Figure 2.14 Spectra of AM waveforms. Spectrum of (a) modulating and (b) modulated waveforms.

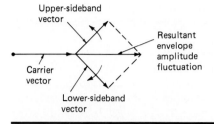

Figure 2.15 AM modulation rotating vector diagram (single-tone sine wave modulation).

The receiver audio output signal power is proportional to the received sideband power, so that the output signal-to-noise ratio is maximized by maximizing sideband power. Most transmitters are, however, peak-power- rather than average-power-limited, and it is therefore desirable to relate the sideband power to peak and average power. From Eqs. (2.24) through (2.26),

$$P_{sb} = \frac{P_{avg}}{1 + R_m} \tag{2.27}$$

and

$$P_{sb} = \frac{P_p}{8R_m} \tag{2.28}$$

Transmitter peak-power ratings are usually specified in terms of peak envelope power P_{ep}, which is half the true peak-instantaneous-power rating P_p. We shall henceforth give peak ratings in terms of peak envelope power. The relationships between peak envelope, average, carrier, and sideband power for the amplitude modulation family are summarized in Table 2.1.

DSBSC modulation. Double-sideband suppressed-carrier modulation is identical to full-carrier AM except that the carrier frequency is partially or totally suppressed. For full-carrier suppression the wave is given by

$$x(t) = A\frac{m(t)}{e_p} \cos(2\pi f_c t) \tag{2.29}$$

which is equivalent to AM except that the modulating function is not provided with a dc bias term. When the modulating function changes sign, the modulated carrier makes sudden 180° phase shifts.

Unlike AM, the absolute value of the envelope is anything but an undistorted version of the modulating waveform, and an envelope detector is not a suitable demodulator. The spectrum of the modulated signal is the same as for AM shown in Fig. 2.14 except that the carrier frequency is absent.

TABLE 2.1   Power Relationships for the AM Modulation Family

| Type of modulation | Equation | | Equation |
	For	In terms of	
AM	P_{sb}	P_c	$P_{sb} = P_c/R_m$
		P_{avg}	$= P_{avg}/(1 + R_m)$
		P_{ep}	$= P_{ep}/(4R_m)$
	P_{avg}	P_c	$P_{avg} = P_c(1 + 1/R_m)$
	P_{ep}	P_c	$P_{ep} = 4P_c$
DSBSC	P_{sb}	P_{avg}	$P_{sb} = P_{avg}$
		P_{ep}	$P_{sb} = P_{ep}/R_m$
DSB with pilot carrier	P_{sb}	P_{avg}	$P_{sb} = P_{avg}(1 - P_c/P_{avg})$
		P_{ep}	$= P_{ep}\left(1 - \sqrt{P_c/P_{ep}}\right)^2 /R_m$
	P_{ep}	P_{sb} and P_c	$P_{ep} = (\sqrt{R_m P_{sb}} + \sqrt{P_c})^2$
SSB	P_{sb}	P_{avg}	$P_{sb} = P_{avg}$

Since all the power is now in the sidebands, the sideband power is equal to the average power:

$$P_{sb} = P_{avg} = \frac{A^2}{2} \frac{E[m^2(t)]}{e_p^2} = \frac{A^2}{2R_m} \tag{2.30}$$

Since the maximum value of $m(t)/e_p$ is 1, the peak power is

$$P_p = A^2 = 2R_m P_{sb} \tag{2.31}$$

where the last expression was obtained by solving Eq. (2.30) for A^2 and substituting. The peak envelope power is therefore

$$P_{ep} = R_m P_{sb} \tag{2.32}$$

Again, the power relationships are summarized in Table 2.1. It will be noted from this table that the sideband power is always greater for a given peak envelope or average power for double sideband (DSB) than for AM, since no power is wasted in transmission of the carrier. For synchronous detection, the output signal-to-noise ratio is proportional to the sideband power, and DSB is therefore more efficient than AM.

While DSB can be synchronously demodulated without a carrier, a pilot carrier is sometimes added as an aid to synchronous detection. The carrier has values between full AM and zero. In the general case, a DSB signal with pilot carrier is given by

$$x(t) = A\left(c + \frac{m(t)}{e_p}\right) \cos(2\pi f_c t) \tag{2.33}$$

The relationships between peak envelope, average, sideband, and carrier power can be solved by means similar to those used for AM and DSBSC, and the results are summarized in Table 2.1.

Single-sideband modulation. Full-carrier AM consists of a carrier plus upper and lower sidebands. In SSB, both the carrier and one sideband are removed so that only the upper or lower sideband remains. The three common methods of SSB generation are the filter method, the phase-shift method, and the Weaver method. Today the filter method is used almost exclusively in analog circuit implementations while the phase-shift and Weaver methods are finding favor in digital circuit implementations.

In the filter method an AM or DSBSC signal is generated and the resultant signal is bandpass-filtered to remove one sideband and the carrier (see Fig. 2.16). In the phase-shift method a complex, baseband single-sideband audio signal is generated by synthesizing a quadrature (Q) component which leads (or lags) the in-phase (I) component by 90° (see Fig. 2.17). This audio SSB signal is then complex-mixed to the desired IF carrier frequency. In the Weaver method the center frequency of the audio bandpass is half-complex-mixed to zero frequency so that the upper (or lower) audio sideband extends

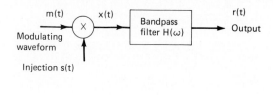

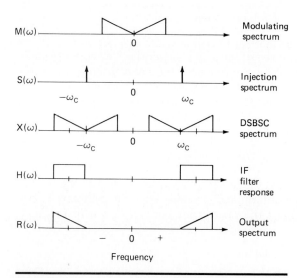

Figure 2.16 The filter method of SSB modulation.

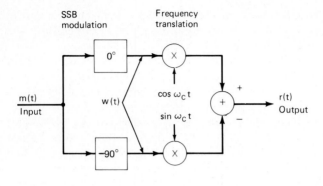

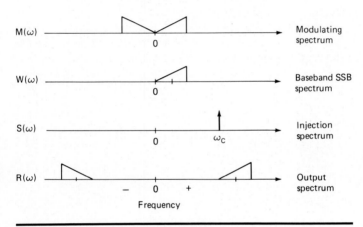

Figure 2.17   Phase-shift method of SSB modulation.

over equal positive- and negative-frequency bandwidths. The opposite audio sideband is removed by low-pass filtering both the I and Q components (see Fig. 2.18). This avoids the need for a wideband 90° phase shifter (Hilbert transformer) as required for the phase-shift method. The resultant complex, audio, single-sideband signal is then translated by a complex mix to the desired IF carrier frequency.

SSB waveforms.   It is readily apparent that the SSB frequency spectrum is the single-sided audio spectrum translated to an RF or IF frequency. While the modification of the signal spectrum is quite simple, the modification of the signal time waveform and envelope are quite complex. This is most easily seen by studying the phase-shift method shown in Fig. 2.17, where the output is:

$$r(t) = m(t) \cos \omega_c t - \hat{m}(t) \sin \omega_c t$$
$$= \underbrace{\sqrt{m^2(t) + \hat{m}^2(t)}}_{\text{SSB envelope}} \cos \left[\omega_c t + \phi(t) \right] \qquad (2.34)$$

where $\hat{m}(t)$ is the Hilbert transform of $\dot{m}(t)$, and $\phi(t)$ is the four-quadrant arctangent given by

$$\phi(t) = \arctan[-\hat{m}(t), m(t)] \tag{2.35}$$

Since all the power is in the single sideband,

$$P_{\text{sb}} = P_{\text{avg}} \qquad P_c = 0 \tag{2.36}$$

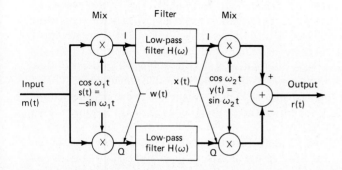

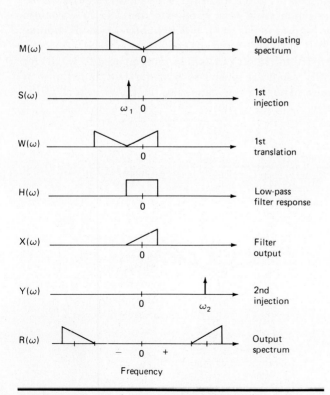

Figure 2.18 Weaver method of SSB modulation.

Peak-to-average-power ratio.   If $m(t)$ is a single sine wave tone, $\cos \omega_a t$, the Hilbert transform, is $+\sin \omega_a t$ and the SSB envelope is a constant. Moreover, the SSB waveform is a sine wave, so that the peak-to-average-power ratio of the SSB signal is equal to that of the modulating waveform. While the peak-to-average-power ratio of SSB modulation is never smaller than the modulating function, it can be much greater. An extreme case is a wideband square wave modulating function which alternates periodically between plus and minus 1 and for which the peak-to-average-power ratio R is unity (0 dB). However, the Hilbert transform of an ideal square wave has infinite peaks, and therefore the peak-to-average-power ratio for ideal square wave SSB modulation is infinite, as shown in Fig. 2.19. Any practical SSB modulation system, however, is bandwidth-limited, and R for these systems is finite. A square wave modulating function is of some interest in that it approximates, to a degree, an infinitely clipped audio waveform.

Most SSB systems have a ratio of high-frequency to low-frequency cutoff of no more than 13 to 1, for which the peak-to-average ratio for square wave modulation is 8 dB.

For waveforms of fluctuating amplitudes, such as speech, however, audio clipping reduces the peak-to-average-power ratio of the SSB waveform, as shown in Fig. 2.20. The results will depend on the bandwidth and phase linearity of the postmodulation IF filter, and the results shown must be viewed as typical. Results for symmetrical peak clipping of the SSB IF waveform and refiltering are also shown in Fig. 2.20. It will be noted that IF clipping is more effective for SSB modulation and can reduce the SSB peak-to-average-power ratio by 6.5 dB, for 18 dB of clipping, as compared to 4.0 dB for audio clipping. The SSB results are much less dramatic than those shown in Fig. 2.8, largely because of the narrow bandwidth and sharp cutoff of the postclipping IF filter.

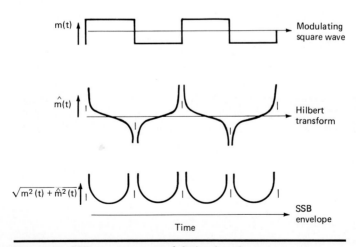

Figure 2.19 SSB square wave modulation functions.

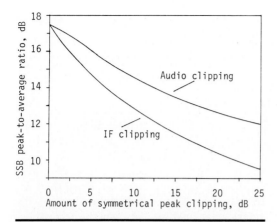

Figure 2.20 The effect of audio and IF peak clipping on the peak-to-average-power ratio of SSB signals (no preemphasis; preclipping audio bandwidth is 70 to 12000 Hz, postmodulation and post-IF-clipping bandwidth is 300 to 3200 Hz).

SSB with pilot carrier. In some cases a low-level pilot carrier is retained as a phase reference for synchronous SSB demodulation. The average power P_{avg} is the sum of the sideband power P_{sb} and the carrier power P_c:

$$P_{avg} = P_{sb} + P_c \tag{2.37}$$

while the peak envelope power P_{ep} is obtained from the sum of the peak sideband voltage and the peak carrier voltage or

$$P_{ep} = (P_{ps}^{1/2} + P_c^{1/2})^2 \tag{2.38}$$

where P_{ps} is the peak envelope power of the SSB signal without the pilot carrier.

Amplitude modulation equivalent. Amplitude modulation equivalent consists of SSB with a carrier of substantial amplitude added so that the signal can be demodulated using a conventional envelope detector while occupying only half the bandwidth of conventional AM. The carrier level is typically set so that P_{ps} does not exceed the carrier level, as discussed in greater detail in Chap. 4. The average and peak envelope power are the same as for SSB with pilot carrier since only the relative magnitude of the carrier is different.

Demodulation of the AM family

The demodulated audio output average-signal-to-noise density ratio $(\overline{S}/N_0)_{AF}$ for all of the amplitude modulation family is

$$\left(\frac{\overline{S}}{N_0}\right)_{AF} = \frac{P_{sb}}{N_{or}} \tag{2.39}$$

where P_{sb} is the total sideband power, and N_{or} is the RF noise-power spectral density, both referred to the receiver input.

SSB demodulation.   Demodulation of an SSB signal is accomplished by mixing the received RF signal to audio. The average audio signal output power $\overline{S}$ is proportional to the RF input sideband power while the audio output noise density is proportional to the RF input noise density, thus giving Eq. (2.39). For analog circuit implementations, the filter method of SSB demodulation is used almost exclusively. Here the IF signal is filtered to pass only the desired sideband and is then mixed to audio. If the mixer injection frequency and phase are exactly correct, the reconstructed audio wave shape will match the original modulating function. However, since there is no absolute phase reference in the case of SSB, the demodulated wave will not generally have the proper phase relationships between the frequency components, and the waveform may be severely distorted even though the power spectrum is unchanged. For voice communications these phase non-linearities have no effect on intelligibility. In addition, there will be errors in the output frequencies because of injection frequency errors and Doppler shifts. Shifts of ±5 Hz have little effect on speech subjective quality or intelligibility. For shifts between ±5 and ±50 Hz the quality suffers but intelligibility is not degraded significantly. The approximate AI reduction factor F due to a frequency offset is shown in Fig. 2.21 [1, 12]. The AI for a frequency shift of Δf is given by

$$AI(\Delta f) = F(\Delta f)AI(0) \tag{2.40}$$

where $AI(\Delta f)$ is the AI for a frequency shift of Δf.

AM and DSBSC can be detected by SSB demodulation of either the upper or lower sideband but in so doing there is a 3-dB reduction in the output

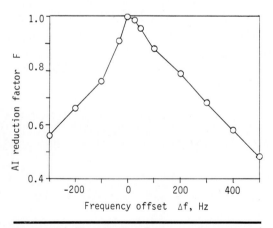

Figure 2.21 AI reduction factor vs. frequency offset.

signal-to-noise-density ratio because of the loss of the coherent opposite sideband.

DSBSC demodulation.   A DSBSC signal can be demodulated coherently by multiplying the IF signal by a recreated carrier of the proper frequency and phase and then low-pass filtering the result. Under these conditions the demodulated signal will be a faithful reproduction of the modulating function. Multiplying the DSBSC signal of Eq. (2.29) by a synthesized carrier, we have

$$x(t) \cos (2\pi f_c t) = A \frac{m(t)}{e_p} [\tfrac{1}{2} + \tfrac{1}{2} \cos (4\pi f_c t)] \tag{2.41}$$

After low-pass filtering we obtain the demodulated output as

$$y(t) = \frac{A}{2e_p} m(t) \tag{2.42}$$

The required carrier for demodulating can be recovered either by using a frequency doubler or a Costas loop, described in the following paragraphs.

Frequency-doubler DSB demodulation.   A frequency-doubler demodulator is shown in Fig. 2.22. The received DSBSC signal is first squared in a frequency doubler. By squaring Eq. (2.29), we obtain

$$
\begin{aligned}
y(t) = x^2(t) &= A^2 \left(\frac{m(t)}{e_p} \right)^2 \cos^2 (2\pi f_c t) \\
&= A^2 \left(\frac{m(t)}{e_p} \right)^2 [\tfrac{1}{2} + \tfrac{1}{2} \cos (2\pi 2 f_c t)]
\end{aligned}
\tag{2.43}
$$

While the original DSBSC waveform had abrupt 180° phase flips, there are no phase flips in the frequency doubler output since 180° phase change of the input signal corresponds to 360° at the doubler output. The dc output component is removed by the second harmonic filter. This filter will also provide a flywheel or ringing action to provide a second harmonic component

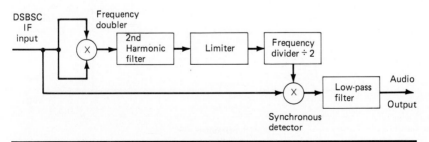

Figure 2.22   Frequency-doubler DSBSC demodulator.

for periods when the signal may be zero. The filter output is limited or clipped to form a square wave which in turn drives a frequency divider to provide the synthesized carrier cos $(2\pi f_c t)$, which is used to synchronously demodulate the DSBSC signal. The filter action could also be provided by a phase-locked loop, as discussed below [9, 10].

Costas-loop DSB demodulator.   If the DSBSC signal includes a pilot carrier, the carrier can be recovered by using a very narrow phase-locked loop locked to the carrier. Since a phase-locked loop locks at 90° with respect to the input carrier phase, a 90° phase shifter is required in order to obtain an in-phase recovered carrier, which can be used for synchronous demodulation, as shown in Fig. 2.23. In the absence of a carrier there are sudden 180° phase shifts, and the phase-locked loop will continually break lock and relock. To avoid this, a phase deflipper is added in the loop so that the sense of the loop is reversed every time the signal phase changes 180°, thus avoiding loss of lock during phase flips using a Costas-loop DSBSC demodulator, as shown in Fig. 2.23 [11].

AM demodulation.   AM or AME can be demodulated either by a synchronous detector or by an envelope detector. Synchronous detection gives maximum demodulation efficiency and gives the full performance indicated by Eq. (2.39). In order to achieve this performance, the recovered carrier must contain very little noise. It can be recovered by the circuit shown in Fig. 2.23 with the phase deflipper removed.

AM and AME can also be demodulated at IF using a simple envelope detector. At carrier-to-noise ratios below 0 dB there is appreciable loss in detection efficiency and the performance of Eq. (2.39) can no longer be achieved. However, for AM speech modulation the audio output signal-to-noise ratio will generally be too low to be useful before the carrier-to-noise ratio reaches 0 dB, and therefore a synchronous detector does not improve AM voice demodulator performance significantly.

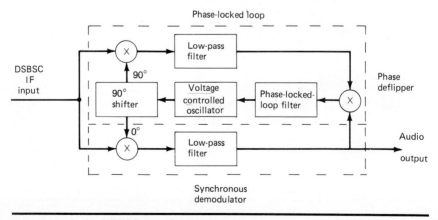

Figure 2.23   Costas DSBSC demodulator.

The angle modulation family

Angle modulation is the second classical analog modulation system. Here the phase angle $\theta(t)$ of a reference carrier of frequency ω_c is varied under control of the modulating function while the amplitude A of the signal is constant. This modulated waveform can be expressed as

$$x(t) = A \cos [\omega_c t + \theta(t)] \tag{2.44}$$

In phase modulation (PM) the phase $\theta(t)$ is made to vary in direct proportion to the modulating waveform. Sine wave phase modulation can be decomposed into an in-phase carrier which is DSB-modulated by even cosine harmonics plus quadrature DSBSC sidebands of odd sine wave harmonics, as shown in Fig. 2.24. For small peak deviations the primary sources of phase deviation are the fundamental quadrature sidebands, while the smaller in-phase sidebands, which are cosine-wave-modulated by the second harmonic, remove most of the amplitude modulation introduced by quadrature sideband modulation. For larger phase deviations there are higher-order sidebands of significant amplitudes. If the modulating function is

$$\theta(t) = \beta \sin (\omega_m t) \tag{2.45}$$

where β is the peak phase deviation, then

$$\begin{aligned}
x(t) = A[&J_0(\beta) \cos (\omega_c t) + 2J_1(\beta) \sin (\omega_m t) \sin (\omega_c t) \\
&+ 2J_2(\beta) \cos (2\omega_m t) \cos (\omega_c t) + 2J_3(\beta) \sin (3\omega_m t) \sin (\omega_c t) \cdots]
\end{aligned} \tag{2.46}$$

where $J_n(\beta)$ is the Bessel function of the first kind of the nth order. For very small peak deviations the RF spectrum is largely contained within twice the audio bandwidth, as with AM. For peak phase deviations greater than 45° this approximation is grossly inadequate and second- and higher-order sidebands of significant amplitude are present.

Instantaneous frequency. If the total angle of the wave is $\phi(t)$ (the argument of the cosine) where

$$\phi(t) = \omega_c t + \theta(t) \tag{2.47}$$

then the instantaneous radian frequency $\omega(t)$ is defined as the rate of change of phase or:

$$\omega(t) = \frac{d\phi(t)}{dt} = \omega_c + \frac{d\theta(t)}{dt} \tag{2.48}$$

For a constant carrier frequency the instantaneous frequency is equal to the carrier frequency. However, for many waveforms there is no simple relationship between the instantaneous frequency and the frequency spectrum. The former is time-dependent and has only a single value at a given instant, while the true frequency spectrum is independent of time and can be composed of

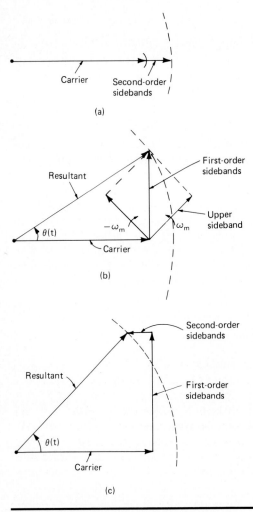

Figure 2.24 Rotating vector representation of a sine-wave-modulated FM signal. (*a*) $\theta(t) = 0$; (*b*) $\theta(t) = \frac{1}{2}$ radian; (*c*) $\theta(t) = 1$ radian.

many frequency components. Instantaneous frequency is a useful concept but should not be confused with the frequency spectrum.

Frequency modulation.   In frequency modulation the instantaneous frequency $\omega(t)$ is made to vary in direct proportion to the modulating function so that

$$\omega(t) = \omega_c + cm(t) \qquad (2.49)$$

where c is a constant.

At high signal levels both FM and PM offer improvement in the receiver output signal-to-noise ratio when compared with AM. There is an IF carrier-to-noise ratio below which the full output signal-to-noise ratio improvement can no longer be maintained. This IF carrier-to-noise ratio is called the FM improvement threshold. The signal and noise characteristics of the FM system can therefore be divided into two primary regions: above and below the improvement threshold.

The receiver IF bandwidth B required to pass the significant spectrum components depends upon the amount of output signal distortion that can be tolerated [13]. One widely used rule of thumb is Carson's rule,

$$B = 2(\Delta f + b) \tag{2.50}$$

This rule allows rejection of all spectrum lines which contribute less than 1 percent of the total power of the FM spectrum. For high values of m, $(\Delta f >> b)$, the value of B approaches $2\Delta f_{max}$. It has been empirically determined that for communications quality voice modulation, a suitable rule is

$$B = \max [2\Delta f, 2b] \tag{2.51}$$

where max [ ] is the larger value of the two arguments.

For minimum bandwidth systems the IF bandwidth can be set at $2b$ and the peak deviation Δf can be equal to b.

The threshold $(C/N)_{IF}$ value lies between 7 and 10 dB and is often considered to be a lower limit for acceptable FM system performance. However, for voice communications, speech intelligibility is adequate, even when the $(C/N)_{IF}$ is several dB below threshold.

A completely rigorous expression describing the entire below-threshold region, for the sine wave modulation case, is not available. Frutiger [14], however, has developed an equation which allows accurate determination of the audio frequency (AF) output signal-to-noise ratio $(S/N)_{AF}$, for sine wave modulation at $(C/N)_{IF}$ values greater than 4 dB. Frutiger's equation is

$$\left(\frac{S}{N}\right)_{AF} = \frac{\frac{3}{2}m^2(B/b)(C/N)_{IF}}{1 + 0.9(B/b)^2(C/N)_{IF} \exp[-(C/N)_{IF}]/(1 - \exp[-(C/N)_{IF}])^2} \tag{2.52}$$

where B is the IF bandwidth, b is the audio bandwidth, and m the modulation index, as defined by

$$m = \frac{\Delta f}{b} \tag{2.53}$$

where Δf is the peak instantaneous frequency deviation. Equation (2.52) has been employed to develop the set of $(S/N)_{AF}$ vs. $(C/N)_{IF}$ curves, illustrated in Fig. 2.25 where the curve parameter is B/b and the deviation ratio m is equal to 1 for all curves. These curves can be adapted to calculate the sine wave audio output signal-to-noise ratios for other values of the modulation index, by adding $20 \log_{10}(m)$ to the value of $(S/N)_{AF}$ read from the curves.

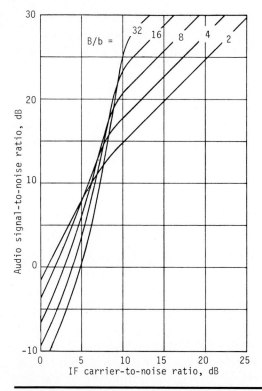

Figure 2.25 Output signal to noise at baseband as a function of input-carrier-to-noise ratio for sine wave modulation. The parameter is B/b. The deviation ratio m = 1.0. For other deviation ratios, add 20 log (m) to the ordinate values.

Voice-modulation FM systems

The FM curves shown in Fig. 2.25 are for sine wave modulation. The output signal-to-noise ratio will be lower with voice modulation since the peak-to-average-power ratio of speech is higher than that of a sine wave. The output signal-to-noise ratio as read from Fig. 2.25 must be reduced for voice modulation by the factor

$$\frac{\text{Peak-to-average-power ratio of speech}}{\text{Peak-to-average-power ratio of sine wave}}$$

It is clear from this that peak clipping of the voice modulating waveform will improve the output signal-to-noise ratio for a fixed peak frequency deviation since it reduces the peak-to-average-power ratio of the modulating waveform.

In calculating the intelligibility of speech, it is necessary to know the shape of the audio output noise spectrum. Above the FM improvement threshold the output noise is f^2 noise, while well below threshold the noise tends to be white. The transition from f^2 to white noise is rather sudden. Near the FM improvement threshold the output noise is made up of two additive components. One is the f^2 gaussian noise, which is inversely proportional to the carrier-to-noise ratio above the FM improvement threshold. The other is white impulse noise, which increases very rapidly with a reduction in the input carrier-to-noise ratio. These two components contribute equally to the output noise when the output signal-to-noise ratio is 3 dB below the straight-line extension of the above threshold curve. This point will be referred to as the "3-dB FM improvement threshold."

In calculating intelligibility, we switch from f^2 to white output noise at the 3-dB FM improvement threshold in lieu of calculating the exact shape of the output noise spectrum.

We are now in a position to calculate the intelligibility of an FM voice system. The procedure is as follows:

1. Assume sine wave modulation of the transmitter with the same peak frequency deviation as will be obtained with voice modulation.

2. Look up the output signal-to-noise ratio for the given input carrier-to-noise ratio using Fig. 2.25 with corrections for the actual modulation index.

3. Subtract from the sine wave output signal-to-noise ratio in dB obtained in step 2 the difference between the peak-to-average-power ratio of the speech waveform in dB obtained from Fig. 2.8 and the 3-dB peak-to-average-power ratio of a sine wave to obtain the voice output signal-to-noise ratio.

4. Look up the articulation index on an appropriate intelligibility curve for the proper premodulation preemphasis and bandwidth, using a curve for f^2 noise when above the 3-dB FM improvement threshold and for white noise when below this threshold.

5. Repeat the above procedure for various carrier-to-noise ratios to obtain an intelligibility curve.

The intelligibility of two FM systems has been calculated by the above method, and the results are shown in Figs. 2.26 and 2.27. Both systems have $+6$ dB/octave preemphasis above 500 Hz, a lower audio cutoff frequency of 200 Hz, 21 dB of audio clipping, a predetection IF bandwidth of twice the peak frequency deviation, and a conventional FM detector. The first system has a peak frequency deviation equal to the upper audio cutoff frequency ($m = 1$), as shown in Fig. 2.26. The second system has a peak frequency deviation equal to twice the upper audio cutoff frequency, as shown in Fig. 2.27. The premodulation voice processing for these sample calculations was picked so as to optimize intelligibility under poor signal conditions.

The threshold of intelligibility (AI = 0.3) for the narrower band system ($m = 1$) requires 1 dB less carrier power than for the wider band systems ($m = 2$), and it is desirable to use an audio bandwidth of between 2 and 3

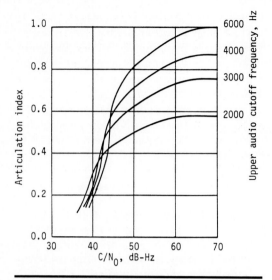

Figure 2.26 Articulation index vs. carrier-power-to-noise power density (C/N_0) for a modulation index of 1.0 (m = 1.0). Preemphasis: +6 dB/octave above 500 Hz; lower audio cutoff: 200 Hz; audio clipping: 21 dB (R_m = 7 dB); modulation index: $m = \Delta f/b = 1$; IF bandwidth: $2b$.

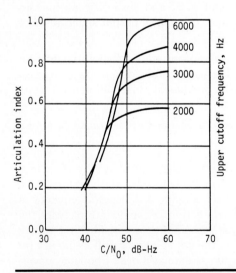

Figure 2.27 Articulation index vs. carrier-power-to-noise-power density ratio (C/N_0) for a modulation index of 2.0 (m = 2.0) with preemphasis and audio clipping. Preemphasis: +6 dB/octave above 500 Hz; lower audio cutoff: 200 Hz; audio clipping: 21 dB (R_m = 7 dB); modulation index: $m = \Delta f/b = 2$; IF bandwidth: $4b$.

kHz for the former. All systems achieve the threshold of intelligibility well below the FM improvement threshold. Thus, if usable intelligibility under weak signal conditions is the primary criterion, a modulation index of 1 should be used. At this low modulation index there is little or no benefit from the use of FM threshold extension techniques.

Comparison of voice-modulation systems

In the previous sections we developed the tools necessary for the calculation of the intelligibility of a wide range of voice communication systems. Modulation theory gives the audio signal-to-noise ratio, given the link signal-to-noise ratio and amplitude statistics of speech, while the articulation index provides a method of calculating the intelligibility, given the audio signal-to-noise ratio. We have used these tools to compare the various modulation systems under typical conditions, to exemplify the results which are obtainable.

The intelligibility for unprocessed voice modulation is shown in Figs. 2.28 and 2.29. The audio bandwidth is 300 to 3000 kHz, and there is no preemphasis or clipping of the audio modulating signal or of the IF or RF signal. The curves show the performance for SSB, DSBSC, AM, and FM. FM curves are shown for peak frequency deviations of 3 and 6 kHz. In each case, the receiver IF bandwidth is equal to twice the peak frequency deviation. Figure

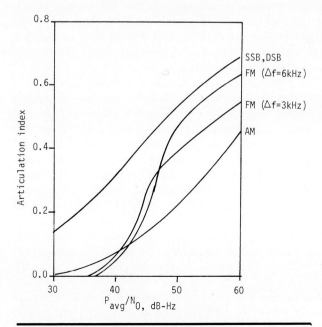

Figure 2.28 AI vs. P_{avg}/N_0 for unprocessed speech modulation (300- to 3000-Hz audio bandwidth).

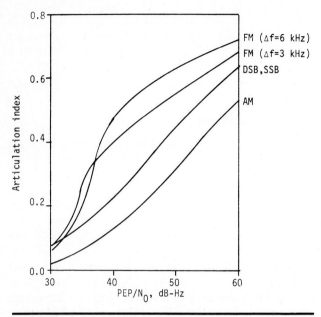

Figure 2.29 AI vs. PEP/N_0 for unprocessed speech modulation (300- to 3000-Hz audio bandwidth).

2.28 shows the articulation index as a function of the RF average signal-power-to-noise-power-density ratio P_{avg}/N_0, while Fig. 2.29 shows AI vs. the peak envelope signal-power-to-noise-density ratio, P_{ep}/N_0. SSB modulation is most efficient for average-power-limited transmitters, while FM is most efficient for peak-power-limited transmitters.

The intelligibility for processed voice modulation is shown in Figs. 2.30 and 2.31. The audio bandwidth is again 300 to 3000 Hz, but here the speech waveform has been preemphasized by +6 dB/octave above 500 Hz, and clipped to reduce the audio peak-to-average-power ratio to 7 dB. In the case of SSB, the clipping, whether done at audio or IF, reduces the final RF peak-envelope-to-average-power ratio to 7 dB. This processing represents a reasonable compromise between quality and efficiency for links which must be operated frequently under marginal signal conditions. Again, SSB is generally best for average-power-limited transmitters, while FM is generally most efficient for peak-power-limited systems.

These results are summarized in Table 2.2. Most power amplifiers have both peak and average power limits, and which one actually limits performance is determined by the peak-envelope-to-average-power ratio of the RF signal waveform.

If the transmitter is average-power-limited, then preemphasis and clipping reduce the required power by 4 dB for SSB, DSBSC, and FM and by 11 dB for AM. If the transmitter is peak-power-limited, preemphasis and clipping reduce the required power by 11 dB for SSB, DSBSC, and AM and

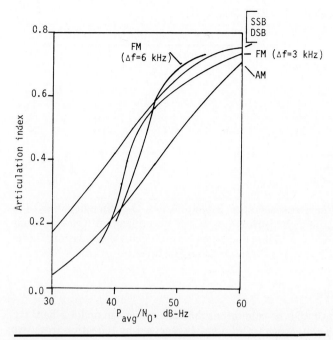

Figure 2.30 AI vs. P_{avg}/N_0 for preemphasized and clipped speech modulation (300 to 3000 Hz).

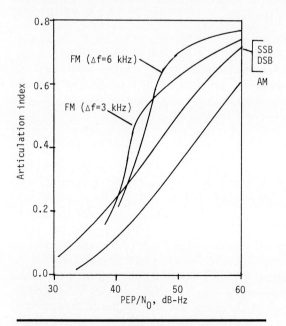

Figure 2.31 AI vs. PEP/N_0 for preemphasized and clipped speech modulation (300 to 3000 Hz).

TABLE 2.2   Comparison of Voice-Modulation Systems*

Modulation type	RF bandwidth, kHz	Signal-to-noise-density ratio at AI = 0.3			
		Unprocessed speech		Processed speech	
		P_{avg}/N_0	PEP/N_0	P_{avg}/N_0	PEP/N_0
SSB	3	39	53	35	42
DSBSC	6	39	53	35	42
FM(Δf = 3 kHz)	6	45	45	41	41
FM(Δf = 6 kHz)	12	46	46	42	42
AM	6	54	59	43	48

* See text for conditions.

by 4 dB for FM. For processed speech modulation, the efficiency of SSB is better or nearly equal to FM. In addition, SSB occupies half the RF bandwidth and, as we shall see, is less disturbed by multipath propagation; therefore, SSB provides the best performance on HF links.

Multipath propagation

Multipath propagation is the rule rather than the exception on long-haul HF links. In multipath propagation the signal is received by reflection from two or more ionospheric layers. The distances traveled by the paths are different, resulting in time delays between the received signals. The delayed signals may tend to cancel or reinforce each other. For two-path propagation, a received sine wave $x(t)$ is of the form

$$x(t) = \sin 2\pi f t + \rho \sin [2\pi f(t - \tau)] \tag{2.54}$$

where τ is the multipath differential time delay and ρ is the relative voltage of the delayed path. The frequency response of the medium is periodic in frequency f, with a period Δf given by

$$\Delta f = \frac{1}{\tau} \tag{2.55}$$

Multipath differential delays range between 1 and 5 ms, so that deep frequency-selective fade troughs are typically separated by 200 to 1000 Hz. The peak-to-trough power ratio in two-path selective fading is $(1 + \rho)^2/(1 - \rho)^2$, and multipath propagation can cause 6-dB reenforcement at peaks and complete cancellation in troughs. Articulation index calculation for two equal paths indicates that multipath selective fading has only a small effect on SSB intelligibility, as shown in Fig. 2.32. Here the total average power is the same with and without fading, implying that the path loss for each of the two paths is 3 dB more than on the single nonfading path. While SSB is affected only slightly by multipath fading, the attenuation of the carrier in AM and FM introduces severe distortion in demodulation, causing significant degradation in intelligibility when the carrier falls in the fading trough.

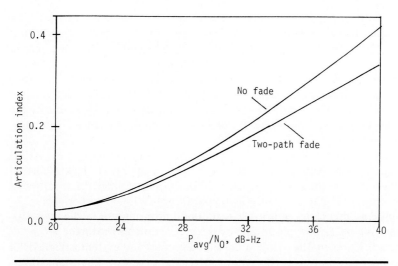

Figure 2.32 AI vs. average-signal-power-to-noise-density ratio for SSB with and without two-path multipath (two equal paths with 1.66-ms differential delay).

Thus, all things considered, SSB is superior to the other types of modulation under adverse HF propagation conditions.

We have addressed the intelligibility for the classical modulation systems under typical conditions. The general method of analysis presented, however, applies to a wide range of conditions. The examples presented are useful as a general guide but it is often desirable to derive results for the particular case under study.

2.2 Colocated System Design

When a transmitter and receiver are operating simultaneously in close proximity, there are several ways in which receiver operation may be degraded. Considering receiver limitations, the most severe degradation is receiver burnout, or more likely, opening of a protective antenna relay. A second is desensitization or blocking caused by overload of the receiver front-end circuits. Somewhat related is cross modulation, which is a transferal, due to receiver nonlinearity, of transmitter modulation to that of the received signal. Reciprocal mixing may occur, a phenomenon that utilizes a strong out-of-band signal to heterodyne local oscillator noise sidebands into the receiver IF passband. Finally, higher-order mixing products, discussed in Chap. 3, "Receiver Design," may result in spurious responses to strong unwanted signals. Transmitter limitations that may degrade colocated receiver operation include harmonic and intermodulation distortion products and broadband noise components that fall within the receiver passband.

A special problem may arise when two transmitters are in operation at the same time in the vicinity of a receiver. First, coupling between the two transmitting antennas transfers some of the power from one transmitter to the other. This transferred power is reflected to the power amplifier output where it intermodulates with its signal to create new frequencies, one of which may fall within the receiver passband. This phenomenon is known as "back-intermodulation." Second, these two transmitted signals, even if they do not create back-intermodulation, may create IM distortion in the receiver front end. Since the same two frequencies are involved, these distortion products also have the same frequencies as those produced by back-intermodulation.

All these degraded reception effects are made worse when there is a strong coupling between transmitter and receiver antennas; hence it is important to reduce the coupling between them as much as possible. Practically this means maintaining as much physical separation as allowed and orienting the receiving antenna to place it as close to a null or minimum in the transmitting antenna pattern as permitted by the constraints of the site.

Figure 2.33 shows the elements of a communication system designed for simultaneous operation of the transmitter and receiver. The main differences between it and a simple half-duplex installation are the use of separate transmitting and receiving antennas, a preselector and/or adaptive canceler to reduce the level of the transmitter at the receiver input, and a postselector to reduce exciter noise and distortion products. The power amplifier may also be designed for lower noise and distortion output. Typically this might be accomplished by heavier filtering of the PA output.

Quasi-minimum-noise considerations

In determining the amount of acceptable interference to a receiver from a colocated transmitter, it is useful to consider to what extent naturally occurring noise levels limit the sensitivity of the receiver. In the absence of other noise sources, thermal noise sets a lower limit to receiver sensitivity. The

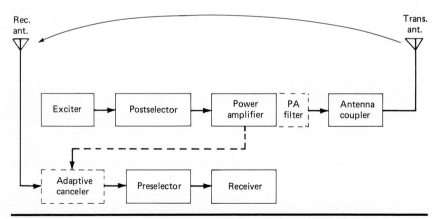

Figure 2.33 Elements of a communication system designed for simultaneous operation of the transmitter and receiver.

magnitude of this noise density is kT_0-W/Hz bandwidth, where k is Boltzmann's constant and T_0 is the absolute temperature in kelvin. Any practical receiver adds noise beyond the thermal limit, and the ratio of its noise output to that which would result from thermal noise alone is the receiver noise figure. Beyond this, naturally occurring atmosphere and galactic sources as well as artificially created radio interference, contribute additional noise. Although these levels can vary widely with location and time, it is useful to lump them together and define quasi-minimum noise (QMN) as a practical minimum-noise design level. This level, expressed in dB, varies approximately log linearly from about 53 dB above thermal at 2 mHz to about 21 dB above thermal at 30 mHz. QMN serves as a floor to limit receiver sensitivity, for no matter how efficient the antenna, the signal-to-noise ratio is ultimately limited by the ratio of the field strength of the signal to that of the QMN. The antenna need only be efficient enough to ensure that the level of QMN delivered to the receiver is about equal to, or exceeds slightly, the receiver noise as determined by its noise figure. In fact, when a nearby transmitter is operating, it is desirable that the receiving antenna be as inefficient as permissible to limit the power coupled from the transmitter. QMN also functions as a useful limit of allowable transmitter interference to the receiver, as will be shown.

Simultaneous operation of one transmitter with one or more receivers

This is perhaps the most common simultaneous operation scenario. Interference to the receiver is due to performance limitations in both the receiving and the transmitting system. Receiving system limitations are caused by its nonlinearities, finite dynamic range, and synthesizer broadband noise and spurious outputs. Performance degradation is manifested in a number of different ways such as:

1. Overload and distortion in the adaptive canceler and/or the preselector
2. Receiver blocking, cross modulation, and intermodulation
3. Spurious mixer products
4. Reciprocal mixing of receiver synthesizer noise and spurious outputs into the IF passband by the transmitter signal
5. Transmitter broadband noise and spurious outputs
6. Transmitter harmonics and IM products

Each of these factors will be considered in turn.

Overload and distortion in the adaptive canceler.   An adaptive canceler operates by utilizing a sample of the transmitter output to cancel the transmitter signal induced in the receiving antenna. It does this by adjusting the phase and amplitude of the transmitter sample such that it is equal and opposite in phase to that picked up by the receiving antenna. Typically this may be done by deriving an in-phase and quadrature-phase signal from the transmitter sample and adjusting the amplitude and polarity of each, such that when recombined, the resulting signal has the same amplitude but opposite phase to that arriving from the receiving antenna. In producing the proper amplitude and phase of the canceling signal, care must be taken not to produce distortion products. Attenuators using positive-intrinsic-negative (PIN) diodes, although perhaps the lowest-distortion solid-state amplitude-control devices, are not immune to distortion generation when signal levels are very high, as for example when the transmitting and receiving antennas are aboard an aircraft. For this reason, applications for adaptive cancelers are presently somewhat limited, although current development work may lead to wider usage in the future. They have the advantages of being capable of broadband operation and, when combined with automatic fast-nulling circuitry, being useful for ECCM operation.

Overload and distortion in the preselector.   Modern HF receivers are generally designed with an untuned, broadband antenna input. The only protection against strong signals within the receiver's tuning range is an overload relay that typically operates at a level of around 0 dBw (1W). Thus when a receiver must operate simultaneously with a nearby high-powered transmitter within the receiver's tuning range, a frequency-selective receiver preselector may be employed to prevent the receiver overload relay from opening up and preventing reception. The preselector must have sufficient out-of-band signal-handling capability to prevent internal damage to itself, and it must have sufficient selectivity to protect the receiver from the effects of the transmitter signal. A purely passive preselector using no semiconductor components or magnetic core inductors would produce no distortion. Using varactor diodes for tuning, or PIN diodes for switching tuning elements, introduces a potential for distortion. Since varactor diodes introduce much more distortion than PIN diodes, they are seldom used as tuning elements of a preselector.

A preselector has a selectivity specification, a maximum voltage rating, and a distortion specification. A typical selectivity rating might be 40-dB minimum attenuation at 10 percent away from the passband. A 10 percent minimum frequency spacing between colocated transmitter and receiver is typical in many HF communication systems. If the receiver can withstand an interfering signal of -20 dBw, the allowable available transmitter power picked up by the receiving antenna is then $+20$ dBw or 100 W.

The allowable maximum voltage across the input terminals of the preselector might typically be 200 V rms, at 10 percent away. The maximum available power from the receiving antenna is then $P = E^2/4R_{ant}$. For a 50-ohm antenna, $P = (200)^2/(4 \times 50) = 200$ W.

Cross modulation in the preselector might be specified as a modulation transfer ratio for a certain level of interfering input. A typical specification might be a modulation transfer ratio of 0.316 (-10 dB) for a 50-V, 30-percent modulated interfering signal 10 percent from resonance. The available power from an antenna at which this occurs is then $P = E^2/4R_{ant} = 50^2/(4 \times 50) = 12.5$ W. This is much lower than the power the preselector can handle, 200 W, without damage. At an input level of 12.5 W ($+11$ dBw) the level of the preselector output is -29 dBw. To determine whether the system cross modulation is governed by the preselector or receiver, the receiver cross-modulation performance at an input level of -29 dBw must be known.

Receiver blocking, cross modulation, and intermodulation. All three of these effects are due to nonlinearities in the preselector and receiver. Most modern HF receivers use no RF amplification before the first mixer. The output of the mixer feeds a narrowband IF filter, protecting the rest of the receiver from interference by off-tune signals. Hence the first receiver mixer, and, possibly the following crystal filter, are primarily responsible for interference produced by the presence of the transmitting signal.

A typical good-quality HF receiver may have a third-order out-of-band intercept point (IP or ip) (see Chap. 3 for the definition of intercept point) of 0 dBw. The onset of blocking may be defined as the 1-dB compression point, and for a typical receiver with no RF amplification, the 1-dB compression point occurs at about 10 to 15 dB below the intercept point or around -10 to -15 dBw. When third-order nonlinearity predominates, the modulation transfer ratio

$$\frac{m'}{m} = \frac{4P_c}{P_{ip}}$$

where m' is the transferred modulation percentage, m is the modulation percentage of the interfering signal, P_c is the interfering power level that causes the specified modulation transfer ratio, and P_{ip} is the out-of-band intercept point. Setting $m'/m = 0.1$, as for the preselector, and $P_{ip} = 1$ W (0 dBw), $P_c = P_{ip}(m'/m)/4 = 1 \times 0.316/4 = 0.079$ W or -11 dBw. Since this is higher than the preselector output (-29 dBw) at the input level ($+11$ dBw) at which the preselector cross-modulates the specified amount, the preselector is the limiting factor in cross-modulation performance in this example. Nonetheless, it does provide for 22-dB greater interference-handling capability over that of the receiver alone.

Spurious mixer products. A receiver mixer produces not only the desired sum or difference frequency between the signal (f_1) and the synthesizer (f_2), but a multitude of products having frequencies of $|mf_1 \pm nf_2|$. For a given m, n, and f_2, other values of f_1 can be found that produce the same IF as when m and n are unity, as discussed in Chap. 3. Generally, the lower m and n, the stronger is the spurious response. Ideally such spurious responses should be no greater than the noise level in the IF bandwidth. A typical well-designed mixer might meet this criterion with an unwanted signal up to -40 dBw. If a preselector having 40-dB attenuation to the unwanted signal precedes such a mixer, the unwanted signal level from the receiving antenna could have a level up to 0 dBw.

Reciprocal mixing of receiver synthesizer noise into the IF passband.   When
a strong out-of-band signal feeds the receiver mixer, it can heterodyne noise
sidebands of the receiver synthesizer or local oscillator into the IF passband.
As shown in Fig. 2.34, this process, known as "reciprocal mixing," can appreciably degrade the signal-to-noise ratio if the interfering signal is sufficiently
strong or if the noise sidebands of the receiver synthesizers are not sufficiently attenuated.

Suppose we were to determine the level of an interfering signal that will
heterodyne synthesizer broadband noise into the IF passband at the same
level as that of the equivalent received noise consisting of that due to the
receiver noise figure plus QMN. Suppose that to minimize interference, the
receiving antenna system is such that the QMN noise level delivered to the
receiver equals the receiver noise level. This would result in an increase in
effective receiver noise figure of 3 dB. A typical receiver noise figure might
be 12 dB, so that the sum of receiver noise and QMN is 15 dB above thermal.
The synthesizer noise sidebands vary with distance from their output frequency, but typically fall off to a shelf level which is more or less constant
beyond a certain frequency separation. This separation may vary depending
upon the loop bandwidth of the synthesizer, which is a function of the loop
settling time (see Chap. 9). In any case, assume the separation is adequate
to ensure that the noise shelf has been reached. A typical good synthesizer
design might have a noise-power density (noise power per hertz bandwidth)
150 dB below the carrier, or as usually expressed, -150 dBc/Hz.

Since the thermal noise level at room temperature is about -204 dBw/Hz,
the equivalent receiver noise is 15 dB above this or -189 dBw/Hz. To heterodyne this amount of noise into the receiver IF requires an interfering sig-

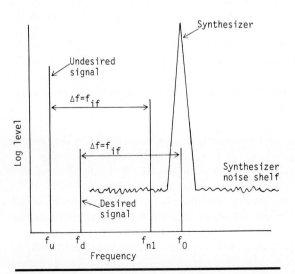

Figure 2.34   Reciprocal mixing mechanism.
$f_{if} = f_0 - f_d = f_{n1} - f_u$.

nal 150 dB stronger, or -39 dBw. If the receiver front end is broadband, this is the level of interference that will cause the equivalent receiver noise to increase 3 dB. Note that if the preselector of the previous example is used, 40 dB of attenuation is provided for an interfering signal 10 percent away. Preceding the receiver with such a preselector increases the allowable level of the interfering signal a like amount, to $+1$ dBw. If the interfering transmitter has a power of 1000 W ($+30$ dBw), 29-dB attenuation is required between the transmitter output and the preselector input to reduce the interference to this level.

Transmitter broadband noise.   Most HF transmitters consist of an exciter followed by a power amplifier. Modern HF solid-state amplifiers operate broadband, without tuned circuits that would progressively attenuate noise at frequencies away from the signal. Hence noise from the exciter and PA can extend over a wide range, as shown in Fig. 2.35, unless some selective filtering is provided. Noise from the exciter comes primarily from two sources, synthesizer noise sidebands that are translated to the transmitted output signal, and broadband amplifier noise following the last IF filter in the exciter. The noise contribution from each of these sources must be added to determine the overall noise level.

Suppose the exciter synthesizer has the same S/N_0 characterization as that used in the receiver in the previous example, and suppose the mixer signal output level is -40 dBw. Then its output noise-power-density level is 150 dB below this, or -190 dBw/Hz. Suppose further that the noise figure of the entire amplifier chain following the mixer is 10 dB. Then its equivalent noise input is -194 dBw. Since noise powers add, the equivalent noise level at the amplifier input is -188.5 dBw/Hz, so that the S/N_0 ratio is 148.5 dB/Hz. Now suppose the transmitter output is 1 kW ($+30$ dBw). Then the

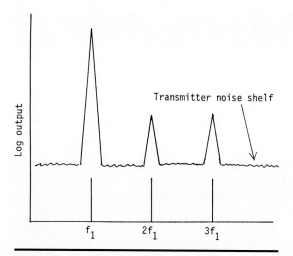

Figure 2.35   Transmitter output spectrum.

output noise-power density is −118.5 dBw/Hz. Since the noise-power density is presumed to exist at the receiver frequency, no receiver selectivity can aid in reducing it. To reduce the transmitter noise level to the equivalent receiver noise level, including QMN, of −189 dBw/Hz, 70.5 dB of attenuation is required between the transmitter output and the receiver input. This attenuation is the sum of space loss, antenna gains, and antenna mismatch losses.

Next consider the effect of using a passive postselector. To obtain quantitative results, we will assume that the postselector has 40-dB attenuation 10 percent away from resonance, that the exciter output level is −10 dBw, the postselector loss on-frequency is 5 dB, and the PA noise figure following the postselector is 15 dB. Since the mixer output level was −40 dBw, the gain to the postselector output is $-5 + [-10 - (-40)] = 25$ dB. Hence the noise output of the postselector is -188.5 dBw/Hz $+ 25 - 40 = -203.5$ dBw/Hz at 10 percent away from resonance. This is so much less than the equivalent input PA noise ($-204 + 15 = -189$ dBw/Hz) that it may be neglected. The PA gain for 1-kW output is $30 - (-15) = 45$ dB. Thus the PA output noise level is $-189 + 45 = -134$ dBw/Hz, which is 15.5 dB less than if no postselector were used. Hence, for the same level of transmitter noise at the receiver input, 15.5-dB less attenuation or 55-dB attenuation is required. If we wish the effects of transmitter broadband noise and that due to reciprocal mixing to be the same, 26-dB additional selectivity must be added after the PA.

Transmitter harmonics and IM products.   When the transmitter output signal contains more than one frequency, intermodulation products between the various frequencies can be formed. With two frequencies f_1 and f_2, the IM products and harmonics are located at $|mf_1 \pm nf_2|$, where m and n are any integers, including zero. The amplitude of these products is determined by the amount and kind of nonlinearity. Class A amplifiers, for example, can have lower distortion levels than that of class AB amplifiers, and generally their higher-order products drop off in amplitude at a higher rate. Because of the lower signal levels in the exciter, it is seldom the limiting factor in determining the transmitter distortion. This is even more true if a postselector is used to attenuate wideband noise and harmonics. Since solid-state amplifiers are inherently broadband, solid-state PAs seldom employ tuned circuits. To attenuate harmonic and sum intermodulation products, low-pass or bandpass filters are used instead. The filters are often arranged to cover a frequency range of about $\sqrt{2}$. This ensures that at the lowest edge of the band in use, there is enough spectral space to gain sufficient attenuation to the second harmonic, which then lies at a frequency ratio of $\sqrt{2}$ beyond the upper edge of the band in use. Levels of distortion in the transmitter are such that it is seldom considered feasible to attenuate harmonics and sum intermodulation distortion products to the same level as transmitter broadband noise, say in a 3-kHz bandwidth. Considering the previous example, even without the postselector, the output noise density of −118.5 dBw/Hz corresponds to a noise power in a 3-kHz bandwidth of −83.7 dBw, or a level −113.7 dB below the 1-kW transmitter rated output. Harmonic levels are specified at a level considerably higher, with the expectation that a colocated receiver will not simultaneously operate at transmitter harmonic frequencies. Specified harmonic levels vary, depending upon application, but second and third harmonic requirements may typically range between 40 and 90 dB below the fundamental frequency.

Simultaneous operation of more than one transmitter with one or more receivers

When two nearby transmitters are operating simultaneously, in addition to the receiver problems caused by each transmitter operating independently, an additional source of potential interference is caused by back-intermodulation distortion produced by two transmitters coupling to each other and/ or by IM distortion produced in the preselector or receiver, as shown in Fig. 2.36.

In the case of two transmitters, like the IM products produced by a single power amplifier, the distortion level depends on the degree of amplifier nonlinearity, and again, class A amplifiers show considerably less back-IM distortion than class AB amplifiers. Besides the problem of IM distortion generation, power coupled between transmitters appears as reflected power and may result in power turndown by standing wave ratio (SWR) protection circuits. The presence of the two strong transmitter signals at the receiver or preselector input can also produce IM products, the level of which depends

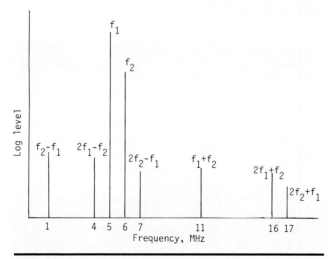

Figure 2.36 Low-order intermodulation products from two frequencies.

upon the input signal levels and the intercept points (see Chap. 3) for the various orders of distortion.

At any rate, the location of transmitter harmonics and intermodulation frequencies is predictable since they occur at integral multiples of the sums and differences of the two transmitter frequencies, e.g.,

$$|mf_1 \pm nf_2|$$

for all integer values of m and n, including zero.

In principle, then, it is possible to determine sets of transmitter frequencies f_1 and f_2 and the receiver frequency f_3 such that f_3 avoids transmitter harmonic and intermodulation frequencies. IM products do not fall between the transmitter frequencies. Hence it is possible to operate the receiver between the transmitter frequencies without interference if transmitter harmonic regions are avoided, and as long as the separation from such transmitter frequencies is sufficient to avoid cross-modulation, IM products of each transmitter separately, transmitter broadband noise, and reciprocal mixing noise. Similarly, there are gaps between different orders of IM products that might also be used by the receiver.

Under conditions where it is difficult or impossible to avoid interference because of back-IM products, further filtering may be employed at the PA output to reduce those products. Reduction of back-IM products is helped both by the additional reduction in fundamental power coupled to the PA from the other transmitter and by the further reduction of generated IM products by the selectivity of the filter.

2.3   ECCM Design Considerations

One of the reasons for renewed interest in HF communications, particularly by the military services, is their use as a backup system for satellite communications. To provide a measure of privacy, secrecy and antijam capability, several schemes for spectrum-spreading the signal have been proposed. Two basic types of spread-spectrum signals have gained wide acceptance. One of these involves using a pseudo-noise (PN) code operating at high speed to switch the carrier phase at rates typically in the megahertz range. This produces a white-noise-like signal occupying several megahertz of bandwidth. Because of the wide bandwidth, the power density of this direct-spread signal is quite low, creating a minimum amount of interference to conventional narrowband signals in the band.

The second type of spread-spectrum signal in wide use utilizes frequency hopping over the band to spread the spectrum. The frequency-hopping rate may vary from a few per second to thousands per second. Where the RF band occupancy is high, such as in the HF band, this is often the preferred ECCM method, because by proper choice of frequencies, strong fixed-channel stations in the band and interference to friendly signals can be avoided.

A combination of the two methods, using a limited amount of direct-sequence bandspreading along with frequency-hopping, may also be employed.

Since the subject of this book is single-sideband systems and circuits, a comprehensive discussion of ECCM communication is beyond its scope, but those aspects that touch upon the design of SSB radio equipment often employed in ECCM communication will be covered. However, a discussion of modems and ECCM controllers, including selection of frequency-hop sequences and synchronization, is beyond the scope of this book. Some useful introductions to spread-spectrum techniques are given in Refs. 21 through 23.

Frequency-hopping single sideband

When frequency hopping is employed, there exists the possibility of direct transmission of the analog SSB voice signal without digital encoding. While not providing the voice privacy of which digital encoding is capable, there may be applications where hopping the analog signal alone is sufficient.

Several potential problems exist when an attempt is made to frequency-hop an analog voice signal. To some extent these are common to all frequency-hopped signals, but those most directly applicable to analog SSB voice transmission are synthesizer switching speed, phase discontinuities, and AGC.

During the time the synthesizer is switching from one frequency to another, the analog voice signal is lost. The effect this has on voice intelligibility depends both upon the percentage of time that the signal is lost and the length of time of the lost segment. Ideally the length of time of a lost segment should not exceed that of the shortest voice sound, or phoneme. Practically, this means that the longest gap should not exceed about 20 to 40 ms. The percentage of time that the signal is lost should not exceed about 20 percent, or the signal will sound excessively chopped up. If, then, 20 ms represents the frequency transition period and this occurs 20 percent of the time, the hop rate is 10 per second, represented by 80-ms segments of the voice signal separated by 20-ms gaps.

It is, of course, possible to design synthesizers to switch frequencies much faster than 20 ms, and this then raises the possibility of faster SSB voice frequency hopping. In the laboratory, using the same synthesizer for the transmitter and receiver, it is possible to demonstrate excellent SSB voice transmissions using hop rates of thousands per second. In practice, however, when separate transmitter and receiver synthesizers are used, very close tracking of the phase of the two oscillators must occur or there will be corresponding phase discontinuities in the SSB voice signal when switching frequencies. These are not of great importance at low hop rates with considerable dead time between the hop periods, because the correlation between adjacent speech signals on either side of the dead period is small. As the dead period becomes shorter, however, the correlation between adjacent transmitted speech segments increases. Phase discontinuities in the signal tend to destroy this correlation.

Even if the transmitter and receiver synthesizers track phase perfectly, phase discontinuities in the demodulated speech may result from differences in the propagation of the different hop frequencies. The problem is particularly severe with skywave propagation, where differences in propagation paths can completely destroy any phase coherence of the signal between hops.

The third problem with a hopping SSB voice signal is that of varying received signal strength at the different hop frequencies. Again the problem is worst for skywave or for any multipath propagation. This problem is also more severe at high hop rates. It is very desirable to have the AGC stabilize in a short fraction of the on-time of the hop period. At the same time, it is desirable to have the AGC remain constant during the on-time so as not to further modulate the signal envelope, and also have it be capable of fast readjustment to the required AGC voltage for the next hop period. At low hop rates, the AGC design need not be much different than for conventional SSB voice receivers, but at high hop rates, the attack time would have to be much faster, and the problem of rapid readjustment of the AGC voltage up or down, as required for the next hop period, is more severe.

Thus, although further experimentation with higher hop rates for specialized communication scenarios might lead to different conclusions, for general-purpose HF analog voice SSB communications, hop rates higher than around 10 per second are impractical.

Where the excision of the portion of the speech between frequency hops is objectionable, a method exists to eliminate this dead period at the expense of more circuit complexity, a total time delay of at least two hop periods, and a wider transmitted bandwidth, as follows. The speech wave is divided into segments equal to the hop period. Each segment in turn is filtered, sampled, digitized, and stored. The stored digitized speech segment is then read out of memory at a faster rate to correspond with the on-time of the hop period. It is reconverted to an analog signal, filtered, and used as the baseband signal to modulate the transmitter during the on-time of its hop period. Meanwhile the next speech segment is similarly processed. Since the stored speech is read out faster than it was stored, all its frequency components are increased by the ratio of the total hop period to the hop-period on-time, so that if there is a 20 percent dead time, the bandwidth of the transmitted signal is increased by a ratio of 1/0.8, or an increase of 25 percent. At the receiver, the analog signal is again sampled, digitized, and stored. It is then read out of memory at a rate corresponding to the total hop period and reconverted to an analog signal. The reconstructed segment then occupies the same time span as the original, and the speech frequencies return to their correct pitches. In the meantime the next component speech signal is being received, digitized, and stored. This procedure can virtually eliminate the speech signals otherwise lost during the synthesizer switching time. The phase discontinuity problem still exists, but at low hop rates is not likely to be severe.

Equipment design considerations

When designing radio equipment for frequency hopping, factors that must be taken into account beyond that of conventional equipment design include:

1. Synthesizer switching speed
2. Spectrum splatter
3. Receiver AGC
4. Bandwidth of receiver front end
5. Bandwidth of transmitter amplifier stages
6. Antenna and antenna coupler bandwidth

Synthesizer switching speed. The required synthesizer switching speed depends upon the maximum hop rate desired. In order to preserve the maximum amount of energy per hop, it is desirable to have the synthesizer settle quickly at the new frequency after the command to change frequency is given. If 1-dB loss in energy is allowable, the maximum switching period is about 20 percent of the hop period. Synthesizer switching speed is discussed in Chap. 9, "Synthesizers for SSB."

Spectrum splatter. Spectrum splatter is a transient phenomenon that occurs when the frequency is changed. For a pulse of constant amplitude A and length T, the spectrum has the form

$$G(f) = AT \frac{\sin \pi Tf}{\pi Tf} \tag{2.56}$$

If such a pulse modulates a constant frequency f_1, the spectrum $G(f)$ is translated to f_1, with f in the expression for $G(f)$ replaced by Δf, where $\Delta f = f - f_1$. If f_1 changes each time period, as in a frequency-hopping signal, the spectrum becomes the sum of the spectra of all the pulses. If the frequencies are produced by switching back and forth between a pair of oscillators, there will generally be no phase correlation between them, and the spectrum around each hopping frequency will drop off as $1/\Delta f$ as given above. This is typical of the spectrum of a discontinuous function. If the function itself is continuous, but has a discontinuous first derivative, the spectrum drops off as $1/(\Delta f)^2$, and in general, continuity of the function and its first m derivatives guarantees that the spectrum will eventually drop off as $1/(\Delta f)^{m+1}$. However, the frequency separation at which the ultimate dropoff first occurs may vary so that for a given transition time between adjacent hopped frequencies and a given Δf, the spectrum may not always be lower for the transition having the highest number of continuous derivatives.

Phase continuity results if the same oscillator is used to generate a changing frequency without stopping and restarting each time the frequency is changed. However, the slewing of the oscillator adds to the generated spectrum. Also, if the frequency must be changed very frequently, it may be necessary to widen the frequency-control-loop bandwidth to a point where synthesizer wideband noise is excessive. It then may become necessary to switch alternately between a pair of synthesizers, each of which is allowed an entire hop period to stabilize at the new frequency. As indicated above, this leads to a $1/\Delta f$ spectrum roll off. In order to produce a faster spectrum rolloff, pulse shaping may be used. Its disadvantage, of course, is that it reduces not only the spectral components, but also the total power in the pulse. For example, a cosine squared (or raised cosine) pulse shape as shown in Fig. 2.37 has the spectrum

$$G_1(f) = \frac{AT}{2} \frac{\sin \pi Tf}{\pi Tf[1 - (Tf)^2]} \tag{2.57}$$

By comparison with the spectrum of a rectangular pulse [Eq. (2.56)], the average amplitude of the raised cosine pulse is half that of the rectangular pulse of the same peak amplitude A and time duration T. A comparison of the spectra of the two pulses shows that except for the factor ½ from the cosine squared pulse, the two numerators are the same. Comparing the denominators, it is seen that the cosine squared pulse spectrum eventually drops off as $1/f^3$ [or $1/(\Delta f)$ for a pulse-modulated sine wave]. This agrees with the conclusion drawn from the fact that the function and its first derivative are continuous for a single raised cosine pulse. At $Tf = 0.5$ the denominator of the rectangular pulse is 0.5π, while that of the raised cosine pulse is $0.5\pi(1 - 0.25) = 0.375\pi$. Relative to their amplitudes at $f = 0$, the cosine pulse spectrum at $Tf = 0.5$ is 1.5 times greater than that of the rectangular pulse, illustrating that for close-in spectra, the modulating waveform with the higher number of continuous higher-order derivatives may not have the

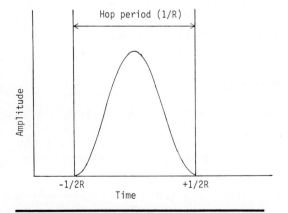

Figure 2.37 Raised cosine window.

highest attenuation. At $Tf = \frac{5}{2}$, however, the denominator of the rectangular pulse is $5\pi/2$, while that of the raised cosine pulse is $5\pi/2[1 - 2.5^2] = 5\pi/2[-5.25]$. Thus the relative amplitude of the raised cosine pulse at $Tf = \frac{5}{2}$ is a factor of 2.625 lower than that of the rectangular pulse, and its phase is inverted as well.

Many other pulse modulation shapes may be used. A compehensive analysis of the spectrum of a number of these is discussed in Ref. 24. Most of those in the cited reference, however, were evaluated on the basis of the spectral width of the main lobe and the strength of close-in spectral side lobes rather than on their ultimate rate of spectral dropoff.

Shaping the pulse may be done at any point in the transmitter where its shape will not be further distorted before transmission. Thus, in an exciter employing frequency translation, it should not be done before stages having selective circuits at their output, since these can stretch the shaped pulse so that its amplitude is not zero when the synthesizer changes frequency. Suitable places for the shaper would be just before or just after the last mixer that translates the IF frequency to the RF band, as shown in Fig. 2.38.

The shaper is basically a modulator. The desired modulating waveform may be stored in a read-only memory (ROM) that is read out to a digital-to-analog (D/A) converter synchronously with changes in frequency. Compensation can be made in the stored waveform for modulator nonlinearities and any D/A converter output filtering required.

Shaping is also desirable in the front end of a hopping receiver. A process similar to that in the exciter can create spectrum splatter at the desired signal frequency from undesired signals on nearby frequencies. In the presence of a strong off-tune signal at its input, when a rectangular pulse of oscillator voltage is applied to the mixer, a rectangular modulated pulse of the translated undesired signal results at the mixer output, displaced from the IF by the amount of its frequency offset from the desired frequency. The spectrum of such a pulse can extend to the IF passband, where it interferes with the desired signal. Preshaping the RF, by modulating it before or just after the mixer but before IF selectivity, as shown in Fig. 2.39, with a pulse shape like that of the exciter has the same effect on reducing the spectrum produced by the interference as it does on the exciter spectrum.

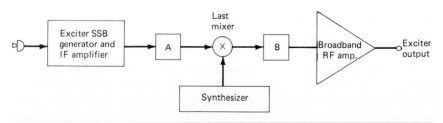

Figure 2.38 Exciter hopping pulse shaping modulator may be located at points A or B

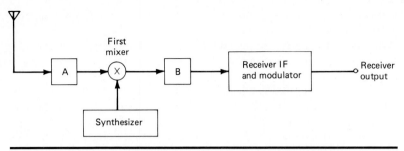

Figure 2.39 Receiver hopping pulse shaping modulator may be located at points *A* or *B*.

Receiver AGC. Because of the differing atmospheric attenuation at different frequencies, a received frequency hopping signal is subject to change in amplitude from hop to hop. It is desirable to level out these changes in amplitude before detection. A simple way to do this for a constant amplitude data signal is by means of a limiter. For a weak signal, limiting degrades the signal-to-noise ratio slightly, but the simplicity of the method commends its use where the ultimate performance is not required.

If the best possible weak-signal performance is required, AGC must be used and adjusted to its proper level on a hop-by-hop basis. In the usual closed-loop feedback type of AGC, this requires that the AGC loop stabilize within a small fraction of the dwell period. Normally the RF pulse will be shaped to reduce the spectral splatter, and the detector and its matched filter will be designed to give the best output signal-to-noise ratio with that shaped pulse. A fast-acting AGC will try to undo this shaping. What is needed is a way to preset the AGC at each hop frequency so that the pulse shape is retained and the output is constant from hop to hop. The proper gain control voltage for each frequency can be approximated by averaging the required AGC voltages for past dwell periods on that frequency. This could be accomplished as follows. An AGC storage memory location is provided for each frequency. Initially it is zeroed. The AGC time constant is such that it allows the proper AGC voltage to be reached at the end of the dwell period. This value is digitized and stored. At the next frequency location the AGC voltage again starts from zero and its final value is stored, and so on for all frequencies. The next time the same frequency is encountered, the stored AGC voltage for that frequency is applied. However, the AGC voltage is allowed to readjust itself up or down. At the end of that dwell period the final AGC voltage is averaged with the initially applied value and stored as the new value for that frequency. This method gives the most weight to the most recent AGC value, and weighs preceding sample values less and less the further they are removed from the present sample. When the receiver gain is controlled in this manner, on a hop-by-hop basis, each controlled stage must have a rapid response time so that the gain can be stabilized quickly each hop period.

Bandwidth of receiver front end.   HF receivers that employ broadband front ends are favored for ECCM since there are no RF circuits that need to track the hopping signal. As will be seen in Chap. 3, this fits in well with modern receiver design unless a preselector is used. If a preselector is employed, either it must be a broadband type that covers all the hopping frequencies in one band, or it must be capable of tuning rapidly between frequencies. For slow hopping speeds, relay-switched tuning elements can be used, but rapid frequency changes require the use of electronic rather than mechanical tuning. A further discussion of preselectors is found in Chap. 8.

Bandwidth of transmitter amplifier stages.   Broadband amplifier stages are preferred for ECCM, again because there are no RF-tuned circuits that need to track the hopping signal. Fortunately wideband amplifiers are easily designed using solid-state amplifiers. However, a problem that occurs with broadband amplifiers is that wideband noise is amplified together with the signal, as discussed in Sec. 2.2. Since this noise can cause interference to nearby receivers, it is desirable to suppress it. Much of this noise may be suppressed by a postselector placed between the exciter and power amplifier. At this power level, often in the range 0.1 to 1 W, the power is low enough that a common design for the postselector and preselector may be used. As for the preselector, the design may be either broadband to cover all the hopping frequencies in one band, or narrowband to tune rapidly between frequencies. For further attenuation of noise outside the hopping band, a wideband filter covering just the hopping band might be used at the transmitter output.

Antenna and antenna coupler bandwidth.   A broadband antenna is desirable for ECCM transmission, since this eases the burden on the antenna coupler. The antenna SWR can be further reduced by using wideband matching networks.

When the antenna bandwidth is narrow, it is desirable to tune it with the coupler to present the proper load to the power amplifier. If the hop rate is low, such a coupler may be digitally tuned using fast-acting relays. The limited lifetimes and response times of relays make it desirable to look for better switches. The solid-state switch offering the most promise is the PIN diode, because of its fast switching speed, relatively low distortion, and almost unlimited lifetime if operated within its ratings. Some of the biggest problems to date in employing PIN diodes for couplers are their limited power-handling capability, the high dc voltage required to back-bias "off" diodes, and the relatively high forward current for the "on" diodes. The switching of these high voltages and currents to the diodes at fast hop rates and the RF interference caused by the sudden application and removal of these high voltages and currents is also a potential problem. With currently (1987) available PIN diodes it is possible to construct frequency hopping couplers in the 100- to 1000-W range, depending upon the antenna impedance characteristics.

A further discussion of antenna couplers is given in Chap. 16.

2.4 Communication-Link Design

System design tradeoff considerations

There are many factors which can be "traded off" in the process of arriving at the most effective system design for HF communications. Some of the parameters in the system design which can be varied in the tradeoff process are listed here:

- Signal-to-noise-density ratio for required quality of service, i.e., voice quality or data bit error rate (BER), SN_0R_R, dB-Hz

- Data transmission rate R, bits/s

- Transmit-power-amplifier output level P_t, dBW

- Transmit-antenna coupler loss L_c, dB

- Transmit-antenna gain, "takeoff" angle, and efficiency G_t, dB

- Receive-antenna gain G_r, dB

- Receiver noise figure

- Modulation type and parameters

- Demodulation and processing type and parameters

- Source and channel coding types and level

- Propagation loss (groundwave vs. skywave mode) L_p, dB

- Miscellaneous cabling, distortion, and intermodulation losses L_m, dB

- Received external (atmospheric and artificially created) noise density N_0, dBW/Hz

Illustrations of specific tradeoffs are given in several of the references; see Refs. 25 through 27, for example.

The received external noise can generally be assumed to be independent of the receive-antenna gain, based on an approximately uniform distribution of noise in the space surrounding the receive antenna. Furthermore, good receiver design will provide a receiver noise figure such that the noise internal to the receiver can be neglected compared with the rather high level of external HF noise. Using the above-defined symbols for the terms, it is readily apparent that the *available* signal-to-noise-density ratio at the input to the receiver, SN_0R_A, is (in decibel notation):

$$SN_0R_A = P_t - L_c + G_t - L_p + G_r - L_m - N_0 \quad \text{dB-Hz} \quad (2.58)$$

Thus, the objective of HF system design is to choose the system parameters such that SN_0R_A equals or exceeds the required signal-to-noise density SN_0R_R a sufficient percentage of the time (over the distribution of environmental and temporal factors to be considered) such that the desired system reliability can be achieved with reasonable confidence. The choices of parameter values such as required quality of service, data-transmission rate, modulation, demodulation, processing and error-correction coding types, and configurations all impact the required SN_0R_R for the service to be provided.

Many of the system design factors (that is, equipment performance parameters) are described and analyzed in detail elsewhere in this text. Guidelines for HF antenna design and/or characterization can be found in several of the references (Refs. 26 and 28 through 31, as examples). The topic of HF radiowave propagation is fairly complex and is treated extensively in Refs. 32 through 35.

Use of propagation/link-performance predictions (forecasts)

An overview of prediction techniques is provided by several of the references (see Ref. 36, for instance). Methods of HF radiowave propagation and link-performance predictions can be categorized for practical application purposes by the type of computational tools employed: manual methods, micro/minicomputer-based methods, and large, mainframe-computer-based methods. Examples of these categories are discussed here. Only the latter method is actually illustrated in the system design example given.

Manual methods were the first-used approach to radiowave propagation predictions. These methods generally employ charts, nomographs, and/or tables of propagation and noise statistical parameters. Use is made of overlays on a specially constructed map of the earth so that geographical (latitude and longitude) effects on propagation can be taken into account by laying out the great-circle propagation path. Examples of manual propagation-prediction techniques are given in Refs. 25, 32, 33, and 37 through 40. Graphical presentations of expected atmospheric radio noise are available [41] for use in manual link analysis. These data are also employed in the form of a data base in the automated methods using computers. Manual methods are rarely used for commercial design of HF communications systems because of the length of time and expense of manual effort required to consider the multitude of possible design combinations, especially for a system or network with a large number of possible point-to-point or mobile-terminus paths.

In recent years, simplified approaches to computer prediction of ionospheric-mode(s) propagating frequencies, maximum usable frequency (MUF), and, to some extent, propagation loss have been developed. These tools are intended more for operational (day-by-day) use than for large-system design applications. In general, they were developed for military applications, although they are now widely applied to other uses as well. They can be employed on minicomputers or even on desk-top microcomputer-based processors. The primary examples of these small-computer-based tools are the computer programs MINIMUF and PROPHET [42, 43]. (Because of their original government development and the wide proliferation of a number of versions of these programs, especially MINIMUF, applications support for their use may be difficult to obtain.)

The current U.S. standard large-computer propagation and system-performance prediction program is IONCAP, developed by the U.S. Department of Commerce [26]. Other versions of large, mainframe computer programs for the same purposes are available elsewhere from international agencies (see Ref. 37, for example).

Example of system design

As an example of a typical HF SSB system design process, a circuit from Cedar Rapids, IA, to Hong Kong is considered. This circuit has a great-circle path length of nearly 12,500 km (about one-third the circumference of the earth), demonstrating the potential of HF SSB systems for long-haul communications. It illustrates the care and tradeoffs required in selecting power levels, antenna types, frequency assignments, and operational procedures/tools for a long-haul circuit. As one might expect, reliable ionospheric sky-wave communications are not always available on a circuit of this type, and operating frequencies and contact times must be selected judiciously.

The propagation- and performance-prediction tool chosen in illustrating the design process is the IONCAP computer program. There are several "methods" of analysis available in using this program, which provide versatility in the types and forms of outputs available from the analysis, only a few of which are illustrated here. Also, some data-reduction/presentation tools which make use of the IONCAP outputs are utilized here to facilitate rapid processing and condensation of the outputs into summarized form. (These latter tools have been developed within Rockwell International Corp. for on-line and off-line application of a microcomputer terminal to the reduction process.)

The IONCAP program method chosen to begin the system design in this case is called Method 16. The first step is to run some sample month and sunspot-number combinations for hypothetical ideal "isotropic" antennas (i.e., antennas with uniform gain in all directions of spherical space). Thus, the antennas are first modeled as lossless radiators (collectors) having a constant gain vs. elevation angle and azimuth angle of 0 dBi (gain relative to that of a reference isotropic antenna). Knowing that this path length is quite long (just over 12,000 km) and that a minimum of three maximum-length (4000-km) "hops" will normally be required, a relatively high power level of 10 kW is initially assumed.

Also, since long hops are involved, the trial operating frequencies are initially chosen in the 8- to 26-MHz portion of the band, rather than in the 2- to 10-MHz spectrum normally associated with short path lengths. If higher or lower frequencies are required, the initial predictions will indicate this by the occurrences of MUFs outside the chosen band for some times of day (TOD) and/or month-sunspot combinations.

Another input factor to be chosen in the performance analysis is the required signal-to-noise-density ratio SN_0R_R. The value of SN_0R_R used in the analysis must be chosen very carefully, with due consideration for fading and atmospheric-noise effects on the demodulation integrity/fidelity, as a few dB variation in its value can cause a substantial variation in the predicted (and experienced) system performance. The required value is derived from the earlier Sec. 2.1 results as follows. Assume that 90 percent intelligibility of words from a 256-word vocabulary is required, which is adequate for operator-to-operator ("order-wire") communications. From Fig. 2.1, this requires an articulation index of approximately 0.36. From Fig. 2.32 (extrapolated), SSB operations with speech preemphasis in the presence of two-path multipath fading requires a P_{avg}/N_0 of approximately 41 dB-Hz for an AI of 0.36. In systems analyses, transmitted power levels (and hence received signal power levels) are usually specified in terms of peak envelope power. In comparing Figs. 2.29 and 2.30, it is noted that, for an AI of 0.36, the difference between the required PEP/N_0 and P_{avg}/N_0 is 7 dB. Thus, using the results from Sec. 2.1, the required value to be used here is given by

$$SN_0R_R = PEP/N_0 = 41 + 7 = 48 \text{ dB-Hz} \qquad (2.59)$$

(This is also the value specified in the IONCAP user's manual [26] for operator-to-operator-quality grade of service for 90 percent intelligibility of related words for nondiversity, SSB, suppressed-carrier communications.)

If higher-quality commercial-grade voice communications or high-speed digital-data transmission is to be provided, a significantly higher value of SN_0R_R must be used in the analysis to provide a realistic system-performance prediction. The specification of SN_0R_R for representative data systems is beyond the scope of this section; examples for typical data-modulation schemes are given in Refs. 26, 27, and 44.

Another input parameter to be chosen judiciously is the approximate level of artificially created electrical (RF) noise density at the receiving sites. A value of -148 dBW/Hz (specified at 3 MHz, with a known rolloff in level with increasing frequency) is used in this system design example. This is typical of levels experienced in rural or suburban locations [26]. Thus, the location assumed here is that of a typical station situated at the outskirts of a residential area, away from large industrial plants and heavily traveled highways. [Somewhat higher (typically $+12$-dB) levels are experienced in industrial urban areas and lower (typically -16-dB) values are found in remote, unpopulated areas.] Atmospheric noise tends to dominate at the lower frequencies and at nighttime, while artificial noise can dominate at the higher frequencies, especially in daytime. It is readily apparent that the predicted performance of the system is directly dependent on the *total* RF noise density (atmospheric and artificial) N_0 at the receiver site. The IONCAP program contains a data base of expected atmospheric-noise levels as a function of location (latitude and longitude), season of year, and time of day. It sums the expected atmospheric-noise level for a receiver location with the value of artificially made noise at the frequency of the calculation, based on the value specified at 3 MHz.

Typical values of the month and sunspot-activity level must be chosen for the initial analysis, as conducting the analysis for all possible month-sunspot combinations is excessively lengthy and expensive and unnecessary. Predictions for June and December (the solar solstice months) and for sunspot number (SSN) values of 10 and 130 essentially "bracket" the expected variations in propagation conditions and are adequate for system design purposes [44]. A slightly more conservative value for maximum SSN of 110 is used in this example. Also, predictions for an SSN of 60 are included to represent the long-term solar-cycle average conditions. The maximum practical time interval between times of day for which the analysis is performed is 4 h. Because the circuit under consideration is a difficult one and careful, detailed selection of TOD for reliable operations is required, the example analysis is conducted here for all 24 h of the day (at intervals of 1 h).

As described above, initial system-performance predictions are made using Method 16 for isotropic antennas at both locations. Figure 2.40 shows a sample tabulated output for this case for one month (June) and one SSN (10) for three selected hours of the day ("universal time," or UT, which is the same as "Greenwich mean time," or GMT). (In some of the figures which follow, the time is also indicated by LMT, the "local mean time" at the transmitter.) The results shown in the first full column of the figure are for the MUF frequency, indicated on the top line of the column for each TOD. The results for the "frequency of optimum transmission/traffic," or FOT (nominally about 85 percent of the MUF), are shown in the second column. The results for each even integer frequency from 8 to 26 MHz are shown in the remaining columns in each TOD block.

Several calculated results are tabulated for each frequency for each hour. MODE indicates the skywave propagation mode (layer) for the transmit-end hop and the receive-end hop, respectively. Similarly, ANGLE indicates the wave-path "takeoff angle" (elevation angle) for the two ends of the path. (There may be other hop modes in addition to those indicated at the transmitter and receiver, especially for a path of this great length.) DELAY is the calculated value of propagation time, in milliseconds, for the path of the modes shown. F DAYS is the probability that the specific frequency listed will be exceeded by the predicted MUF, indicating the fraction of days in the month that propagation by these modes is expected (in a statistical sense) at a given frequency for the tabulated time of day. LOSS is the median system loss in dB for the most reliable mode, and DBU is the median field strength expected at the receiver location in dB above 1 μV/m. S DBW and N DBW are, respectively, the median signal and noise-power-density levels expected at the receiver input terminals in dB above a watt. The difference between these values is the available signal-to-noise-density ratio, shown as SNR, in dB-Hz.

The results of primary interest are the communications reliability values (REL) listed in the last line in each TOD block. Each of these values is essentially the probability that the required SN_0R_R of 48 dB-Hz will be exceeded (provided) by the available SN_0R_A over the month, for this TOD for the frequency listed. The calculated result termed RPWRG is the required dB power gain in the system needed to obtain SN_0R_R for a specified percent of time (REQ. REL), 90 percent in this figure. It is seen that only at the frequencies where the predicted reliability, REL, is already moderately high is

```
                         METHOD 16    IONCAP  78.03    PAGE   5

            JUN                      SSN =  10.
CEDAR RAPIDS,IA TO HONG KONG                AZIMUTHS        N. MI.         KM
42.00 N    91.50 W - 22.00 N   114.10 E   334.45   20.23  6709.6  12425.3
                               MINIMUM ANGLE   1.0  DEGREES
ITS- 1 ANTENNA PACKAGE
XMTR   2.0  TO  30.0  CONST. GAIN  H   0.00 L    0.00 A    0.0  OFF AZ    0.0
RCVR   2.0  TO  30.0  CONST. GAIN  H   0.00 L    0.00 A    0.0  OFF AZ    0.0
POWER =  10.000 KW  3 MHZ NOISE = -148.0 DBW  REQ. REL = .90  REQ. SNR = 48.0


  UT   MUF

13.0 13.7 11.9  8.0 10.0 12.0 14.0 16.0 18.0 20.0 22.0 24.0 26.0 FREQ
     F2F2 F1F2  EF2 F1F2 F1F2 F2F2 F2F2 F2F2 F2F2 F2F2 F2F2 F2F2 MODE
      5.4 10.0  1.0 10.0 10.0  4.3  8.1  8.1  8.1  8.1  8.1  8.1 ANGLE
     14.0 14.0 14.0 14.0 14.0 14.0 12.0  3.0  1.0  8.1  8.1  8.1 ANGLE
     44.2 43.5 42.6 43.3 43.6 44.2 44.0 43.8 43.8 44.3 44.3 44.3 DELAY
     415. 302. 177. 260. 311. 420. 376. 368. 384. 434. 434. 434. V HITE
      .50  .82 1.00  .97  .81  .43  .08  .00  .00  .00  .00  .00 F DAYS
     149. 152. 159. 156. 151. 151. 179. 221. 276. 334. 335. 335. LOSS
      21.  17.   6.  12.  18.  19.  -8. -49. **** **** **** **** DBU
    -109 -111 -119 -115 -111 -110 -139 -181 -235 -294 -294 -294 S DBW
    -162 -159 -152 -156 -160 -163 -166 -168 -170 -171 -172 -173 N DBW
      54.  48.  33.  41.  49.  53.  27. -13. -65. **** **** **** SNR
      20.  26.  28.  27.  25.  21.  47.  87. 139. 183. 182. 181. RPWRG
      .61  .50  .02  .18  .52  .59  .15  .00  .00  .00  .00  .00 REL


14.0 15.0 13.0  8.0 10.0 12.0 14.0 16.0 18.0 20.0 22.0 24.0 26.0 FREQ
     F2F2 F1F2  EF2 F1F2 F1F2 F2F2 F1F2 F1F2 F1F1 F1F1 F1F1 F1F1 MODE
      5.2 10.0  1.0 11.5 10.0  7.8  3.9  3.9  3.9  3.9  3.9  3.9 ANGLE
     12.0 14.0 14.0 14.0 14.0 14.0 10.0  3.0  1.0  3.9  3.9  3.9 ANGLE
     44.6 43.7 42.7 43.4 43.4 44.6 43.5 43.4 43.6 43.4 43.4 43.4 DELAY
     478. 325. 181. 275. 275. 462. 319. 319. 350. 308. 308. 308. V HITE
      .50  .90 1.00 1.00  .98  .74  .24  .02  .00  .00  .00  .00 F DAYS
     145. 147. 159. 154. 152. 142. 161. 199. 261. 357. 371. 371. LOSS
      25.  22.   6.  13.  17.  28.  10. -27. -88. **** **** **** DBU
    -105 -107 -119 -113 -111 -101 -121 -159 -220 -317 -330 -330 S DBW
    -164 -161 -151 -156 -160 -163 -166 -168 -170 -171 -172 -173 N DBW
      60.  55.  32.  42.  49.  62.  45.   9. -50. **** **** **** SNR
      14.  19.  28.  24.  25.  12.  29.  64. 124. 219. 218. 217. RPWRG
      .72  .63  .01  .22  .51  .75  .44  .03  .00  .00  .00  .00 REL


15.0 16.0 13.9  8.0 10.0 12.0 14.0 16.0 18.0 20.0 22.0 24.0 26.0 FREQ
     F2F2 F1F2  EF2  EF2 F1F2 F1F2 F2F2 F2F2 F2F2 F2F2 F2F2 F2F2 MODE
      5.0  9.8  1.0  1.0  9.0  9.6  5.0  4.3  4.3  4.3  4.3  4.3 ANGLE
     10.0 14.0 14.0 14.0 14.0 14.0 10.0  3.0  4.3  4.3  4.3  4.3 ANGLE
     44.4 43.8 42.7 42.7 43.4 43.8 44.4 44.1 44.7 44.7 44.7 44.7 DELAY
     452. 338. 183. 190. 285. 339. 453. 437. 527. 527. 527. 527. V HITE
      .50  .82 1.00 1.00  .96  .81  .50  .14  .02  .00  .00  .00 F DAYS
     142. 145. 157. 149. 146. 145. 142. 161. 220. 265. 312. 342. LOSS
      30.  25.   8.  18.  23.  25.  30.  12. -47. -91. **** **** DBU
    -101 -104 -117 -109 -105 -104 -104 -120 -180 -225 -272 -302 S DBW
    -166 -163 -151 -156 -160 -163 -166 -168 -170 -171 -172 -173 N DBW
      65.  59.  34.  47.  55.  59.  65.  48. -10. -53. -99. **** SNR
       9.  15.  25.  14.  15.  15.   9.  26.  84. 127. 173. 188. RPWRG
      .80  .70  .02  .45  .65  .71  .80  .50  .00  .00  .00  .00 REL
```

Figure 2.40 Sample IONCAP Method-16 system performance prediction tabulation.

the calculated value of RPWRG nominally 10 dB or less. Thus, proper choice of operating frequency is a necessity. The meanings of the remaining parameters tabulated in Fig. 2.40 are explained subsequently, as needed for the system design process.

Figure 2.41 is an IONCAP Method 24 tabulation of the voice communications reliability summary for selected frequencies from 6 to 25 MHz for all 24 h of day for June with the sunspot number value of 60. This summary is for the case of 0 dBi transmit and receive antennas and for a nominal transmit power of 10 kW. It is apparent that the frequency of maximum reliability

```
                        METHOD 24    IONCAP 78.03    PAGE    1

               JUN                    SSN =   60.
CEDAR RAPIDS, IA  TO  HONG KONG                AZIMUTHS           N. MI.        KM
42.00 N   91.50 W -  22.00 N   114.10 E    334.45    20.23    6709.6   12425.3
                              MINIMUM ANGLE     1.0   DEGREES
ITS- 1 ANTENNA PACKAGE
XMTR    2.0   TO   30.0   CONST. GAIN  H    0.00 L     0.00 A    0.0  OFF AZ      0.0
RCVR    2.0   TO   30.0   CONST. GAIN  H    0.00 L     0.00 A    0.0  OFF AZ      0.0
POWER =  10.000 KW   3 MHZ NOISE = -148.0 DBW    REQ. REL = .50   REQ. SNR = 48.0

                    FREQUENCY / RELIABILITY
```

GMT	LMT	MUF	FOT	6	8	10	12	14	16	18	20	22	25	MUF
1.0	18.9	17.9	.02	.00	.00	.00	.04	.01	.09	.16	.07	.01	.00	.14
2.0	19.9	17.7	.01	.00	.00	.00	.00	.01	.00	.10	.03	.01	.00	.11
3.0	20.9	17.7	.00	.00	.00	.00	.00	.00	.00	.09	.03	.01	.00	.02
4.0	21.9	17.2	.00	.00	.00	.00	.00	.00	.00	.02	.01	.00	.00	.01
5.0	22.9	16.2	.00	.00	.00	.00	.00	.00	.01	.04	.00	.00	.00	.00
6.0	23.9	15.2	.00	.00	.00	.00	.00	.00	.02	.01	.00	.00	.00	.01
7.0	.9	14.4	.00	.00	.00	.00	.00	.01	.03	.00	.00	.00	.00	.01
8.0	1.9	13.5	.00	.00	.00	.00	.00	.04	.02	.00	.00	.00	.00	.02
9.0	2.9	12.8	.00	.00	.01	.00	.12	.10	.01	.00	.00	.00	.00	.14
10.0	3.9	12.4	.00	.00	.03	.00	.16	.08	.00	.00	.00	.00	.00	.22
11.0	4.9	12.5	.02	.00	.00	.05	.13	.11	.01	.00	.00	.00	.00	.20
12.0	5.9	14.3	.07	.00	.00	.00	.10	.38	.16	.02	.00	.00	.00	.35
13.0	6.9	15.7	.63	.00	.00	.00	.54	.80	.76	.53	.20	.01	.00	.76
14.0	7.9	16.2	.70	.00	.00	.06	.61	.70	.81	.62	.35	.05	.00	.81
15.0	8.9	17.3	.78	.00	.00	.00	.58	.72	.72	.89	.66	.20	.00	.77
16.0	9.9	18.2	.79	.00	.00	.00	.50	.71	.79	.80	.49	.03	.00	.79
17.0	10.9	18.8	.81	.00	.00	.00	.52	.67	.80	.83	.65	.00	.00	.82
18.0	11.9	19.1	.80	.00	.00	.00	.30	.59	.76	.83	.16	.01	.00	.76
19.0	12.9	19.1	.77	.00	.00	.00	.08	.52	.71	.77	.14	.01	.00	.19
20.0	13.9	16.9	.00	.00	.00	.00	.00	.00	.02	.07	.05	.00	.00	.04
21.0	14.9	18.2	.08	.00	.00	.00	.00	.00	.23	.50	.16	.00	.00	.49
22.0	15.9	18.4	.00	.00	.00	.00	.00	.00	.06	.18	.25	.05	.00	.38
23.0	16.9	18.7	.02	.00	.00	.00	.00	.00	.14	.12	.16	.03	.00	.16
24.0	17.9	17.3	.02	.00	.00	.00	.00	.02	.10	.14	.02	.00	.00	.12

Figure 2.41 Sample IONCAP Method-24 communication reliability summary tabulation.

(FMR) varies significantly with the diurnal cycle. Also, the reliability is much higher for some times of day than for others. Figures 2.42*a* and *b* are graphical representations of the diurnal variation in maximum reliability and frequency of maximum reliability for this sunspot value for June and December, respectively. The maximum reliability plotted here is the largest value of reliability selected for each hour from tables such as shown in Fig. 2.41, for the FMR. (For this to be meaningful, it is assumed that some form of "adaptive" communications system is employed which utilizes automatic connectivity and optimum frequency selection.) It is seen that the reliability is higher for a longer interval of the day during June than during December. In general, these reliabilities are considered marginally or unacceptably low, so that some improvement in the system design is required to provide an acceptable system.

Further system analysis and design

The most practical way to improve the performance of this hypothetical system is to increase the transmit- and receive-antenna gains for the frequencies and takeoff angles of interest. It is seen from Fig. 2.40 and other similar tables (not shown) that the most-usable frequencies are in the range of 6 to

22 MHz and that the required takeoff angles are typically 15° or less at these frequencies. To indicate a possible solution, Fig. 2.43 shows a tabulation and graph of the gain vs. takeoff angle and frequency for a typical horizontal log-periodic-array (LPA) antenna. This type of antenna has high gain at low takeoff angles and medium to high frequencies, as needed for this path.

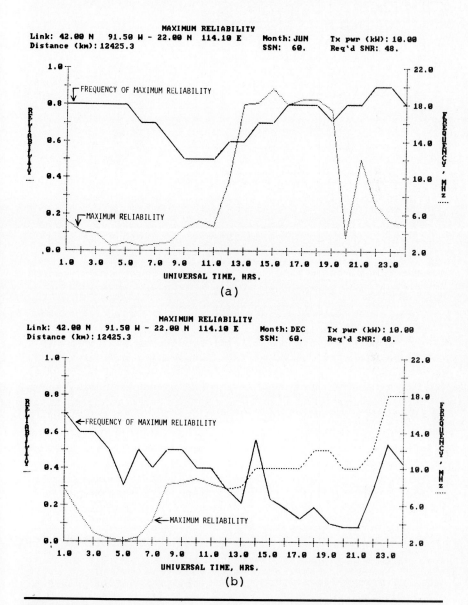

Figure 2.42 Sample computer-generated graph from IONCAP Method-24 data, showing maximum reliability and frequency of maximum reliability (FMR) for (*a*) June and (*b*) December. SSN = 60 for both.

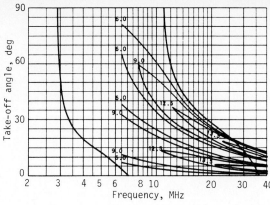

Figure 2.43 Gain vs. takeoff angle for a typical log-periodic-array antenna usable from 6 to 30 MHz. *(Left)* Graph; gain contours in decibels above an isotropic radiator; *(Below)* tabulation.

(This pattern and several others are stored on computer magnetic tape and are available for use in IONCAP analysis. In addition, IONCAP has the capability of calculating and tabulating the gain vs. frequency and takeoff angle for any antenna which can be modeled by one of several available configurations. In either case, IONCAP uses the specified antenna pattern results in the system-performance predictions.) Since fixed (ground) stations in residential or semirural areas are assumed, LPA antennas mounted at about 50 ft (15.2 m) in height appear to be a practical solution to the increased-gain requirement. If cost, real estate requirements, or vulnerability to icing and high winds rule out this type of antenna, some other choice must be made and a reduction in reliability and/or flexibility may result. This is typical of the tradeoffs which must be made in HF systems design.

The remainder of the system analysis is for the assumed configuration of LPA antennas at both ends of the circuit. Figure 2.44 shows a sample reliability summary table for the same conditions present in Fig. 2.41, but with LPA antennas employed. It is apparent that the additional 15 dB or more of system gain results in a significantly improved SN_0R_A for this circuit. Figures 2.45a and b plot the maximum reliability and FMR for the same conditions as in Figs. 2.42a and b, but with the improved antennas. These improvements result in a circuit which is usable for operator-to-operator-

```
                        METHOD 24      IONCAP 78.03    PAGE    1
              JUN                      SSN =  60.
CEDAR RAPIDS,IA TO HONG KONG                  AZIMUTHS         N. MI.         KM
42.00 N    91.50 W  - 22.00 N   114.10 E    334.45    20.23   6709.6   12425.3
                             MINIMUM ANGLE    1.0  DEGREES
ITS- 1 ANTENNA PACKAGE
XMTR    2.0  TO   30.0   237B-3 50 FT H   0.00 L    0.00 A    0.0  OFF AZ    0.0
RCVR    2.0  TO   30.0   237B-3 50 FT H   0.00 L    0.00 A    0.0  OFF AZ    0.0
POWER =  10.000 KW   3 MHZ NOISE = -148.0 DBW   REQ. REL = .50   REQ. SNR = 48.0

                 FREQUENCY / RELIABILITY
```

GMT	LMT	MUF	FOT	6	8	10	12	14	16	18	20	22	25	MUF
1.0	18.9	17.9	.18	.00	.00	.00	.03	.13	.34	.48	.41	.14	.00	.47
2.0	19.9	17.7	.14	.00	.00	.00	.00	.10	.22	.42	.26	.10	.00	.48
3.0	20.9	17.7	.00	.00	.00	.00	.00	.00	.15	.40	.17	.10	.00	.33
4.0	21.9	17.2	.00	.00	.00	.00	.00	.00	.08	.20	.11	.04	.00	.21
5.0	22.9	16.2	.00	.00	.00	.00	.00	.00	.15	.21	.03	.01	.00	.14
6.0	23.9	15.2	.00	.00	.00	.00	.00	.04	.13	.10	.00	.00	.00	.15
7.0	.9	14.4	.00	.00	.00	.00	.00	.18	.17	.03	.00	.00	.00	.19
8.0	1.9	13.5	.01	.00	.00	.00	.18	.26	.15	.00	.00	.00	.00	.28
9.0	2.9	12.8	.08	.00	.00	.09	.45	.31	.04	.00	.00	.00	.00	.43
10.0	3.9	12.4	.12	.00	.01	.11	.46	.28	.02	.00	.00	.00	.00	.51
11.0	4.9	12.5	.16	.00	.02	.14	.51	.34	.04	.00	.00	.00	.00	.49
12.0	5.9	14.3	.38	.00	.00	.18	.46	.69	.35	.12	.02	.00	.00	.61
13.0	6.9	15.7	.93	.00	.00	.02	.88	.97	.95	.84	.53	.06	.00	.96
14.0	7.9	16.2	.96	.00	.00	.06	.91	.96	.97	.92	.72	.19	.00	.98
15.0	8.9	17.3	.98	.00	.00	.00	.92	.95	.99	.90	.50	.01	.00	.96
16.0	9.9	18.2	.98	.00	.00	.00	.90	.95	.98	.96	.77	.11	.00	.96
17.0	10.9	18.8	.98	.00	.00	.00	.68	.95	.98	.97	.83	.02	.00	.95
18.0	11.9	19.1	.98	.00	.00	.00	.58	.92	.97	.96	.20	.03	.00	.90
19.0	12.9	19.1	.96	.00	.00	.00	.15	.88	.95	.91	.18	.03	.00	.39
20.0	13.9	16.9	.01	.00	.00	.00	.00	.04	.37	.34	.30	.08	.00	.42
21.0	14.9	18.2	.64	.00	.00	.00	.00	.03	.77	.85	.36	.00	.00	.83
22.0	15.9	18.4	.20	.00	.00	.00	.00	.01	.58	.59	.64	.24	.00	.79
23.0	16.9	18.7	.44	.00	.00	.00	.00	.03	.61	.63	.49	.21	.00	.56
24.0	17.9	17.3	.27	.00	.00	.00	.00	.28	.63	.49	.23	.04	.00	.51

Figure 2.44 Sample reliability summary tabulation with LPA antennas added, for June, SSN = 60.

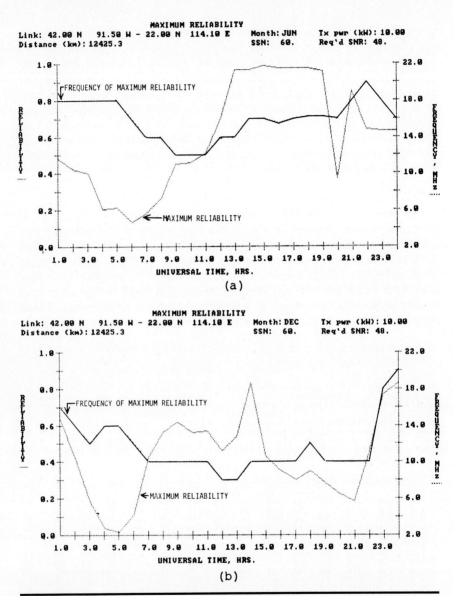

Figure 2.45 Sample computer-generated graphs of maximum reliability and FMR with LPA antennas added for (*a*) June and (*b*) December. SSN = 60 for both.

quality voice communications about 5 h of the day for June, SSN = 10, and 8 h of the day for June, SSN = 110. The diurnal availability for the month of December is somewhat less. Contacts between the two stations would have to be very carefully scheduled and would last for only 1 or 2 h daily during the winter months, for all SSN values. Some means of automatic frequency selection would be essential to successful operations. If additional hours of contact and/or a higher SN_0R_A are required, the system designer must consider the cost and value of adding more transmitter power to the system. Since the present level is assumed to be 10 kW, a further increase in power output level would be quite expensive. The designer and the user representative must carefully trade off the benefits to be gained by further power increases vs. increased costs and make a decision judiciously before proceeding.

Frequency-management techniques

Tables such as those shown in Figs. 2.40 and 2.41 are of value in manually selecting the operating frequency to try first when contact is attempted or in selecting frequency presets for automated operations, and they illustrate the variability of the FMR with the many HF propagation factors. These results clearly demonstrate the need for some form of frequency-management technique for selecting the optimum frequency and terminal configuration in HF communications operations. In general, a complete frequency-management system (FMS) includes the following functional elements to some degree:

1. Preparatory and/or "on-line" propagation and performance prediction algorithms and programs
2. A control mechanism, including an "engineering-order-wire" (OW) function
3. Channel evaluation and/or sounding and noise monitoring
4. Selective calling and a frequency-scanning receiver, if automatic connectivity is required
5. On-line performance monitoring and adaptation

Figure 2.46 represents some of the relationships among these functions in the complete HF-link call process, as discussed below. The optimum combination of the five functional elements and the implementation of each is dependent upon the overall system requirements and the available funding. That is, frequency-management capability, and hence system effectiveness, must be traded off against capital and operational costs. When optimized data transmission is required, some form of adaptive data terminal, having variable modulation and coding types and rates in its library, is highly desirable.

Propagation/performance predictions.   Considerations for propagation predictions were discussed previously. Computer, microprocessor, data-base, propagation-prediction, and supporting-sensor technologies are evolving very rapidly [42, 43, 45]. For instance, it is now possible to receive continuous broadcasts of solar, ionospheric, and geomagnetic data from satellites, using a simple earth-terminal receiver [46], which can be utilized in refining

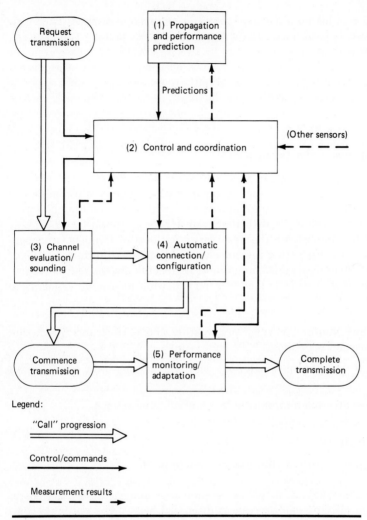

Figure 2.46 Functional representation of frequency management process for HF communications.

propagation predictions. Clearly, near-real-time propagation predictions will become an essential part of HF frequency management in the near future, as they are already being employed in some experimental HF systems.

Control mechanism. The degree of sophistication and cost of the frequency-management control mechanism will vary greatly from one system to another. For the simplest operations, voice calls (QSY) on one or two fixed frequencies are employed. In other, more advanced systems, the control mechanism is built into the automatic-connectivity-function implementation. Thus, once a connection is established, it is possible to automatically pass additional control information between stations using the same signaling equipment and formats as used in automatically establishing the link.

Channel evaluation and sounding.   The core of transmission performance and throughput optimization, especially in a dynamic and stressed environment, is the channel-evaluation process. The rationale for the development of real-time channel evaluation (RTCE) techniques is simple: Significant improvements in the use of the HF propagation medium can be achieved only if a communicator, or HF systems controller, using a specific path at a given time has access to real-time data on the path parameters rather than having to rely on frequency predictions which can be subject to appreciable errors [47]. But further development and guidance in RTCE subsystem design and selection is needed. MIL-STD-188-100 [48] and MIL-STD-188-317 [44], for example, are intended to be used in the design and installation of new military HF radio communications systems, subsystems, and equipment. However, they do not provide specifications of acceptable limits of certain parameters introduced by the ionospheric propagation channel or designations of methods and techniques for measuring those parameters. Most notably lacking from definition and specification are the channel parameters of multipath time-delay profile and rms spread, (Doppler) frequency profile and rms spread, and fading depth and rate [49, 50]. These, coupled with the burst characteristics of atmospheric and other impulsive noise, determine the ultimate performance of higher-speed ($>$ 75-bits/s) data transmission over the HF circuits. Indeed, for trans-auroral paths, it has been shown that all of these factors are important for transmission rates as low as 75 bits/s, a standard teletype channel rate [51]. Although the types of radio equipment under consideration are not the cause of these channel-induced parameters, the effects of the parameters in defining an "irreducible" BER for data transmission must be taken into account in the HF system design and operation (e.g., see Refs. 26 and 27).

A wide variety of channel-evaluation techniques have been designed and experimented with in the past. Vertical-incidence and oblique-incidence ionospheric sounders, while popular in the past, are expensive to purchase because they utilize separate RF equipment from that employed for communications (see Refs. 52 through 54 for examples). Generally, they require trained interpretation of the resultant ionograms to determine the optimum frequency. The current trend is to utilize the system's RF equipment (employed for communications) as the primary tool for probing or sounding the channel, with high-speed, digital signal processors added at the terminal to extract useful channel parameters from the received IF or baseband signal. One example is an advanced link quality analyzer (ALQA), currently under development by Rockwell International, which measures many HF parameters and is compatible with an existing automatic-connectivity subsystem for conventional, processor-controlled HF radios [51, 55].

Automatic connectivity.   Provision of automatic connectivity is perhaps the key building block in advanced HF systems design and implementation. The primary function of automatic connectivity is to quickly and reliably bring two or more stations into HF communications with each other, without the need for manual trial-and-error optimum-frequency searching. Two examples of practical automatic-connectivity subsystems currently being fielded are SELSCAN™ [56] and RACE [57]. The SELSCAN™ system provides automatic connectivity within 10 s of call initiation; details of SELSCAN™ design, operation, and performance are provided in Sec. 2.5.

Performance monitoring.   The degree of complexity required for on-line performance monitoring varies greatly with the intended application of the HF system. Ordinary voice circuits are adequately monitored by the users themselves, who can readily detect when the SN_0R_A deteriorates sufficiently to require a change in operating frequency or configuration. For high-speed data transmission, the situation is different—often the users are not directly monitoring the quality of the output or the channel conditions. Several schemes for automatic, on-line HF data-transmission performance monitoring have been devised and tested. Some of these employ measures of analog signal distortion in the demodulator (similar to the "eye pattern" used in wireline communications). Others operate with a parallel "pseudo-error"-generation device or algorithm at the demodulator, to detect in advance when the channel is deteriorating. With a larger number of HF data circuits now employing forward-error-correction (FEC) coding, error-detection-and-correction (EDAC) coding, or automatic repeat request (ARQ) operation, it is practical to monitor the performance by using the error-detection circuitry. Especially with the advent of soft-decision decoding techniques, the trend will be toward using the BER indicator as the primary on-line performance-monitoring method.

It should be noted, however, that such performance monitors will not necessarily provide a meaningful indication of which channel parameter(s) are contributing to the degraded BER performance. Hence, reversion to a channel-evaluation technique must likely be employed to determine what form of adaptation is required (frequency or terminal configuration) to recover from the situation. For practical purposes, there is no universal on-line performance monitor applicable to the wide variety of HF communications waveforms currently employed. The selection of the technique(s) to use will be dependent on the form of modulation and coding chosen for data transmission in the overall system design.

2.5   Automatic Connectivity

Design considerations

Microprocessor technology has allowed electronic equipment designers to implement relatively complex logical control and data processing functions as an integral part of modern equipment designs. The powerful capability of the microprocessor has opened the door for automation of HF SSB communications equipment and the logical starting point is in the area of automatic connectivity. Establishing the link is by far the most difficult part of using HF and requires time, knowledge, skill, and coordination on the part of the user/operator.

The basic concept of automatic connectivity is relatively simple. An analogy which may be helpful in visualizing and analyzing an HF automatic-connectivity system is a modern telephone system. The idea is for the operator (caller) to be able to initiate a call by inputting the identification code (telephone number) of the station to be called and letting the automatic HF system (telephone central office) perform the frequency selections and data-transmission exchanges (telephone trunk selection/connections) necessary to complete the communications link with the designated second station.

HF automatic connectivity can be defined as a series of automated events which begin as the result of an operator's initiating action or an external system input at one station and end with that station and a second designated station ready for communications traffic exchange on a commonly shared, currently propagating HF channel.

Automatic connectivity can be achieved through the proper combination of the following functions:

1. Scanning of preset channels

2. Selective calling

3. Channel propagation evaluation (sounding)

4. Control and interface logic (microprocessor)

The block diagram in Fig. 2.47 shows the major functional elements of an automatic communications processor (ACP).

The incorporation of preset channels allows rapid selection of any of several assigned operating frequencies. Sequentially advancing an HF receiver through a selection of preset channels at regularly timed intervals is a simple receiver-scanning technique which allows a single HF receiver to provide samples of the channel activity on multiple predetermined frequencies within the HF band. Scanning rates must be selected to allow a minimum sampling period on each channel. The sampling period is dependent on the data format and coding redundancy factors chosen. HF receiver tune time and synthesizer settling time must be added to the minimum sampling period to obtain the total dwell period.

Selective calling provides a means of station identification via data transmission and reception of station addresses or identification codes. A data modulator/demodulator is required to provide address and other command data exchange between two automatic HF stations. The data modem design selected must be compatible with the bandpass characteristics of the HF radios with which it is intended to operate. In addition, the data format must provide a means of synchronization under scanning conditions.

Channel propagation evaluation data provide the basis for quick and accurate automatic channel selection. Sufficient data should be measured and

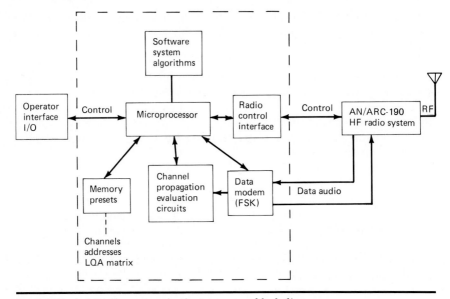

Figure 2.47   Automatic communications processor block diagram.

stored for several key stations on each preset channel in use to provide a working data base of near-real-time propagation information from which a high probability of successful channel selections can be made. Such a channel propagation data base is the key to quick and accurate selection of the proper channel in order to establish a good quality link in the shortest time possible.

A microprocessor or other data-processing mechanism is required to provide the data manipulation, coordination, radio remote control, and operator input/output (I/O) interfaces necessary to make meaningful use of the other three basic functions. It is, of course, the software which ultimately determines the coordination of the hardware functions and defines the final operational characteristics of the system.

As may be expected, there may be many different design approaches which will provide acceptable performance, and thus the intent here is not to go into the details of a specific design approach but rather to point out the parameters which must be dealt with in the design of an automatic-connectivity system. In order to design an automatic communications system, it is necessary to define the desired performance characteristics in terms of the critical system parameters. The following is a representative list of some of the major system parameters which must be considered:

1. Receive vs. transmit scan timing relationship

2. Scanning rate

3. Address data word format

4. Synchronization

5. Data modulation scheme

6. Data rate

7. Data error rate performance

8. Data error correction scheme

9. Address recognition reliability

10. Address recognition false alarm rate

11. Number of address code combinations

12. Address coding scheme

13. Coded address length

14. Sounding measurements

Examination of the above list of critical parameters should lead one to recognize the dependence of each parameter on the others. For example, scanning dwell time is directly related to the transmitted data rate, the number of bits in the address data word format, the redundancy factors introduced by the data error correction method chosen, and the synchronization scheme used. The length of the address data word, on the other hand, is a function of the address coding scheme and the number of address code combinations allowed as well as the synchronization scheme used. Designing to minimize the address word length may seem to be a move in the right direction but consideration of the false alarm rate performance, which worsens as the word length decreases, forces the definition of a minimum acceptable word length.

The solutions must be practical compromises reached by a process of trading off the interactive effects of each of the critical parameters with respect to the others. Some basic assumptions and a few key arbitrarily chosen parameters serve as the starting point for the first iteration.

Automatic-connectivity system implementation example

The pioneering approach used by Rockwell-Collins in the development of its SELSCAN™ automatic communications system (ACS) involves the addition of an automatic communications processor to an existing HF radio system. Additional details of the early developmental assumptions and performance tradeoffs may be found in Ref. 56.

The microprocessor-based ACP acts as a smart remote control device for the HF radio system and incorporates the additional circuitry and software required to accomplish automatic connectivity.

The SELSCAN™ ACS uses an asynchronous receiver scanning approach that eliminates the need for time-of-day clocks. This approach does not require the transmitter to scan, thus offering compatibility with fixed-station HF systems which use large slow-tuning transmitters as well as aircraft or vehicular HF systems with narrowband antennas and slow-tuning antenna couplers.

When not in a communications link, the ACP causes the HF radio's receiver to scan a number of preset channels dwelling for 0.5 s on each channel. Receive audio is fed to the ACP where an internal frequency shift keying (FSK) data modem listens for recognizable data. The ACP mutes the receive audio to the operator while scanning to avoid unnecessary distraction to the operator.

The FSK address data word format provides TO and FROM synchronization preambles which allow rapid word synchronization for scanning compatibility and identifies the address being transmitted as that of the station "TO" which the transmission is directed or that of the station "FROM" which the transmission is being made.

Sounding is accomplished by using a FROM address data word format as the transmitted sounding signal. This provides a signal with known characteristics upon which channel propagation evaluation measurements [called link quality analysis (LQA) by Rockwell-Collins] can be made by each receiving ACP as its scanning receiver dwells on the channel being sounded. The sounding signal also contains the address of the transmitting station which allows the receiving ACP to store the LQA data in matrix form, referencing the transmitting station's address and the channel on which the sounding transmission was received.

Calls are initiated by selecting the desired preset address and keying the system. The ACP takes over and automatically executes the following sequence of events:

1. Automatic channel selection
   - Looks up the called address in the LQA data base
   - Ranks the channels according to the available data
   - Chooses the highest ranking channel for the first connectivity attempt
   - Tunes receiver to the selected channel
   - Listens for other traffic before transmitting
   - If channel not available, chooses alternate channel per the channel selection algorithm and repeats the above two steps
   - If channel is available, tunes transmitter

2. Automatic link establishment
   - Transmits call
   - Waits for response
   - If no response within time limit, selects alternate channel and repeats call
   - If response received, transmits confirmation, unmutes audio, alerts operator that link is established

Each of the three link establishment transmissions, the call, the response, and the confirmation, contains a TO and a FROM portion. The calling station waits long enough to allow the responding station to tune its transmitter and transmit a response before going on to an alternative channel.

The sequence of events at the called station is as follows:

1. Scanning
   - Operator's audio muted
2. Call received
   - TO address recognized during scan dwell on calling channel
   - Scanning stopped on calling channel
   - FROM address decoded
   - Transmit tune cycle initiated
   - Response transmitted to caller
   - If no confirmation received from caller, returns to scan
   - If confirmation received, unmutes audio, displays caller's address, alerts operator of call received

To disconnect the link, the operator may return the system to the scan mode, which again mutes the operator's receive audio, or the system will automatically disconnect following a time out with no key activity.

Some further insight may be gained by examining some of the system tradeoffs and resulting critical parameters chosen by Rockwell-Collins for its SELSCAN™ ACS.

1. *Receive vs. transmit scan timing relationship.* The SELSCAN™ system is based on an asynchronous receiver scanning approach which does not require the transmitter to scan. When a call is initiated, a channel is automatically chosen and the transmitter tuned on that frequency. The call is transmitted for a long enough period of time to ensure that the scanning receiver at the called station will have an opportunity to dwell on the calling frequency at some point during the call transmission.

Since the frequency is automatically chosen based on near-real-time propagation data (sounding results), the probability is high that connectivity will be achieved on the first call attempt. If contact is not achieved, an alternative frequency will be chosen and the transmitter will be retuned to the new frequency for another call. Transmitter system tuning is minimized with this approach, and timing is not critical, which means transmitting systems with long tune times may be used.

2. *Scanning rate.* The scanning rate selected is two channels per second. This is based on a minimum sampling period of 320 ms, allowing an additional 180 ms for receiver tuning, synthesizer settling time, AGC settling time, and remote control timing uncertainties.

3. *Address data word format.* The address data word format chosen contains 32 bits divided into four 8-bit characters. The first character is a synchronization character which also contains TO and FROM information. The last three characters are coded address characters with embedded synchronization bits.

4. *Synchronization.*   Scanning is asynchronous. Data word synchronization is provided by the unique characteristics of the first character of the data word with respect to the last three characters. This scheme provides the capability to synchronize on the 32-bit words starting at any point in a continuous transmission, thus meeting the requirements for scanning compatibility. The need for bit synchronization is avoided by performing a digital correlation at 8 times the bit rate.

5. *Data modulation scheme.*   The data modem design was selected for simplicity, the ability to meet the minimum error rate performance requirements, the ability to operate with up to 100-Hz frequency error, the ability to perform under HF multipath conditions, scanning compatibility, and the desire to be compatible with existing unsophisticated SSB voice and/or low-speed data transmitting and receiving equipment. A four-tone FSK data modulation scheme was chosen.

6. *Data rate.*   The transmitted data rate is 300 bits/s.

7. *Data error rate performance.*   The data error rate performance using an FSK modulation scheme at 300 bits/s and a simple two-out-of-three error correction scheme was determined to be sufficient to support the desired address recognition reliability.

8. *Data error correction scheme.*   A simple method of statistical error correction using the natural redundancy of the repetitive address data words was chosen for its ease of implementation and effectiveness against typical HF burst-type interference. The method votes on the content of each bit position from three consecutive address data words to construct a best two-out-of-three corrected data word.

9. *Address recognition reliability.*   Since this system was intended for establishing voice and slow-speed data communications links, the address recognition reliability was chosen to be 99 percent under signal-to-noise conditions which would just support voice communications [approximately 13-dB signal-plus-noise-to-noise [$(S + N)/N$] ratio in a 3-kHz bandwidth].

10. *Address recognition false alarm rate.*   False alarms are considered a serious threat to an automatic system where transmitters are keyed and transmissions are made without operator interaction. An arbitrarily chosen number of months between false alarms allowed calculation of the minimum number of bits for the coded address word. The final design far exceeds the initial minimum requirements because of other tradeoffs which increased the coded address length, resulting in a false alarm rate which is measured in years rather than weeks or months of continuous 24 h/day operation.

11. *Number of address code combinations.*   The number of possible address code combinations is 46,656 using three alphanumeric characters and allowing any combination of the 26 uppercase alpha characters and the numbers from 0 through 9.

12. *Address coding scheme.*   A three-character alphanumeric address code was chosen over a purely numeric code because of the possible human factors relationship of the alphanumeric characters code assignments to existing voice call signs and the potential for minimization of call sign cross-reference (telephone book) materials. Abbreviated 6-bit American Standard

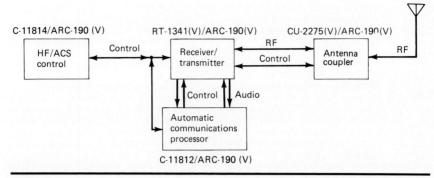

Figure 2.48 AN/ARC-190(V) HF SSB automatic communications system.

Code for Information Interchange (ASCII) characters were used to minimize the address character length prior to coding.

13. *Coded address length.* The addition of two synchronizing overhead bits to each 6-bit address character resulted in an 8-bit byte for each of the three address characters plus a similar 8-bit byte for the synchronizing preamble character, for a total of 32 bits in the coded address word.

14. *Sounding measurements.* The FROM address word containing the transmitting station's address is used as the transmitted sounding signal. Signal-to-noise ratio and multipath delay distortion measurements are made on the received signal. Relative channel quality numbers are derived and stored in the LQA data matrix according to the channel number on which the transmission was received and the FROM address decoded from the received signal.

While the ACS concept is simple, the performance of such a system is dependent on the quality of the design of the different hardware functional elements and the details of the software design which integrate these functions and others into an operational system.

The ACS system shown in Fig. 2.48 is built around the U.S. Air Force AN/ARC-190(V) airborne HF radio system and is capable of either manual or fully automatic operation.

REFERENCES

1. K. D. Kryter, "Methods for the Calculation and Use of the Articulation Index," *J. Acoust. Soc. Am.,* vol. 34, 1962, pp. 1689–1697.
2. K. D. Kryter, "Validation of the Articulation Index," *J. Acoust. Soc. Am.,* vol. 34, 1962, pp. 1698–1702.
3. L. L. Beranek, "The Design of Speech Communication Systems," *Proc. Inst. Radio Eng.,* vol. 35, 1974, pp. 880–890.
4. H. R. Bertscher and J. C. Webster, "Intelligibility of UHF and VHF Transmissions at Fifteen Representative Air Traffic Control Towers," *J. Acoust. Soc. Am.,* vol. 28, 1956, pp. 561–564.
5. Harvey Fletcher, *Speech and Hearing in Communications,* D. Van Nostrand, Princeton, NJ, 1953.
6. N. R. French and J. C. Steinberg, "Factors Governing the Intelligibility of Speech Sounds," *J. Acoust. Soc. Am.,* vol. 19, 1947, pp. 90–119.

7. *American National Standard Methods for the Calculation of the Articulation Index,* ANSI 53.5-1969, American National Standards Institute, New York, 1969.
8. J. C. R. Liklider and I. P. Pollack, "Effects of Differentiation Integration and Infinite Peak Clipping upon the Intelligibility of Speech," *J. Acoust. Soc. Am.,* vol. 20, 1948, pp. 42–51.
9. F. M. Gardner, *Phase Lock Techniques,* John Wiley & Sons, New York, 1966.
10. W. C. Lindsey, *Synchronization Systems in Communication and Control,* Prentice-Hall, Englewood Cliffs, NJ, 1972.
11. J. P. Costas, "Synchronous Communications," *Proc. IRE,* vol. 44, 1956, pp. 1713–1718.
12. J. F. Nickerson and D. K. Weaver, Jr., *A Study of the Effect of Frequency Translation Error on the Intelligibility of Speech in the Presence of Noise,* unpublished internal document of the Electronics Research Laboratory Endowment and Research Foundation, Montana State College, Bozeman, MT, January 1959.
13. S. C. Plotkins, "FM Bandwidth as a Function of Distortion and Modulation Index," *IEEE Trans. Commun. Tech.,* vol. 15–3, June 1967, pp. 467–470.
14. P. Frutiger, "Noise in FM Receivers with Negative Frequency Feedback," *Proc. IEEE,* vol. 54, November 1966, pp. 1506–1520.
15. A. Acampora and A. Newton, "Use of Phase Subtraction to Extend the Range of a Phase-Locked Demodulator," *RCA Rev.,* December 1966, pp. 557–599.
16. B. R. Davis, "Equivalent Variable Center-Frequency Amplifiers," *Radio Electron. Eng.,* vol. 27, December 1964, pp. 381–388.
17. V. L. Bykov, "Improving the Threshold Properties of the FM Receiver by Means of a Frequency Divider," *Telecommun. Radio Eng.,* vol. 20, October 1965, pp. 14–19.
18. K. K. Clarke and D. T. Hess, "Frequency Locked Loop FM Demodulator," *IEEE Trans. Commun. Tech.,* vol. 15-4, August 1967, pp. 518–524.
19. H. Akima, "Theoretical Studies on Signal-to-Noise Characteristics of an FM System," *IEEE Trans. Space Electron. Telem.,* vol. 9, December 1963, pp. 101–108.
20. H. Haberle, "Theoretical Comparison of Modulation Systems in Satellite Communications," *NTZ-Commun. J.,* vol. 6, no. 3, 1967, pp. 110–112.
21. R. C. Dixon, *Spread Spectrum Systems,* John Wiley & Sons, New York, 1976.
22. R. C. Dixon (ed.), *Spread Spectrum Techniques,* IEEE Press, Piscataway, NJ, 1976.
23. W. E. Sabin, "Spread Spectrum Applications in Amateur Radio," *QST,* vol. 67, July 1983, pp. 14–19.
24. F. J. Harris, "On the Use of Windows for Harmonic Analysis with the Discrete Fourier Transform," *Proc. IEEE,* vol. 66, January 1978, pp. 51–83.
25. Gerhard Braun, *Planning and Engineering Shortwave Links,* Heyden & Son, London, 1982, pp. 15–77 and 124–252.
26. L. R. Teeters, J. L. Lloyd, G. W. Haydon, and D. L. Lucas, *Estimating the Performance of Telecommunications Systems Using the Ionospheric Transmission Channel: Ionospheric Communications Analysis and Prediction Program User's Manual (IONCAP),* NTIA Rep. 83-127 (PB84-111210), U.S. Dept. of Commerce, National Telecommunications and Information Administration, Institute for Telecommunication Sciences, Boulder, CO, July 1983.
27. C. C. Watterson, *Methods of Improving the Performance of HF Digital Radio Systems,* NTIA Rep. 79–29 (PB80-128606), U.S. Dept. of Commerce, National Telecommunications and Information Administration, Institute for Telecommunication Sciences, Boulder, CO, October 1979.
28. Gerald L. Hall (ed.), *The ARRL Antenna Book,* 14th ed. (and subsequent editions), American Radio Relay League, Newington, CT, 1982.
29. R. C. Johnson and H. Jasik, *Antenna Engineering Handbook,* 2d ed., McGraw-Hill, New York, 1984.
30. L. A. Moxon, *HF Antennas for All Locations,* Pitman Press (for the Radio Society of Great Britain), Bath, U.K., 1982.
31. M. F. Radford, "High Frequency Antennas," Chap. 16 in A. W. Rudge et al. (eds.), *The Handbook of Antenna Design,* vol 2, Peter Peregrinus (for the IEE), London, 1983, pp. 663–724.
32. P. David and J. Voge, *Propagation of Waves,* Pergamon Press, New York, 1969.
33. Kenneth Davies, *Ionospheric Radio Propagation,* Natl. Bur. Std. Monograph 80, U.S. Government Printing Office (for the U.S. Dept. of Commerce), Washington, DC, Apr. 1, 1965.
34. Karl Rawer, *The Ionosphere: Its Significance for Geophysics and Radio Communications,* Frederick Ungar, New York, 1957.
35. E. W. Pappenfus, Warren B. Bruene, and E. O. Schoenike, *Single Sideband Principles and Circuits,* McGraw-Hill, New York, 1964, pp. 13–20.
36. J. A. Betts, *HF Communications,* American Elsevier, New York, 1967, pp. 8–16, 84–94.
37. *CCIR Interim Method for Estimating Sky-wave Field Strength and Transmission Loss at*

Frequencies between the Approximate Limits of 2 and 30 MHz, CCIR-Report 252-2, in *New Delhi Assembly, 1970/1974,* ITU-CCIR, New Delhi, 1970/1974. See also *Second CCIR Computer-based Interim Method for Estimating Sky-wave Field Strength and Transmission Loss at Frequencies between 2 and 30 MHz,* CCIR Doc. 6 1070-E, Draft Supplement to CCIR-Report 252-2, submitted to XIV Plenary Assembly, Kyoto, 1978.

38. George Jacobs and Theodore J. Cohen, *The Shortwave Propagation Handbook,* 2d ed., CQ Publishing, Hicksville, NY, 1982.

39. Stanley Leinwoll, *Shortwave Propagation,* J. F. Rider, New York, 1959.

40. P. N. Saveskie, *Radio Propagation Handbook,* TAB, Blue Ridge Summit, PA, 1980.

41. *World Distribution and Characteristics of Atmospheric Radio Noise,* CCIR-Report 322, in *1963 Geneva Assembly,* ITU-CCIR, Geneva, 1964. (Revised in 1974 as CCIR-Report 322-1.)

42. Robert B. Rose and J. N. Martin, *MINIMUF-3.5: Improved Version of MINIMUF-3, A Simplified HF MUF Prediction Algorithm,* Tech. Doc. NOSC TD 201, U.S. Naval Oceans Systems Center, San Diego, Oct. 26, 1978.

43. Robert B. Rose, "PROPHET—An Emerging HF Prediction Technology," in John M. Goodman (ed.-in-chief), *Effect of the Ionosphere on Radiowave Systems,* U.S. Government Printing Office, Washington, DC, 1982. (Book based on IES '81 Ionospheric Effects Symposium, Alexandria, Va, Apr. 14–16, 1981.)

44. *Standards for Long-Haul Communications: Subsystems Design and Engineering Standards and Equipment Technical Design Standards for High Frequency Radio,* U.S. Military Standard MIL-STD-188-317, Dept. of Defense, Washington, DC, Mar. 30, 1973.

45. M. Daehler, *An HF Communications Frequency-Management Procedure for Forecasting the Frequency of Optimum Transmission,* NRL Memorandum Rep. 5505, U.S. Naval Research Laboratory, Washington, DC, Dec. 31, 1984.

46. J. A. Joselyn and K. L. Curran, "The SESC [Space Environment Services Center] Satellite Broadcast System for Space Environment Services," paper 4-1 in *IES '84 Proceedings: The Effects of the Ionosphere on C^3I Systems,* published in 1985; available from National Technical Information Service, Springfield, VA, as document ADA 163622. (Book based on IES '84 Ionospheric Effects Symposium, Alexandria, VA, May 1–3, 1984.).

47. M. Darnell, "Channel Evaluation Techniques for Dispersive Communications Paths," in J. K. Skwirzynski (ed.), *Communication Systems and Random Process Theory,* Sijthoff and Noordhoff, Alphen aan den Rijn, The Netherlands, 1978, pp. 425–460. (Book based on NATO Advanced Study Institute Series E, No. 25, Darlington, UK, Aug. 8–20, 1977.)

48. *Common Long-Haul and Tactical Communications Systems Technical Standard,* U.S. Military Standard MIL-STD-188-100, Dept. of Defense, Washington, DC, Nov. 17, 1976.

49. David H. Bliss, "Channel Characteristics and Anomalies," Sec. 5.1 in Charles A. Harper (ed.-in-chief), *Handbook of Electronic Systems Design,* McGraw-Hill, New York, 1980, pp. 5-15 through 5-18.

50. L. W. Pickering, "The Calculation of Ionospheric Doppler Spread on HF Communications Channels," *IEEE Trans. Commun.,* vol. COM-23, May 1975, pp. 526–537.

51. David H. Bliss, "Automated Channel Evaluation for Adaptive HF Communications," in *HF Communication Systems and Techniques '85,* IEEE Conference Pub. 245, London, 1985, pp. 37–41.

52. R. B. Fenwick and T. J. Woodhouse, "Real-Time Adaptive HF Frequency Management," paper 5 in V. J. Coyne (ed.), *Special Topics in HF Propagation,* NATO-AGARD Conference Proceedings 263, 1979 (document ADA080855), published for NATO-AGARD by Technical Editing and Reproduction, London, 1979. (Book based on Symposium of the Electromagnetic Wave Propagation Panel, Lisbon, Portugal, June 1, 1979.)

53. L. E. Hoff and R. L. Merk, *Performance Measures for an Automated Navy Tactical Sounder System (NTSS),* NOSC Tech. Rep. 409 (ADA072198), U.S. Naval Ocean Systems Center, San Diego, July 1, 1979.

54. Bodo W. Reinisch and Klaus Bibl, *Ionospheric Research Using Digital Ionosondes,* U.S. Air Force Geophysics Laboratory Tech. Rep. 83-0184, University of Lowell, Lowell, MA, July 1983.

55. David H. Bliss, "A New HF-Link Parameters/Quality Approach," in *MILCOM '83 Conference Proceedings,* IEEE, Washington, DC, 1983, pp. 530–534.

56. James V. Harmon, "Automatic Connectivity for Low-Speed Data Communications Systems," in *Recent Advances in HF Communication Systems and Techniques,* IEEE Colloquium Digest 1979/48, IEE, London, 1979, pp. 13–18.

57. S. M. Chow et al., 'RACE'—*An Automatic High-Frequency Radio Telephone System for Communications in Remote Areas,* CRC Rep. 1338-E, Communication Research Centre, Canadian Dept. of Communications, Ottawa, Canada, December 1980.

3

Receiver Design

David B. Hallock

High-frequency single-sideband receivers have evolved from the rudimentary superheterodyne of the 1920s to today's sophisticated multiple-conversion and frequency agile receiver having optimum design with respect to the interlocking aspects of sensitivity, intermodulation, dynamic range, selectivity, and many other criteria. This evolution has been possible because of advances in all areas of receiver design ranging from components to circuit details. This chapter will present the results of this evolution in receiver design with emphasis on the circuits, components, and techniques that are important for single-sideband reception.

3.1 Introduction

The block diagram and circuit of any receiver is strongly if not totally determined by the available components. Wave-filtering components having sufficient selectivity to select SSB signals are available only with fixed center frequency designs. Therefore, the standard receiver design for HF SSB has become the superheterodyne which uses frequency translation to convert the HF signal to a fixed intermediate frequency where selectivity is practically obtainable. The modern superheterodyne receiver will typically use several intermediate frequencies to obtain selectivity for image and spurious signal rejection in addition to sideband selection. An advantage of the superheterodyne is that the majority of the gain needed to amplify picowatt signal levels to the level needed for human audibility can be constructed and controlled in the fixed-IF circuits. Constant-frequency amplifiers are generally better behaved in the areas of gain stability, noise figure, and distortion.

3.2 HF Receiver Requirements

The technical, physical, and cost requirements of receivers are as varied and complex as there are applications and users. However, there are several basic requirements plus service and special needs which commonly enter into the design of a receiver, be it simple or complex. It is helpful and necessary to understand the basis for the technical needs and to know the range of values to be expected in each parameter. First, the basic requirements will be examined.

Sensitivity

HF receiver sensitivity is commonly expressed as the number of microvolts necessary to achieve some value of signal-to-noise ratio at the output. More specifically, the signal level is measured in open-circuit generator voltage together with a generator source resistance. Closed-circuit voltage, or the voltage across the receiver input terminals, is sometimes used to specify sensitivity. This is technically imprecise since the receiver input resistance is then an undefined variable, which makes the power flowing into the receiver input an unknown. Figure 3.1 illustrates the generator and receiver input circuit model. If R_{in} is exactly equal to R_g, the receiver is accepting the generator's available power ($V_{oc}^2/4R_g$) and V_{in} is one-half of V_{oc}. But, if V_{in} were to be specified for sensitivity, the power flowing into the receiver could theoretically approach infinity if R_{in} were to be allowed to approach zero.

Industry jargon often calls open-circuit voltage "hard" and closed-circuit voltage "soft." It is "harder" to achieve a certain output signal-to-noise ratio with one hard microvolt than it is with one soft microvolt. A source of confusion is that most signal generators are calibrated in terms of the closed-

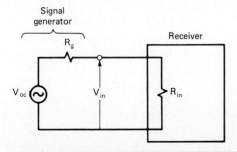

Figure 3.1 The closed-circuit input voltage V_{in} is a function of the open-circuit generator voltage V_{oc}, the generator resistance R_g, and the receiver's input resistance R_{in}.

circuit voltage across a load resistance equal to the generator source resistance. The open-circuit voltage is then twice the indicated value. Often a 6-dB attenuator is added at the generator output so that the indicated voltage can be read directly as open-circuit voltage. Typical HF receiver sensitivity for a 10-dB output signal plus noise-to-noise ratio lies in the region of 1.0 μV, open circuit, for a nominal 50-ohm source resistance. Sensitivity is a function of bandwidth, since the signal (for test purposes) is a single frequency which occupies no bandwidth while the noise fills the receiver's bandwidth.

The open/closed voltage specification confusion is eliminated when sensitivity is stated in terms of available signal power, for example, dBm, decibels with respect to 1 mW. This is unambiguous and also appears directly on signal generator displays. (In this chapter, we will use the more common abbreviation, dBm, for the precise designation, dBmW.) A typical sensitivity power level of -113 dBm is equivalent to 1.0 μV, open circuit, for 50-ohm source resistance.

Noise figure

The ratio of the available signal-to-noise ratio at the input of a receiver (or any two-port network) to the available signal-to-noise ratio at the output is named "noise figure" when given as a decibel ratio and "noise factor" when expressed as a power ratio. (For a complete and basic foundation of "noise factor," see Friis—Ref. 1.) Noise figure is independent of bandwidth because the available noise powers are from the same bandwidth and cancel when the ratio is taken. HF SSB receivers have noise figures in the 12- to 17-dB region, which is all that is usually necessary because of the generally high level of atmospheric noise prevalent at HF. An important exception occurs in special receiving systems with antennas which are very inefficient. This results in available signal and noise powers commensurate with the self-noise of the receiver. In these systems, RF gain is usually required to reduce the noise figure.

The interrelation of noise figure and sensitivity is readily done when the receiver's effective noise bandwidth is known because the overall system is linear. If, for example, a certain signal level produces a 10-dB output signal-to-noise ratio and the receiver has a 15-dB noise figure, the available input-signal-to-noise ratio must be 25 dB, the sum of output ratio and noise figure. The noise power available from a room temperature source ($+290$ K) is kTB, where k is Boltzmann's constant (1.38×10^{-23} W·s/K), T is the absolute temperature, and B is the bandwidth. An easily remembered fact is that in a 1-kHz bandwidth, the available noise power is -144 dBm. (A negative gross of dBm's!) For an SSB receiver bandwith of 3 kHz, the noise is about 5 dB greater (10 log [3 kHz/1 kHz]) or -139 dBm. In our example the signal power is 25 dB stronger than the noise power, and so is -114 dBm. For a 50-ohm signal source, the corresponding open-circuit generator voltage is about 0.9 μV. Note that we did not know or mention the receiver's input resistance, it being sufficient only to know the source resistance and the resulting noise figure together with the noise bandwidth.

Intermodulation distortion

When two relatively large signals combine in a nonlinear stage to produce one or more new frequencies, the results are termed "intermodulation distortion," or IMD. In a receiver, we are concerned with distortion from signals both within and outside the intermediate frequency bandwidth, and so will refer to in-band and out-of-band intermodulation distortion, respectively. For a first-cut explanation, the output of the receiver can be considered to be an ascending power series of the input such as:

$$E_{\text{out}} = A_0 + A_1 E_{\text{in}} + A_2 E_{\text{in}}^2 + A_3 E_{\text{in}}^3 + \cdots \tag{3.1}$$

When E_{in} is replaced by the sum of two sine waves in this series, it is found that new frequencies are produced which occur at spacings equal to the difference between the original pair of signals. If it so happens that the IMD frequency is within the receiver's bandwidth, a signal is heard that is, in reality, not present. For example, if a receiver is tuned to 10 MHz and there are two large signals at 4 and 14 MHz also present, the difference frequency 10 MHz may be generated somewhere in the receiver by nonlinearity. This example is termed "second-order" IMD because it arises predominantly from the A_2 term in the power series. It is readily eliminated by passive filtering at the receiver input since the large signal frequencies are much different from the desired signal frequency.

When the A_3 term in the series is included in the computation of distortion products, it is found that intermodulation frequencies of the form $2f_2 - f_1$ and $2f_1 - f_2$ are generated, f_1 and f_2 being the large signal frequencies. These are called "third-order" IMD and can be very difficult to reduce in level because the undesired signals can be very close to the passband frequencies and even within the passband. Third-order IMD is also generated by the higher odd-order terms of the series. In our 10-MHz receiver example, suppose there are two large signals at 11 and 12 MHz. The second harmonic of 11 MHz minus the 12-MHz signal is exactly 10 MHz. Likewise, the second harmonic of a 9-MHz signal minus another 8-MHz signal will produce 10-MHz IMD. Higher odd-order IMD products are also sometimes specified and are of concern in receiver design. When three or more strong signals are present, the possible number of interference combinations grows astronomically (Chap. 14).

Fortunately, well designed solid-state receivers have sufficient signal-handling capability to be useful with normal on-the-air signal strengths. It is typical to have two signals 80 to 100 dB above the receiver's sensitivity level produce intermodulation products less than the sensitivity level.

Intercept point

The concept of intercept point, developed by McVay (Ref. 2), wraps the IMD performance of a receiver into one number. If we plot the two-signal output level and the distortion level in dBm vs. the two-signal input level in dBm as shown in Fig. 3.2, we find that the second-order distortion increases two decibels for each decibel increase in both input signal levels. [This is also predictable from the series expansion of Eq. (3.1).] Further, a 3-dB increase is found for third-order distortion when both signals are increased 1 dB. In general, there will be an n-dB increase in nth-order IM for each dB of input signal increase. If the receiver did not limit, the distortion products would increase until they equaled the output signal level. This point is called the "second-" or "third-order intercept," respectively. If output power is used as the dimension, the term "output intercept" is used. Receivers are usually specified in terms of input intercept, using the input signal level.

Useful relationships exist between IMD level, signal level, and the intercept point. For second-order intercept the input intercept is:

$$_2I_{in} = \text{Input} + \Delta \tag{3.2}$$

where Input is the two-tone signal level per tone in decibel units such as dBm, and Δ is the ratio between the two-tone level and the IMD level in decibels.

The third-order input intercept is found from

$$_3I_{in} = \text{Input} + \frac{\Delta}{2} \tag{3.3}$$

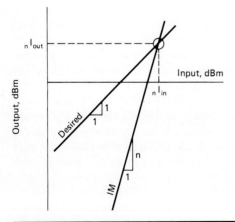

Figure 3.2 The intercept point is at the intersection of the desired output power and the IM output power lines.

Generally, the nth-order input intercept is equal to

$$_N I_{in} = \text{Input} + \frac{\Delta}{N - 1} \qquad (3.4)$$

The third-order input intercept for a high-grade commercial HF SSB receiver is in the $+20$- to $+35$-dBm region, with intercepts below 0 dBm being on the low-performance side. Second-order input intercept values are higher, $+50$ to $+70$ dBm being typical.

Dynamic range

The simplest definition of dynamic range is just the ratio between the maximum signal that the receiver is capable of handling before overloading and distorting and the minimum signal producing a useful signal-to-noise ratio. This is the in-band dynamic range and would be 120 dB for a 1-V to 1-μV input ratio. It is a function of the receiver's bandwidth and the effectiveness of the automatic gain control circuits.

A more useful measure of dynamic range is the ability of a receiver to receive weak desired signals in the presence of strong out-of-band signals. If a pair of strong signals has an intermodulation product which lies in the receiver passband, sensitivity will be degraded by the interfering signal. Since the ear can recognize a desired signal at or somewhat below the receiver ambient noise level, one way to specify dynamic range is to state how far above the equivalent input noise level is each signal of a two-signal set whose IMD is equal to the input noise level. This definition of IM dynamic range is a function of the receiver's bandwidth since the noise power is proportional to bandwidth as defined by the expression

$$N = kTBFG \qquad (3.5)$$

where F is the noise factor and G is the receiver gain. Referred to the input, the noise power is just $kTBF$. This product expression is more easily handled by working with power in decibel units. Suppose the receiver's third-order input intercept point is Δ dB above the input noise. Since the third-order IMD slope is 3 (see Fig. 3.2), the per-signal input level of a two-signal set producing IM at the noise level is $\Delta/3$ below the intercept. The third-order IMD dynamic range (abbreviated DR$_3$) is the difference between the per-signal level of the two-signal set and the input noise level. In equation form:

$$\text{DR}_3 = \frac{2(_3 I_{in} - kTBF)}{3} \quad \text{dB} \qquad (3.6)$$

where $kTBF$ is understood to be expressed in decibel power units. A receiver having a 14-dB noise figure, 3-kHz noise bandwidth, and third-order input intercept of $+20$ dBm will have a dynamic range of:

$$DR = \frac{2[+20 - (-144 + 5 + 14)]}{3} = 96.7 \text{ dB}$$

From a practical standpoint, an off-frequency pair of signals, each having a level of -28.3 dBm, will produce a third-order intermodulation product which is equal to the receiver's input self-noise level of -125 dBm. With an antenna connected to the receiver, it is likely that the -125-dBm product will be further masked by external noise. However, the undesired signal level will not have to rise appreciably above -28 dBm before the IM interference is heard since the absolute power level of the product rises 3 dB for each decibel of undesired level increase.

Dynamic range can also be limited by noise sidebands present on the injection power to the first mixer. This effect, called "reciprocal mixing," was mentioned in Chap. 2 and is often noticed at colocated transmitter-receiver sites. Figure 3.3 illustrates the process which translates noise into the intermediate frequency when a strong off-frequency signal which is ideally spectrally pure is translated to the IF output together with the injection sideband noise. The translated signal frequency is then outside the IF passband while a portion of the noise spectrum lies within the passband. The mechanism in the mixer is simply preservation of instantaneous phase in the time domain as the injection vector is randomly advanced and retarded causing similar perturbation of the IF vector. When the off-frequency signal is close to the receiver's tuned frequency, 100 kHz away for example, the amplitude of the noise at the IF center may exceed the receiver self-noise. When the injection spectrum is known from measurement, it is readily possible to calculate the magnitude of reciprocal mixing by remembering that the IF spectrum is a recreation of the injection spectrum. If the injection noise is 100 dB below carrier at 100 kHz away from the injection frequency, then the IF noise due to reciprocal mixing will also be 100 dB below the IF carrier level at the mixer output.

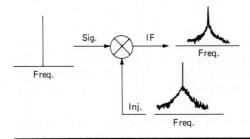

Figure 3.3 The mixer injection spectrum is heterodyned by a strong off-frequency pure signal into a spectrum offset from the IF and having noise sidebands identical in ratio to those of the injection.

3.3 Topology

Although the superheterodyne is ubiquitous in commercial HF receiver art, it is helpful to understand some of the alternative SSB receivers.

Historically, the first receiver type that could now be considered a candidate for solid-state design was the regenerative detector. This receiver consists of an oscillator whose feedback is adjusted to be just beyond the verge of oscillation for SSB or CW reception. The antenna is coupled to the oscillator's tuned circuit, and headphones or an audio amplifier are connected in the collector or drain circuit to listen to detected audio. Since the received signal tends to injection-lock the weak oscillator, SSB voice signals are distorted although CW signal reception is satisfactory.

The tuned radio frequency (TRF) receiver is a step above the regenerative design. The TRF topology consists of multiple synchronously tuned circuits separated by amplifiers to increase the signal level. Detection of SSB signals is accomplished by heterodyning the amplified signal with a local oscillator whose frequency is equal to the suppressed carrier of the SSB signal. The oscillator must be well shielded from the receiver input to avoid gain suppression by amplifier overload. The TRF receiver lacks the selectivity necessary for single-signal reception, meaning that rejection of the unwanted sideband is not possible when tunable HF filters are used. One specialized use for the TRF design is for a fixed tuned receiver where crystal filters are used for selectivity.

Another simple form of HF receiver is the homodyne or direct-conversion receiver. This receiver uses a conversion mixer preceded by some RF selectivity to heterodyne SSB or CW signals directly to audio frequency, using a carrier frequency local oscillator for mixer injection. A low-pass filter for SSB or a bandpass filter for CW directly follows the mixer to provide selectivity. This selectivity is less costly to implement than the bandpass filter used in a superheterodyne and is integrable into small size using either analog active filter or charge switching filter technology. Most or all of the receiver's gain is obtained in the AF amplifiers following the audio filter. This presents a challenge in audio amplifier design since noise and hum pickup must be kept very low. Another design and construction problem with the homodyne is leakage of the local oscillator into the RF filter and thence into the mixer. The mixer acts as a phase detector between the leakage and injection signals. If the oscillator has mechanical or electrical frequency instability, the resulting frequency modulation will cause audio output from the mixer. Also, since the RF selectivity is insufficient to reject the undesired sideband, this receiver has no unwanted sideband rejection. Despite these drawbacks, the direct-conversion receiver performs well, considering its simplicity, and is a practical design for hobby use.

Sideband selection can be obtained in a homodyne receiver by separately mixing the incoming signal with a local oscillator split into two paths having a 90° relative phase difference (Ref. 3). The resulting in-phase and quadrature audio channels are then phased-shifted a relative 90° with wideband networks and combined vectorially to output either the upper or lower sideband (USB or LSB). Low-pass selectivity then provides the receiver's major selectivity element. The ratio of desired to undesired sideband response in decibels may be found from

$$R = 10 \log \frac{1 + 2G \cos \phi + G^2}{1 - 2G \cos \phi + G^2} \quad \text{dB} \tag{3.7}$$

where G is the ratio of the I and Q channel voltage gains at the summing point and ϕ is the total phase error from 90° in the RF and audio phase shifters. With practical circuits, ratios of 30 dB are possible, which is low performance when compared to the 60 dB or more available with good band-pass filters in the superheterodyne.

The superheterodyne receiver, whose block diagram is shown in Fig. 3.4, is capable of providing excellent selectivity by using fixed-frequency filters after conversion of the signal to IF. The conversion is done with mixers whose injections are generally obtained from synthesizers having a stable reference source. In simpler designs, crystal or LC oscillators can provide adequate frequency stability. The various signal path blocks shown in Fig. 3.4 perform the following functions:

Input filter	Provides bandpass or low-pass selectivity to prevent first-mixer overload and spurious signal response.
First mixer	Converts the signal frequency to the first intermediate frequency, which may be either lower or higher than the signal frequency.
Crystal filter	Provides the first narrowband selectivity element in the receiver. Protects the following amplifier from overload by off-frequency large signals and attenuates the second-mixer image response. Also called a "roofing filter."
First IF amplifier	Provides gain and low noise figure as the first stage in the IF section. An IF amplifier may directly follow the first mixer when sensitivity is paramount.
Second mixer	Heterodynes the first IF to a new frequency where the major amount of the receiver's selectivity can be obtained with minimum cost.

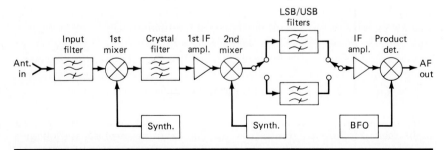

Figure 3.4   The superheterodyne uses multiple heterodyning and filtering to select the desired sideband.

LSB/USB filters	High-performance bandpass filters with 2- to 3-kHz passbands used for lower or upper sideband selection. A single filter may be used in low-cost designs.
IF amplifier	An integrated circuit or distributed component amplifier which provides a major amount of the receiver's gain. Includes gain control elements and selectivity to reduce wideband noise.
Product detector	Heterodynes the IF signal to audio using injection from the following beat frequency oscillator (BFO).
BFO	Provides injection power for the product detector. May be frequency-coordinated with the second-mixer injection to allow use of a single IF filter for LSB or USB selection.

The audio circuits following the product detector may contain functions in addition to gain and power output generation. Audio selectivity may be incorporated especially as the IF selectivity is narrowed by filter selection for CW. Syllabic rate-detection squelch circuits will also be found in the audio section. Squelch and other audio processing circuits are discussed in Chap. 6. Audio compression may be necessary in some designs, although that function is better accomplished with automatic gain control ahead of the product detector.

Historically, the frequency plan of the superheterodyne was first implemented with downconversion to successively lower frequencies where low-cost and high-performance selectivity could be obtained. This resulted in the requirement for high-performance and costly input filter selectivity to reject the image frequency. For example, a first conversion from 20 to 3 MHz using a 23-MHz injection would have an image response at 26 MHz which must be reduced with selectivity. The more recent availability of very-high-frequency (VHF) crystal filters using overtone-mode quartz crystal resonators has changed the frequency topology of modern HF receivers almost exclusively to upconversion schemes (Ref. 20). For example, the first IF might be 50 MHz, with the second IF as low as 455 kHz. The first injection for this case might range from 52 to 80 MHz for a signal range of 2 to 30 MHz, the first conversion being termed a "high-side difference mixer." Sum mixing would require an injection frequency span from 48 to 20 MHz. In either case, the image frequency band lies well above 30 MHz and so is readily filtered by fixed tuned bandpass or low-pass filters. This upconversion and broadband approach has great advantages in component cost, accuracy, and performance. It will be examined in detail in Sec. 3.4, Frequency Schemes.

3.4 Frequency Schemes

The optimum frequency scheme or plan for the HF superheterodyne involves tradeoffs between performance, circuit complexity, and cost. In this section we will discuss topics which influence the designer's choice of IF and injection frequencies, with emphasis on the spurious responses which are inherent in any scheme.

IF selection

The first important choice in selecting a frequency scheme is the determination of the intermediate frequency. As we have just seen, the upconverting superheterodyne is the primary topology for HF SSB use, so the IF must be above the highest signal frequency, or generally above 30 MHz. Crystal filters in production quantity are available up to about 150 MHz, with the cost increasing with frequency. There are several discrete frequency choices which may offer cost advantages because of high-volume usage by equipment in other services. These include:

45 MHz, used in cellular radiotelephones

70 MHz, a standard military IF for ultrahigh-frequency (UHF) equipment

75 MHz, the marker beacon frequency in civil aviation

These and other "round number" IF frequencies may not be optimum when the overall frequency scheme, including that in the synthesizer, is considered. One long-used IF at 109.35 MHz was based on the references used in a two-loop, sliding divisor synthesizer, the standard frequency, and the ease of multiplying the standard to get injection frequency for second-IF conversion.

The effects of IF upon receiver performance can be conflicting. As the IF is increased, the susceptibility of the receiver to spurious responses will diminish. These responses will be described in detail in the next section. An upconverting first mixer with a 45-MHz IF can be used to illustrate one class of spurious responses. If a relatively large signal at 22.5 MHz produces second harmonic distortion in the mixer, the resulting 45-MHz signal will directly enter the IF. For an upper signal limit of 35 MHz as set by the stopband of a low-pass filter before the mixer, a 75-MHz IF would reject the second harmonic spurious but would be susceptible to third harmonic interference. To reject third harmonics, an IF above 105 MHz would be required. As the IF is increased, however, the first-injection-carrier-to-noise ratio will generally degrade since the synthesizer must generate higher frequencies with constant step size. This means that reciprocal noise mixing (refer to Sec. 2.2) with strong off-frequency signals will become more noticeable as the IF rises. The apparent stopband selectivity of the overall IF will also be degraded as synthesizer noise enters the IF passband. Also, if receiver operation down to near zero frequency is required, the injection noise sidebands will directly enter the IF through mixer imbalance.

Intermediate frequencies above the readily available crystal filter range are not normally used in HF SSB receivers. Lumped or distributed constant LC filters, surface acoustic wave (SAW) transversal filters, SAW resonator filters, and chemically etched thin resonator filters all have practical problems with low Q, high insertion loss, and power-handling capability.

Spurious responses

The desired output frequency of an ideal mixer consists of the sum or difference of the signal and injection frequencies. The real mixer may also produce an identical output frequency when the input signal is at any one of numerous frequencies. This reality may be examined in detail by considering a general expression for the output of a mixer:

$$m\text{SIG} + n\text{LO} = \text{IF} \tag{3.8}$$

In this equation m and n are signed integers defining which harmonics of the signal (SIG) and local oscillator (LO or injection) can add or subtract from one another to produce an IF output. Depending upon the frequency scheme, m and n may be both positive, alternately positive or negative, but never both negative. In a receiver, the mixer is followed by narrowband selectivity (the crystal filter), so that the only mixing products of concern are those equal to the desired IF.

An example of a particular spurious response is helpful in seeing how Eq. (3.8) applies to a mixer. Illustrated in Fig. 3.5 is a mixer which upconverts the 2- to 30-MHz HF range to 100 MHz by adding a 98- to 70-MHz local oscillator to the signal. The plus signs at the signal and local oscillator ports indicate the sign of that addition. Thus, the desired mixing process has $m = +1$ and $n = +1$. Suppose that the desired signal is at 24 MHz, so that the local oscillator is set at 76 MHz to produce the desired IF of 100 MHz by summation. Further, suppose that there is a large undesired signal at 26 MHz which can easily reach the signal port through wideband filters to create second harmonic distortion in the mixer. The local oscillator also creates the second harmonic of 76 MHz in the mixer. For these harmonics, the arithmetic of Eq. (3.8) becomes $2 \times 76 - 2 \times 26 = 100$; that is, the second harmonic of the 76-MHz injection mixes subtractively with the second harmonic of the undesired 26-MHz signal to produce the 100-MHz IF. This IF signal passes through the receiver's IF, detection, and audio circuits and appears as an output even though the receiver indicates that it is tuned to 24 MHz rather than the undesired 26 MHz. This example response is sometimes referred to as a "2 by 2 response," corresponding to the magnitudes of m and n in the order of signal and local oscillator, respectively. It is also called a "fourth-order spurious response" because the sum of the harmonic magnitudes is 4.

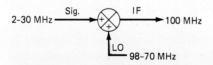

Figure 3.5 An example mixing scheme in which the HF signal is added to a backward-tuning local oscillator to produce a 100-MHz IF.

Another example of spurious responses, the "crossover," may be found in the foregoing example when the receiver is tuned to 25 MHz. Then the local oscillator is at 75 MHz, and its second harmonic mixes with the second harmonic of 25 MHz to again generate the 100-MHz IF. This case is called a "crossover response" because the desired and undesired signal frequencies are equal. If the frequencies are exactly 25 and 75 MHz, the resultant IF vector voltage is only perturbed by a constant amplitude and phase change due to the spurious response. When the 25-MHz signal is an SSB signal with varying instantaneous frequency, the crossover response causes in-band distortion in the audio output if the mixer is poorly designed. Fortunately, this example response can be very well suppressed with well-designed balanced mixers.

Determination of spurious response locations can be an intuitively difficult task without some kind of aid. Equation (3.8) can be expanded into a simultaneous set by using the subscripts d for desired responses and u for undesired responses:

$$m_d \text{SIG} + n_d \text{LO} = \text{IF} \tag{3.9a}$$

$$m_u \text{UND} + n_u \text{LO} = \text{IF} \tag{3.9b}$$

In the second equation of this set UND represents the undesired spurious response which may or may not cross the desired frequency SIG. If UND = SIG, i.e., if there is a crossover response, a graphical aid may be constructed by equating the set to give

$$\text{SIG} = \text{LO} \, \frac{n_u - n_d}{m_d - m_u} \tag{3.10}$$

This is the equation of a straight line on axes of SIG and LO passing through the 0,0 origin and having a slope of $(n_u - n_d)/(m_d - m_u)$. Using the prior upconversion example, it can be seen that $m_d = +1$, $n_d = +1$, $m_u = -2$, and $n_u = +2$, so that SIG = LO/3. This slope of ⅓ line is plotted in Fig. 3.6 together with a dotted line representing the relations between the signal and local oscillator which produces a 100-MHz IF. The intersection at SIG = 25 MHz is, as shown before, the frequency at which the IF produced by the desired SIG + LO response is indistinguishable from the undesired -2SIG $+ 2$LO response.

This type of crossover graph may be further generalized by considering both sum and difference mixing and finding the line slopes for higher-order responses. Reference 4 contains a chart useful for up to ninth-order responses.

The use of the crossover chart is not restricted to the fixed-IF example. It sometimes happens in receivers and often in complex frequency synthesizer schemes that all three mixer port frequencies are varying and are related by some independent variable. If the relationship is linear, the desired mixing line is straight; otherwise it is curved. The intersections still give the crossover points at which multiple responses occur.

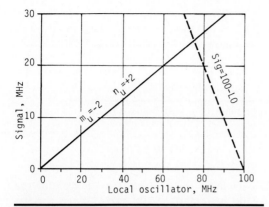

Figure 3.6 A spurious crossover response graph showing the loci of the fourth-order 2 × 2 responses for a sum mixer (solid line) and the intersecting dotted line of an upconverter with 100-MHz IF.

The general simultaneous equation set may be manipulated in almost endless ways to create graphs, pocket calculator routines, and computer programs fulfilling special needs. For example, the simultaneous equations may be normalized by one of the input frequencies to form a spurious graph with frequency ratio coordinates (see Ref. 5). Another variation is to express the undesired response frequency separation from the desired in percent (Ref. 6). This is useful for finding how far away a noncrossing response is from the signal frequency. Spurious response separation can also be plotted vs. signal frequency by defining the ordinate to be Δ_{freq}, the algebraic difference between undesired and desired response frequencies. This presentation succinctly displays the entire response picture, both crossing and noncrossing.

Internal signals

Another source of undesired response interference is that emanating from sources within the receiver. These responses do not depend upon external signals and are often called "birdies" because of their characteristic sound as the receiver is tuned. In an HF receiver it is practically impossible to avoid having oscillators within the tuning range of the receiver. The internal frequency standard, operating in the 3- to 10-MHz region for best stability, is an example of such an internal source. The only way to avoid in-band internal signals is to shield and filter to the point of inaudibility, a difficult task if low-cost, open, printed circuit board construction is used. High-performance receivers require shielding of signal generator quality to avoid unusable frequencies.

The frequency scheme itself should be analyzed to avoid building in birdies that can be avoided without other penalty. In Fig. 3.7, for example, a second mixer and IF are added to the 100-MHz upconverter scheme to allow

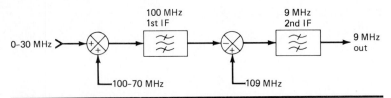

Figure 3.7   A frequency scheme having a 100-MHz first IF followed by a 9-MHz second IF has the second injection at 109 MHz to avoid an internal spurious beat with leakage from the first injection.

adding selectivity at the 9-MHz second IF. There are two choices for the injection frequency into the second mixer, 91 or 109 MHz. When the 91-MHz frequency is used, leakage from the first injection at 82 MHz (corresponding to a signal frequency of 18 MHz) could pass around or through the 100-MHz crystal filter, enter the second mixer, and produce the 9-MHz IF. This situation is avoided by picking a 109-MHz second injection so that the first injection can never be 9 MHz away from the second injection. The frequency inaccuracy of the second injection is partially canceled by the other injection inaccuracies such that the overall stability of the receiver is equal to the frequency standard.

When harmonics of the injection sources are considered, it becomes difficult to foresee the many internal spurious signals which may be generated. This analysis problem is similar to that for spurious responses and is readily attacked with computer programs which methodically plod through all the combinations and present only those which can pass through the IF selectivity. Knowing the oscillators, harmonics, and circuit paths responsible for the birdies, the designer can make appropriate choices of frequency scheme, shielding, and filtering to reduce or eliminate them.

RF selectivity

We have seen that the noncrossing spurious responses can be attenuated by providing selectivity ahead of the first mixer. The question of how much selectivity and how it is to be implemented involves the usual tradeoffs between cost, complexity, and performance. One response which must be attenuated to a great degree is the image. In our 100-MHz IF sum upconverter example the image moves from 198 to 170 MHz as the signal tunes from 2 to 30 MHz. Throughout the world this range is well occupied with large signal sources from television transmitters and other emitters. Typically, a 2- to 30-MHz bandpass filter will be used between the antenna and the first mixer to eliminate the image response, this architecture being termed "wideband." This requires no switching in the receiver input and so is low in cost. In frequency-hopping receivers the fixed-input filter eliminates hopping noise generation which could occur if switched filters interrupted strong CW signals.

The penalty for the wideband architecture is increased spurious responses due to harmonics of HF signals being generated in the mixer. If a receiver tuned to 10 MHz has no selectivity at 5 MHz, a strong signal at 5 MHz with no harmonic energy of its own will produce 10 MHz through mixer distortion. An effective topology is to use *half-octave* filters which are switched as required across the 2- to 30-MHz range. A half-octave filter is a bandpass filter whose passband is about one-half octave wide such as 2 to 3 MHz. These filters and narrower preselection filters are discussed in Chap. 8.

3.5 Block Diagram Design

In this section we will examine some of the techniques for designing an SSB receiver at the block diagram level. This will include the aspects of gain and noise figure distribution, optimization for intermodulation distortion, synthesizer injection noise effects, and automatic gain control.

Level diagrams

A level diagram is a pictorial way of describing any quantity or property in the receiver's signal path so that individual blocks are defined or optimization can be made. For example, we might wish to make a gain distribution diagram to show how a 1-μV signal is amplified throughout the receiver stages to produce a 1-V audio output signal. On the same diagram, the actual voltage, or power level, at each point can also be shown. Knowing the input and output power levels, the cumulative IMD or intercept points can be plotted. Cumulative noise figure is also a useful line item on a level diagram.

Figure 3.8 illustrates the use of a level diagram to describe the gain and noise figure of stages up to the output of the second mixer. The diagram is prepared by filling in the individual stage gain and stage noise figure rows

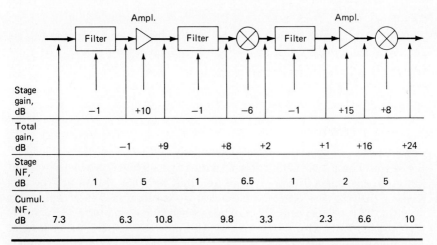

Figure 3.8 A level diagram which describes the gain and noise figure distribution up through the second mixer.

with values which experience or manufacturer's data indicate can be obtained. The total gain and cumulative noise figure rows can then be calculated, the latter using the Friis equation in which F_{in} is

$$F_{\text{in}} = F_A + \frac{F_{\text{out}} - 1}{G_A} \qquad (3.11)$$

the input noise factor (a power ratio) to the stage, F_A is the amplifier or other block intrinsic noise factor (measured as if there were no subsequent noise sources), G_A is the amplifier available power gain (again, a numeric ratio), and F_{out} is the output noise factor terminating the stage. The noise figure, abbreviated NF, is found from the noise factor by

$$\text{NF} = 10 \log_{10}(F) \qquad \text{dB} \qquad (3.12)$$

These calculations are quickly made with a hand calculator having a 10^x or Y^x function in addition to logarithms. An important fact that facilitates computation is that the noise factor of a passive network is the reciprocal of the available gain (see Friis, Ref. 1). In decibels, the passive network noise figure is equal to the loss.

If a great amount of component selection tradeoff studies and comparisons are to be made, a very efficient analysis tool is one of the spread sheet programs for personal computers (Ref. 21). The spread sheet columns can be related by any mathematical expression and become a powerful way of quickly seeing the influence of changes anywhere in the block diagram.

There is one other detail that should be understood before leaving the subject of gain and noise figure diagrams. When calculating noise figure, the precisely correct form of gain is the available power gain as defined by Friis. In equation form:

$$G_{\text{av}} = \frac{P_{\text{out avail}}}{P_{\text{gen avail}}} \qquad (3.13)$$

in which $P_{\text{out avail}}$ is the power available at the output terminals of the stage, i.e, a conjugate match. $P_{\text{gen avail}}$ is the available generator power. The more commonly measured value of gain is transducer gain, which is defined by the ratio

$$G_T = \frac{P_{\text{deliv to load}}}{P_{\text{gen avail}}} \qquad (3.14)$$

in which $P_{\text{deliv to load}}$ is the actual power delivered to a specific test load on the stage. These two definitions of gain are equivalent when the output reflection coefficient is zero, a condition that may not always be true in a receiver cascade. For practical purposes, G_T is often used interchangeably with G_{av}. The error so caused is not large when the second term of Eq. (3.11) is small compared with the first term. Also note that the resistance level at each point in the block diagram need not be known when transducer gain is used. If voltage levels are to be shown, the stage interface resistances need to be accounted for so that the power levels are consistent with the trans-ducer gains.

The level diagram can also be used to compute the input intercept point of the receiver by using a stage-by-stage calculation approach similar to that used for noise figure. In Fig. 3.9, a single stage is defined with a third-order input intercept of $_3I_1$ expressed in power such as milliwatts rather than the usual logarithmic ratio, dBm. Similarly, the input intercept with which the stage is terminated, $_3I_2$, is given in power units. The input third-order inter-cept of the stage plus its termination is

$$_3I_{\text{in}} = \frac{1}{1/_3I_1 + G_1/_3I_2} \qquad \text{power} \tag{3.15}$$

Starting with the output termination of a receiver having infinite intercept watts, this relation can be used to find the cumulative input intercepts at each point in the block diagram. For example, in the cascade of a mixer, amplifier, and crystal filter shown in Fig. 3.10, the individual stage intercepts are shown both in dBm and in milliwatts for clarity. The infinite intercept shown looking into the IF system is assumed to be valid in the stopband of the crystal filter, which precludes the entry of a strong off-frequency signal into the IF. Therefore, the intercept into the filter is $+50$ dBm or $100,000$ mW. Looking now at the input to the amplifier, the cascaded intercept is found from Eq. (3.15) to be 99 mW, which is 19.96 dBm. The mixer gain is -6 dB, which is 0.25 in power ratio. Using that value for gain and the 25-dBm mixer input intercept together with the amplifier input intercept just determined, the total input intercept of 176 mW or 22.45 dBm is found.

This example and Fig. 3.9 illustrate some shortcuts to aid in quickly esti-mating the intercept point of a cascade. A stage terminated in an intercept much larger than its own intercept will have a net input intercept nearly equal to the stage value. Loss in the signal path increases the intercept and, if distortionless, increases the intercept by the amount of the attenuation. The receiver dynamic range as defined in this chapter is not increased by attenuation since the desired signal is reduced by the same amount. The input intercept of a stage will be 3 dB below that of the stage alone when

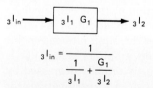

Figure 3.9 Definition of the intercept point cas-cading rule which uses power and power ratios as parameter units.

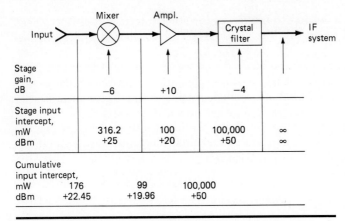

Figure 3.10 Example of a receiver front end to show the calculation of intercept points.

the terminating intercept minus the stage gain is equal to the stage intercept.

Second-order intercept calculations may be accomplished with similar methods except that the cascading equation becomes:

$$_2I_{in} = \frac{1}{(1/\sqrt{_2I_1} + \sqrt{G_1/_2I_2})^2} \tag{3.16}$$

Formulas exist additionally for handling higher-order intercept calculations. Wilson (Ref. 7) gives a concise introduction to this area. In intermodulation distortion calculations it should also be clearly understood that all of the defining equations stem from the straight-line plots of IM vs. signal level as shown in Fig. 3.2. Not all active or passive elements are so well behaved. Doubly balanced diode mixers and bulk quartz crystal filters in particular can be difficult to model with straight-line equations, and departure from the theoretical performance can be expected in practical circuit designs.

Optimization

The receiver attributes of sensitivity and dynamic range are conflicting and cannot be simultaneously increased by manipulation of front-end topology and gain distribution. Noise figure can be improved by adding a low-noise RF amplifier before the first mixer but this reduces the input intercept point by at least the amount of amplifier gain. When amplifier distortion is accounted for, the IM dynamic range of a receiver is actually decreased by adding an RF amplifier in front of the mixer. Sensitivity specifications for some unique applications may require an input noise figure lower than the 12 to 15 dB possible with a mixer-only front end, so that RF amplification is necessary. In some cases it is also necessary to use a low-noise IF amplifier between the first-mixer output and the following filter. When amplifier-mixer cascades are involved, tradeoffs can be calculated to optimize the receiver's performance vs. cost and complexity.

Before examining tradeoff techniques, the reciprocal mixing phenomenon discussed in Sec. 3.1 should be compared to the IM performance of the front end. It is inefficient to suppress IM products below the level of reciprocal mixing noise and, conversely, to produce a synthesized injection source that is purer than needed from an intermodulation standpoint. To make this comparison, some idea or specification of the maximum undesired off-frequency signal strength is needed. Letting the undesired signal power be P_{in}, measured in units of power, and rearranging Eq. (3.3) in terms of power, the following relation is obtained:

$$_3IP = \frac{P_{in}^{3/2}}{P_{im}^{1/2}} \tag{3.17}$$

The equivalent input noise to the receiver comes from the input noise floor, $kTBF$, and the reciprocal mixing noise referred to the input. Letting the total noise N_T be equal to the equivalent input intermodulation power gives an expression for the maximum usable input intercept point:

$$_3IP = \frac{P_{in}^{3/2}}{N_T^{1/2}} \tag{3.18}$$

A numerical example illustrates the calculation of the maximum usable input intercept for a particular case. Suppose we have a receiver with the following characteristics:

Noise figure = 14 dB

Bandwidth = 3 kHz

Injection carrier to noise ratio = 100 dB (100 kHz away and measured in a
3-kHz bandwidth)

With a -20-dBm undesired input signal 100 kHz away from the desired frequency, the noise power due to reciprocal mixing is -120 dBm, or 1×10^{-12} mW. The equivalent $kTBF$ noise is found to be 3×10^{-13} mW, so that the total input noise is 1.3×10^{-12} mW. The input intercept is therefore:

$$_3IP = \frac{(1 \times 10^{-2})^{3/2}}{(1.3 \times 10^{-12})^{1/2}} \tag{3.19}$$
$$= 877 \text{ mW or } +29.4 \text{ dBm}$$

This analysis has ignored the practical fact that the interfering signal may itself have noise sidebands which lie within the passband of the receiver. This noise power available from the antenna acts to further reduce the intercept point needed in a practical sense.

Proceeding now to the problem of optimizing a practical receiver front end in terms of cost and complexity tradeoffs for constant input noise figure and intercept point performance, consider the block diagram shown in Fig. 3.11. The objective is to find the tradeoff relationship between $_3I_1$ and $_3I_2$ while holding $_3I_{in}$ and F_{in} constant. The noise factor F_3 looking into the filter includes the filter loss plus the cumulative noise factor of the receiver's IF system. The filter's input intercept $_3I_3$ is an out-of-band intercept for the filter, the remaining IF stages being protected by the filter stopband attenuation. Application of the Friis noise factor cascade equation to this block diagram gives:

$$F_{in} = \frac{1}{G_1}\left(F_2 + \frac{F_3 - 1}{G_2}\right) \tag{3.20}$$

Also, the intercept cascading equation can be used to relate $_3I_1$ and $_3I_2$:

$$\frac{1}{_3I_{in}} = \frac{1}{_3I_1} + \frac{G_1}{_3I_2} + \frac{G_1G_2}{_3I_3} \tag{3.21}$$

For illustration, let this front end use a doubly balanced diode mixer with 6-dB loss and, neglecting any additive noise, a 6-dB noise figure. For calculation purposes, let the IF amplifier gain G_2 be a variable which does not affect the amplifier noise figure. This is reasonably true for high-performance lossless feedback amplifier circuits. The amplifier noise figure will be 4.77 dB (power ratio of 3), which is representative of a high-dynamic-range VHF feedback amplifier. And let the IF system noise figure be 9 dB, which includes the combined termination loss and insertion loss of the filter plus the cascaded noise of the rest of the IF. Converting all numbers to power ratios and substituting into Eq. (3.20) gives:

$$F_{in} = 4\left(3 + \frac{7.94 - 1}{G_2}\right)$$

Finally, let us ask for a receiver input noise figure of 12 dB, which results in an IF amplifier gain G_2 of 7.22 or 8.58 dB.

Now turning to the intercept cascade equation, let the filter input intercept be 50 dBm (10^5 mW). Equation (3.21) therefore contains input, mixer, and amplifier intercepts as variables. Figure 3.12 shows the results of solving the equation with the input intercept as a running parameter. As can be

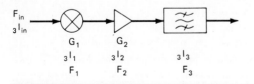

Figure 3.11 A front-end cascade having general values of gain, intercept point, and noise figure for optimization analysis.

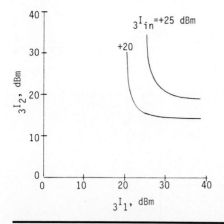

Figure 3.12 Contours of a constant-input intercept for a mixer-amplifier-filter cascade having a 12-dB input noise figure together with gain, intercept, and noise figure constraints.

seen, mixer intercept can be traded for amplifier intercept within a range bounded by the input intercept asymptote on the mixer axis and the input intercept minus the mixer gain (-6-dB) asymptote on the amplifier axis. For a receiver input intercept of 20 dBm, the mixer intercept might be about 21.3 dBm when the amplifier intercept is 20 dB.

A poor design decision would put either the mixer or amplifier input intercepts near asymptotes since the cost of achieving large intercepts is high. The optimum decision can be a complex judgment based on the above analysis applied to the cost, circuit complexity, reliability, and power consumption of the actual circuits involved.

AGC design

The means for providing automatic gain control for the overall receiver are important aspects of the block diagram design for an HF SSB receiver. The receiver is operationally required to have nearly constant audio output as the signal input ranges from the 1-μV region to perhaps 1 V or more and to do so without having loop oscillation or distorting the received signal. A receiver primarily designed to be used by an operator for signal search or monitoring will typically allow an audio output rise of 6 dB or so over the input signal range. A receiver for data signals, on the other hand, can have a very flat output requirement so that the following data-detection circuits have a constant-amplitude input.

Some insight into AGC loop design can be obtained by studying the receiver signal path shown in Fig. 3.13, which includes voltage-controlled attenuators in the RF, first-IF, and second-IF sections. A detector at the output develops a dc output voltage proportional to the IF or AF output

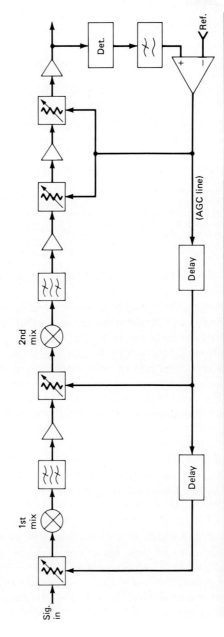

Figure 3.13 A double-conversion receiver has distributed AGC attenuators to prevent stage overload while also causing the output S/N ratio to rise with signal increases.

level. IF detection is normally used because it gives less time delay (more charging cycles per second) and has output even when the product detector audio output frequency is zero. After low-pass filtering, the voltage is compared with a reference such that gain control action commences when the signal input has reached some threshold level such as that causing a 6-dB signal-to-noise ratio. As the input signal rises, attenuators at the end of the IF path are used first, preventing overload of the output stages as they reach their signal amplitude limit. Since attenuators at the input of the receiver are not yet being used, the gain into the first and second mixers does not change and the input noise figure is not materially increased. This results in a very nearly linear increase in output signal-to-noise ratio vs. input signal increase. If all of the attenuation were placed at the receiver's input, the output S/N ratio would rise to the threshold value and stay there (or rise only slightly) as the signal level is increased. The delay blocks represent voltage delay circuits which enable the forward-placed IF and RF attenuators at signal levels which are ideally just in advance of succeeding stage overload or IM level specification limits. As the input attenuator begins to operate with rising signal strength, the output S/N ratio becomes constant with a value ranging from 30 to 50 dB in typical designs. The ultimate S/N ratio is usually limited by the synthesizer phase noise when the IF delays are properly placed.

The amount of dc gain needed in the AGC loop is dependent upon the output rise characteristics previously described. If the audio output as represented by the detected dc voltage is 1 V at threshold and a 6-dB output rise is acceptable for input signals at some maximum level, the dc voltage will rise to 2 V and the differential output will be 1 V. An AGC amplifier gain of only 10 would suffice to cause a 10-V AGC line increase to operate the RF and IF attenuators. On the other extreme, if virtually no output rise is desired, the AGC amplifier is replaced by an operational amplifier integrator whose huge low-frequency gain makes the output as constant as the nonlinearities of the final IF stage and detector will allow. When an integrator is used, it forms part of the low-pass filter which is required to remove envelope audio from the gain control voltage. This can result in unacceptable signal attack time delays unless nonlinear circuits are used.

The dynamics of the AGC loop constitute the most difficult part of the gain control design. An AGC loop is a feedback system having gain which is dependent upon the carrier strength in the forward path. It is entirely possible for the loop to be stable at one value of signal input and be oscillatory for another value of signal. In the reference by W. K. Victor and M. H. Brockman (Ref. 8) it is shown that when the signal level and receiver attenuation are expressed in logarithmic units, the loop becomes a linear servomechanism. This means that the attenuators at each point in the receiver should have a slope which advances at least approximately 1 dB per unit of control voltage throughout the control range. It is points of high slope that contribute to instability, as evidenced by poor transient response to a step in signal input or outright oscillation at a particular input signal level. When the attenuators are logarithmic, the loop gain is constant, and linear servo-mechanism design techniques can be applied to design a stable loop.

The impulse-loading characteristic of the AGC system must be considered in the receiver block design so that overshoot in gain control is not excessive when a strong signal or noise impulse is received. A dual time constant approach has been used to solve the impulse-loading problem. The loop filter is designed to have some transmission at frequencies in the 100- to 300-Hz range such that some gain control can be rapidly applied without causing a large amount of charge in the integrator or low-pass filter. The receiver gain will then rapidly recover after the noise burst or signal impulse has ceased, so that a weak signal can be immediately recognized. This technique is a compromise with envelope distortion caused by envelope frequency appearing on the control voltage to the attenuators.

Another problem associated with the narrow-bandwidth IF filters of the receiver is the absolute time delay incurred by the signal as it passes through the IF. When a rapidly rising signal is at the input, the AGC detector has no output until the signal propagates through the filters. The input stages then may be in overload during the delay time interval. When the signal does reach the detector, the system may overcompensate by reducing the gain more than necessary because of the energy stored in the IF filter. This effect can be practically reduced by using lead compensation on the voltage driving the attenuators ahead of the IF selectivity. The dual time constant filter mentioned above also helps reduce the effects of filter time delay.

A state variable type of AGC loop called "hang AGC" is very often used to obtain rapid recovery of receiver gain after signal cessation while also having very low envelope distortion due to audio on the gain control line. The loop filter is designed to charge rapidly to follow the rising signal input and then to remain at that level after the signal drops. In effect, the receiver gain "hangs" for a preset amount of time. For voice systems the attack time should be in the 2-ms region with a hang time of about 0.3 s followed by a gradual recovery time of up to 1 s. Adaptive circuits can be designed which give shorter hang and recovery time as the signal on-time decreases, thus minimizing impulse loading of the AGC system.

Since a microprocessor is often used elsewhere in an otherwise analog receiver, it is an attractive possibility to consider a digitally closed gain control loop. The output of the AGC detector or even the detected audio can be sampled and processed for average, rms, or peak amplitude determination. After adaptive processing, the gain control is applied with digital-to-analog converters to the various attenuators in the receiver. Alternatively, step-value attenuators can be used as opposed to continuous-function attenuators. The latter generate intermodulation distortion when the control current or voltage is low, which occurs near the minimum attenuation end of the range. Computed AGC can achieve infinite hang time when needed. An example of this would be to return the receiver to a set gain point after a companion transmitter completes its transmission, thereby readying the receiver for an expected signal strength.

3.6   Components

The design of a solid-state SSB receiver is heavily influenced by the available components together with their performance and cost. A thorough knowledge of components is as valuable to the design engineer as are the theoretical design details of receivers. This section will highlight some of the current state-of-the-art components that are applicable to HF receiver design and will show some of the associated circuit design techniques.

Front-end components

It is in the front end that the greatest amount of work and progress is made in the effort to improve intermodulation and sensitivity performance. The input signal to IF mixer, RF or IF amplifiers if used, and first band-limiting filter are the critical components in front-end design.

Mixers

There are two broad classes of frequency mixers used in SSB receivers, passive and active. A passive mixer is generally one which has insertion loss and is often bidirectional, that is, one in which signal conversion can flow in two directions. The prime example of a passive mixer is the diode mixer, and more specifically, the doubly balanced diode mixer. The latter is the most widely available mixing component in the HF-through-microwave region and is obtainable with a variety of performance specifications. Active mixers contain elements having transconductance and therefore have conversion gain. They are almost always unidirectional. Transistors, both bipolar and field effect, form the basis for active mixer designs, which are usually custom-designed for a particular receiving requirement. There can be exceptions to the passive and active classes, the parametric mixer being one example. This type of mixer contains varactor diodes as the active component. Although a varactor does not have transconductance, the parametric mixer can have gain, the added power being obtained by conversion of injection power to IF power (Ref. 9).

In Fig. 3.14 the schematic diagram of a doubly balanced mixer is drawn in two ways. In Fig. 3.14*a*, the conventionally used schematic illustrates the cathode-to-anode connection around the ring of four diodes, often referred to as a "diode quad." The diodes are usually silicon Schottky contact types having low capacitance and charge storage time that are matched for forward voltage drop and reverse capacitance over a wide dynamic range. The transformers use ferrite cores with transmission line winding construction when possible to maximize bandwidth. The combination of diode matching and high transformer coupling coefficients results in typical port-to-port isolation of 30 dB or more. Thus, the injection signal at the LO port is attenuated by 30 dB as it arrives at the RF or IF ports.

The redrawn schematic in Fig. 3.14*b* perhaps more clearly illustrates the

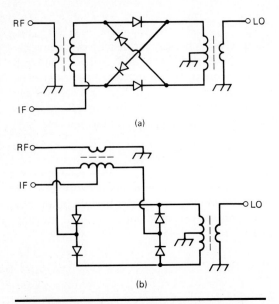

Figure 3.14 Schematic diagrams of the doubly balanced diode mixer. (*a*) Conventional circuit of a doubly balanced diode mixer. (*b*) Redrawn circuit emphasizes the commutation of the RF signal to the IF port by the local oscillator.

switching action of the mixer. At some instant the injection polarity might be such that forward current is flowing downward in the left-hand pair of series diodes. Since the diode forward voltage drops are matched, the potential at the cathode-anode node is zero with respect to ground by virtue of the center tap on the local oscillator transformer. The RF signal voltage appearing across half the RF input transformer therefore is switched to the IF output port. When the injection polarity reverses and the right-hand pair of series diodes is forward-biased, the other end of the RF signal transformer is switched to ground. The IF port then receives the RF signal with opposite polarity, a 180° phase shift. When the switching action is rectangular, the resulting IF spectrum consists only of the sum and difference of the RF and LO frequencies, with the RF and LO being suppressed in the IF output.

When one pair of diodes is forward-current-biased, the other pair is reverse-voltage-biased by the voltage drop of the forward pair. If the RF signal becomes comparable in power to the injection, the switching times become a function of the RF as well as local oscillator signals. This results in single-signal compression and multiple-signal intermodulation distortion. The signal-handling capability can be increased in many ways, usually involving more diodes and injection power. Two or more diodes in series or parallel can be used in each diode position. Resistors can be placed in series with each diode to increase the voltage drop with an attendant increase in conversion loss.

Circuit modifications can increase the diode mixer's signal-handling capability. In Fig. 3.15 each single pair of diodes from Fig. 3.14*b* has been replaced by a sampling quad of four diodes. Note that the diode quads are connected in a series-parallel arrangement rather than in the ring arrangement used in the simple doubly balanced mixer. The RF signal phase-reversing commutation principle is still the same but the resistors in series with each diode quad cause large reverse bias voltage to appear across the nonconducting set. Greater than 30-dBm third-order input intercept points can be obtained with this mixer compared to 20 dBm for the four-diode circuit using 7-dBm injection power. The cost of increased mixer dynamic range is injection power with levels of up to 1 W being used in commercially available mixers.

Another diode mixer improvement is to use square wave as opposed to sine wave injection. This minimizes the diode transition time from conducting to nonconducting states, making the switching more independent of signal level. Upconverting HF mixers with third-order input intercept points of 43 dBm or more have been constructed using square wave drive from transistor-limiting amplifiers having transition time in the 1-ns region.

When a high-dynamic-range mixer is used as the first active stage in a receiver, there can be a very real problem with the noise of the injection entering the mixer, at both RF and IF. This desensitizes the receiver by decreasing the signal-to-noise ratio at the mixer output and is especially noticeable in low-front-end-gain receivers with no RF stage. The extent of this problem is illustrated by considering a -113-dBm input signal to the mixer which is producing a 10-dB output-signal-to-noise ratio. With 6-dB conversion loss, the IF signal power out of the mixer is only -119 dBm and the equivalent noise level is about -129 dBm, neglecting additive sources within the mixer itself. For a mixer-injection-to-IF-port balance of 30 dB, a -99-dBm noise level at the IF would degrade the signal-to-noise ratio by 3 dB. If the injection power is $+30$ dBm for a large mixer, the injection-carrier-to-noise ratio is 129 dB. This large ratio is especially difficult to main-

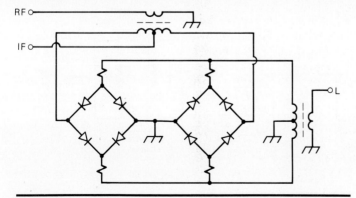

Figure 3.15 A high-level diode mixer using sampling diode quads for signal commutation.

tain when the injection frequency approaches the IF at the low-frequency end of the tuning range.

The injection noise problem can be minimized by a combination of approaches. The obvious improvement is to increase the mixer balance. The noise balance point may not be coincident with balance of second-order IM distortion, however. The bandwidth of the injection amplifier should just cover the necessary band. Low-frequency resonances in the amplifier dc feed circuits should be suppressed to prevent noise generation by high-impedance collector loading. When linear injection amplifiers are used, linearity improvement to reduce second-order distortion will minimize translation of HF noise to VHF within the amplifier. Finally, the voltage-controlled synthesizer oscillator (VCO) should be operated at as high a level as is consistent with tuning range and tuning voltage limitations. This minimizes the amount of injection amplifier gain. It is not advisable to inject the mixer directly from a power VCO since large signal levels entering the mixer would then pass through the RF to injection-port-imbalance and perturb the oscillator.

The doubly balanced mixer is sensitive to reflection of conversion sidebands from its three ports. Intermodulation is especially degraded when reactive sources and loads are present at the RF and IF ports and is a strong function of frequency as the mixer is used over the HF band. The circuit blocks illustrated in Fig. 3.16 cause matched or "50-ohm" terminations to be presented to the mixer at each port (Ref. 11). At the RF port, a complementary low-pass-high-pass filter is used to get a wideband match. The filters are synthesized from Butterworth single-side-loaded prototypes (Ref. 10) and are scaled to have identical cutoff frequencies above the HF range. The open-circuit ends of the filters are paralleled, the result being a constant-resistance node whose bandwidth is limited only by practical consideration of lumped component accuracy vs. frequency. The injection amplifier output is attenuated by about 3 dB for sine wave injection to improve the return loss seen by the mixer. The attenuator would not be used if square wave

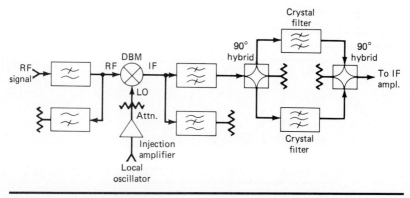

Figure 3.16 Improved IM performance is obtainable when low SWR terminations are used on the mixer ports.

injection were being applied. The circuits in the IF path are necessary to allow the use of a crystal filter directly after the mixer for best IM performance while eliminating the poor termination on the mixer in the stopband of the filter where power is reflected back into the IF port. The desired IF is passed through an *LC* bandpass filter to the following 90° hybrid splitter. Frequencies other than IF are passed to a 50-ohm load via an *LC* band-reject filter. The 90° hybrid has the valuable property that when its output ports are terminated in equal complex reflection coefficients, the input resistance remains 50 ohms. With two reasonably identical crystal filters in the hybrid outputs, the equal-reflection-coefficient condition is satisfied both in the passband and well into the stopband (Ref. 12). The 90° hybrid need not have extremely large bandwidth since the bandpass and band-reject filters can take care of the mixer loading well into the UHF region for an HF-to-VHF upconverting mixer. The crystal filter outputs must be combined in quadrature. A second hybrid may be used for this purpose or, alternatively, simple +45° and −45° L-section matching networks may be used to combine the outputs since the operating bandwidth is set by the crystal filters.

It is possible to construct "termination-insensitive" passive mixers by combining two or more mixers with hybrid transformers such that mixer products are returned to the mixer rather than to the external terminations. Since additional components are present, this type of mixer has greater insertion loss than the simpler doubly balanced type and has not had popularity in HF receiver designs. Reference 13 contains more information on this technique.

Passive mixers can be built with transistor switches substituted for the diodes of balanced mixers. For example, in Fig. 3.17 the field-effect transistors (FETs) are gate-controlled by the local oscillator to cause alternating polarity of the signal to IF path similar to that shown in Fig. 3.14*b*. When fast microwave FETs such as the NEC NE 868299 are used in this circuit input, intercepts of 30 dBmw can be obtained with injection power of well under 1 W. The balance of any mixer using discrete transistors will be poorer than the balance of a diode mixer because of the difficulty of matching the

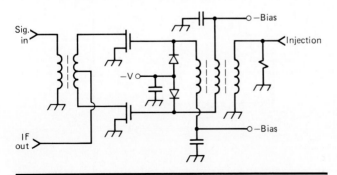

Figure 3.17 Low-gate-capacitance microwave power field-effect transistors may be used as switches in a passive mixer.

rather complex transistor parameters over the operating range. Matching can be greatly improved by integrating the transistors onto one custom chip when it is economically feasible to do so. Passive mixers using four complementary metal-oxide semiconductor/silicon-on-sapphire (CMOS/SOS) transistors in an integrated quad ring can be built having reliable input third-order intercept points of 35 dBm over the HF band in an upconversion (109.35-MHz) receiver (Ref. 20).

A doubly balanced mixer illustrating the use of bipolar medium-power transistors is shown in Fig. 3.18. The circuit is that of a pair of transconductance mixers with emitter resistors added for IM improvement. Resistors in the base and collector leads add loss of ultrahigh frequencies to suppress parasitic oscillations caused by resonances formed by circuit and transistor capacitances together with the leakage reactance of the associated transformers. Injection is applied through a balancing transformer to the bases which are overdriven, resulting in signal switching-action. Collector supply voltage is applied to the output transformer centertap through a parallel resistor-inductor to further suppress oscillation. Although the transistors are operating as injection-controlled signal polarity switches, the impedance ratio between the signal emitters and the IF output collectors results in a modest gain of a few decibels. This can be very desirable when noise figure requirements make the loss of the diode mixer unattractive. Using transistors such as the Motorola MRF 517, this active mixer will give a 3-dB gain, 9-dB noise figure, and +25-dBm input intercept over the 2- to 30-MHz band as an upconverter to the 100-MHz range. This type of mixer is also available in integrated circuit (IC) form, the Motorola MC1596 being a low-level device and the Plessey SL6440 being a high-level receiving mixer (Ref. 21).

Spurious signal responses in mixers are of great concern, especially in the first mixer of a receiver. The magnitude of these responses, whose frequency

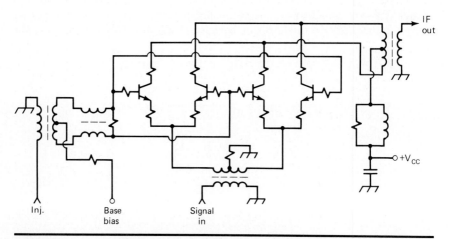

Figure 3.18 A doubly balanced active mixer uses bi-polar transistors in a degenerated version of the balanced transconductance mixer.

determination was discussed in Sec. 3.4, can be estimated in the planning stage of a design when mixer data are available giving the ratio of desired output to spurious output for a 0-dBm or other signal input. At another level, the absolute level of the spurious output in decibel units changes by the difference in input level times the harmonic number of the signal.

When experimental data are not available, the spurious signal suppression of a doubly balanced diode mixer can be calculated from the diode mismatch, forward diode voltage, and transformer unbalances as described by Henderson (Ref. 14).

Amplifiers

The most critical amplifier in an HF receiver is the IF amplifier that follows the mixer, either directly or after a crystal filter. This amplifier must have a low noise figure since it is generally preceded by mixing and filtering components that have loss which add to the IF noise figure. It often must have a high-input intercept point since even when selectively protected by a crystal filter it will experience large off-frequency signals which are not attenuated greatly by a low-loss filter having limited stopband selectivity. Both bi-polar junction transistors (BJTs) and field-effect transistors are used in circuits ranging from simple tuned amplifiers to push-pull designs with transformer-coupled RF negative feedback. As with mixers, a great variety of packaged amplifiers are available in the component market, ranging from units with a 2-dB noise figure to those with +40-dBm output third-order intercept points. Simultaneous low noise and high intercepts are a rare combination, however.

The simplest amplifier for the first IF stage is the FET common-base stage. A representative circuit diagram of this type of amplifier is shown in Fig. 3.19. When a 2N5432 FET is used in this circuit, a 2-dB noise figure is obtainable with a 50-ohm system gain of 9 dB and an output third-order intercept point of +30 dBm when biased at V_{DD} of 12 to 15 V and 50 mA. The input coupling is low reactance, the optimum source resistance being about 50 ohms. The tuned output network is designed for a 450-ohm load on the drain. There are two drawbacks to this circuit: The input impedance

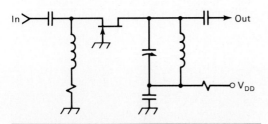

Figure 3.19 A simple grounded-gate FET amplifier can provide 2 dB noise figure in the 100 MHz region.

is about 18 ohms, and it has some gain instability with temperature variation. The latter can be lessened by replacing the source bias resistor with an active constant-current sink. The former mismatch problem is a direct result of the inherent difference in amplifiers between the optimum source resistance for minimum noise and the input resistance. It is difficult to optimally terminate a crystal filter or mixer directly with the common-base or -gate stage, although it is still a practical circuit.

Figure 3.20 illustrates a transformer feedback technique which can be applied to the input of a BJT or FET stage to obtain a simultaneous noise and input impedance match. That is, the input terminal resistance is equal to the optimum source resistance at the input terminal for minimum noise figure. This is accomplished by presenting the optimum source resistance value to the transistor base-emitter or gate-source junction via a tapped autotransformer whose turns ratio N is determined from

$$N = g_m R_{S,\text{opt}} - 1 \qquad (3.22)$$

In this equation, $R_{S,\text{opt}}$ is the optimum source resistance and g_m is the transconductance. The autotransformer is usually made with a large-area ferrite core to minimize flux density for negligible IM distortion. Using the 2N5432 as an example, g_m is $0.05S$ and $R_{S,\text{opt}}$ is 50 ohms, resulting in $N = 1.5$. The input resistance is

$$R_{\text{in}} = \frac{(1/g_m)N^2}{N + 1} \qquad (3.23)$$

which is found to be 18 ohms for the example. If an 18-ohm source is presented to the input, the resistance looking into the transformer from the transistor junction may be computed to be 50 ohms, as desired. The 18-ohm level may be converted to any desired value by additional turns on the transformer or by a reactive matching network. One additional aspect of this circuit is that it may be neutralized for input/output isolation by adding capacitance from drain to source.

When an IF amplifier must provide a low SWR at both input and output for mixer and filter termination, more complicated transformer feedback circuits may be used. One such feedback amplifier shown in Fig. 3.21 uses wide-

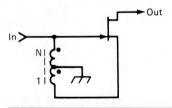

Figure 3.20 AC circuit diagram of a transformer input technique for obtaining simultaneous noise and input match.

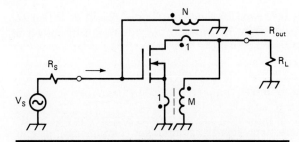

Figure 3.21 A transistor amplifier using both current and voltage feedback can have simultaneously low-input/output SWR together with moderate noise figure and high intercept point.

band transformers to sense drain current and voltage. Only the alternating-current (ac) circuit details are shown using a metal-oxide semiconductor field-effect transistor (MOSFET) as the active component. The design equations for this amplifier which force the input and output SWR to be equal and minimum start with an independent choice of source (R_S) and load (R_L) resistances and the turns ratio M. Then:

$$K = \frac{M^2 R_S}{R_L(M + 1)[(1/g_m) + R_L(1 + 1/M)/M]}$$

$$B = \frac{K}{g_m}$$

$$C = K R_S$$

$$N = \frac{B}{2} + \left[\left(\frac{B}{2}\right)^2 + C\right]^{1/2} \qquad (3.24)$$

$$R_{\text{IN}} = N\left(\frac{1}{g_m} + R_L\frac{1 + 1/M}{M}\right)$$

$$R_{\text{out}} = \frac{M^2}{M + 1}\left(\frac{1}{g_m} + \frac{R_S}{N}\right)$$

$$\text{Transducer gain} = \frac{4 R_S R_L N^2 (1 + 1/M)^2}{(R_S + R_{\text{in}})^2}$$

With large-power MOSFETs this circuit can have impressive performance. A push-pull version which consumed 0.9 A of drain bias current had a 3.6-dB noise figure, a 9.6-dB gain, an input/output SWR of 1.48:1, and an output third-order intercept of +54 dBm.

Other amplifiers are used in the SSB receiver for IF and audio gain. These are discussed in the IF and baseband system sections of this chapter.

Filters

Filter components are used in all sections of the SSB receiver for RF selectivity, IF selectivity, sideband selection, and audio response shaping. The types of filters used are discussed in detail in Chaps. 5 and 8. IF select-ivity is detailed in Chap. 5, while RF preselection filters are discussed in Chap. 8.

IF system components

Filters for sideband selection, low-IF gain-stage components, attenu-ators, and product detectors are employed in the IF system following the front end. High-frequency IF to low-frequency IF mixers are needed as well and can be similar to the passive and active types used in the front end.

IF gain

Depending upon in-band IM distortion requirements and thermal stability, IF gain is obtained either with linear integrated circuits or with discrete component circuits. The choice of integrated circuits is quite narrow if most of the receiver's gain is to be developed in one IC. The Motorola MC1590 has a 50-dB gain at frequencies up to at least 30 MHz and is gain-controlled by voltage applied to one of its pins. Its gain stability as a function of tem-perature is not outstanding, however, with a 10-dB gain change possible over a 150°C temperature range. The Plessey SL600 series of ICs may also be applied to SSB IF systems. Several chips are necessary to get sufficient gain and gain control. There is a definite trend away from military-temperature-range linear IF IC components caused by the economics of low military quantity compared with high consumer product quantity.

When high performance is needed, discrete-component amplifiers are often employed. Typical circuits use BJTs with emitter degeneration and low gain per stage to achieve low IM and thermal stability. Gain control is never done by changing the stage bias when low distortion is needed. The PIN diode is nearly always employed for gain control between BJT stages. Often, several PIN diodes are used in series to get increased linearity at the expense of control range.

Figure 3.22 is a schematic diagram of a discrete-component IF amplifier stage which uses PIN diode attenuation for gain control. Transistors Q_1 and Q_2 form a common-collector, common-emitter pair having high input resis-tance and degeneration by the partially bypassed emitter resistance in Q_2. The gain is set by the ratio of collector-to-emitter resistance and is 26 dB for a representative circuit using 2N2222 medium-level transistors. The IF input series resistance and CR_1, a PIN diode with at least a 1.5-μs charge storage time, form the AGC attenuator. The series resistance in the AGC line is shunted by a capacitor for phase lead compensation. At 450 kHz, this gain block will accept an input level of up to 5 to 10 mV, rms per tone, for 65-dB down relative-output third-order IM distortion.

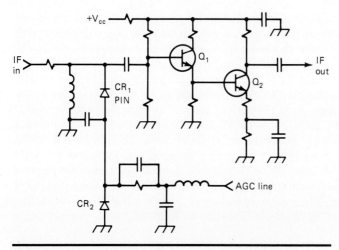

Figure 3.22 Schematic diagram of a discrete-component 450-kHz IF amplifier stage which includes shunt PIN diode attenuation.

Product detectors

A mixer is required at the output of the IF system to convert signals to audio frequency. The injection to the product detector is often called the "beat frequency oscillator" or BFO. A conventional diode balanced mixer can certainly be used for this function with audio taken from the IF port which has response to zero frequency. Because of the normally large difference between IF and AF frequencies, however, a balanced mixer is not needed. For example, a dual-gate MOSFET with IF signal applied to the first gate and injection voltage applied to the second gate will perform well and has gain. Another type of balanced mixer with gain is the 1496/1596 family of linear integrated circuit doubly balanced modulator/demodulators. This circuit is a transconductance mixer similar to the mixer shown in Fig. 3.18 but without degeneration resistors. When operated with a 0.5-V (rms-per-tone) signal level, the IM ratio is below 50 dB.

IF selectivity

In the IF section, the sideband selection and CW narrow bandwidths require filters with high Q resonators. Quartz crystal, mechanical, and, for low performance, piezoelectric ceramic resonator filters for IF use are nearly exclusively procured as purchased items from a large base of manufacturers. When time-delay equalization is required, all-pass delay networks may be placed in the audio section and require coordination with the IF filter characteristics. Chapter 5 contains details of the filters usable in the receiver IF.

The distribution of IF selectivity and gain can degrade the output signal-to-noise ratio if care is not taken to limit the bandwidth immediately ahead of the product detector. In a receiver having the IF bandwidth restricted by the sideband selection filter immediately following the front-end mixer and having the majority of the receiver's gain developed in an amplifier with unrestricted bandwidth, the noise developed by the wideband gain lies in both upper and lower sideband channels. It is translated to audio frequency by the product detector. Although audio selectivity can be added to restrict the bandwidth to equal that from the sideband filter, the excess noise on the unused sideband remains in the audio passband and can degrade the signal-to-noise ratio. The addition of an IF filter directly ahead of the product detector will attenuate the undesired channel noise. The filter need not be especially high performance, needing only to drop the undesired sideband by 10 to 20 dB. An alternative to filtering is an image-canceling product detector using the circuits previously described for the single-sideband homodyne receiver. The relatively narrow IF bandwidth allows accurate formation of the I and Q channels. This can be followed by an "active" audio filter.

A recent trend in HF receiver design is to use digital computation to synthesize the receiver's selectivity, the digital output being converted back to analog with a digital-to-analog converter. (See Chap. 7.)

Baseband components

The audio or baseband (data) section of the receiver must provide the gain and power output to drive output transducers for voice and data lines. Filtering components are also needed in the baseband circuits.

Filtering is normally done with distributed component active filters to attenuate high-frequency hiss from wideband amplification after the IF filters. Analog filter circuits include the Sallen-Key operational amplifier (op-amp) circuits (Ref. 15) as well as the more modern state-variable circuits (Refs. 16 and 17). Switched capacitor integrated circuit components, intended for the telephone industry, are becoming available which offer extremely low shape factors and constant time delay (Refs. 18 and 19). The operating bandwidth of these components is a function of the switch clocking frequency and so is readily varied for operating flexibility.

There are a large variety of audio power output amplifiers available in plastic packages from the consumer industry. If the receiver is to be used in acoustically noisy environments such as vehicles, at least 2 W of audio power is required. Output levels for driving headphones or telephone lines are nominally 0 dBm, with peak power capability of +20 dBm. Ordinary operational amplifiers have sufficient voltage and current swing capability to supply these types of outputs. With feedback, the audio circuit harmonic distortion of the output amplifiers is negligible compared with IF and product detector distortion contributions.

3.7 Design Example

In this section we will study a commercial SSB receiver design by examining the frequency scheme and block diagrams of each section. We will use level diagrams to explain the gain, noise figure, and IM distribution in the RF and IF sections of the receiver. Finally, the AGC system will be described using a level diagram showing signal levels throughout the receiver for several values of input signal.

Frequency plan

Figure 3.23 presents a block diagram showing the triple-conversion process from signal input to audio output. The first conversion produces the sum of the signal and first-injection frequencies to generate a 109.35-MHz first IF. The spurious responses of this conversion are chiefly caused by signal harmonics. The lowest-order spurious response which crosses the desired signal is fourth order (4 times 27.3375 MHz = 109.35 MHz). In this design, sum mixing has been selected to minimize noise on the first injection at the low-frequency end of the signal range where the synthesizer VCO is at its maximum frequency. The tradeoff is that the VCO tuning ratio is greater for low-side compared with high-side injection.

The second injection at 118.8 MHz and the resulting 9.45-MHz second IF is selected for three reasons. The rather high second IF makes it simpler to reject the 128.25-MHz image frequency in the first-IF selectivity. Because 118.8 MHz is on the high side of the first-injection frequency it will not cause an internal birdy by mixing with the variable first injection to generate an IF. Finally, 118.8 MHz is the twelfth harmonic of the synthesizer frequency standard at 9.9 MHz and so is simple to generate.

The second IF uses a crystal filter whose bandwidth, like the first 109.35-MHz filter, is wide enough to simultaneously pass both sidebands. In some receivers, these filters are 12 kHz wide so that a total of four independent sideband channels may be processed by a multiple-channel IF system. The third injection at 9.9 MHz is conveniently obtained from the synthesizer standard. It should be obvious that excellent shielding and circuit bypassing are necessary to prevent the 9.9-MHz signal from reaching the front end of the receiver. Ideally, this internal signal should be inaudible; practically, reduction to a 0.5-μV equivalent level is possible.

Sideband selection is obtained in the 450-kHz output of the third mixer. The indicated filter may actually be several switched filters for differing

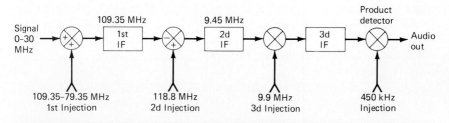

Figure 3.23 Example frequency plan is a triple conversion with sum mixing in the first frequency translation.

bandwidths and center frequencies. Although the block diagram in Fig. 3.23 shows fixed frequencies for the IF at each conversion, it is alternatively possible to shift any one of the injections by an amount equal to the 450-kHz filter bandwidth so as to make a single filter select either sideband. This minimizes filter cost but also means that the filter stopband must be fairly symmetrical to give equal-carrier and unwanted sideband rejection.

Finally, the IF signal is converted to audio by heterodyning with the 450-kHz injection signal in the product detector. When multiple-sideband-selection filters are used, this final injection remains at 450 kHz. When a single filter is used, the 450-kHz injection must move from one stopband edge of the filter to the opposite stopband edge. In simpler receivers, the injection comes from switched crystal oscillators or even an LC variable oscillator which is then often called a beat frequency oscillator. For CW (continuous-wave telegraphy) reception, a variable injection is desired by the operator to lessen listening fatigue by allowing variation of the resulting audio output frequency. The range of the BFO should result in audio frequency from zero to above 1 kHz. A direct digital synthesizer may be used when standard referenced stability is required as for radio teletype reception.

With multiple mixers it is always possible that a combination of injection frequencies will occur which produces one of the IFs or the signal frequency. These internal birdies were mentioned in Sec. 3.4 and are predictable. Table 3.1 shows the results of a simulation in which a line is printed whenever an oscillator combination produces a mixing product lying within the IF passband. Harmonic combinations up through the fifth order are allowed. For example, the first line predictably shows that the first injection enters the IF when the signal frequency is zero. Reception of the 9.9-MHz internal standard is indicated by the second line. Shielding and filtering will reduce these signals (except for the line 1 feedthrough) to the 1-μV (open-circuit) or less equivalent input level.

TABLE 3.1   Internal Spurious Signal Analysis for the Design Example Receiver

```
INTERNAL TWEETS UP TO ORDER 5

LO1 = 79.350 to 109.350
LO2 = 118.800
LO3 =    9.900
IF1 = 109.350
IF2 =    9.450
IF BW=   0.012
```

HARMONICS			LO1	SIGNAL
LO1	LO2	LO3	FREQUENCY	FREQUENCY
1	0	0	109.350	0.000
1	0	1	99.450	9.900
1	0	2	89.550	19.800
1	0	3	79.650	29.700
-1	1	0	109.350	0.000
3	-2	0	82.350	27.000
3	-2	0	79.350	30.000

Hardware

A block diagram of the hardware making up the front end of the HF receiver is shown in Fig. 3.24. Overload protection is required in the antenna input circuit to prevent physical and electrical damage when large signals from colocated transmitters are present. When the overvoltage is sustained, a detector-operated mechanical relay in the overload protector block is opened. Fast limiting for less than 1 ms is obtained with reverse-biased shunt diodes following the input low-pass filter.

Several low-pass and bandpass filters are needed to restrict the range of signals passing through to the first mixer. The low-pass filters primarily reject the first-IF image response, which lies in the band 188.7 to 218.7 MHz, a region with large RF field intensity from broadcast television transmitters. These filters also attenuate first-mixer injection energy that would cause possible interference to VHF receivers. The 0- to 530-kHz low-pass filter is used for low-frequency reception which is low-frequency-limited to about 100 kHz by synthesizer noise on the first injection. The commercial broadcast band is bandpassed by the 0.53- to 1.6-MHz filter to prevent strong HF signals from desensitizing the first mixer. The 1.6- to 30-MHz bandpass filter gives adequate selectivity to meet 80-dB spurious response rejection throughout the HF band with a well designed first mixer. Optionally, half-octave filters could be fitted into the translator assembly to give additional selectivity. These filters are electrically switched with PIN diodes having 1-μs or greater storage time. A second low-pass filter ahead of the mixer further attenuates VHF signals.

The first mixer uses junction field-effect transistors (JFETs) in a singly balanced active mixer circuit having an input intercept of +25 dBm for third-order IM. The injection amplifier associated with this mixer includes bandpass elements to restrict the frequency range to 79 to 109.35 MHz to eliminate low-level signal frequency and VHF noise from the synthesizer. For special very-high-performance systems, a +35-dBm intercept doubly balanced switching MOSFET mixer is employed with added expense and injection power. This mixer must have improved balance plus a quiet injection amplifier to not be desensitized by synthesizer noise. (Refer to Sec. 3.7.) When high-level mixers are used, the power-handling capability and intercept point of the following 109.35-MHz overtone crystal filter becomes important and in some cases a limiting IM factor. In the lower-level first-mixer case, an IF preamplifier is used to improve the noise figure. At the low-signal frequency end, this preamplifier receives both sidebands from the first mixer since there is only matching circuit selectivity between the mixer and amplifier. For example, when receiving 2 MHz, the synthesized injection is at 107.35 MHz and both 109.35- and 105.35-MHz sidebands exit from the mixer. The signal power level is therefore double the expected amount and requires 3-dB additional intercept in the amplifier. When the +35-dBm intercept mixer is employed, a low-loss crystal filter is inserted between the mixer and preamplifier.

Delayed AGC is applied at the RF input to the first mixer and before the

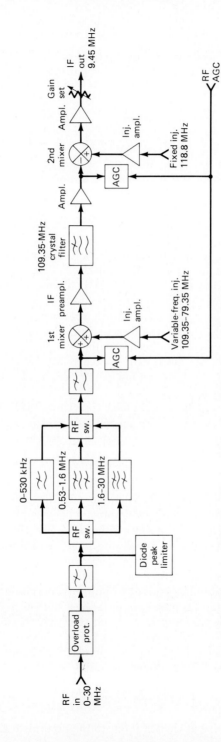

Figure 3.24 Front-end translator is a double-conversion design using 109.35- and 9.45-MHz intermediate frequencies to give improved image reduction in the first-IF crystal filter.

second mixer. The IF amplifiers at 109.35 MHz also isolate the crystal filter from termination impedance change due to AGC that would distort the pass-band shape.

The second mixer is a conventional +7-dBm doubly balanced diode mixer. At this point in the front end, out-of-band strong signal rejection has been obtained with the first crystal filter and the noise figure has been set by the first-mixer and IF preamplifier characteristics. After amplification and a gain adjustment, the resulting 9.45-MHz signal is passed to the IF system. The circuits comprising Fig. 3.24 are packaged in a cast aluminum module with extensive cast-in shielded compartments to eliminate or reduce spurious responses and birdies.

Figure 3.25 shows the blocks of the IF system which include an active FET mixer third conversion to 450 kHz, the switched sideband selection filters, the IF gain, and the product detector. In multiple-channel receivers, this section becomes complex, with the output of the third mixer being split into as many as four independent channel paths. Mechanical filters are used in this example since their size and performance are excellent at 450 kHz. Crystal filters could be used but would be larger in cost and volume at this frequency. The IF amplifier uses emitter degenerated bi-polar transistors to obtain temperature-stable gain and low IM generation. PIN diode attenuators are used for the gain control elements. For cost reduction, a narrowband IF image noise reduction filter is not used before the product detector. The gain distribution before and after the mechanical filters is such that the output signal-to-noise degradation is small. A doubly balanced transconductance mixer integrated circuit is used for the product detector. Printed circuit board construction is used for these circuits.

The remainder of the receiver's audio signal path is shown in Fig. 3.26 along with the AGC detection, hold, and dumping circuits. This receiver has three independent audio outputs for a small built-in speaker, for 600-ohm balanced line driving, and for headphone output. The indicated audio amplifiers contain filtering components to restrict the high-frequency range. A transformer is frequently required for balanced line driving to isolate the receiver from common-mode hum and lightning surge voltages. The AGC circuits provide the features of selectable hang time and time-sequenced dump rates. A portion of the IF signal is amplified and average-value-rectified, then amplified and used to charge an RC low-pass filter whose following amplifier input impedance is high. Thus, the filter charges quickly up to the average signal value with an attack time constant of about 2 ms for SSB and CW. The filter output is compared to a reference voltage, the resulting voltage operating the gain control elements, and the signal strength meter ("S meter"). The gain control vs. voltage must be a stable function if the S meter is to be calibrated in a meaningful way.

The amplified IF signal is also rectified and charges a capacitor having an adjustable decay time. When the signal decreases, the capacitor voltage decreases to a reference value at which a long-time constant-charge dump is switched to begin discharge of the RC low-pass AGC filter. If the signal decrease persists, a second comparator reference is reached and a faster

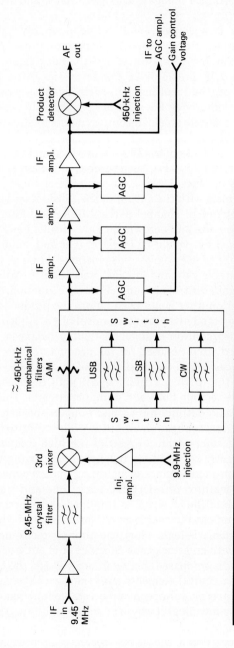

Figure 3.25 Third-conversion and IF amplifier/detector section use mechanical filters at 450 kHz for sideband selection.

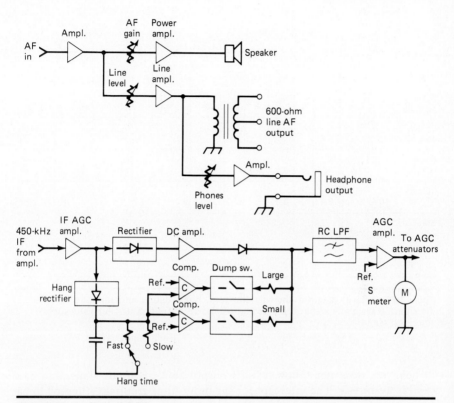

Figure 3.26 Audio and AGC system blocks provide three audio outputs and select-able AGC time constants.

dump is turned on which quickly increases the receiver gain. The time con-stants are determined by operator subjective testing and typically range from 30-ms to 0.3-s hang time and 0.1- to 1-s dump time.

Level diagrams

The level diagram shown in Fig. 3.27 shows the gain, noise figure, and third-order IM intercept points at each point in the front end of the receiver up to the second IF. In designing a receiver, conservative values should be used for the parameters of each stage so that a producible overall design is obtained. The noise figure of passive elements is equal to their loss. The noise figure of the second mixer (doubly balanced diode) is set 0.5 dB higher than its loss to account for small noise sources in the diodes. An adjustable-output attenuator (nominal 3 dB) is used to trim the overall gain to 20 dB to make front-end assemblies interchangeable. IM distortion calculations are not carried past the first-IF filter since selectivity prevents overload in subsequent stages of the IF. The input intercept point for the crystal filter is set at +50 dBm with the caveat that crystal filter intermodulation is very

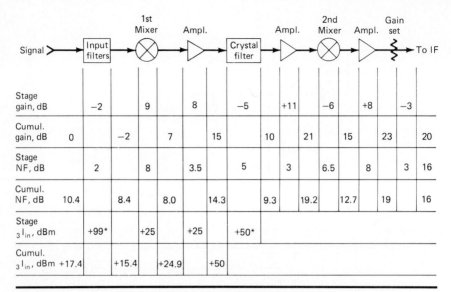

	Input filters		1st Mixer		Ampl.		Crystal filter		Ampl.		2nd Mixer		Ampl.		Gain set	
Stage gain, dB	−2		9		8		−5		+11		−6		+8		−3	
Cumul. gain, dB	0		−2		7		15		10		21		15		23		20
Stage NF, dB	2		8		3.5		5		3		6.5		8		3	16
Cumul. NF, dB	10.4		8.4		8.0		14.3		9.3		19.2		12.7		19		16
Stage $_3I_{in}$, dBm	+99*		+25		+25		+50*									
Cumul. $_3I_{in}$, dBm	+17.4		+15.4		+24.9		+50									

Figure 3.27 A level diagram showing the gain, noise figure, and input intercept distribution from the signal input to the second-IF output. Note: For values with asterisks, see text.

ill behaved, does not follow a 3-dB output to 1-dB input slope, and can exhibit hysteresis. The intercept for the input filter group is estimated to be well above the intercept looking into the mixer and is therefore set at +99 dBm to have little effect on the cascade calculations. All lines of cumulative parameters are calculated using the previously discussed equations for cascaded gain, noise figure, and intercept point.

This front-end design is guaranteed to have a 14-dB noise figure and a +15-dBm third-order input intercept. In production, a typical input noise figure of 12 dB and an intercept of +20 to +25 dBm would be routinely expected.

The gain distribution of the rest of the IF system and the amount of signal attenuation due to automatic gain control is described by a different type of level diagram, as shown in Fig. 3.28. In this diagram, the IF output to the product detector is allowed to rise by 6 dB as the input signal level varies from 1 μV to 2 V. For convenience, the impedance level is kept at the 50-ohm input value throughout the analysis so that true stage power gain can be read off the curves. The lower curve establishes the receiver's net gain by showing how the input equivalent noise power $kTBF$ (−130 dBm) is amplified up to −30 dBm at the product detector input. The upper curve illustrates a maximum gain reduction condition, with a +20-dBm input causing both IF and RF attenuators to be fully used. The middle trace indicates an input signal condition where the IF gain has just started to decrease but no RF attenuation has occurred because of voltage delay in the RF AGC line to the front end. As the signal is further increased, the output signal-to-noise

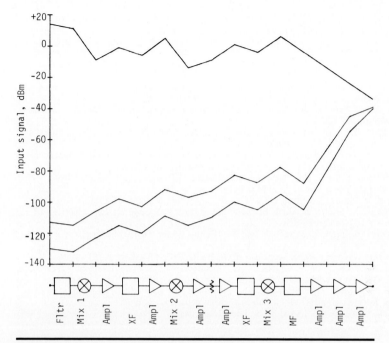

Figure 3.28 The power level for three conditions of signal input is plotted for each stage to plan the gain and AGC distribution.

ratio will increase in proportion to signal level since the input noise figure is relatively unaffected by gain change deep in the IF chain.

This type of level diagram is useful for quick planning of gain distribution prior to detailed noise figure and IM calculations. Adequate sensitivity will be obtained if the signal level at any point is at least 5 dB above the input signal. High gain prior to selectivity can be avoided so that out-of-band IM is minimized. The attack points of AGC throughout the receiver can be distributed to maximize ultimate signal-to-noise ratio without sacrificing distortion.

REFERENCES

1. H. T. Friis, "Noise Figures of Radio Receivers," *Proc. IRE,* vol. 32, July 1944, pp. 419–422. [Note: Equation (15) on Friis' p. 421 is garbled and should read: $F_{ab} = F_a + (F_b - 1)/G_a.$]
2. Franz C. McVay, "Don't Guess the Spurious Level," *Electron. Des. 3,* vol. 15, Feb. 1, 1967, pp. 70–73.
3. D. Norgaard, "The Phase-Shift Method of Single-Sideband Signal Reception," *Proc. IRE,* vol. 44, December 1956, pp. 1735–1743.
4. D. B. Hallock, "Mixer Spurious Charts," Rockwell-Collins Working Paper 4255, May 3, 1966, p. 4. (Available from author, c/o Rockwell-Collins; SASE requested.)
5. Thomas T. Brown, "Mixer Harmonic Chart," *Electron.,* vol. 24, April 1951, pp. 132, 134.
6. W. R. Olson and R. V. Salcedo, "Mixer Frequency Charts," *Freq.,* vol. 4, April–March 1966, pp. 24, 25.
7. Stuart E. Wilson, "Evaluate The Distortion of Modular Cascades," *Microwaves,* vol. 20, March 1981, pp. 67, 68, 70.

8. W. K. Victor and M. H. Brockman, "The Application of Linear Servo Theory to the Design of AGC Loops," *Proc. IRE,* vol. 48, February 1960, p. 234.
9. Paul Penfield, Jr., and Robert P. Rafuse, *Varactor Applications,* The M.I.T. Press, Cambridge, MA, 1962.
10. *Reference Data for Radio Engineers,* 5th ed., Howard W. Sams, Indianapolis, 1968, Chap. 8.
11. Michael Martin, "Stock Components Produce Improved Receiver Design," *Microwaves,* vol. 21, August 1982, pp. 59–61, 103.
12. Reed Fisher, "Twisted-Wire Quadrature Hybrid Directional Couplers," *QST,* vol. 63, January 1978, pp. 21–23.
13. Peter Will, "Termination Insensitive Mixers," *Wescon/81 Conf. Rec.,* Session Rec. 24/3, San Francisco, Sept. 15–17, 1981.
14. Bert C. Henderson, "Predicting Intermodulation Suppression in Double-Balanced Mixers," *Watkins Johnson Tech-Notes,* vol. 10, no. 4, July/August 1983.
15. R. P. Sallen and E. L. Key, "A Practical Method of Designing RC Active Filters," *IRE Trans. Circuit Theory,* vol. CT-2, March 1955, pp. 74–85.
16. Arthur B. Williams, *Electronic Filter Design Handbook,* McGraw-Hill, New York, 1981.
17. L. P. Huelsman and P. E. Allen, *Introduction to the Theory and Design of Active Filters,* McGraw-Hill, New York, 1980.
18. *1984 Linear Supplement Databook,* National Semiconductor Corp., Santa Clara, CA, 1984, pp. S9-1 to S9-53.
19. *Analog and Telecommunications Data Book,* Harris Corp., Melbourne, FL, 1984.
20. William E. Sabin, "Use of Mixers in HF Upconversion Receivers/Exciters," *Wescon/81 Conf. Rec.,* Session Rec. 24/4, San Francisco, Sept. 15–17, 1981.
21. Peter E. Chadwick, "The SL6440 High Performance Integrated Circuit Mixer," *Wescon/81 Conf. Rec.,* Session Rec. 24/2, San Francisco, Sept. 15–17, 1981.
22. P. O'Neil, "Engineering Use of Spreadsheet Languages," *RF Des.,* vol. 8, December 1985, pp. 54–57.

Exciter and Transceiver Design

Sylvan L. Dawson

A single-sideband transmitter system may contain several functional elements, as shown in Fig. 4.1. These include a data terminal, remote control unit, exciter, power amplifier, antenna coupler, and antenna. More elaborate systems may also include switching units, RF output bandpass filters, or control processors. The essential elements, however, are the exciter, power amplifier, and antenna. They may be separate or combined into a single unit, as in a packset.

The exciter is a key component of this system and performs several important functions. It translates one or more baseband input signal(s) to the desired output HF frequency, and drives the power amplifier at the proper level. It provides for different emission modes which may be required such as CW or FSK. Usually it coordinates gain setting and tune cycle operations of the transmitter. It also controls performance parameters such as bandwidth, distortion, frequency stability, and spurious emissions.

This chapter discusses the performance requirements of an exciter, then how its component parts are assembled in an architecture which meets the requirements and performs the needed functions.

A transceiver is an exciter and receiver combined in one functional unit. An exciter and receiver have several internal elements in common such as a frequency synthesizer, IF filters, control circuits, and power supplies. In applications where size is at a premium, such as in airborne or other mobile equipment, a transceiver configuration provides the most efficient use of available space. Transceiver design will also be discussed in this chapter.

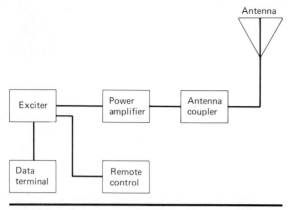

Figure 4.1 Typical single-sideband transmitter system.

4.1 SSB Exciter Output Signal Requirements

Ideally, the RF output from an SSB exciter would be an exact linear translation of the input baseband signal, with no amplitude or phase distortion or added noise, and at exactly the level required by the following PA. Of course, this ideal is not achieved in practice, and the degree to which imperfections in performance can be tolerated determines to a great extent the complexity of the exciter design. It is important, then, to determine the allowable levels of the various forms of distortion of the exciter RF output.

The limits of distortion and noise pollution of a transmitted HF signal are generally set by signal fidelity needs of other communication system components and by government regulatory agencies. System components at the receiving end of a radio link generally place requirements on in-band characteristics of the signal. These are characteristics such as amplitude distortion, phase distortion, in-band intermodulation distortion, and signal-to-noise ratio.

Out-of-band emissions from a transmitter can be in the form of either discrete spurious signals or broadband noise. Discrete spurious signals can be caused by intermodulation distortion, leakage of mixer injections, and harmonics of the transmitted signal. Broadband noise is most commonly caused by amplifier noise and oscillator phase noise on mixer injections. The source of many of the spurious emissions of the transmitter system is the exciter.

Figure 4.2 is a spectral representation of the RF output of an exciter, showing the desired USB signal above f_c, the carrier frequency, and several of the possible unwanted output signals. The LSB signal is not perfectly suppressed and appears at the output. Harmonics of the output USB signal appear around the carrier frequency harmonics, $2f_c$ and $3f_c$. Odd-order IMD products appear around the desired USB signal and its harmonics. Various other spurious emissions may appear because of combining of internal injection signals in output stages. The PA following the exciter will also generate

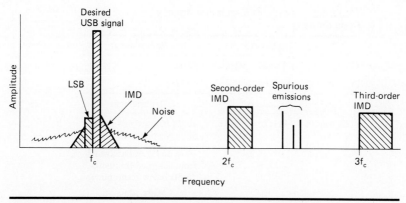

Figure 4.2 Possible spectral components of exciter output.

IMD products. It may provide some selectivity, such as in the output circuit, to help suppress harmonics and similar products. A broadband amplifier, however, will not help in reducing these unwanted outputs. A principal function of the exciter design is to control out-of-band emissions.

Spurious emissions limitations

Governmental regulatory agencies prescribe certain limitations to the levels of spurious emissions allowed from radio transmitters. The International Telecommunications Union (ITU) sets forth regulations observed by member nations governing the level of spurious emissions, frequency assignments, allowable signal bandwidth, and other significant parameters of radio transmission. Regulatory agencies of member nations, such as the Federal Communication Commission, generate their own regulations for internal use within the ITU limitations.

Table 4.1 provides a few of the limitations on radio spurious emissions and frequency tolerances in the HF (generally 2- to 30-MHz) frequency range. The limitations given may not be current, and are provided only as an illustration of the type of legal restriction imposed on transmitters.

In addition to the emissions limitations imposed by regulatory agencies, operational considerations may dictate additional restraints. For example, when transmitters and receivers are located in close proximity, it is not difficult to imagine the interference which could be caused in the receivers by a transmitter which emits the broad spectrum of signals alluded to in Fig. 4.2.

A situation in which a transmitter and a receiver are colocated is shown in Fig. 4.3. The transmitter signal is at frequency f_t at a 1-kW level, +60 dBm. A receiver is simultaneously receiving a signal of frequency f_r of −116 dBm. The transmit- and receive-antenna separation provides isolation of 30 dB. If the acceptable interference level at the receiver input is −126 dBm, the allowable level of transmitter spurious emissions which fall on the receive

TABLE 4.1   Sample of Regulatory Agency Requirements

Frequency tolerance	Requirement
ITU, App. 7—1.6 to 29.7 MHz	20 Hz
FCC, Part 81—1.6 to 27.5 MHz	20 Hz

Spurious emissions	Requirement
ITU, App. 8—9 kHz to 30 MHz	40 db below mean power, 50-mW maximum
FCC, Part 81	50 to 150% of bandwidth from assigned frequency,* 25 dB below mean power
	150 to 250% of bandwidth from assigned frequency, 35 dB below mean power
	250% or more of bandwidth from assigned frequency, 43 dB + 10 log (mean power)

* Assigned frequency is center frequency of assigned bandwidth.

frequency is −96 dBm, or 156 dB below the transmitter output signal. This is a very stringent requirement on the transmitter system. If filtering in the PA and transmitter output filter provide 50 dB of selectivity, the required relative level of spurious signals at the exciter output is −106 dB. It should be noted that this limit applies not only to discrete spurious signals, but to broadband noise as well.

From the above, it is apparent that the range of allowable spurious emissions levels can be quite wide, depending on end-use requirements.

SSB channel characteristics

The exciter, as it processes the baseband input to the final RF output, will add distortion and noise to the signal. A description of these effects and typical allowable levels are discussed below.

In-band intermodulation distortion. Figure 4.4 depicts a typical transmitter output within the confines of the passband. The in-band IMD prod-

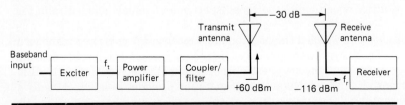

Figure 4.3 Colocated transmitter and receiver.

ucts indicated may interfere with signal components near the same frequency. Multitone data signals are particularly susceptible to this type of interference, because the IMD products can fall into data tone slots.

The in-band IMD can be generated in the baseband audio frequency processing circuits or in any of the IF or RF stages. Even-order and odd-order IMD can both be generated in the baseband circuits. In Fig. 4.4, where the 800- and 900-Hz tones are the only two input signals, the baseband circuits may generate the second-order IMD products of 100, 1600, 1700, and 1800 Hz. Third-order IMD products are 700, 1000, 2400, 2500, 2600, and 2700 Hz; the 700- and 1000-Hz products can also be generated in IF and RF circuits. Higher-order products may also be generated.

RF and IF stages generate IMD products, but only the odd-order products fall in-band; the even-order products fall around harmonics of the RF and IF frequencies, and are outside the passband. These are the stages with the highest signal levels, however, and can be the primary source of in-band odd-order IMD in the exciter.

In a transmitter, the highest levels of in-band IMD are usually generated by the PA, with transmitter IMD limits close to actual PA performance. This requires the exciter in-band IMD to be well below the transmitter requirement, so that the exciter and PA combined will not exceed the limit. If the transmitter IMD limit is -35 or -40 dB relative to either of two equal output in-band signals, the exciter IMD is typically required to be no greater than -50 dB.

Noise.   In-band noise appearing in the output of the exciter, if excessive, will degrade performance at the receiving end of the system. The noise may consist of broadband amplifier noise, discrete hum and power supply ripple components, and phase noise from injection signals. The hum components and phase noise appear by modulating the signal, so are measured when the exciter has an output signal. Typical values of in-band noise, measured in a 3-kHz bandwidth, are -40 to -50 dB from the exciter output.

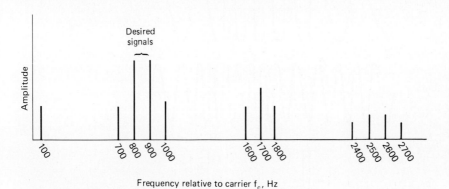

Figure 4.4 Possible in-band intermodulation distortion products.

Amplitude variation.   This is the variation in RF output signal level as a function of baseband input frequency. The passband must be wide enough to accommodate the baseband signal bandwidth. For voice signals, a bandwidth of 2.5 to 3 kHz is commonly used, such as 300 Hz to 3 kHz. This bandwidth and frequency range also accommodates most single- and multitone data terminals producing FSK and differential phase-shift keyed (DPSK) tones. The 3-kHz bandwidth is also consistent with allowances of regulatory agencies for SSB transmissions. (See Refs. 1 and 2.)

The variation of amplitude response across the passband is also an important factor. For voice signals, a variation of 4 to 6 dB is allowable. For data signals, however, data errors may increase at the receiver if a data tone is reduced in amplitude because of excessive amplitude variation in the exciter. A reasonable limit on passband variation for data signals is 2 to 3 dB, with some users requiring even tighter limits.

Time-delay distortion.   The effect of time-delay distortion is important to multitone data signals, as illustrated in Fig. 4.5. The signals in two FSK channels are shown in the exciter output with modulation transitions separated by a time difference t_d. The time difference is caused by variations in group delay across the passband. If the time-delay difference (or time-delay distortion) is a significant part of the time 1/baud (per tone), modulation transitions will occur between clock intervals in the demodulator at the receiver, causing data errors to increase.

Typical data terminals operate at rates to 75 baud/channel, or modulation transitions 13 ms apart. Differential time delays of 500 to 700 μs maximum are normally allowed across that part of the passband occupied by the data signals.

Frequency stability.   The frequency of the exciter output is determined

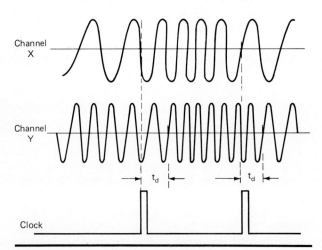

Figure 4.5   Effect of time-delay distortion.

by the various mixer injection frequencies along the exciter signal path. In modern exciters, the injection signals are derived directly from a single reference frequency, or by oscillators which are frequency-locked to a reference signal. In either case, the long-term frequency stability (in ppm) of the exciter output is the same as the reference.

The frequency reference is usually generated by a stable crystal oscillator, when the reference is part of the exciter. When better stability is required, reference oscillators using atomic devices are used. See Chap. 10 for more information on frequency standards.

Voice signals can tolerate frequency errors on the order of 20 Hz before the frequency shift becomes evident to the listener (see Chap. 2, Sec. 2.1). Data signals vary in tolerance of frequency error, but some, utilizing narrow effective bandwidths per channel, may require tighter tolerances. As seen in Table 4.1, regulatory agencies impose limits apart from operational requirements. Typical frequency stability requirements are 0.5×10^{-6}, or 1×10^{-8} for higher-performance equipment.

Phase stability. Voice signals are not affected by phase instability but certain data signals are. An obvious example is a DPSK signal, where data is transmitted by phase shifting successive frames of the DPSK signal. If one or more of the mixer injection signals in the exciter introduces spurious phase changes from frame to frame, data errors may result. A typical allowable amount of short-term phase instability is 6° average per 13 ms, at 75 baud/channel, two channels per data tone (13 ms per frame, 45° phase-shift increments).

Exciter output signal level

Usually, the exciter controls the transmitter output level by controlling the PA input (exciter output) level. Occasionally the transmitter output level control function is located in the PA, but it is easier to control signal levels in low-level exciter stages. Regardless of where the function is located, the desired control characteristics are the same.

The limitation on transmitter power output is normally the peak-power output capability of the PA. For single-frequency signals, the PEP and average power are the same, but for more complex signals the envelope peaks must be controlled so that the PA output is maintained at an optimum level. The transmitter gain control (TGC) and automatic level control (ALC) functions are two methods used to meet this requirement.

The TGC is considered a static gain control, while the ALC is dynamic. The TGC is set when the transmitter is first tuned to a new frequency by inserting a calibrated signal into the exciter output, then adjusting the exciter output level to achieve a particular PA output. To perform this operation, exciter gain is increased or decreased in response to sense signals fed back from the PA. The calibration signal bears a fixed relationship to the peak envelope power during normal operation. However, the TGC alone is not sufficient to control the PA PEP output.

The ALC is a dynamic level control, operating to control the PEP output of the PA. A signal detector in the PA senses the peak signal level, and provides a gain control signal back to the exciter. Its operation is similar to receiver AGC, responding quickly to signal peaks and decaying more slowly when the peaks are reduced. This characteristic is necessary to prevent distorting the transmitter output by modulating it with the envelope of the signal, as discussed in more detail in Sec. 4.3.

Ideally, the ALC action will be minimal, consistent with maintaining the transmitter at maximum output. If ALC action reduces exciter gain excessively on normal signal levels, noise output levels may be high when no signal is present, as during pauses in speech. Also, excessive gain variation due to ALC action causes distortion of the transmitted signal. The resulting sidebands on the output have the appearance of in-band odd-order IMD, with the same disruptive effects on communication.

Other level control techniques are used in exciters. Speech has a notoriously wide dynamic range, and audio compression amplifiers can be used to reduce the range of speech levels at the exciter output. The compression amplifier introduces moderate distortion on the voice signal because of the time constants and gain variation needed to be effective. This is tolerated, however, because it does not affect intelligibility. If ALC is used to perform this function, other signals such as data will be seriously distorted, because ALC acts on all transmitter signals. See Sec. 4.3.

Carrier levels. The carrier is suppressed in normal SSB operation, but it must be reinserted for certain emission modes or for tuning and setting up gain of the transmitter. When the reinserted carrier is used to set gain, its level has a fixed relationship to the PEP of the exciter output in normal operation. For example, if the PA (and perhaps antenna coupler) is to tune up at half-power, the exciter carrier output during the setup or tune cycle will be 3 dB below the rated PEP output. A tune or gain setting level is chosen below full output to avoid PA limiting or operation of protective circuits in the PA or antenna coupler.

An emission mode may require transmitting a pilot carrier at a level, say, 17 dB below transmitter PEP output. This level must be referred to the tune power carrier level used during gain setup. In this example, if that is 3 dB below PEP, the pilot carrier level is set 14 dB lower.

Another commonly used mode requiring a reinserted carrier is the so-called "AM equivalent" (AME). The carrier, in combination with an SSB signal, produces a signal having an envelope which can be received intelligibly by using an envelope detector. Maximum envelope amplitude occurs when the carrier is 6 dB below rated transmitter PEP. When the SSB signal and carrier are equal in amplitude, the PEP of the combined signals is at the rated PEP level. This carrier level is 3 dB below the tune power carrier used above.

An emission mode sometimes requiring a reinserted carrier is single-channel frequency-shift-keyed radio teletype (FSK RTTY). The carrier is reinserted and shifted in frequency around the assigned carrier frequency. A common example of a frequency shift used is ±85 Hz. There is no baseband input; the only signal transmitted is the FSK carrier. Its level will be set to produce full PEP output. If CW operation is required using a keyed carrier, this carrier level must also produce full PEP output.

4.2 Exciter Architecture

A basic exciter block diagram is shown in Fig. 4.6. The baseband input signal enters the baseband processing circuits, then is fed to the modulator, where the first frequency translation takes place. The output of the modulator is the first IF, which is usually chosen to accommodate SSB filter design requirements. After filtering and amplification, the signal is translated again to a second IF which is above the HF range. After filtering in the second IF, the signal is translated down in the output mixer to the desired HF frequency.

The frequency translation scheme described above is the one most commonly used in modern exciters because of its simplicity. By converting up to a last IF which is above the HF range, then down to the desired output frequency, unwanted spurious emissions are greatly reduced or eliminated. These techniques are now practical because of the availability of IF filters, mixers, frequency synthesizers, and amplifiers which will operate satisfactorily at these higher frequencies.

The exciter architecture discussed in this chapter will use the upconversion scheme described. The basic blocks of the exciter will now be discussed in more detail.

Baseband amplifier and signal processing

The function of the baseband-signal-processing section is to receive the baseband input and do the necessary amplification, impedance changing, filtering, or other processing before it is modulated up to the first IF.

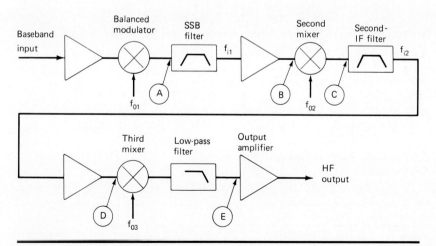

Figure 4.6 Basic exciter block diagram.

A block diagram of a typical baseband amplifier is shown in Fig. 4.7. It has a 600-ohm line audio input which may range from -30 to $+10$ dBm, and a microphone input as low as -55 dBm. Each of these inputs passes through a gain-controlled amplifier. The purpose of the microphone amplifier is to compress the wide amplitude range of normal voice signals into a narrower range, to increase average power output of the peak-limited (in the PA) transmitter. The desired effect is to maintain the average transmitter power output within 6 dB of the PEP output, when the microphone is used. Compression amplifiers are discussed further in Chap. 6. Preemphasis techniques are discussed in Chap. 2, Sec. 2.1.

The function of the line-leveling amplifier is not to compress the range of the input signal, but to maintain a long-term, relatively constant output level, so that occasional peaks are at the desired PEP level. The input range for which leveling is desired will be 10 to 15 dB.

The output of the line-leveler and microphone amplifiers are connected one at a time by a switch into the output amplifier. This amplifier drives the output at the level and impedance needed by the modulator. Noise and IMD generated in these circuits should not be significant (see Sec. 4.3), with IMD well below -60 dB if amplifiers and other components are properly applied.

Filtering may be needed at this point to remove noise components below approximately 200 Hz, or noise at twice the first IF which could be mixed

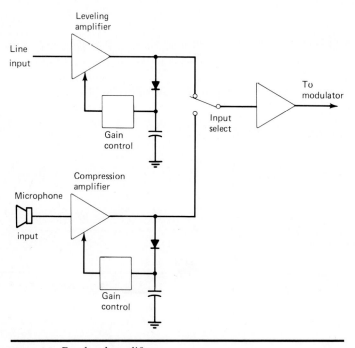

Figure 4.7 Baseband amplifier.

into the modulator. These possibilities should be considered in the circuit design to determine if such filtering is needed.

If additional speech processing is desired, Chap. 6 describes several other techniques.

Balanced modulator

The function of the balanced modulator is to modulate an injection signal with the baseband input from the baseband amplifier, generating a double-sideband, suppressed-carrier IF signal. The diagram in Fig. 4.8 illustrates the process. The baseband signal into the modulator is f_b; the output IF signal has an upper-sideband signal $f_{01} + f_b$, and a lower-sideband signal $f_{01} - f_b$. The injection signal, or carrier at f_{01}, is suppressed below the two sideband levels by the balanced modulator action. This is the conventional and most widely used method of producing the two SSB (USB and LSB) signals: An IF filter following the modulator will then select the desired sideband and provide additional carrier rejection.

Suppression of the carrier in the output of the balanced modulator should be in the 35- to 45-dB range and is achieved in the modulator by combining equal amplitude and opposite polarity injection signals. Careful design of printed circuit board layouts is needed to maintain isolation between modulator output circuits and injection signals, to avoid compromising the inherent modulator balance.

The filtering following the modulator selects the desired sideband in the above method. An alternative method uses phase shifting and combining techniques to produce an SSB output without filtering. It is used primarily

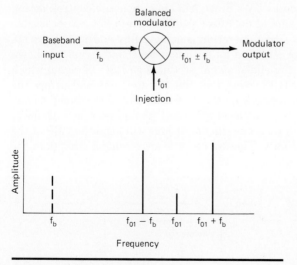

Figure 4.8 Balanced modulator output.

when selection of the desired sideband by filtering is not desirable because of impractical filter bandwidth requirements, excessive time-delay distortion, etc. This modulator is discussed in Sec. 4.3.

SSB IF filter and amplifier

The SSB filter and IF amplifier section of the exciter are depicted in Fig. 4.9. The double-sideband signal from the balanced modulator passes through an amplifier then the SSB filter. The filter output contains only the selected USB or LSB signal, which passes through additional amplifier stages to achieve the desired output level.

The characteristics of the SSB filter, because it is the most sharply selective in the exciter signal path, control the amplitude and delay characteristics of the exciter passband. The SSB filter also controls the level of the unwanted sideband, and carrier suppression. For a complete discussion of SSB filters, refer to Chap. 5.

The stages following the filter not only provide amplification but also the gain control of the exciter, and the reinsertion of carrier when needed. The gain control functions, from earlier discussions, are the TGC and ALC. Referring again to Fig. 4.9, the important thing to note is the relative position of TGC, ALC, and the carrier reinsertion function. As discussed earlier, TGC is set up using a reinserted carrier of known level relative to PEP. The AME and pilot carriers, when enabled by the operating mode, are preset relative to the tune power level, and thus are fixed relative to rated PEP once TGC is set. The gain from the point of carrier reinsertion should not be disturbed, once set, until the next tune cycle. For this reason, the TGC function follows the point of carrier reinsertion, while ALC precedes it.

ALC acts to control the level of the SSB signal itself and carriers intended to produce full PEP, such as CW. Since ALC is a dynamic control, acting only after TGC is set, it should not affect the AME and pilot carrier levels.

Independent-sideband (ISB) operation is achieved by adding a complete signal-processing path for a second independent baseband signal, as shown in Fig. 4.10. In this case the added signal produces an LSB IF signal which is combined with the USB IF. Note that the IFs are combined before the ALC- and TGC-controlled stages, so the ALC acts on the combined signal. Another point to note is that the level of each IF should now be 6 dB lower than would be the case for only one sideband. This will keep the PEP of the combined signal within limits. The use of peak-level-control circuits in the

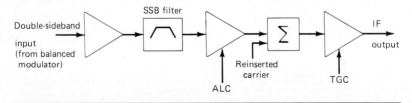

Figure 4.9 IF filter and amplifier.

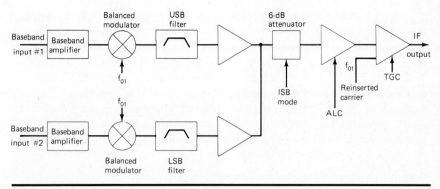

Figure 4.10 Independent sideband generation.

baseband-processing section (line levelers, microphone compression) is advantageous in ISB operation, because it prevents one of the sideband signals from depressing the other by ALC action. For example, a strong voice signal in the USB channel will not depress or modulate a data signal in the LSB channel. The 6-dB reduction in IF level occurs before the point of carrier reinsertion, to avoid affecting carrier levels.

Four-channel ISB operation is sometimes required for very-high-capacity communications links. The arrangement of the four IF channels is shown in Fig. 4.11. The inboard channels are arranged as in two-channel ISB operation, but the outboard channels have separate subcarriers, f_A and f_B. The injection signal into the modulator for the upper outboard channel is at frequency $f_B = f_{01} + 6.29$ kHz, and the injection into the lower outboard channel is $f_A = f_{01} - 6.29$ kHz. Thus the lower outboard signal is an USB signal referenced to its subcarrier f_A, and the upper outboard signal is an LSB signal with respect to *its* subcarrier f_B. The frequency spacing of the subcarriers from f_{01} used here is from current U.S. Department of Defense requirements.

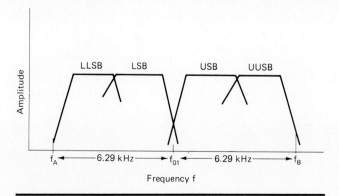

Figure 4.11 IF filter passband arrangement for four independent sidebands.

The designer should note that other subcarrier frequencies may be required in a particular case.

The selectivity requirements are more severe for four-channel ISB operation than for SSB or two-channel ISB operation. For example, a filter used in this application has -2-dB passband edges at 250 and 3100 Hz from the carrier, and a -60-dB response at 3550 and -250 Hz. This places the passband edges of adjacent inboard and outboard channels a maximum of 90 Hz apart, requiring the very rapid falloff in response provided by the -60-dB specification. The filters required are discussed in more detail in Chap. 5.

Output frequency translator and amplifier

The purpose of this section of the exciter is to translate the output signal of the IF amplifier to the final desired output frequency and amplify it to the required level. Figure 4.12 illustrates the process. The signal from the IF amplifier output is translated up to a second high IF in the second mixer. It is filtered to remove the injection signal and unwanted mix products, then mixed down to the desired HF output frequency in a third mixer with a variable-frequency injection input. The output of this mixer is passed through a low-pass filter with cutoff frequency above 30 MHz to remove the injection signal and sum mix product, then is amplified to the required level.

The result of passing the first-IF signal through the second mixer is illustrated in Fig. 4.13. The input signal from the first IF at frequency f_{i1} mixes with the injection signal f_{02} to produce the output signals shown. Not only are the two sidebands produced ($f_{02} + f_{i1}$, $f_{02} - f_{i1}$), but also sidebands around harmonics of the injection, f_{02}. The injection signal itself and its har-

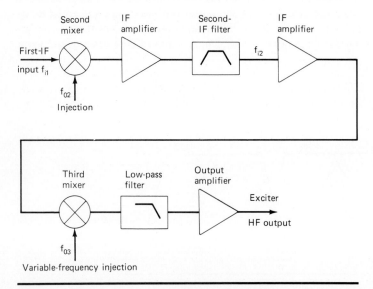

Figure 4.12   Output frequency translator and amplifier.

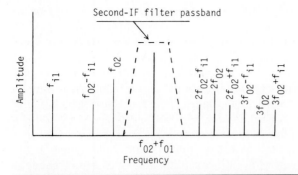

Figure 4.13 Second-mixer output signals relative to second-IF filter passband.

monics are also present in the output, even though it may be a high-quality doubly balanced mixer. The second-IF filter attenuates the unwanted products enough that they will not result in excessive spurious emissions in the exciter output.

An example may be a doubly balanced diode mixer with injection signal f_{02} of 90 MHz at a level of $+13$ dBm. The first-IF input f_{i1} of 501 kHz is at -11-dBm PEP. The mixer conversion loss (per sideband) is 6 dB, and the rejection to the injection signal as it appears at the mixer output is 30 dB. The levels of the more important mixer output products can then be tabulated as shown in Table 4.2. The desired signal in Table 4.2 is the sum product, $f_{i1} + f_{02}$. The others may cause spurious signals in the exciter output, so must be reduced by the second-IF filter.

The second-IF filter has a passband wide enough to pass signals in the first-IF passband without adding significant additional selectivity or time-delay distortion. If the signals will be both USB and LSB, for example, the filter must be wide enough to pass both. It must also have enough selectivity to effectively eliminate the unwanted mixer output signals listed in Table 4.2. A typical filter used for the second IF is a four-pole crystal filter, with a center frequency of approximately 90 MHz. The -2-dB passband is 20 kHz,

TABLE 4.2   Mixer Output Product Levels

Mixer output signal frequency	Mixer output level, dBm	Frequency, MHz
Injection, f_{02}	-17	90
Sum product, $f_{02} + f_{i1}$	-17 (PEP)	90.501
Difference product, $f_{02} - f_{i1}$	-17 (PEP)	89.499
Injection second harmonic, $2f_{02}$	-22	180
Injection third harmonic, $3f_{02}$	$+ 3$	270
Injection fourth harmonic, $4f_{02}$	-23	360
Injection fifth harmonic, $5f_{02}$	$- 1$	450

and the -60-dB stopband is 100 kHz wide. At 500 kHz below the passband, the selectivity is -70 dB.

To continue with the above example, it will be assumed that the mixer output signals are amplified by 7 dB in a broadband amplifier, then passed through a filter with selectivity characteristics as described above. The signals at the output of the filter, assuming a 4-dB passband loss, can then be tabulated as shown in Table 4.3. Note that the injection signal, which is only 500 kHz from the desired signal, is now -70 dB in relative level, and the unwanted difference product at 1 MHz away is -70 dB from the desired signal. These unwanted signals will now appear as spurious signals in the exciter output at these relative levels, since they are too close in frequency to be filtered out, once the second-IF filter output signal is converted down to the desired HF frequency.

The filter output signal is amplified and fed into the output mixer at a level of -1 dBm. This mixer is also a doubly balanced diode mixer with an injection level of $+23$ dBm, at a frequency below 90 MHz. The mixer output level of -7 dBm passes through a 30-MHz low-pass filter to remove the injection frequency f_{03}, and is then amplified to the proper exciter output level. There will be further discussion of the IMD, spurious signal, and noise characteristics of the output translator in the next section.

Gain distribution, IMD, and noise

This section discusses methods of analyzing IMD and noise and determining proper gain distribution.

In-band IMD. As a multitone signal propagates through the exciter from baseband input to RF output, each stage along the path contributes to the level of output in-band IMD. The problem is to maintain the signal level at critical points in the signal path at optimum levels, so that undue amounts of IMD are not generated by over driving particular circuit elements, or that signal levels are not too low, raising the output noise level and making inefficient use of amplifiers. A method will be described which establishes signal levels at components which are critical because of their IMD characteristics, then accounts for the contribution of each of these critical components to the total exciter output IMD.

Refer again to Fig. 4.6, the exciter signal path. Certain critical points in

TABLE 4.3   Filter Output Signal Levels

Filter output signal frequency	Level, dBm	Frequency, MHz
Injection, f_{02}	-84	90
Sum product, $f_{02} + f_{i1}$	-14	90.501
Difference product, $f_{02} - f_{i1}$	-84	89.499
Injection second harmonic, $2f_{02}$	-89	180
Injection third harmonic, $3f_{02}$	-64	270
Injection fourth harmonic, $4f_{02}$	-90	360
Injection fifth harmonic, $5f_{02}$	-68	450

the path are identified. The first critical point, A, is the input to the first-IF filter. The filter is critical because, as signal level is increased, preceding components (amplifier, modulators) will produce less IMD if they are properly used. It will be assumed that the IMD characteristics at A are not only due to the input signal to the filter, but also to the cumulative effect of preceding circuits. The next critical point, B, is the input to the second mixer, because the mixer has a definite IMD characteristic related to the injection level available, which is relatively inflexible. Point C is the input to the second-IF filter, which has definite upper limits on the signal level which can be applied. Point D is the output mixer, and E is the output amplifier, which will have IMD limitations because of the output power level. At each of the critical points selected, the signal level is determined by the IMD characteristics of that component, including the contribution of all circuitry back to the preceding critical point. The signal levels used will be the level per tone of a two-tone signal which produces the rated exciter PEP output.

An example will illustrate the method. The output requirement for the exciter will be assumed to be $+20$-dBm PEP, with in-band third- and higher-order IMD products each suppressed to at least a -50-dB relative level. Considering the IF filter at point A, the allowable IMD level will be set at -65 dB. For the IF filter to be used, an input limit of -23 dBm/tone will be assumed.

The mixer at B is a doubly balanced diode mixer with an injection level of $+13$ dBm, so an input third-order intercept of $+18$ dBm will be assumed. (See material on mixers in Sec. 4.3.) Input signal levels 35 dB lower, -17 dBm/tone, will produce third-order products (in the mixer and preceding circuits back to A) of -70 dB. Point C, the second-IF filter, has a maximum input level of -10 dBm/tone, which is expected to produce third-order products suppressed to -65 dB. Note here that neither of the IF filters can be characterized in terms of an input intercept. The IMD characteristics of mechanical or crystal filters are not predictable by an intercept concept, which requires empirically determining the allowed signal level at the desired IMD level. This is discussed further in Chap. 5.

Next is the output mixer D, which is a doubly balanced diode mixer with an injection level of $+17$ dBm, resulting in a third-order input intercept of 25 dBm. The input signal level will be set 35 dB lower at -10 dBm/tone, producing third-order products suppressed to -70 dB. Finally, the output amplifier, at E, must provide the output power of $+20$-dBm PEP, or $+14$ dBm/tone. If the output intercept of the amplifier is $+44$ dBm, it will contribute third-order IMD products of -60 dB.

The operating conditions that have been established at each of the critical points can now be tabulated and the gain distribution and total IMD performance determined. In Table 4.4, the signal levels and third-order input intercepts are entered; then net gain between critical points is obviously the difference in signal levels. The IMD generated at a critical point is entered, and the last column is a running total of the IMD level at each point. This is obtained by adding the IMD generated at a point to IMD input levels from preceding circuits. Figure 4.14 shows a curve which facilitates adding the

TABLE 4.4   Exciter Gain and IMD Performance

Critical point	Signal level, dBm/tone	Net gain, dB	Input 3d-order intercept, dBm	IMD-generated, dB	Sum of IMD products, dB
A	−23		...	−65	−65
		6			
B	−17		+18	−70	−61.1
		7			
C	−10		...	−65	−56.9
		0			
D	−10		+25	−70	−55.3
		−6			
E	−16		+14	−60	−51.3
Output	14 dBm	30			

IMD components. The larger of the two components being added is normalized to 0 dB. The relative level of the other, lower level intersects the curve at a point representing the amount in dB by which the sum exceeds the referenced level. This curve adds the two components in phase, such as is most likely to occur in a broadband circuit. The designer may not wish to use this worst-case approach when considering IMD component additions in filters, because of their phase-shift characteristic which makes in-phase addition unlikely.

The bottom entry in the last column of Table 4.4 shows that the −50-dB level required will be met. These entries would also show where large increases in IMD occur, indicating circuits which may need optimization or perhaps where the design is too conversative. The process can, of course, be refined to add as many other significant points in the signal path as desired.

The gain conditions used should correspond to maximum gain. TGC or ALC action should only reduce the above levels. IMD caused by PIN diode

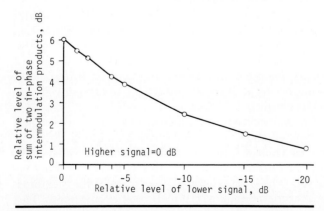

Figure 4.14   In-phase sum of two identical-frequency IMD products.

attenuators commonly increases just at turn-on and should be checked against the allowable levels established in Table 4.4 at the appropriate critical point.

Out-of-band spurious signals. Spurious signals which are outside the exciter passband, i.e., 20 kHz and further off the output carrier frequency, will be generated between the output of the last-IF filter and the exciter output. The allowable level of these signals at the exciter output will depend on how much additional selectivity is available in the PA, and the transmitter output spurious signal limitations. The PA may have suboctave filters providing selectivity primarily at harmonics, or more selective bandpass circuits, or may be broadband with no selectivity. The transmitter spurious signal output limitations may be those of a regulatory agency, or more severe requirements imposed by interference considerations with colocated receivers.

Referring again to Fig. 4.6, the IF amplifier following the filter will generate second-, third-, and higher-order products, but they will be clustered around harmonics of the IF (neglecting in-band products). A simple low-pass filter in the output of the amplifier should reduce these products to the point that they can safely be ignored.

The output mixer generates spurious signals which are calculated as sum products, such as second and third order, of a two-tone in-band signal, and as harmonics of these signals. If the two equal-level in-band signals into the mixer are at frequencies f_1 and f_2, the so-called "second-order sum product" in the mixer output is at frequency

$$(f_1 - f_{03}) + (f_2 - f_{03}) = f_1 + f_2 - 2f_{03} \tag{4.1}$$

which is actually a fourth-order mixer product. For example, if $f_1 = 90.501$ MHz and $f_2 = 90.502$ MHz, and the desired output carrier frequency is 2 MHz, then $f_{03} = 88.500$ MHz, and the second-order sum product frequency at the mixer output is 4.003 MHz. The desired output frequencies due to f_1 and f_2 are 2.001 and 2.002 MHz, respectively. Similarly, the third-order sum products at the mixer output are actually sixth-order mixer products, whose frequencies are given by

$$2(f_1 - f_{03}) + (f_2 - f_{03}) = 2f_1 + f_2 - 3f_{03} \tag{4.2a}$$

and

$$(f_1 - f_{03}) + 2(f_2 - f_{03}) = f_1 + 2f_2 - 3f_{03} \tag{4.2b}$$

Some of the more troublesome spurious signals generated in the mixer are tabulated in Table 4.5 using levels which may occur in a doubly balanced diode mixer. The injection level is $+17$ dBm and IF input level -10 dBm, with frequencies f_1, f_2, and f_{03} as above. Output signals outside the 2- to 30-MHz range are not considered.

The output amplifier is also a source of out-of-band IMD. The amplifier will be assumed to have a third-order input intercept of $+14$ dBm and sec-

TABLE 4.5   Mixer Output Levels

Mixer output signal	Level, dBm	Frequency, MHz
Desired signals	−16	2.001, 2.002
Second-order sum product	−78	4.003
Second harmonics	−84	4.002
	−84	4.004
Third-order sum products	−89	6.004
	−89	6.005
Third harmonics	−98	6.003
	−98	6.006

ond-order input intercept of +35 dBm. Table 4.6 lists the contribution of the mixer products to the exciter output spurious, the amplifier contribution, and the total. The two contributing sources are assumed to add in phase. The levels shown in Table 4.6 for mixer contribution are for the mixer output referred to the amplifier output (add amplifier gain to mixer output levels shown in Table 4.5).

In the above example, the mixer is a significant contributor to the third-order products, while the amplifier controls the second-order IMD levels.

There are other spurious signals which can be generated, formed by the second-mixer injection frequency f_{02} leaking into the output mixer. These spurious signals are at frequencies

$$f_s = mf_{02} + nf_{03}$$

where f_s is the spurious frequency, and m, n arc positive or negative integers. Figure 4.15 is a plot of output frequencies vs. desired output frequency for the above example. Shown are the fourth-, fifth-, sixth-, and seventh-order products of the two injection frequencies used in the above example. The results will be different for different frequency schemes, so the designer should check each case. The possible leakage paths for the injection signal at f_{02} and its harmonics include the second-IF filter as well as across inadequate shielding and filtering. The designer should also find that using "high-side" injection, where both f_{02} and f_{03} are above the second IF, will produce fewer potential spurious signals.

Noise.   The in-band noise output of the exciter consists of noise from amplifiers and other active circuits in low-level stages, hum and power sup-

TABLE 4.6   Mixer Contribution Levels

Exciter output signal	Output mixer contribution, dBm	RF amplifier contribution, dBm	Combined level, dBm
Desired signal levels	. . .	+14	+14
Second-order sum product	−48	−36	−35.4
Second harmonics	−54	−30	−29.5
Third-order sum products	−59	−60	−53.9
Third harmonics	−68	−56	−54

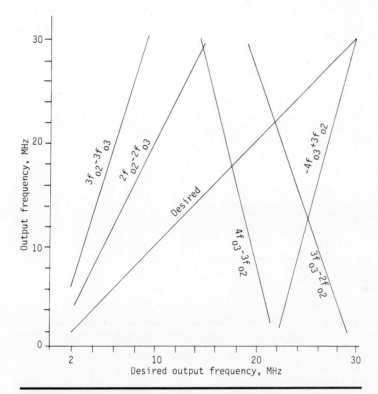

Figure 4.15 Spurious output signals caused by combining of two injection signals, f_{02} and f_{03}.

ply ripple components induced on the signal, and phase noise transferred to the signal from mixer injections. The noise from low-level stages should not be significant if the baseband and low-level IF stages are properly designed (see the material on baseband components in Sec. 4.3). Hum components may be induced in the signal by the magnetic fields of power transformers or blowers. The most common problem is hum induced in the control line of a voltage-controlled oscillator in the frequency synthesizer. Physical separation and the use of steel or other magnetic shielding will reduce the effect. Adjacent equipment in a cabinet can also be a source of interfering fields.

Phase noise on mixer injections affects both in-band and out-of-band noise, because it is primarily associated with the variable-frequency oscillator (VFO) injection of the output mixer. The phase noise on the VFO is transferred directly to the signal passing through the mixer and is not reduced or affected by mixer balance. Figure 4.16 shows an injection signal f_{03} with phase noise around it. A mixer input at frequency f_{i2} produces an output at f_{HF} which has the phase noise transferred to it. Typical levels of the phase noise, relative to the VFO level, may be -50 dB in a 3-kHz band around f_{03}, -90 dB at 10 kHz removed either side, and -110 removed

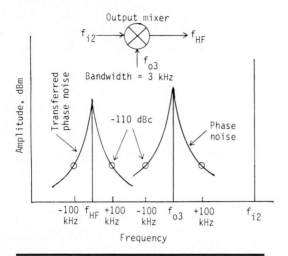

Figure 4.16 Transferral of phase noise on variable-frequency injection f_{o3} to mixer output signal.

100 kHz, all measured in a 3-kHz bandwidth. If the in-band noise from low-level stages is at least −60 dB, phase noise will be the predominant source of in-band noise, which is usually the case. If the exciter output is at +20 dBm, the out-of-band noise output due to phase noise will be at −90 dBm, at 100 kHz off-frequency.

Another source of out-of-band noise in exciters is the intrinsic noise of amplifiers between the output of the second-IF filter and exciter output. Figure 4.17 shows their effect. The IF amplifier, with a noise figure of 3 dB, produces noise at the exciter output at a level of −106.5 dBm (in a 3-kHz bandwidth). The output amplifier, with a noise figure of 4 dB, produces a noise output of −105 dBm. The combined output from these two sources is −102.7 dBm. The other components in the signal path, i.e., low-pass filters and mixer, are considered to produce no excess noise above thermal noise. The output noise level of −102.7 dBm is 36.6 dB greater than thermal noise and will be broadband in character, assuming a flat frequency response from

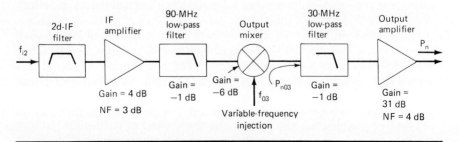

Figure 4.17 Noise sources in exciter output stages.

2 to 30 MHz. This compares with the -90 dBm due to phase noise, making phase noise predominate at 100-kHz frequency separation. Phase noise continues to decrease at greater frequency separations, but is dominant to wide frequency separations.

Excess noise, P_{n03}, on the VFO in the 2- to 30-MHz range may require high-pass filtering in the VFO path. If this noise level is at -120 dBc (3-kHz bandwidth), for example, and mixer balance reduces it another 25 dB, the level at the mixer output would be -145 dBc, or -128 dBm for a VFO level of $+17$ dBm. It will be assumed a small amount of filtering is used and the contribution of P_{n03} in the exciter noise output is insignificant.

If the exciter is to be used in a transmitter which is colocated with receivers, the noise output of -110 dBc may be excessive. Obviously, the VCO in the frequency synthesizer should be as clean as possible. Amplifier noise should be kept insignificant by using low-noise amplifiers and keeping gain as low as possible. It may be necessary to add selectivity to the output amplifier to reduce off-frequency noise, which is complex and costly.

4.3 Circuit Components

Circuit components in this context are functional entities such as modulators, amplifiers, and gain control elements. The circuit components discussed are critical in some way to exciter performance.

Baseband components

The signal-to-noise ratio established at the baseband signal input, of course, must exceed the desired exciter output signal-to-noise ratio. The input S/N ratio is set by the level of signal applied to the input of an amplifier, and the intrinsic noise level of that amplifier.

Figure 4.18a shows a typical balanced, transformerless line input amplifier. The potentiometer R_1 is a termination for the line as well as a gain control. The amplifier is a JFET input operational amplifier with low input noise voltage and currents and excellent common-mode rejection. It will be assumed in this example that the equivalent input noise current of the operational amplifier is 0.01 pA/(Hz)$^{1/2}$, and the equivalent input noise voltage e_n is 25 nV/(Hz)$^{1/2}$. In a 3-kHz bandwidth the noise current induces insignificant noise voltage in the source impedance of 50K ohms ($<0.1\ \mu$V), while the amplifier noise voltage is 1.4 μV.

If the line input level in this example is a minimum of -30 dBm, $e_s =$ 24.4 mV and 12.2 mV will appear at the amplifier input. The S/N will then be

$$\text{S/N} = 20 \log \left[\frac{12.2 \times 10^{-3}}{1.4 \times 10^{-6}} \right] = 79 \text{ dB}$$

This is certainly an adequate signal-to-noise ratio if the requirement on the exciter output is, say, 50 dB.

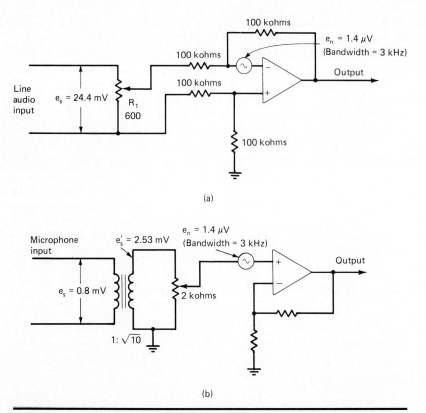

(a)

(b)

Figure 4.18 (*a*) Establishment of signal-to-noise ratio at the baseband line input amplifier. (*b*) Use of input transformer to improve signal-to-noise ratio.

This amplifier could also be considered for use with a low-level input signal such as from a dynamic microphone. If the typical microphone input is -55 dBm at an impedance of 200 ohms, the signal e_s is only 0.8 mV. This signal, applied directly to the above amplifier, would produce an S/N ratio of 49 dB. If a higher S/N ratio is needed, an input transformer to the amplifier could be used which steps up the input voltage. Figure 4.18*b* shows a transformer with a 2K- to 200-ohm impedance ratio which provides such a stepup. The secondary signal voltage is applied to the amplifier input, at full gain, giving an S/N ratio of 65 dB. This result provides an excellent S/N ratio even on this low-level input.

Distortion caused by the above amplifier will be very low. Total harmonic distortion, with a voltage gain of 10 or less, should be less than 0.03 percent (<-70 dB). Second- and higher-order IMD products will be similarly suppressed.

Compression amplifiers and line-leveling amplifiers. Compression amplifiers and line-leveling amplifiers are similar in that they are automatic-gain-controlled amplifiers, with the gain controlled so as to maintain constant output. The difference between the two is the range of gain change and time constants of the gain control action.

Figure 4.19 illustrates an automatic-gain-controlled amplifier. The transistor Q_1 is a JFET which acts as a variable resistor. The output of the amplifier is detected, and the dc voltage stored in capacitor C_1. The gain control amplifier varies the gate voltage of Q_1, maintaining a constant output by the action of R_1 and Q_1 operating as a variable voltage divider. The voltage across C_1 builds up quickly, following signal peaks, and decays through R_2.

The purpose of a line-leveling amplifier is to make minor adjustments in baseband amplifier gain to compensate for small changes in input line level. This is desirable to keep the transmitter operating at full-rated PEP. The range of gain adjustment will be 10 to 15 dB. The attack time (charge time of C_1) must be fast to respond to signal peaks, on the order of 5 ms. But the decay time (discharge of C_1 through R_2) must be slow enough that the gain does not follow the signal envelope. To do so would introduce distortion, as discussed later for ALC operation. Since the line input signals may be data as well as voice, it is important that distortion not be introduced by the line leveler. The decay time should be relatively long, 5 to 20 s.

The purpose of the microphone compression amplifier is to maintain a high average transmitter power output with a wide swing of input voice signal levels. This means the attack time and decay times are both relatively fast to follow the dynamics of normal speech. Compression amplifiers are discussed more fully in Chap. 6.

Voice-operated transmit keying. Voice operated keying (VOX) is a method for keying the exciter without operating a separate push-to-talk or other keying switch. It is especially useful when the user is patched in from a telephone line and does not have access to a key switch.

A VOX keying circuit is shown in Fig. 4.20. The transmit audio is passed through a variable-gain amplifier then detected. The resulting dc voltage is applied to the positive $(+)$ input of a voltage comparator. When this input is more positive than the dc voltage applied to the negative $(-)$ input, the

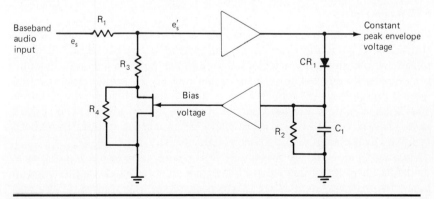

Figure 4.19   Automatic gain control audio amplifier.

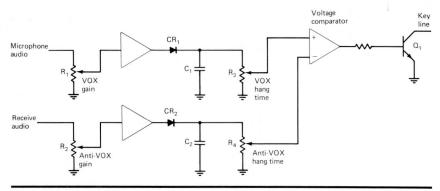

Figure 4.20   Circuit for voice-operated transmitter keying.

comparator output turns on Q_1, pulling the key line down to the (in this case) transmit condition.

The dc voltage applied to the negative input of the comparator is derived from the receive audio output, which is most readily available in a transceiver. This is an "anti-VOX" function to prevent false keying on microphone pickup of a speaker output. Both the VOX and anti-VOX amplifier/detector have gain controls R_1 and R_2 to allow the user to adjust for proper keying operation.

Associated with the VOX and anti-VOX detectors are decay-time adjustments R_3 and R_4. The purpose of these adjustments is to vary the "hang" time of the keying operation. When the transceiver is keyed and the voice input ceases, the adjustment of R_3 determines how long the exciter will remain keyed with no voice input. It should be long enough that the key line is not released on short pauses or spaces between words. The anti-VOX hang time is also adjustable and should be long enough that the circuit sensitivity does not quickly increase, causing keying on background noise. The adjustment range of the hang times should cover 0.2 to 5 s.

SSB modulators

Balanced modulator.   By far the most popular form of SSB modulator is the balanced modulator, used in conjunction with an USB or LSB IF filter to remove the unwanted sideband. Two popular types of balanced modulators are the doubly balanced diode mixer and an integrated circuit implementation (an industry standard, type 1496) of a switching-type modulator. The latter combines excellent carrier suppression, linearity, and moderate gain. These will not be discussed further here; numerous descriptions of both types are available in manufacturers' data sheets.

Phasing modulator.   Occasionally it is desirable to use a phasing-type modulator because of inadequate filter frequency response, excessive group delay distortion, or some other shortcoming of the balanced modulator and filter technique.

A simplified block diagram of the phasing modulator is shown in Fig. 4.21. The baseband signal is applied to two balanced modulators, with the signal applied to one shifted from the other by 90°. The injection signal to one of them is also shifted from the other by 90° using digital circuits. The outputs of the two balanced modulators are then combined, resulting in the cancellation of one of the sidebands because the components of that sideband in the two modulator outputs are out of phase.

The output signal of modulator A can be represented as:

$$e_{OA} = K_A V_1[\cos (\omega_c + \omega_1)t + \cos (\omega_c - \omega_1)t] \tag{4.3}$$

and of modulator B as:

$$
\begin{aligned}
e_{OB} &= K_B V_1 \left\{ \cos \left[\left(\omega_c t + \frac{\pi}{2} \right) + \left(\omega_1 t + \frac{\pi}{2} \right) \right] + \cos \left[\left(\omega_c t + \frac{\pi}{2} \right) - \left(\omega_1 t + \frac{\pi}{2} \right) \right] \right\} \\
&= K_B V_1[\cos (\omega_c - \omega_1)t - \cos (\omega_c + \omega_1)t]
\end{aligned}
\tag{4.4}
$$

where K_A, K_B = constants of proportionality between modulator output and baseband input
V_1 = peak baseband voltage
ω_c = modulation injection angular frequency
ω_1 = baseband signal angular frequency

It is obvious that, if $K_A = K_B$, adding together the above two modulator output signals, Eqs. (4.3) and (4.4), will result in cancellation of the upper sideband, $\omega_c + \omega_1$. If it is desired to remove the lower-sideband signal, take the difference of e_{OA} and e_{OB} by shifting one of them by 180°.

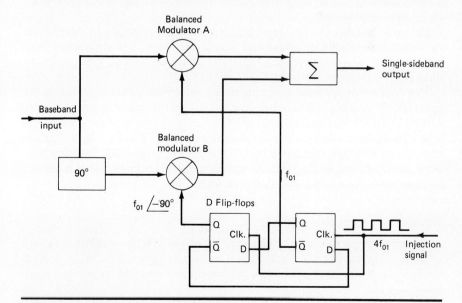

Figure 4.21 Phase-shift-type SSB modulator.

The effect of imperfect 90° phase shift in the baseband signal path to modulator B or the injection signal will be found by adding phase errors δ and Δ, respectively, to Eq. (4.4):

$$
\begin{aligned}
e_{OB} &= K_B V_1 \left\{ \cos \left[\left(\omega_c t + \frac{\pi}{2} + \Delta \right) + \left(\omega_1 t + \frac{\pi}{2} + \delta \right) \right] \right. \\
&\quad \left. + \cos \left[\left(\omega_c t + \frac{\pi}{2} + \Delta \right) - \left(\omega_1 t + \frac{\pi}{2} + \delta \right) \right] \right\} \\
&= K_B V_1 \left\{ - \cos \left[(\omega_c + \omega_1) t + \Delta + \delta \right] + \cos \left[(\omega_c - \omega_1) t + \Delta - \delta \right] \right\}
\end{aligned} \tag{4.5}
$$

Combining the outputs of the two modulators gives

$$
\begin{aligned}
e_O &= e_{OA} + e_{OB} \\
&= V_1 [K_A^2 + K_B^2 + 2 K_A K_B \cos (\Delta - \delta)]^{1/2} \sin \left[(\omega_c - \omega_1)t \right. \\
&\quad \left. + \tan^{-1} \left(\frac{K_A + K_B \cos (\Delta - \delta)}{K_B \sin (\Delta - \delta)} \right) \right] + V_1 [K_A^2 + K_B^2 - 2 K_A K_B \cos (\Delta \\
&\quad + \delta)]^{1/2} \sin \left[(\omega_c + \omega_1)t - \tan^{-1} \left(\frac{K_A + K_B \cos (\Delta + \delta)}{K_B \sin (\Delta + \delta)} \right) \right]
\end{aligned} \tag{4.6}
$$

This is the general expression for the combined modulator outputs. The amount of suppression, α, of the unwanted sideband ($\omega_a + \omega_1$) is given by:

$$
\alpha = 10 \log \left(\frac{K_A^2 + K_B^2 - 2 K_A K_B \cos (\Delta + \delta)}{K_A^2 + K_B^2 + 2 K_A K_B \cos (\Delta - \delta)} \right) \tag{4.7}
$$

This expression can be used to evaluate the effects of amplitude imbalance and phase-shift errors.

Figure 4.22 shows the degree of suppression of the unwanted sideband for various combinations of phase and amplitude error. For simplicity, it is assumed that only the baseband signal has phase-shift error, and amplitude imbalance is given as the ratio K_A/K_B.

The greatest problem in designing phase-shift modulators is providing for accurate 90° phase difference between the baseband inputs to the two modulators. This will not be further explored here, but there are now some excellent techniques available which are described in Refs. 3 and 4. The 90° phase shift of the injection signal can be quite accurately controlled by using flip-flops, as illustrated in Fig. 4.22. At injection signals below 1 MHz, it should be possible to maintain a 90° shift well within 1°.

Transmitter gain control methods

Transmitter gain control. The function of the TGC is to adjust the overall gain of the exciter and PA during a tuneup or gain-setting cycle, so that a reference carrier level produces a predetermined transmitter power output level.

Figure 4.23 illustrates a circuit for achieving this function. In general, the

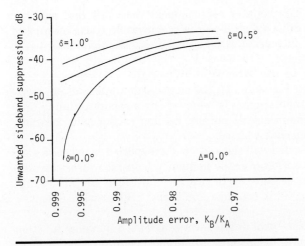

Figure 4.22 Suppression of unwanted sideband vs. amplitude error.

PA generates a control voltage V_c which is positive and proportional to output power (when driven by a single-tone signal). A gain control circuit then adjusts gain in small steps at a set rate until the output power is properly set. In the diagram, V_c is detected in a dual-voltage comparator as being above or below the reference voltages V_{RU} and V_{RL}, which correspond to the upper and lower limits, respectively, of V_c at which gain-setting action stops. The width of the window set by V_{RU} and V_{RL} may, for example, correspond to 0.5 dB in power output.

If V_c is above V_{RU}, a countup command is applied to a counter, and a clock

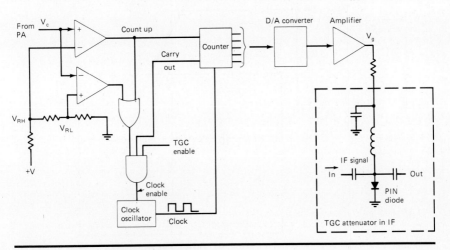

Figure 4.23   Transmit gain control circuit.

oscillator is activated. The counter counts up at the clock rate and the counter outputs, which drive a digital-to-analog converter, cause the analog voltage V_g to increase, increasing attenuation in a PIN diode attenuator located in the IF amplifier. If V_c is below V_{RL}, the counter will count down, decreasing attenuation in the attenuator. When the gain-change action causes V_c to fall between V_{RU} and V_{RL}, the clock oscillator is shut off, stopping the counter. The enable signal is removed (by a separate timing process) and the counter maintains its output, holding exciter gain constant, until reappearance of the enable signal.

The range of TGC needed will depend on the expected worst-case gain variation of the PA and exciter over the frequency range, as well as the variation in interconnect losses between the exciter and PA. If the TGC range is, say, 15 dB, then an 8-bit counter (256 steps) will provide adequate resolution.

Automatic level control.   Automatic level control is a dynamic function which operates while the transmitter is in normal operation. The primary function of ALC is to prevent overdriving the PA on signal peaks. To achieve this, a peak detector in the PA feeds an analog voltage back to the exciter for adjusting gain in the IF amplifier. This voltage, V_{ALC}, is generated only when the PA output exceeds a predetermined level, which corresponds to its maximum allowable PEP.

As seen in Fig. 4.24, the circuit concept is very simple. V_{ALC} is applied to an amplifier, causing the voltage V_a to increase, increasing attenuation in the PIN diode attenuator in the IF amplifier. The capacitor C_1 discharges or decays slowly through R_1 and the PIN diode when V_{ALC} drops, letting the gain increase.

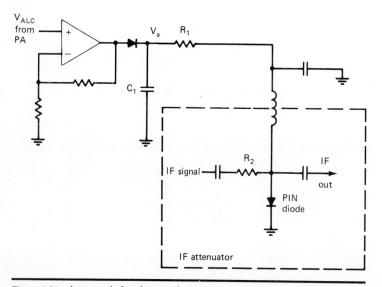

Figure 4.24   Automatic level control circuit.

An important consideration is the effect of the ALC action in producing distortion in the transmitter signal. V_{ALC} follows the signal envelope, assuming fast attack and decay times of the PA detector circuit. If the voltage V_a is also allowed to follow the signal envelope, as for a multitone signal, amplitude modulation distortion results. The time constant R_1C_1 must be long enough to reduce this distortion to acceptable levels.

Figure 4.25a illustrates a two-tone signal in the PA output and the action of V_a in following the envelope. A variation $\Delta V_a(t)$ occurs, causing a change in IF gain ΔG,

$$\Delta G = K\Delta V_a(t) \tag{4.8}$$

where ΔG is the change in voltage gain in the attenuator, and K is a constant for a narrow part of the gain control range.

Figure 4.25b illustrates how the resulting change in gain of the PIN diode attenuator would amplitude-modulate each tone of the IF signal as it passes through the attenuator.

If the peak amplitude of the IF input signal is A, then

$$\Delta A = A\Delta G = AK\Delta V_a(t) \tag{4.9}$$

If $\Delta V_a(t)$ is approximated as a sawtooth wave form, it can be represented as

$$\Delta V_a(t) = \Delta V_a \left(\frac{1}{2} - \frac{1}{\pi} \cos \omega_m t - \frac{1}{2\pi} \cos 2\omega_m t \cdots \right) \tag{4.10}$$

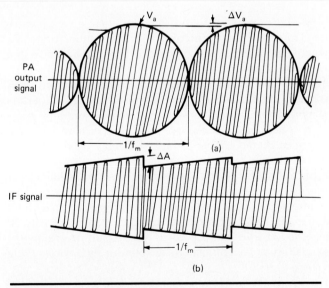

Figure 4.25 (a) How ALC gain control voltage V_a tends to follow signal envelope. (b) Modulation of IF signal by ALC voltage variations.

The modulation index of an amplitude-modulated signal is the envelope voltage divided by the unmodulated signal, or carrier, voltage:

$$m = \frac{(A_{pk} - A_{min})/2}{(A_{pk} + A_{min})/2} = \frac{\Delta A}{2A} = \frac{\Delta G}{2} \tag{4.11}$$

from Eq. (4.9) or

$$m(\omega_m) = \frac{K}{2} \Delta V_a \tag{4.12}$$

The relative level of the sidebands at $\pm \omega_m$ produced because of amplitude modulation of the signal passing through the attenuator can now be calculated as

$$\frac{m}{2} = \frac{K \Delta V_a}{4\pi} \tag{4.13}$$

An example may be $K = 0.1/\text{volt}$, and $\Delta V_a = 0.1$ V. Then $m = 0.005/\pi$, and the level of upper and lower envelope frequency sidebands is $0.005/2\pi$, or -62 dB. This will be the approximate amplitude of the sidebands, depending on the accuracy of the approximation of the waveform of $\Delta V_a(t)$ as a sawtooth. It should also be taken into account that K will change over the range of V_a. It was also assumed in the above discussion that the modulation process was inefficient enough that it was not regenerative.

Mixers

Mixers can be either active or passive. By far the most common are passive doubly balanced diode mixers. They are obtainable from manufacturers in a compact package whose characteristics are specified. They are available in a wide range of characteristics, and have evolved into a highly developed art. Active mixers, on the other hand, are not readily available as such but must be individually designed. There seems to be no real advantage in performance to be gained by their use, except for elimination of an amplifier stage because of their gain. Therefore, the discussion of mixers here will deal entirely with performance characteristics of passive doubly balanced diode mixers.

Of the several important characteristics of the mixer, one is the balance or isolation from one port to another. Figure 4.26 shows the balance parameters usually specified. These and other mixer characteristics are controlled and specified using standard impedance terminations on each port, usually 50 ohms. In HF exciters the LO-to-IF and LO-to-RF port isolations are important because of the possibility of coupling noise or spurious signals appearing on the injection to these ports.

The signal level at which the mixer can operate is determined primarily by the injection or local oscillator level. The RF input compression point

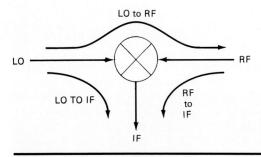

Figure 4.26 Mixer balance parameters.

depends on the LO level, but for HF applications, the IMD characteristics are usually the most important consideration.

In general, IMD characteristics of a doubly balanced diode mixer are related to the LO and RF input levels, assuming proper terminations (50 ohms on all ports). Under these conditions it has been found that mixer spurious levels can be estimated to a fair degree of accuracy (see Refs. 6 and 7). Table 4.7 lists the spurious frequencies and their predicted levels, based on the difference ΔP between the LO and RF input power levels. The spurious

TABLE 4.7   Predicted Mixer Spurious Levels

Order of harmonic		Spurious
LO	RF	level, dB
1	1	0 dB (desired)
1	2	$\Delta P - 41$
1	3	$2\Delta P - 28$
2	1	-35
2	2	$\Delta P - 39$
2	3	$2\Delta P - 44$
3	1	-10
3	2	$\Delta P - 32$
3	3	$2\Delta P - 18$
4	1	-35
4	2	$\Delta P - 39$
5	1	-14
5	3	$\Delta P - 14$
6	1	-35
6	3	$\Delta P - 39$
7	1	-17
7	3	$2\Delta P - 11$

SOURCE: Bert C. Henderson, "Predicting Intermodulation Suppression in Double-Balanced Mixers," *Watkins-Johnson Tech-Notes,* vol. 10, no. 4, July/August 1983. (Reprinted by permission.)

frequencies f_s are found from

$$f_s = mf_{LO} \pm nf_{RF} \tag{4.14}$$

where m and n are the integers in the LO and RF columns, respectively. The levels stated are relative to the desired IF port output signal level. Note that the spurious levels associated with higher harmonics of the LO are still relatively high. An example is the calculation of relative spurious levels of a mixer having an RF input of -10 dBm at 9 MHz and an LO level of $+13$ dBm at 100 MHz. The products for $m = 3$, $n = 1$ are at 291 and 309 MHz. From Table 4.7, the estimated suppression of these products is only -10 dB from the desired IF output.

Table 4.7 does not predict two-tone IMD levels such as in-band third-order IMD. These can be predicted by estimating the input third-order intercept of the mixer as being 5 to 10 dB higher than the LO level. For a $+13$-dBm LO the estimated input third-order intercept is $+18$ dBm. For an RF input of -10 dBm/tone, the in-band third-order IMD appearing at the IF output will be -56 dB, relative to the desired IF output level.

The above predictions of spurious levels in mixer outputs should be used only to aid in selection of a mixer for a particular application, using actual measurements to make the final choice.

Proper termination of the LO, RF, and IF ports is important in properly using the diode mixer, the IF and RF ports being most critical. At the IF output, a very broadband termination is particularly important in high-performance mixers to prevent the unwanted image frequency and higher-order products from reflecting back into the mixer. These reflected products remix with the mixer inputs, increasing IMD output levels.

4.4 Introduction to Transceivers

Exciter and receiver functions are combined into one unit, a transceiver, when size or cost is of paramount importance. Airborne radios, packsets, and vehicular mobile are just a few applications where the transceiver finds wide application. Radio operation in these cases is typically simplex, i.e., transmitting and receiving alternately on a single frequency. (Occasionally, dual frequencies are used.) Some flexibility may be sacrificed in selecting operating modes or conditions, such as independent sideband, extra receiver bandwidths, etc. Performance may also be sacrificed to save power or space.

The receiver and exciter have several functional elements in common, such as power supply, frequency synthesizer, frequency standard, control circuits, and front panel controls. Circuit components, such as IF filters, mixers, and amplifiers, also perform functions common to both transmit and receive operations. These will be discussed further.

Since the transceiver is alternately an exciter and receiver, there are potential problems because of transmit-to-receive and receive-to-transmit timing, transmit signals desensitizing receiver circuits, etc. These will also be discussed.

4.5   Transceiver Architecture

The unique features of transceiver architecture are the functions shared between the transmit and receive operations. The key to a simple, compact transceiver design is to make use of common elements to the maximum extent possible, consistent with meeting performance requirements.

The power supply, frequency synthesizer, and control functions are obviously shared between transmit and receiver operations by using common supply voltages, one frequency scheme for both operations, and similar control methods. Circuit elements can also be shared, such as amplifiers, mixers, and filters. Components which are capable of bilateral signal flow, such as filters and diode mixers, are particularly useful.

Figure 4.27 shows a block diagram of a typical transceiver which helps to illustrate these points. In the exciter path, the baseband signal enters the left-hand side through baseband amplifier and processing circuits into the balanced modulator. The signal then progresses through the rest of the familiar exciter signal path to the output. Along the way it passes through amplifier stages, as shown, which are switched into the signal path.

For operation as a receiver, the received signal enters on the right, passing through a broadband "roofing" filter into the mixer M_3. This mixer is used as a bilateral circuit element, with the receiver signal passing back through it in the opposite direction of the transmit signal. The signal passes through another bilateral circuit device, the second-IF filter, then into a receive IF amplifier. The mixer M_2 is also used as a bilateral device, mixing the receive signal down to the first or lowest IF. Signal flow progresses through the first-IF filter, another bilateral circuit element. The output of this filter is switched into the receive IF amplifier and detected, and the resulting audio signal is amplified and applied to the output terminals.

For detailed design considerations of individual sections of the transceiver, refer to Chap. 3 and previous sections of this chapter. Some considerations unique to transceiver design will be discussed here.

IF filter and amplifier

The IF amplifier and filter section is considered here to contain the transmit balanced modulator and IF amplifier, receive detectors and IF amplifiers, and the first-IF filter. A block diagram is shown in Fig. 4.28.

Considering the receive signal path, in addition to filtering to select the proper sideband (or other passband), the IF amplifiers must provide enough gain to drive the detectors at the proper level. Gain on the order of 60 dB could be required in the IF amplifier between the IF filter and detectors. AGC is used in this amplifier to maintain constant levels into the detectors. The transmit-IF amplifier, on the other hand, may have little gain, and no automatic gain control requirement. The functions of the two amplifiers are quite different, not lending themselves to sharing functions. The IF buffer amplifiers (to the second mixer) in the transmit and receive paths are both relatively low gain, and are switched on and off to change signal direction.

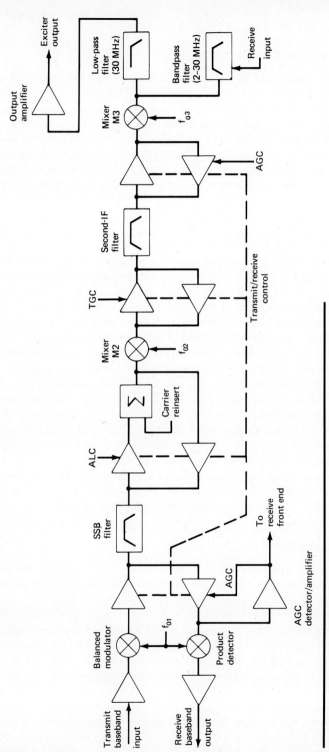

Figure 4.27 Transceiver block diagram.

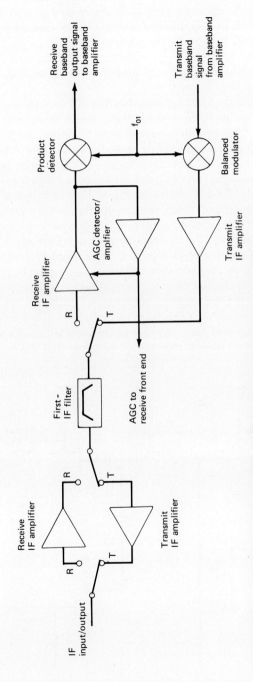

Figure 4.28 Transceiver IF amplifier and filter.

There are, of course, many methods of switching the IF filter into the proper signal path. One simple method is shown in Fig. 4.29, where FETs are biased on and off in response to control voltages applied to their gates. Bias voltages V_T and V_R turn on the appropriate FETs in the transmit and receive signal paths. Resistors R_T provide proper terminations for the filter. If FETs are not appropriate to the IF amplifiers being used, diode switches or some other form may be used.

Although not indicated on the block diagram of Fig. 4.28, it may be desirable to use a single circuit element for the transmit modulator and receive product detector. The designer may want to trade off the complexity of switching the circuit against providing two separate circuits. A technique for using the switching-type IC modulator (type 1496/1596) may be considered where the balanced inputs and outputs are separated into baseband and IF inputs and outputs. This is shown in Fig. 4.30, where one of the inputs receives transmit baseband audio, and the appropriate output is the modulator IF output with suppressed carrier. The input has capacitor bypassing which is effective only at IF, not degrading the baseband signal. The other input to the IC is the receive IF signal. On this input is a high-pass filter. The appropriate output contains the recovered audio signal, and has a low-pass filter to remove the injection f_{01}. Careful layout of circuit components is required to achieve good performance, especially in terms of transmit carrier suppression.

It should also be noted that, because of the crowded component layouts common to transceiver design, care should be taken that the receive IF out-

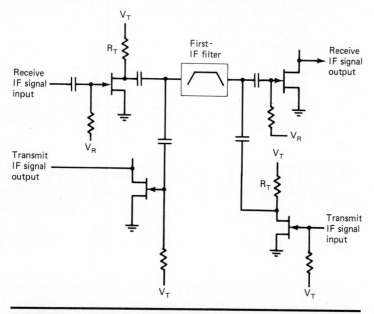

Figure 4.29   A switching method for the first-IF filter.

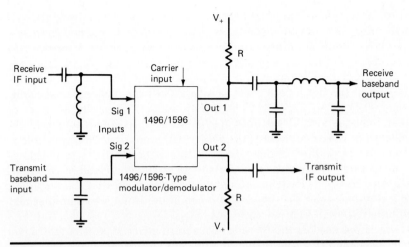

Figure 4.30 Transmit/receive application of 1495/1596-type modulator/demodulator.

put is well isolated from the IF filter's input (receive-side) circuitry. Because of the high gain usually needed in the receive IF amplifier, it is easy for passband amplitude variation to be increased over that of the filter alone by output IF signal leaking back and combining with the filter input IF signal, causing partial cancellation or addition. The output IF signal, having passed through the IF filter, undergoes rapid phase shifts with respect to the filter IF input signal, across the passband. For example, if the IF output signal appearing at the filter input is 20 dB lower than the filter input signal, it will introduce 1 dB of additional amplitude variation at those passband frequencies where it is out of phase with the input.

IF-to-RF translator

The IF-to-RF translator has some characteristics to consider which differ from the IF amplifier. Figure 4.31 shows how the translator might be config-

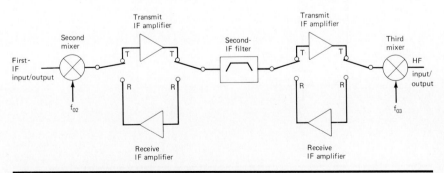

Figure 4.31 Switching IF amplifiers in frequency translator.

ured to accommodate transmit and receive functions. The mixers and second-IF filter are bilateral elements, with the amplifiers switched to reverse signal flow. The IF amplifiers used here are operating at VHF (around 100 MHz) and so will not be amenable to simply biasing on and off as for the first-IF amplifiers. The inputs and outputs of the amplifiers can be switched in and out of the signal path, such as with PIN diodes. One possible configuration is shown in Fig. 4.32. The isolation across the switches must be greater than the sum of the amplifier gains, at all frequencies within the bandwidth of the amplifiers, or instability will occur. It may be possible to use only one amplifier, if the gain each way is nearly the same. A small amount of gain adjustment, in the form of an attenuator, could be combined into one of the diode switches. It should be determined that the amplifiers used are stable under the switched-out condition. If not, the amplifier may need to have power removed when not in use.

The switches used on the HF side of the third mixer M_3 will handle higher signal levels, requiring that they have sufficient on current and voltage back-bias for the expected signal levels. Since they are switching signal frequencies down to 2 MHz, they must also have sufficiently long carrier lifetimes.

There are alternatives to the switching methods discussed here, of course. One which has been used is shown in Fig. 4.33, where the third mixer is an active mixer and not bilateral. The signal flow through the second and third mixer and second-IF filter is reversed by transmit/receive switches as shown,

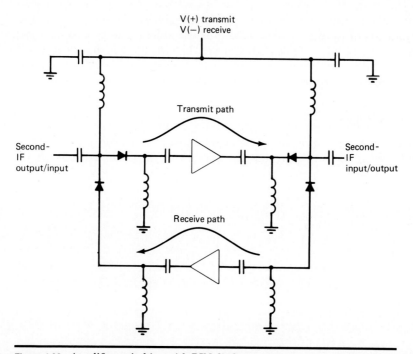

Figure 4.32 Amplifier switching with PIN diodes.

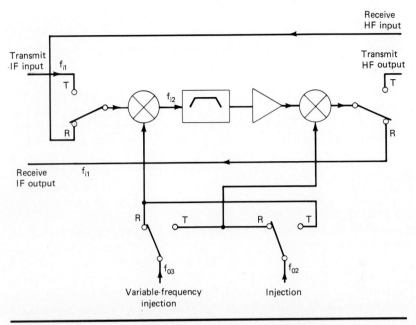

Figure 4.33 Alternative switching scheme for frequency translator.

and the injection signals to the two mixers are switched. This method requires that the isolation between the two injection signals across the switches be very high to eliminate generation of spurious signals, as discussed in Sec. 4.2 and Chap. 3.

Filter-saving frequency scheme

If the transceiver has a requirement to operate in upper sideband or lower sideband, but not independent sideband, then a frequency scheme using only one first-IF filter may be considered. The scheme uses one SSB filter in the first IF. The desired sideband is selected in the second IF by proper choice of the second injection frequency, f_{02}.

Figure 4.34 illustrates the frequency scheme. An USB filter is used in the first IF. In the second mixer, the USB signal is translated by f_{02} to an USB which falls in the passband of the second-IF filter, and is transmitted as an USB signal. If the operating mode is LSB, the injection frequency of the second mixer is changed to f'_{02}, which is above the second-IF filter passband. The difference product now falls in the second-IF filter, which is inverted from the original USB signal, becoming an LSB signal. It is then transmitted as an LSB signal. In receive, the same process operates in reverse.

The advantage of the above scheme is obviously the saving of an IF filter and associated switching circuits, but at the expense of devising the means to change the injection frequency f_{02}. Note also that different receive and

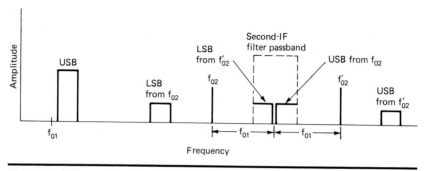

Figure 4.34 Filter-saving-frequency scheme.

transmit spurious signals will be generated for f_{02} and f'_{02}, and should be taken into account.

CW and RTTY modes

Sometimes transmission and reception of CW or RTTY signals or both are required in an SSB transceiver. There are alternative approaches to generating the transmit signals and receiving them, and deciding which to use depends on the complexity of the approach in each case.

A CW signal can be generated either by reinserting a keyed carrier at f_{01} or by keying an audio signal. If it is required that the emitted signal be at an assigned carrier frequency, using a reinserted carrier is the preferred approach. If the emission mode allows a keyed audio signal, a keyed audio oscillator can be used. The latter simplifies the receiver operation because it is tuned to the assigned carrier frequency and no BFO is required to receive the keyed audio-modulated signal.

Controlling the emission bandwidth of the CW signal requires shaping the keyed signal envelope, or possibly a narrow filter. Rise and fall times of the envelope of 5 to 10 ms may be sufficient to meet emission limits. A narrow IF filter inserted in the keyed carrier path with a passband of approximately 300 Hz provides positive control.

In reception, if the CW signal is at the carrier frequency, one of the injections in the receiver must be offset enough to produce an audio tone (assuming the receive tuning is to remain at the assigned carrier frequency, as in a transceiver). It may be more convenient to offset f_{03}, placing the received CW signal in the upper or lower sideband. The normal USB filter could be used, or a narrow CW filter switched in with a passband centered on the displaced carrier frequency. For example, if f_{03} were displaced by 800 Hz, the center of the passband of the receive CW filter would be required to be displaced to 800 Hz higher than the first-IF carrier frequency f_{01}. If it is desired to displace f_{01} to produce the audio tone, a CW filter would be centered at f_{01}, because the SSB filter will not pass the signal.

The transceiver is sometimes required to incorporate a single-channel

RTTY mode, using an FSK signal. If operation of the RTTY channel in SSB mode is allowed, a two-tone audio generator keyed by the teletype (TTY) mark/space input will suffice. An oscillator which switches from a "mark" to a "space" frequency in response to the TTY input will produce the necessary FSK signal in the SSB passband.

If the emission mode requires the shifted frequencies to be on each side of the assigned carrier frequency, the above approach may not be acceptable. A more straightforward approach is to insert the FSK signal in the first IF, shifting each side of f_{01}. A crystal oscillator which is "pulled" between the mark and space frequencies is a method of generating the FSK signals. Figure 4.35 shows a crystal oscillator operating in a frequency range which is more conducive to being pulled, then divided by a fixed ratio to the first-IF frequency. A mark/space input signal is shown which changes the capacitance of a voltage-controlled capacitor, thus changing the oscillator frequency. For example, if the mark frequency is 500.085 kHz and the divide ratio is 20, the oscillator frequency is 10.0017 MHz. The required pull range for 170-Hz shift is 340 ppm, well within the capability of such an oscillator. Minor temperature compensation may be required to bring the frequency stability within requirements. If compensated to 5×10^{-6}, frequency error would be 2.5 Hz. Also shown in Fig. 4.35 is a filter in the signal path to the IF, which may be required to control spurious emissions.

Another approach to generating the FSK signal, if the frequency synthesizer is capable of it, is to shift the injection signal f_{01}. This has the advantage of not introducing additional frequency error since it is locked to the transceiver frequency standard. The transition time between mark and space frequencies must be fast, however, on the order of 1 ms for data rates of 75 baud.

To receive the FSK signal, it is converted to an audio FSK signal then detected in a phase-locked loop or filter-type discriminator. If the FSK signal is received in the SSB mode, the receiver output is audio and is fed to the FSK discriminator and detected, and the appropriate mark/space signal sent to the TTY printer.

If the received signal is a shifted carrier, the required audio signal is generated by shifting one of the injection signals in the receive path. For example, the variable-frequency injection f_{03} could be shifted by 2 kHz, placing

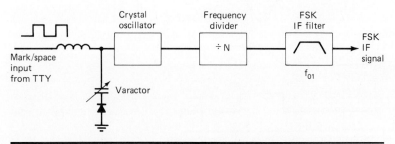

Figure 4.35 Method of generating IF FSK signals centered at f_{01}.

the signal in the USB passband, resulting in the required audio output. A separate IF filter could be used instead of the normal USB filter, if better selectivity is needed. Or the injection to the product detector, f_{01}, could be shifted to produce the audio output. In this case, the signal would require filtering by a separate IF filter, because the signal will not pass through the USB (or LSB) filter. Either approach will produce the same result.

Transmit/receive switching

In switching from the transmit to receive condition in a transceiver, the receive circuits must be ready for normal operation quickly so as not to disrupt a received signal. This means that power must be applied to receive circuits, frequency changes required in any of the injection signals made, and gain of the receiver initialized before a usable baseband output is produced. If the signal to be received is voice, then the time allowed may be 0.1s or longer. If an FSK or other data signal is to be received, the allowable time may be on the order of 10 to 20 ms.

A common problem which occurs concerns the receive AGC circuit. When in the transmit mode, transmit signals are present in the IF amplifier section which will generate high AGC levels, reducing receive gain when switched back to the receive mode. Disabling the receive-IF amplifier when in the transmit mode is usually a necessary step, but other precautions are necessary. At the top of Fig. 4.36 it is shown how the transmit signal is expected to decay in the output of the IF, particularly the IF filter. The filter "rings out" for a period of time t_1 and produces a short signal in the receive IF when

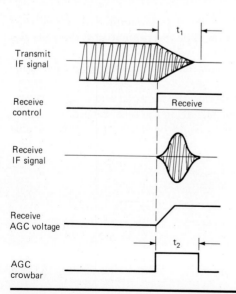

Figure 4.36 Transmit-to-receive timing and AGC crowbar operation.

the receive circuits are reactivated. The result is that the receive AGC responds to the signal, decreasing the receive gain and desensitizing the receiver for a period of time determined by the AGC decay time. A method of defeating this effect is to "crowbar" the AGC control voltage at the AGC holding capacitor for a period of time t_2, which assures that the filter has completely dissipated its stored energy. Mechanical SSB filters (seven-pole design) with group delay of 900 μs may require t_2 to be on the order of 10 ms, depending on the transmit signal level in the filter.

Transients caused by changing bias conditions on amplifiers as they are turned on can also generate a receive IF signal which generates AGC voltage. This can be minimized by making coupling capacitors only as large as needed for the IF signals. The AGC crowbar will also nullify the effects of these transients.

In switching from receive to transmit, the transmit circuits must be ready to transmit quickly because a key signal may be applied simultaneously with the baseband input. If the input signal is data, keying to the transmit mode may be required in less than 10 ms.

At the top of Fig. 4.37 is shown the application of the key signal, putting the transceiver in the transmit mode. The exciter output is shown building up during time t_a. It is during this time that circuit gains must stabilize and injection signals change, if necessary, to the correct frequencies. As mentioned previously, the time allowed for t_a may be less than 10 ms. At the bottom of Fig. 4.37 is shown an undesirable transient "spike" in the exciter output caused by the rapid application of bias voltages. Such a transient

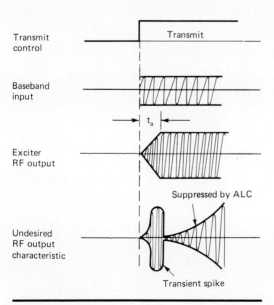

Figure 4.37 Receive-to-transmit switching effect on transmit signals.

could cause the transmitter ALC circuit to reduce transmitter gain in the same way AGC acted to reduce receive gain. These transients can be eliminated by shaping turn-on voltages and controlling size of coupling capacitors.

REFERENCES

1. "Part 81—Stations on Land in the Maritime Service and Alaska Pacific Fixed Stations," in *Rules and Regulations,* Federal Communications Commission, U.S. Government Printing Office, Washington, DC, 1985.
2. "Appendix 8—Table of Maximum Permitted Spurious Emission Power Levels," in *Radio Regulations,* International Telecommunications Union, Geneva, Switzerland, 1982.
3. Raymond E. Cook, "Cascaded Active Circuits Yield 90-degree Phase Difference Networks," *Electron. Des. News,* vol. 18, Apr. 5, 1973, pp. 52–56.
4. Alan G. Loyd, "90 Degree Phase Difference Networks," *Electron. Des.,* vol. 24, Sept. 13, 1976, pp. 90–94.
5. E. W. Pappenfus, W. B. Bruene, and E. O. Schoenike, *Single Sideband Principles and Circuits,* McGraw-Hill, New York, 1964, p. 34.
6. Bert C. Henderson, "Predicting Intermodulation Suppression in Double-Balanced Mixers," *Watkins Johnson Tech-Notes,* vol. 10, no. 4, July/August 1983.
7. Bert C. Henderson, "Mixers: Part 1," *Watkins Johnson Tech-Notes,* vol. 8, March/April 1981.

IF Analog Filters

Joseph A. Vanous

Intermediate frequency filters are used in SSB receivers and exciters to shape the desired signal spectrum and to reduce the unwanted signals. Unwanted signals are created by the mixing process when a signal frequency is mixed, or translated, to a different frequency. The desired signal may be shaped by filter design to conserve bandwidth and to prevent adjacent channel interference. Filters also protect receiver stages from overload by strong signals on nearby frequencies. In addition, the filtering must not unduly alter the characteristics of the modulated signal. These alterations show up as distortion in the frequency domain (intermodulation and harmonic distortion) or in the time domain (signal delay differences). These effects must be minimized.

The SSB IF filters differ from other bandpass filters because they are offset from the carrier frequency and have a nonsymmetrical attenuation response. These filters are designed to pass one sideband such as USB and reject LSB. Other IF filters have the signal frequency centered in the passband and are used to reduce spurious signals generated by the mixers. Such filters have a symmetrical response.

5.1 Passband and Stopband Characteristics

Since bandpass filters share certain common characteristics, it is desirable to define the various terms associated with them. A diagram of these is shown in Fig. 5.1.

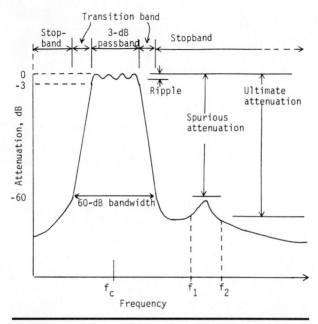

Figure 5.1 Common amplitude characteristics of a band-pass filter.

Passband.   The passband defines the limits of the desired signal modulation and is usually defined between the 3 dB (or half-power points) referenced to the highest peak between these limits. Often, other attenuation points are given such as, 1 or 0.5 dB. This occurs when the overall exciter or receiver 3-dB passband is specified, and the attenuation at 3 dB is then partitioned among all the filters in the signal path.

Passband ripple.   This is the variation in signal level or response across the passband. It is defined as the difference in amplitude between the minimum response and the maximum response values. The difference is stated in dB and can range from a few tenths of a dB to 3 dB or more.

Transition band.   This term is loosely defined but generally includes the region between the 3- and 60-dB points. It is often defined as being monotonic, i.e., a smooth transition. It can also be specified as a region where the attenuation is some lesser amount than that existing in the stopband.

Stopband.   The stopband is the region beyond the transition band. A specified amount of attenuation is often stated for specific frequencies in the stopband. These usually correspond to images and injection signals. See Chap. 3 for a discussion on image frequencies.

Spurious attenuation.   Many filters have spurious responses in the stopband. The locations of these are sometimes defined by a frequency band

and the expected minimum attenuation levels. They are usually above the passband in crystal filters.

Ultimate attenuation.   This is specified as an attenuation in the stop-band region where the attenuation can be expected to remain greater than this level.

Intermodulation distortion.   The in-band intermodulation distortion is specified for exciters and receivers, and the out-of-band intermodulation distortion primarily for receivers. This is described in detail in Sec. 5.4. The level of the two tones is specified for a given third-order distortion, product level. For example, for a two-tone level of -25 dBm/tone, the third-order distortion product could be specified as no greater than -60 dB down (-85 dBm).

Insertion loss.   The insertion loss of a filter is the loss in available power, in dB, that occurs when the filter is inserted between the source and load. It is defined as $10 \log (P_{\text{available}}/P_{\text{load}})$ and can be measured as $20 \log (E_1/E_2)$, as shown in Fig. 5.2. The maximum amount of power delivered to a load occurs when the source and load are matched. This level can be considered the reference of 0 dB. With the filter inserted, the loss occurring is the insertion loss in dB and is measured over the specified filter passband. When the source impedance differs from the load, a transformer can be used to obtain the reference voltage E_1.

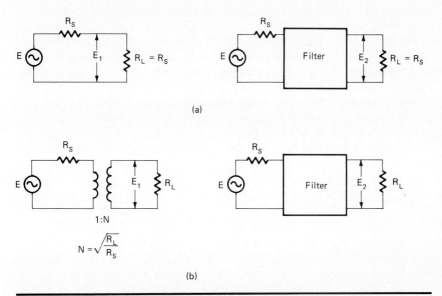

(a)

(b)

Figure 5.2 Method of determining insertion loss of filters: (*a*) when load and source impedances are matched ($R_L = R_S$); (*b*) when impedances are different ($R_L \neq R_S$). Insertion loss (in decibels) $= 20 \log (E_1/E_2)$.

Shape factor.   The shape factor of a filter is a figure of merit which is usually specified as the ratio of the 60-dB bandwidth to the 3-dB bandwidth. At times other numbers are used. For example, a 6-dB bandwidth may be used to provide a 60- to 6-dB ratio.

Delay distortion.   Phase linearity is specified as a time delay across the filter passband. Ideally, a constant delay across the passband would provide linear phase shift with signal frequency change. The variation in the time delay is called "delay distortion" and is described further in Sec. 5.5.

Most *LC* tuned circuits and crystal and mechanical filters have amplitude characteristics that fall within the following major classifications:

1. Butterworth maximally flat passband response

2. Chebyshev (sometimes spelled Tchebycheff) equal ripple response

3. Gaussian response

4. Bessel response

Many other types of responses exist. Another variation of the Chebyshev has equal ripple in the passband and equal attenuation minima in the stopband. These are also called "elliptic-function filters." This filter has the steepest response in the transition band but at the expense of rising attenuation lobes in the stopband. Other responses include equal-ripple delay, transitional, Legendre, and minimum-insertion-loss filters. Each of these has its special characteristics. The majority of filters for general application, however, use responses 1 and 2.

The Butterworth has a maximally flat amplitude response at the center of the passband and exhibits a gradual increase in attenuation near the 3-dB point, as shown in Fig. 5.3. It provides reasonable selectivity and is monotonic in both the passband and stopband.

The Chebyshev filter has equal ripple in the passband. The response extends closer to the 3-dB point and does not have the gradual attenuation of the Butterworth in this region, especially for ripples of 0.1 dB or greater. In the transition region, Fig. 5.4*a,* a sharper monotonic attenuation provides

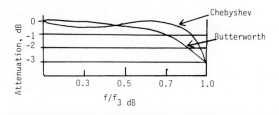

Figure 5.3 Passband comparison between Butterworth and Chebyshev, $n = 3$. In-band response of the Chebyshev is wider.

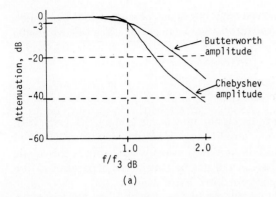

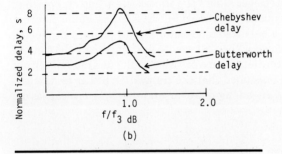

Figure 5.4 Comparison between Butterworth and Chebyshev filters, $n = 5$. (a) Selectivity plot showing steeper Chebyshev response; (b) delay characteristics showing greater delay variation for the Chebyshev. *Note:* Both (a) and (b) represent half the passband.

more selectivity for the same number of poles. In the limiting case when the passband ripple is zero, the response becomes a Butterworth. It becomes apparent that the allowance of a little ripple in the passband causes a great difference in the selectivity of a filter.

In general, for the Butterworth and Chebyshev, the more poles used, the sharper the attenuation transition at the 3-dB point. This type of characteristic results in a higher time-delay variation at that point. Figure 5.4b illustrates the difference between delays of a five-pole Butterworth and a five-pole 0.1-dB ripple Chebyshev. Since the Chebyshev has this sharper attenuation at 3 dB (Fig. 5.4a), the delay variation is greater. Both exhibit a saucer-shaped delay across the passband.

The gaussian filter has a relatively flat delay out to and beyond the 3-dB points, but has a slowly increasing attenuation characteristic in the stopband. The Bessel filter has the flattest delay and has similar attenuation characteristics. These two-filter responses are not widely used because of their poor selectivity. However, in applications where an impulse or step function signal must be preserved with low levels of ringing and overshoot, the constant time delay of these filters may be necessary. See the discussion on noise blankers in Chap. 6.

5.2 Filter Arrangements

In SSB systems, information transmission may occur in the USB, LSB, ISB, or four-channel ISB. In addition, amplitude modulation may be transmitted as USB with carrier or amplitude modulation equivalent. Since this mode customarily uses the USB filter, it will not be considered separately. More information on this mode is contained in Chaps. 2 and 4.

In USB operation, the most widely used form of SSB in the HF band, the USB filter in the exciter or receiver allows the transmission and reception of signals above the carrier frequency, as shown in Fig. 5.5. The audio is mixed with the carrier injection in a balanced modulator (for an exciter), producing a double-sideband output which is then filtered to pass only the USB signals. Then this IF frequency is translated once or twice to the desired RF output frequency. In this case, it is presumed that the translation preserves the carrier-to-signal relationship, i.e., an increase in audio frequency causes an

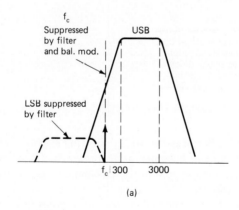

(a)

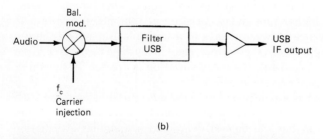

(b)

Figure 5.5 Relationship between USB, suppressed carrier, and opposite sideband. (*a*) Selectivity response; (*b*) USB exciter circuit block diagram.

increase in RF frequency. For example, assume that the carrier frequency, although suppressed, is 2.0 MHz. The actual signals transmitted would be 2.000300 through 2.003000 MHz. In some equipment designs, a sideband reversal occurs so that an LSB filter is needed for USB transmission.

An example of bandwidth requirements for equipment can be obtained from a military standard specification (see Ref. 1). This specification concerns the requirement for an HF tactical digital information link. The overall receiver or exciter passband amplitude response is stated as not more than (NMT) -2 dB between 450 and 3050 Hz, and NMT -3 dB at 300 Hz. The -60-dB attenuation frequencies are $+4400$ and -400 Hz. The negative sign indicates that the frequency is on the low-frequency side of the carrier. Since these are overall requirements, the 2- to 3-dB passband response has to be partitioned between all filters in the signal path. The 60-dB selectivity will have to be obtained primarily from the USB filter. The LSB is similarly specified except that the numbers will be negative since they are referenced to the carrier frequency. Typically, 10 to 30 dB of carrier attenuation can be expected of the SSB filter. Since at least -50 dB is usually required, the difference has to come from the carrier null in the balanced modulators.

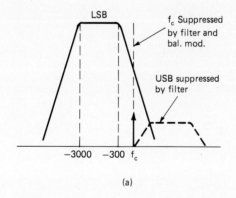

(a)

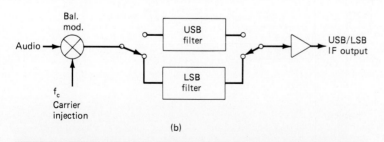

(b)

Figure 5.6 Relationship between LSB, suppressed carrier, and opposite sideband. (a) Selectivity response of LSB; (b) block diagram shows filter switching allowing either USB or LSB operation in exciter. Only one is in use at a time.

In the LSB mode, only the frequencies below the carrier are transmitted. It should be noted that LSB is not the predominant mode of transmission in the HF range. When it is used, it is usually in addition to USB. Consequently, when equipment has USB and LSB (without ISB), the same audio and balanced modulator is used for both with the filter switched to provide one or the other sideband, as shown in Fig. 5.6.

ISB uses both the USB and LSB modes simultaneously to transmit and receive two types of signals which can be completely independent of each other. Or the same information can be transmitted in both sidebands simultaneously to enhance the transmission link reliability. The use of ISB requires two separate audio channels, modulators, and filters in the trans-

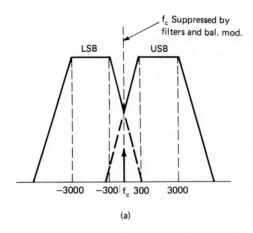

(a)

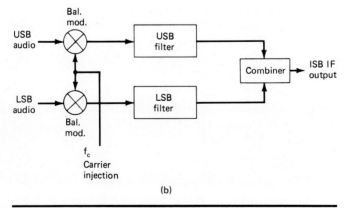

(b)

Figure 5.7 Independent sideband operation. (*a*) Selectivity response of both USB and LSB; (*b*) ISB exciter block diagram using separate channels allowing use of both simultaneously or each separately.

mitter, and two filters, IF amplifiers, product detectors, and audio amplifiers in the receiver. Refer to Fig. 5.7.

In the four-channel ISB mode of operation, filters are arranged as shown in Fig. 5.8. The USB and LSB modes in the four-channel configuration are the same as described for ISB and use a common carrier frequency injection. The outer channels designated lower LSB (LLSB) and upper USB (UUSB) have additional subcarrier injections that are specified a fixed difference

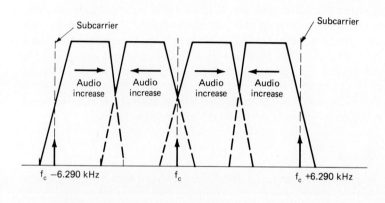

(a)

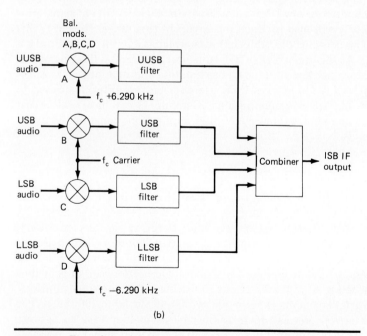

(b)

Figure 5.8 Four-channel independent sideband operation. (a) Selectivity response of four filters; (b) block diagram showing four independent audio and balanced modulator circuits.

from the carrier injection frequency. The military standard frequency separation is $f_c \pm 6.290$ kHz.

Note that the outer sideband filters have the passband frequencies inverted with respect to the inner sidebands. This method provides the least amount of interference between the four modes of operation when all are in use simultaneously. Four separate audio amplifiers, modulators, and filters are required in the transmitter, and four separate channels are also required in the receiver.

Another military standard (see Ref. 2) defines the selectivity characteristics for a four-channel radio as NMT -2 dB between 250 and 3100 Hz and not less than -40 dB at 50 and 3250 Hz. In addition, the attenuation shall not be less than 60 dB at 3550 Hz and higher frequencies and at $f_c -250$ Hz and lower frequencies. This is stated for USB but applies to the other filters also.

This selectivity is extremely difficult to meet because the transition band is defined at the 40-dB as well as the 60-dB attenuation points.

5.3 Filter Types

Selectivity is a basic requirement for SSB receivers and exciters. Many options appear to be available for the equipment designer when specifying selectivity at the various IF frequencies. For high-performance radios, the range quickly narrows for SSB filtering. The use of mechanical and crystal filters predominates for low IF frequencies up to 500 kHz. Digital signal processing (Chap. 7) will also produce selectivity in this range. However, this method involves complex digital techniques, which is a totally new approach to IF filtering. At the other higher IF frequencies, the crystal filter possesses a clear advantage because of its low insertion loss and high degree of selectivity. Bandpass *LC* filters have their use also, but are often restricted to low-pass and high-pass configurations. Ceramic filters have a low-cost advantage in some applications. SAW filter applications generally lie in the VHF/UHF range.

LC filters

The *LC* bandpass filter is seldom used as an IF filter in HF receivers and exciters. In order to achieve the narrow passband and sharp skirt selectivity required for SSB filtering, extremely high inductor Q's are necessary. Mechanical and crystal IF filters utilize Q's of 10,000 or more, which are not attainable with coils.

Nevertheless, single- or double-tuned circuits are often used to provide a high impedance for amplifier stages or to further attenuate some spurious. Small single-layer solenoids can provide coil Q's in the 50 to 100 range. The use of iron or ferrite cores can decrease the coil size and increase the Q's into the 100 to 300 range. Toroidal inductors will also exhibit such low losses.

For higher Q's (up to 1000), helical resonators can be used (see Ref. 3). Although optimal use for these resonators lies in the VHF and UHF ranges, practical use extends down into the HF region. The helical resonator is a single-layer solenoid or helix enclosed in a circular or square highly conductive shield.

The achievable Q for a given size using copper for the coil and shield is determined from the following equation:

$$Q = 60S(f_0)^{1/2} \tag{5.1}$$

where S = the length of the square side, in
f_0 = the resonant frequency, MHz

For example, a helical coil inside a 2-in copper shield at 25 MHz can be expected to have a Q of $(60)(2)(25)^{1/2}$, or 600. The length of the enclosure would be $(2)(1.6)$, or 3.2 in. The large-volume $(2)(2)(3.2)$ or 12.8 in^3 for a single inductor precludes its use inside a receiver or exciter.

Mechanical filters

The mechanical IF filter for radio equipment has been in use since the mid to late 1940s, although the concept was developed earlier. The mechanical filter achieves selectivity by converting the electrical signal to mechanical vibrations that are passed through a network of high-Q resonators and coupling elements and then are converted back to electrical signals. In the disc-wire type of mechanical filter, the disc resonators are coupled together with wires. The electrical analogy of this filter is composed of inductively coupled parallel-tuned circuits in a ladder configuation. Transducers used for the mechanical-electrical conversion are either the magnetostrictive-ferrite or the piezeoelectric-ceramic type. The result is a highly selective bandpass filter that is stable under a wide range of environmental conditions.

Mechanical filters provide excellent selectivity characteristics. Their high Q-resonators have values that are typically about 20,000. Figure 5.9a illustrates the selectivity characteristics of a representative SSB 455-kHz mechanical filter. Note that the carrier frequency is attenuated by 20 dB. Typically, 10 to 30 dB of carrier attenuation can be provided.

The design range of the disc-wire type of mechanical filter is shown in Fig. 5.10. The percent bandwidth of center frequency extends from 0.1 to about 10 percent over a frequency range of 60 to over 500 kHz. Low-frequency narrowband mechanical filters using flexure-mode resonators composed of iron-nickel alloy bars extend the range down to 3 kHz, with percent bandwidths ranging from 0.2 to 1.5 percent. However, for SSB operation, Fig. 5.10 is representative of filter designs extending from 250 to 500 kHz.

The disc-wire filter is designed to approximate a 0.1-dB Chebyshev passband characteristic. Because of termination variations, manufacturing processes, and other variables, a conservative 1-dB ripple specification is typically assigned, although variations can be held to 0.5 dB.

Shape factor is a function of the number of discs or resonators used. For example, a nine-disc-resonator 455-kHz filter has a 60- to 3-dB shape factor of 1.6 to 1. High-performance voice-bandwidth mechanical filters have been

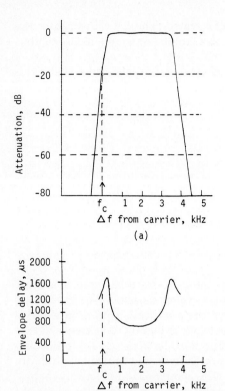

Figure 5.9 Mechanical filter characteristics. (*a*) Amplitude response; (*b*) time-delay response.

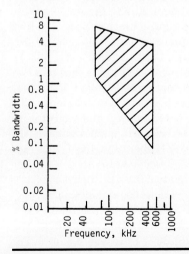

Figure 5.10 Percent bandwidth vs. frequency for disc-wire mechanical filters.

made with shape factors as low as 1.2 to 1. However, for SSB filters, the shape factor is often indirectly determined by other specification requirements and is usually not explicitly stated. The delay distortion, when specified, and the required 60-dB attenuation points can effectively determine the shape factor.

The envelope delay characteristic is specified as a differential delay between passband frequencies (see also Sec. 5.5). Figure 5.9 shows the amplitude and delay characteristics of a 2.7-kHz bandwidth filter that meets the requirements of a military standard specification (see Ref. 1). When the delay differential is specified out to the amplitude response edge, the manufacturer is forced to increase the passband limits. Note that in Fig. 5.9 the delay begins to increase rapidly near the 3-dB amplitude response points. Consequently, in this application the width of the passband amplitude response was increased to meet the delay requirement. This usually poses no problem since the passband amplitude response limits are stated as a minimum in most applications. For example, in Fig. 5.9, the upper amplitude response is stated as not less than 2 dB at 3050 Hz and the differential delay as 500 μs out to 3050 Hz. To meet this delay, the upper 2-dB response was increased to 3400 Hz. It was necessary to make the shape factor ratio smaller since the required 60-dB points remained the same. This can be done by increasing the number of resonators, varying the symmetry of the stopband response, or adding attenuation poles through use of wire bridging between nonadjacent resonators.

The intermodulation distortion of mechanical filters does not follow the third-order intercept rule. Why this is so is not clear. In his book *Mechanical Filters in Electronics* (see Ref. 4) Robert A. Johnson shows the results of a number of 450- to 455-kHz filter intermodulation distortion measurements. The in-band third-order intercept line plotted on log paper has a slope that averages 2.44 for filters with pizeoelectric-ceramic transducers and 1.93 for those with magnetostrictive-ferrite transducers. For out-of-band signals, the slope for those transducers averages 2.08 and 1.85, respectively. In Sec. 5.4, it is shown that the slope for well-behaved devices is 3.0 for the third order. Accurate prediction of the distortion performance from one filter to another is not possible since the variation of the individual filters measured varied from 3.1/1 to 1.7/1. From the data presented, the ceramic transducer filters, in general, have less distortion that the ferrite types.

Although the actual changes in distortion with varying signal levels may be difficult to predict, the distortion does decrease with decreasing signal level. Furthermore, specific distortion limits can be maintained by manufacturers, and the user can expect the distortion levels to be no more than the specified amount.

An example of the distortion occurring at various output levels is given in Table 5.1. The measurements were taken on a 455-kHz filter which has a 2.7-kHz 2-dB bandwidth and a 3-dB insertion loss. The load and source impedance levels are 2000 ohms in parallel with 30 pF.

Mechanical filters are remarkably free of spurious responses in the stopband, compared with crystal filters. This is because of the filters' ladder con-

TABLE 5.1   In-Band Third-Order Intermodulation Distortion
Measurements on a 455-kHz Mechanical Filter

Output signal level across 2000 ohms, V/tone	Third-order IM distortion below each tone, dB	
	Low side	High side
0.50	−55	−55
0.25	−60	−60
0.13	−71	−71
0.06	−79	−80

figuration employing input and output electrical tuned circuits and transducer resonators which reduce the effects of spurious modes of vibration of
the interior resonators. Consequently, the attenuation far-off-frequency can
be expected to remain about 70 to 90 dB down and becomes a function of
the circuit layout rather than the filter characteristic.

Mechanical filters have source and load terminations, each consisting of a
capacitor in parallel with a resistor. The values of these components depend
on the type of transducer used and the bandwidth of the filter. Older filter
designs used magnetostrictive-wire transducers that were self-terminating.
These filters still required an external tuning capacitor and a terminating
resistor of 100 K ohms or greater. They also exhibited high insertion losses.
For the newer ferrite and ceramic transducer types, the user must work
closely with the manufacturer in specifying the type of termination desired.
A wide variety of options are available, including unbalanced and balanced
circuits, input and output circuits capable of carrying low-level dc currents
(5 mA), circuits with dc blocking, etc. Once the impedance is determined,
the user's circuit must duplicate the values to prevent additional insertion
loss and, more important, increased passband ripple. The filters are most
sensitive to capacitance changes, and tolerances of ± 2 percent are usually
specified. Drive levels are dependent upon the intermodulation requirements. Although some SSB mechanical filters are capable of being driven up
to 10 Vrms without damage, the input voltage max level may be more like
1.0 Vrms. In low-level applications, the distortion of the amplifier stages may
become the deciding factor on the actual signal levels that can be used. In
receivers, large amounts of wideband amplification ahead of the filters invite
third-order intermodulation problems.

Insertion loss can vary from 2 to 15 dB and is dependent upon the number
of resonators, bandwidth, and transducer type. For example, the filter shown
in Fig. 5.9 has a 3-dB insertion loss.

Mechanical filters possess excellent temperature and aging characteristics.
Frequency shifts over temperature are parabolic and are about 5 ppm/°C.
At 455 kHz, this results in a center frequency shift of 116 Hz over a ±50°C
temperature range. Over a 20-year period, the filters are stable within 50
ppm. The center frequency shift would be less than 23 Hz for a 455-kHz
filter.

Crystal filters

The crystal filter has been used as an SSB filter by the Bell System since the 1930s (see Ref. 5). That type provided the band selection necessary for the SSB frequency division multiplex voice channels. Their use in radio equipment followed, as SSB equipment came into wide use.

Crystal filters attain selectivity by the use of quartz crystals that act like highly selective tuned circuits. The crystals have extremely high Q's which can range from 10,000 to over 100,000. They utilize the piezoelectric effect of crystalline quartz. Originally, natural or mined quartz was used, but in recent times, cultured quartz has been developed and is used exclusively. The material is cut and precision-ground into blanks. The dimensions and the angle of cut of the material determines the resonant frequency and mode of vibration. This type of filter is characterized by low insertion loss, sharp skirt selectivity, and a high degree of temperature stability. Whereas mechanical filters are limited to approximately 600 kHz as an upper limit, crystal filters range from a few kilohertz to over 250 MHz. Refer to Fig. 5.11. A new ion-etching technique (see Ref. 6) enables crystal filters to operate up to 500 MHz. Percent bandwidths can range from 0.01 to 10 percent of center frequency.

Crystal filters are either the discrete crystal type or the monolithic type. Filters which use discrete crystal blanks require additional inductors, transformers, and capacitors in lattice-type networks to achieve the bandpass characteristic. These are capable of operation from a few kilohertz to 100 MHz. The monolithic filter uses a quartz wafer as a substrate with deposited electrodes to form resonators. This type of construction eliminates the internal components necessary for the discrete type. This unique construction results in a smaller package, lower cost, and higher reliability. Monolithics have been designed to operate from 10 to over 100 MHz.

A single crystal behaves as a tuned circuit, as shown in Fig. 5.12. It has a

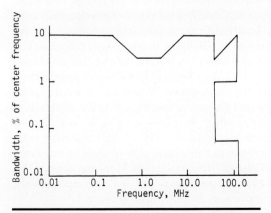

Figure 5.11 Crystal filter percent bandwidth vs. frequency.

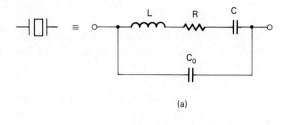

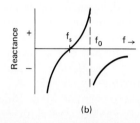

Figure 5.12 Properties of a quartz crystal. (*a*) Equivalent electrical circuit diagram; (*b*) frequency response of the crystal circuit. *L*, motional inductance; *C*, motional capacitance; *R*, energy loss resistance; C_0, capacitance of electrodes and holder.

series resonant frequency determined by *L* and *C* followed by a parallel resonance caused by the capacitance of the coupling plates or electrodes. Occasionally, a single crystal is used as a filter when a fixed frequency, such as a mixer injection, requires a small amount of additional spurious attenuation. Since it is a two-terminal device, it is easily adapted into a circuit.

The source and terminating impedances of crystal filters consist of a resistance and possibly a parallel capacitance. The values of the resistances vary over a wide range, from a few hundred ohms at 50 MHz and above to over 100,000 ohms at 10 KHz. In general, the higher the frequency, the lower the impedance level. The capacitive reactance is greater than the resistance and is specified to accommodate the stray capacitance in the circuit application. The exception is at the 50-ohm impedance level. When filters are designed for use above 30 MHz, it is advantageous to specify a 50-ohm source and load impedance. With such a termination, it becomes a simple task to measure insertion loss and amplitude characteristics in the lab since RF voltmeters and signal generators operate at this impedance level. The filter test fixture requires only input and output RF connectors. More important, circuit design is simplified since diode quad mixers and hybrid amplifiers are usually specified with 50-ohm input and output impedances.

Spurious responses in a crystal filter are usually a function of the number of poles. These occur above the bandpass frequency because of spurious response modes of the crystals. Figure 5.13 illustrates typical response curves for a 21-MHz IF filter in two-, four-, six-, and eight-pole configurations. The two-pole filter will have spurious responses at the −25- to −30-dB level a few hundred kilohertz above the passband. With the eight-pole configuration, the responses have been suppressed below the 70-dB level.

In some circuits, a two-pole filter will provide sufficient selectivity following, for example, a mixer stage. If the injection frequency and image frequency fall on the low side of the filter, the spurious region on the high side can thus be tolerated. If high-side injection is necessary, the injection can be placed outside the spurious area. Most often, frequency schemes are chosen based on other factors, and filters with the desired characteristics are then specified. By noting these filter response characteristics, some advance planning may allow the use of a simpler filter in particular applications.

The third-order intermodulation distortion in crystal filters does not follow the third-order intercept line. Consequently, the distortion products

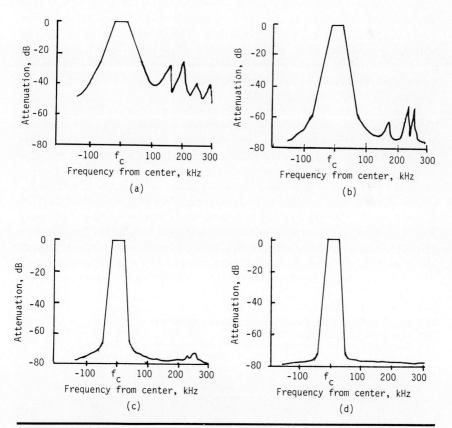

Figure 5.13 Typical response curves of 21-MHz monolithic crystal filters. (a) Two-pole; (b) four-pole; (c) six-pole; (d) eight-pole.

cannot be predicted at various signal levels based on one distortion measurement. Thus, the intercept equation (5.13) cannot be used with any validity, and the designer must resort to actual measurements at the signal levels over which the filter is expected to operate. Distortion in crystal filters can occur at low as well as high operating levels. At low drive levels, intermodulation can be due to high starting resistance caused by crystal surface contamination, scratches, plating defects, etc. The high-drive-level causes may include nonlinear resonance and parametric excitation of other modes. The low-level causes can be controlled in the manufacturing process. However, the high-level problems apparently are not well defined or completely understood at this time.

Nevertheless, crystal filters do provide consistent and predictable results at the design range levels. The examples of signal levels and resulting distortion product measurements on crystal filters given in Tables 5.2 and 5.3 can guide the designer toward reasonable operating levels.

Table 5.2 lists measured values taken on a 24-crystal, 450-kHz, high-performance filter which has a 1-dB passband of 250 to 3100 Hz and a 4-dB insertion loss. The filter source and load impedance is 2000 ohms in parallel with a 33-pF capacitor. The output level is in millivolts/tone across the load impedance. For this filter, the third- and higher-order distortion products are specified not to exceed -60 dB below each tone of a 50-mV/tone or less signal level, measured at the output terminals. The table indicates a distortion margin of approximately 7 dB.

Table 5.3 shows distortion levels measured on a 105-MHz IF crystal filter. This six-pole filter has a 0.5-dB bandwidth of 25 kHz and an insertion loss of 5 dB. The input and output impedances are 50 ohms and the levels are specified in dBm. The tones are 10 kHz apart, centered in the passband. The measurements show evidence of probable phase modulation cancellation as indicated by the level difference between the low- and high-side products.

Out-of-band intermodulation distortion may be considerably less than the in-band levels. For this type of test, both test frequencies are out-of-band and spaced so that the third order falls inside the passband. The reference signal level is the voltage across a 50-ohm load (maximum available power). Because the test signals are out-of-band, the selectivity of the crystal resonators tends to reduce the levels across them. Therefore, the distortion effects

TABLE 5.2   In-Band Third-Order Intermodulation Distortion Measurements on a 450-kHz Crystal Filter

Signal output level across 2000 ohms, mV/tone	Third-order intermodulation distortion below each tone, dB	
	Low side	High side
30	-68	-68
40	-68	-69
50	-67	-67
60	-68	-69
79	-68	-68

TABLE 5.3   In-Band Third-Order Intermodulation Distortion
Measurements on a Six-Pole 105–MHz Crystal Filter

Signal output level at 50 ohms, dBm/tone	Third-order intermodulation distortion below each tone, dB	
	Low side	High side
0 (0.22 V/tone)	−50 dB	−55 dB
−5 (0.12 V/tone)	−63	−60
−10 (0.07 V/tone)	−65	−63

are often decreased. For filters using ferrite impedance transformers, the ferrite material can become a source of distortion, especially at the higher levels.

SAW filters

The surface-acoustic-wave filter is an inherently simple and rugged device that provides a bandpass characteristic from electrodes deposited on a piezoelectric substrate. These electrodes form an interleaved (interdigital) pattern on the substrate and serve as transducers. When an RF signal is applied to one transducer, an electric field is generated, causing acoustic waves at the RF frequency to propagate along the surface to the opposite transducer. The waves generate an electric field which produces an output voltage. The bandpass characteristics are controlled by the choice of substrate material and the electrode interleaved pattern. The fabrication process requires the highly developed manufacturing techniques of the semiconductor industry. Because of the high initial design costs but low manufacturing costs, the filters are widely used in the high-volume consumer market such as TV sets where the unit cost can be reduced to a few dollars.

SAW filters can be designed to operate from about 10 to over 1000 MHz. Percent bandwidth can vary from a few percent to about 50 percent. The choice of substrate material affects the temperature coefficient, frequency range, and insertion loss. Widely used materials include quartz and lithium niobate. The insertion loss of SAW filters is high, generally ranging from 10 to 25 dB. However, new techniques have produced filters with losses as low as 2 and 3 dB.

The advantages of the SAW filter include practically constant time-delay characteristics across the passband (linear phase), a flat amplitude response, extremely good shape factor (1.2/1), and small size.

Disadvantages include the presently high insertion loss, difficulty in producing narrow-bandwidth filters (below 1 percent fractional bandwidth), and design cost. But even though their cost may be high in small volume, the SAW filters' special characteristics find application in radar systems and high-performance communication equipment, primarily in the VHF/UHF range.

5.4   Intermodulation Distortion

Intermodulation distortion is extremely important in radio systems that transmit and receive data. When nonlinearities exist in amplifiers, mixers, and filters, distortion products are generated. If a single tone is transmitted in-band, only harmonics are generated, which in the case of IF frequencies, are out-of-band and easily attenuated. If two or more tones are transmitted, in-band intermodulation distortion products are created about the transmitted tones (in addition to out-of-band products about the harmonics.) Since data transmission usually involves closely spaced audio tones, predicting distortion levels becomes a necessity in radio design.

In general, the nonlinearities in a transfer function of an amplifier can be expressed as a power series about a zero-signal operating point:

$$i = K_0 + K_1 e + K_2 e^2 + K_3 e^3 + K_4 e^4 + K_5 e^5 \tag{5.2}$$

The K_0 and $K_1 e$ represent the linear transfer. The terms with powers of 2 to 5 represent the nonlinearities that create the distortion products.

A two-frequency signal is represented by:

$$e(t) = A_1 \cos \omega_1 t + A_2 \cos \omega_2 t \tag{5.3}$$

where A_1 and A_2 = the amplitudes of the signals
$\omega_1 = 2\pi f_1$ and $\omega_2 = 2\pi f_2$
f_1 and f_2 = the signal frequencies

Substituting for e in Eq. (5.2) produces the following terms which are grouped in terms of distortion product orders:
The fundamentals components are:

$$(K_1 A_1 + \tfrac{3}{4}K_3 A_1^3 + \tfrac{3}{2}K_3 A_1 A_2^2 + \tfrac{5}{8}K_5 A_1^5 + \tfrac{15}{4}K_5 A_1^3 A_2^2 + \tfrac{15}{8}K_5 A_1 A_2^4) \cos \omega_1 t$$
$$(K_1 A_2 + \tfrac{3}{4}K_3 A_2^3 + \tfrac{3}{2}K_3 A_1^2 A_2 + \tfrac{5}{8}K_5 A_2^5 + \tfrac{15}{4}K_5 A_1^2 A_2^3 + \tfrac{15}{8}K_5 A_1^4 A_2) \cos \omega_2 t \tag{5.4}$$

The second-order components are:

$$(K_2 A_1 A_2 + \tfrac{3}{2}K_4 A_1^3 A_2 + \tfrac{3}{2}K_4 A_1 A_2^3) \cos (\omega_1 \pm \omega_2)t$$
$$(\tfrac{1}{2}K_2 A_1^2 + \tfrac{1}{2}K_4 A_1^4 + \tfrac{3}{2}K_4 A_1^2 A_2^2) \cos 2\,\omega_1 t \tag{5.5}$$
$$(\tfrac{1}{2}K_2 A_2^2 + \tfrac{1}{2}K_4 A_2^4 + \tfrac{3}{2}K_4 A_1^2 A_2^2) \cos 2\omega_2 t$$

The third-order components are:

$$(\tfrac{3}{4}K_3 A_1^2 A_2 + \tfrac{5}{4}K_5 A_1^4 A_2 + \tfrac{15}{8}K_5 A_1^2 A_2^3) \cos (2\omega_1 \pm \omega_2)t$$
$$(\tfrac{3}{4}K_3 A_1 A_2^2 + \tfrac{5}{4}K_5 A_1 A_2^4 + \tfrac{15}{8}K_5 A_1^3 A_2^2) \cos (\omega_1 \pm 2\omega_2)t$$
$$(\tfrac{1}{4}K_3 A_1^3 + \tfrac{5}{16}K_5 A_1^5 + \tfrac{5}{4}K_5 A_1^3 A_2^2) \cos 3\omega_1 t \tag{5.6}$$
$$(\tfrac{1}{4}K_3 A_2^3 + \tfrac{5}{16}K_5 A_2^5 + \tfrac{5}{4}K_5 A_1^2 A_2^3) \cos 3\omega_2 t$$

The fourth-order components are:

$$(\tfrac{1}{2}K_4 A_1^3 A_2) \cos (3\omega_1 \pm \omega_2)t$$
$$(\tfrac{3}{4}K_4 A_1^2 A_2^2) \cos (2\omega_1 + 2\omega_2)t$$

$(\tfrac{1}{2}K_4 A_1 A_2^3) \cos (\omega_1 \pm 3\omega_2)t$

$(\tfrac{1}{8}K_4 A_1^4) \cos 4\omega_1 t$ (5.7)

$(\tfrac{1}{8}K_4 A_2^4) \cos 4\omega_2 t$

The fifth-order components are:

$(\tfrac{5}{16}K_5 A_1^4 A_2) \cos (4\omega_1 \pm \omega_2)t$

$(\tfrac{5}{8}K_5 A_1^3 A_2^2) \cos (3\omega_1 \pm 2\omega_2)t$

$(\tfrac{5}{8}K_5 A_1^2 A_2^3) \cos (2\omega_1 \pm 3\omega_2)t$

$(\tfrac{5}{16}K_5 A_1 A_2^4) \cos (\omega_1 \pm 4\omega_2)t$ (5.8)

$(\tfrac{1}{16}K_5 A_1^5) \cos 5\omega_1 t$

$(\tfrac{1}{16}K_5 A_2^5) \cos 5\omega_2 t$

The fundamental components can be considered the first order; the second-order components contain the second harmonics $2f_1$ and $2f_2$ (dropping the 2π constant) and the sum and difference of the fundamentals $f_1 + f_2$ and $f_1 - f_2$. The third order contains the third harmonics of the signals, $3f_1$, $3f_2$, and the third-order products $2f_1 + f_2$, $2f_1 - f_2$, $f_1 + 2f_2$, and $f_1 - 2f_2$, each of which represents a single frequency. The same applies to the fourth and fifth orders.

A considerable amount of information can be obtained from this expansion. The primary concern, although not the only one, has to do with the in-band components. However, out-of-band components are of interest too, especially in broadband amplifier applications. Grouping the frequencies in increasing frequency order shows which components are in-band and which are out-of-band. To show the actual frequency positions of the various orders, numbers are assigned to the fundamental pair. Let $f_1 = 2.0$ MHz and $f_2 = 2.1$ MHz. Although separated by 100 kHz, let us assume that the frequencies are in-band. Table 5.4 shows the frequency positions.

A number of observations can be made from Table 5.4 for the parameters assumed for this example:

1. All the frequencies shown, except the fundamentals, are caused by the nonlinearity of the device (K_2, K_3, K_4, K_5 coefficients).

2. Only the odd orders (third, fifth) show up around the fundamental frequencies and only these are in-band. Although in this case the frequency separation was exaggerated to simplify the table, the frequency spacing would normally be from 100 Hz to 3 kHz.

3. The frequency difference Δf between all the distortion components in any harmonic region is the same and is equal to the Δf frequency spacing of the fundamental signals.

4. Note that the second-order product falls between the two second harmonic frequencies. The relative level of the second order and second harmonic can be calculated.

TABLE 5.4   Distortion Products Illustrating the Sequence of Orders and Harmonics

Region	MHz	Frequency components	Orders/harmonics
Audio and VLF region	0	dc	
	0.1	$f_2 - f_1$	Second order
	0.2	$2f_2 - 2f_1$	Fourth order
Fundamental region (in-band)	1.8	$3f_1 - 2f_2$	Fifth order
	1.9	$2f_1 - f_2$	Third order
	2.0	f_1	Fundamental
	2.1	f_2	Fundamental
	2.2	$2f_2 - f_1$	Third order
	2.3	$3f_2 - 2f_1$	Fifth order
Second harmonic region	3.9	$3f_1 - f_2$	Fourth order
	4.0	$2f_1$	Second harmonic
	4.1	$f_1 + f_2$	Second order
	4.2	$2f_2$	Second harmonic
	4.3	$3f_2 - f_1$	Fourth order
Third harmonic region	5.9	$4f_1 - f_2$	Fifth order
	6.0	$3f_1$	Third harmonic
	6.1	$2f_1 + f_2$	Third order
	6.2	$2f_2 + f_1$	Third order
	6.3	$3f_2$	Third harmonic
	6.4	$4f_2 - f_1$	Fifth order
Fourth harmonic region	8.0	$4f_1$	Fourth harmonic
	8.1	$3f_1 + f_2$	Fourth order
	8.2	$2f_1 + 2f_2$	Fourth order
	8.3	$f_1 + 3f_2$	Fourth order
	8.4	$4f_2$	Fourth harmonic
Fifth harmonic region	10.0	$5f_1$	Fifth harmonic
	10.1	$4f_1 + f_2$	Fifth order
	10.2	$3f_1 + 2f_2$	Fifth order
	10.3	$2f_1 + 3f_2$	Fifth order
	10.4	$f_1 + 4f_2$	Fifth order
	10.5	$5f_2$	Fifth harmonic

5. Note also that the two third-order products fall between the two third harmonics. The relative levels of the third-order products and the third harmonics can be calculated.

6. The orders fall between the harmonics in the fourth and fifth harmonic regions.

7. Knowing the sequence of the distortion products can be very helpful when attempting to identify the products on a spectrum analyzer.

The preceding analysis is based on a simple analytical model where only amplitude modulation distortion occurs, and only one stage is involved. If the signal undergoes a small phase shift in addition to the amplitude change, then phase modulation distortion will occur also. In AM distortion, all the distortion products have a positive sign. In low-level phase modulation, the same odd-order components can be generated but have a negative sign (180° out-of-phase) for the lower-sideband products and positive (in-phase) for the upper-sideband ones. Consequently, the resulting sidebands will be unequal, with the lower-sideband amplitudes smaller and the upper-sideband amplitudes greater. Generally, in low-level class A stages this effect is minor.

The same effect can result as the signal passes through tuned circuits, filters, and additional stages. Phase shifting of the distortion products will create unequal product amplitudes.

Product levels

The relative amplitude levels between the second harmonic and the second order can be determined from Eq. (5.5). The equation for the second-order frequency is:

$$(K_2 A_1 A_2 + \tfrac{3}{2}K_4 A_1^3 A_2 + \tfrac{3}{2}K_4 A_1 A_2^3) \cos (\omega_1 \pm \omega_2)t$$

and for the second harmonic:

$$(\tfrac{1}{2}K_2 A_1^2 + \tfrac{1}{2}K_4 A_1^4 + \tfrac{3}{2}K_4 A_1^2 A_2^2) \cos 2\omega t$$

Assume that the amplitude of the two signals [Eq. (5.3)] are $A_1 = A_2 = 1$. The ratio of the amplitude coefficients of the second order and the second harmonic, after combining the K_4 terms, becomes:

$$\frac{\text{Second-order amplitude}}{\text{Second harmonic amplitude}} = \frac{K_2 + 3K_4}{\tfrac{1}{2}K_2 + 2K_4} \tag{5.9}$$

If the K_2 is much greater than the K_4, i.e., second order predominates over the fourth, then the ratio reduces to:

$$\frac{\text{Second-order amplitude}}{\text{Second harmonic amplitude}} = \frac{K_2}{\tfrac{1}{2}K_2} = 2 \tag{5.10}$$

Thus it is seen that the second-order amplitude is twice the amplitude of the second harmonic (6 dB greater).

The relative amplitude levels of the third-order and third harmonic components can also be determined in the same manner using Eqs. (5.6). As before, let $A_1 = A_2 = 1$, and combining the K_5 terms together, the ratio becomes:

$$\frac{\text{Third-order amplitude}}{\text{Third harmonic amplitude}} = \frac{\tfrac{3}{4}K_3 + \tfrac{25}{8}K_5}{\tfrac{1}{4}K_3 + \tfrac{25}{16}K_5} \tag{5.11}$$

If the K_3 term is much greater than K_5, then the ratio reduces to:

$$\frac{\text{Third-order amplitude}}{\text{Third harmonic amplitude}} = \frac{\tfrac{3}{4}K_3}{\tfrac{1}{4}K_3} = 3 \tag{5.12}$$

In this case, the third-order component is 3 times the amplitude of the third harmonic (9.5 dB greater).

These relative levels are shown graphically in Fig. 5.14. Note that the in-band third order and out-of-band third order have the same magnitude. This is evident from Eq. (5.6), where the third-order frequencies $2\omega_1 \pm \omega_2$ and $\omega_1 \pm 2\omega_2$, which represent the in-band and out-of-band third orders, have the same amplitude coefficients.

The levels of the second- and third-order products with respect to the fundamental frequency levels can be calculated by using the intercept point equation. It should be noted that this analysis represents an ideal condition and does not take into account possible phasing alterations which would change these relationships.

Intercept point

The intercept point method is used for predicting third-order intermodulation product levels for nearly linear circuits such as class A amplifiers, mixers, etc. The third-order output intercept is the point where the two-tone output signal level crosses over the third-order distortion that is created. This is a theoretical point and lies above the device's compression point (where the level begins to depart from linearity and starts to limit). This is described in Chap. 3. Because the third-order products are created by the power-of-3 coefficients, a 10-dB change in the two-tone signal output will cause a 30-dB change in the third-order distortion. However, referenced to the desired output level, the change in distortion is only 20 dB. When a device has distortion products that follow the intercept line, it is considered "well behaved."

The graph shown in Fig. 5.15 illustrates the intercept concept (see Ref. 7).

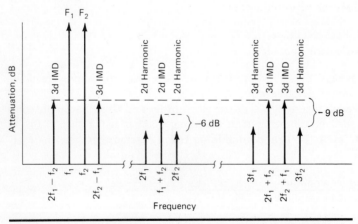

Figure 5.14 Frequency spectrum of a two-tone signal showing the relative levels between second order and second harmonic, and third order and third harmonic.

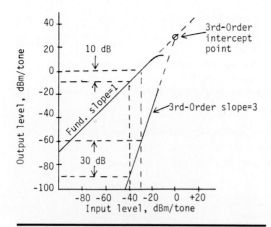

Figure 5.15 Third-order intercept line. A 10-dB change in output (or input) produces a 30-dB change in third-order distortion.

Another useful tool is the equation for the third-order intercept which can be derived from Fig. 5.15:

$$\text{OPI}^3\text{P} = P_0 + \frac{\text{IMD}}{2} \tag{5.13}$$

where OPI^{3}P = third-order output intercept, dBm
  P_0 = output level/tone, dBm/tone
  IMD = third-order intermodulation distortion ratio below each output tone, dB

Rearranging the equation for IMD, which is the quantity usually desired, produces:

$$\text{Third IMD} = 2(\text{OPI}^3\text{P} - P_0) \tag{5.14}$$

For example, if an amplifier has an OPI^{3}P of 30 dBm and is driven to produce an output level of -5 dBm/tone, the third-order intermodulation distortion is $2[30 - (-5)]$ or 70 dB below either -5-dBm tone.

The intercept point can be referenced to the input signal instead of the output. Circuits which have losses, such as mixers, have input intercept points (IPI^{3}P) specified. The IMD calculated from the input signal level will be the IMD at the output. The output level will be the input level reduced by losses of the circuit.

The second-order intercept point is sometimes specified for mixers and amplifiers. It becomes useful in calculating the second-order out-of-band signal for broadband circuits which have no selectivity. The equation for the second-order intercept point is:

$$\text{OPI}^2\text{P} = P_0 + \text{IMD} \tag{5.15}$$

or

$$IMD = OPI^2P - P_0 \qquad (5.16)$$

where OPI^2P = second-order output intercept point dBm
$\quad P_0$ = output level/tone, dBm/tone
$\quad IMD$ = second-order intermodulation distortion below each output tone, dB

Since the second order is created by the second-power coefficients, a 10-dB change in signal level will cause a 20-dB change in the second-order distortion. Referenced to the output level, the distortion increase is only 10 dB, as shown by the equation.

5.5   Envelope Delay Distortion

Distortion through time delay

The SSB signal can be distorted by a varying time delay across the passband as well as by a changing amplitude characteristic. When a signal passes

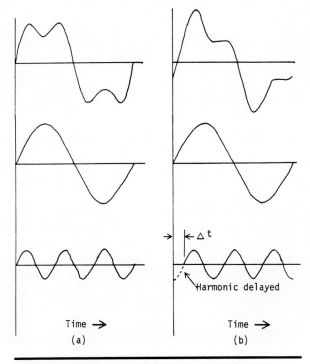

Figure 5.16 Effect of signal delay on composite waveform. (a) Fundamental and third harmonic in phase; (b) harmonic delayed by amount Δt. Top curve in each: resultant waveform; middle: fundamental; bottom, third harmonic.

through a filter, a time delay occurs because of the phase shift caused by the circuit reactances. If this delay is not constant with frequency, amplitude distortion of the signal will result. This is made obvious by examining a plot of two frequency components as shown in Fig. 5.16. In Fig. 5.16a, both the fundamental and the third harmonic start at time zero, resulting in the composite signal shown. If both signals are delayed an equal amount of time, this relationship will not change. If the third harmonic is delayed an amount Δt with respect to the fundamental, as shown in Fig. 5.16b, the composite signal is distorted with respect to the original waveform. Consequently, in order to maintain envelope integrity, the delay for all modulated signal frequencies must be the same.

The envelope delay can be expressed as an equation relating phase shift to frequency. Mathematically, the delay is equal to $-d\phi/d\omega$ where ϕ is in radians and ω is in radians/second. For incremental differences, the following equation applies and the minus sign is omitted:

$$T = \frac{\Delta\phi}{360\Delta f} \tag{5.17}$$

where $\Delta\phi$ = change in phase, deg
$\quad\quad \Delta f$ = change in passband frequency, Hz
$\quad\quad T$ = envelope delay, s

In order to obtain a constant envelope delay T, the phase shift must be directly proportional to the frequency change. Any deviation from linearity will cause a change in the time delay or delay distortion. Figure 5.17 helps to illustrate the equation. The steeper the phase-shift slope, the greater the total delay.

The term "group delay" is sometimes used in place of "envelope delay." Group delay is a telephone circuit term that applies to the delay of groups of audio frequencies. In RF circuit applications the terms "envelope delay" and "group delay" are used interchangeably.

Envelope delay distortion is usually specified as a differential time delay

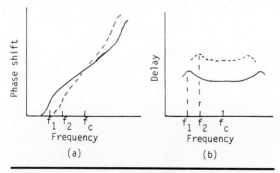

Figure 5.17 Phase-delay characteristics. (a) Phase-shift vs. frequency response, (b) steeper phase curve produces a greater delay.

between tones in the passband. In multitone data transmissions, a certain amount of delay distortion is tolerated. For example, a 16-tone digital data transmission system in common use allows a 500-μs differential delay between passband tones of 815 and 3050 Hz for the receiver and also for the transmitter.

Figure 5.18 illustrates a typical delay characteristic of a USB filter. The differential delay is the difference between the minimum point of the delay and the delay at some specified passband frequencies. In the graph, this is shown as a differential delay boundary. The actual delay curve is shown to be less than the specified amount. If the delay curve is unsymmetrical, the worst-case frequency is used to determine the Δ.

The total delay for a receiver or exciter is specified as a maximum within the passband frequencies. In Fig. 5.18, the total delay can be determined for any frequency since the y ordinate is scaled as total delay. The other filters in the signal path cannot be neglected since they also contribute delay. However, in SSB equipment the greatest delay, both differential and total, occurs in the low-frequency SSB filters. The other IF filters in the signal path can be considered to contribute about 10 percent of the overall amount. Consequently, the delay of the other filters must be subtracted from the delay characteristics that are specified for the SSB filter.

Total delay is obtained from Eq. (5.17) provided the measurement is made between the audio input and the RF of an exciter or the RF input and the audio output of a receiver.

Another specification that occasionally must be taken into consideration is the delay slope distortion. When specified, it is stated as a (Δ delay)/ (Δ freq.) ratio that must be met between the differential delay frequencies. In Fig. 5.18, the delay distortion could be specified not to exceed 150 μs for any 100-Hz frequency increment between 600 and 3000 Hz. The intent of this requirement, probably, is to control the delay ripple. For most filters the in-band delay ripple is minor, but the problem is created at the passband edges. Here the delay can have a sharp slope which exceeds the slope spec-

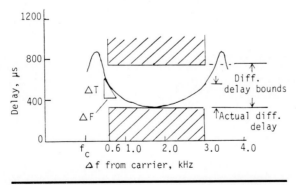

Figure 5.18 Typical delay characteristics of a USB filter with differential delay specified across the passband frequencies.

ification but still meets the differential delay. The problem can be resolved two different ways. One choice for the designer is to widen the passband and thereby lower the slope. This approach forces a decrease in the shape factor ratio since the 60-dB attenuation bandwidth is probably specified. The result is an increase in filter complexity and cost. The alternative is to equalize the delay to produce a relatively flat delay response over the passband frequencies. This approach requires additional circuitry either at the IF or the audio frequencies, but is often used.

Delay equalization

The total delay through a receiver or exciter is the sum of the individual delays, most of which occur in the bandpass filters. This additive characteristic of the delay makes it possible to compensate any undesirable variation by adding a delay with an opposite slope characteristic as shown in Fig. 5.19. Equalizing the delay increases the total delay through the equipment. The total delay is not a critical element and in most systems can be tolerated. Some difficulties may be encountered in receiver AGC loops which contain filters with large amounts of time delay. Loop instability can occur and must be corrected.

A very convenient method of equalization utilizes the all-pass filter as a delay equalizer. This type of filter provides a flat amplitude-frequency response and a prescribed phase-shift-frequency or delay characteristic. This is precisely the characteristic that is needed for compensation.

The all-pass filter delay equalizer can be a first- or a second-order design. The first-order equalizer has a delay that is maximum at dc and consequently has limited usage. It can be used to compensate a low-pass filter, for example. The second-order equalizer has a delay that can be positioned anywhere in the passband. In addition, the amplitude response can be made constant and independent of the delay chosen. The characteristics of a first- and second-order equalizer are shown in Fig. 5.20. The width of the delay curve in Fig. 5.20*b* is a function of the peak delay time. The greater the delay,

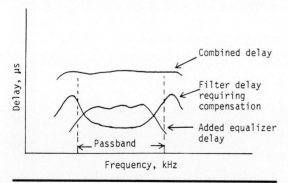

Figure 5.19 Delay equalization of a bandpass filter.

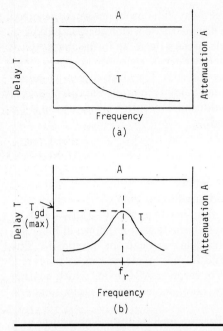

Figure 5.20 Delay and amplitude characteristics. (*a*) First-order all-pass equalizer; (*b*) second-order all-pass equalizer.

the narrower the delay response becomes. The delay curve can be considered to possess a Q factor similar to tuned circuits.

The second-order all-pass transfer function in the complex frequency plane S is given by (see Ref. 8):

$$T(S) = \frac{S^2 - \omega_r S/Q + \omega_r^2}{S^2 + \omega_r S/Q + \omega_r^2} \tag{5.18}$$

where ω_r is the pole resonant frequency in radians per second, and Q is the pole Q.

From this equation, the group delay is derived as:

$$T_{gd} = \frac{2Q\omega_r(\omega^2 + \omega_r^2)}{Q^2(\omega^2 - \omega_r^2) + \omega^2\omega_r^2} \tag{5.19}$$

By letting $\omega = \omega_r$ in Eq. (5.19), the delay at ω_r becomes:

$$T_{gd,max} = \frac{4Q}{\omega_r} = \frac{2Q}{\pi f_r} \tag{5.20}$$

$T_{gd,max}$ is in seconds, f_r in hertz, and Q is a dimensionless number. When the Q is greater than 2, the peak delay occurs at ω_r (or f_r) for all practical purposes. For Q's less than 2, the peak value will be slightly lower in frequency. Most of the Q's will range from about 1 to 20.

The two variables, T_{gd} and f_r, are known quantities. For example, a certain amount of delay is described at a specific frequency. Using Eq. (5.20), a value for Q is calculated. Then this value of Q is used in Eq. (5.19) to determine the delay of other values of f (converted to ω by multiplying the frequency by 2π) in the passband. Thus, one delay response is obtained with its peak at f_r.

More than one delay equalizer section is often required. The number of equalizer sections required to compensate a particular delay curve can be roughly approximated from (see Ref. 8):

$$N = 2 \, (\Delta BW) \, (\Delta T) + 1 \tag{5.21}$$

where ΔBW = the bandwidth of interest, Hz
ΔT = the delay distortion over ΔBW, s

For example, to compensate a delay distortion of 500 μs in a 2700-Hz bandwidth may take $(2)(2.7 \times 10^3)(0.5 \times 10^{-3}) + 1$ or 4 equalizer sections.

Equalizing a delay curvature is a tedious task. The delay to be compensated is first plotted as a function of the passband frequency. Then, starting at the point of minimum delay, the additional Δ delay required to make this point equal to the delay at the delay specification edges is determined from the graph. The frequency at this point is also noted. Then these two values are used in Eq. (5.20) to calculate Q. This Q value is used in Eq. (5.19) to determine the delay at other frequencies in the passband. These values are then plotted on the graph, and a composite curve is drawn by adding the new delay to the original. At one of the resulting curve dips, another estimate is made as to the amount of delay necessary to bring its level up with the delay just calculated. The frequency of this new delay point is noted and the computation process is repeated. This process continues until a satisfactory composite delay curve is obtained. Figure 5.21 illustrates the equalizer delay

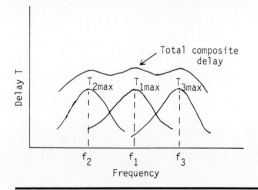

Figure 5.21 Equalizer delay curvature obtained from three equalizer sections.

curvature based on three equalizer sections. An iterative process will be necessary varying f_r and Q of each section to create a better fit.

The preceding method can be simplified by normalizing the delay and the frequency. Tables of normalized values for various Q's can then be established to speed the graphics. Programmable calculations can also be utilized to solve Eq. (5.19) for the desired frequencies and Q's.

Once the resonant frequencies (f_r) and the corresponding max delays (T_{gd}) are determined, the equalizer sections must then be designed and added to the radio equipment. The equalization can be accomplished either with passive or active filters. For passive circuits, a bridged T network functions as a delay equalizer. This type of circuit, shown in Fig. 5.22, exhibits a second-order delay response. Its all-pass characteristic is a function of inductor Q and may require additional amplitude correction. When a number of such sections are necessary, it can be difficult to implement because of interaction between sections and the need for trimming adjustments.

The use of active RC filters at audio makes the design approach much simpler. In this type of circuit the delay is determined by a choice of resistors and capacitors. The flat amplitude response is independent of the delay. One version of the second-order active filter is shown in Fig. 5.23 (see Ref. 8). The values of R and C are arbitrarily chosen, and A corresponds to the gain. The maximum delay ($Q > 2$) is related to the components by (see Ref. 8):

$$R_2 = \frac{T_{gd,max}}{2C} \tag{5.22}$$

and the resonant frequency f_r corresponding to the maximum delay by:

$$R_{1b} = \frac{R_2}{(\pi f_r T_{gd,max})^2 - 2} \tag{5.23}$$

and

$$R_{1a} = \frac{R_2}{2}$$

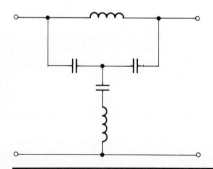

Figure 5.22 Bridged T network which has second-order delay characteristics.

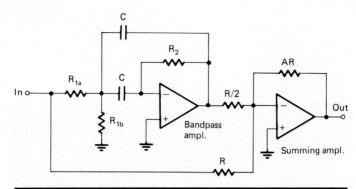

Figure 5.23 Active all-pass delay equalizer section ($0.7 < Q < 20$).

Other active RC all-pass circuits can also be used. The circuit shown in Fig. 5.23 illustrates the relative simplicity of designing an active equalizer.

In order to compensate for passband delay, a number of such sections must be used in cascade. Each section is designed for one $T_{gd,max}$ and its corresponding f_r. The overall gain can be made unity by adjusting each section for a gain of 1. The equalizing sections can then be added to the receiver or exciter audio amplifier stages at some convenient location.

For the designer who wants to bypass the trial-and-error method of equalizing delay, it should be noted that commercial equalizers are available. Some manufacturers of mechanical and crystal filters also design delay equalizers at audio and at the IF frequencies to the user's specifications. Computer programs for delay equalization are also available (see Ref. 9).

Acknowledgment. The author wishes to acknowledge the valuable suggestions of Robert A. Johnson, Rockwell International, who kindly reviewed the sections of the chapter on filter types and delay.

REFERENCES

1. *Subsystem Design and Engineering Standards for Tactical Digital Information Link (TADIL-A)*, U.S. Military Standard MIL-STD-188-203-1, Naval Publications and Forms Center, Philadelphia, Sept. 10, 1982.
2. *Standards for Long Haul Communications*, U.S. Military Standard MIL-STD-188-317, Naval Publications and Forms Center, Philadelphia, Mar. 30, 1972.
3. A. I. Zverev, *Handbook of Filter Synthesis*, John Wiley & Sons, New York, 1967.
4. Robert A. Johnson, *Mechanical Filters in Electronics*, John Wiley & Sons, New York, 1983.
5. T. H. Simmons, Jr., "The Evaluation of the Discrete Crystal Single-Sideband Selection Filter in the Bell System," *Proc. IEEE*, vol. 67, January 1979, pp. 109–115.
6. B. d'Albaret and P. Siffert, "Recent Advances in UHF Crystal Filters," *36th Annual Frequency Control Symposium*, Argenteuil, France, 1982. (Available from Defense Technical Information Center, Alexandria, VA, Doc. AD/A-130,811.)
7. Franz C. McVay, "Don't Guess the Spurious Level," *Electron. Des. 3*, vol. 15, Feb. 1, 1967, pp. 70–73.
8. Arthur B. Williams, *Electronics Filter Design Handbook*, McGraw-Hill, New York, 1981.
9. *Super Filsyn Version 4.5*, DGS Assoc. Santa Clara, CA, 1980. (Availabe from DGS Associates, 1353 Sartia Way, Santa Clara, CA., 95051.)

6

Speech Processing, Squelch, and Noise Blanking

William E. Sabin

6.1 Speech Processing

The human voice does not utilize the SSB power amplifiers very well. The 15-dB peak-to-average ratio, or 24-dB dynamic range, means that a high-power amplifier which handles the peaks well is just "loafing" most of the time. Unless the amplifier and power supply are marginal, much greater power can be transmitted if the deficiencies of speech can be improved. The usual case is that amplifiers which will handle the peaks well are capable of higher average levels than natural speech provides. The central idea is that the weaker components which we will emphasize in this section contribute much to the intelligibility.

Audio processing

The two methods of audio processing are clipping and compression. In the clipper the audio signal, after 10 to 20 dB of additional amplification, is simply sliced off at the required level. It is "memoryless" in that the action at any one time does not affect subsequent actions. The strong syllabic peaks, which occur from 5 to 10 times per second, are thus instantly reduced. The weaker parts which lie between the peaks are clipped much less and are therefore relatively stronger. The resulting truncated wave is then high/low-pass-filtered to remove low/high-frequency distortion products, and then converted to SSB. The clipper generates significant amounts of audible harmonic and intermodulation distortion, but emphasizes weaker speech elements effectively. Many of these are high-frequency components which are important. The distortion reduces the effectiveness appreciably since it degrades the improvement in intelligibility.

In a compressor the peaks are limited by gain reduction, and the behavior after a peak differs from the clipper. The amplifier gain does not restore immediately but is allowed to recover more slowly in a controlled exponential manner. It has memory. On subsequent peaks the amount of gain reduction required may therefore be much less. The result is that the compressed signal has less distortion but tends to reduce the weaker elements which lie between peaks, especially those which immediately follow the peaks, and therefore tends to be less effective. Some of this reduction in effectiveness is ameliorated by the lower distortion. Compressors are widely used to maintain a constant output level despite variations in voice level. Figure 6.1 illustrates the differences in the two methods.

There are alternative ways of performing audio processing of the memoryless variety which reduce the distortion by eliminating harmonic distortion. This reduction in distortion increases the effectiveness. These methods will be treated in detail after other subjects have been introduced.

Speech clipping

To put the subject of speech clipping into perspective, we discuss the most important basic factors which influence the design and use of such circuitry. The actual circuit designs will be covered in later sections. Of particular interest here is the speech waveform and its relationship to the SSB signal. This relationship changes in some rather peculiar ways as a result of the speech processing operations. It is necessary to understand these changes so that the SSB system can be designed to function properly with the speech processing operational. The central idea is that the transmitter must be kept linear while processing is going on, to prevent splatter, and must be as free as possible of excessive background noise and intelligibility degradation due to distortion. But we find, in a PEP-limited system, that certain SSB waveform effects can reduce the effectiveness of the speech processing because they introduce envelope peaks which partially restore the original peak-to-average ratio.

The equation of an upper sideband signal is given as

$$f(t) = g(t) \cos \omega_c t - h(t) \sin \omega_c t \tag{6.1}$$

where $g(t)$ is the audio input waveform, $h(t)$ is the Hilbert transform of the audio waveform, and ω_c is the RF signal frequency in radians/second. (Chapter 2 discusses this signal in much more detail.)

To find the envelope of this SSB wave, we draw a line through the peak values of Eq. (6.1) as discussed in Fig. 1.2. This envelope is given by

$$f(t) \text{ (env)} = \sqrt{\frac{g(t)^2 + h(t)^2}{2}} \tag{6.2}$$

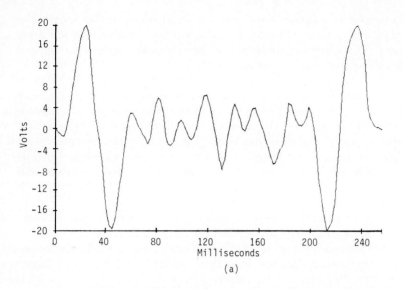

(a)

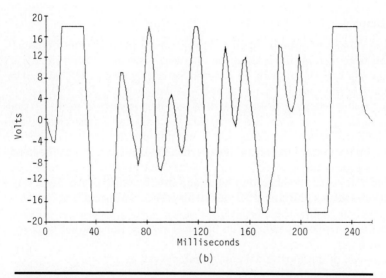

(b)

Figure 6.1 Computer-generated graphs showing (*a*) a 0.5-s sample of speech which has been subjected to (*b*) 10 dB of clipping (unprocessed) and (*c*) 10 dB of compression (100-ms decay time constant). The compression of weaker components after the peaks is visible.

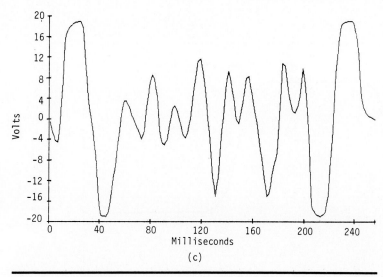

Figure 6.1 *(Continued)*

Of particular interest at this point is the shape of the $h(t)$ wave. It is derived from $g(t)$ in the following manner:

1. Find all the spectral components of $g(t)$. In terms of complex exponentials there are elements at positive frequencies and similar elements at negative values of frequency, as shown here:

$$A \cos \omega t = \frac{A}{2} e^{j\omega t} + \frac{A}{2} e^{-j\omega t} \qquad (6.3)$$

2. Change the phase angle of all positive-frequency components by $-90°$.

3. Change the phase angle of all negative-frequency components by $+90°$.

4. Convert this modified spectrum back to the time domain to get $h(t)$.

In terms of analog circuit design, we operate on the analog audio signal and apply a 90° phase lag. Circuitry to do this is discussed in Chap. 4. Digital implementations are discussed in Chap. 7.

The operation described above produces waveform distortion which can result in detrimental peaking of the envelope. To see how this happens, consider Fig. 6.2, which shows a computer-generated plot of a 300-Hz square wave input signal which has been subjected to various degrees of low-pass filtering and then subjected to the Hilbert Transform operation. The SSB envelope is then generated using Eq. (6.2). The bandpass filter in the SSB exciter would eliminate harmonics above the ninth (2700 Hz). As the waveform $g(t)$ is made less square, the peakiness of $h(t)$ and therefore of the SSB signal is reduced, as shown in the illustration. As the peaking is reduced, the

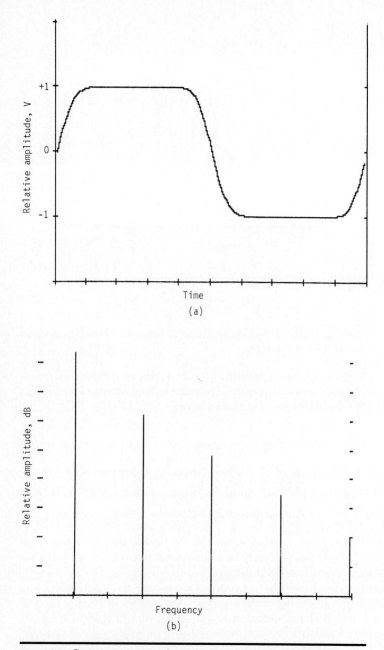

Figure 6.2 Computer-generated graphs showing (*a*) a 300-Hz low-pass-filtered (linear phase) square wave, (*b*) its spectrum up to 2700 Hz, (*c*) its Hilbert transform, and (*d*) the SSB envelope (positive half only). In (*e*) through (*h*), similar results for (*a*) through (*d*), respectively, after additional filtering, are shown. The reduction in peaks of the SSB wave are visible in (*h*).

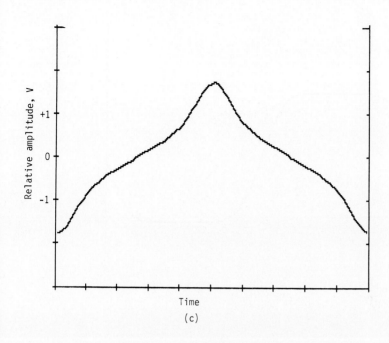

Time

(c)

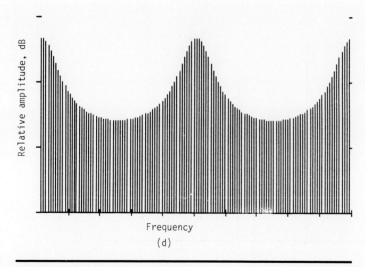

Frequency

(d)

Figure 6.2 (*Continued*)

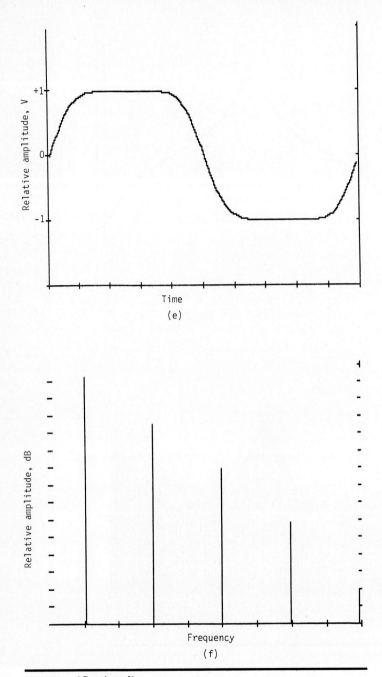

Time

(e)

Frequency

(f)

Figure 6.2 (*Continued*)

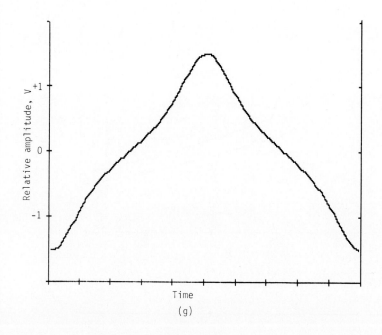

(g)

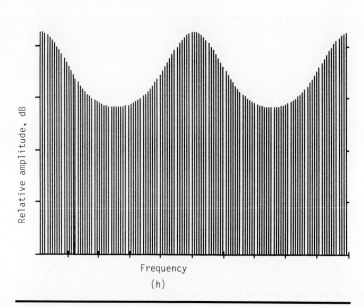

(h)

Figure 6.2 (*Continued*)

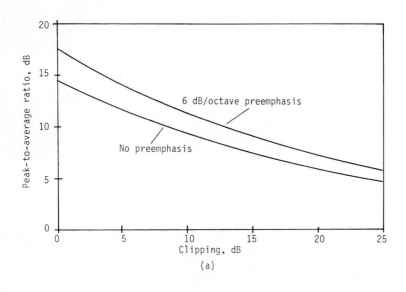

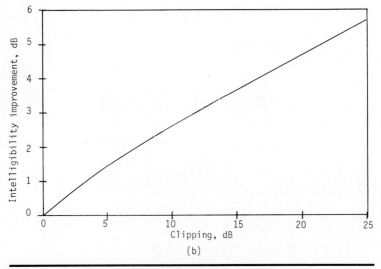

Figure 6.3 Computer-generated graphs showing performance of an audio clipper. (*a*) The peak-to-average ratio of the audio signal; (*b*) the improvement in intelligibility in white noise.

tendency to overdrive the linear amplifiers is reduced and the average power in a peak-limited system is at the same time increased.

The importance of this discussion, in the present context, is that audio speech clipping can produce the results just described. The speech signal contains strong components at the lower audio frequencies, and clipping of this signal can produce approximately the kind of square wave signal described above. Speech compression, on the other hand, produces a more "rounded" signal which is less prone to this effect.

The long-term spectrum of speech shows that above 500 Hz there is a roll-off of high-frequency power spectral density of about 6 dB/octave. Preemphasis of these frequencies at 3 dB/octave has been shown (Ref. 1) to improve intelligibility. Also, as mentioned previously, speech has a peak-to-average ratio of about 15 dB. It happens that preemphasis increases the peak-to-average ratio somewhat, partially offsetting the advantage of preemphasis (see Fig. 6.3a). However, it has been found experimentally (Ref. 1) that preemphasis, followed by speech clipping, leads to an overall improvement, especially if deemphasis is used at the receiver. Clipping tends to suppress the higher-frequency formants (harmonics of certain speech sounds) which are needed; preemphasis helps to restore them.

After the speech clipper, a low-pass/high-pass filter attenuates distortion products at low and high frequencies. This filter may introduce nonlinear phase shift of the speech spectrum and therefore some waveform distortion in the audio signal. But a consideration of the trigonometry involved in Eq. (6.1) shows that no additional distortion of the SSB wave is produced by these filter phase shifts. This assumes, of course, that audio stages and modulators are not overdriven by the possibly peaky audio waveform. Also, if the filters exhibit overshoots to a fast-changing signal, that could add additional peaks to the waveform.

However, it is possible that the processed audio wave will produce envelope peaking of the SSB wave because of its squareness, as previously described. Therefore we filter the audio signal at low and high frequencies to no more than the necessary bandwidth to minimize this degrading effect.

An additional point is that a squared-off low-frequency audio signal, upon being filtered, is subject to a "repeaking" effect. That is, if a square wave has amplitude equal to 1.00, the fundamental component out of the filter has amplitude 1.27, or $4/\pi$ (2.1 dB). This effect has an important influence on gain settings for the entire transmitter because the voice dynamics are quite

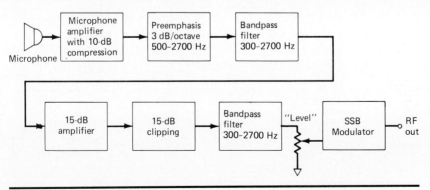

Figure 6.4 Block diagram of an audio speech processing system employing compression and clipping. Careful filter design reduces distortion products and SSB envelope peaking.

different from the steady tone used to make transmitter adjustments. As a result, serious overloading of linear amplifiers can result. Transmitter design can easily guard against this effect, and others previously described, using a concept mentioned in earlier chapters, automatic level control, (ALC) to be discussed later. Still, the repeaking effect increases the peak-to-average ratio, and this degrades the speech processing effectiveness.

The curves of Fig. 6.3 show the peak-to-average ratio of the audio signal (not the SSB envelope) and the intelligibility improvement of the SSB signal. These results are quite useful and inexpensive to achieve using simple circuitry. The distortion and the SSB envelope peaking are the main drawbacks. These can be greatly reduced at a somewhat higher cost, as will be described later. The block diagram of the processor is shown in Fig. 6.4.

Speech compression

The discussion of audio clipping was used to introduce some of the basic considerations of speech processing. This section on audio compression will build on that base and show how the two methods differ. As mentioned before, audio compressors are used mostly to provide an output which is invariant from one talker or microphone distance to another. However, they can also be used to improve somewhat the intelligibility of speech. Figure 6.1 showed the difference in the way the signal is modified by the two methods. We now consider the operation of the compressor.

Figure 6.5 shows a block diagram of a speech compressor. The compression is usually accomplished by a variable-gain integrated circuit amplifier such

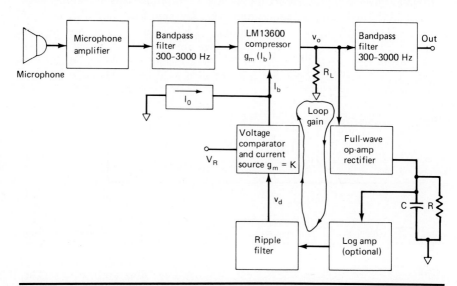

Figure 6.5 Block diagram of a speech compressor. A control current i_b reduces amplifier gain. Full-wave rectification catches both positive and negative excursions. The loop gain path is indicated.

as the National LM13600, used here as an example. The output voltage is full-wave-rectified (so that both positive and negative excursions of speech will be detected) using op-amp detector circuits, and if v_d is greater than a reference voltage V_r, then current i_b, which controls transconductance g_m, decreases and the gain is reduced in the manner shown in Fig. 6.6a. This action occurs while the magnitude of the input signal continues to increase. But when the input level starts to decrease, the diodes go out of conduction because of the voltage v_d stored on the capacitor C. The gain control loop is then in an open state, and voltage v_d falls exponentially with time constant RC until such time that the diodes start to conduct again. During this fall time the amplifier gain increases, and if v_d becomes less than V_r, the maximum gain is restored. Thus there are two situations to consider, the closed-loop state and the open-loop state.

For the closed-loop case the output signal is found from the following equation:

$$v_o = v_i g_m(i_b) R_L \tag{6.4}$$

where $g_m(i_b)$ is a function of a bias current i_b as shown in Fig. 6.6a. Note the log-log relationship. Using the points marked on the graph, the equation for the straight line is given by

$$\log g_m = \left[\frac{d - b}{c - a} \right] \log i_b + \left[\frac{bc - ad}{c - a} \right] = M \log i_b + B \tag{6.5}$$

Using Eqs. (6.4) and (6.5) and Figs. 6.5 and 6.6, we find the output in logarithmic form as follows:

$$\log v_o - M \log [I_0 - K(v_o - V_R)] = \log v_i + B + \log R_L \tag{6.6}$$

where $v_o > V_r$ (the closed-loop mode). Figure 6.6b shows the response, using realistic circuit values as shown. The response slope is not constant but flattens out, indicating an increase in the loop gain path indicated in Fig. 6.5. This effect is shown also in Eq. (6.7), which shows the loop gain increasing as v_o increases (large input signal):

$$\frac{d(\log v_o)}{d(\log v_i)} = \frac{1}{1 + \dfrac{Mkv_o}{I_o - K(v_o - V_R)}} = \frac{1}{1 + (\text{loop gain})}$$
$$v_o = V_R \tag{6.7}$$

The output changes 6 dB for a 33-dB input change (the compression is 27 dB). To achieve a very small output change, a very large value of loop gain (high K) would be needed. This can create difficult problems with loop stability, especially at large values of input signal. If there is some time delay (phase shift) in this loop due to the filtering of the control signal, overshoots and instability could result. "Gulping" is a term used to describe a situation

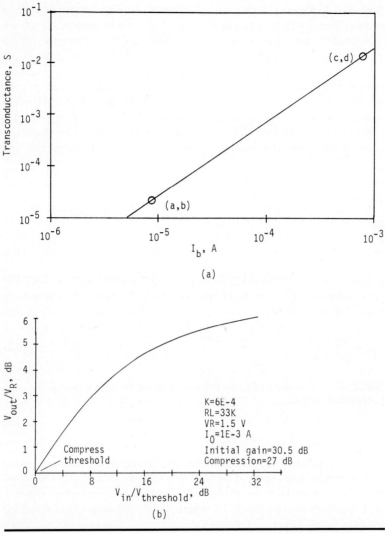

(a)

(b)

Figure 6.6 Computer-generated graphs showing gain control characteristics. (a) The almost logarithmic effect of i_b on the transconductance of a National LM16300 amplifier. (b) The audio output vs. input of the compressor circuit, showing the output flattening at large input values, indicating high loop gain.

where an overshoot in i_b shuts off the output signal until v_d can decay (via RC) sufficiently to recover. Also, any slight audio signal on i_b will modulate the output signal and produce some distortion; therefore the v_d line must be adequately filtered. So the design goals are as follows:

1. Restrict, by filtering, the low- and high-frequency ends of the input signal. Restricting low frequencies makes the v_d line easier to filter.

2. Make the loop response fast enough to follow the syllabic rises in the voice signal (as filtered in step 1) so that saturation of the amplifier does not occur. To aid in this, design the amplifier with adequate "headroom," or large-signal handling ability.

3. Low-pass-filter the v_d line to reduce ripple, but not to such an extent that step 2 is violated, or to such an extent that gulping occurs.

4. Post-filter the audio output signal to remove as many low- and high- frequency distortion products as possible.

These four requirements obviously interact and possibly conflict, and a combination of experimental, analytical, and simulation analyses must be performed to achieve a working design.

A better design can be obtained, at greater cost, if a logarithmic amplifier is inserted as suggested in Fig. 6.5. This reduces loop gain variations and improves dynamic response. Op-amp design literature for these circuits is ubiquitous. See Ref. 2, for example.

After a peak has occurred, v_d falls off because of the discharge of RC. As Fig. 6.1 shows, the speech which immediately follows the peak is compressed but the compression decreases with time. This effect becomes more noticeable as RC becomes small. As a result, the weaker speech elements are enhanced. At the same time, the signal becomes more distorted because of the modulation of signal amplitude by v_d. As RC becomes small, the compressor acts more like a clipper.

It has been found (Ref. 1) that with a 0.5-s recovery time and 10 dB of compression, a 1- or 2-dB improvement in intelligibility is obtained. Compare this with Fig. 6.3b. The combination of compression (10 dB) and clipping (20 dB) has been found to be useful (the compressor helps to maintain a more constant average level into the clipper). Finally, Ref. 3 notes that if the gain control is applied in a balanced manner to a push-pull gain control amplifier, the effect of ripple voltage on v_d is reduced (but some intermodulation effects can still be created).

RF clipping

We have seen that there are two problems with audio processing. One is the amount of distortion which accompanies audio clipping (a more effective method than compression for intelligibility improvement), and the other is the peakiness of the SSB envelope due to the Hilbert Transform phenomenon. RF clipping, and a form of audio processing which is mathematically equivalent to RF clipping, help to resolve these problems.

We first discuss true RF clipping as shown in the block diagram of Fig. 6.7. A high-speed diode circuit slices the RF cycles in a memoryless manner. The diodes are in shunt with a high-impedance tuned circuit, and the amplifier is essentially a current source. The peak signal currents are diverted to the low-impedance diodes. High-conductance RF diodes are needed to get a flat envelope when clipping (see Ref. 4). Any Hilbert peaks present are also

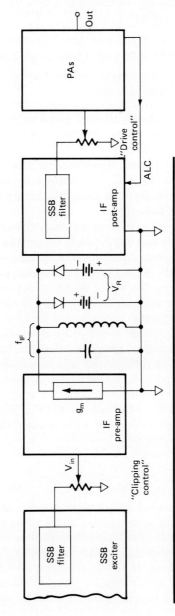

Figure 6.7 Block diagram of an RF clipper circuit.

clipped. There are some initial conditions at the beginning and end of diode conduction which involve the charge and current in the tuned circuit, but at RF frequencies these are quickly resolved and cause no problems in the circuit performance. The degree of clipping, in dB, is the decrease in output of a single-tone signal when the diodes are introduced. An exception to this for a speech or multitone signal will be noted shortly. The Hilbert peaks are not recreated after the clipping process if the envelope delay after clipping is fairly constant.

Because the nonlinear clipping occurs at an RF frequency, any harmonic distortion products which are generated are at multiples of the RF frequency and can easily be filtered out. Thus, only intermodulation products of those voice frequencies which are simultaneously present and which are within the output filter passband are present. This filter must be capable of rejecting intermodulation products (mostly of higher order) which are close to the desired passband and which would constitute adjacent channel splattering. For heavy clipping (20 dB or more) the third-order IM products are about 9 dB below each tone of a two-equal-tone signal. Speech signals can often approximate such a two-tone signal for short periods of time. The absence of harmonic distortion greatly improves the intelligibility of the processed signal. Figure 6.8 shows this improvement, which should be compared with the effects of audio clipping.

Figure 6.7 also reveals some of the main problems with RF clipping. One is that the circuit must be added to the RF signal path. Another is that an additional high-quality bandpass filter (crystal or mechanical) must be added. These make this approach expensive and also somewhat difficult to retrofit to existing equipment. The additional RF gain added to the signal

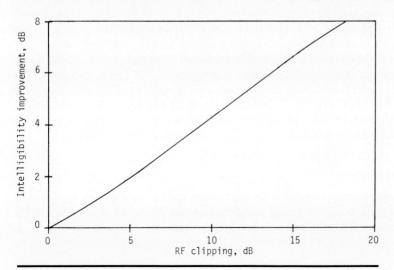

Figure 6.8 Computer-generated graph showing improvement in speech intelligibility for RF clipping.

path can create vulnerability to various kinds of spurious signals and instability unless special care is taken to shield and filter the RF clipper assembly.

Another problem is that when the clipped envelope is bandpass-filtered, a repeaking effect just like the one described in audio clipping occurs. If a two-equal-tone signal is infinitely clipped, the peak envelope output level after postfiltering is 2.1 dB greater than the clipped envelope. Of course, the amount of repeaking depends on the voice constituents present at any one time and is therefore a variable quantity. This means that the amplifiers after the clipper can flat-top unless they are protected by ALC. For this reason, ALC should be considered an important ingredient in any speech processor approach. Of course, the ALC should be applied to a stage which follows the clipper, rather than precedes it, in order to be effective. Also, if a single-tone signal is used to set up the RF amplifier signal levels, this adjustment is not correct for the speech signal dynamics encountered because of repeaking. See Ref. 4 for further discussion. The results shown in the plot of Fig. 6.8 are corrected for this effect. Measurements verify that with 20 dB of clipping, the peak-to-average ratio of speech, including the repeaking effect, is about 9 dB.

Experience with RF clipper units has shown that if a high-quality second filter is used and if the amplifier stages after the clipper are carefully designed, using ALC, to prevent even very slight flat topping, a very-high-quality narrowband signal can be transmitted with 20 dB of clipping and very high "talk power" and excellent intelligibility. The second-IF filter contributes to this cleanliness. The two filters must have well-matched passbands for best quality of speech sound. The overall response should be sufficiently flat to minimize response peaks. The intermodulation distortion does not create a "mushy" sound, but rather a crisp and clean effect which is pleasant sounding, even when the received signal is strong. Preemphasis of the audio signal at 3 dB/octave is sometimes suggested to improve the result. It is desirable, though, to use a noise-canceling microphone.

Two adjustments are required: a gain control ahead of the clipper to set the degree of clipping and one after the clipper to set the output level. The correct output level is that which produces the required ALC action on voice peaks. The ALC recovery time constant should be short (e.g., 100 ms), so that the average power will be reduced as little as possible. The ALC reduces the effectiveness of RF clipping slightly, but this cannot be helped.

RF compression

The most common form of RF compression is ALC. It is widely used to control the peak levels in power amplifiers and is discussed thoroughly in the PA chapters. We will mention briefly one way that ALC is used to provide speech processing. The discussion will perhaps suggest similar methods to the reader.

As indicated in Fig. 6.9, a control signal, proportional to the SSB envelope, is developed in a PA which is applied to an early stage in such a way that the peak envelope level is regulated. Think of it as envelope feedback. This

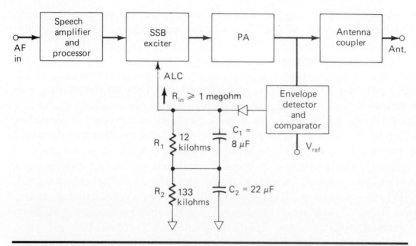

Figure 6.9 Block diagram and simplified schematic diagram of an ALC circuit which provides a small measure of speech intelligibility enhancement.

control is usually developed on voice peaks. If the control has a short recovery time constant, some enhancement of the speech signal occurs between the syllabic peaks. Figure 6.9 shows a diode/RC circuit which has been used to maintain a slowly varying average level with a 3.0-s time constant (R_2, C_2) and also a faster varying level (R_1, C_1) with a 0.1-s time constant. The voltage across the short time constant decays between syllabic peaks, allowing the SSB envelope to increase, and provides a small amount of speech processing.

The proportion of control voltage which is fast-varying is determined by the ratio $R_1/(R_1 + R_2)$. Choose C_1 and C_2 to satisfy the time-constant requirements. This ratio should be such that about 3 dB of gain fluctuation occurs between syllabic peaks. The slowly varying voltage across C_2 constitutes a simplified transmit gain control (TGC) voltage (see Chap. 4 for a discussion of TGC). In order to determine the quantities involved, it is necessary to make a plot of RF output v. control voltage for the intended system. The driver circuit for the RC network should have a very low output impedance so that the capacitors can be charged quickly and the control voltage can therefore follow the fast-rising syllabic peaks. Of course, there should be very little time delay within the complete control loop so that overshoots (gulping) do not occur. Also, if the control loop is not designed properly, transient flat topping, with splatter, can occur on voice peaks because the envelope peaks are not properly restrained. Just as we found with the audio compressor, wide variations in ALC loop gain can be difficult to deal with. The gain control function should be free of abrupt changes and should be as logarithmic as possible.

Baseband envelope clipping

We have seen that RF clipping is superior to audio clipping for two reasons: There is less harmonic distortion (therefore greater intelligibility), and the envelope peaks created by the Hilbert Transform are also clipped, thereby increasing the average power. With certain precautions and at a slightly greater cost and complexity than audio clipping, the same results can be obtained in an audio processor.

If an SSB envelope which has been clipped and filtered is frequency-translated to baseband, the resulting audio signal may then be fed into an SSB modulator to create an SSB signal which has the same envelope as the first SSB signal. That is, the SSB envelope is invariant with respect to frequency translation, even if the translation is down to baseband and back up to some different RF frequency. However, the baseband signal does not have an "envelope," strictly speaking, because the RF wave associated with an envelope is not present. But recall that in Eq. (6.2) the audio signal and its Hilbert Transform accomplish this quite well. From previous discussion regarding the Hilbert Transform it can be seen that if a signal is accurately Hilbert-transformed repeatedly, the signal changes from $g(t)$ to $h(t)$ to $-g(t)$ to $-h(t)$ and so forth, with the respective wave shapes preserved. So if an SSB envelope is demodulated and remodulated, the envelope shape is reproduced. The requirement is that the Hilbert Transform be done accurately.

The unit can be external to the transmitter and plug into the microphone jack.

Figure 6.10 shows a block diagram of an RF clipper which clips at some low RF frequency. A single local oscillator performs the upconversion and downconversion. The relative phase of the two injections is not important for correct operation. The audio output must not overload the amplifiers and SSB modulators in the transmitter, though. Because large peaks have been removed by the clipper, this problem is well solved.

Figure 6.11 shows another, cheaper approach. An SSB envelope is generated at baseband by creating the square root of the sum of the squares of the audio signal and its Hilbert Transform [see Eq. (6.2)]. The resulting envelope voltage is used to limit the desired audio $g(t)$, or I (in-phase) component, in a gain control amplifier (LM13600). The resulting audio is mathematically equivalent to that produced by the circuit shown in Fig. 6.10. This circuit has been patented by R. L. Craiglow and F. W. Werth for the Rockwell-Collins Co. (Ref. 5) and is used in production line equipment.

Lincompex processing

A major complaint regarding speech processing is that the natural amplitude variations which one expects to hear are "washed out," creating an unpleasant effect for nontechnical users. The Lincompex system (for "Linked Compression and Expansion," developed by the British Post Office in the 1960s; see Ref. 6) encodes the audio amplitude levels at the transmitter and sends them on an auxiliary channel. The receiver decodes this information and reconstructs the original signal. However, the improvement in intelligibility is preserved during the process, and the received signal is "telephone quality." Since the auxiliary channel contains information regarding the absolute short-term amplitude of the speaker's voice, the receiver output

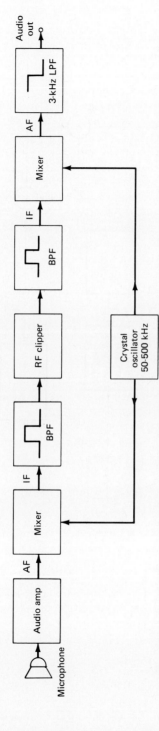

Figure 6.10 Block diagram of a baseband processor which uses RF clipping. The audio signal is converted to SSB, clipped, filtered, and converted back to baseband. Upon subsequent conversion to SSB, the envelope characteristics of the RF clipper are retained.

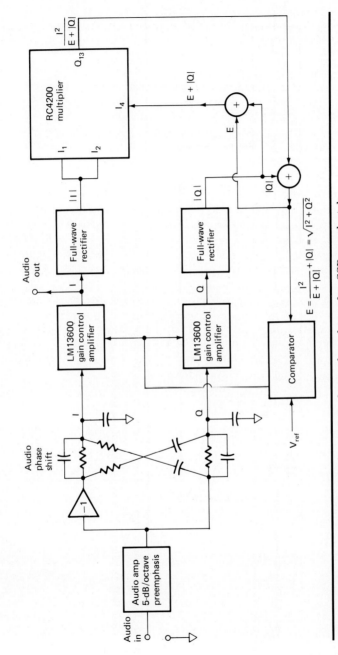

Figure 6.11 Baseband processor which generates the envelope shape of an SSB wave by taking the square root of the sum of squares of the audio signal and its Hilbert Transform. The envelope waveform then controls the gain of an amplifier which provides the audio output signal.

also has the same amplitude if the equipment is properly adjusted. Therefore, the received signal is transparent to fading and path loss. Receiver AGC helps this process and prevents receiver overload. The control information is usually sent at reduced amplitude so that more speech power will be available in a peak-power-limited system, but of course some "talk power" is sacrificed. Because of the companding, the background microphone noise usually associated with speech processors is reduced. This permits larger amounts of compression (30 to 40 dB) to be used.

Figure 6.12 shows a block diagram of a Lincompex transmitting unit which uses FM at about 2900 Hz for the amplitude information. The VCO frequency is proportional to the amplitude in dB and has a sensitivity of about 0.5 dB/Hz. Therefore the transmitter and receiver must both have very excellent frequency stability to prevent excessive amplitude dropoff at the receiver. Doppler shift due to relative motion of the transmitter and receiver would also create problems. The time delays assure that the envelope information is well coordinated with the compressed speech. Digital implementations of Lincompex have been suggested (Refs. 7 and 8) which reduce the frequency stability requirements and provide some automatic calibration at the receiver.

Figure 6.13 is the receiver demodulator. The constant-volume amplifier helps (along with AGC) to eliminate amplitude variations prior to volume expansion. The antilog amplifier complements the log amplifier at the transmitter. Under weak-signal conditions the FM channel can be contaminated with noise, though, and some degradation can occur. But since the channel is very narrowband, this effect is reduced.

6.2 Squelch

Many users of SSB equipment want the receiver to be activated only when the desired signal is present, even though it may be noisy and contaminated with interference. In conventional AM and FM the presence of a carrier sig-

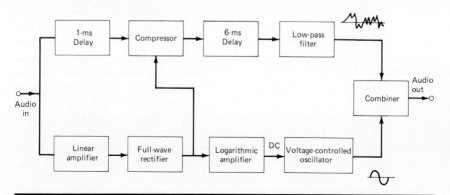

Figure 6.12 Block diagram of a Lincompex modulator. The VCO provides the FM auxiliary signal which contains the original amplitude variations.

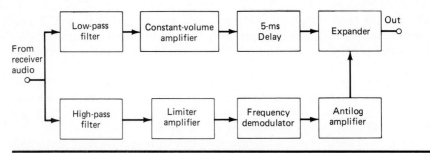

Figure 6.13 Block diagram of a Lincompex demodulator. The expander restores the original amplitude variations, as conveyed by the subband FM signal.

nal can be determined, and this can be used to operate a squelch gate. The carrier conveys no speech information, but it is a 1-bit message which says "signal present" or "signal not present." In SSB, where there is usually no carrier, the voice signal itself must be recognized unambiguously in the presence of noise and interference. The time needed to recognize a voice signal must be short enough that very little speech information is lost, but long enough that false triggering on transient noise pulses is minimized. These conflicting requirements have led to a great deal of effort to discern the unique characteristics of SSB speech which a squelch can recognize and which will optimize its performance in the presence of noise, fading, and interference. Also, quite often the squelch must be tolerant of frequency mistuning of, say, a hundred hertz or so.

One useful property of speech is its long-term spectral distribution, which shows a strong peak in the area of 500 to 600 Hz and a 6-dB/octave rolloff. However, the short-term spectrum over a period of a hundred milliseconds or so will at different times show a somewhat different distribution.

A comparator is adjusted for balance with "white," or uniform, noise. The voice signal then unbalances the comparator. Once triggered, the audio remains gated on for about 2s so that annoying rapid on/off toggling will not occur. This is improved by providing hysteresis so that the pull-in level is 6 to 10 dB higher than the dropout level. A problem with this approach is that a beat note at low frequency causes false trigger. A high-pitch note will prevent, or lock out, desired response to a speech signal. Certain kinds of unvoiced, or fricative, speech sounds have mostly high-frequency components which do not properly actuate the squelch. If these are the opening sounds, the squelch will tend to miss them. Also, certain types of pulses may not have a flat spectrum, causing false trigger. In addition, it is necessary to be able to preset both transmitter and receiver frequencies to within a hundred hertz or so to be sure the squelch will work properly. With synthesizer control, this is no problem. Despite its faults this approach has been used very successfully in production equipment.

A second property of speech is the low-frequency "syllabic" variations. These are in the range of 1 to 10 Hz or so. Figure 6.14 shows a schematic

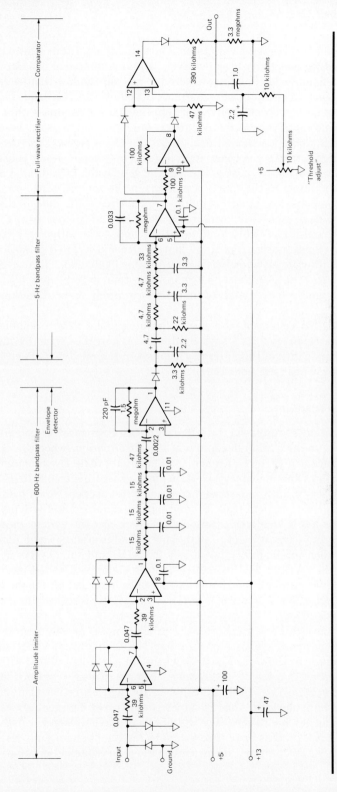

Figure 6.14 Schematic diagram of a squelch which detects syllabic modulation of a speech signal.

237

diagram which utilizes these variations. The signal is amplitude-limited with diodes to reduce sensitivity to signal level, bandpass-filtered at 600 Hz, envelope-detected, and then bandpass-filtered to recover the low-frequency syllabic variations which amplitude-modulate the 600-Hz speech band. That is, the bursts of speech spectral energy within the 600-Hz bandpass filter vary at the syllabic rate. Noise and CW carriers are relatively weak in these syllabic frequency components. Also, slight mistuning of receiver frequency is less detrimental than some other approaches. This simple circuit is used in a production receiver. Because of the limiting action, all of the desired information is contained in the time fluctuations in the zero crossing—in other words, in the phase variations. A more complex circuit also detects the syllabic variations in a passband centered at 2200 Hz and compares the results of the two bands. The two sets of variations tend to be either in phase or 180° out of phase most of the time, that is, either correlated or anticorrelated. The full-wave rectification corrects for this likelihood. The use of correlation reduces the sensitivity to signals other than desired speech signals, since noise and many types of interference rarely have this kind of coincidence.

In mobile SSB systems a pilot carrier has been found to be a reliable way to detect the signal (Ref. 9). A special filter passes only the carrier frequency. Since the bandwidth of this filter is very narrow, the pilot carrier can be 10 to 15 dB below peak envelope power.

6.3 Noise Blanking

The elimination of impulsive interference in an SSB receiver contributes substantially to the quality of communication in situations where the source of interference cannot be controlled, such as in a mobile environment and near power lines and machinery. Certain pulse-generating transmitters such as HF over-the-horizon radars send complex pulse packets which present a somewhat special problem (Ref. 10) and have become an international nuisance. There has been a great deal of effort to perfect the various means of making a receiver transparent to these kinds of interference, which not only degrade speech intelligibility but affect the AGC and thereby desensitize (paralyze) the receiver. In this section the discussion is directed mostly at noise blanking, in which the receiver signal path is turned off for the duration of the pulse. The absence of a carrier in SSB systems makes this method especially effective.

Impulse noise differs from ordinary random noise in two respects. Its short-term spectrum is phase-coherent and has an amplitude variation and autocorrelation, as shown in Fig. 6.15, which are a function of its width and its edge slopes. As a result, the received voltage is nearly proportional to bandwidth (within the limits indicated in the figure), rather than to the square root of bandwidth. Also, the pulse power is very high for a short time and then falls quickly to zero. The duty cycle of these pulses is usually less than, say, a few percent or so. For example, automobile ignition pulses are from 3 to 10 ns in duration (at the source; they are stretched in the process

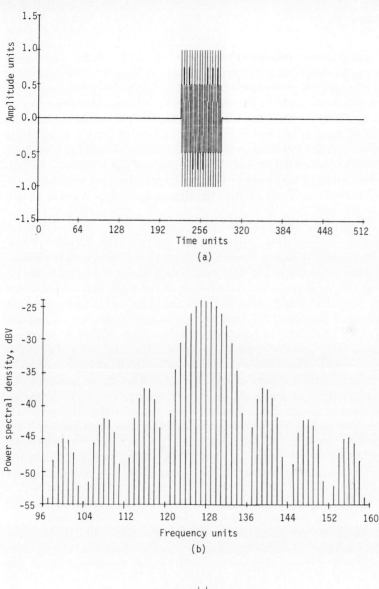

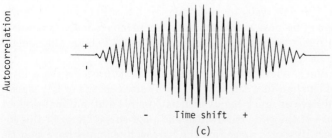

Figure 6.15 Computer-generated graphs showing (*a*) a narrow repetitive RF noise pulse, (*b*) its one-sided spectrum, and (*c*) its autocorrelation function.

of being radiated by the vehicle), and for an eight-cylinder four-stroke engine the pulse rate is roughly rpm/15 pulses per second. Other artificially produced sources emit pulses in the 0.1- to 10-µs range. These characteristics are sufficiently different from the speech signal and noise that they may be exploited by the noise blanker in ways which do not seriously degrade the desired signal. Speech can be interrupted for about 10 percent or so of the time with an acceptable (usually) loss of articulation, as discussed in Chap. 2. Other types of interference, such as lightning and pulse packets, are sufficiently similar to speech both in time and spectrum that they are more difficult to blank. Amplitude limiting or clipping can help somewhat in this case.

A signal or pulse entering a receiver encounters at some point a bandpass filter which rejects undesired signals and interference. If an RF pulse of narrow but finite width is passed through this filter, the time output is the convolution of the pulse shape and the impulse response of the filter, or, equivalently, the output spectrum is the product of the pulse spectrum and the frequency response of the filter. If the pulse spectrum is essentially flat across the filter passband, the time output is approximately the impulse response of the filter. This impulse response causes the output pulse energy to be delayed by an amount equal to the slope of the filter phase shift, to be elongated in time to about twice the reciprocal of the bandwidth, and to be reduced in amplitude (the time-power product is fixed by the energy of the pulse). Also, multiple-response echoes, called "ringing," occur which are separated in time by about the reciprocal of the filter bandwidth and which must often also be blanked. The relative amplitudes of these responses are determined by the shape of the filter transition band and its differential phase delay (the two are related). Figure 6.16 illustrates these points and also shows that a rounded-response, linear-phase filter is a better choice for the bandpass filtering of RF impulses. This filter may not be optimal in terms of eliminating undesired signals, though, so a conflict appears which must be resolved in the receiver design which employs a noise blanker.

At this point the discussion centers on a particular technique for noise blanking, called the "in-band" blanker because the noise pulse energy is in the frequency band closely adjacent (10 to 50 kHz) to the desired signal. The emphasis is not on circuit details but on general principles which can be applied in many different ways by the designer. The discussion is for the most part qualitative because a detailed and very involved analysis requires more space (and rigor) than is feasible here. Figure 6.17 shows the generic block diagram to be discussed.

The noise amplifier follows the RF translator and is preceded by a filter which is much wider than that required for the desired speech or CW signal. This filter should have as much bandwidth as possible and minimal ringout responses. Because of the wide bandwidth and poor shape factor of this filter, the signal path IF stages preceding the narrow filter must have as little gain and as much signal-handling ability as possible in order to minimize the chances of spurious signal generation in these stages. Refer to Chap. 3 for a detailed discussion of this subject. A further important point is that the input impedance of the noise amplifier must be constant with respect to sig-

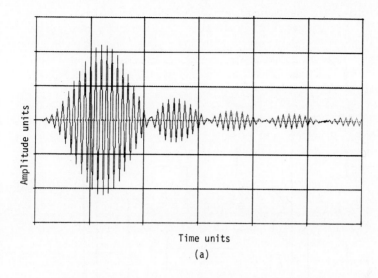

Time units

(a)

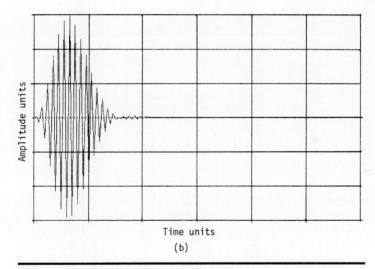

Time units

(b)

Figure 6.16 Computer-generated graphs showing response of a bandpass filter to a narrow pulse of RF energy. A Chebyshev and a Bessel filter are compared: (*a*) four-pole, 0.5-dB Chebyshev; (*b*) four-pole Bessel.

nal and noise spike levels so that intermodulation will not be generated by a nonlinear impedance. There are two ways to help this: Use a MOSFET input stage and operate its gate terminal at a very low impedance level (this reduces signal levels at the input gate). Noise figure for this stage is relatively less important, so considerable noise mismatch is tolerable. The wide bandwidth of the filter magnifies the amplitude of the noise pulses and makes them much narrower than would be the case for a narrow filter, as previously

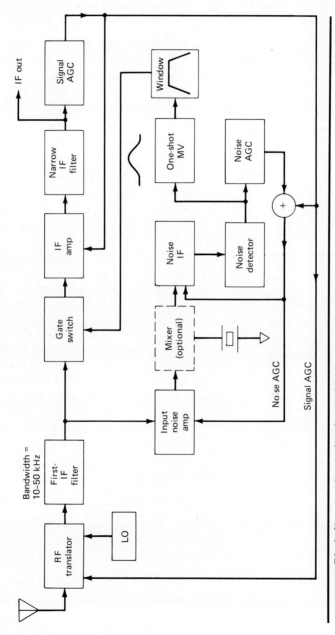

Figure 6.17 Block diagram of an in-band noise blanker.

discussed, and this helps to get more noise spike into the noise amplifier. The signal IF amplifiers which precede the gate switch, however, must handle the large noise spikes and must have a low noise figure. This conflict creates a difficult design problem which can be solved only by minimizing the gain and by using a power amplifier with low noise figure. Amplifiers after the gate switch do not have the noise spike, and this eases the design problems of these stages. The use of the wide filter does make the signal path more difficult, and a degradation of receiver noise figure may have to be accepted if strong signal performance is a major specification. Very often this is a mild penalty. From this discussion, the tradeoff choices are readily apparent. For example, a narrower filter will widen the noise pulses (this may be quite acceptable in a speech SSB application) and make the circuit design easier.

Following the noise amplifier, an envelope detector provides a pulse which actuates a retriggerable monostable flip-flop which provides an output as long as the noise pulse lasts and can be quickly ready to provide another pulse if it is needed. This method has been found to be very helpful in production equipment in reducing interference from HF radar pulse packets. We can now estimate the required gain in the noise channel. Suppose we want to blank a spike whose power in a 3-kHz bandwidth at the antenna is equal to a desired -115-dBm signal. If the RF translator has 15-db gain and if the first IF filter has a 50-kHz bandwidth, the spike level at the noise amplifier input is $-115 + 15 + 20 \log (50/3) = -76$ dBm, or 112 μV at 500 ohms. The flip-flop requires about 3 V to trigger, so the voltage gain needed, including rectification, is 27,000. Three stages at 30 per stage will suffice. Some of the gain can be at dc after rectification. Often, especially in upconversion receivers (see Chap. 3), a frequency conversion to a much lower IF frequency is performed, as indicated in the block diagram.

The gate switch attenuates the signal path by at least 50 dB. Figure 6.18

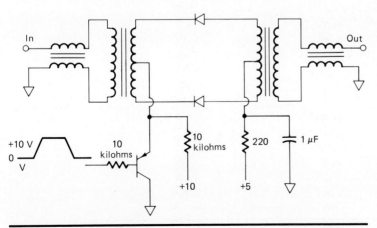

Figure 6.18 Schematic diagram of a noise blanker gate switch. The switch is singly balanced to reduce the leakage of gate pulse energy into the signal path.

shows a typical example. It is singly balanced with respect to the blanking pulse so that the spectrum of the blanking pulse itself will introduce less noise into the signal path. In addition, the blanking pulse should be "windowed," or shaped as indicated in the figure, to attenuate IF frequency components. Despite these precautions the blanking pulse can intermodulate with undesired signals to produce interference in the desired passband. Figure 6.19 shows how the product of a blanking pulse and an off-frequency carrier creates the problem. The windowing of the blanking pulse reduces this effect; for an excellent discussion of windowing, see Ref. 11.

A serious problem with the in-band noise blanker is that undesired signals within the passband of the wide filter can trigger the gate circuit, cutting off the signal path. To minimize this, AGC is derived from the impulse detector and applied to the noise amplifier as shown in the Fig. 6.17 block diagram. Then normal signals will be restricted to levels which do not affect the gate switch. This AGC must not come on too quickly, though, because noise spikes will make AGC and will not attain enough amplitude to operate the gate. For this reason, the AGC attack time is made very slow, perhaps 10 to 20 ms, so that the noise impulses will produce the desired output. The leading edges of normal speech signals, both desired and undesired, will also often trigger the switch momentarily, but a considerable amount of this can be tolerated if less than about 5 percent or so. The rejection of speech signals can be much improved by postdetection filtering; a filter which rolls off below 3 kHz will be less affected by the greater low-frequency speech energy. Also, the AGC recovery must be fairly fast, say 50 ms or so, so that rapid repetitions of pulses can be blanked. The dual-time-constant AGC idea described in the section on ALC would work well in a blanker.

A further problem is that strong undesired signals make noise channel AGC and therefore reduce the effectiveness of the blanker for weaker spikes. This can be improved by deriving at least part of the noise channel AGC from the normal AGC which is generated after the narrow filter. Since this

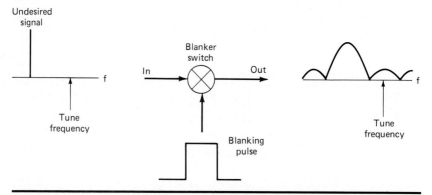

Figure 6.19 The intermodulation of a blanking pulse and an out-of-band undesired signal produces an in-band interference.

filter greatly attenuates, stretches, and delays impulses, the impulse is blanked before the normal AGC can react significantly. This approach was patented by S. L. Dawson for Rockwell Corp. (Ref. 12). To prevent excessive blanking by out-of-band signals, as described in the previous paragraph, some of the noise AGC should be derived in the manner discussed there. Also, as the desired signal becomes large, the need to blank is reduced; this method aids in this if it is implemented properly.

In order for the pulse to be properly blanked, the gate switch must be fully opened at the time that the pulse arrives at the switch in the signal path. This timing becomes more critical as the first-IF bandwidth becomes wider, and also as the blanking pulse is windowed, as we have already discussed. The windowing creates a time delay in the blanking pulse which must be matched in the signal path. One author (Ref. 13) uses a glass acoustical delay line. Another approach for short delays is to use a cascaded multiple-resonator filter. The value of the delay can be determined from the low-pass prototype from which the tuned filter is derived (Ref. 14).

The methods discussed so far are adequate for SSB speech systems. For high-speed data systems the blanking width must be much less, to prevent data loss. To accomplish this, a separate wideband noise-sensing receiver is often used as the noise channel. This receiver is tuned to a relatively unused frequency. Its wide bandwidth assures a very large noise spike, relative to the incidental signals which may also be present in the noise-sensing receiver. The wide bandwidth greatly reduces the amount of noise amplification needed (Ref. 15). The noise and signal path time delays are carefully coordinated.

REFERENCES

1. R. L. Craiglow et al., *A Study of the Effects of Elementary Processing Techniques on the Intelligibility of Speech in Noise,* Collins Radio Res. Rep. CCR 201, 1963.
2. D. F. Stout and M. Kaufman, *Handbook of Operational Amplifier Circuit Design,* McGraw-Hill, New York, 1976, Chap. 17.
3. E. W. Pappenfus, W. B. Bruene, and E. O. Schoenike, *Single Sideband Principles and Circuits,* McGraw-Hill, New York, 1964, p. 330.
4. W. E. Sabin, "RF Clippers for SSB," *QST,* vol. 51, no. 6, July 1967, pp. 13–18.
5. R. L. Craiglow and W. F. Werth, Speech Processor for Processing Analog Signals, U.S. Patent 4,410,764, Oct. 18, 1983.
6. *Proceedings,* vol. III, International Radio Consultative Committee (CCIR) XIII Plenary Assembly, Geneva, 1974.
7. S. M. Chow et al., *Syncompex, a Voice Processing System for Low Cost HF Radio Telephony,* Communications Research Centre, Canadian Dept. of Communications, Ottawa, Canada, 1980.
8. V. R. DeLong, "Digital Lincompex" (private communication; copies not available).
9. Barry Manz, "SSB Technology Fights Its Way into Land-Mobile Market," *Microwave & RF,* vol. 22, August 1983, pp. 72–80.
10. Bradley Wells, "The Russian Woodpecker: A Continuing Nuisance," *Ham Radio,* vol. 17, November 1984, pp. 37–45.
11. F. J. Harris, "On the Use of Windows for Harmonic Analysis with the Discrete Fourier Transform," *Proc. IEEE,* vol. 66, January 1978, pp. 51–83.
12. S. L. Dawson, Noise Blanker, U.S. Patent 4,479,251, 1984 (assigned to Rockwell International).

13. W. Gosling, "Impulsive Noise Reduction in Radio Receivers," *Radio & Electron. Eng.,* vol. 43, May 1973, pp. 341–347.
14. H. J. Blinchikoff and A. I. Zverev, *Filtering in the Time and Frequency Domain,* John Wiley & Sons, New York, 1978.
15. R. H. Sternowski, "Noise Blanking at the Antenna Input of a Communication Receiver," Master's thesis, Iowa State University, Ames, IA, 1977.

Digital Signal Processing

Marvin E. Frerking
Richard A. Groshong

7.1 Introduction

The concept of digital signal processing is relatively new compared with that for analog techniques, and although the mathematical techniques have been developed for some time, it was only during the late 1970s that integrated circuit technology progressed to the point where it became economical to replace many of the analog circuits in SSB equipment with digital processing hardware. In some cases digital processing techniques yield superior performance to their analog counterparts. For example, a filter with no differential time delay is easily built. In other cases, for example dynamic range, the analog techniques are presently superior because of the limited number of bits that can be practically obtained in an analog-to-digital (A/D) converter. In still other cases, digital techniques are capable of performing functions not previously practical or economical using analog techniques. For example, speech processors and modems can be realized in relatively few chips and can be included in a receiver or transmitter.

As discussed in other chapters, SSB can be generated either by filtering techniques or by phasing techniques to eliminate the unwanted sideband. The filtering technique has dominated analog equipment design because of the difficulty in obtaining wideband phase shifters and accurate amplitude balance across the audio spectrum. These difficulties are easily overcome using digital techniques, and consequently the phasing technique has been predominantly used to date in digital SSB radio design.

There are several key concepts which are used in digital SSB radio design. Since they are essential to understanding the radio implementations to follow, we shall pause briefly to review them. It is not the purpose here to provide a general treatment of digital signal processing techniques, and it is assumed that the reader is familiar with sampling techniques, Z transforms, and digital filtering theory. (See Refs. 1 through 5.) Only techniques which are rather directly applicable to SSB are reviewed here.

One of the key concepts in digital signal processing as applied to radio communications is that of analytic or complex signals. An ordinary or real signal if represented in the frequency domain has symmetrical positive and negative frequencies. For example, a signal $e_1 = A \cos 2\pi f_0 t$ has a spectrum point at both f_0 and at $-f_0$. If one displays the signal on a spectrum analyzer, of course only the positive portion is displayed. The negative component is nevertheless present, and if we mix the signal with another signal $e_2 = B \sin 2\pi f_1 t$, both sum and difference frequencies will be generated. In complex signal representation it is possible to obtain signals with one-sided or nonsymmetrical positive and negative sideband structures. It is also possible to keep track of which components are positive and which components are negative. The complex signals which exist in the computer, while represented in complex mathematical form, behave precisely as predicted by the mathematical theory and can be processed, translated, phase-shifted, etc., without the attendant restrictions of real analog signals. Once the signals have been processed or manipulated as desired, they can be converted into real signals by digital-to-analog converters or used directly by other digital processors. The most important function performed by digital signal processing is normally filtering, and this is discussed in detail in Sec. 7.4. Two types of filters are used: infinite impulse response, or IIR, filters, which provide characteristics similar to analog filters such as the Butterworth or Chebyshev types, and finite impulse response, or FIR, filters. FIR filters, as will be seen later, can be constructed with no differential time delay and in some cases provide an improvement in performance not achievable with analog filters. Digital techniques can also be used to provide mixers, oscillators such as a BFO, AGC loops, phase shifters, etc., so that nearly all the functions required for single-sideband equipment can be implemented digitally.

The primary limitation at the present time is the dynamic range which can be achieved by the analog-to-digital and the digital-to-analog converters. Additional limitations result from the processing speed required to perform the filters. Thus a practical system currently includes a combination of analog and digital circuits. The analog circuits are used for the relatively wideband signals and the digital circuits are used for the narrowband functions such as the final filtering and detection. A significant advantage of digital circuits also results from the availability of broadband audio phase shifters which can be achieved by the Hilbert Transformer. This makes it practical to produce and use complex signals, which can be of considerable advantage for SSB modulation and demodulation.

The use of digital signal processing thus encompasses considerably more than filtering alone. An SSB radio employing digital signal processing may require a considerable number of high-speed processing elements, and the amount of data to be transferred within the radio as well as synchronization of the processors, may become a formidable problem. Several techniques which can be used to manage this problem are discussed in Sec. 7.10. Several of the processing elements available at the time of this writing are also discussed. Sampling and data conversion are discussed in Sec. 7.2, filtering in Sec. 7.4, detection methods in Sec. 7.5, and modulation in Sec. 7.9.

The remainder of this introduction discusses briefly the mathematics of complex signals which is essential to an understanding of digital receiver/exciter structures which are then briefly treated.

Mathematics of complex signals

The area of digital signal processing which relates to complex signals and the concept of positive and negative frequencies is often not well understood and leads to much confusion in signal processing. An attempt will, therefore, be made here to convey a sufficient understanding to the reader so that the techniques described subsequently can be understood. A real signal, say, $f(t)$ = $\cos \omega_0 t$, is normally considered to be a positive frequency and can be displayed on a frequency spectrum analyzer. If it is in the RF region, it can be transmitted and occupies a definite position in the electromagnetic spectrum. A real signal of this type can be represented by two rotating vectors in the complex plane, as shown in Fig. 7.1.

Since the vectors rotate in opposite directions, the imaginary component resulting from the sum of the vectors is always zero. Therefore, the signal can be transmitted on a single circuit. The Fourier transform of this signal is, of course, composed of identical positive and negative components of the form

$$F[\cos \omega_0 t] = \pi\delta(\omega - \omega_0) + \pi\delta(\omega + \omega_0) \tag{7.1}$$

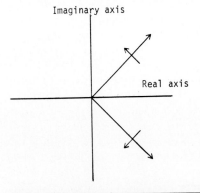

Figure 7.1 Phasor representation of real signal.

A real signal is always composed of symmetrical positive and negative frequencies, although in some cases they may be of opposite sign, e.g.,

$$F[\sin \omega_0 t] = j\pi\delta(\omega + \omega_0) - j\pi\delta(\omega - \omega_0) \tag{7.2}$$

It is possible to represent a signal which has only positive or only negative frequencies if we allow two circuits and represent it in the form $f(t) = I(t) + jQ(t)$. This is shown in Fig. 7.2. In this case $I(t) = \cos \omega_0 t$ and $Q(t) = \sin \omega_0 t$. We note here that the $I(t)$ component taken by itself still has a positive and a negative component as before, as does the $Q(t)$ component. The explanation is that when taken together in the form $I(t) + jQ(t)$, the negative spectral components cancel each other while the positive frequency components reinforce each other. Complex signals of this type are referred to as "analytic signals."

It is often desirable in SSB equipment to begin with a real two-sided signal such as the audio from a microphone and convert it to a one-sided signal by eliminating either the positive or the negative components. The signal can then be frequency-converted without producing unwanted sidebands.

A real two-sided signal, say, $f(t)$, can be converted into a one-sided signal. First, all the components of $f(t)$ are shifted in phase by 90°. Let this signal be represented by $\hat{f}(t)$. If the shifted component is multiplied by j (where $j = \sqrt{-1}$) and added to the original signal, an analytic signal is created which has only the positive frequencies of the original function. Thus if $f(t)$ has a frequency spectrum $F(\omega)$ as shown in Fig. 7.3a, the complex signal $f(t) + j\hat{f}(t)$ has a spectrum as shown in Fig. 7.3b. Interestingly, the signal $f(t) - j\hat{f}(t)$ has a spectrum consisting of the negative frequencies of $f(t)$. We shall see more of positive and negative frequencies later. In general, we represent a complex signal in the form $I + jQ$, where I can be thought of as the in-phase component and Q the quadrature component.

Another very useful concept in digital signal processing is that of frequency translation. This is based on the Fourier frequency translation theo-

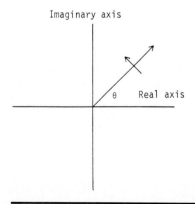

Figure 7.2 Phasor representation of positive frequency.

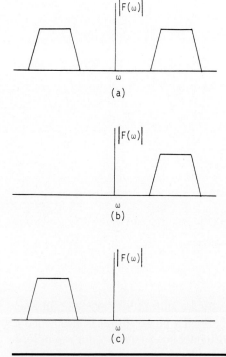

Figure 7.3 (a) Frequency spectrum of real audio signal. (b) Frequency spectrum of signal $f(t)$ + $j\hat{f}(t)$. (c) Frequency spectrum of signal $f(t)$ − $j\hat{f}(t)$.

rem which states that if a signal $f(t)$ has a frequency spectrum $F(\omega)$, the signal $e^{j\omega_0 t}f(t)$ has a frequency spectrum $F(\omega - \omega_0)$. Thus all components in the original signal are translated up in frequency by a value f_0 (where $\omega_0 = 2\pi f_0$). The theorem holds whether the signal is real or complex. If it is real, both the positive and negative sidebands are increased by a value f_0, and multiplication by $e^{j\omega t}$ results in a complex signal.

From the Euler identity

$$e^{j\omega_0 t} = \cos \omega_0 t + j \sin \omega_0 t \tag{7.3}$$

the output of a frequency translator has the form

$$e^{j\omega_0 t}(I + jQ) = (\cos \omega_0 t + j \sin \omega_0 t)(I + jQ) \tag{7.4}$$

$$= (I \cos \omega_0 t - Q \sin \omega_0 t) + j(I \sin \omega_0 t + Q \cos \omega_0 t) \tag{7.5}$$

Thus a complex mixer can be implemented as shown in Fig. 7.4.

A third technique is that of shifting the phase of a signal by 90°. This is normally done on a real signal. The phase shifter delays all components by

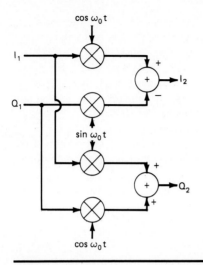

Figure 7.4 Block diagram of complex frequency translator.

90°; consequently all positive frequencies are shifted by $-90°$ and all negative components are shifted by $+90°$. Such a phase shifter is also called a "Hilbert Transformer." For a signal with only one frequency, for example, $e = A \cos \omega_0 t$, the phase shift can be realized by providing a delay of a quarter-cycle, as shown in Fig. 7.5a. If the signal consists of a band of frequencies, however, the phase shift is a perfect 90° only at the center frequency. A bet-

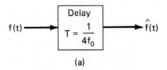

(a)

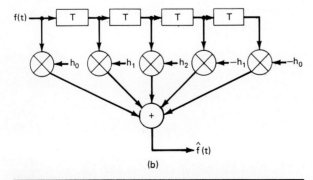

(b)

Figure 7.5 (a) Narrowband phase shifter; (b) 90° phase shifter.

ter phase shifter can be obtained using the implementation shown in Fig. 7.5*b*. Here each block T represents one sample time delay in a digitized signal. The signal multipliers are h_0, h_1, . . . , etc. The phase shifter can be made as broadband as necessary by using additional delays. The values for the h's are optimized for the bandwidth and sample rate used. Section 7.4 discusses this form of FIR filter in more detail; however, it is interesting to note that the coefficients have odd symmetry about the center. If the total number of taps is odd, the even tap weights are normally zero.

Complex signals are sometimes translated in frequency so that the center of the frequency spectrum is at zero. This allows the lowest possible sample rate to be used since the analytic signal is then composed of both positive and negative frequencies. After filtering, the signal can again be translated to the normal position in the audio spectrum.

Digital receiver/exciter concepts

The concepts discussed in the previous paragraphs will now be used to illustrate the design of both digital SSB exciters and receivers. We shall return later to those ideas and develop them in more mathematical detail, particularly as related to limitations imposed on digital radio performance. There are, of course, many different ways in which an exciter or receiver can be configured, and only a few are illustrated here to show the concepts.

The block diagram of a digital SSB exciter is shown in Fig. 7.6. The audio signal must be low-pass-filtered to remove frequencies greater than half the sample frequency of the analog-to-digital converter. A sample rate in the range of 16 to 32 kHz may be found to be appropriate. The digitized audio signal can then be compressed or limited using a fast envelope detector in a digital speech processor; or analog processing can be used prior to the A/D. The signal is then passed through a bandpass filter to form the I component of a complex signal and through a similar bandpass filter having a built-in 90° phase shifter to form the Q component. The filters are identical except for the values of the multipliers. The resulting complex signal $I + jQ$ has a one-sided frequency spectrum. This signal is translated to an IF frequency by multiplication by

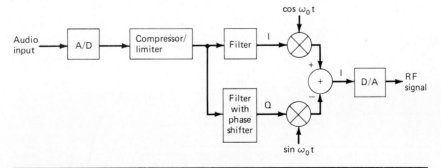

Figure 7.6 Block diagram of digital exciter.

$$e^{j\omega_0 t} = \cos \omega_0 t + j \sin \omega_0 t \tag{7.6}$$

The resulting signal is shown in Fig. 7.7. This signal is then converted to an analog signal by the D/A. In this case only half the complex mixer is used because it is not necessary to compute the Q component. The case shown results in USB transmission. If the sum of the two components from the sine and cosine multipliers had been used, the lower sideband would have resulted.

An independent sideband exciter can be constructed as shown in Fig. 7.8. The LSB and USB circuits are shown independently for clarity. These functions can be combined by moving the adder and subtracter to the outputs of the compressor/limiters. The resulting configuration is shown in Fig. 7.9.

The sampling process results in the spectrum repeating at harmonics of the sampling frequency. The harmonic spectrums must be removed by an analog filter following the D/A. In reality the D/A does not provide a series of impulses equal to the sample values, but rather holds the sample value until the next sample time. This results in the sample and hold function which acts as a filter.

If the sample rate is too low, this filtering action may result in attenuation of the upper portion of the audio band. For this reason as well as to reduce the requirements of the analog filter which eliminates the harmonic spectrums, it may be desirable to add an interpolation filter ahead of the D/A to increase the sample rate.

An interpolation filter is a filter operating at an output (higher) sample

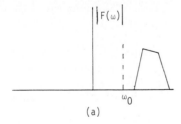

(a)

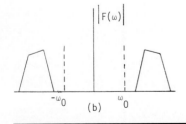

(b)

Figure 7.7 (a) Frequency spectrum of complex translated signal $I + jQ$. (b) Frequency spectrum of I component only.

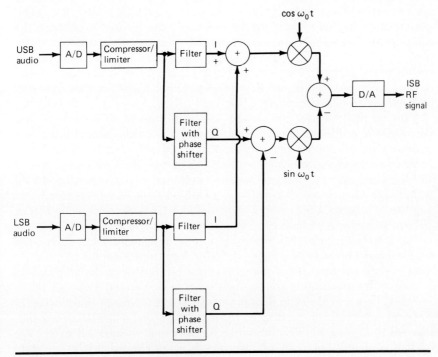

Figure 7.8 Block diagram of ISB exciter.

rate which should be integrally related to the input sample rate. The additional required input samples are taken to be zero. The bandwidth of the interpolation filter is chosen to provide sufficient attenuation of the harmonic spectra in the original signal.

The design of digital SSB exciters requires a considerably greater depth of knowledge than presented here. However, it is intended that this tutorial introduction will give the reader a basic idea of how digital signal processing techniques can be used to perform the function of a digital exciter. There

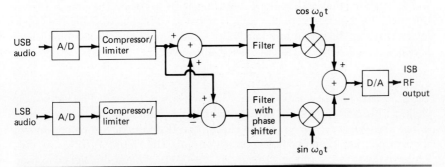

Figure 7.9 Block diagram of ISB exciter with common filters.

are, of course, many different ways of developing a digital exciter. For example, the filtering rather than phasing technique can be used to generate the SSB signal. The signals can then be filtered at an intermediate digital frequency rather than at baseband. The latter implementation does not require the use of 90° phase shifters, so that the use of IIR filters is more convenient. Several techniques which can be used to develop signals for a four-channel SSB exciter are also discussed in Sec. 7.9.

A digital SSB receiver can also be designed in many different ways, and the reader is cautioned not to assume that the methods described here are optimum for all applications. Again, the approaches can be divided into phasing methods and filtering methods to separate the sidebands. As with the digital exciters the phasing methods become more practical using digital techniques because good broadband phase shifters can be realized and amplitude balance is not upset by the digital system. Systems using FIR or IIR filters can be used; however, FIR filters are easier to design if a 90° phase shifter is to be included. FIR filters can also be designed without differential time delay, which may be an advantage for data transmission.

At the present time one of the most severe limitations on digital receivers is the limited precision in the analog-to-digital converters. Although 16-bit precision is practical within digital processors at the time of this writing, 8- to 12-bit converters, depending on the sampling speed, must be used to digitize the analog signal. This limitation dictates to a considerable extent the present configuration of digital receivers. It is anticipated that as the state of the art improves, sampling will progressively move closer to the antenna port of the receiver. The economics of currently available processors which are competitive with analog techniques also seriously limit the bandwidth of practical digital filters. This imposes a further constraint on the configuration of the receiver and also dictates the use of a fairly sharp analog filter preceding the A/D.

The AGC system of a digital receiver is severely impacted by the limited dynamic range of the A/D converter, and is discussed further in Sec. 7.6.

A block diagram of one implementation of a digital SSB receiver is shown in Fig. 7.10. The function of analog-to-digital conversion using IF sampling is discussed in Sec. 7.2 and will not be described here other than to indicate that IF sampling allows the sampling rate to be determined by the bandwidth of the signal rather than requiring it to be twice the actual IF frequency. The digitized signal is then translated to baseband using the translation theorem discussed previously in this section. Since the sampled signal is real, translation requires only two multipliers:

$$x(n)e^{j\omega_0 t} = x(n) \cos \omega_0 t + jx(n) \sin \omega_0 t \tag{7.7}$$

Thus $I = x(n) \cos \omega_0 t$ and $Q = x(n) \sin \omega_0 t$, where $t = nT$. The value ω_0 is chosen to beat the center of the desired sideband to zero (not the frequency of the carrier). It is convenient to choose the IF frequency to be one-fourth the sample rate. Then $\cos \omega_0 nT$ takes on only the values 1, 0, -1, 0, etc., while $\sin \omega_0 nt$ takes on the values 0, 1, 0, -1, etc. The multipliers can then be replaced by inverters and multiplexers.

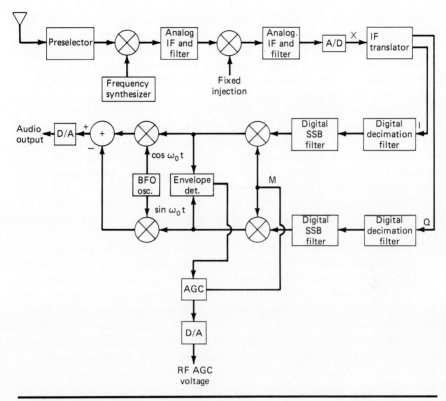

Figure 7.10 Block diagram of digital SSB receiver.

The sampling rate should now be reduced to the lowest possible value prior to narrowband filtering. This minimizes the number of taps required in the SSB filters. This is accomplished by the decimation filter, which reduces the bandwidth to perhaps 8 kHz. A 16-kHz sample rate can then be used in the narrow SSB filters. If FIR filters are used, approximately 64 taps are required to obtain a good passband response. In this case the I and Q filters are identical since no 90° phase shifter is required. The level of the signal is next adjusted by the AGC multiplier M, and the BFO beats the signal up in frequency by the amount that it was beat below zero in the IF translator. A value of the order of 1700 Hz is appropriate for voice bandwidth signals. Since a real output signal is required, again, only two multipliers are required for the translator. The digital BFO oscillator must generate both $\cos \omega nT$ and $\sin \omega nT$. An accumulator keeps track of the accumulated phase value $\theta(n + 1) = \theta(n) + \Delta$, where $\theta = \omega nT$. Δ determines the BFO frequency. A lookup table for the sine and cosine along with an interpolation routine can be used to find the actual values. The AGC may be quite complex because of the limited dynamic range of the A/D, as discussed previously.

The block diagram in Fig. 7.10 shows a single-channel SSB receiver. Recall that in this case the frequency synthesizer is programmed to beat the desired sideband below baseband so that the signal occupies a frequency range of about ± 1.4 kHz, and the I and Q filters are identical. Another implementation is also possible in which the carrier frequency is at zero and the USB corresponds to positive frequencies while the LSB corresponds to negative frequencies. This implementation is more conducive to building an independent sideband receiver.

A block diagram of an ISB SSB receiver is shown in Fig. 7.11. Here the SSB filter in the Q channel includes a 90° phase shifter. The outputs of the filters can then be subtracted to extract the upper sideband and added to extract the lower sideband. The AGC is not shown here and is considerably more complex than the signal-channel AGC. This results since two AGC detectors are desirable with separate digital gain multipliers. A single RF gain control voltage must be used which is determined by the larger of the ISB signals.

It should be pointed out that the information presented here is tutorial in nature and that considerably more in-depth knowledge is required to design digital SSB equipment. Indeed, unexpected results often occur as a result of aliasing, quantization effects, nonlinearities, etc., and a thorough analysis and simulation is recommended prior to undertaking the design of digital SSB equipment.

The sections following in this chapter will explain more thoroughly some of the concepts, limitations, and advantages of digital signal processing.

7.2   Sampling and Data Conversion

Since the input and output signals of most radio communications systems are analog, the first and last steps in a digital radio must be converting between analog and digital forms. At the RF side of this transformation,

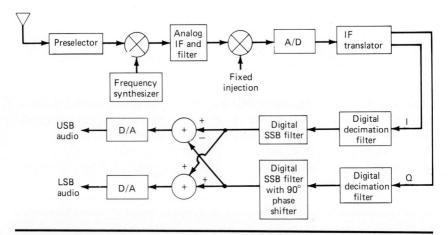

Figure 7.11 Block diagram of independent-sideband receiver.

there are stringent demands for linearity and dynamic range. In the transmitter, the modulated digital RF or IF signal must be converted to analog form with very low distortion and noise so as not to contaminate the radio frequency spectrum with unwanted emissions which destroy the usefulness of other channels. In the receiver, the wideband analog RF or IF signal must be converted to digital form without introducing noise and distortion which will fall back on the desired signal channel and make it unusable. To maintain good orthogonality between assigned frequency channels, both in the transmitter and the receiver, requires extremely good linearity and resolution in the RF or IF A/D and D/A converters. Indeed, the linearity and resolution of high-speed A/D and D/A converters presently limit the achievable performance of digital radios. They are by far the most critical subsystems in digital radio implementations, and it is therefore often necessary to reduce the bandwidth and range of signal amplitudes at the RF/IF analog-to-digital interface by analog RF/IF signal conditioning.

The sampling theorem

"Sampling" refers to the process of periodically extracting the value of the analog waveform. Once the analog value is extracted, it must be converted to a digital value or number (A/D conversion) that can be processed mathematically.

In order to understand the sampling theorem, we consider a special type of sampling, namely, impulse sampling. Impulse sampling replaces the continuous analog signal by a train of impulses occurring at the sample times, with the area or "weight" of each impulse equal to the original signal amplitude at those sample times. This process can be described by the following equation:

$$s(t) = x(t)i(t) \tag{7.8}$$

where $x(t)$ is the original continuous signal, and $i(t)$ is the impulse train given by

$$i(t) = \sum_{k=-\infty}^{\infty} \delta(t - kT) \tag{7.9}$$

The sampled signal is simply the original signal multiplied by a train of unit impulses, and results in the convolution of the two corresponding frequency spectra. Figure 7.12 shows the frequency spectrum of a unit impulse train consisting of equispaced frequency δ functions, an arbitrary bandlimited signal spectrum, and the resulting spectrum from the convolution of the two. We can see that the bandlimited signal spectrum repeats at every multiple of the sample frequency which is the reciprocal of impulse train period. The information contained in any one of these frequency bands is sufficient to describe the input signal.

If the sampling frequency in the example shown in Fig. 7.12 is reduced, a

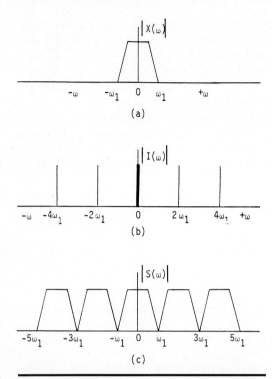

Figure 7.12 Frequency domain illustration of the impulse sampling process: (*a*) bandlimited signal spectrum; (*b*) unit impulse train spectrum; (*c*) spectra resulting from the convolution of (*a*) and (*b*).

distortion due to aliasing results. Figure 7.13 illustrates this effect. Aliasing distortion occurs when the corresponding frequency spectra overlap. This distortion cannot be removed once it has occurred, and must be avoided or reduced to an acceptable level in practice.

This brings us to the result of the sampling theorem. That is, the sampling frequency must be at least twice the bandwidth of the desired signal to avoid aliasing distortion and loss of information due to the sampling process. Sampling at twice the bandwidth of the desired signal is said to be "sampling at the Nyquist rate." In practice, it is usually necessary to sample at a rate somewhat higher than the Nyquist rate to allow for finite transition bandwidths in the antialias filters.

Bandpass and harmonic sampling

Digital radio implementations typically require the sampling of a receiver intermediate frequency signal. Assuming the IF has been bandlimited by a filter of some type, as indicated in Fig. 7.14*a*, it is not necessary to sample this IF at twice the highest frequency component of the signal, although there may be advantages in doing so. If the IF band is located between adjacent integer multiples of the total IF bandwidth, the sample frequency is only required to be twice the bandwidth of this signal (which can be considerably less than the highest-frequency component). Under these conditions bandpass or harmonic sampling can be used to efficiently digitize the IF signal. If the IF band does not fall within the above constraint, bandpass sampling can still be used, but the sample frequency will necessarily be greater than twice the IF bandwidth to prevent aliasing.

Bandpass or harmonic sampling is simply the result of the convolution of the IF frequency spectrum with the spectrum associated with the repetitive sampling impulse, as shown in Fig. 7.14b. The sampled baseband output spectrum will be an undistorted representation of the IF signal provided there is no aliasing. Aliasing is avoided as long as the IF spectra of Fig. 7.14c do not overlap.

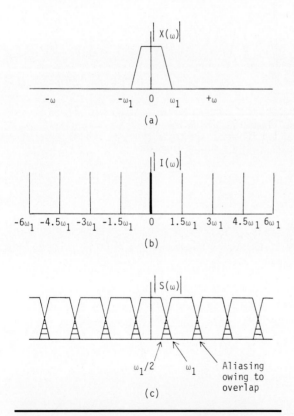

Figure 7.13 Frequency domain illustration of aliasing: (a) bandlimited signal spectrum; (b) unit impulse train spectrum; (c) overlapping spectra resulting from the convolution of (a) and (b).

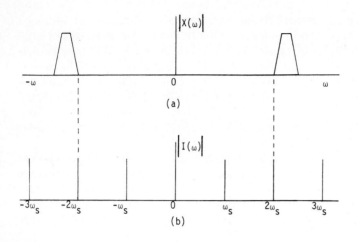

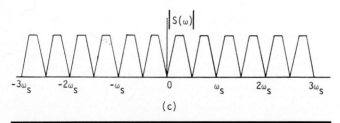

Figure 7.14 Frequency domain illustration of the harmonic sampling process: (*a*) bandlimited IF signal spectrum; (*b*) sampling sequence spectrum; (*c*) spectra resulting from the convolution of (*a*) and (*b*).

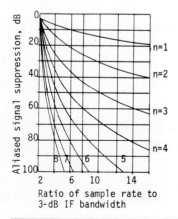

Figure 7.15 Minimum aliased signal suppression vs. the ratio of sampling frequency to 3-dB low-pass filter bandwidth. The parameter *n* is the number of poles required for a 1-dB ripple Chebyshev filter.

Antialias filter requirements

An antialias filter is required to bandlimit the input signal prior to sampling. A filter is also required following D/A conversion. In a digital transceiver, these filters may be a bidirectional IF filter and an active audio output or microphone input filter. In order to avoid aliasing completely, a filter with infinite out-of-band rejection would be required. With all practical filters, only finite out-of-band rejection can be obtained. A curve of minimum suppression of an out-of-band aliased signal as a function of the sample frequency and the number of poles in the antialias filter is shown in Fig. 7.15. Note that even with an eight-pole, 1-dB ripple, Chebyshev filter, the sample frequency must be 4 times the 3-dB bandwidth or twice the Nyquist rate for 80-dB suppression. Thus, regardless of how good the digital filtering is that follows, the filter must be very good if the sample frequency is to be kept within a factor of 2 of the Nyquist rate.

Data converters

The A/D converter is a device or functional block that accepts an analog value and produces its digital equivalent value. The D/A converter, on the other hand, performs the reverse operation. Many types of data converters are available to perform these operations, each with varying degrees of resolution, speed, and distortion.

Distortion sources in A/D and D/A converters

A/D and D/A converters introduce the following types of noise and distortion:

- Quantizing noise produced by an ideal quantizer
- Nonlinearities due to nonuniform quantizing step sizes
- Aliasing of signal frequencies which are outside of the Nyquist bandwidth (already discussed)
- Signal bandwidth spreading due to sampling aperture jitter
- Analog signal distortion due to nonlinear input or output impedance
- Digital noise pickup on the analog lead

Quantizing noise.   Quantizing noise is the most fundamental type of distortion in a data converter. The total quantizing noise N_q for an ideal converter is

$$N_q = \frac{\Delta^2}{12R} = \frac{(V_{pp}/2^b)^2}{12R} \quad \text{watts} \tag{7.10}$$

where Δ is the voltage step size, R is the input resistance, V_{pp} is the peak-to-peak voltage range, and b is the number of bits of resolution.

Ideally, this noise is spread uniformly over the Nyquist bandwidth of $f_s/2$ where f_s is the sample rate and the quantizing noise density N_{0q} is therefore

$$N_{0q} = \frac{N_q}{f_s/2} = \frac{(V_{pp}/2^b)^2}{6f_sR} \qquad \text{watts/hertz} \tag{7.11}$$

The decrease in noise density with increasing sample rate is shown in Fig. 7.16. Thus, the quantizing noise density decreases by 6 dB for every bit of resolution added to the converters and by 3 dB for every doubling of the sample rate. The signal-to-noise ratio can be increased by increasing the sample rate and then digitally filtering the signal back to the bandwidth corresponding to a lower sampling rate. This is called "oversampling."

The maximum sine wave signal power $S_{\max}$ that the converter can handle without overload is

$$S_{\max} = \frac{\frac{1}{2}(V_{pp}/2)^2}{R} = \frac{\frac{1}{8}V_{pp}^2}{R} \qquad \text{watts} \tag{7.12}$$

The maximum signal-to-noise ratio is therefore

$$\frac{S_{\max}}{N_q} = \frac{3}{2}\,2^{2b}$$
$$= 6.02b + 1.75 \qquad \text{dB} \tag{7.13}$$

A useful measure of normalized dynamic range is the maximum sine wave signal-to-quantizing-noise density ratio given by

$$\frac{S_{\max}}{N_{0q}} = \frac{3}{4}\,2^{2b}f_s$$
$$= 6.02b + 10\log_{10}(f_s) - 1.25 \qquad \text{dB} \tag{7.14}$$

The conventional definition of dynamic range is the normalized dynamic range $(S_{\max}/N_{0q})$ divided by the IF passband bandwidth. Figures 7.17 and 7.18 show the sine wave signal-to-quantizing-noise ratio and the normalized dynamic range for ideal converters.

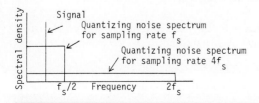

Figure 7.16 Reduction in quantizing noise density by oversampling.

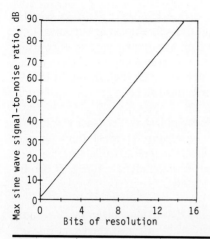

Figure 7.17 Maximum sine wave signal-to-quantizing-noise ratios for ideal data converters.

Nonlinearities. In practice, data converter quantizing steps are not of equal size, and this nonlinearity increases the quantizing noise and introduces discrete distortion products. Not only does this increase the amount of noise, but much of the distortion producing noise will be concentrated in discrete low-order distortion products. The type and amount of distortion depend on the type of converter and on the tolerances of the various converter components.

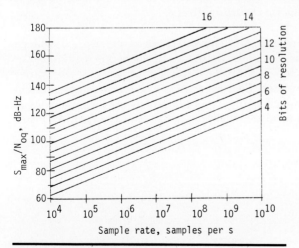

Figure 7.18 Normalized dynamic range vs. sampling rate for various sizes of data converters.

Nonlinearity correction.   The nonlinear A/D converter distortion can be reduced by using lookup table correction at the A/D converter output so that the true mean or center value of the analog quantizing step is outputted when the input voltage falls in this range. This arrangement is shown in Fig. 7.19. Note that the lookup table must be driven by all the bits out of the A/D converter, but that the table output words need to have greater resolution than the A/D converter.

The least significant bit must have less weight than the least significant bit of the A/D output, while the most significant bit must have enough weight to correct the largest error. In general, the lookup table must be continuously updated to correct for temperature-dependent errors and can be implemented by random access memory (RAM).

Aperture jitter.   In addition to the noise and distortion caused by the quantizing amplitude errors, there is noise induced by jitter at the exact instant of sampling. This source of distortion is called "aperture jitter," and causes, in effect, phase modulation of the received waveform. If the jitter or error in the sampling instant is independent from sample to sample, a sine wave component in the signal generates a white noise component in the output. The ratio of the sine wave signal power (C) to the aperture noise density that it generates (N_{0a}) is

$$\frac{C}{N_{0a}} = \frac{f_s}{8\pi^2 f_0^2 \sigma_a^2} \tag{7.15}$$

where f_s is the sampling frequency, f_0 is the signal frequency, and σ_a is the rms time jitter in the sampling (see Ref. 6). This is also of the form of the normalized dynamic range usually expressed in dB-Hz. Note that this normalized dynamic range is inversely proportional to the square of both the signal frequency f_0 and the rms aperture jitter σ_a.

Parametric distortion.   In flash A/D converters, there are $2^b - 1$ voltage comparators driven in parallel by the input signal, where b is the number of bits of resolution. These comparators have an input capacitance that varies with the applied signal voltage. Because there are so many comparators in parallel, the input capacitance is quite large and can distort the input voltage waveform significantly unless the driving impedance of the flash A/D con-

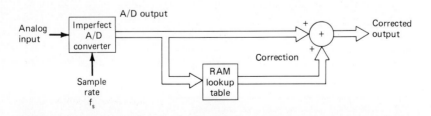

Figure 7.19   Block diagram of A/D converter with linearity correction.

verter-driving amplifier is quite low. Therefore, low-impedance A/D converter-driving amplifiers are generally required.

Converter noise.   For high-resolution A/D converters, the smallest quantizing step size is frequently so small that the noise figure of the voltage comparators becomes an issue. For example, consider an A/D converter with 16 bits of resolution, a peak-to-peak range of 2 V, and an input impedance of 50 ohms. The mean square noise contributed by the smallest quantizing step is −88 dBm. If the comparators have a bandwidth of 50 MHz and a noise figure of 10 dB, the thermal noise at the comparator input is −88 dBm or just equal to the quantizing noise. Thus, it is very difficult to design high-speed, single-stage A/D converters with high resolution, even considering only the noise figure problems in the voltage comparators. This problem is partially solved by the use of multistage A/D converters.

D/A converter zero-order hold distortion.   Most D/A converters are zero-order hold devices. That is, the analog output of the converter is held at a level corresponding to a digital value applied to the converter for an entire sample period. A zero-order hold D/A converter has a frequency response of

$$|H(\omega)| = \left| \frac{\sin(\omega T_s/2)}{\omega T_s/2} \right| \qquad (7.16)$$

where T_s is the hold period or the reciprocal of the sample frequency. This results in a gradual output frequency rolloff which may not be desirable in certain instances. For example, if the output passband width is one-fourth the sample frequency, a passband tilt of approximately 1 dB must be tolerated. This rolloff can be eliminated by adding a digital compensation filter prior to D/A conversion. The compensation filter frequency response must be

$$\frac{1}{|H(\omega)|} = \left| \frac{\omega T_s/2}{\sin(\omega T_s/2)} \right| \qquad (7.17)$$

over the desired frequency range.

Impulse sampling of the D/A converter output can also be used to reduce the hold period and consequently the rolloff. Although the rolloff in the desired passband region is reduced, this method increases the high-frequency content of the D/A converter output and places more stringent requirements on the output filter.

7.3   Sampling Rate Reduction

Sampling at a high rate is often advantageous because it reduces the requirements of the antialiasing filter preceding the A/D converter. It also reduces the quantization noise density from the A/D converter. In cases of this type it is advantageous to reduce the sample rate prior to narrowband filtering.

It is also often advantageous to perform filtering in several stages, reducing the sample rate between stages as the bandwidth is reduced.

Reducing the sampling rate is often referred to as "decimation." The rate of reduction is normally done in integer values and is equivalent to resampling the signal at a lower rate. This results in the spectrum being repeated at harmonics of the lower sample frequency, and consequently the bandwidth must be reduced to half the lower sampling frequency prior to decimation. This is illustrated in Fig. 7.20. Figure 7.20b shows the input spectrum which repeats at intervals of $3f_0$. The decimation filter which operates at the higher sample frequency eliminates the frequency components above $f_0/2$ so that aliasing will not occur after the sample rate is reduced. The out-

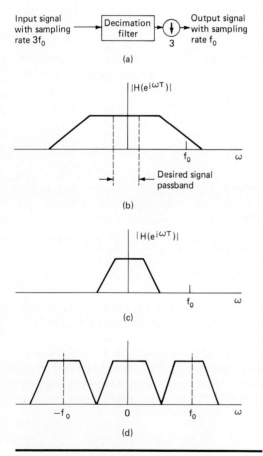

Figure 7.20 (a) Block diagram of decimation filter; (b) frequency spectrum of input signal; (c) frequency response of decimation filter; (d) frequency response of output signal.

put signal can now be further filtered with sample rate f_0, which requires less computation. Decimation is particularly effective for FIR filters since only the output samples which are actually used need to be computed.

Occasionally it occurs that a signal is grossly oversampled to reduce the quantization noise associated with an A/D converter. A very simple FIR decimation filter can then sometimes be used in which all the multiplier coefficients are unity. Only an adder, accumulator, and counter are required to implement a filter of this type, called a "boxcar filter," as shown in Fig. 7.21.

The Z transform of a box car filter is given by

$$H(Z) = \sum_{k=0}^{N} h(k)Z^{-1} = \frac{Z^{-N} - 1}{Z^{-1} - 1} \tag{7.18}$$

and the frequency response is

$$|H(e^{j\omega T})| = \left| \frac{\sin(\omega NT/2)}{\sin(\omega T/2)} \right| \tag{7.19}$$

where T is the input sample period.

7.4 Digital Filtering

The use of digital filtering is one of the major reasons for using digital signal processing techniques in single-sideband equipment, and digital filters offer several significant advantages over analog filters. One of the most obvious is that once the filter is designed each unit performs identically, which eliminates the tuning, tweaking, and testing often required for analog filters. In addition, since the characteristics of the digital filters are determined by the values of the multipliers in the program, it is possible to store the values for many filter bandwidths in a given processor or even to download the coefficients when it is desired to change the filter bandwidth.

Another advantage, in some cases, if FIR filters are used is that the filters can be designed with no differential time delay. This is discussed further in the following section. Finally, because there is no production variation, it is possible to consider filter types which are difficult to handle with analog techniques because of component tolerances.

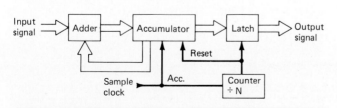

Figure 7.21 Block diagram of box car filter.

FIR filtering

A finite impulse response filter transfer function consists of only zeros, compared with the pole-zero structure of infinite impulse response filters. The transfer function of the FIR filter has the form

$$H(Z) = \sum_{n=0}^{N-1} h(n)Z^{-n} \qquad (7.20)$$

where $h(n)$ is the impulse response represented by N coefficients of the filter. A block diagram of two equivalent forms of FIR filters is shown in Fig. 7.22. Since the current filter output depends only on a finite number of past and present input values, it is sometimes referred to as a "tapped delay line filter" or a "transversal filter."

FIR filters have several advantages which make them a good choice in digital transceivers. Computer tools are available to readily design FIR filters with arbitrary frequency or time response characteristics (see Ref. 7). The filters are normally designed to have symmetrical or antisymmetrical coefficients about the center of the filter. This is a sufficient condition to produce a filter with no delay distortion. Since there is no feedback, the filters are absolutely stable, and there are no limit cycles. Furthermore, the absence of feedback results in a considerable computational savings if the sample frequency is to be decimated following the filter, since only the output samples required at the decimated rate need be computed.

It is relatively easy to incorporate a Hilbert Transformer in an FIR filter so that the phase of the output is shifted by 90° from a similar filter without a Hilbert Transformer. This allows phasing of the signals to generate or demodulate single-sideband signals.

It can be shown that if the impulse response of a low-pass filter is $h_{\mathrm{LP}}(t)$,

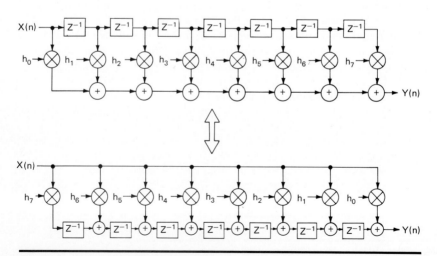

Figure 7.22 Equivalent FIR filter structures.

with a frequency response $H_{LP}(f)$, the frequency response of a filter with an impulse response $h_{LP}(t) \cos \omega_0 t$ or $h_{LP}(t) \sin \omega_0 t$ is given by

$$|H_{BP}(f)| = \tfrac{1}{2}|H_{LP}(f - f_0)| + \tfrac{1}{2}|H_{LP}(f + f_0)| \tag{7.21}$$

which is a bandpass filter centered at f_0. The phase response of the filter obtained by multiplying the impulse response by $\sin \omega_0 t$ is 90° out-of-phase from the filter obtained by multiplying by $\cos \omega_0 t$. Since the impulse response of an FIR filter consists of N coefficients, $h(n)$, these values can be multiplied by

$$\sin \omega_0 \left(n - \frac{N}{2} + \frac{1}{2} \right) T_s \qquad \text{or} \qquad \cos \omega_0 \left(n - \frac{N}{2} + \frac{1}{2} \right) T_s$$

for $n = 0, 1, \ldots, N - 1$, to perform the transformation where T_s is the sample time.

Thus a pair of filters can be designed for the I and Q channels in a digital transceiver which includes a Hilbert Transformer. Using a design program, such as that described in Ref. 7, it is also possible to design an FIR filter simply to implement a Hilbert Transformer.

The primary disadvantage of FIR filters is that a large number of taps can be required to achieve a sharp cutoff. The approximate number of taps required by a particular design can be estimated (see Refs. 5 and 12) by the equation

$$N = \frac{-10 \log_{10} (\delta_1 \delta_2) - 15}{14 F_T / F_s} + 1 \tag{7.22}$$

where N = number of taps
$\quad F_T$ = transition bandwidth
$\quad F_s$ = sample rate
$\quad \delta_1$ = passband peak per unit ripple voltage
$\quad \delta_2$ = stopband voltage attenuation

After the number of taps is estimated and the full precision filter coefficients are computed by the design program, overflow scaling and quantization effects must be evaluated. Overflow scaling is required in most filter designs implemented in fixed-point signal processors. For example, a typical processor might be capable of representing numbers from $+1$ to -1 in 16-bit 2's complement fractional form. In these implementations, care must be taken to avoid intermediate or final values in the overall computation that exceed ± 1. Even though a particular filter design produces a maximum sine wave gain of 1 throughout the passband, the filter output can often exceed a value of ± 1 for arbitrary input waveforms. This is especially true in very-high-performance sharp-transition bandwidth filters such as SSB filters. In general, the worst-case gain is computed by summing the absolute value of all the filter coefficients:

$$\text{Worst-case gain} = \sum_{n=0}^{N-1} |h(n)| \tag{7.23}$$

To prevent overflow, all the coefficients can be scaled so that the worst-case gain is slightly less than unity, or the filter input value can be scaled by the reciprocal of the worst-case gain. Both of these methods result in some degradation of the overall signal-to-noise ratio because of quantization effects, since the maximum sine wave signal power through the filter has been reduced.

There are three primary quantization effects which can affect the performance of the FIR filter. Input quantization noise is determined by the input data word length and the signal level through the FIR filter delay registers. This noise is white and uniformly distributed over the Nyquist bandwidth. It is computed in the same way that the A/D converter noise is computed. That is, the total input quantizing noise σ_i^2 is

$$\sigma_i^2 = \frac{\Delta_i^2}{12R} \qquad \text{watts} \tag{7.24}$$

where Δ is the resolution determined by the value of the least significant bit of the fixed-point word and R is the assumed resistance. This noise is directly affected by the overflow scaling method.

Roundoff noise is another quantization effect and is a result of errors in the filter computation due to truncations following the coefficient multiplications and the final filter output accumulation. It is uniformly distributed white noise and is, therefore, computed as above. For example, if each multiplication is truncated, in an N-tap filter, the total roundoff noise is

$$\sigma_r^2 = \frac{N\Delta_r^2}{12R} \qquad \text{watts} \tag{7.25}$$

where Δ_r is the minimum step size following the truncation.

Many digital multiplier/accumulators today provide a very large accumulator word length so that full precision products can be accumulated. In this case, σ_r^2 is zero and the roundoff noise corresponds to a single filter output truncation such that

$$\sigma_a^2 = \frac{\Delta_a^2}{12R} \qquad \text{watts} \tag{7.26}$$

The maximum signal-to-quantization-noise ratio of the FIR filter is then $S_{\max}/N_q$, where $S_{\max}$ is the maximum sine wave signal power determined by the input level and the gain of the overflow scaled filters and N_q is the total noise power consisting of σ_r^2 or σ_a^2 and that portion of σ_i^2 which is not attenuated by the filter.

The final quantization effect, coefficient quantization, is a function of many filter design variables and is difficult to predict. Coefficient quantization does not add to the overall noise power of the filter, but does affect the overall response of the filter.

Since the filter coefficients are represented by a finite number of bits in a particular machine implementation, the filter's impulse response and consequently the frequency response will be affected. In some cases, a high-performance SSB filter's stopband requirements may not be met in a fixed-point implementation without factoring the filter into smaller cascade filters requiring less stopband attenuation in each of the cascade sections.

The frequency response of a 64-tap SSB filter, operating at a 16-kilosample/s rate and using 16-bit coefficient values, is shown in Fig. 7.23. Figure 7.24 shows the same filter response when the filter coefficients are reduced to 13-bit precision. Note that the original 60-dB stopband requirements cannot be met by the reduced coefficient filter.

If the original N-tap filter transfer function is factored so that zeros can be optimally paired to break the original filter into two or more cascade sections, the coefficient quantization effect can be reduced with a slight increase in roundoff noise resulting from an additional accumulator truncation for each section. In general, the polynomial of order $N - 1$ is factored using a good root-finder program. The roots are then grouped to evenly distribute each filter section's gain and response requirements, and the new coefficients are calculated. The factoring procedure results in an overall increase of one tap computation for a total of $N + 1$ taps compared to the original filter's N taps.

Infinite impulse response filters

Infinite impulse response filters are distinguished from FIR filters in that feedback is present. This results in the presence of poles in the transfer func-

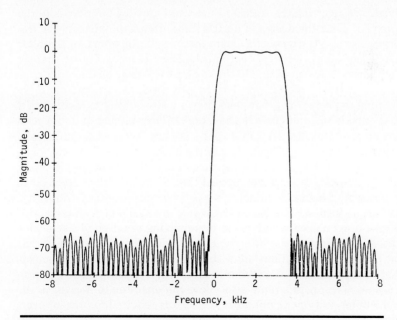

Figure 7.23 Computer-generated graph showing 64-tap sideband FIR filter response using 16-bit coefficients.

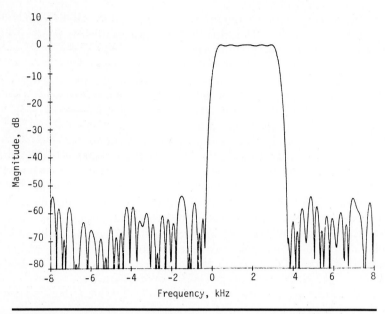

Figure 7.24 Computer-generated graph showing 64-tap sideband FIR filter response using 13-bit coefficients.

tion which are not present in FIR filters. Normally IIR transfer functions are derived by converting the transfer functions of analog filter types to the digital domain. Thus the design of an IIR filter often approximates the frequency response of a Butterworth, Chebyshev, or elliptic filter. An IIR filter can be designed to have a sharper cutoff frequency for a given order than an FIR filter; however, it has generally the same phase-delay characteristics as the analog filter from which it was derived. IIR filters tend to require more careful scaling to prevent overflow, and they are also subject to oscillation if any pole is outside the unit circle in the Z plane. The presence of limit cycles must also be carefully studied. Limit cycles are low-level oscillation usually in the order of the least significant bits of the digital word. IIR filters can be equalized if necessary to minimize the delay distortion. However, if this is required, the complexity may well exceed that of an FIR filter designed to perform the same function.

A number of excellent IIR design programs are available in the marketplace. These programs generally begin by inputting the desired filter characteristics and determine the filter type and order by interacting with the operator. Some of the programs allow the operator to determine the effects of truncated coefficients and arithmetic as well as to scale the filter to prevent overflow. Several programs also allow the operator to designate the order of the filter sections to minimize the scaling required to prevent overflow. Limit cycles are also identified in some cases.

It is not the purpose of this discussion to describe specific filter design programs or to redevelop the theory of IIR digital filter design, which is treated in a number of excellent texts (see, for example, Refs. 1 through 3) on the subject. A brief description of a common implementation of digital IIR filters is presented here, along with an overview of the bilinear transform method of converting an analog filter transfer function to a digital transfer function.

An analog low-pass filter transfer function of the Butterworth or Chebyshev type can generally be written in the form

$$H(S) = \frac{K}{S_p^n + a_1 S_p^{n-1} + a_2 S_p^{n-2} + \cdots + a_n} \tag{7.27}$$

Tables are available in the literature listing the coefficient values [1]. Standard methods are also given to convert the transfer functions to bandpass or bandstop filters.

Several methods can be used to approximate the digital transfer function $H(Z)$ from the analog transfer function $H(S)$. The most common of these are the impulse invariant method and the bilinear transform. The impulse invariant method guarantees that the digital filter will have the same impulse response as the analog filter at the sample times. Thus the digital filter also has the same phase response as the analog filter. This method is quite good so long as the frequencies of interest are well below half the sampling frequency. As this condition is approached, the frequency response of the digital filter deviates considerably from that of the analog filter. For this reason, the bilinear transform method is more widely used.

The bilinear transform produces considerably better results and is implemented by making the following substitution for S in the analog transfer function:

$$S = \frac{2}{T} \frac{Z - 1}{Z + 1} \tag{7.28}$$

It can also be shown that the digital frequency corresponding to a given analog frequency value is given by:

$$\omega_d = \frac{2}{T} \tan^{-1} \frac{\omega_a T}{2} \tag{7.29}$$

where T = sampling time
$\quad \omega_d$ = digital frequency
$\quad \omega_a$ = analog frequency

Thus, if a specific cutoff frequency is desired in the final digital filter, the analog filter from which the digital filter is realized must have a cutoff frequency given by

$$\omega_a = \frac{2}{T} \tan \frac{\omega_d T}{2} \tag{7.30}$$

A digital filter can be realized in many different configurations. In general the overflow characteristics are different for each configuration and it may be worthwhile to investigate the scaling requirements of several configurations. Among the configurations used are the direct form, the canonic form, the cascade form, and the parallel form. Block diagrams for these forms are given in the references cited. The transfer functions are of the form:

$$H(Z) = \frac{a_0 + a_1 Z^{-1} + a_2 Z^{-2} + a_3 Z^{-3} + a_4 Z^{-4}}{1 + b_1 Z^{-1} + b_2 Z^{-2} + b_3 Z^{-3} + b_4 Z^{-4}} \tag{7.31}$$

Often the transfer function is factored into two-pole sections, as given below, and implemented as cascaded bi-quad sections such as shown in Fig. 7.25 using the canonic form (this configuration tends to be more tolerant of truncated arithmetic than a single realization of the entire filter):

$$H(Z) = \left[\frac{a_{10} + a_{11} Z^{-1} + a_{12} Z^{-2}}{1 + b_{11} Z^{-1} + b_{12} Z^{-2}} \right] \left[\frac{a_{20} + a_{21} Z^{-1} + a_{22} Z^{-2}}{1 + b_{21} Z^{-1} + b_{22} Z^{-2}} \right] \tag{7.32}$$

A bi-quad section requires five multiplications and four additions which must be performed during each sample time. It should be noted that arithmetic overflow is a serious problem because, with 2's complement arithmetic, overflow from the largest positive number results in the largest negative number.

Optimum pairing of the poles and zeros of the transfer function can reduce the scaling required between sections to prevent overflow.

It should also be noted that since IIR filters utilize feedback, oscillation is possible if the poles are outside of the unit circle on the Z plane. Even for a stable filter, however, limit cycle oscillations can occur with truncated arithmetic. These low-level oscillations, which may be in the order of the least significant bits, result because for specific low-level signals the truncation results in a pole apparently moving to the unit circle causing oscillation. Information concerning limit cycles is given by several of the IIR filter design programs.

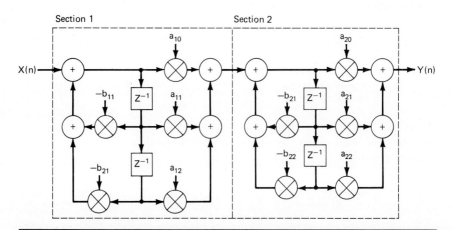

Figure 7.25 Block diagram of cascaded bi-quad filter sections.

7.5 SSB Detection

Product detectors

Conventional analog product detectors are heterodyne detectors (mixers) which combine two input signals (IF and BFO) to produce a difference frequency at audio or baseband. The sum frequency, IF, and BFO frequency are removed from the mixer output by relatively simple low-pass filters.

A single frequency component of an SSB signal, at complex baseband, can be represented as

$$Y(t) = Ae^{j\omega_0 t} = A(\cos \omega_0 t + j \sin \omega_0 t) = I(t) + jQ(t) \tag{7.33}$$

and as quadrature components

$$I(t) = \text{Re}\{Y(t)\} \tag{7.34}$$

$$Q(t) = \text{Im}\{Y(t)\} \tag{7.35}$$

In one implementation of a digital receiver, the desired sideband is translated to baseband and selected by filtering. The digital product detector must take the filtered complex baseband input, perform the BFO translation, and convert the complex result to real audio.

Complex signal translation can be accomplished by multiplying the input SSB signal $Y(t)$ by a complex BFO signal $e^{j\omega_b t}$ for USB or $e^{-j\omega_b t}$ for LSB and outputting only the real or imaginary part, as shown in Fig. 7.26. If $Y(t)$ is sampled at $t = nT_s$ at a rate $f_s = 1/T_s$:

$$f(nT) = [Ae^{j\omega_0 nT_s}][e^{\pm j\omega_b nT_s}] \tag{7.36}$$

$$= Ae^{j(\omega_0 \pm \omega_b)nT_s} = A[\cos(\omega_0 \pm \omega_b)nT_s + j \sin(\omega_0 \pm \omega_b)nT_s] \tag{7.37}$$

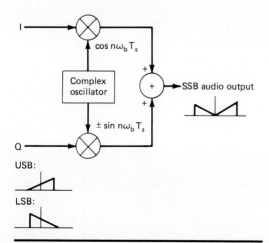

Figure 7.26 Digital product detector and BFO.

where

$$\mathrm{Re}\{f(nT)\} = A \cos(\omega_0 \pm \omega_b)nT_s \tag{7.38}$$

The analysis shown above illustrates the cancellation of the undesired mixer product (either the sum or difference) and assumes perfect amplitude and phase balances of the input and the BFO. However, there are always distortions which produce some errors in the amplitude or phase balance of both. This error results in imperfect cancellation of the undesired mixer product which shows up as a spurious distortion product. This distortion (see Ref. 8) can be expressed as the following ratio:

$$\frac{\text{Undesired product}}{\text{Desired product}} = \frac{a^2 + b^2 - 2ab \cos (\Delta + \delta)}{a^2 + b^2 + 2ab \cos (\Delta - \delta)} \tag{7.39}$$

where a and b are proportionality constants such that the in-phase input I can be modeled as aI and the quadrature component Q can be modeled as bQ (these constants take into account amplitude imbalance in both the input signal and the digital BFO signal), Δ is the BFO phase error (relative to 90°), and δ is the input phase error between I and Q components (relative to 90°).

In general, the amplitude and phase balances of the complex input can be made nearly perfect by proper digital design. However, any error in the BFO algorithms will contribute to amplitude and phase imbalances, and the algorithm complexity will increase as the required distortion levels decrease. Two BFO algorithms are presented below. Each has advantages and disadvantages in terms of speed, memory requirements, and accuracy which must be weighed in each machine implementation.

BFO generation

One method of implementing a complex oscillator for digital BFO generation uses a phase accumulator driving a sine and cosine algorithm or generator. The output of the sine and cosine algorithm is then the sin $\omega_b nT$ and cos $\omega_b nT$ values which are used in the product detector, as shown in Fig. 7.26.

The phase accumulator represents the $\omega_b nT$ modulo 2π quantity used to compute sin $\omega_b nT$ and cos $\omega_b nT$. The value is obtained by simply incrementing a phase angle θ by an amount Δ at each sample time. If the sample frequency is f_s,

$$\Delta = \frac{2\pi f_b}{f_s} \quad \text{radians} \tag{7.40}$$

A sine and cosine generator can be implemented using lookup tables and interpolation. The following algorithm utilizes the trigonometric identities below to provide the required complex oscillator outputs:

$$\sin (A + \delta) = \sin A \cos \delta + \cos A \sin \delta \tag{7.41}$$

and

$$\cos (A + \delta) = \cos A \cos \delta - \sin A \sin \delta \tag{7.42}$$

If δ is made small, the following approximations can be made:

$$\sin (A + \delta) \simeq \sin A + \delta \cos A \tag{7.43}$$

and

$$\cos (A + \delta) \simeq \cos A - \delta \sin A \tag{7.44}$$

The sine and cosine generators use the above approximation and identity to calculate

$$\sin (X) = \sin (Y) + \delta \cos (Y) \tag{7.45}$$

and

$$\cos (X) = \cos (Y) - \delta \sin (Y) \tag{7.46}$$

where

$$X = \omega_b nT \tag{7.47}$$

$$Y = \text{nearest quantized lookup table value less than } \omega_b nT \tag{7.48}$$

and

$$\delta = X - Y \tag{7.49}$$

In general, it is desirable to limit the size of the lookup table. The algorithm presented normalizes the input angle $(0 \le \theta \le \pi/2)$ and corrects the sign of the sine or cosine after computation by using the following rule:

$$\text{Sign of sin } (\omega_b nT) = \text{sign of } \omega_b nT \tag{7.50}$$

and

$$\text{Sign of cos } (\omega_b nT) = \text{sign of } \left\{ \frac{\pi}{2} - \text{ABS}(\omega_b nT) \right\} ; \ -\pi < \omega_b nT \le \pi \tag{7.51}$$

where ABS is the absolute value. A single table can be used for both sine and cosine functions since $\cos \theta$ is equal to $\sin (\pi/2 - \theta)$ over the range $0 \le \theta \le \pi/2$.

The distortion performance for several table sizes are shown in Table 7.1. The distortion values listed were computed assuming a complex translator implementation where both sine and cosine envelope and phase error values are taken into account.

TABLE 7.1   Distortion Performance of Translator Using Trigonometric Approximated Sine and Cosine Generators ($\pi/2$ Normalization)

sin/cos Table length N	Total translator distortion	
	dB	%
4	-28	4
8	-40	1
16	-52	0.25
32	-64	0.06
64	-76	0.016
128	-88	0.004

The sine and cosine generator can also be implemented without large lookup tables by using an algorithm based on a series expansion. The method is characterized by an increase in accuracy as the number of terms in the series increases and requires a normalization of the input angle and a sign correction after the sine and cosine are computed, as described previously.

The most common series expansion is the Maclaurin series, which is just a special case (expansion about zero) of the familiar Taylor's power series as illustrated below:

$$\sin (x) = x - \frac{1}{3!} x^3 + \frac{1}{5!} x^5 - \frac{1}{7!} x^7 + \cdots \tag{7.52}$$

$$\cos (x) = 1 - \frac{1}{2!} x^2 + \frac{1}{4!} x^4 - \frac{1}{6!} x^6 + \cdots \tag{7.53}$$

As the angle increases, the error increases rapidly. The distortion performance for several expansion lengths was calculated for a complex translator implementation and is summarized in Table 7.2.

7.6   Digital AGC Methods

Automatic gain control provides the same overall function in a digital receiver as in a purely analog receiver. However, there can be significant differences in the design approach used, because of receiver hardware differ-

TABLE 7.2   Distortion Performance of Translator Using MacLaurin Series Sine and Cosine Generators ($\pi/2$ Normalization)

Order of polynomial represented by series		Total translator distortion	
Sine	Cosine	dB	%
3	4	-28	4
5	6	-52	0.25
7	8	-82	0.008

ences. For instance, more gain is generally required before the digital IF filter in the digital receiver in order to drive the A/D converter at a satisfactory level. This means that appreciable AGC must be applied before the digital IF filter. In addition, because of the envelope delay associated with a high-performance digital filter, special techniques must be used to provide an AGC with adequate speed, while still controlling overshoot. A digital receiver block diagram illustrating a typical AGC processor interconnection was shown in Fig. 7.10.

The AGC processor operates on the digital IF signal components to provide a desired gain control value to a D/A converter, which, in turn, controls the attenuators in the IF translator, and consequently the signal level at the A/D converter. It also provides a digital gain multiplier to control the signal level at the audio output D/A converter.

The desired receiver gain distribution, or analog vs. digital receiver gain, is selected on the basis of a system level analysis. The maximum analog translator gain must be great enough so that the quantizing noise of the A/D converter does not degrade the receiver noise figure or sensitivity below the desired limit. As the signal level increases above the sensitivity level, the analog gain should not be decreased by AGC action until an adequate signal-to-noise ratio is obtained. As the signal level increases still further, the analog AGC should hold the signal level at the A/D converter essentially constant. In addition, adequate "headroom" at the A/D converter and D/A converter must be provided to avoid saturation during normally high peak-to-average-voltage ratio periods of the desired signal.

Strong signals which fall outside the narrowband digital filter bandwidth, but inside the analog IF translator bandwidths, can overload or saturate the A/D converter. This results in the generation of in-band intermodulation distortion products and can result in significant degradation of the desired signal. If large signal levels are detected at the A/D converter, the receiver gain may have to be redistributed by reducing the preconversion analog gain and increasing the digital gain to maintain the desired signal output level. This will, however, reduce the desired signal-to-quantization-noise ratio.

7.7 Digital Squelch

Chapter 6 presented various methods of implementing the SSB squelch function. Nearly any squelch which can be implemented with analog circuitry can also be implemented digitally since the bandwidths are relatively low and the filter requirements are generally modest. One of the advantages of digital signal processing may well prove to be the ability to realize a signal delay while the squelch decision is being made. This should allow a longer averaging time in the squelch detector without losing the first syllable of the message while the squelch decision is being made.

One of the more widely used squelch circuits for single sideband compares the energy in the lower and upper portions of the audio band, as indicated previously. A block diagram of this circuit, implemented digitally, is shown in Fig. 7.27. A two-pole low-pass filter with a 1.2-kHz cutoff may be appropriate, while the high-pass filter has a cutoff in the order of 1.8 kHz. Two FIR filters may be used. FIR filters have the advantage that the delayed signal is also available in the filter, eliminating the need for a separate delay. The Hilbert Transformer produces a 90° phase shift for the detectors. A transformer with 8 to 12 taps may suffice. The detectors perform an approximation of the function $\sqrt{I^2 + Q^2}$ by taking the absolute value of the larger of I or Q and adding 0.4 times the absolute value of the smaller. A smooth window function such as a Hamming window can be used as the squelch gate, or a simple on/off threshold can be used.

7.8 Speech Compression

Over the years there have been many approaches used to increase the effective "talk power" of SSB transmissions. Chapter 6 presented various methods of speech processing which can be used to accomplish this. Each approach has distinct advantages and disadvantages. From a performance viewpoint, RF speech processing has often provided the best results. A digital compressor can be implemented to operate on the instantaneous speech modulation envelope and provide the same effect as RF processing. The compressor time constants can be varied to provide speech compression or clipping. A block diagram of the compressor is shown in Fig. 7.28. The real audio input signal is phase-shifted 90° in the Hilbert Transformer so that the instantaneous envelope of the signal can be computed from the in-phase I and quadrature Q components. The envelope $E(n)$ is then used to generate a multiplier $M(n)$ which scales the delayed signal on a sample-by-sample basis.

A signal path delay is provided to prevent hard limiting during transient responses and thereby eliminate "clicks" normally encountered in closed-loop or analog systems.

The envelope detector can approximate the $\sqrt{I^2 + Q^2}$ by taking the absolute value of the larger of I or Q and adding 0.4 times the absolute value of

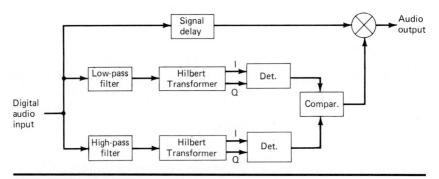

Figure 7.27 Block diagram of digital squelch.

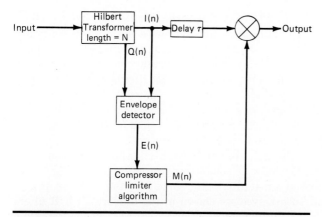

Figure 7.28 Block diagram of speech compressor/limiter processing.

the smaller. The compressor algorithm can adjust the multiplier value using the following recursive equation:

$$M(n) = [1 - K]M(n - 1) + \frac{KE_{\text{Desired}}}{E(n)} \qquad (7.54)$$

where K is a positive constant less than 1, $M(n - 1)$ is the previous multiplier value, and E_{Desired} is the desired output envelope level.

The time constant of the compressor is then

$$\text{TC} = -\frac{T_s}{\ln(1 - K)} \qquad (7.55)$$

where T_s is the sample period or $1/f_s$.

Thus the time constant can be varied by changing the factor K. As K tends toward 1, the time constant is reduced and the compressor will operate as a clipper. In general, the time constant must be somewhat larger than the Hilbert Transformer envelope delay of $N/2$ sample periods. A speech compressor requires a fast-attack, slow-release characteristic, and, thus, two values of K are used depending on whether the compressor multiplier is increasing or decreasing.

This example simply illustrates the advantage of digital signal processing in that flexibility is obtained by using sophisticated mathematical algorithms which are difficult to implement with analog circuitry.

7.9 SSB Modulation

SSB modulation techniques are discussed in detail in Chap. 4 and briefly in Sec. 7.1 using digital signal processing. These techniques as well as several others used to produce four-channel SSB are examined in more detail here.

SSB signals are often generated by filtering techniques in the analog domain because of the difficulty in obtaining wideband phase shifters and maintaining exact amplitude balance as required by phasing techniques. These limitations are largely overcome with digital systems, and consequently phasing methods for SSB generation tend to dominate with digital signal processing techniques.

The filtering techniques can, of course, also be implemented with digital filters; however, the processing load may be higher than for the phasing techniques. One of the basic methods of SSB generation is shown in Fig. 7.6. Here the signal is passed through two bandpass filters, one of which contains a 90° phase shift. Typical bandwidth characteristics are shown in Fig. 7.29a. The amplitude response of a real filter is the same for either positive or negative frequencies, and both halves are shown in the drawing. If FIR filters are used, it is convenient to begin with a low-pass filter as shown in Fig. 7.29b and transform it to a bandpass filter as described in Sec. 7.4. This can be accomplished by multiplying each of the low-pass coefficients $h(n)$ by a cosine function such that

$$h_c(n) = h(n) \cos \omega_0 \left(n - \frac{N}{2} + \frac{1}{2} \right) T_s \qquad n = 0, 1, \dots, N - 1 \qquad (7.56)$$

where ω_0 is the desired angular frequency shift. In this case $\omega_0 = 2\pi (1500)$. A companion filter which has a 90° phase offset relative to the first can be obtained by using a sine function multiplication, such that

$$h_s(n) = h(n) \sin \omega_0 \left(n - \frac{N}{2} + \frac{1}{2} \right) T_s \qquad n = 0, 1, \dots, N - 1 \qquad (7.57)$$

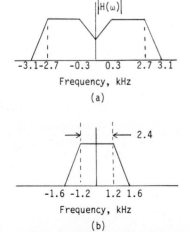

Figure 7.29 (a) Typical SSB filter characteristics; (b) low-pass source filter frequency response.

Care must be exercised in the low-frequency region if the filters are not used as a complex pair because the overall characteristic of each filter is produced by the overlapping positive and negative responses and the response at -300 Hz should be in the order of 60 dB down. The resulting I and Q outputs from the filters represent a positive-frequency spectrum and, as shown in Fig. 7.6, may be translated to the digital IF frequency.

Another technique known as the "Weaver method" first translates the audio signal down by about 1600 Hz, forming a complex signal with unsymmetrical positive and negative parts (see Fig. 7.30). The resulting signal can then be low-pass-filtered and no 90° phase shifter is required in the filters. This technique results in a low computation rate and is also more amenable to the use of IIR filters. The second full-complex mixer translates the SSB signal to the digital IF. The circuit shown in Fig. 7.30 can also be used to generate the upper-upper sideband or the lower-lower sideband for a four-channel exciter by using an ω_1 which is 2π (6100 Hz) greater or lower than that used for the LSB and USB translators, and all four signals are summed prior to applying to the D/A converter. The filter characteristics will, in general, be more severe for a four-channel system, however. The spectrum generation using the Weaver method is shown in Fig. 7.31.

As shown in Sec. 7.1 (see Fig. 7.9), a considerable savings can be realized in a two-channel ISB exciter using the phasing method. This results because for a 90° phase-shifted pair derived from a real signal the representation $I + jQ$ gives the positive frequencies and $I - jQ$ gives the negative frequencies. An examination of the block diagram shown in Fig. 7.8 reveals that by interchanging the order of filtering and summation one pair of filters can be eliminated. We first consider the component from each of the audio inputs. In each case, the audio signal is passed through a filter, and the outputs of the two filters are added together. Obviously the signals could have been added first and then passed through a single filter.

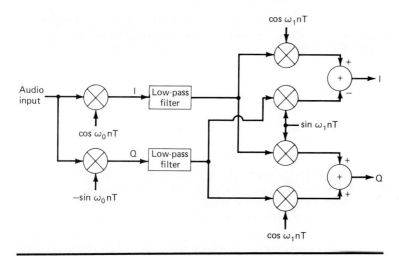

Figure 7.30 Weaver method for SSB generation.

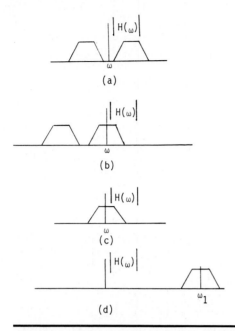

Figure 7.31 (*a*) Input audio spectrum; (*b*) audio spectrum of complex signal after first mixer; (*c*) audio spectrum of complex signal after filters; (*d*) frequency spectrum of signal after final mixer.

In the case of the Q components each audio input is passed through a filter incorporating a 90° phase shifter. The outputs of the filters are then subtracted. An equivalent result could have been obtained by first subtracting the signals and then passing them through a single filter which incorporates a 90° phase shifter. The results of these modifications are shown in Fig. 7.9.

A brief discussion of the conversion of complex signals into real signals at the D/A converter will now be given. In general, if one component (either I or Q) of a complex signal is applied to an D/A converter, all the positive-frequency components of the complex signal are also duplicated on the negative side and all the negative-frequency components of the complex signal are duplicated on the positive side. This can occasionally lead to interesting results if the complex signal has low-level residual spurious signals on the undesired side. These effects can be avoided by using a circuit such as shown in Fig. 7.32 which includes a full-complex mixer, as compared with the circuit shown in Fig. 7.6 which uses only half the mixer.

The circuit shown in Fig. 7.32 selects only the positive-frequency components of the complex spectrum and outputs a real signal with the positive components duplicated on the negative side. In this case, any residual negative-frequency components in the complex spectrum are not outputted.

The D/A converter normally operates as a sample and hold circuit, holding one value until the next sample is available. This can cause a significant droop in the upper frequency response of the audio spectrum. A low sample rate also limits the maximum frequency to which the signal can be translated by the digital mixer. Consequently it is often necessary to increase the sample rate by interpolation prior to translation or application to the D/A converter. This can be accomplished by supplying an integral number of zero samples between the actual signal values and following the process with a low-pass filter operating at the higher sample frequency. The filter removes the components of the signal caused by harmonics of the lower sample rate and provides a clear spectrum for application to the D/A converter.

7.10 Digital Hardware

Thanks to large-scale integration (LSI), digital hardware is rapidly becoming available for real-time digital signal processing applications. Integrated signal processing chips, high-speed multiplier/accumulators, and fast, large-word-length A/D converters are just a few of the devices that are seeing applications in digital transceivers. As the level of integration and operating

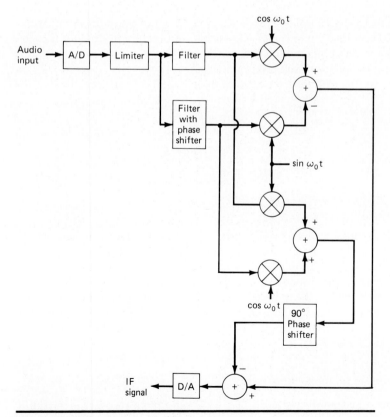

Figure 7.32 Block diagram of digital exciter with complex frequency translator.

speed of these devices increases, more and more analog circuitry will be eliminated in communications equipment designs.

A signal processor must perform a variety of functions in a digital transceiver, and, in some respects, must have the capabilities of a general-purpose microprocessor. However, the demands of handling real-time sampled data force specialized architectures and processing techniques to be used.

Processing requirements

The previous sections discussed various algorithms for a digital transceiver implementation. For example, a signal processor used in this application must provide frequency translation by either half complex multiplication or full complex multiplication, where

$$y(n) = X(n)e^{j\omega_0 nT} \tag{7.58}$$

or

$$y(n) = [I(n) + jQ(n)]e^{j\omega_0 nT} \tag{7.59}$$

Generation of the complex exponential involves the computation of trigonometric functions, namely, sine and cosine, and is also required for the various modulation and demodulation functions.

Filtering, decimation, and phase shifting are provided by either FIR filters computed by the difference equation

$$y(n) = \sum_{k=0}^{N-1} h(k)x(n - k) \tag{7.60}$$

or by IIR filters where

$$y(n) = \sum_{k=0}^{N} a(k)x(n - k) - \sum_{k=1}^{N} b(k)y(n - k) \tag{7.61}$$

Automatic gain control, receiver squelch, and speech compression all require a decision-making capability as well as arithmetic functions such as addition, subtraction, multiplication, and division. The AGC processor may also require a logarithmic function to be computed.

In this application, the most predominant function to be computed is the multiplying and adding operation. The various trigonometric, logarithmic, and division operations can all be obtained from algorithms based on fast multiplication (see Refs. 9 through 11).

Signal processor architecture

In general, a fast hardware multiplier, as opposed to a software algorithmic multiplier, is required by a signal processor to be of any value for moderate bandwidth processing. Typical integrated signal processors use Harvard-type architectures with separate data and program space and multiple internal data busses to allow simultaneous instruction prefetch and execution. Today, multiply and add (MAD) rates ranging from 5 to 20 million MADs per second can be obtained using 16-bit fixed-point arithmetic. A typical integrated digital signal processor block diagram is shown in Fig. 7.33.

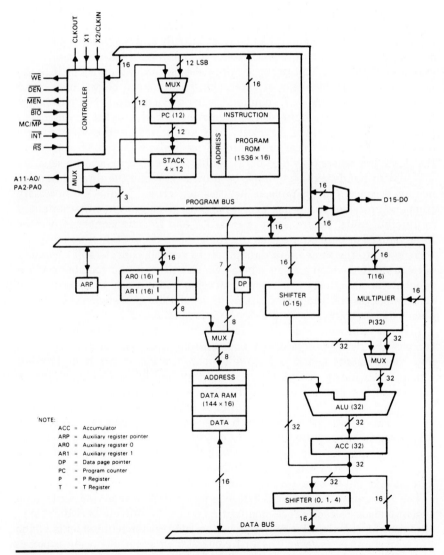

Figure 7.33 Block diagram of a typical, single-chip, integrated signal processor. *(Used with permission of Texas Instruments, Inc.)*

Multiprocessor environment

The use of digital signal processing techniques for SSB receivers and transmitters frequently requires the use of several signal processing units working together synchronously, and indeed the data flow within the equipment may be one of the more difficult aspects of the design. Two major techniques are discussed here and of course an almost infinite number of variations are possible. The techniques could be further broken down into data-driven systems or systems with a master controller which provides synchronization.

Perhaps the simplest way to interconnect multiprocessors is simply to connect them to one another as indicated by signal flow block diagrams (see, for example, Fig. 7.9). Each unit can be reset initially and the programs written so that after reset each processor waits for input data before commencing execution. When the first processor produces output data, it sends it to the next processor in the chain, etc. Resynchronization can be provided by an interrupt to the processor, if required. Either serial or parallel data transfers are used. In general, a buffer is required either internal to the processors or physically between them. In most cases an interconnection to a control microprocessor in the receiver or transmitter is also required. In some cases the signal processors provide a port suitable for this but in others a separate buffer with handshake logic must be provided. While the direct interconnection is conceptually simple, difficulties may arise if feedback is necessary from one processor to another or if inputs to a given processor are computed in different units. If care is not exercised, I and Q components can become interchanged or data points from interpolation or decimation filters may not correspond to the same input data point. In general, considerable ingenuity is required to develop a clean scheme which will start and remain synchronized. It is sometimes necessary to develop code in one processor which accommodates the timing requirements in another processor. This should obviously be avoided to the greatest extent possible.

Another approach to data transfer is to use a common data bus to interconnect the signal processors. A bus controller can then manage the data flow requirements and also provide synchronization as required. The bus structure obviously provides more flexibility and expansion capability in equipment but in some cases at the expense of additional hardware. The block diagram of a bus-controlled digital radio is shown in Fig. 7.34. The system can be data-driven with each processor commencing execution when it receives all the required inputs. In a system of this type it may be necessary to provide multiple input ports with first-in first-outs (FIFOs) for each processor to identify the particular data type and sequence. Provision for detecting an out-of-sync condition and resynchronization may be necessary.

The bus controller program can also be written to read and write data synchronously to each processing unit as well as to provide periodic resynchronization signals. This may reduce the I/O register requirements of the processing units; however, the bus controller program obviously becomes tied to the specific data rates as well as being somewhat dependent on the software in the individual processing units.

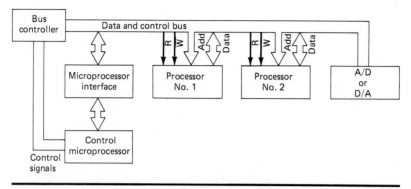

Figure 7.34 Block diagram of bus-oriented data structure.

A parallel cascadable data flow system has also been proposed in which all data flows through each processor. A tag accompanies each data word to identify for which processor the data is intended. All other processors simply pass the data along without acting on it. The tag obviously can be expanded to identify the type of data, source, processing requirements, etc.

As very-large-scale integration (VLSI) continues to expand, the character of SSB radios will no doubt be shaped considerably by the availability of data flow systems and interface capabilities.

REFERENCES

1. William D. Stanley, Gary R. Dougherty, and Ray Dougherty, *Digital Signal Processing,* Reston Publishing, Reston, VA, 1984.
2. Andreas Antoniou, *Digital Filters Analysis and Design,* McGraw-Hill, New York, 1979.
3. Alan V. Oppenheim and Ronald W. Schafer, *Digital Signal Processing,* Prentice-Hall, Englewood Cliffs, NJ, 1975.
4. Ronald E. Crochiere and Lawrence R. Rabiner, *Multi-Rate Digital Signal Processing,* Prentice-Hall, Englewood Cliffs, NJ, 1983.
5. Lawrence R. Rabiner and Bernard Gold, *Theory and Application of Digital Signal Processing,* Prentice-Hall, Englewood Cliffs, NJ, 1975.
6. Walter Kester "Test Video A/D Converters under Dynamic Conditions," *EDN,* vol. 27, Aug. 18, 1982, pp. 103–112.
7. Digital Signal Processing Committee of the IEEE Acoustics, Speech, and Signal Processing Society (eds.), *Programs for Digital Signal Processing,* IEEE Press, Piscataway, NJ, 1979.
8. E. W. Pappenfus, W. B. Bruene, and E. O. Schoenike, *Single Sideband Principles and Circuits,* McGraw-Hill, New York, 1964.
9. P. W. Baker, "Parallel Multiplicative Algorithms for Some Elementary Functions," *IEEE Trans. Comput.,* vol. C-24, March 1975, pp. 322–325.
10. David F. Freeman, "Equal Ripple Approximation for Envelope Detection," *IEEE Trans. Acoust., Speech, & Signal Proc.,* vol. ASSP-26, no. 3, June 1978, pp. 254–156.
11. Fred Ruckdeschel, "Functional Approximations," *BYTE Mag.,* vol. 3, November 1978, pp. 34–46.
12. L. R. Rabiner, J. F. Kaiser, O. Herrmann, and M. T. Dolan, "Some Comparisons between FIR and IIR Digital Filters," *Bell Syst. Tech. J.,* vol. 53, February 1974, p. 308.

8

Preselectors and Postselectors

Bill D. Hart

Although wideband receiver front ends are seeing increasing use, they cannot handle situations with very strong off-channel signals. Passive tuned circuit filters are still needed to protect against cross-modulation, intermodulation, damage, and other interference effects. The trend is toward separately packaged preselector filter units using sophisticated tuning and control methods. Selectivity, noise figure degradation, and maximum interference voltage are important constraints. It is possible to design filters with an optimal tradeoff of these parameters for given component limitations. With some forethought in the filter design, several preselectors can be driven by the same antenna in a multicoupling configuration.

The same filters or similar circuits can be employed as postselectors to filter the transmitter signal before final power amplification, thus reducing its out-of-band noise and spurious emissions which could interfere with nearby receivers.

8.1 Purpose and General Description

Receiver preselector filters

A receiver preselector is a passive, tuned filter used between the antenna and the receiver input. It provides additional selective filtering which prevents or reduces the numerous interference and damage problems resulting from colocation of transmitters and receivers, as discussed in detail in Chap. 2. The interference problems which preselectors reduce include intermodulation, cross modulation, reciprocal mixing, desensitization, spurious and image responses, and circuit overload damage. These problems occur when adequate antenna separation is not available, for instance aboard aircraft, ships, vehicles, and transportable communication shelter units, or in crowded fixed-station sites. It is common to find isolation between two HF antennas on an aircraft of less than 6 dB at many frequencies. Figure 8.1 shows that coupling between two whip antennas is significant at appreciable distances, perhaps as great as 1000 ft (300 m). When these users need multiple radio installations, or when several users are in close proximity, simultaneous transmitter and receiver operation (SIMOP) nearly always requires the selectivity of tuned circuits.

Receivers have historically included tuned circuit stages at the input to attenuate out-of-band undesired signals. Research has improved mixer dynamic range (Chap. 3) and synthesizer noise levels (Chap. 9) to the point where receivers are now produced with wideband input stages. They cover their entire frequency ranges with no retuning of filter elements and provide adequate performance for many users. Omitting tuned circuit filtering is economical and permits the operating frequency to be changed rapidly. The dynamic range of the best wideband receivers is still not adequate, however, for sites where there are strong interfering signals.

Exciter postselector filters

Exciter postselectors are very similar to receiver preselectors. They filter the transmitter signal between the low-level exciter stages and the power ampli-

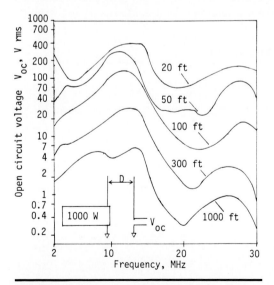

Figure 8.1 Voltage on receiving antenna at varying distances from transmitter. Antennas are 32-ft vertical whips over "good" ground; $\sigma = 10^{-2}$ S/m.

fier to reduce emissions which could interfere with nearby receivers. They reduce transmitted broadband noise, spurious signals, and in some cases harmonics.

Postselector design is in many respects similar to that for preselectors. A filter can be configured for use as both a preselector and a postselector in a transceiver installation. Postselectors differ from preselectors in that the available desired signal level is much higher, so the emphasis is on in-band intermodulation instead of noise figure. There are no large out-of-band signal voltages to stress components.

Adding a postselector has a small impact on transmitter design. The postselector may include an amplifier so no net loss is incurred and the power amplifier drive level is maintained. An allowance for postselector gain variation vs. tuned frequency must be made in the design of ALC or TGC loops, either by having sufficient margin for variation or by correcting the gain from a lookup table. A postselector's tuning time may delay the tuning of the power amplifier or antenna coupler while they wait for a stable RF signal.

Research continues into improvements in noise and linearity in transmitters. Such improvements could eventually reduce the need for postselectors, but at the current level of technology a filter still improves colocation performance.

Typical preselectors

Modern preselectors typically have one to four bandpass resonators automatically tuned to the radio operating frequency. They are usually packaged as separate units because it is not economical to provide the basic transmit-

TABLE 8.1   Example Preselector Specifications

Characteristic	Unit A	Unit B
Frequency range, MHz	2–32	2–30
Number of bands	4	2
Number of resonators	3	2
Tuning method	Capacitor servo	Diode switch
Tuning time (typical), s	1	0.01
Impedance (nominal), ohms	50	50
Impedance out-of-band	50–150 pF	2 or 0.5 μH
Operating RF input @ 10% frequency separation, V_{rms}	200	140
Protection limit, V_{peak}	500	500
Selectivity @ 10% frequency separation, dB	47	40
Minimum passband, kHz	12	6
@ dB points, dB	2	1
Filter loss, dB	6	10
Loss with amplifier, dB	0	
Total noise figure, dB	12	12
Transmit intermodulation below each tone, dB	46	40
Intermodulation test tone level, V_{rms}	1.58	0.56

ting and receiving equipment with additional selectivity which, although sometimes vital, is required only in a minority of installations.

The principal performance specifications for two tunable preselection filters are given in Table 8.1. The values include an allowance for variation over the operating frequency range, temperature, and other environmental conditions.

Suboctave bandpass filters

A bank of fixed-tuned suboctave-width bandpass filters is a limited form of preselector and postselector filtering. The design of such filters is covered in standard references [1, 2]. The appropriate filter is typically diode-switched into the signal path by the receiver tuning control circuits.

Half-octave filters (high/low passband frequency ratio = 1.4) can usually provide adequate suppression of second-order IM interference because, as shown in Fig. 8.2, one undesired signal producing the IM must be at least a full octave away (no closer than half or twice the desired frequency). A second-order IM product will be reduced 1 dB for each dB of attenuation the filter has at f_2.

The 2- to 32-MHz band is covered by eight half-octave filters, which are typically smaller than a tunable filter covering the band. Narrower filters may be desired, but the number of filters required goes up rapidly and a tunable design soon becomes advantageous. The number of fixed filters needed, in terms of the band limits to be covered and filter corner frequencies, is:

$$N = \frac{\log \text{ (band-high/band-low)}}{\log \text{ (filter-high/filter-low)}}$$

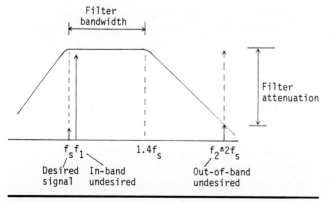

Figure 8.2 Worst-case frequencies for second-order intermodulation in half-octave filter. Second order product is $f_2 - f_1 = fs$.

For example, with 15 percent bandwidth filters, 20 filters would be required to cover the 2- to 30-MHz band.

8.2   Design Considerations for Preselectors

A preselector contains many circuits besides the basic RF filter. This section describes some of the supporting circuitry associated with overload protection, signal amplification, and frequency tuning, and some practical limitations on the components and circuits which the filter employs.

Overload protection

The preselector may be exposed to several sources of electrical energy on its input terminals, which it should be able to withstand even if operation is temporarily interrupted. These include large RF signals inside or outside the filter passband, static charges, and transients induced by nearby lightning strokes. Several techniques should be considered to protect the filter from these overloading voltages. Some of these are illustrated in the design examples, Figs. 8.10 and 8.11.

A static discharge resistor of 100K ohms or more should be placed across the input terminals if there is no other dc path. Spark-gap or ionization-tube surge protectors may be effective in shunting the transients induced by nearby lightning strokes. Semiconductor surge protectors, if used, should be very carefully checked for intermodulation distortion at the largest specified level of undesired signals.

Protecting the filter from overload by large RF signals usually requires a detector and monitor circuit. If the monitor senses an overloading signal, it can disconnect the filter from the input or alter the filter response to prevent absorption of excess power. Shunting a filter resonator with a resistance will lower the resonant Q factor. With most filter designs the resulting mismatch will lower the power absorbed from the antenna and the shunting resistor does not have to dissipate very much undesired power. A discharge device such as a neon lamp can perform this same function if the maximum filter voltage levels happen to coincide with its breakdown voltage and if the resulting output level is acceptable.

Both rapid and long-term protection is required. An overload monitor sensor will have some actuating time constant and the disconnect device will take time to operate. A fast relay, for example, will require at least a millisecond to operate. Surge protection from zeners, voltage clamp circuits, or discharge devices is necessary to protect amplifiers and the receiver during this interval. On the other hand, disconnecting or detuning is essential to prevent overheating of surge protection devices.

Both in-band and out-of-band RF signals can overload the filter. Out-of-band signals develop a large voltage across the input without actually dissipating much power because the filter input impedance is mostly reactive at out-of-band frequencies. In-band signals cause overload at much lower voltages because the power is transferred with low loss to all filter sections and to the output.

It is desirable for the protection circuit to restore normal operation when the overloading signal goes away. This is a great convenience for the operator, since occasional momentary overload conditions do not disable the equipment or require manual reset.

The filter should be automatically disconnected from the antenna when power is turned off and the automatic overload circuits can no longer protect it.

Amplifiers

A passive preselection filter's loss adds directly in dB to the receiver noise figure (neglecting output mismatch). A better system noise figure can be achieved if the filter is followed by a low-noise amplifier which restores the received signals to near their original level or higher. If the overall preselector unit has unity gain, then the receiver AGC threshold and S-meter calibration are undisturbed. The noise figure of the amplifier must be much lower than that of the receiver to minimize the system degradation.

The amplifier must also have good dynamic range in order to handle undesired signals within the preselector bandwidth. These could cause odd-order intermodulation products to fall within the receiver passband. The filter attenuation curve reduces the desired signal somewhat and out-of-band undesired signals much more. The net effect is to improve the third-order intercept point, relative to the amplifier alone. The gain of the amplifier, of course, causes larger signals to be applied to the receiver.

In very lossy filters, it may be advantageous to place an amplifier between sections of the filter to compromise between noise and distortion. It must be located where considerable selectivity has been achieved, to protect the amplifier, but before too much loss has occurred.

Proper design of the filter and amplifier require a systematic analysis of the system noise figure and intermodulation intercept, considering the cascaded system of filter, amplifier, and receiver. These topics were treated in more detail in Chap. 3 and are illustrated in Example 8.2 of Sec. 8.4.

Tuning methods

Passive filters may be tuned by varying an inductance or capacitance, or both. The most common tuning elements are switched capacitors, servo-driven variable capacitors, and varactor (variable capacitance) diodes.

Tunable cavities are often used at VHF and UHF for high performance, particularly for very-low-loss designs, but become huge at lower frequencies and are almost never used in the HF band.

Because of the large ratio of high- to low-frequency limits often encountered, it is usually not practical to tune the entire range in one band. For example, the 2- to 30-MHz HF band would require variable elements with more than a 225:1 ratio, and have a 15:1 variation in impedance. Band switching of inductors is used with variable tuning capacitors, or vice versa, to obtain a realistic tuning ratio while reusing the tuning elements. One-octave or two-octave bands are commonly used, so that the 2- to 30-MHz unit uses two to four bands.

In servo-tuned units, wafer switches or relays are suitable for band switching. High-reliability vacuum relays are available that operate in milliseconds and can switch kilovolts of RF. Fast-tuning units used in ECCM applications will need fast relays or diode switches. These units will accumulate a huge number of retuning cycles and may need special relay designs to obtain adequate life. Diode switches can provide faster band switching, but stray effects may be hard to control when switching inductors.

Variable inductors are sometimes used for tuning but are generally limited to slow manually or electromechanically tuned designs. Two common forms of mechanically variable inductors are those with movable tuning slugs and roller coils. Rapid-tuning, electronically variable inductors based on gradual magnetic saturation have problems with intermodulation and temperature drift which prevent their widespread use.

The filter shown in Fig. 8.3 uses switched capacitors for tuning. If each capacitor is half as large as the previous one (binary weighting), equal steps of capacitance are available up to the total. A larger number of tuning elements will provide finer tuning steps. The tuning control must convert operating frequencies to switch combinations which add up to the right capacitance.

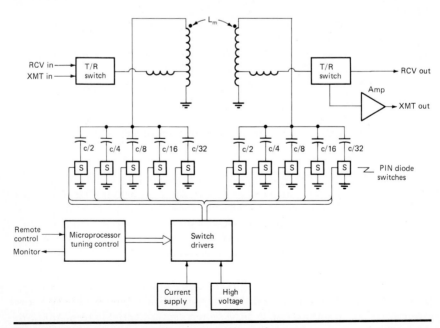

Figure 8.3 Block diagram of PIN-switch-tuned preselector.

Although the scheme is conceptually simple, the control algorithm or the actual component values or both will have to be adjusted for stray effects. The inductors will be found to have a significant amount of capacitance effectively in parallel with them, determined by their self-resonant frequency. Great care must be taken to keep the lead length of the capacitors small or the lead inductance will cause a frequency-dependent error in the effective capacitance values. Lead inductance is a greater problem in low-reactance resonators. The switch circuit can also cause an alteration of the effective capacitance. All these effects must be minimized or the tuning algorithm becomes quite involved with corrections to the capacitance values at each new tuned frequency.

Filters could also be tuned with switched inductors, but this is less commonly done. Switched inductors are harder to design because they add in series, requiring switches to operate at floating RF potentials. The open-state capacitance of the switches and their capacitance to ground can resonate with unused inductor sections and affect the filter tuning. Inductors are usually large and expensive compared to capacitors, and must be optimized for low dissipation rather than for ease of switching. Inductor switching is usually restricted to band changes.

PIN diode switching

Positive-intrinsic-negative layered diodes are commonly used to switch RF circuits. The relevant diode specs are on-state resistance, off-state (reverse-bias) capacitance, reverse-bias resistance, noise, intrinsic carrier lifetime, and breakdown voltage.

A possible PIN diode switch for tuning capacitors is illustrated in Fig. 8.4. The driver circuit switches between a low-voltage, high-current supply which turns the diodes on, and a high-voltage, low-current supply which back-biases the diodes to turn them off. Two diodes are usually required to provide the switching current path and to isolate the bias circuits, which could create undesired resonances. A switched inductor may not always need the second diode.

A diode will not be properly switched off if it has a significantly lower back-bias resistance than the other one, and therefore much less of the bias voltage. This can cause unacceptable mistuning and loss in the resonator. Large resistances across the diodes or a single resistor connected to a supply of half the total voltage is usually needed to assure equal voltage division. These resistors increase the resonator dissipation and must be made as large as practical. It should be noted that high-value carbon resistors have a lower effective resistance to RF (the value in parallel with the equivalent capacitance) than to dc. This is due to the distribution of capacitance between carbon granules which effectively finds a shorter path through the granular array and partially shunts the resistive contacts.

The second diode is effectively in parallel with the first for the RF signal current and can be utilized to lower the overall switch resistance, with proper precautions as discussed below. The bypass capacitors must be large with

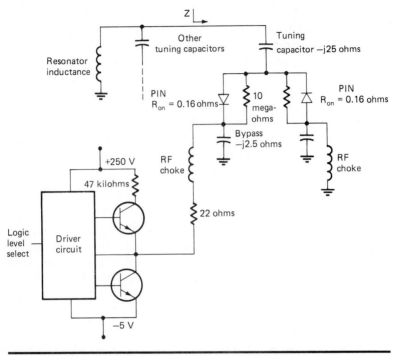

Figure 8.4 PIN diode switch with the driver and bypassing.

respect to the tuning capacitor, but do not need stable RF characteristics. It is sometimes possible to series-resonate the bypass capacitor in the lowest band and thus achieve a low impedance where it is needed most. The effect of this frequency-dependent bypass on the total tuning reactance should be checked.

Because of the large switching voltages, it is often impractical to make the bypass capacitor reactance smaller than the diode resistance, which leads to a somewhat surprising requirement. Both ends of the diode switch must have the same bypassing impedance if we are to benefit from the conduction of both diodes. For example, in the circuit shown in Fig. 8.4 the total impedance presented to the tuned circuit is $0.08 - j26.25$, representing a capacitor with $Q = 328$. If we replace one bypass circuit with a direct ground connection, the impedance becomes $0.16 - j25.01$ and the Q drops to 158. This is because essentially all the RF current is flowing in the grounded diode and we no longer have the second diode resistance in parallel.

The switching diodes can generate noise which is significant in receiver preselectors because it degrades the noise figure. This noise level is usually related to the back-bias leakage current of the diodes. The current and the noise increase very rapidly because of avalanche multiplication as the breakdown voltage is approached, and it is usually necessary to use a large voltage derating factor.

Varactor tuning

Varactors are semiconductor diodes which have been optimized for a variation in the effective capacitance of the junction as the dc reverse-bias voltage is changed. A typical range of tuning capacitance per diode is 5 to 25 pF for small varactors which are commonly used at VHF and UHF frequencies. Some very large varactors are being made for the low-HF-frequency range, although their loss goes up at higher frequencies. The frequency tuning range is set by the ratio of maximum to minimum capacitance (including strays).

Varactor-tuned filters are used for their small size and low control (tuning) power in circuits which have moderate signal levels and a moderate tuning range. VHF and UHF receivers have used them extensively, but they are less common in the HF band.

A fundamental limitation on varactor-tuned filters is the intermodulation caused by the variation in junction voltage when a large signal is applied. The varactor is inherently and necessarily a nonlinear device. Even-order distortion is greatly reduced by the back-to-back circuit shown in Fig. 8.5, where the signal increases the voltage across one diode while decreasing that on the other. In general, all distortions are reduced by using more varactors in series or parallel combinations so that the signal swing on each varactor is reduced.

The impedance feeding the tuning voltage to the varactors affects the per-

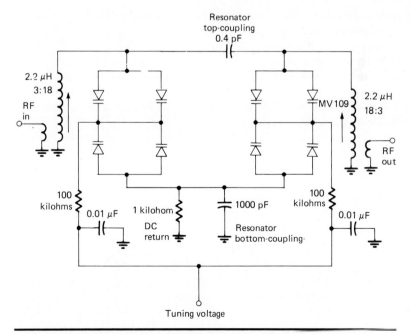

Figure 8.5 Varacter-tuned filter. Frequency range: 20 to 33 MHz; loss: 2 to 3 dB; tuning voltage: 5 to 27 V; 3-dB bandwidth/f_0: 6.5 to 7.5 percent.

formance. A resistor will lower the resonator Q. A very high resistance seems to cause more intermodulation distortion than a high reactance feed (such as a resonant choke). Large out-of-band signals tend to detune the resonator because of their effect on the varactor voltages. This can lead to oscillation at a low frequency, determined by the time constant of the tuning voltage feed circuit.

As a rule of thumb, the circuit should be expected to operate with a peak-to-peak resonator RF voltage no more than half the minimum dc tuning voltage. If all the tuning range is not needed, the minimum tuning voltage can be increased. The out-of-band available power should be less than 25 mW/varactor when the small 25-pF varactors are used.

It is usually necessary to buy varactors in sets matched at three or more points on their capacitance-vs.-voltage curve, or at least to use parts all from the same lot. This is to assure that the tuning of all sections of the filter track together as the tuning voltage varies.

Resonator loss

The most important limitation on the performance of a filter design is the resonator dissipation. A low dissipation (high Q) allows the designer to improve other design tradeoffs. It is generally constrained by the volume available for the resonator and the materials suitable for the operating frequency range. Reference 3 is a good introduction to RF component limitations.

At frequencies up to a few megahertz, low-permeability ferrites are attractive for physically small designs. High-permeability ferrites are not sufficiently temperature-stable and cause unacceptable tuning drift. At the top of the HF band, powdered iron and similar materials are suitable. Toroidal and cup-core forms are popular. Any magnetic material can cause distortion due to nonlinearities in its magnetization curve, particularly if operated at high flux densities, as would be done to obtain physically small inductors. A test should be made for intermodulation distortion at the largest operating levels of received interfering signals or in-band transmit signals. Refer to Chap. 17 for a discussion of intermodulation tests.

Helical resonator cavities [4, 5] are carefully proportioned coil and cavity assemblies which provide the highest unloaded Q for an air-core inductor in a given volume. They can be operated as high-Q coils below their self-resonant frequency. Their equivalent parallel capacitance must be included in the filter design. The Q when optimum proportions are used is estimated from:

$$Q_u = 60Sf_0^{1/2}$$

where S = side of square cavity, in
f_0 = frequency, MHz

Dielectric materials in a high-Q resonator, including structural pieces, should be chosen with caution because they can increase the dissipation. The choice of materials generally becomes more critical with increasing frequency. The loss depends on the product of the dissipation factor (loss tangent) of the material and the fraction of the resonator capacitance which is effectively within that material. Coil supports should avoid, when possible, high-field-strength regions, including the inside of the coil. For a given mechanical configuration and operating frequency, the product reduces to dielectric constant $\times$ dissipation factor, both of which can be found in handbooks [6]. For example, glass-epoxy board, nylon, and phenolics (Bakelite) and any kind of hygroscopic materials should be avoided. Teflon, polyethylene, and polystyrene are usually good materials, if suited to the environment. Ceramics, any organic material, and other circuit board materials should be chosen with caution and carefully specified, because good materials are available but apparently similar materials may have much higher dissipation.

Capacitor losses, while lower than those of most inductors, can still significantly increase resonator dissipation. Switching of tuning elements introduces some resistance, particularly if PIN diode switching is used.

8.3 Filter Design

Topology

The choice of a filter topology is strongly influenced by the requirements for switching and controlling the tuning elements. Most variable elements and switching circuits should have one side referred to chassis ground; for example, diode switch biases, varactor control voltages, and mechanically tuned capacitors. If both ends of a tuning element are "RF hot," additional isolating RF chokes are required. The stray capacitance to ground of these isolation circuits and of the component mountings must be absorbable into the filter topology. If the strays are not in parallel with capacitors of the filter model, they can form parasitic resonances and undesired low-pass/high-pass sections, and the expected response may not be obtained.

Grounded elements rule out lattice and series-arm, shunt-arm ladder filters but fit well in the coupled-resonator model. It places one end of each resonator inductor and capacitor near RF ground, and all nodes can have a capacitor to ground, which means that stray capacitances to chassis and component mountings are easily absorbed into the design. The coupled-resonator form is suitable for filters with a fractional bandwidth less than about 10 percent, which covers most preselector and postselector applications. Below about 1 percent, high losses and tuning drift become severe.

Mathematically, coupled-resonator filters are usually derived from a low-pass prototype ladder filter, although it is also possible to derive exact equations for the response of low-order coupled-resonator filters. Converting a low-pass prototype to a "classical" bandpass gives a series-arm, shunt-arm ladder filter with a response having geometric symmetry (not arithmetic symmetry). The total bandwidth at any attenuation is exactly proportional to that of the prototype, but the high and low frequencies at a given attenuation will not have the same separation from f_0.

Conversion from the classical ladder form to coupled-resonator implementation uses impedance transformation networks to change alternate series and parallel resonators into all-series or all-parallel resonators with coupling elements. Several forms of coupling can be used, as discussed in the next section. These transformations are exact only at one frequency but are usable over a frequency range which is suitable for most preselectors.

Resonator coupling methods

The design procedures for coupled-resonator filters give the desired resonator coupling coefficients rather than element values. The coupling can be implemented in many ways, such as those shown in Fig. 8.6 or Ref. 7. The most common are mutual inductance, top C, and bottom L. Mutual inductance may be provided by a link winding or an aperture between resonator compartments. End resonator loading to the source and load terminations may be provided in a similar manner, as shown in Fig. 8.7. The form with the termination coupled by a large reactance to the top of the resonator tank is often preferred over the tapped divider form when large off-resonance input or output impedance is needed for multicoupling applications (Sec. 8.7).

Inductive coupling models may be converted using the equations given in Fig. 8.8. Input and output couplings to a given resonator should not be made through the same element (e.g., both being taps on the coil) as this couples the signal past the resonator and its selectivity is reduced.

Note that each resonator must have its component values altered from the nominal used in the resonant frequency equation, in order to account for the detuning effects of the coupling or end-loading reactances on both sides. The corrected value for one coupling is shown in each figure. For example, the center resonator in a three-resonator top-C coupled filter must be corrected for each coupling capacitor and uses a main capacitor of value $C - 2C_t$.

There is a frequency variation inherent in each of these methods which shows up in response plots as a passband tilt and a greater stopband attenuation on one side of resonance than the other (after accounting for geometric symmetry). This is related to the single-frequency transformations used in deriving the coupled-resonator form from ladder-form bandpass filters. The tilt may not be significant within a narrow passband. The asymptotic behavior at very high and low frequencies is determined entirely by the coupling methods between resonators and at the input and output [8]. It is usually necessary to choose a combination of coupling methods throughout the filter to obtain the best compromise stopband tilt for the application.

A performance loss occurs in tunable filters if the optimum coupling and end-loading values cannot be maintained as the resonator is tuned across the band. Couplings of the same type as the tuning element (e.g., top-C between variable capacitors), which would probably be chosen to control tilt, will cause this problem. It also arises when the resonator Q_u varies appreciably over the band, as with helical resonator inductors. The ratio of load resis-

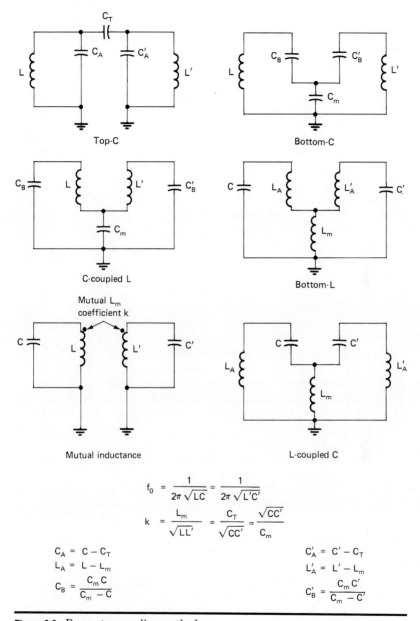

Figure 8.6 Resonator coupling methods.

tance to resonator reactance will determine which of the end-loading methods shown in Fig. 8.7 will have the most acceptable variation in Q_t. Overcom-
ing these variations can tax the ingenuity of the designer. The effect can
sometimes be alleviated with more complex matching networks at the ends
of the filter, as shown in Fig. 8.3, with tailored-curve variable capacitors such

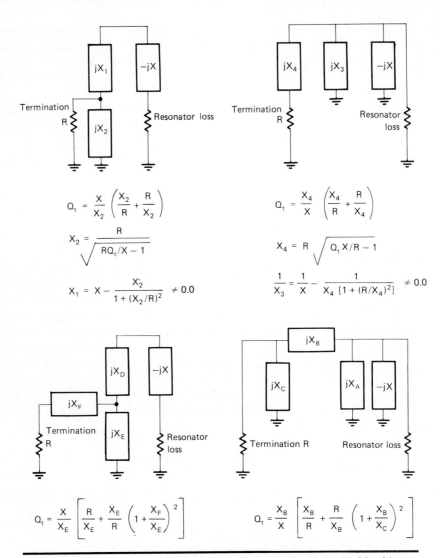

$$Q_t = \frac{X}{X_2}\left(\frac{X_2}{R} + \frac{R}{X_2}\right)$$

$$X_2 = \frac{R}{\sqrt{RQ_t/X - 1}}$$

$$X_1 = X - \frac{X_2'}{1 + (X_2/R)^2} \neq 0.0$$

$$Q_t = \frac{X_4}{X}\left(\frac{X_4}{R} + \frac{R}{X_4}\right)$$

$$X_4 = R\sqrt{Q_t X/R - 1}$$

$$\frac{1}{X_3} = \frac{1}{X} - \frac{1}{X_4\,[1 + (R/X_4)^2]} \neq 0.0$$

$$Q_t = \frac{X}{X_E}\left[\frac{R}{X_E} + \frac{X_E}{R}\left(1 + \frac{X_F}{X_E}\right)^2\right]$$

$$Q_t = \frac{X_B}{X}\left[\frac{X_B}{R} + \frac{R}{X_B}\left(1 + \frac{X_B}{X_C}\right)^2\right]$$

Figure 8.7 Resonator input and output loading methods. *Note:* (1) Matching range $X/Q_t < R < XQ_t$; (2) X is the nominal total resonator reactance, either inductive or capacitive; (3) all subscripted X_i must have signs opposite X; (4) equations are approximate, with fractional errors on the order of $1/Q_t^2$; (5) error partially depends on whether resonator loss is actually where shown.

as shown in Example 8.1 of Sec. 8.4, or by combinations of resonator coupling methods, as in Fig. 8.5.

Filter types

The best prototype for most preselector applications is the Cohn minimum-loss (min-loss) filter. Other prototypes are useful when they provide some

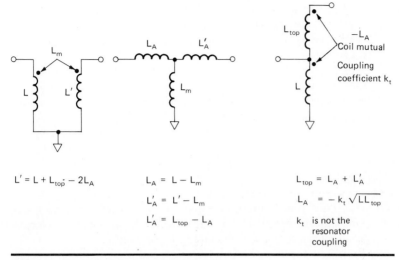

$$L' = L + L_{top} - 2L_A$$

$$L_A = L - L_m$$
$$L'_A = L' - L_m$$
$$L'_A = L_{top} - L_A$$

$$L_{top} = L_A + L'_A$$
$$L_A = -k_t \sqrt{LL_{top}}$$

k_t is not the resonator coupling

Figure 8.8 Equivalent forms of coupled coils.

characteristic which is not controlled by the min-loss design. The min-loss, with its simple design procedure, should be calculated first in any case to provide a basis for comparing with other designs.

The min-loss prototype is appropriate when designing for the lowest center frequency loss consistent with a specified stopband width. The theory developed by Cohn and others [9–11, 13, 14] explicitly trades off resonator dissipation factor (or Q), selectivity at some point on the skirt (e.g., 40 dB), and midband filter loss to give a design which is optimum for these three parameters. It does not try to control passband shape, but generally gives good results in preselector applications. The min-loss has other good properties, as discussed below, which may make it a good choice even when the lowest loss is not required.

Lossless filter prototypes such as Chebyshev, Butterworth, and Bessel give their theoretical response shapes when the elements have infinite Q. Filters implemented with the lossless prototype values but lossy elements are called "pseudo-exact" designs, and their response shapes vary with the element loss. With plots of these responses [12] or a good computer program for network analysis, a designer can iteratively find a tradeoff among selectivity, ripple, passband width, and midband loss. Equation (6.3-15) in Ref. 15 provides a useful way to estimate the tradeoff between loss and normalized q (element Q_u divided by bandwidth) for any pseudo-exact prototype. Selectivity and loss are closely tied to passband width and ripple in this design method. If the passband is not a critical aspect of the design, its central place will hinder the design tradeoff process.

Predistorted Butterworth and Chebyshev designs are available to maintain the theoretical shape in the presence of element loss. This is done with impedance mismatch [high voltage standing wave ratio (VSWR)] and increased passband loss, and is rarely applicable to preselector design.

A min-loss design may not be chosen in an application requiring a relatively wide and flat passband. The passband width is not specified in the min-loss design process. It has a ripple which is greatest at the edge of the passband and becomes quite large for filters with several resonators and low loss. If these characteristics are not satisfactory, then a low-ripple (e.g., 0.1-dB) Chebyshev or Butterworth pseudo-exact design may be the best choice. The loss obtained will not be the lowest achievable, but the penalty is often small. A side benefit is sometimes a better VSWR.

Each resonator of the min-loss filter has equal loss (in dB). For an equally terminated filter, this results in an equal-element low-pass prototype. In the case of a one- or two-pole doubly terminated filter, the Cohn filter is also the Butterworth pseudo-exact filter. The Cohn has some advantages over many others. All resonators have nearly equal voltages for a midband signal, and it has a large in-band power-handling capability. No resonator is more sensitive to tuning adjustment than the others, which helps with temperature stability, ease of alignment, and tracking in a tunable filter.

When optimizing a receiving system for a very low noise figure, it is sometimes found that improvement is obtained by allowing some impedance mismatch between the filter and its load (an RF amplifier, for instance) and reoptimizing the selectivity/loss tradeoff. This "optimum noise matching" has been taken into account in an extension of the Cohn theory [13, 14]. The improvement usually turns out to be a fraction of a decibel and is unimportant for typical HF preselector designs, but can be more significant at higher frequencies.

In many cases the coupling values for any of the filter types discussed will differ by 10 percent or less. Then the unavoidable variations inherent in a tunable filter, as discussed earlier, make the choice of prototype a moot question. In practice, the calculated design is a simplified model which omits many real component effects. The designer must use it as a starting point, then measure and adjust the experimental model until its response is acceptable according to the performance specifications.

Min-loss design procedure

The design of equally terminated minimum-loss filters is covered in Ref. 15. A design procedure for doubly terminated, coupled-resonator filters where all resonators have the same unloaded Q is summarized here. It is not required that the resonators be implemented with the same element values.

Given the following:

f_0 = resonant frequency

f_H = a frequency above resonance with specified attenuation

f_L = frequency below resonance with same attenuation as f_H

$f_0^2 = f_L f_H$

$B = f_H - f_L$ bandwidth at the specified attenuation

N = number of resonators

L_0 = midband insertion loss, dB

Q_u = unloaded resonator Q

Q_t = "terminal Q," the Q of a lossless resonator loaded only by the terminating

resistance on one side

Q_L = $Q_u Q_t/(Q_u + Q_t)$, resonator Q with its loss and termination

r = Q_t/Q_u, dissipation to loading ratio; also the prototype filter's series element

normalized resistance

k = resonator-to-resonator coupling

The filter will have geometric symmetry, except for the effects of the coupling as discussed earlier, and thus only two of the four frequencies (f_0, B, f_H, and f_L) at a given attenuation level may be chosen arbitrarily. The fractional bandwidth at the selectivity specification point is needed:

$$\frac{B}{f_0} = \frac{f_H}{f_0} - \frac{f_0}{f_H} = \frac{f_0}{f_L} - \frac{f_L}{f_0}$$

The design procedure begins with two of these three specifications: selectivity requirement, insertion loss, and unloaded resonator Q. The designer selects a filter with an acceptable number of resonators, midband loss, and off-frequency attenuation. The curves shown in Figs. 8.9a through c represent the response of doubly terminated Cohn filter prototypes (equal-element pseudo-exact) on a normalized frequency scale and provide a quick means of determining the design tradeoffs. The prototype curves can be extended at $6N$ dB/octave but a coupled-resonator implementation eventually departs from the prototype shape.

Then the following approximate equations are used to design the couplings (they are accurate for filters with low midband loss):

$$r = \frac{L_0}{4.343N} \qquad \text{(accurate if } L_0 < 2N \text{ in dB)}$$

$$Q_t = rQ_u$$

$$k = \frac{1}{Q_t}$$

Implementation consists of setting the component values to obtain these coupling and loading values, as shown in Figs. 8.6 through 8.8. All resonator-to-resonator coupling coefficients are k and each end termination is chosen to obtain Q_t.

8.4 Design Examples

The following design examples illustrate the use of the filter design formulas and curves and the resonator coupling techniques. The second example is also used to illustrate the design tradeoffs between noise figure and distortion which the preselector design engineer must make. These examples are

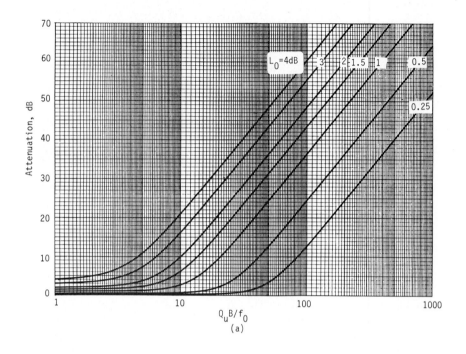

(a)

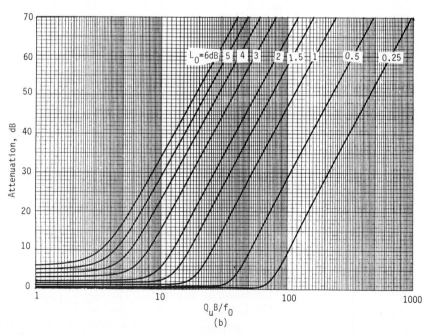

(b)

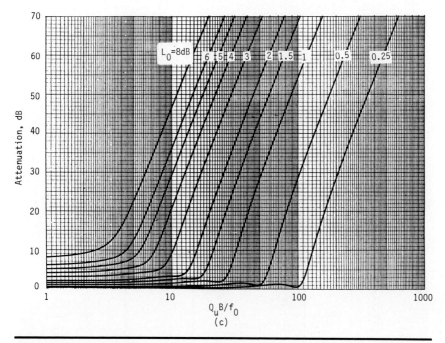

Figure 8.9 (*a*) Attenuation of two-resonator Cohn filter; (*b*) attenuation of three-resonator Cohn filter; (*c*) attenuation of four-resonator Cohn filter.

intended as "first-pass" studies which the designer would use for initial feasibility and tradeoff study but which do not include margins for variations in temperature and production part tolerances.

Example 8.1: Tunable Preselector We are designing a receiver and need a tunable preselector to offer as an accessory. It should provide 20 dB of absolute attenuation for signals 5 percent away from the tuned frequency. The space available requires us to use toroid inductors, and their unloaded Q_u will be 200.

solution We start with the following equations:

$$B = \left(1.05 - \frac{1}{1.05}\right) f_0 = 0.098 f_0$$

$$Q_u \frac{B}{f_0} = 200 \times 0.098 = 19.5$$

Referring to Fig. 8.9*a*, we find that a two-resonator filter will give us the required 20-dB attenuation with a midband loss of about 2.0 dB. Then we calculate:

$$r = \frac{2.0}{4.343 \times 2} = 0.230$$

$$Q_t = 0.230 \times 200 = 46.0$$

$$k - \frac{1}{46.0} = 0.022$$

The filter is illustrated in Fig. 8.10. The input coupling will be provided by a capacitance to the top of the resonator in order to obtain a suitable out-of-band input impedance for multicoupling. In order to maintain reasonably constant input loading and therefore the required Q_t, we will make this a variable capacitor section tied to the tuning shaft. The capacitance vs. rotation of the sections of this capacitor can be tailored to obtain the desired loading. The resonator coupling will be "bottom L." The output loading will be provided by a link winding on the second inductor, with a turns ratio as needed to obtain Q_t, in conjunction with the receiver input impedance. We will choose a maximum total resonator capacitance of 4 times the minimum resonator capacitance in order to tune octave frequency bands. Pick a minimum capacitance, including strays, of 50 pF at 4

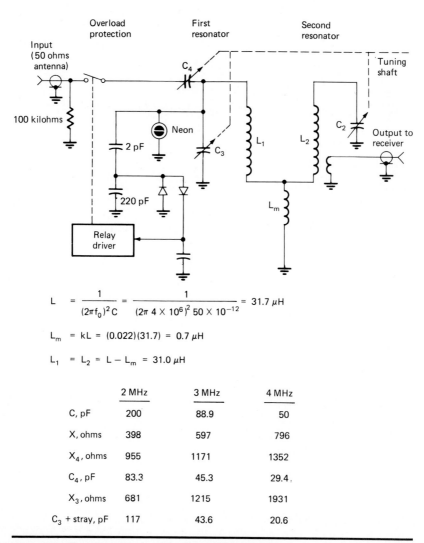

$$L = \frac{1}{(2\pi f_0)^2 C} = \frac{1}{(2\pi\, 4 \times 10^6)^2\, 50 \times 10^{-12}} = 31.7\ \mu H$$

$$L_m = kL = (0.022)(31.7) = 0.7\ \mu H$$

$$L_1 = L_2 = L - L_m = 31.0\ \mu H$$

	2 MHz	3 MHz	4 MHz
C, pF	200	88.9	50
X, ohms	398	597	796
X_4, ohms	955	1171	1352
C_4, pF	83.3	45.3	29.4
X_3, ohms	681	1215	1931
C_3 + stray, pF	117	43.6	20.6

Figure 8.10 Two-resonator tunable filter of Example 8.1.

MHz. The inductors can be calculated as shown in Fig. 8.10. The capacitors are calculated from the equations for X_3 and X_4 in Fig. 8.7. The capacitors must be calculated at several frequency points within the band to establish their tracking curves. The inductors and input capacitor may be switched to cover additional frequency bands, while the main tuning capacitors are reused.

Example 8.2: Fixed Preselector An 18-MHz receiver needs a filter to protect it from a nearby foreign broadcast transmitter only 2 percent from the center of the band. The receiving antenna signal is 50 V and the receiver can operate with 1.0-V undesired signals. Resonators with $Q_u = 525$ can be obtained by using cavities containing helical resonator coils operated below their self-resonance. The receiver has a 14-dB noise figure, and a low-noise pre-amp (noise figure 5 dB) is being considered because the antenna is not efficient and there is loss incurred in distributing the signal to several receivers. The preselector should be designed for multicoupling.

solution The 2 percent separation gives a normalized frequency variable of

$$\frac{Q_u B}{f_0} = 525 \left(1.02 - \frac{1}{1.02} \right) = 20.8$$

We need $20 \log(^{50}\!/_1) = 34$-dB overall reduction in the undesired signal, which is the total of filter attenuation and amplifier gain. This gain will depend on the noise figure goal. We will guess the filter in-band loss to be 4.5 dB and try for a 12-dB system noise figure. The Friis noise figure equation [16] is used, as discussed in Chap. 3 and Ref. 20 of this chapter, to find the noise figure of the cascaded stages. All values must be converted from dB to power. Remember that the filter noise figure is equal to its loss (neglecting mismatch effects) because the filter contributes thermal noise, as well as attenuating the signal power. We start with:

$$F_R = 25 \quad \text{(14 dB receiver noise)}$$

$$F_A = 3.2 \quad \text{(5 dB amplifier noise)}$$

$$F_F = \frac{1}{G_F} = 2.8 \quad \text{(4.5 dB filter noise)}$$

$$F_{\text{sys}} = 15.8 \quad \text{(12 dB)}$$

$$= F_F + \frac{F_A - 1}{G_F} + \frac{F_R - 1}{G_F G_A} = 2.8 + \frac{3.2 - 1}{0.35} + \frac{25 - 1}{0.35 G_A}$$

Solving for the gain gives $G_A = 9.8$ or about 10 dB. Then we need a filter attenuation of $34 + 10 = 44$ dB.

Filters with various numbers of resonators and 44-dB attenuation at this frequency are checked on the plots of Fig. 8.9. It is decided that three resonators give the best hardware/loss tradeoff:

n	L_0, dB
2	8 (out of valid range)
3	4.3
4	3.7

We note that the passband is fairly flat out to a normalized bandwidth of 3 or so. This indicates that we may be able to use a fixed tuned filter with a tunable receiver if our band of interest is no wider than

$$B = \frac{3f_0}{Q_u} = \frac{3 \times 18}{525} = 0.103 \text{ MHz}$$

This possibility should be checked by a circuit analysis program before committing to the design. Passband tilt could be a problem, depending on the coupling methods.

We next calculate the filter coupling and loading:

$$r = \frac{4.3}{4.343 \times 3} = 0.330$$

$$Q_t = 525 \times 0.330 = 173$$

$$k = \frac{1}{173} = 0.0058$$

The filter is illustrated in Fig. 8.11. Figure 8.12 shows the insertion loss response of the filter. Coupling is obtained by an aperture in the wall between each resonator and the next. The aperture dimensions can be determined experimentally, using the coupling measurement technique discussed in Sec. 8.5. The input and output end loading is obtained with a small capacitor or a probe inserted into the top of the resonator cavity. This provides capacitive coupling to balance the inductive coupling between resonators and improves the stopband symmetry. A slight tilt remains, but the result is very close to the original design values. This form of coupling also presents a high input impedance for good multicoupling, as shown in Fig. 8.13.

The Friis equation is now used to check the system noise figure. Filter:

$$F_F = 2.7 \quad (4.3 \text{ dB})$$
$$G_F = 0.37 \quad (-4.3 \text{ dB})$$

Amplifier:

$$F_A = 3.2 \quad (5 \text{ dB})$$
$$G_A = 10 \quad (10 \text{ dB})$$

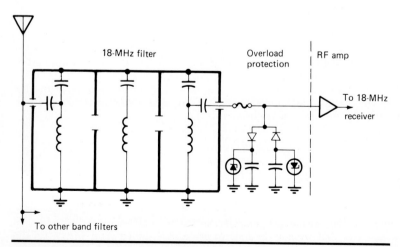

Figure 8.11   Three-resonator fixed filter of Example 8.2.

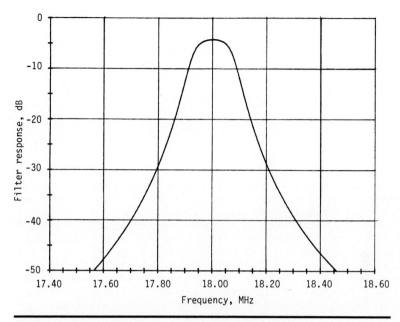

Figure 8.12 Frequency response of fixed filter of Example 8.2.

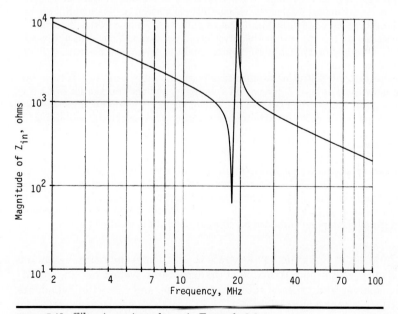

Figure 8.13 Filter input impedance in Example 8.2.

Receiver:

$$F_R = 25.1 \quad (14 \text{ dB})$$

System noise figure:

$$F_{\text{sys}} = F_F + \frac{F_A - 1}{G_F} + \frac{F_R - 1}{G_F G_A}$$

$$= 2.7 + \frac{3.2 - 1}{0.37} + \frac{25.1 - 1}{(0.37)(10)} = 15.0 \quad (11.8 \text{ dB})$$

The new system noise figure is 11.8 dB, which is a significant improvement over the original receiver noise figure if the system is used with an inefficient antenna system or in a low-noise location.

Next we should consider what we have done to the intermodulation intercept point. Assume the receiver's third-order intercept point is $+15$ dBm and the amplifier input intercept is $+13$ dBm. As discussed in Chap. 3 and Refs. 17 and 20, the intercept points should be adjusted one to one by the gains and losses in order to refer them to a new point in the system, and when expressed in milliwatts, they will, in the worst case, combine like resistors in parallel. In this example, we will find the combined intercept point of the receiver and amplifier at the amplifier input:

$$I_{\text{sys}} = \left[\frac{1}{I_A} + \frac{G_A}{I_R} \right]^{-1} = \left[\frac{1}{20} + \frac{10}{32} \right]^{-1} = 2.7 \text{ mW or 4.4 dBm}$$

Referring this to the filter input gives an input intercept of $4.4 + 4.3 = 8.7$ dBm for signals near the peak of the preselector passband. It is assumed that the filter has no distortion because it uses no ferrous materials. The amplifier is not contributing much distortion, but its gain significantly increases the distortion in the receiver for signals within the preselector passband. This situation would improve if we let the system noise figure equal the original receiver noise figure and used less amplifier gain.

The out-of-band distortion performance is considerably improved. If the interfering signals are at least 2 percent off-frequency, and the third-order distortion of the receiver follows the expected 3:1 rate of change, the filter will increase the intercept point at a rate of ⅔ dB for each dB of *relative* selectivity, obtaining

$$8.7 + \tfrac{2}{3}(44 - 4.3) = 68 \text{ dBm}$$

which is a very respectable value. The value will increase for greater frequency separations. Actually, one interfering tone will have to be separated twice as far as the other from the operating frequency in order to produce an in-band third-order product (e.g., $f_0 = 2f_2 - f_1$). It will be attenuated much more, improving the intermodulation performance much more than that calculated above.

The numbers in Example 8.2 illustrate the tradeoffs the receiving system designer must go through to arrive at an acceptable system design, considering the sources and types of interference, noise, and distortion which are most critical in each application.

8.5 Implementation Considerations

Operating voltages

The midband rms voltages in the min-loss filter can be estimated from the loaded Q_L values, reactance at resonance X_0, and power P flowing through the filter:

$$Q_L = \left[\frac{1}{Q_\ell} + \frac{1}{Q_u} \right]^{-1} = Q_u \frac{r}{1 + r}$$
$$V^2 = Q_L X_0 P$$

This estimate is approximate and is valid only at resonance. It will usually be found that some resonator has more voltage at frequencies near the edge of the passband. For farther out-of-band signals the selectivity improves through each resonator. The equal-loading property of the min-loss filter assures that the in-band voltages will be approximately equal. Other filter designs such as Butterworth may have some resonators with extremely high in-band voltages. It is advisable to use a circuit analysis program to determine the voltage-vs.-frequency curve for each resonator before setting component ratings. Such a plot for Example 8.2 is shown in Fig. 8.14, for an antenna signal of 1 V into a matched load.

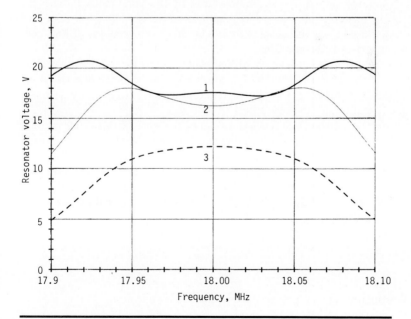

Figure 8.14 Resonator voltages in Example 8.2.

Measuring *Q* and coupling

It is desirable to measure the assembled unloaded resonator's Q_u to verify that all the losses have been accounted for, even if the components were measured. For comparison and combining components, it is best to work with measurements as dissipations ($d = 1/Q$) because the dissipations add numerically. This leads more quickly to an intuitive grasp of where the losses are than does working with Q values.

The in-place measurement is based on Dishal's methods [18, 19]. The simplest equipment setup uses a stable RF generator having a fine-tune adjustment, a frequency counter, and a sensitive RF voltmeter. A network analyzer with a sweep display is more convenient, if available. The generator and voltmeter are each very lightly coupled to the resonator with a "sniffer" probe, loop of wire, or one of the filter-terminating methods at an extremely high Q_t. The insertion loss when the resonator is coupled between generator and meter should be no less than 30 dB to avoid lowering the Q being measured. Adjacent resonators and terminations are disconnected (opened or shorted as appropriate) when measuring a single resonator.

The signal generator is tuned for a peak voltmeter reading, and then tuned above and below to find the frequency separation between the 3-dB (71 percent voltage) frequencies. We use the equation

$$d = \frac{1}{Q} = \frac{F_{3H} - F_{3L}}{F_0}$$

End-resonator loaded Q_L can be measured by the same method, with the termination reconnected and other resonators still disconnected. Then Q_t can be calculated from the measurements to check the accuracy of link-coupled or tapped-coil terminations.

A vector impedance meter provides another means for determining Q by reading the 45° phase points, which are nearly coincident with the 3-dB points. The high impedance of this instrument makes it easy to use with less instrument loading on the resonator.

The coupling between two resonators can be measured in a similar manner by lightly coupling the generator to one and the meter to the other. All other resonators or terminations are removed (open or short circuit as appropriate for the topology). The two resonators are carefully tuned to the same frequency. For useful values of coupling between the resonators, a double-resonance peak will be obtained. The separation between the peaks is measured and *k* is computed:

$$k = \frac{F_H - F_L}{F_0}$$

8.6   Control

A tunable preselector filter must be kept tuned to the same frequency as its associated receiver. Synthesized receivers will have logic level binary or binary coded decimal (BCD) frequency information. The preselector will take this information and convert it to the necessary switching or servo positioning signals its filter tuning elements need. Conversions and calculations can be done by a microprocessor.

In electromechanical servo-tuned filters it is necessary to obtain a feedback of the tuning element position (Fig. 8.15). Potentiometers or shaft encoders may be used. The digital information giving operating frequency must be converted into a code or voltage specifying where in the tuning band the elements are to be positioned. The servo system drives the tuning elements to the position where the feedback matches the desired value.

Dither sensing tunes the filter to a sample of the desired RF frequency. It senses the direction to tune by varying the filter's tuned frequency rapidly back and forth (dithering) a small amount and determining which direction increases the level of the RF signal. When properly tuned, no increase is found in either direction. Tuning dither can be provided by a varactor or small diode-switched capacitor. Dither tuning is not a widely applicable method because it cannot be used with receive-only equipment and is relatively slow.

Switched-element tuning also requires conversion of the frequency information (Fig. 8.3) to select the proper tuning element switches for each frequency. This conversion is sufficiently complex to require a microprocessor or a very large lookup table. In the simplest case, with binary-weighted tuning elements, the square of the frequency must be calculated. In practice, there may be several stray effects to compensate in the selection of elements. Often it is simpler to perform interpolation in the microprocessor between entries of a lookup table which has the frequency-squared curve and the major stray effects precomputed.

8.7 Multicoupling

The need frequently arises to operate several receivers from one antenna. Signal preamplifiers and power splitters allow this to be done with minimal degradation of noise figure, but such devices may not be able to handle large interfering signals. If a preselector is needed on a single receiver, it is also needed on a multiple-receiver connection. A single preselector cannot be used unless the receivers always operate on very closely spaced frequencies. Therefore we must connect several preselector inputs to the antenna and are faced with the problem of assuring satisfactory performance.

This situation is very difficult to analyze because the input impedance of each preselector filter varies as it is measured across the frequency band and is also different for each frequency it may be tuned to. The two methods of attack are worst-case analysis and statistical simulation. Worst-case analysis can often suggest a configuration which looks promising, although the worst-case degradation is large. Then statistical analysis of many randomly chosen combinations of tuned frequencies can tell whether 90 or 99 percent of the cases are acceptable.

As an example, consider a preselector tuned to some frequency in the mid-

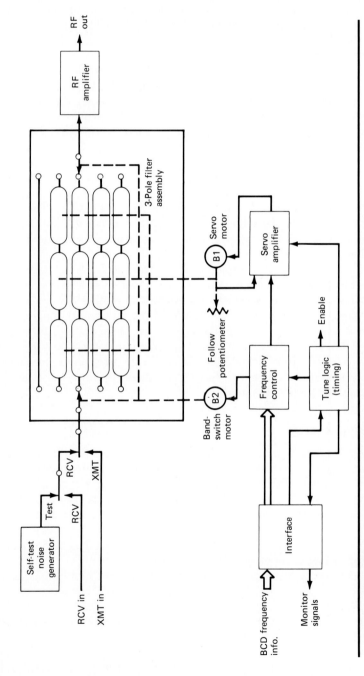

Figure 8.15 Block diagram of servo-tuned preselector.

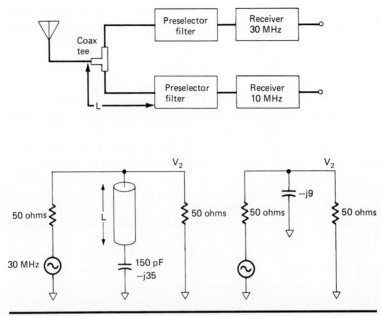

Figure 8.16 Worst-case multicoupling analysis for two units.

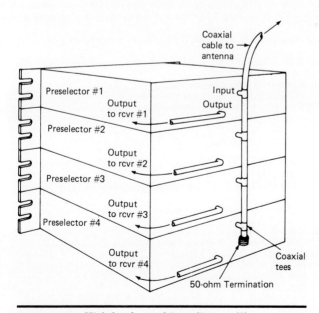

Figure 8.17 High-level multicoupling with preselectors.

dle of the HF band and which has an input impedance above its operating frequency modeled by a 150-pF capacitor (Fig. 8.16). Let us analyze the degradation it causes a second unit tuned to 30 MHz with an input impedance on frequency of 50 ohms. At 30 MHz the capacitance has a reactance of 35 ohms. If there is a 1.5-ft (0.46-m), 50-ohm, 66 percent velocity coax between the capacitance and the common connection point, the transmission line effect transforms the 35 ohms to 9 ohms of reactance. It is shunting the 50-ohm input to the second preselector, which sees a 10-dB loss compared to having the antenna unshared.

This type of analysis leads to the rule of thumb that if the input impedance off-frequency is capacitive, the coax length to the tee connection must be as short as possible. If the input impedance is always inductive off-frequency, a small coax length may improve the performance, but a long coax will cause bad degradation at some frequency.

If many units are connected together, a useful starting point is a daisy chain of tee connections, all with short coax lengths, and a resistive termination at the end (Fig. 8.17). The best termination may not be the coax impedance, and the best location may not be at the end of the chain, since the system is full of mismatched impedances. This model can be varied to study the effects of coax lengths, termination impedance, and of inserting reactances between the units.

REFERENCES

1. Anatol I. Zverev, *Handbook of Filter Synthesis,* John Wiley & Sons, New York, 1967.
2. W. H. Hayward, *Introduction to Radio Frequency Design,* Prentice-Hall, Englewood Cliffs, NJ, 1982, Chaps. 2 and 3.
3. James K. Hardy, *High Frequency Circuit Design,* Reston Publishing, Reston, VA, 1978, Chap. 2.
4. ITT, *Reference Data for Radio Engineers,* 6th ed., Howard W. Sams, Indianapolis, 1975, pp. 24-28 to 24-30 (material on helical resonators).
5. Zverev, op. cit., Chap. 9, material on helical resonators.
6. ITT, op. cit., pp. 4-28 to 4-31 (material on dissipation factors).
7. ITT, op. cit. p. 8-25, Fig. 28, and p. 9-2 (material on coupling circuits).
8. William E. Sabin, "Designing Narrow Band-Pass Filters with a BASIC Program," *QST,* vol. LXVII May 1983, pp. 23–29.
9. Seymour B. Cohn, "Direct Doupled Resonator Filters," *Proc. IRE,* vol. 45, February 1957, pp. 187–196.
10. Seymour B. Cohn, "Dissipation Loss in Multiple-Coupled Resonator Filters," *Proc. IRE,* vol. 47, August 1959, pp. 1342–1348.
11. Jesse J. Taub, "Design of Minimum Loss Bandpass Filters," *Microwave J.,* vol. 6, November 1963, pp. 67–76.
12. Robert L. Sleven, "Pseudo-exact Bandpass Filter Design," *Microwaves,* vols. 11 and 12, August 1968 through July 1969 (appeared in eight parts).
13. R. W. Carroll and D. B. Hallock, "Application of the Minimum-Loss Filter to Optimum Receiver Input Design," Collins Radio Co. Working Paper WP-8521, August 1965.
14. R. W. Carroll, "Synthesis of Optimal Receiver Preselectors," Collins Radio Co. Working Paper WP-8522, August 1965.
15. Herman J. Blinchikoff and Anatol I. Zverev, *Filtering in the Time and Frequency Domains,* John Wiley & Sons, New York, 1976, Sec. 6.3.
16. H. T. Friis, "Noise Figures of Radio Receivers," *Proc. IRE,* vol. 32, July 1944, pp. 419–422. [Note: Equation (15) on Friis' p. 421 is garbled and should read: $F_{ab} = F_a + (F_b - 1)/G_a$.]

17. Hayward, op. cit., Chap. 6.
18. M. Dishal, "Alignment and Adjustment of Synchronously Tuned Multiple-Resonant-Circuit Filters," *Proc. IRE,* vol. 63, November 1951, pp. 1448–1455.
19. Hayward, op. cit., Sec. 3.4.
20. W. E. Sabin, "A BASIC Approach to Calculating Cascaded Intercept Points and Noise Figure," *QST,* vol. LXV, October 1981, pp. 21–24.

9

Synthesizers for SSB

Donald E. Phillips

William R. Weaverling

This chapter will deal with frequency synthesizers appropriate for medium- and high-performance HF SSB radios. Space limitations preclude a thorough treatise on synthesizer design, many aspects of which are covered in the literature (see Refs. 6, 10, 14, 17, and 19, for example). We will concentrate on tuning speed, phase noise, spurious output signals, and the generation of small frequency steps needed in the HF band. The most important phase-locked loop configurations will be discussed; newer, all-digital techniques for producing small steps will be introduced, and the methods of combining these with traditional loops will be shown.

The method of analysis is, we believe, unique. Most of the literature on synthesizers presents either a detailed mathematical analysis of single loops or a discussion of multiloop synthesizers that have already been designed. Here, we will concentrate on the important middle ground, where it is assumed that the individual building blocks exist to build a loop and the designer must understand in detail the overall loop properties and the way loops relate to each other. Block diagrams will be used extensively; the blocks that make up a loop will be assigned terminal characteristics and analyzed. Computer analysis will be extensively used. Graphic results will be shown for each configuration, and it will become clear why certain arrangements are preferred and what level of complexity is required to produce the desired output.

9.1   Receiver-Synthesizer Relationship

Overall frequency scheme

Synthesizer design requires coordination with the receiver or transmitter frequency schemes, which should be created together to optimize important tradeoffs in the choice of all frequencies. Figure 9.1 shows a receiver scheme that will be used as a design example throughout this chapter. This design is typical of a modern, high-performance upconverter type like those discussed in Chap. 3. The first IF at $f_1 = 109.35$ MHz is commonly used and is high enough to reduce the first-mixer spurious responses but low enough that crystal filters at f_1 are available. The second IF at $f_2 = 10.7$ MHz gives the designer a wide choice of available crystal filters, and f_3 at 455 kHz makes a wide selection of mechanical, ceramic, or crystal filters usable.

The synthesizer is required to produce frequencies f_4, f_5, f_6, and the 455-kHz product detector injection f_3 with certain specifications on the level, frequency stability, purity, and tuning time. If the receiver interference rejection specifications require a narrow filter for f_1, then f_4 must provide all the frequency variation with f_5 fixed. If a wider IF at f_1 can be permitted, the synthesizer design can provide coarse variations in f_4 and fine variations in f_5; here we assume all of the variation must be in f_4.

Most SSB synthesizers use a phase-locked loop to produce f_4, for its built-in filtering, economy, flexibility, and producibility rather than direct analog synthesis. This chapter initially features all PLLs, but later includes other digital techniques.

Mixer injection choices

The choice of high- or low-side receiver first-mixer injection involves both receiver and synthesizer design tradeoffs which need to be made before considering the synthesizer in more detail. Assuming that a PLL will be used to provide f_4 (Fig. 9.1), the choice will depend upon the frequency range of the VCO, the divider and frequency control capabilities, the phase noise allowed for f_4, and the spurious levels allowed in the first receiver mixer.

The frequency ratio of the VCO is less for high-side injection. Lower VCO tuning ratios mean easier VCO design, assuming that the frequency does not go too high for the available circuit components. High-side injection with a

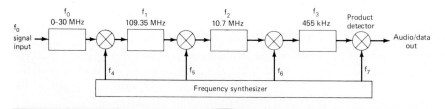

Figure 9.1   Relationship of the receiver to the synthesizer.

1.27 ratio (139.35/109.35) is preferred when only this factor is considered, although low-side injection with a 1.38 ratio is also possible. Ratios become difficult in the 1.5 to 1.75 range and impossible above about 2.0. To cover higher ratios, it is necessary to bandswitch either whole oscillators or the frequency-determining components of one oscillator.

Phase noise originating in the VCO is usually lower at the high-frequency end of any given VCO tuning range, partly because of the higher varactor diode Q at higher tuning voltages. Low-side injection would provide lowest VCO noise near 109.35 MHz (receive frequencies near 0 Hz), while high-side injection would provide lower VCO noise near 139.35 MHz (receive frequencies near 30 MHz). However, the lower tuning ratio required with high-side injection might counteract this effect since the varactor diode tuning voltage would not have to go as low.

The divider upper frequency limit and the range and direction of counts available may also help determine whether f_4 is above or below 109.35 MHz. For high-side injection using a PLL, the divide ratio N will increase as receive frequency increases, while for low-side injection N will decrease. With microprocessor control, either choice may be acceptable. The need to control N with mechanical switches or to retrofit the synthesizer into older equipment may influence the decision, since dividers using both variable-modulus prescalers and counters are easier to implement as downcounters, with N increasing as channel frequency increases.

In the first receiver mixer, high-side-injected difference mixing typically results in lower levels of spurious responses (see Chap. 3). When very low VCO phase noise at low receiver input frequencies is needed, and the first-receiver-mixer spurious responses are low enough, low-side injection would be the proper choice. For the design example in this chapter we have chosen high-side injection with f_4 ranging from 109.35 to 139.35 MHz.

Synthesizer configurations

SSB synthesizers may use one or many PLLs, depending upon the required noise, spurious, and settling time requirements. Small frequency increments are needed for SSB (100 Hz or less), which result in a correspondingly low reference frequency for a single PLL. A loop with such a low reference would have a bandwidth of 5 Hz or less, and would not reject noise, mechanical vibration, magnetic field, and power supply ripple components in the audio frequency range. Also, SSB is more sensitive to phase noise than conventional AM; multiple-loop methods must therefore be used.

Section 9.2 describes loops with improved performance, which generate coarse (100-kHz) steps in the "output" loop providing f_4 (the variable injection), and with fine frequency steps mixed into the loop from a separate source. Section 9.3 descrbes the highest-performance two-loop schemes for generating coarse steps. Section 9.4 then describes methods of generating fine frequency increments, including special techniques to obtain wider bandwidth with small frequency steps in single or dual loops.

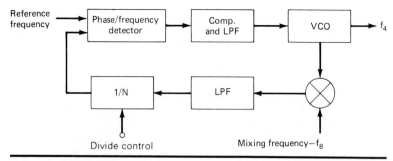

Figure 9.2 Basic elements of a PLL to produce f_4.

9.2 Generating Coarse Frequency Steps in the Output Loop

The output loops providing f_4 in these examples will use a 100-kHz reference to allow the loop bandwidth to cover audio frequencies. Fine frequency steps are supplied through a loop mixer. The basic components (Fig. 9.2) will be discussed in sufficient detail for analytical purposes, and the same principles will then apply to later designs described in this chapter.

Basic PLL design

The VCO tuning curve (frequency vs. control voltage V_c) is basic to loop design. A VCO and its tuning curve are shown in Fig. 9.3. The 109.35- to 139.35-MHz operating range is tuned with a V_c ranging from 5 to 13 Vdc (with a maximum VCO range of 105 to 142 MHz and a maximum V_c range of 3.0 to 13.5 Vdc). The slope at any point is designated as K_v in megahertz/volt, which decreases with increasing frequency. It is especially important to know the extremes of K_v, as well as the extreme frequency limits past the desired operating range. The latter are important because under transient conditions when the loop is tuning, V_c could go above 13 Vdc or below 5 Vdc. This could create problems if, for example, the loop divider ceased operation above 150 MHz or the VCO stopped running below $V_c = 2$ Vdc. Also, it is necessary to know the tuning curve over the temperature range to be encountered. K_v plays a key role in many loop characteristics and must be a stable, repeatable parameter.

The PLL shown in Fig. 9.2 has a mixer between the VCO and the variable divider. The mixer allows introduction of fine frequency increments through the mixing frequency f_8, and can reduce the divider input frequency and count ratio. A low-pass filter (LPF) at the mixer output reduces interference from the mixer input signals. An IF amplifier would be used, if necessary, to drive the divider.

The frequency divider divides the VCO or mixer output frequency by

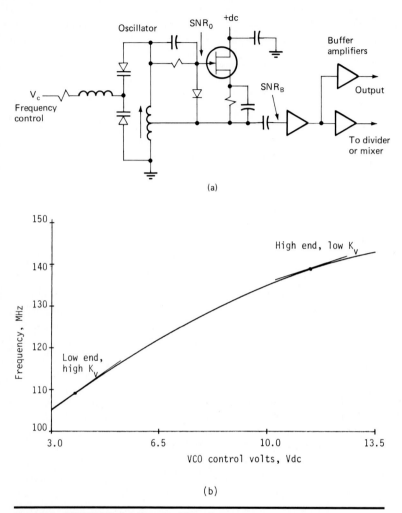

(a)

(b)

Figure 9.3   FET VCO. (*a*) Circuit; (*b*) tuning curve.

some integer value N, resulting in f_D which is applied to one of the phase detector inputs. The divider usually consists of a digital programmable counter, with a variable-modulus prescaler to extend the upper frequency limit.

The phase detector produces a voltage related to the phase difference between the reference input f_{R1} and the divider output f_D. The digital phase detectors discussed in this chapter develop a variable duty-ratio rectangular wave error signal composed of both ac (v_c) and dc (V_c) components. Phase/frequency detectors are usually used to ensure rapid locking from an unlocked condition.

Two types of phase/frequency detectors are shown in Fig. 9.4. Because of some confusion in the literature about phase detector terminology (such as "edge-triggered," etc.), we will adopt the following functional definitions, regardless of the hardware used. A "phase/frequency detector" (discriminator) is any phase detector having a strong off-frequency sense, to ensure rapid capture. All phase detectors used in this chapter are of the phase/frequency type.

A "proportional phase detector" has a phase range of 2π radians, as shown in Fig. 9.4a (Refs. 1 and 2). The phase difference between the inputs (horizontal axis) causes the output rectangular wave to vary its duty ratio. This wave is filtered and becomes the VCO control voltage (vertical axis), so that the phase difference is roughly proportional to the VCO frequency. The slope of the phase-sensitive region is K_p in volts/radian. If this phase difference exceeds the 2π range, causing a loss-of-lock (LOL) condition, the additional frequency detection provides a strong error signal to move the VCO in the proper direction until phase lock occurs. Frequency detection in the proportional detector is shown by the horizontal lines at either limit, instead of a repeating sawtooth function. If the detector output swing is insufficient for the required V_c range, it may be amplified by a switching level shifter which has less noise than an analog "op-amp" amplifier.

A proportional detector is intended for use in a type 1 PLL, which means that there is only one integrator (the VCO frequency-to-phase conversion) in the open-loop transfer function. When used without lead-lag compensation, the proportional detector results in the highest tuning speed and minimum overshoot, but this requires careful loop gain adjustment, with prepositioning of the VCO control voltage if necessary.

A "differential phase/frequency detector" has a phase range of 4π radians, as shown in Fig. 9.4b (Ref. 3). The phase difference results in a voltage that varies on either side of some zero-phase center voltage. Frequency detection occurs because of the net dc shift in the sawtooth wave. An ac component exists when the phase difference is nonzero, but nearly disappears at the center operating point. This reduces the reference frequency filtering requirements. A differential phase/frequency detector is intended for use with a compensated integrator circuit, resulting in a type 2 PLL.

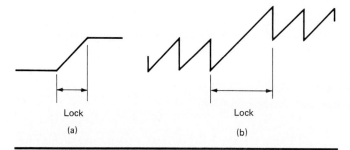

Lock   Lock

(a)   (b)

Figure 9.4 Phase/frequency detector average output voltage vs. phase difference. (a) Proportional 2π lock range; (b) differential 4π lock range.

The type 2 loop has higher gain at lower frequencies because of the added integrator, which tends to reduce noise at these frequencies, to reduce post-tuning drift due to component instabilities, and to tune more rapidly than a lead-lag-compensated type 1 loop. But it will tune more slowly than an uncompensated type 1 loop and may have more noise at some Fourier frequencies (Δf from carrier) because of the use of an op-amp integrator.

Type 2 loops will generally be used in our examples because of the reduced reference filtering requirements and the general availability of differential phase detectors as integrated circuits. Other types of phase detectors or combinations of types have been used, but the two discussed here are found most often in SSB synthesizers.

The low-pass filter plays a crucial role in loop stability, dynamics, and spectral purity of f_4. Its purpose is to reduce the loop reference frequency component, its harmonics, and high-frequency random noise on the VCO control voltage, without introducing enough phase shift to cause loop instability or poor dynamic characteristics. The term "LPF" used here does not include any compensating or integrator networks, which, of course, may have some additional filtering effect. LPF types include passive and active RC filters, which generally have the largest phase shift, high-order elliptic LC filters with less phase shift, and sample/hold types having the least phase shift. Sample/hold filters are most practical at reference frequencies below 5 kHz, and can be used with either proportional or differential phase/frequency detectors. Active RC filters using wideband op-amps are practical up to 100 kHz, where the attenuation requirement is not too severe. High-order elliptic LC filters are most useful at 100 kHz and above, where the inductance values are smaller.

Loop compensation circuits (Fig. 9.5) are also important. A type 1 uncompensated loop is partially shown in Fig. 9.5a. A switching limiter amplifier is used to provide the required V_c range. If a type 1 loop is unstable or underdamped because of insufficient phase margin, it may be stabilized with an RC lead-lag network (Fig. 9.5b). A type 2 loop, by definition, requires an integrator compensated for stability (Fig. 9.5c). A "charge pump" (Fig. 9.5d) combines the two phase detector outputs digitally to feed a single-ended network whose dynamic characteristics may differ from that shown in Fig. 9.5c in the amount of lag (or delay) contributed to the loop, depending upon whether the charge pump has a voltage or current output. Linearity in the zero-phase center region is more difficult to achieve with digital combining. The op-amp integrator is used in our type 2 loop examples to ensure greater linearity through zero phase, and consequently better control of loop dynamics.

Direct- and reverse-count mixer loops with variable dividers

As shown in Fig. 9.6 and Table 9.1, the VCO output is combined with a mixing frequency which lowers the divider input frequency (or loop IF), resulting in a lower division ratio N compared to a loop with no mixer. The lower

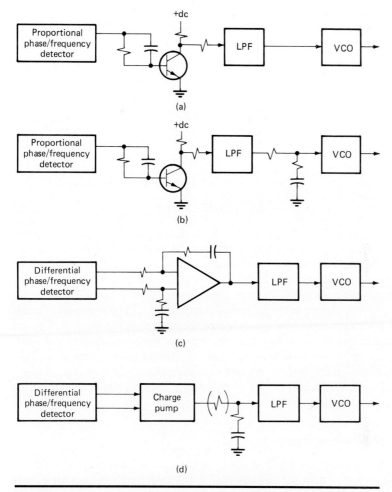

Figure 9.5 Compensation circuits. (*a*) Uncompensated loop; (*b*) lead-lag network; (*c*) dual-input integrator; (*d*) charge-pump integrator.

N ratio reduces reference noise multiplication, and a wide loop bandwidth helps suppress VCO noise. The 100-kHz reference results in 100-kHz steps. Finer steps enter through the mixing frequency.

If the mixing frequency is lower than the VCO frequency (low-side injection), the VCO frequency rises with increasing N, resulting in a "direct-count" loop. If it is higher than the VCO frequency (high-side injection), the VCO frequency is lowered by raising N, resulting in a "reverse-count" loop.

The usefulness of the reverse-count design lies in its ability to minimize loop bandwidth changes as the loop is tuned. Referring again to the VCO characteristic, Fig. 9.3*b*, the slope of the VCO curve (K_v) decreases as fre-

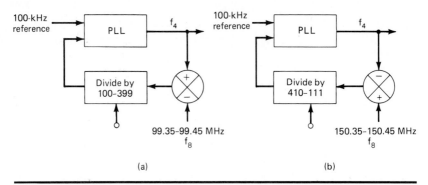

Figure 9.6 Loops with mixers and 100-kHz reference signals. (*a*) Direct count;
(*b*) reverse count.

quency increases. Since loop bandwidth is proportional to Kv/N, the bandwidth varies less in the reverse-count loop because K_v and N vary in the same direction. With proper VCO design and choice of IF tuning ratio (i.e., maximum-to-minimum ratio of N), it is possible to achieve nearly constant bandwidth over a wide VCO range, which then allows a wider stable bandwidth, as will be shown in the following paragraphs. This is especially important for wideband, fast-hop synthesizers where every possible microsecond must be removed from the tuning time. Other schemes are available to optimize bandwidth over a wide tuning range, but these usually involve switching integrator component values and can add considerable complexity and more noise to the loop. Further comparisons between these loops will be made in the following analysis.

Frequency domain analysis

The next step after the VCO is the LPF design. A Cauer (elliptic) LPF is often used to minimize phase shift within the loop bandwidth, with a large suppression of reference frequency sidebands, and can be easily built with small RF inductors and capacitors, with the first notch at 100 kHz and

TABLE 9.1   Loop parameters for Fig. 9.6

Parameters	Direct count	Reverse count
Reference frequency, kHz	100	100
VCO frequency f_4 range, MHz	109.35–139.35	109.35–139.35
Mixing freq f_8 range, MHz	99.35–99.45	150.35–150.45
N division range	100–399	410–111
Loop IF range, MHz	10.0–39.9	41.0–11.1
Phase-frequency detector	Differential	Differential
Loop type	2	2
LPF, 45° at, kHz	10	10
Integrator lead corner, kHz	1	2.5
Integrator gain	0.5	0.7

another notch at 200 kHz to help attenuate the first two harmonics. When the LPF phase characteristics are known, the open-loop response can be obtained and adjusted for stability and eventually for transient performance.

The open-loop responses of the direct- and reverse-count loops are shown in Figs. 9.7a and b (dashed lines). In the direct-count loop, the open-loop bandwidth (at 0-dB gain) varies considerably from the high to low ends of

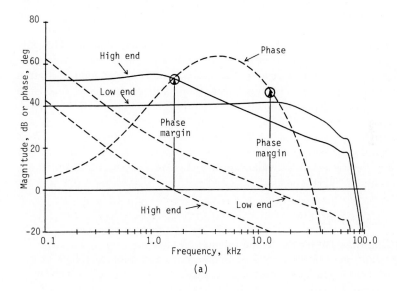

(a)

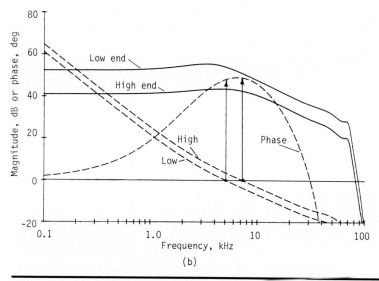

(b)

Figure 9.7 Loop frequency responses for Fig. 9.6. (a) Direct count; (b) reverse count. — Closed-loop response; --- open-loop response.

the VCO range, because K_v and N change in opposite directions, gain being proportional to K_v/N. The phase rises because of the integrator lead compensation, and then falls off rapidly because of the LPF (total loop phase shift is shown including the 180° inversion for negative feedback). The phase margin (phase at 0-dB gain) falls within the peak of phase. The compensation parameters were chosen for transient performance, to be described later. The smaller variations in the reverse-count loop are quite noticeable.

The open-loop response is the product of all the functions around the loop, including the phase detector gain K_p in volts/radian, the VCO gain K_v in hertz/volt, the divide function $1/N$, the frequency-to-phase conversion $1/s$ (the La Place integration), the LPF, and compensation, if used. The only time delay is the logic propagation delay, which is negligible in this case. Transport lag is not inherent in a PLL (Refs. 4 and 5), although it is often assumed in some "charge pumps" (Fig. 9.5c) and sample/hold filters. In these cases, an exact response is more accurate than an assumed delay (Ref. 6, Sec. 5.3).

The closed-loop responses in Fig. 9.7 also show that the reverse-count loop has less bandwidth variation, actually overcompensated with the high end of the band having a slightly wider bandwidth. The sharp cutoff of the Cauer LPF is seen at 70 kHz.

Time domain analysis

The settling time variations in the two approaches are even more dramatic (Fig. 9.8). Tuning is from 109.35 to 139.35 MHz and back to 109.35 in two periods of 3 ms each. The direct-loop compensation parameters were optimized for similar settling times in both directions.

Transient phase error (Fig. 9.8b) is the phase difference between the slewing VCO and a steady-state signal with the same phase as the final value of the VCO phase. For clarity, plotting is omitted for very large phase errors. Phase error is easily measured by mixing the VCO output with a phase-stable signal generator, both synchronized to the same frequency standard. The computer analysis includes nonlinear VCO gain, op-amp slew rate and voltage limiting, and phase detector characteristics. Not included are the effects of post-tuning drift caused by some types of capacitors and varactor diodes having charge penetration effects. Varactor diodes may also cause post-tuning drift because of thermal variations as their dissipation changes with frequency.

The direct-count loop takes almost 2 ms to reach 1 radian of error, while the reverse-count loop only takes 0.7 ms.

"Instantaneous frequency" error (Fig. 9.9) is computed vs. time. The downward "points" are transitions through zero frequency error due to the slightly underdamped loop. Although an "instantaneous frequency" settling time is often specified, it is more difficult to measure, being the derivative of the phase error measurement. Where rapid settling time is required, as in frequency-hopping systems, the phase-settling time specification is usually more appropriate. Since a rapidly changing frequency has a transient spread

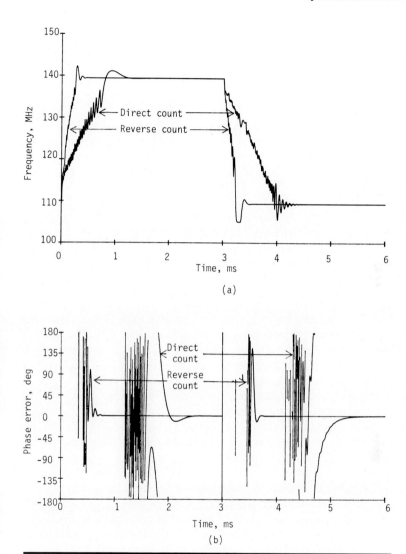

Figure 9.8 Transient responses for Fig. 9.6. (*a*) Absolute frequency; (*b*) phase error. Switching occurs at 0 and 3 ms.

to its spectrum, the signal is useful when the phase is stable, even before the instantaneous frequency reaches the system steady-state bandwidth. Since this frequency-error analysis does not represent a *physical reality,* it should not be used as a firm design goal, which can result in costly overdesign, but rather as a most useful graphical analytical *tool* for optimizing loop settling time as long as the final evaluation is done on a phase-settling basis (Ref. 7).

The curves are accurate enough to speed up the early stages in the design process and give the designer added insight about the interrelationships of the basic loop parameters.

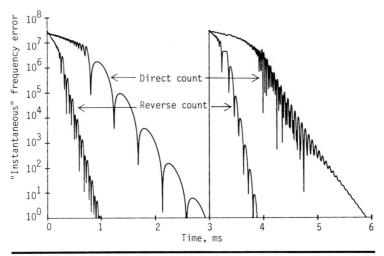

Figure 9.9 "Instantaneous" frequency error for Fig. 9.6.

The effect of compensation on transient performance is not what one would expect. Its usual purpose is to lower the loop bandwidth for stability or noise reasons (discussed under noise analysis). "Lagging", for either type 1 or type 2 loops, not only reduces the bandwidth with a corresponding increase in settling time, but also causes the loop to lose lock for large-frequency jumps, which further increases the settling time. Therefore, the total settling time is increased approximately as the *square* of the bandwidth reduction. Prepositioning of the VCO control voltage results in faster settling, more because of the gain reduction without lagging than the prepositioning itself.

In our example, frequency overshoot of the VCO driving the first receiver mixer can degrade the receiver performance whenever a large step is taken in a downward direction, especially in a frequency-hopping system. If the injection frequency passes through the receiver first intermediate frequency, it leaks through the mixer with enough power to excite the receiver IF filter, creating a large momentary signal and possibly upsetting the AGC system. If the signal frequency hopped from 30 to 2 MHz the first receiver mixer injection frequency would change from 139.35 to 111.35 MHz, just 2 MHz short of the IF at 109.35 MHz. Compensated loops inherently overshoot unless extremely overdamped. In fact, a type 2 second-order loop with a damping factor of 1 allows a 6 percent overshoot, which in the above case would be just short of reaching the IF. Since most loops designed for speed are somewhat underdamped and the LPF phase shift tends to increase the overshoot, this can be a significant design consideration. Even uncompensated type 1 loops must be carefully designed to control overshoot.

Figure 9.10 shows an enlarged overshoot area for the reverse-count loop. The original design overshoots past the receiver IF, hitting it twice (curve *A*). This occurs even for smaller frequency jumps (curve *B*). Narrowing the bandwidth and increasing the damping of the loop (curve *C*) reduces the overshoot at a considerable increase in settling time.

Prepositioning the VCO control voltage can greatly reduce the overshoot while maintaining faster settling (curve *D*). This requires precise voltage control. Prepositioning after the LPF results in even less overshoot, but some filtering may be necessary to prevent high-frequency noise from entering the VCO via the prepositioning circuit.

Another solution is windowing or blanking (between the oscillator and the receiver first IF), which may also be used for hopping spectrum control. However, very high attenuation is required to eliminate the effect of overshoot.

Loop noise sources

All noise levels in this chapter are normalized to a 1-Hz bandwidth. The various noise sources in a phase locked loop are now defined as shown in Fig. 9.11, with numerical examples for the reverse-count loop.

"Frequency standard noise" is that in the 5-MHz frequency standard sine wave output, with a typical noise level of -140 dBc for a simple fundamental crystal oscillator. If the reference divide-by-50 lowered this noise by 34 dB (20 log 50) to -174 dBc, the loop would multiply this by 52 dB to -122 dBc (Fig. 9.12). "Fourier frequency" is frequency-offset from the carrier.

"Digital reference noise" is defined here as originating in all sources after the VCO and before the phase detector combined output. This includes the mixer, IF amplifier, loop divider, reference divider, phase detector (but not voltage noise sources from the phase detector output to the VCO output, which is forward-path noise, discussed later), and the frequency standard itself. The term "digital" refers to the fact that these sources cause phase

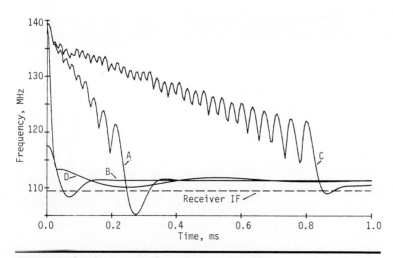

Figure 9.10 Synthesizer overshoot across receiver IF.

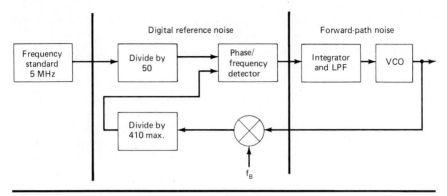

Figure 9.11 PLL noise sources.

jitter on the edges of the digital waveforms that appear at the output of the phase detector. The closed-loop effect on all reference noise is that of an LPF.

Careful measurements with a 100-kHz reference, divided from the frequency standard with high-speed HCMOS logic, indicate a noise level of −160 dBc at the reference frequency. The loop multiplies this by 52 dB (20 log 410) at the low end to −108 dBc, as shown in Fig. 9.12 (solid line). After 5 kHz, the loop rolls off noise because of this source until the loop filter corner near 70 kHz eliminates this noise from the VCO output.

"Forward-path noise" includes noise voltage sources from the phase detector output to the VCO, and the VCO phase noise itself. The loop response is basically low-pass (with one exception) to the noise voltage, and

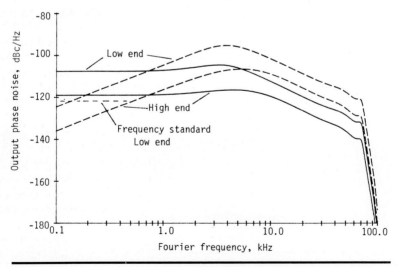

Figure 9.12 Noise sources (except the VCO) for loop in Fig. 9.6*b*. — Digital reference noise; --- forward-path noise before LPF and before the integrator.

high-pass to the VCO noise. The equivalent output phase noise is N times the voltage divided by Kp.

The loop response to noise voltages after the integrator and before the LPF in Fig. 9.12 was computed for a prepositioning op amp after the integrator. A total op-amp noise of 14 nV was assumed, consisting of 4 nV from a 5534 op amp, plus resistor noise. Noise voltages at the phase detector output and integrator input have a similar effect except without the low-frequency roll-off. Note that the noise of a single op amp is noticeably higher than the total standard and digital reference noise, which clearly indicates the need for lower-noise op amps or linearized high-voltage charge pumps.

"VCO noise" is plotted in Fig. 9.13 (the dashed lines apply to a circuit described later which has a 1.0-MHz reference). The open-loop VCO noise is predominantly phase noise close to the carrier, falling off with increasing Δf until near 1 MHz it reaches the "buffer noise" shelf (broadband amplifier noise), which is uncorrelated additive noise. The following equation (derived from Ref. 8) is useful to describe the basic form of VCO noise-to-signal ratio (NSR) (even though it omits shot noise and varactor diode parametric effects):

$$\text{VCO NSR} = 10 \log \left\{ \text{NSR}_b + \text{NSR}_o \left[\left(\frac{f_o}{2Q\Delta f} \right)^2 + \frac{f_a}{\Delta f} \right] \right\} \qquad \text{dBc} \qquad (9.1)$$

where Q = loaded Q (including all circuit losses, but no Q multiplication)

NSR_b = noise-to-signal-power ratio at the first buffer amplifier input (Fig. 9.3a)

NSR_o = noise-to-signal-power ratio at oscillator device input (Fig. 9.3a)

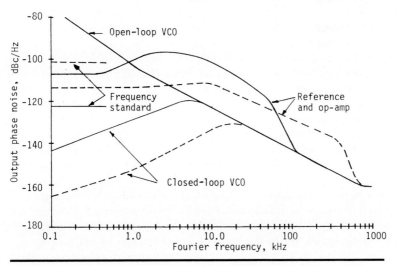

Figure 9.13 VCO noise and total noise in loops of Fig. 9.6b and 9.15. — 100-kHz reference; --- 1-MHz reference.

f_o = oscillator frequency

Δf = frequency separation (Fourier frequency) from f_o

f_a = upper frequency corner of extra 3-dB/octave slope (typically about 1000 Hz)

Note that the signal-to-noise ratios are inverted to simplify adding the two noise powers. Above $\Delta f = f_o/2Q$ (700 kHz in Fig. 9.13, assuming equal SNRs for the buffer and oscillator), the noise flattens out to a "shelf" of -162 dBc/ Hz, which depends on the buffer amplifier noise figure and the signal power at its input. The active-device noise figure in the VCO depends upon its input source impedance, which varies rapidly on either side of the carrier. Therefore, it is difficult to optimize oscillator operating conditions to minimize the noise figure as is done in low-noise amplifier designs. At frequencies lower than noise shelf corner, the sidebands become correlated phase noise, with a slope of -20 dB/decade. The slope increases to -30 dB/decade below a corner frequency f_a because of additional low-frequency noise sources (Ref. 9, Chap. 5). f_a is shown at a typical value of 1 kHz. Additional noise sources with steeper slopes at very low frequencies are not shown here.

Parametric effects in the varactor tuning diodes cause a noise level which is greater than their effect on tank Q would predict. This "varactor noise" and tuned circuit Q are the major factors in determining phase noise. There is a compromise between the noise shelf and close-in noise, since more power drawn from the tank reduces the loaded Q. To achieve a high carrier-to-noise ratio in the VCO, the buffer must have a low noise figure and a large signal-handling ability, and the oscillator should have a high level of available power in its LC tank.

In Fig. 9.13, the closed-loop VCO phase noise is also shown, where the high-pass filtering effect of the loop increasingly (because it is a type 2 loop) reduces the VCO noise at lower frequencies as the loop gain increases. Above the loop bandwidth, the VCO noise is unaffected.

The combination of all loop noise sources, or total closed-loop noise output, in Fig. 9.13 is shown as "Ref & op-amp." The multiplied digital reference noise predominates up to 700 Hz. Then the op-amp (forward-path) noise predominates, peaking at 3 kHz and rolling off to the LPF corner at 70 kHz, where it drops rapidly. Then the VCO noise is the major source until the -162-dBc noise shelf at 700 kHz is reached.

This example illustrates that a low-noise VCO does not guarantee a low-noise output over much of the Δf range. Even more important are the digital reference noise, the size of the loop multiplication ratio N, and the op-amp noise. Any additional noise from the loop-mixing frequency must be considered if it is higher than the closed-loop output noise shown. This loop could be improved from a noise standpoint by reducing reference noise sources and op-amp noise, and changing the overall frequency scheme to lower N.

If the tuning speed can be degraded, noise levels can be reduced by narrowing the bandwidth to 1500 Hz, where the op-amp noise would peak at -101 dBc and roll off above 1500 Hz. The VCO contribution would move up at 1500 Hz, but the VCO and reference noise combined would still be less than the op-amp contribution. The large noise bulge to about 24 dB above the VCO curve in the 5-kHz bandwidth design would be cut down to about 8 dB above the VCO curve with the narrower 1500-Hz bandwidth.

A type 1 loop with a low-noise switching amplifier and passive LPF (as in Fig. 9.5a) can reduce the forward path noise to almost the reference level, while allowing even faster tuning time than the example shown.

Loop mixer spurious signals

While a loop mixer has the advantages of lowering N and providing a convenient means of combining loops, the biggest disadvantage is the presence of unwanted discrete spurious signals in the mixer output. Since the VCO, which provides the LO input to the mixer, must vary over a 30-MHz range for this example, the ratio of mixer input frequencies varies enough to allow spurious as low as fifth order to cross over the IF output; seventh- and ninth-order crossovers are also present.

The fifth-order spurious crossovers at the mixer output are illustrated in Fig. 9.14a, with the synthesizer IF at 33.1 and 33.2 MHz and the mixing frequency varied from 150.35 to 150.45 MHz.

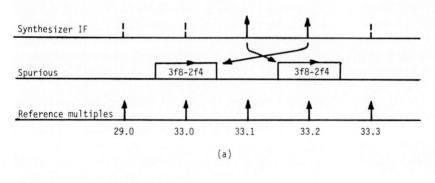

(a)

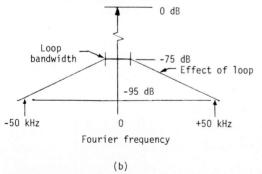

(b)

Figure 9.14 Mixer spurious in loop of Fig. 9.6b. (a) Spurious beating with reference harmonics; (b) loop filtering effect on spurious.

This corresponds to the receiver bands 23.1 to 23.2 and 23.2 to 23.3 MHz. Because the synthesizer IF moves in 0.1-MHz steps, the $3f_8-2f_4$ fifth-order spurious mixer output never falls right on the IF signal; it ranges from 50 to 150 kHz above when the IF is at 33.1 MHz and 250 to 150 kHz below when the IF is at 33.2 MHz. However, these spurious signals beat just as effectively with other harmonics of the reference, as shown. This occurs in the digital divider mechanism itself (Ref. 6, pp. 15 to 23).

Typical fifth-order spurious suppression for a properly terminated doubly balanced mixer with a -10-dBM signal at the RF port is 69 dB. A digital divider converts the discrete spurious signal into two FM sidebands, 6 dB lower. (A single sideband represents combined AM and FM modulation, and the AM sidebands are removed by clipping.) The resulting spurious at the divider output is $-69 - 6$ dBc divided by N, or -125 dBc, the beat note ranging from 50 kHz to 0, as the spurious crosses over any reference harmonics. Inside the loop bandwidth (Fig. 9.14b), the loop multiplies the spurious levels by N (20 log 331 = 50 dB) to -75 dBc, the same degree to which they were lowered by the divider, except for the 6-dB SSB to DSB conversion loss due to the divider. Outside the loop bandwidth, the spurious signals are attenuated by the low-pass effect of the loop.

Other spurious production mechanisms exist, such as leakage from either end of the divider to the other, leakage around the IF filter, and leakage between loops, both conducted and radiated. The degree to which the spurious signals are actually seen in the synthesizer output depends on the close-in phase noise performance of the whole synthesizer. In the design example above, -75-dBc spurious at $\pm$ 5-kHz separation due to the output loop mixer would be below the phase noise of most synthesizers in a 3-kHz noise bandwidth.

If low-side *receiver* mixer injection (below 109.35 MHz) had been chosen, the resulting *synthesizer* mixer loop with moderate values of N would produce a third-order crossover because of the higher variation in the ratio of mixer input frequencies (lower frequency divided by the higher). In a typical mixer this third-order spurious can be held to about -35 dB below the IF output, resulting in a possible -41-dBc spurious at the synthesizer output, allowing for mixer compression and converting to double sideband. In this example, with a 109.35-MHz first IF, the spurious crossover would occur at 5.325 MHz in the HF band. To achieve lower spurious levels, the output loop can be used for a purpose other than producing frequency increments, as described in Sec. 9.3.

9.3   Generating Coarse Frequency Steps with Combining Loops

Loop configuration

Figure 9.15 shows a unity gain ($N = 1$) combining first loop mixed with a second divider loop generating 1-MHz increments. The finer frequency steps are provided via the combining loop's high variable reference from another

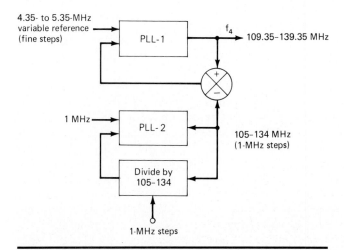

4.35- to 5.35-MHz
variable reference
(fine steps)

PLL-1

f_4

109.35–139.35 MHz

1 MHz

PLL-2

105–134 MHz
(1-MHz steps)

Divide by
105–134

1-MHz steps

Figure 9.15 Two-loop approach with improved mixer and noise performance.

circuit in the synthesizer. The problem of low-order loop mixer spurious output signals has been eliminated because as loop #2 steps from 105 to 134 MHz, the loop 1 VCO also moves upward, remaining above the loop #2 output by the value of the loop #1 reference. This keeps the ratio of the two mixer inputs nearly constant at approximately $105/109.35 = 0.96$, a value where lower-order spurious outputs are not troublesome. A combining loop sometimes has an N greater than 1, to alleviate tracking problems, but with a low fixed ratio.

The price paid for this excellent mixer performance is complexity. If the loop #1 output f_4 ever gets below the mixer image frequency (f_2 − variable reference), loop #1 will latch up on this wrong mixer sideband. To prevent this, the loop #1 VCO is coarsely tracked by the control voltage from loop #2, which keeps loop #1 in a safe range. The two VCOs must have similar tuning characteristics so that f_4 and f_8 keep the correct relationship across their respective bands. An alternative is to generate the tracking voltage with a D/A converter and curve shaper driven by the loop #2 frequency control lines; a programmable read-only memory (PROM) and D/A combination can also be used.

Loop analysis

The loop #2 bandwidth is held narrower than that for loop #1, and will control the transient performance of the combination, which is an order of magnitude faster than the loops with 100-kHz reference described in Sec. 9.2. The Bode plots are similar, at correspondingly higher frequencies. The frequency overshoot problem also exists in the coarse-step loop. However, noise and spurious levels do not change proportionally, and will be described in more detail.

Noise analysis

In the two-loop combination shown in Fig. 9.15, the loop #1 output noise level will depend primarily on loop #2 because of its higher multiplication of reference noise.

The loop #2 digital reference noise, shown in Fig. 9.16, is lower than that in Fig. 9.12 for the 100-kHz reference, both derived from the same 5-MHz frequency standard. This implies that broadband noise in digital dividers is not reduced in proportion to the division ratio, perhaps because of the sampling effect described in Ref. 6, pp. 75 to 81. Measurements with HCMOS logic, operating from low-noise power sources and good RF construction techniques, indicate that the digital reference noise of -160 dBc at 100 kHz rises to only -157 dBc if divided down to only 1 MHz, and to -145 dBc at 5 MHz. Direct measurement is difficult, and the stated values have mostly been inferred by reducing noise from all other sources and knowing the values of loop parameters accurately. New measuring methods should lead to improved analysis and design techniques in the next few years (Ref. 11).

The forward-path (op-amp) noise before the LPF is greatly reduced by the wider loop bandwidth. However, the 5-MHz frequency standard typical noise of -140 dBc in this scheme will result in an output noise of -102 dBc, which is higher than the -114-dBc digital reference noise (all levels referred to the VCO output frequency at the high end of the band). Therefore, it is now helpful to use a lower noise frequency standard or a crystal filter after the frequency standard to achieve the overall performance shown in Fig. 9.13 (dashed lines).

Thus, the choice of reference frequency has a great effect on synthesizer noise. The narrowband slow-tuning synthesizer with large N piles up noise

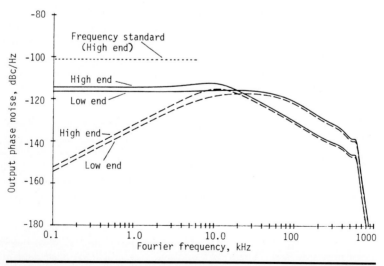

Figure 9.16 Noise sources (except the VCO) for loop #2 in Fig. 9.15. — Digital reference noise; --- forward-path noise before LPF.

near the carrier, but uses the narrow bandwidth and LPF to roll off the noise before it contaminates adjacent signals. Lower audio frequencies are contaminated with a high noise level, and the loop is very susceptible to external disturbances such as vibration, magnetic fields, and power supply ripple. The wideband, low-N synthesizer reduces noise and vibration effects and tunes fast, but requires clean reference sources and low-noise hardware for its benefits to be fully realized.

9.4   Generating Fine Frequency Increments

Phase-locked loop methods

The generation of fine frequency increments involves the application of the same principles that have been discussed in connection with coarse-increment loops. Reference frequencies must be high to provide loop bandwidths wide enough to meet the required tuning time specification. Division ratios (N) must be held low to keep multiplied digital reference and frequency standard noise low enough to meet the required phase noise specification, within the loop bandwidth of the loop (or loops) that will translate the fine increments to the output.

For small increments such as 1 to 10 Hz, it is necessary to generate steps at higher frequencies and larger increments, which are then divided to obtain the smaller steps; this also reduces the noise contribution from the fine-increment generator. The VCO and divider frequency ranges are critical design considerations. $N = 1$ (or at least low-fixed-N) combining loops are frequently required to raise the output of the fine-increment section to a frequency that will interface with the coarse loops. These principles are best illustrated by the following two examples that interface with the designs shown in Figs. 9.6b and 9.15, respectively.

Generating fine increments with two loops.   In Fig. 9.17, loop #3 gener-

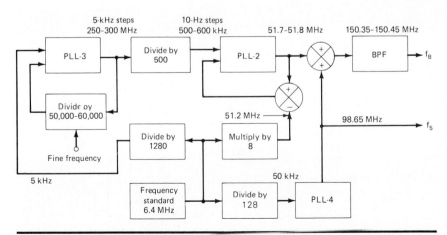

Figure 9.17   Loops to provide 10-Hz steps to the coarse loop in Fig. 9.6b, and the second receiver injection in Fig. 9.1.

ates a 250- to 300-MHz signal with 5-kHz steps; this reference is high enough to provide a 250-Hz loop bandwidth and tuning time (end to end) of 20 ms. Though N_3 maximum is 60,000, the output of loop #3 is divided by 500, for a net multiplication of only 60,000/500 = 120. Because the signal at the divide-by-500 output is translated (not multiplied) to the synthesizer output, noise contributions by loop #3 are low. The range of the loop #3 VCO is 50 MHz in order to produce the 100-kHz range required by the loop in Fig. 9.6b. The sole function of loop #2 is to translate the 500- to 600-kHz signal to 51.7 to 51.8 MHz, to be used in the final translation to 150.35 to 150.45 MHz.

Also illustrated is the use of fixed frequencies 51.2 MHz (eighth harmonic of the 6.4-MHz frequency standard) and 98.65 MHz, to be used as the second receiver injection (Fig. 9.1). Making maximum use of such available signals to minimize complexity is a major and challenging aspect of multiloop synthesizer design. Loop #2 also demonstrates a potential problem with $N = 1$ translating loops. The 51.7-to 51.8-MHz VCO must be stable enough over the required operating temperature range, on an open-loop basis, so as not to drift more than 500 kHz below 51.2 MHz, or the loop will latch up past the mixer image frequency. Thus, there is a practical limit on how small the reference frequency can be relative to the VCO frequency; the limit is 0.5 to 1 percent for a temperature-compensated VCO. Therefore, it may not be possible to make the translation in one loop, from the low-frequency range where the finest steps are generated to the required frequency (500 to 600 kHz and 150.35 to 150.45 MHz, in the example). Another reason might be a lack of the required fixed frequency signals of sufficient stability and spectral purity.

Generating fine increments with three loops. Figure 9.18 shows a method of generating the 4.35- to 5.35-MHz signal with 10-Hz steps to interface with the two-coarse-loop approach of Fig. 9.15. Loop #3 acts as an $N = 1$ combining loop for signals from loops #4 and #5. Loop #5 generates 10-

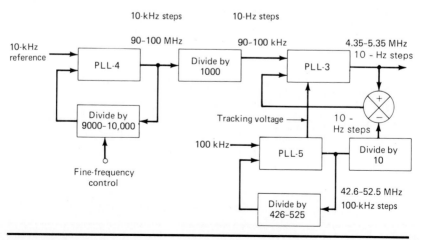

Figure 9.18 Loops to provide 10-Hz steps to the coarse loops in Fig. 9.15.

kHz steps across the 4.26- to 5.25-MHz range, which is translated by loop #3. The net worst-case multiplication of 100-kHz reference noise is only $N_{5,\text{max}}/10 = 525/10 = 52.5$ or $20 \log 52.5 = 34$ dB. Loop #5 must track the loop #3 VCO to prevent loop #3 from latching up past the image when loop #5 makes its largest steps. This tracking voltage could also be provided by an outside source such as a microprocessor that also controls the division ratios.

The finest 10-Hz steps are provided by loop #4, where the VCO produces 10-kHz steps across the 90- to 100-MHz range. This is divided by 1000 to produce 10-Hz steps over the 90- to 100-kHz range, which acts as a reference for loop #3, where it is converted to the desired 4.35- to 5.35-MHz range. The net worst-case multiplication of 10-kHz reference noise is only 10,000/1000 or 20 dB. Unity gain loop #3 and loop #1 (in Fig. 9.15) provide no additional multiplication.

The settling time can be estimated for loops in these frequency ranges as 50 to 200 reference periods (depending on loop type). For loop #4 (the slowest in this scheme), which has a 10-kHz reference, this would be 5 to 20 ms, which is adequate for dial-tuned SSB radios. The division by 1000 will reduce this settling time by a small amount, but not by 1000 because of the exponential characteristic of loop settling. Loops #3 and #5 would be about 10 times faster because of the higher references.

The "difference-loop scheme" shown in Fig. 9.19 (Ref. 12) uses two loops with references that differ by the smallest desired increment, in this case 100 Hz. Loop #2 tunes in 10-kHz steps, with the output f_8 always above f_4. For steps in f_4 of 10 kHz, only N_2 changes, tuning the 114.3- to 144.3-MHz range in 3000- 10-kHz steps. The loop #1 VCO is coarsely tracked by the loop #2

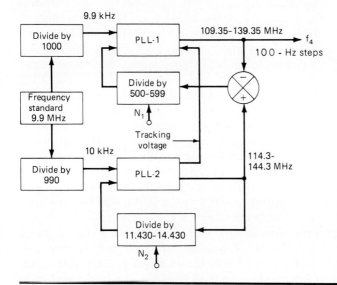

Figure 9.19   Difference-loop synthesizer.

tuning voltage, and its divider N_1 is changed at the same time as N_2 for 100-Hz steps. The *difference* in the frequency changes of the two loops appears at f_4. Since the smallest changes in N are the same for both dividers, $\Delta f_4 = \Delta N \times 10 \text{ kHz} - \Delta N \times 9.9 \text{ kHz} = \Delta N \times 100 \text{ Hz}$. N_1 increments from 500 to 599, while N_2 increments 99 counts. At the next 100-Hz increment, N_1 recycles by 99 back to 500, and N_2 decreases by 98, and the cycle repeats.

This economical scheme has been used effectively for SSB synthesizers, in spite of the higher phase noise close to the carrier caused by large values of N_2 multiplying the 10-kHz digital reference noise, the slower tuning time of 20 ms, and tuning transients on the 100-Hz increments. The latter results from the fact that generation of each 100-Hz step requires tuning both loops simultaneously, with the settling of loop #1 dependent on the settling of loop #2; therefore, the two opposing transients cannot cancel completely, causing large transients for even the smallest steps. The resulting audio noise can be muted if necessary while tuning. This scheme is at its best in low-cost, channelized HF radios.

The examples shown in Figs. 9.17 through 9.19 illustrate the complexity of generating small steps at even modest high frequencies using phase-locked loops. Multiloop VHF technology is required, just as in the coarse-increment sections of the synthesizer. As medium-scale-integration (MSI) and LSI circuit technologies have advanced in the mid-1980s, digital methods have become available to generate small frequency increments up to at least a few megahertz. These methods are examined in the next sections.

Direct digital synthesis

Direct digital synthesis (DDS), in contrast to the previously described indirect synthesis techniques, combines rapid phase-continuous frequency switching with closely spaced frequency increments. Notwithstanding its problems of comparatively high spurious frequency content and low output frequency range, the design has many applications when combined with wideband PLLs. The circuits are highly digital in nature, which leads to production economies.

A simplified block diagram for a direct digital synthesizer is shown in Fig. 9.20. A clocked phase accumulator creates a sawtooth wave in digital (numeric) form. The accumulator most significant bit (MSB) is an actual rectangular wave, which can be used directly. Alternatively, the digital sawtooth can be used to address a read-only memory that stores sine wave sample values, which can be converted to a sine wave voltage by a D/A converter and LPF (Refs. 13 and 14). It should be apparent that arbitrary waveforms may be generated by appropriate storage in the ROM, and that the accumulator itself can produce other waveforms, such as triangular.

The accumulator output frequency $F_o = K_1 F_b$, where K_1 is the binary frequency control word, and F_b (base frequency) $= F_c/2^n$ (F_c is the accumulator clock frequency, and n is the number of binary stages in the accumulator). Decimal and other schemes have been used (Ref. 15), but binary accumula-

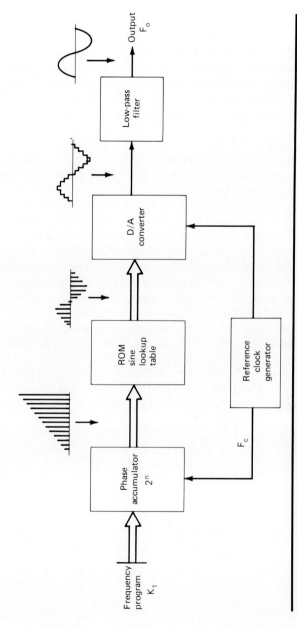

Figure 9.20 Direct digital synthesizer with sine lookup table.

tors are the simplest and most efficient, and can be effectively controlled if the radio has a microprocessor.

The accumulator output (MSB or carry) has an average frequency equal to the desired F_o, and is spurious-free if K_1 is an integer power of 2. Noninteger powers of 2 have zero crossings that ideally would have to occur between clocks. Since there can be no output except on a clock, the outputs will then occur on the nearest clock, resulting in a spurious modulation as the output phase moves with the clock for awhile, then jumps ahead or behind one clock period to "catch up." The ratio of spurious amplitude to accumulator output is approximately equal to the output-to-clock frequency ratio.

The sine ROM and D/A converter greatly reduce these spurious signals by creating a sine wave with zero crossings that can occur between clocks at the desired times for each output frequency. These correct zero crossings are detected when the sine wave is finally converted to a rectangular wave again. The spurious levels in this approach depend upon the number of bits in the sine table input and output, and glitches in the D/A converter. Efforts to predict the quantization error levels using statistical methods usually result in levels that are much higher than measured. Fairly good correlation seems to result from a Fourier transformation of the complete sine table, which for a 10-bit table predicts spurious levels of -72 dBc. Typical spurious levels of -65 dBc have been achieved with a low-glitch D/A converter, up to 1- or 2-MHz output, and a clock frequency of 8 to 10 MHz.

A synthesizer using a DDS for fine increments is shown in Fig. 9.21, where loop #1 combines 1-MHz steps from loop #2 with the fine increments $\Delta f_{\min}/$ 10 on the loop #1 reference. Loop #3 raises the DDS frequency to the 10.35- to 11.35-MHz range where loop #1 will track properly with loop #2. The two divide-by-10 circuits at the loop #1 reference lower the phase detector operating frequency to the 1.035- to 1.135-MHz range, while maintaining the

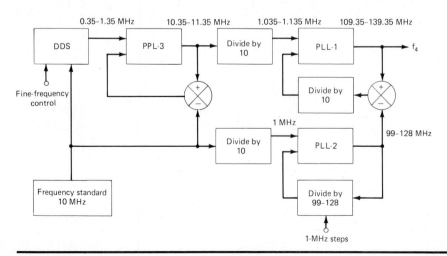

Figure 9.21 Synthesizer with fine steps produced by a DDS.

10.35- to 11.35-MHz range at the mixer output. Thus the net division from the DDS to the output f_4 is unity, and the smallest output frequency increments are those of the DDS.

The 10-MHz clock for the DDS requires a BCD or some decimal form of accumulator. If the more usual and efficient binary accumulator is used, a clock generator PLL would be required (between the frequency standard and the DDS) to provide a power-of-2 clock, such as 10.48576 MHz for 10-Hz increments.

A DDS output can also be mixed up to a higher frequency and used with the loops shown in Fig. 9.6.

Fractional division

Like the DDS, fractional division (Ref. 6, pp. 196 to 202, and Ref. 18) deals with noninteger relationships and corresponding spurious problems. The difference is in the relationship between the frequency increment and the input and output frequencies. The DDS is intended for a fixed input frequency, with equal frequency increments in the output. A fractional divider has a constant output frequency with equal frequency increments in the input. This presents a difficulty in using a sine ROM, as the accumulator size would then have to vary with the division ratio.

In order to use a constant-size accumulator, most fractional dividers use some form of analog bridge to balance out the spurious components. Figure 9.22 shows how a fractional divider could be used in a single-loop synthesizer. In spite of the 100-kHz reference, very small frequency increments are possible, such as 1 Hz, but at the price of a wide spectrum of spurious signals.

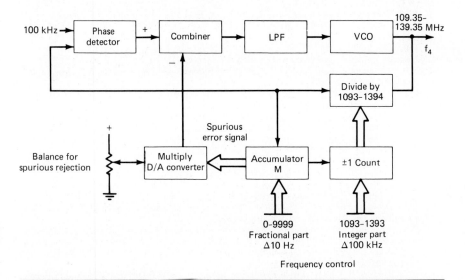

Figure 9.22 Single-loop synthesizer with fractional division.

The fractional part M of the total divide ratio programs an accumulator which alters the main divider count N at intervals to obtain the correct average total count in the loop. The accumulator also creates a spurious modulation error signal, which is converted to an analog signal of polarity opposite to the modulation on the desired signal, and combined at the phase detector output. The degree of spurious reduction is related to the degree of balance, affected by component variations with temperature and aging. Uncorrected spurious signals at the phase detector would be approximately $1/N$, but multiplied by N at the VCO output, so the output spurious depends primarily on the degree of balance.

Since more than a 20- or 30-dB reduction is difficult to maintain with wide temperature variations and other tolerances, fractional division is usually used with a very narrow loop bandwidth to filter the spurious signals, and much of the advantage of a high reference frequency is lost.

REFERENCES

1. J. J. Andrea, Phase Locked Loop with Digitalized Frequency and Phase Discriminator, U.S. Patent 3,431,509, Mar. 4, 1969 (assigned to Rockwell International).
2. R. C. Debloois and N. E. Hogue, Digital Frequency-Phase Discriminator Circuit, U.S. Patent 3,866,133, Feb. 11, 1975 (assigned to Rockwell International).
3. J. M. Laune, Digital Frequency and/or Phase Detector Charge Pump, U.S. Patent 3,714,463, Jan. 30, 1973 (assigned to Motorola).
4. D. M. Mitchell, "Pulsewidth Modulator Phase Shift," *IEEE Trans. Aerospace Electron. Syst.,* vol. AES-16, no. 3, May 1980, pp. 272–278.
5. W. E. Sabin, "Phase Relations in the Frequency Divider and Phase Detector of a Locked Digital Frequency Synthesizer," Rockwell-Collins Working Paper WP3881, 1974.
6. W. F. Egan, *Frequency Synthesis by Phase Lock,* John Wiley & Sons, New York, 1981.
7. M. A. Caloyannides, "An Analytic Evaluation of Synthesizer-Switching Performance Loss," Rockwell-Collins Working Paper WP81-3005, 1981.
8. E. A. Janning, "A Low Noise Oscillator," Master's thesis, University of Cincinnati, Cincinnati, 1967.
9. W. P. Robins, *Phase Noise in Signal Sources,* IEE Telecommunications Series 9, Peter Peregrinus, London, 1982, Chap. 5.
10. U. L. Rohde, *Digital PLL Frequency Synthesizers,* Prentice-Hall, Englewood Cliffs, NJ, 1983, Fig. 2-12.
11. Hewlett-Packard, Spectrum Analyzer System model HP3047A.
12. R. D. Tollefson, Frequency Synthesizer, U.S. Patent 3,588,732, June 28, 1971 (assigned to Rockwell International).
13. W. J. Melvin, Digitalized Tone Generator, U.S. Patent 3,597,599, Aug. 3, 1971 (assigned to Rockwell International).
14. J. Tierney, "Digital Frequency Synthesizers," in Gorski-Popiel (ed.), *Frequency Synthesis: Techniques & Applications,* IEEE Press, Piscataway, NJ, 1975, pp. 121–149.
15. L. B. Jackson, Digital Frequency Synthesizer, U.S. Patent 3,735,269, May 22, 1973 (assigned to Rockland Systems Corp.).
16. C. J. Byrne, "Properties and Design of the Phase-Controlled Oscillator with a Sawtooth Comparator," *Bell Syst. Tech. J.,* vol. 41, March 1962, pp. 559–602.
17. F. M. Gardner, *Phaselock Techniques,* 2d ed., John Wiley & Sons, New York, 1979.
18. G. C. Gillette, "The Digiphase Synthesizer," *Freq. Tech.,* vol. 7, August 1969, pp. 25–29.
19. J. Noordanus, "Frequency Synthesizers—A Survey of Techniques," *IEEE Trans. Commun. Tech.,* vol. COM-17, no. 2, April 1969, pp. 257–271.
20. D. E. Phillips, "HF Frequency Synthesizer Adaptive to Various Tuning Time and Frequency Increment Requirements," in *Proc. of 32nd Annual Symposium on Frequency Control,* Electronic Industries Association, Washington, DC, 1978, pp. 373–377. (Symposium held in Atlantic City, NJ, May 31–Jun. 2, 1978.)
21. M. J. Underhill, "Wide Range Frequency Synthesizers with Improved Dynamic Performance," *Radio Electron. Eng.,* June 1980, pp. 291–296.

22. J. Vlack and K. Singhal, *Computer Methods for Circuit Analysis and Design,* Van Nostrand Reinhold, New York, 1983.

23. A. B. Williams, *Electronic Filter Design Handbook,* McGraw-Hill, New York, 1981.

24. C. E. Wheatley and D. E. Phillips, "Spurious Suppression in Direct Digital Synthesizers," in *Proc. of 35th Annual Symposium on Frequency Control,* Electronic Industries Association, Washington, DC, 1981, pp. 428–435. (Symposium held in Philadelphia, PA, May 27–29, 1981.)

10

Frequency Standards for Single Sideband*

Marvin E. Frerking

The application of precision frequency control has played an important role in establishing single sideband as a reliable means of radio communications. The crystal oscillator thus provides one of the vital links required for the implementation of SSB. As will be seen subsequently, the crystal oscillators used for SSB are often required to maintain a higher degree of accuracy than those used in many other applications.

The material covered in this chapter deals primarily with crystal oscillators in the frequency stability range required for SSB equipment operating at HF or VHF frequency bands. The design of higher-precision frequency standards such as might be used for microwave SSB links is beyond the scope of this book, and the reader is referred to the references listed at the end of this chapter. Thus, both temperature compensated crystal oscillators and crystal ovens of the type used to achieve a frequency stability in the ppm range are addressed. Since the quartz crystal itself plays such a vital role in determining the oscillator performance, a section is included discussing many of the characteristics of the crystal itself. A brief sketch is also included presenting a historical review of frequency control in SSB equipment.

---

* Much of the material in this chapter is taken from M. E. Frerking, *Crystal Oscillator Design and Temperature Compensation,* Van Nostrand, New York, 1978, and appears by courtesy of the Van Nostrand Company.

10.1   Historical Notes on Frequency Stability

Historically, one of the most effective frequency control schemes for general receiver coverage has been to use a crystal oscillator in combination with a variable LC oscillator. The LC oscillator, often in the 1- to 3-MHz range, had a tuning range of a few hundred kilohertz to perhaps 1 MHz. The permeability tuned oscillator (PTO), developed by Hunter, Hodgin, Mifflin, and others at Collins Radio served this function well and was used for over 30 years in the manufacture of communications receivers and transceivers. The PTO uses a Colpitts oscillator in which the inductor is tuned by means of a ferrite core on a special lead screw with a linearization cam. As a result, the PTO has a very linear tuning range and also possesses an inherent frequency stability of approximately $\pm$ 200 ppm. The PTO has now been displaced by frequency synthesizers in modern communications equipment. One of the early frequency synthesizer designs using discrete tuning steps controlled by a tuning knob was used in the Collins 651S receiver. This receiver tuned in 100-Hz increments. As frequency synthesizer hardware continued to improve, frequency synthesizers with 10- and even 1-Hz steps came into use. These designs give the impression of continuous tuning.

The crystal oscillators used for SSB communications vary considerably in frequency stability, depending on the application. For military applications requiring an accuracy of about 1 ppm, crystal ovens were first used. These units were relatively large, consumed considerable amounts of power, and unfortunately required a warmup time to stabilize. The introduction of the varactor tuning diode during the late 1950s, however, soon made temperature compensation of crystal oscillators practical and eliminated the warmup time. Recent improvements in crystal ovens have reduced the warmup time to about 2 min, and a few designs have allowed the use of an oven at a somewhat lower cost than a temperature-compensated crystal oscillator (TCXO).

10.2   Crystal Oscillator Design

The design of precision crystal oscillators is somewhat unique in that not only must the circuit oscillate, but it must also possess a high degree of frequency stability as the environment changes and over long periods of time. A considerable portion of this chapter is, therefore, devoted to showing how to achieve a high degree of frequency stability from the oscillator.

Basically a crystal oscillator can be thought of as an amplifier and a feedback network. The crystal is placed in the feedback network in a position where it has a large effect on the phase shift. When the oscillator is turned on, the amplitude of oscillation builds up at a frequency where the phase shift around the loop is a multiple of 360° and the loop gain is greater than unity. The amplitude continues to increase until saturation or limiting effects reduce the loop gain to unity. If a frequency does not exist where the phase-shift requirement is satisfied and the loop gain is greater than unity, oscillation will not take place. A crystal oscillator is unique in that the impedance of the crystal changes so rapidly with frequency that all the other components in the oscillator can be considered to be of constant reactance, that reactance being calculated at the nominal frequency of the crystal. Variations in the oscillator components do, of course, have a secondary effect on the phase shift, and the frequency of oscillation then adjusts itself so that the resulting impedance change of the crystal exactly compensates for the phase change caused by the oscillator component.

The application of these principles combined with the circuits listed in this chapter and in the references at its end allows the design and understanding of many of the frequency standards used in single-sideband equipment.

Crystal oscillators have been designed from a few kilohertz to several hundred megahertz with frequency stabilities ranging from several hundred parts per million to parts in 10^{10}. The frequency region from 3 to 5 MHz is very desirable for the design of temperature-compensated crystal oscillators, although other frequencies can be used, and many reference oscillators have been built in this range for frequency synthesizers.

An AT-cut quartz resonator is often used for SSB equipment. This resonator, if optimized for stability in a particular temperature range, can have a frequency stability of about ± 1 ppm over a limited temperature range of 0 to 50°C and about ± 15 to ± 20 ppm over -55 to $+105$°C. Improved frequency stability is normally obtained by the use of temperature compensation or temperature control in a crystal oven.

Quartz crystals

The quartz crystal itself plays such an important role in the design of precision crystal oscillators that the designer should become familiar with the fundamentals of the crystal prior to undertaking an oscillator design. This section, therefore, summarizes many of the important characteristics of

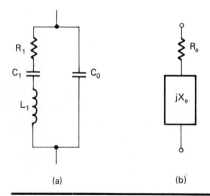

(a)   (b)

Figure 10.1 (a) Approximate equivalent circuit of a quartz crystal. (b) Impedance representation of a quartz crystal.

TABLE 10.1   Typical Crystal Parameter Values

Frequency, MHz	Cut	Overtone	C_0, pF	C_1, pF	L_1	R_1, Ω
2	AT	1	4	0.012	520 mH	100
3	AT	1	3.2	0.011	256 mH	20
5	AT	1	5.0	0.020	51 mH	7
10	AT	3	5.0	0.0025	102 mH	20
30	AT	3	6	0.0026	11 mH	20
4	SC	3	3.3	0.0002	7.9 H	300
10	SC	3	3.5	0.00027	940 mH	60

quartz crystals. For more information the reader is referred to the many excellent discussions in the literature, especially Refs. 1 through 3.

A quartz crystal possesses an extremely high Q, it has a very stable resonant frequency, and is also small in size and available at reasonable cost. A quartz crystal utilizes the piezoelectric properties of quartz. If a stress is applied to the crystal in a certain direction, an electric field appears in a perpendicular direction. The converse is also true, so that if an electric field is applied across the crystal, a small mechanical deformation will result. In a quartz crystal resonator a thin slab of quartz, called the "crystal blank," is placed between two electrodes. An alternating voltage applied to these electrodes causes the crystal to vibrate at the frequency of the applied voltage. If this frequency approaches a natural resonance in the blank, the amplitude of the deflection becomes relatively large. The mechanical vibration causes charges to be induced in the electrodes and greatly influences the impedance observed between the electrodes.

The electrical equivalent circuit of the crystal is shown in Fig. 10.1. The inductor is associated with the mass of the crystal, the capacitor C_1 is associated with the stiffness of the quartz, and R_1 with the loss in the quartz as well as in the mounting structure. The capacitor C_0 is due to the quartz dielectric material between the two electrodes, but also includes the stray capacitance of the crystal mounting structure. C_0 is often in the 3- to 5-pF range, while C_1 may be on the order of 0.01 pF for a fundamental-mode AT-cut resonator. A list of typical equivalent circuit values is given in Table 10.1.

The equivalent circuit shown in Fig. 10.1a can be simplified to that shown in Fig. 10.1b at any specific frequency. A reactance-vs.-frequency plot of the equivalent circuit is given in Fig. 10.2. The portion circled on this plot is

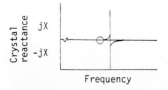

Figure 10.2   Reactance vs. frequency for a quartz crystal.

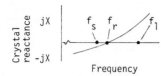

Figure 10.3 Expanded portion of crystal reactance near resonant region.

expanded in Fig. 10.3. The corresponding equivalent resistance is shown in Fig. 10.4.

Several frequencies are marked on these figures. The first of these is f_s. This is the frequency where the motional arm consisting of R_1, L_1, and C_1 is series resonant and is given by:

$$f_s = \frac{1}{2\pi \sqrt{L_1 C_1}}$$ (10.1)

The second point, f_r, is where the crystal is purely resistive. It is different from f_s because of the presence of C_0 and for practical purposes can be considered to be equal to f_s. The third point, f_L, is the frequency at which the crystal is resonant with an external capacitor C_L. If Δf is the frequency shift between f_L and f_s, it can be shown [1] that

$$\frac{\Delta f}{f_s} = \frac{C_1}{2(C_0 + C_L)}$$ (10.2)

where Δf = frequency shift $f_L - f_s$
  C_1 = motional capacitance, pF
  C_0 = crystal holder capacitance, pF
  C_L = external load capacitance, pF

In the equivalent circuit shown in Fig. 10.1b, jX_e has a value equal to, but opposite in sign to the reactance of, C_L at a frequency f_L. The antiresonant frequency of the crystal (the peak in Fig. 10.2) is the frequency where the motional arm is resonant with C_0. This can be found by setting $C_L = 0$ in Eq. (10.2) and setting $\Delta f = f_a - f_s$. It is given by:

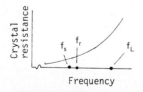

Figure 10.4 Equivalent resistance of crystal near resonant region.

$$f_a = f_s \left(1 + \frac{C_1}{2C_0}\right) \tag{10.3}$$

The equivalent resistance R_e of the crystal in the region between series and antiresonance is given by:

$$R_e = R_1 \left(\frac{C_L + C_0}{C_L}\right)^2 \tag{10.4}$$

provided $|X_{c0}[C_L/(C_L + C_0)]| >> R_1$ is true, where $X_{c0} = -1/2\pi f_s C_0$.

It is often quite convenient to calculate the reactance of the crystal as a function of frequency using Eq. (10.2). This will be discussed further in Sec. 10.4.

The crystal is normally operated between series and antiresonance so that the reactance of the crystal is either zero or inductive.

The properties of the crystal may be varied considerably by the angle at which the blank is cut from the raw quartz and by the mode of vibration. This topic is primarily a concern of the crystal manufacturer and will not be discussed in detail here. (An excellent treatment of crystal resonator design is given in Ref. 3.) But several properties of crystal resonators *are* of concern to the designer of crystal oscillators and will be discussed in the following paragraphs.

Load capacitance

From Fig. 10.3 it can be seen that the frequency of the crystal will vary to some extent depending on the reactance that the crystal must present to the circuit. It is important that the crystal be plated to frequency at the load reactance value at which it will be used in the oscillator circuit. Several load conditions have become standard and are nearly always used. Among these are 20, 30, and 32 pF. These crystals must be used in parallel resonant oscillators to operate on frequency. Another common load condition is series resonance, where the crystal is purely resistive, and has a value R_1. Crystals of this type must be used in series resonant oscillators if they are to operate at the specified nominal frequency.

Resistance

The resistance of a crystal is specified at the rated load capacitance, and usually does not differ greatly from the series resistance R_1. It may vary considerably from unit to unit, however, and it is important to assure that the the oscillator will function properly with a crystal which has a resistance as large as the specification allows. The maximum allowable resistance for a given crystal type may vary from about 40 ohms for VHF crystals to over 500K ohms for audio frequency crystals.

Rated drive level

"Drive level" refers to the power dissipated in the crystal. The drive level specification should be reasonably duplicated in the oscillator.* The drive level ratings vary from 5 μW below 100 kHz to about 10 MW in the 1- to 20-MHz region for fundamental crystals. Precision crystals normally operate at considerably lower drive levels in the 10- to 50-μW region. This leads to greater stability since the frequency effect of drive level is reduced at low drive levels, as is the aging rate. The frequency effect of drive level is less predominant in SC-cut crystals than in AT cuts.

Frequency stability

The frequency stability of a quartz crystal is limited primarily by its temperature coefficient and the aging rate. Common temperature specifications are ± 0.0025 percent from -55 to $+105°C$ for wide-temperature-range units or ± 0.001 percent over a 10°C range for oven crystals. The frequency-vs.-temperature characteristics of a given crystal are determined by the angle at which the crystal is cut from the raw quartz bar, and typically the manufacturer can cut a given angle plus or minus a few minutes of arc. Tighter tolerances are available by selection. Figure 10.5 shows the frequency-temperature-angle characteristics of typical AT-cut crystals. The points of zero slope are called the "lower" and "upper turning point temperatures."

The aging rate of a crystal is caused primarily by a gradual mass transfer to or from the crystal blank and by stress relaxation. The cleaning of the

---

* At the time of this writing, consideration is being given to specifying the drive current rather than the power dissipation since this more nearly determines the amplitude of displacement.

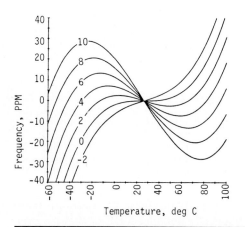

Figure 10.5 Frequency-temperature-angle characteristics of AT-type quartz resonators.

unit and the seal of the holder are thus extremely important. Aging rates in the order of parts in 10^9 to a few parts in 10^8 per week are typical for precision oscillators used in SSB equipment. This requires considerable care, and glass or coldweld enclosures are often used.

Other factors

A number of other factors are also of concern to a crystal oscillator designer and the reader is referred especially to Refs. 1 through 3 for a more detailed treatment. Among these are the finishing tolerance, Q, stiffness, spurious modes, pin-to-pin capacitance, vibration susceptibility, and others. It should also be noted that quartz crystals can be used on odd mechanical overtones, notably the third and fifth. If these are used, it is often necessary to use a trap in the oscillator to ensure oscillation on the desired mode. If this is not done, it is necessary to ensure that the resistance of the fundamental mode and lower overtones is considerably higher than that of the desired mode.

Oscillator circuits

A large number of crystal oscillator circuits have been used in various applications, and it is beyond the scope of this chapter to discuss even the majority of these circuits. A very comprehensive treatment will be found in Refs. 1, 2, and 4. Since a large number of oscillators for SSB have used the Pierce or Colpitts circuits, they will be discussed in more detail here.

These circuits have the same RF equivalent circuit, but with the ac ground at different points. The ac ground in the Colpitts is at the collector while in the Pierce it is at the emitter. Practically, since the biasing resistors and the stray capacitance fall across different elements, the circuits may perform considerably differently. Both circuits can be made to perform well over the 1- to 20-MHz frequency range; however, the Pierce circuit generally operates better at very low or very high frequencies. The Pierce circuit has been used in the frequency range extending beyond 60 MHz; however, above the 30- to 60-MHz range the grounded-base (Butler) circuit may be more appropriate to use.

The Pierce circuit is generally easier to design than the Colpitts. It is less prone to spurious oscillations and squegging and in some cases possesses superior stability. A significant disadvantage is the fact that neither pin of the crystal can be grounded. The Colpitts oscillator, on the other hand, does allow one side of the crystal to be grounded. Also, since the collector may be tied directly to the supply voltage, it can be operated from lower supply voltages without using an inductor to feed the collector.

A number of crystal oscillators have also been designed using logic gates and integrated circuit oscillators. The performance of these circuits varies greatly and generally tends to be inferior to that obtained using a well-designed transistor stage. For this reason, crystal oscillators used in SSB equipment often use a transistor oscillator. Gate oscillators are treated in

Refs. 1, 2, and 4. Gate oscillators having the best frequency stability often use a single gate with a π network containing the crystal.

Pierce oscillator.   A schematic diagram of the Pierce oscillator is shown in Fig. 10.6. The conditions for oscillation are satisfied in the following manner. The basic phase-shift network is composed of C_1, C_2, and the crystal, which looks inductive. The capacitors are normally large enough to effectively swamp out the transistor input and output impedances. Under these conditions, if the crystal resistance is not too large, the following explanation is applicable. The frequency of oscillation adjusts itself so that the crystal is inductive and resonant with the series combination of C_1 and C_2. Since the inductive reactance of the crystal is larger than the capacitive reactance of C_1, the current I_1 lags the voltage e_2 by 90°. The voltage e_1, being developed across C_1, lags I_1 by 90°, making it 180° behind e_2. Now, since C_2 is resonant with the resulting reactance from C_1 and the crystal, the collector of the transistor looks into a resistive load. This being the case, the collector voltage e_2 is in phase with the current generator in the transistor which is 180° out of phase with the base voltage e_1. The total phase shift around the loop is, therefore, 360°. If either of the capacitors C_1 or C_2 changes slightly with temperature, the frequency of oscillation shifts so that the change in crystal reactance restores the phase balance. When the circuit is turned on, if the conditions for oscillation exist, the amplitude builds up until saturation takes place and the loop gain is reduced to unity. Depending on how the transistor is biased, saturation may take place by the base-to-emitter junction being cut off during part of the RF cycle or by the base-to-collector junction becoming forward-biased during part of the RF cycle. Generally the former results in better stability while the latter gives better amplitude control. Limiting effects are difficult to analyze mathematically; however, a good treatment of them is presented in Ref. 2.

A small-signal analysis can be used to determine the conditions necessary

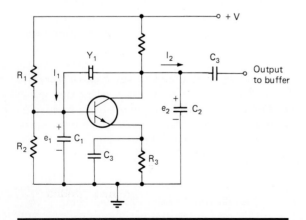

Figure 10.6   Pierce oscillator schematic diagram.

for the onset of oscillation. Reference 1 presents a treatment based on the y parameters of the transistor. It is shown that for oscillation to take place

$$g_{fe}X_1X_2 \geq R_e + K_1 \qquad \text{(gain equation)} \tag{10.5}$$

$$X_1 + X_2 + X_e = 0 + K_2 \qquad \text{(phase equation)} \tag{10.6}$$

where g_{fe} = real part of the transistor forward transfer admittance, sometimes referred to as the "transconductance"

$$X_1 = \frac{-1}{\omega C_1}$$

$$X_2 = \frac{-1}{\omega C_2}$$

R_e = effective crystal resistance
X_e = crystal reactance

K_1 and K_2 are corrective terms which produce only secondary effects if the previous assumptions are fulfilled [see Ref. 1, Eqs. (7-13) and (7-14)].

It can be shown that to a first approximation, loading of the output manifests itself as an effective increase of the crystal resistance, given by $\Delta R_e = X_2^2/R_L$, where R_L is the load resistance. The loading due to the bias resistors results in a $\Delta R_e = X_1^2/R_\rho$, where R_ρ is the equivalent resistance of R_1 and R_2 in parallel. To a first approximation, at frequencies well below the cutoff, the transconductance is given by:

$$g_{fe} = 0.04 I_e \text{ mhos} \tag{10.7}$$

where I_e is the emitter current in milliamperes (mhos are also known as siemens, abbreviated S).

It is normally desirable to design an oscillator so that the gain is 2 to 3 times greater than that required for oscillation with a maximum resistance crystal to allow for production variations.

The oscillator is normally trimmed to frequency by placing a variable reactive element such as a varactor or trimmer capacitor in series with the crystal.

If the Pierce oscillator is used with overtone crystals, it is necessary to prevent oscillation on the fundamental mode. This can be done by placing an inductor in parallel with C_1 or C_2 with appropriate dc blocking. The resulting combination should be resonant below the desired overtone, but above the next lower odd overtone. Thus at the lower overtone the reactance of the parallel circuit changes sign and becomes inductive. As can be seen from Eq. (10.5), X_1 and X_2 must be of like sign for oscillation to take place.

Colpitts oscillator. The Colpitts oscillator has been widely used because of its circuit simplicity and excellent frequency stability. The ac equivalent circuit is the same as that for the Pierce oscillator, but with the ac ground point moved from the emitter to the collector. Equations (10.5) to (10.7) can be used to predict oscillation provided the loading assumptions are accounted for. Because the loading and biasing configuration is different than for the

Pierce oscillator and because stray capacitance on the base falls across the crystal, Colpitts circuits may behave considerably differently. The base biasing resistors also effectively shunt the crystal, and they must be made as large as possible. Using an FET transistor allows the use of a very large bias resistor which is an advantage particularly at low frequencies.

A schematic diagram of a Colpitts crystal oscillator is shown in Fig. 10.7. This circuit can be thought of as an emitter follower driving a capacitive tapped tank circuit. The frequency of the oscillator adjusts itself so that the crystal is inductive and resonant with the series combination of C_1 and C_2. The Colpitts oscillator is more prone to squegging than the Pierce circuit and it may be necessary to choose C_2 and R_3 to prevent this effect. If the Colpitts oscillator is used to operate with the crystal on its third overtone, an inductor must be placed across C_1 or C_2 to produce a resonant frequency between the fundamental and the third overtone. Appropriate dc blocking must, of course, be provided.

10.3 Temperature Control

The frequency stability of a crystal oscillator is primarily determined by the quartz crystal. A graph showing the temperature characteristics of the crystal for several angles of cut is shown in Fig. 10.5. Temperature effects on other oscillator components result in additional frequency changes of a few ppm over a wide temperature range for a well-designed circuit. Since the requirements of SSB are often in the 1-ppm range, a considerable improvement in performance is required. Temperature control or temperature compensation are the primary means by which the frequency stability can be improved. Temperature control to achieve a frequency stability in the ppm range is relatively straightforward and requires less test labor than temperature compensation. However, temperature control has the following disadvantages: (1) A warmup stabilization period is required after turn-on, (2) the

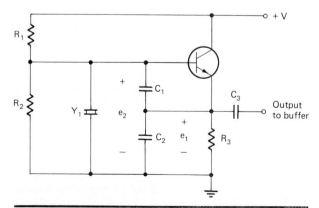

Figure 10.7 Colpitts oscillator circuit.

power consumption is higher than for temperature compensation because of thermal loss, (3) the size of the units may be larger than that required for temperature compensation because of the amount of thermal insulation required, (4) the reliability may be reduced because of thermal cycling if the unit is frequently turned on and off, and (5) the aging rate is increased because of the higher operating temperature of the crystal. In some applications these characteristics may be of little concern. For example, in a fixed station installation, power consumption and size may be secondary to cost.

Temperature-controlled crystal oscillators can be built with extremely high frequency stability in the region of parts in 10^8 to parts in 10^9 over a wide temperature range. Oscillators of this type are beyond the scope of this chapter since the requirements of SSB are generally much less severe.

A variety of crystal ovens can be used to achieve frequency stabilities from a few parts per million to a fraction of a part per million. In the 1- to 5-ppm range a number of commercial ovens are available which can be placed over the crystal or into which the crystal can be inserted. The warmup time is usually not critical in these applications and may be in the 5- to 15-min range. Often, only the crystal is in the oven, with the other oscillator components exposed to the ambient temperature. A higher-performance oscillator with a frequency stability of a few parts in 10^7 can be achieved by placing the oscillator stage itself along with the crystal in the oven. The oven in some cases may consist of a metallic shell around the components to be temperature-controlled or in some cases a small block of metal to which the crystal and oscillator components are mounted. The heater may be a power transistor which is attached to the oven. The warmup time may vary considerably with the size of the oven and the amount of warmup power used.

With considerable power, in the 10- and 30-W region, and a small oven, the stabilization time can be reduced to the 2- to 3-min region even for a turn-on temperature of $-55°C$.

The crystal characteristics over the temperature range can be described by a cubic equation of the form

$$\frac{\Delta f}{f} = A_1 (T - T_0) + A_2(T - T_0)^2 + A_3(T - T_0)^3 \tag{10.8}$$

where T_0 is an arbitrarily chosen reference temperature, usually selected to be in the 20 to 30°C range and A_1, A_2, and A_3 are constants for a given angle of cut and reference temperature T_0. For an AT-cut crystal and $T_0 = 25°C$, $A_1 = -5.08 \times 10^{-6}\Delta\theta$, $A_2 = -0.45 \times 10^{-9}$, and $A_3 = 108.6 \times 10^{-12}$. Here $\Delta\theta$ is the angle in degrees from the angle producing a zero slope at 25°C (see Ref. 7). Figure 10.5 shows these characteristics for AT-cut crystals.

It is desirable to operate the crystal oven at the upper turning-point temperature where the crystal has a zero slope or as near as possible to the turning point. In a precision oven, the temperature is adjusted to match the turning-point temperature of the particular crystal used. For a frequency standard of lesser stability, an error of several degrees may be tolerated. It can be shown from Eq. (10.8) that the crystal slope as a function of distance from the turning-point temperature is given by

$$S = 2A_2(T - T_p) + 3A_3[(T^2 - T_p^2) - 2T_0(T - T_p)] \qquad (10.9)$$

where S = slope of curve, ppm/°C
$\quad T$ = temperature, °C
$\quad T_p$ = turning-point temperature, °C

For an AT-cut crystal with an 85°C turning point, the slope is about 0.2 ppm/°C if the oven is 5°C off the turning point. An oven must then hold the crystal temperature to within ±0.5°C to achieve a ±0.1-ppm frequency stability.

The schematic diagram of a typical oven temperature control circuit is shown in Fig. 10.8. The heating element is the power transistor Q_2. This transistor is attached directly to the oven block or to the crystal. The temperature sensor is a thermistor R_{T1}, which is also attached to the oven and very near the heater transistor. A significant problem in crystal ovens is that of temperature gradients. Crystals are quite sensitive to minute temperature differences between the pins and between the pins and the crystal case. When the crystal is operated at its turning-point temperature, the frequency-vs.-temperature characteristic of the cubic curve can be completely masked by temperature gradients. Therefore, it is good practice to provide a metal block or enclosure to equalize the temperature. This becomes increasingly more important in high-precision oscillators in the parts per 10^8 region where two heaters are often used, one on each side of the oven.

The circuit shown in Fig. 10.8 works in the following manner. When the oven is cold, at turn-on, the thermistor RT_1 has a high resistance causing V_1 to exceed V_{ref}. This causes the output of the operational amplifier V_3 to go

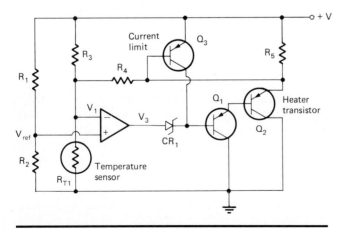

Figure 10.8 Schematic diagram of temperature control circuit.

low, turning on Q_1 and Q_2. The power dissipated by Q_2 heats the oven, and when it reaches the set temperature determined by V_{ref}, the thermistor resistance decreases to the point where V_1 approaches V_{ref}. At that point the voltage V_3 increases, which reduces the power in Q_2. The oven stabilizes when the heater power is equal to the thermal loss at the operating temperature. The resistor R_4 is used to provide negative feedback which limits the gain. If the gain is too high, thermal oscillations will occur because the heater and/or oven becomes too hot before the temperature sensor cuts down the power. If the gain is too low, inadequate temperature control will result over the ambient temperature range. The transistor Q_3 in connection with R_5 can be used to limit the current during warmup to a safe value.

The steady-state power is a function of the thermal loss, which consists primarily of the heat flow through the insulation and the loss in the wires going into the oven. The approximate heat loss for a crystal oven with foam insulation can be calculated using the formula:

$$P = \frac{\lambda A \Delta T}{L} \tag{10.10}$$

on each of the six surfaces and for each of the wires going into the oven. Here

λ = thermal conductivity of the wire or insulation
A = cross-sectional area for volume under consideration
L = length of the thermal path or wire length
ΔT = difference between oven and ambient temperature

Depending on the size of the oven, ambient temperature, and insulation used, a thermal loss in the region of 1 to 5 W may be expected.

10.4 Temperature Compensation

Advantages

The frequency stability of a crystal oscillator can be greatly improved by temperature compensation, and the resulting stability is adequate for many SSB applications. The resulting crystal oscillators, with an accuracy in the ± 1-ppm range, are fairly inexpensive, operate on low power, and stabilize very quickly after turn-on. A temperature-compensated crystal oscillator can be packaged in 2 or 3 in^3 (33 to 50 cm^3) using conventional components.

Methods of temperature compensation

The frequency-vs.-temperature curves for AT-cut quartz crystals are shown in Fig. 10.5 for various angles of cut. The crystal is not the only contributor to frequency changes, and the other oscillator components affect the frequency, but to a much smaller degree. The overall uncompensated frequency stability of the oscillator is then approximately the same as that shown in the crystal curves. To temperature-compensate a crystal oscillator, such as the circuit shown in Fig. 10.6, a varactor is normally placed in series with the crystal Y_1, where it has a maximum effect on the frequency. DC blocking capacitors are used so that a bias voltage can be applied to the varactor through large-value resistors which have no effect on the RF signal. The varactor bias voltage applied at any given temperature is the value required to pull the crystal by exactly the amount, but in the opposite direction that it has drifted in temperature. If the varactor voltage is carefully developed as a function of temperature, a resulting frequency error of parts in 10^7 can be obtained.

Many methods have been devised to develop the required varactor bias voltage as a function of temperature. The majority of these methods fall into three categories: (1) analog resistor thermistor compensations, (2) digital temperature compensation, and (3) microcomputer temperature compensation. A detailed treatment of temperature compensation is beyond the scope of this book, and the reader is referred to Ref. 1 for more detailed information. A brief summary of the methods in common use is given here to provide a reasonable understanding of how they work.

Analog temperature compensation. The method of analog temperature compensation was developed during the late 1950s by D. G. Newell and G. R. Hykes at Collins Radio for use over a wide temperature range. (See Ref. 8.) The method uses a network consisting of several thermistors and resistors to develop a voltage curve which is the mirror image of the crystal curve. A considerable number of network variations have been used to provide advantages in one situation or another. The network shown in Fig. 10.9 is fairly typical and has been used on over 50,000 TCXOs covering the temperature range from -55 to $+75°C$.

The thermistor resistance values are chosen so that the network achieves a reasonable degree of independence of adjustment between the cold temperature region and the room temperature region, and also between the hot

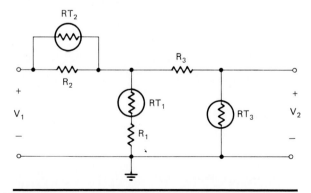

Figure 10.9 Analog temperature compensation network.

temperature region and the rest of the curve. It is not difficult to show that the network transfer function is given by:

$$\frac{V_2}{V_1} = \frac{RT_3(R_1 + RT_1)(R_2 + RT_2)}{(R_1 + RT_1)(R_2 + RT_2)(R_3 + RT_3) + R_2RT_2[(R_1 + RT_1) + (R_3 + RT_3)]}$$

(10.11)

where the thermistor resistances are approximately given by:

$$RT = RT(T_0) \exp\left[B\left(\frac{1}{T} - \frac{1}{T_0}\right)\right]$$

(10.12)

Here $RT(T_0)$ is the nominal thermistor resistance at the reference temperature, T_0 usually taken to be 298 K (25°C), B is the thermistor exponential temperature coefficient, and T is the temperature, kelvin.

For precision temperature compensation, the thermistor values are usually taken from stored tables derived from measured values. It is not surprising that the computer has been used to aid in the initial selection of the resistors to minimize the number of temperature runs required.

A considerable latitude exists in the computer program and in the accuracy with which it predicts the resistance values. At one extreme, the required varactor voltage as well as the thermistor resistances are first measured at temperatures spaced 10 to 20°C apart. The computer then determines the resistance values giving the minimum error in some sense. An initial strategy may be desirable to calculate resistance values approximately to avoid local minima in the optimization program. One such strategy is to assume initial values and using Eq. (10.11) solve for R_2 to obtain the desired voltage V_2 at the coldest temperature, for R_1 to obtain it at room temperature, and for R_3 to obtain it at the highest temperature. This procedure can be iterated until exact values of V_2 are obtained at each of the three temperatures with one set of resistances. An optimization program such as the steepest-descent algorithm can then be used to improve the values using additional temperature points. More elaborate networks than the one shown in Fig. 10.9 can be effectively handled with computer programs.

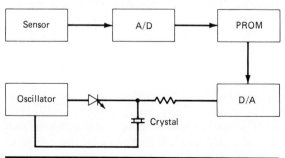

Figure 10.10 Digital temperature compensation circuit.

One of the most difficult problems, however, seems to be finding a global minimum for the resistor configuration. TCXOs designed with the aid of computer programs have been produced with frequency stabilities in the order of a few parts in 10^7.

Another program strategy is to measure only the required varactor voltages over the temperature range and predict the thermistor resistances from prestored tables. This procedure requires less data-taking, but sacrifices some accuracy in the process.

A still easier process is simply to use the constants for the particular crystal being used, from manufacturers' data, and predict the varactor voltage. This can be done by using the constants A_1, A_2, and A_3 in Eq. (10.8) to calculate $\Delta f/f$ at a given temperature T. The value of $\Delta f/f$ can be used in connection with Eq. (10.2) and the nominal load capacitance C_L to find the reactance change necessary to pull the crystal back on frequency. The reactance change is then used in the varactor equation to find the required voltage. The varactor capacitance is represented by an equation of the form

$$C = \frac{K}{(V + V_0)^n}$$

where K, V_0, and n are determined for the particular varactor used. Obviously this procedure results in additional errors, but if carefully done, a frequency stability of several ppm can be obtained. Experimental tweaking can then be done to improve the frequency stability. At the time of this writing most TCXOs are manufactured using analog networks in which the components are adjusted with the aid of computer programs, with the amount of final tweaking dependent on the frequency stability required. The difficulty of compensation increases considerably beyond ± 1 ppm.

Digital temperature compensation.   Digital techniques are quite amenable to temperature compensation and eliminate much of the skill required to determine the component values in an analog network. At the present time an integrated circuit designed for temperature compensation is not available and the cost of the MSI parts exceeds the component cost of the analog network. Digital compensation can easily be automated, however, which reduces the labor cost. The block diagram of a digital compensation circuit is shown in Fig. 10.10. In this circuit the temperature sensor develops a voltage which approximates a linear function of temperature. A temperature-dependent current source or a poorly biased transistor are both possible choices. This voltage is digitized by the A/D converter. The digital word is then used as the address to a PROM which has been programmed to contain the required correction voltage at every temperature. The output of the PROM is then converted to an analog voltage by the D/A converter and applied to the varactor. A detailed description of a digitally compensated crystal oscillator (DCXO) is given in Ref. 1, along with an analysis of the digital word size required.

In practice it is desirable to use enough bits so that the frequency errors due to the digital system are small compared with the required frequency tolerance. This allows most of the tolerance to be used for temperature tracking and for the frequency retrace characteristics of the crystal.

The PROM can be programmed by a test station which reads the address and simultaneously provides a tracking or searching voltage which determines the proper word to apply to the D/A converter. In practice, it is not necessary to check every temperature during compensation and the test station can interpolate between points 5 to 10°C apart.

Microcomputer temperature compensation.   Another technique which can be used for temperature compensation is microcomputer temperature compensation. A block diagram is shown in Fig. 10.11. This circuit appears to be more complex than the DCXO in Fig. 10.10; however, the microcomputer offers several advantages.

One of the major advantages is that an *RC* oscillator such as an astable multivibrator can be used for the temperature sensor if the resistor is a thermistor. The microcomputer can then measure the period of oscillation to determine the temperature in digital form. A second advantage is the convenience of using 8-bit memory words. The microprocessor can then unpack the memory as required to achieve a 9- or 10-bit word if desired. The microcomputer can also perform interpolation, so that a smaller number of memory words are required.

It is probable that microcomputers with (on-chip) electronically erasable and programmable read-only memory (EEPROM) will soon be available which will make this technique very attractive compared to the DCXO. The availability of nonvolatile RAMs may also soon make the microcomputer temperature-compensated crystal oscillator easier to compensate. As in the case of the DCXO, it is not necessary to provide compensation data at every temperature, and the test station can perform interpolation from a relatively small number of temperature points.

Basically the microcomputer goes through a never-ending loop in which it reads the temperature, searches the table for the two closest data points,

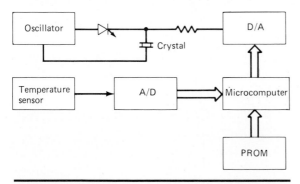

Figure 10.11 Microprocessor temperature-compensated crystal oscillator.

interpolates between them, and outputs the calculated voltages. The use of microcomputers holds the promise of ultimately producing improved accuracy over the analog compensated crystal oscillators. This results because sufficient bits can be used so that nearly all the frequency error is due to retrace errors in the crystal and the oscillator reactive elements.

REFERENCES

1. M. E. Frerking, *Crystal Oscillator Design and Temperature Compensation,* Van Nostrand Reinhold, New York, 1978.
2. B. Parzen and A. Ballato, *Design of Crystal and Other Harmonic Oscillators,* John Wiley & Sons, New York, 1983.
3. V. E. Bottom, *Introduction to Quartz Crystal Unit Design,* Van Nostrand Reinhold, New York, 1982.
4. R. J. Matthys, *Crystal Oscillator Circuits,* John Wiley & Sons, New York, 1983.
5. R. Bechmann, "Frequency-Temperature-Angle Characteristics of AT-Type Resonators Made of Natural and Synthetic Quartz," *Proc. IEEE,* vol. 44, No. 11, November 1956, pp. 1600–1607.
6. M. E. Frerking, "Methods of Temperature Compensation," in *Proc. of the 36th Annual Symposium of Frequency Control,* National Technical Information Service, Springfield, VA., 1982, pp. 564–570. (Symposium held in Philadelphia, PA, June 2–4, 1982; sponsored by the U.S. Army Electronics Research and Development Command.)
7. A. Ballato, "Doubly Rotated Thickness Mode Plate Vibrators," in W. P. Mason and R. N. Thurston (eds.), *Physical Acoustics Principles and Methods,* Academic, New York, 1977, Vol. 3, Chap. 5, pp. 115–181.
8. G. R. Hykes and D. G. Newell, "A Temperature Compensated Frequency Standard," in *Proc. of the 15th Annual Frequency Control Symposium,* National Technical Information Service, Springfield, VA., 1961, pp. 297–317.

Digital Control

Steven J. Harmening

Remote control of modern HF communications equipment substantially increases user applications for this equipment. And the addition of a few parts using microprocessor technology can provide remote control in an economically feasible way. The purpose of this chapter is to provide some basic understanding of remote control and its applications. This includes a description of some of the basic elements of remote control, a design example of a remotely controllable HF receiver, and a description of a current central communications site.

11.1 Overview

Remote control is a means of operating equipment at a location different from the equipment. The distances involved can vary from a few feet to thousands of miles. The distance requirements influence the type of physical interface required and the speed of the control system. The physical interface defines the types of control lines necessary to connect the equipment to the control device. Longer distances usually use fewer control lines (serial control) and slower speeds. The shorter distances can use more lines (parallel control) and achieve faster control rates. Primary areas for the application of remote control are:

1. Extended local control

2. Control between separated sites

3. Electronic countermeasure (ECM)/ECCM operations

Extended local control

Extended local control is implemented with the radio equipment and controlling device at the same site. It separates the radio operator from the communications equipment to provide an operator environment free from equipment noise. It also allows for consolidation of equipment into one area and facilitates equipment cooling and maintenance. Extended local control is widely used in airframe installations where the control unit is in the cockpit area and the radio equipment is located in the equipment bay. Many military applications use extended local control when equipment needs to be close to the operator to provide mobility in emergency situations. Because of the limited distances in extended local control, many types of physical interfaces may be used. Serial interfaces can be used at higher data rates and parallel control can be used for extremely short distances where a very fast data rate is required.

Control between separated sites

Remote control is essential at large communications sites where the receiving and transmitting pieces of equipment are separated by several miles to avoid the problems of receiver overloading. A typical site would have the receiving equipment and the control unit located at the same site and the transmitters located at another site. A serial control format is preferred with this type of control system because of the distances involved. This requires fewer control lines between the separated sites. The transmitters are usually connected to the controller via phone lines. A modem is used to send the audio and control data to the transmitters.

It is also feasible in some applications to have the control unit, receivers, and transmitters located at separate sites several miles from each other. In this case modems are used for both the receiving and transmitting sites for the audio and control data. A minicomputer or mainframe is usually used in large communications sites to provide the remote control. This allows software to be written to aid in the operation of the communications site. The software can provide frequency management for the operators by preventing more than one transmitter from transmitting on the same frequency. It can also provide for the automatic logging of the frequencies used by the operators. Section 11.5 will demonstrate these and other functions which can be implemented on a central computer in a communications site.

ECM/ECCM operations

Remote control has many applications in the ECM/ECCM field. Receivers can be controlled to scan frequencies for the purpose of monitoring signals. It is also useful in a non-ECCM environment where emergency frequencies can be scanned for distress calls. Transmitters and receivers can be controlled to provide antijam (AJ) capabilities. In one type of AJ system the receiver and transmitter are hopping through pseudo-random frequencies to avoid signal jamming. Fast receiver and transmitter responses are required when implementing this type of remote control. A control scheme that will allow buffering of the frequency data is necessary. This frequency data is stored in the equipment until an execute command is received. This command consists of one or two characters for a serial control or a pulsed line for parallel control. The command instructs the equipment to change to the next frequency in the buffer. This type of remote control is usually done in an extended local control environment. The speed required of the control system and the possibility of radiating the hopping information on the control lines necessitate the need for extended local control. For this reason, fiber optics is becoming popular for this type of remote control. It also is not affected by electromagnetic interference (EMI) as a wire system is.

Remote control was seen as a desirable feature when the first commercial radio equipment appeared on the market. The first form of remote control was through parallel wire control. This type of control required large bundles of wires and was limited to relatively short distances.

In the late 1950s Collins Radio Co. used available telephone technology and created a dial pulse encoding scheme to remotely control its Universal Radio Group (URG) radio equipment line. The dial pulse control is operated over ordinary telephone lines. The equipment is capable of decoding commands for antenna, frequency, and mode selection on up to 10 preset channels. Each preset contains antenna, frequency, and mode information.

In the mid-1960s Collins developed a product line and control scheme that used a synchronous phase-shift-keyed (PSK) modulation at 4800 Hz for control and monitoring. This scheme was called the Collins Control and Communications System (CCCS). It is a computer-based scheme, and the processors send out 36-bit control words. The equipment automatically returns a 36-bit monitor word after receiving the control word. It also has addressing capability and up to 32 pieces of equipment can be placed on a common bus. The bus consists of three lines for control, monitor, and clock.

In the early 1970s the Collins HF-80 series of equipment was developed, which uses RS-232 for its remote control interface. It can operate from 75 to 19.2K baud. The basic control word is five characters long, with the first character containing the equipment address and the rest the control data. Each character has 8 bits with an optional 1 or 2 stop bits. Each control word can request a monitor word response from the equipment. The monitor word is returned in the same format as the control word.

The current remote technology at Collins employs the use of embedded microprocessors in the equipment. The software provides the ability to implement many different types of control schemes.

11.2 Control Formats

Remote control

To aid in the understanding of remote control, let us assume we have the design requirement which is shown in Fig. 11.1: a simplified radio that has four mode lines and four frequency lines. Each of the mode lines is controlled

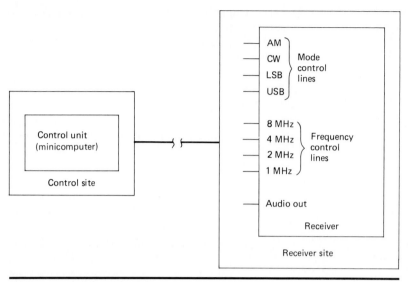

Figure 11.1 Separated site design requirement.

independently, and the frequency lines are controlled with a BCD code. The system is required to operate with the remote controller at a separate site. To implement this design, we need to define the following:

1. A data format for the control bits

2. Physical interface for the control connection

3. Type of data transmission: serial or parallel

Because of the potentially long distances required in separated sites, we will choose serial data transmission. The next thing to consider is the data definition of the control bits, which describes how the control bits are used. Some of the typical ways to define control bits are:

1. Binary

2. Binary coded decimal

3. ASCII

For the design example shown in Fig. 11.1, we will use binary code for the mode control bits. One bit will be used for each mode line. This will require 4 bits to control the radio mode. Since the frequency information used by the radio is in BCD, we will use it. To control frequency and mode will require 8 bits, as shown in Fig. 11.2.

Now that we have defined the control bits, we need to choose the type of serial interface. This defines the electrical and mechanical requirements of the connection between the radio and the remote controller. The main physical interfaces used for remote control are:

1. EIA RS-232C

2. EIA RS-422/449

3. IEEE Standard 488

4. MIL-STD-1553

5. Frequency shift keying

EIA RS-232C. This is an Electronic Industries Association (EIA) standard for interface between data terminal equipment and data communications equipment. It defines the signal names, pin numbers, and electrical line parameters. The electrical signals are bi-polar and range between $+3$ V, $+25$ V (for a space) and -3 V, -25 V (for a mark). The maximum speed is 20,000 bits/s with a line length limit of 15 m. Remote control using RS-232C is usually implemented with an asynchronous format with 7 or 8 data bits/character. It is also defined as a one-on-one control bus. When used with radio equipment that can be connected in parallel to the same control and monitor lines, a problem arises in tri-stating the equipment on the monitor line. Only one bus driver can be turned on at a time. The RS-232 line drivers available are not tri-statable, and a relay or electronic switch is needed to turn the line drive on and off. RS-232 has an advantage in that it is a common interface to nearly all data modems.

EIA RS-422/499. RS-422 is an electrical specification for a balanced voltage interface. The RS-422 driver is a low-impedance (100 ohms or less) balanced voltage source. It produces a differential voltage across the interconnecting cable to the RS-422 receiver. The use of the balanced interconnection eliminates any common-mode noise. RS-449 specifies the mechanical characteristics that implement RS-422. The maximum speed of the RS-422 is 10 million bits/s. The speed at which the data is sent controls the recommended line length. At speeds below 100,000 bits/s a line length of 1200 m or less is recommended. At 10 million bits/s the length of the line is down to 15 m. The use of a balanced line provides better noise immunity for the data signal. There are a number of line drivers and receivers that will interface digital signals to the balanced RS-422 lines. Some of the drivers are tri-statable to allow for bussing of the monitor line.

IEEE Standard 488. The IEEE-488 is sometimes referred to as the "general-purpose interface bus" (GPIB). It was developed by Hewlett-Packard and is used extensively in the field of automatic test equipment control.

Bit 8	Bit 7	Bit 6	Bit 5	Bit 4	Bit 3	Bit 2	Bit 1
8 MHz	4 MHz	2 MHz	1 MHz	AM	CW	LSB	USB

Figure 11.2 Control character.

It is a parallel interface using eight data lines and eight control lines. The data transfer is byte (8 bits)-serial or bit-parallel using an asynchronous interface. The data transfers are controlled by three handshake lines: DAV (data valid), NRFD (not ready for data), and NDAC (not data accepted). The remaining five control lines are used for other bus activity. On one bus there can be a maximum of 15 devices. One of these is called the "talker" (controller) and the other 14 are "listeners" (test equipment or radio equipment). The addressing of the equipment is part of the data message format. The maximum data rate is 1 Mbyte/s. The bus length is up to 20 m. The bus protocol is rigidly defined and somewhat complicated. However, there are many LSI devices on the market that make this interface easy to implement.

MIL-STD-1553.   This is a control bus defined by the military to be used for navigation and weapons systems. Some of the devices placed on the bus can be radio equipment. Data is transmitted over a pair of wires (or fiber optic cables) at a 1-MHz rate using Manchester II bi-phase signals. Control of the data on the bus is in accordance with the rules of this standard and can be implemented directly from a host processor or through a dedicated bus controller. This standard defines a bus with four levels of redundancy. Three words are defined as command word, data word, and status word. Each is 20 bits long and uses 3 bits for start synchronization and 1 bit for parity. Remote terminals (radio equipment) are controlled by the command word, which contains the remote terminal address (5 bits), subaddress (5 bits), the number of data words (5 bits), and a receive/transmit bit. The receive/transmit bit defines the command word as a control word which will be followed by the number of data words (control information) or the number of words to be sent back (monitor data). The status word contains system information that is used by the host controller. Remote terminals may be directly coupled to the main bus by using a pair of 55-ohm isolation resistors. These resistors are incorporated in the equipment that is connected to the bus. This type of stub is limited to 30 cm or less in length. Transformer coupling may be used to stub up to 6 m. This bus provides good noise immunity and is useful where high reliability and dual redundancy are needed. At this writing there are a few chip sets available to interface to this bus. Fiber optics is currently becoming popular for use in military applications. MIL-STD-1773 is a proposed new specification for military fiber optic data buses. It is basically a fiber optic version of MIL-STD-1553.

FSK.   Sending digital information (square waves) over long distances requires large bandwidth. This problem can be remedied by converting these signals into audio tones. FSK uses two frequencies, one for the mark tone and the other for the space tone. This is the technique used by most low-speed commercial modems. As the data goes into the modem in serial digital form, the modem generates a sine wave that shifts between the mark and space tones. In remote control applications where high speed is not required (up to 300 baud), there are a number of LSI chips available to generate FSK signals.

For the example shown in Fig. 11.2, we will use RS-232C. This is a widely used interface and will work with most modems. It also serves as a standard interface to a number of minicomputers or mainframe computers that could be used as the control device. Because we are using a serial data transmission, the problem now becomes how to handle the transfer of data from the serial form to the parallel form.

There are many devices on the market that will accept a serial input and provide a parallel output such as universal asynchronous receiver/transmitters (UARTs), which are available for use in discrete logic design or for microprocessor applications. The UART serial signal is usually in an asynchronous format which is sent without a common system clock line, and the time between characters can be random. The data synchronization uses a start bit and a stop bit along with the data bits. Figure 11.3 shows an asynchronous character definition. A bit is defined as a logic high level or a logic low level, or may be referred to as a "mark" (high level) and a "space" (low level). The speed at which the UARTs work is specified in baud rate. In serial data communications, baud rate is the reciprocal of the time of one bit period. For example, a bit time of 3.333 ms is equivalent to 300 baud. The typical baud rates used are: 75, 110, 150, 300, 600, 1200, 2400, 4800, 9600, and 19,200. The UART devices can be programmed to generate 5, 6, 7, or 8 data bits and a parity bit with odd or even or no parity.

The design example shown in Fig. 11.1 now looks like the system shown in Fig. 11.4. The UART is set for 8 data bits. With it (and some control logic to route the bits to the hardware) and the data definition, the radio can be controlled. However, we still have the problem of completing the connection between the radio and the remote controller. This can be done by running wires between the sites or using existing phone lines. The example shown in Fig. 11.4 uses phone lines, which require the use of a modem. The following is a brief description of modems.

Modems

"Modem" is an acronym for *mo*dulator/*dem*odulator. There are three general classes, low speed up to 600 bits/s, medium speed up to 2400 bits/s, and high speed up to approximately 10,000 bits/s. The low-speed modems use FSK for the modulation. Complex modulation techniques are used as the modem speed increases. Phase-shift keying is an example of this type of modulation, in which the phase angle of the carrier wave is varied to represent different bit values to the receiver. There are two basic communication

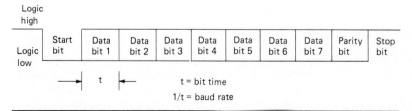

Figure 11.3 Asynchronous character.

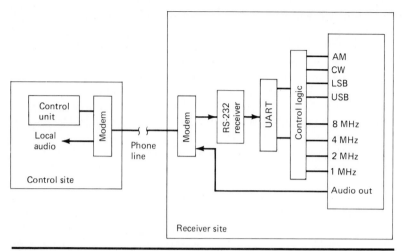

Figure 11.4 Completed radio control scheme.

modes, half-duplex and full duplex. In half-duplex, data can only go in one direction at a time. In full duplex, communications can go both directions at the same time. An example of full-duplex communication is a conventional telephone. The Bell 103 series modem has become a pseudo standard. It operates full duplex on a phone line at speeds up to 300 bits/s. It uses two sets of tones within the bandwidth of the phone lines (300 to 3400 Hz). The low band uses a 1070-Hz tone as a space and 1270-Hz as a mark. The high band uses a 2035-Hz tone as a space and 2225-Hz as a mark. Standards are available from the International Telegraph and Telephone Consultative Committee (CCITT) that define this type of data communications. It should be noted that the modems are specified in bits per second and not baud. Because of the modulation techniques used in modems, the baud rate and the bits per second are not always the same. In higher-speed modems, 2, 3, or 4 data bits may be sent in one baud period.

The completed radio control scheme is shown in Fig. 11.4. The controller sends the control character through the modem and a phone line. The remote interface has a modem, a UART, and some discrete logic control that takes the received control character and outputs it to the radio to control mode and frequency. Section 11.3 describes a method of remote control used on a Rockwell-Collins receiver that is now in production.

11.3 Digital Interface Techniques

There are many advantages to using microprocessor technology when designing new radio equipment. The microprocessor is used to replace the discrete control logic. It can also be used to control the remote interface in the radio equipment. Because of the processing ability, a versatile remote control interface can be designed. This section describes a new receiver that has been designed and developed at Rockwell-Collins using microprocessor technology.

Figure 11.5 shows a block diagram of the central processing unit (CPU) and the hardware on the CPU bus. The CPU used is an Intel 80188. It is in a 68-pin leadless (approximately 1 in^2) hermetic chip carrier. It also has a number of on-chip peripherals, which conserves board space. It has an internal clock generator (crystal is external), three general-purpose programmable timers, and an interrupt controller. The CPU also supplies chip selects for the ROM, RAM, and seven I/O ports. It has an internal 16-bit data bus and an 8-bit external data bus. This gives the speed of a 16-bit processor and the ease of interface of an 8-bit processor. The program is stored in three 27128 (16K $\times$ 8) EPROMs. This gives a total ROM memory size of 48K bytes. There are 4K bytes of RAM for variable storage which is battery-backed-up. This allows for the retention of channels (presets) and for restoring the last operating state of the receiver on powerup. For remote control the CPU interfaces to an Intel 8251A universal synchronous-asynchronous receiver/transmitter (USART) which can be programmed for 5- to 8-bit characters. It will run up to 19.2K baud and can operate in full duplex. The CPU controls the following receiver functions:

1. IF/audio, RF translator, synthesizer

2. Front panel

3. Eight-channel analog-to-digital port

4. Preselector port

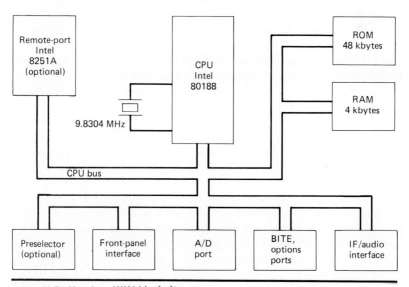

Figure 11.5 Receiver CPU block diagram.

5. Built-in test equipment (BITE)

6. Remote port

The IF/audio board contains three digital signal processing chips plus an RF translator, and the frequency synthesizer. The signal processing chips contain their own algorithms for digital signal processing. The signal processing chips are given mode and frequency information from the CPU. The CPU supplies frequency band information to the RF translator. The synthesizer receives an encoded serial bit stream from the CPU every time the frequency changes.

The front panel contains a key pad, liquid crystal displays (LCDs), and mode control switches. The key pad and mode switches are connected in a matrix and generate an interrupt to the CPU every time a switch is depressed. The CPU scans the matrix to determine which switch is closed. The main function control switches on the front panel are "Channel," "BFO," "Frequency," "Normal," "Program," "Enter," and "Local/Remote." The two LCD displays are controlled by the CPU. One displays frequency, channel, and BFO, and can also display 16 characters of ASCII text; the other displays mode and operating status. The operating status includes a bar graph of the audio channel output and the RF input signal levels. The CPU obtains the bar graph data from the signal processing chips.

The eight-channel A/D port is used to digitize the RF gain and the squelch pots on the front panel. The audio lines are inputted through the A/D and then displayed as a level on the front panel bar graph. The remaining A/D lines are used for the BITE.

The preselector port is optional and provides a latched BCD encoded representation of the current frequency. It also provides a tune-start pulse that can be used to indicate when this frequency information has changed.

There is extensive BITE used in this receiver, which is started from the front panel or from the remote controller. The signal processing chips have their own BITE routines which are initiated by the CPU. There are a number of electrically controlled loopback tests that can be run by the CPU to check signal flow. The A/D port has the essential test signals for the digital signal processing chips which can be read and verified by the CPU.

The remote interface has the option of being either RS-232 or RS-422. Both ports use the standard recommended connector. However, they use other pins on the same connector to define four address strapping pins. This strapping allows for the setting of 15 different addresses. This allows more than one receiver on a common bus. When the RS-422 option is installed, an integrated circuit driver is used which can be tri-stated. For RS-232, the driver circuit is built from discrete components which will allow for tri-stating. Sometimes, on a tri-state monitor bus, problems can arise because the tri-stated line might look like a continuous start bit to the controller. This will cause a framing error at the controller and may cause system problems. If this happens, a pull-down resistor is needed somewhere on the bus to provide a mark state. The baud rate is selectable from 75 to 19.2K baud by a dip switch on the CPU card. The baud clock frequency is generated (16 times baud rate) by selecting a suitable crystal for the CPU clock which can be divided down by one of the CPU's internal programmable timers. The USART is programmed for 7-bit characters with odd parity and 1 stop bit. This allows the use of ASCII characters for the control data definition.

The optional features of the receiver are controlled by an option ROM. This ROM is read by the CPU on powerup and indicates to the CPU which options are installed in a particular receiver.

The program was written using PASCAL as the primary programming language. Some time-critical functions required the use of assembly language routines. The CPU card has a test/debug connector. During software development and testing, a software debug card was installed on this connector. The card contains RAM and a debug monitor program. The software for the radio was compiled, linked, and located on an IBM personal computer (PC). The software was then downloaded into the RAM of the debug card. The debug monitor provides the ability to examine, change, run, and single-step the program. The software was written using state-driven routines. The high-level state diagram is shown in Fig. 11.6. The two primary

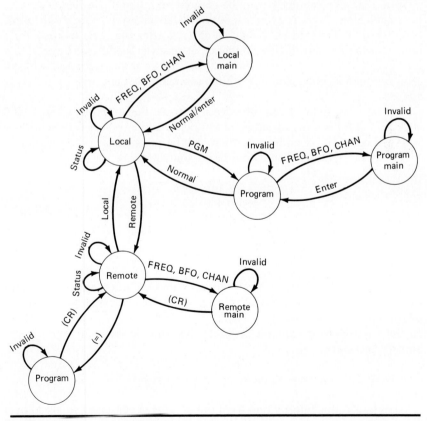

Figure 11.6 Software state diagram.

states are local and remote. The local/remote switch determines which state is active. When the local state is active and a function switch (FREQ, BFO, CHAN) is depressed, the state changes to the local main state. This state inputs the remaining switch depressions, and if they are a valid command (terminated by the enter switch), the radio hardware is set accordingly. Each state has a decision table which contains an event and an action. For example, in the local state if the event was a decimal switch (0 to 9), the action is to ignore the switch. If the event was the FREQ switch, the action is to enter the local main state. A few of the low-level hardware interface routines were written in 80188 assembly language because of the timing requirements of the hardware.

When the receiver is in the remote state, any device capable of generating ASCII characters with odd parity and one stop bit may be used as a controller. The control characters make a word description of the command. This makes the commands human-readable and easy to use and understand. The control word may be spelled out, but only the first two characters will be used by the CPU. A space is used to separate commands from the command variables. The command will be executed when a carriage return (CR) is received by the CPU.

More than one command may be entered on a line if they are separated by a semicolon. There is a limit of 80 characters allowed before a (CR) must be entered. A line feed (LF) may be entered after the (CR) to allow for a human-readable copy of the commands. A receiver is addressed by sending UNIT XX (00 to 15). Once this is sent, the receiver addressed will accept commands until another UNIT command is sent with a different address.

Address 00 is defined as a broadcast address. For example, when UNIT 00; TEST (CR) is sent, all receivers will perform the test regardless of their strapped address. On address 00 there will be no response returned by any of the receivers. Some of the other basic commands are:

MODE	(AM, USB, LSB, ISB, CW)
AGC	(SLOW, FAST, OFF)
BW	(6000, 3200, 1000, 300)
RF XXX	(Sets RF gain from 00 to 256 steps)
BFO	(FIXED, VAR$\pm$XXX)
CHANNEL XX	(Selects preset channel 00 to 99)

The receiver can store up to 100 preset channels. Each preset contains a frequency, MODE, AGC, and BFO information. To program a preset (or any programmable function) the = sign is used. For example, to program preset 10 (all the following examples assume that the receiver unit number has already been sent):

PRESET 10 = FR 20000.00,AM,AGC SLOW,BFO FIXED (CR)

To obtain status information from the receiver, a command followed by a ? can be used. For example, to find what frequency the receiver is on, send

FR? (CR). When the TEST ? is received, the CPU will execute its BITE programs. The results of the BITE are displayed to the subassembly level that failed. Also displayed are additional codes that can tell the test technician which test failed and the data that caused the failure.

The receiver can scan a list of programmed channels from a start number to a stop number. For example, to scan a list of channels:

```
DWELL 0.5 (CR)
SCAN 10,22 (CR)
```

This command will cause the receiver to start at channel 10 and increment to channel 22 and then repeat. The receiver will stop on each channel for 0.5 s dwell time. This will continue until the operator stops the scan or the stop scan signal on the rear panel goes to an active state.

The receiver can search a range of frequencies with a specified increment and dwell time. For example, to search a range of frequencies:

```
INCREMENT 10.0 (CR)          Increment frequency kHz
DWELL 1.0 (CR)               Dwell time, s
SEARCH 2000.0,16000.0 (CR)   Frequency range
```

The operator can assign a set of channels to a group and have the receiver scan that group. There can be up to 10 groups with 20 channels in each group. For example, to assign and scan a group:

```
GROUP = 5,1,7,9,11,23,45 (CR)
GROUP 5 (CR)
```

The first command assigns group number 5 to have channels 1, 7, 9, 11, 23, and 45. The second command will start the scan of group 5.

When the receiver is in local mode, the remote port is still monitored. The Receive Data Read output of the USART is connected to one of the CPU interrupt control lines. All the remote activity is monitored during local operation. However, only the unit and ? commands are used and the others are ignored. When the unit command is received, it is stored. This allows the receiver to respond to any ? commands that are received from the remote controller. If a ? command is received when the receiver is in local, the response will be the normal response for the type of ? command followed by the word LOCAL.

This section has shown how an embedded microprocessor in radio equipment can be used to implement a remote control scheme. The microprocessor provides many advantages in the remote control by making the equipment easy to implement and maintain.

11.4   Remote Controllers

To remotely control a radio usually requires that more than one control character be sent. This group of characters is called a "control word." These are usually divided into functions such as mode, frequency, and so on. After receiving a control word, the radio equipment usually responds with a monitor word. When more than one piece of equipment needs to be controlled by one control unit, the equipment is connected to a common control bus. This is accomplished by providing a control scheme that will allow each piece of equipment to have a different address. The basic types of controllers are:

1. Dedicated controller

2. Multiple-unit controller

3. Front panel simulator

4. Central processor

The dedicated units control one piece of equipment. Most dedicated controllers operate in the extended local mode of operation. A typical example of this is the control head used in the cockpit of an aircraft.

Multiple-unit controllers are used to control more than one piece of equipment. They have some provision that allows them to select the address of the equipment to be controlled and they usually control equipment of the same type. The equipment is connected to the controller via a common control and monitor bus. Some of the more sophisticated multiple-unit controllers, ones that use processors, can control different types of equipment.

Some remote controllers are made to look like the front panel of the equipment they are controlling. This makes it easy for an operator who is familiar with the equipment to remotely control the equipment without learning a new procedure. These controllers may be of the dedicated or the multiple-unit type. The multiple controllers will differ from the radio front panel by the addition of an address selection switch.

Many controllers in larger communications sites are mainframes or minicomputers. At these sites the operator controls the equipment with a keyboard and cathode ray tube (CRT) terminal. The keyboard is used to enter commands, and the equipment status is displayed on the CRT. Employing a central processor as a controller provides many advantages through the use of software. An example of this type of remote control will be described in Sec. 11.5.

One of the problems that can be encountered in remote control is the handling of data errors between the controller and the equipment. In most systems this is the responsibility of the remote control unit. To solve this problem, a way of detecting the errors is needed. Most equipment, including the controller, uses a UART for serial control. The UARTs currently available have internal communications error checking which is made available to the user. These are parity error, framing error, and overrun error. Most UARTs are double-buffered. This gives a full character time before the character must be removed from the UART to prevent an overrun error. When the equipment being controlled detects a UART error, it can set an error bit in its monitor status. When the controller reads the status and detects this error bit it can resend the control information.

There are many types of control schemes used in remote control systems. Each of these systems has its unique way of controlling data errors. In some the controlled equipment does not perform any error checking and will only echo the control characters it receives. The controller handles these systems by sending a control character and then waiting for the equipment to echo that character back. If the control character is echoed correctly, the controller sends the next character. If the echoed character is in error, the same control character is resent.

In other systems the equipment has internal error checking and will send back a single character. The controller sends the complete control command and then waits for the equipment to respond with an "acknowledge" character. If the acknowledge is not received by the controller, it will repeat the control command. In some systems this acknowledge may not be in the form of a character but may be a hardwire that uses a logic level for the acknowledge.

In some systems the equipment can return a monitor response of its current status. A scheme can be used whereby the controller sends the command and then sends a monitor request for status. The controller then compares the monitor response with the command sent to verify that the equipment performed the control command.

The introduction of computer technology to the field of remote control has greatly increased user application. This is true for dedicated remote controllers as well as for the more sophisticated communications sites.

11.5   Communications Site

Rockwell-Collins in Cedar Rapids, IA, has a modern HF communications control site which is an example of remote control implemented in extended local control. The station is in two adjacent rooms. One contains all the radio equipment and the other the operators and control consoles. The station is staffed continuously. It is engaged in several different types of HF communications. It is licensed as an experimental high-frequency research station, an aeronautical flight test station, and a limited coast-maritime station. The traffic it handles includes communications and phone patching to aircraft, drill rigs, and tankers on the high seas. The station also serves as a "testbed" for the research and development of new HF communications equipment.

In the operator control room there are four consoles. Each is equipped with a CRT and a keyboard. The CRT displays a main menu with eight functions. These are:

1. Equipment control

2. Radio station log

3. Scratch pad

4. Propagation forecast
5. SELSCAN
6. Information retrieval
7. Operator sign-on
8. Data/time set

The equipment control function allows the operator to control the radio equipment. The system can control up to 10 transceivers and their associated antenna switching matrix. Figure 11.7 shows the CRT screen displaying the equipment control status. Each numbered horizontal row of data is associated with one transceiver. The column labeled FREQ shows all of the selected frequencies. The next columns show antenna number and azimuth. The rotatable antennas have their present position displayed. The next column, labeled MOD, displays the equipment mode U = USB, L = LSB, I = ISB, A = AM, and C = CW. The column labeled GN is the receiver RF gain setting. This function provides thirty-two 3-dB steps of attenuation. The column labeled AGC contains the current AGC setting O = OFF, S = SLOW, F = FAST. The status block is a display of conditions which are true when * is displayed and not true when . is displayed. They correspond to the performance sensors built into the HF-80 radio equipment. The labels for each column are vertical and represent:

LPE Low-power enable
LVE Low-voltage enable
HVE High-voltage enable

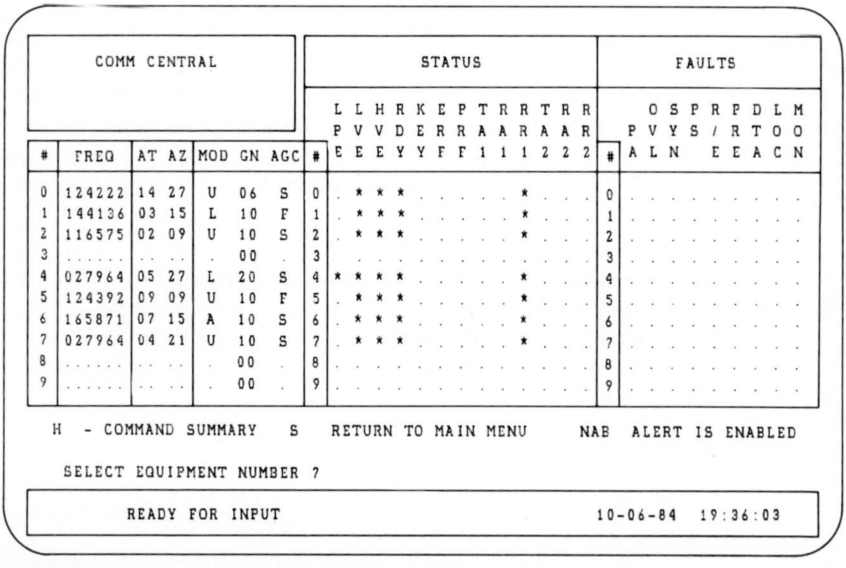

COMM CENTRAL | STATUS | FAULTS

#	FREQ	AT	AZ	MOD	GN	AGC
0	124222	14	27	U	06	S
1	144136	03	15	L	10	F
2	116575	02	09	U	10	S
3	......	..	..	.	00	.
4	027964	05	27	L	20	S
5	124392	09	09	U	10	F
6	165871	07	15	A	10	S
7	027964	04	21	U	10	S
8	......	..	..	.	00	.
9	......	..	..	.	00	.

#	LPE	LVE	HVE	RDY	KEY	ERF	PRF	TA1	RA1	RR1	TA2	RA2	RR2
0	.	*	*	*	.	.	.	.	.	*	.	.	.
1	.	*	*	*	.	.	.	.	.	*	.	.	.
2	.	*	*	*	.	.	.	.	.	*	.	.	.
3		.	.	.	.	.	.	.	.	.	.	.	.
4	*	*	*	*	.	.	.	.	.	*	.	.	.
5	.	*	*	*	.	.	.	.	.	*	.	.	.
6	.	*	*	*	.	.	.	.	.	*	.	.	.
7	.	*	*	*	.	.	.	.	.	*	.	.	.
8	.	.	.	.	.	.	.	.	.	.	.	.	.
9	.	.	.	.	.	.	.	.	.	.	.	.	.

#	PA	OVL	SYN	PS	R/E	PRE	DTA	LOC	MON
0	.	.	.	.	.	.	.	.	.
1	.	.	.	.	.	.	.	.	.
2	.	.	.	.	.	.	.	.	.
3	.	.	.	.	.	.	.	.	.
4	.	.	.	.	.	.	.	.	.
5	.	.	.	.	.	.	.	.	.
6	.	.	.	.	.	.	.	.	.
7	.	.	.	.	.	.	.	.	.
8	.	.	.	.	.	.	.	.	.
9	.	.	.	.	.	.	.	.	.

H - COMMAND SUMMARY S RETURN TO MAIN MENU NAB ALERT IS ENABLED

SELECT EQUIPMENT NUMBER 7

READY FOR INPUT 10-06-84 19:36:03

Figure 11.7 Equipment control menu.

RDY Transmitter ready

KEY Transmitter keyed

ERF Exciter RF output

PRF Power amplifier output

TA1 Transmitter audio input, channel #1

RA1 Receiver audio output, channel #1

RR1 Receiver RF Input, channel #1

TA2 Transmitter audio input, channel #2

RA2 Receiver audio output, channel #2

RR2 Receiver RF input, channel #2

The block labeled FAULT is similarly displayed and labeled according to the following definitions:

PA Power supply fault

OVL Receiver input overload

SYN Frequency synthesizer fault

PS Power supply fault

R/E Receiver exciter fault

PRE Preselector fault

DTA Data transmission error detected by transceiver

LOC Local/remote switch in local

MON Monitor switch on

The information displayed in the status and fault blocks gives enough detail to isolate malfunctions to unit level in all cases and to circuit card level in many cases.

In Fig. 11.7 inverted video is used on the equipment number to indicate which equipment is selected. All subsequent commands will operate on this selected equipment. All commands are initiated with a single keystroke. For operating convenience, a HELP screen is available which lists the commands. After the first keystroke, a prompt appears on the screen to help the operator complete the command. Invalid entries are detected by the console processor and reported to the operator on the bottom line of the CRT along with an audio beep. An assurance tone tells the operator when a command has been executed. The following is a list of the operator commands:

A Antenna number (00—drop antenna)

B No answer back (NAB) alert, enable/disable

E Equipment number (0 to 9)

F Frequency

G RF attenuation

H This menu

K   "Key" radio

L   Radio station log

M   Mode (u—upper, l—lower, a—AM, f—FM)

O   Output power

S   Return to main menu

T   AGC (f—fast, s—slow, o—off)

U   "Unkey" radio

V   Voltage (o—off, l—low-enabled, 2—high and low)

Z   Antenna azimuth (00, 03, 06, 09, 12, 15, 18, 21, 24, 27, 30, 33, 36)

<   Antenna lockout

>   Antenna unlock

Critical safeguards to prevent damage to the system hardware are implemented in the equipment control software. Whenever an antenna is selected, the master equipment control processor checks the frequency of the associated transmitter to make sure it is within the range of the requested antenna. If not, the antenna selection is automatically refused. Conversely, whenever the frequency is changed, an antenna band check is performed and the antenna is disconnected if the new frequency is out of band.

The station log function provides some automatic logging for the station operators. The computer system relieves the operator from entering information such as date, time, frequency, mode, power, and antenna. In addition, the computer checks the log for accuracy and prompts the operator to correct errors which are detected. Call signs are automatically checked against a list of authorized users to prevent unauthorized access to the service. The data base computer prints a hard copy of the log and saves copies on the disk. The disk copies are used to generate user billing and other reports at monthly intervals.

The scratch pad function provides a bulletin-board type of capability on the operator CRT. When selected, any operator can view the information stored there by all operators. Likewise, all operators can add or delete information in the scratch pad. It is used primarily by the operators to list pending traffic.

The propagation forecast function provides quick frequency propagation information to the operators. The station uses a program developed at the Naval Ocean Systems Center called MINIMUF. MINIMUF uses mathematical modeling of the ionosphere to calculate the maximum usable frequency (MUF) and frequency of optimum transmission (FOT). This technique eliminates the need for periodic updates with empirical data from ionospheric soundings.

The SELSCAN^{TM} is not an integral part of the station system but rather a peripheral using the console processor as a smart terminal. This operation is discussed in Chap. 2. The information retrieval function is used primarily as a telephone directory and for automatic telephone dialing. Telephone numbers which are dialed are automatically transferred to the radio log. It is used to provide rapid access to frequently used reference information. The operator sign-on function is used by the operator to sign on duty. All subsequent radio logs entered on the operator's console will automatically include the operator's unique identification code until he or she signs off again. The date and time set function are used for the setting of the master clock/calendar.

An overall block diagram of the computer hardware is shown in Fig. 11.8. It is a multiuser system with four operator consoles. The computational workload is spread among seven separate computers: one in each console, an antenna matrix controller, a master equipment controller, and a data base computer. This configuration was chosen to achieve high performance at minimum cost. The console computers consist of a Rockwell RM-65 modular computer system with high-resolution CRT and high-reliability Hall-effect keyboards. The master equipment control processor and clock also use the RM-65 modular computer system components but the card cage is 16 slot instead of 8 slot as in the console system. The data base computer is an IBM PC with dual floppy disk drives, CRT, and 80-column printer. The antenna matrix controller is a Delta, Model MCU8, which uses a 6502 CPU. The radio equipment is from the Collins HF-80 series of fixed-station equipment. The consoles and master equipment control processors communicate over a 2400-baud RS-232 line. The remote transceiver located in Newport Beach, CA, is controlled via leased telephone lines. The remote transceiver is con-

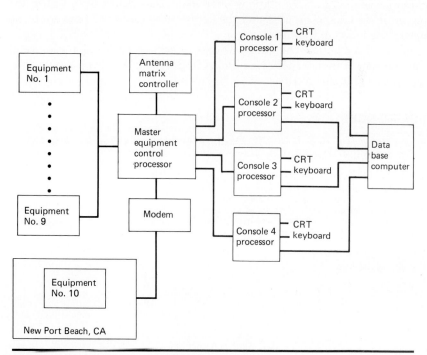

Figure 11.8 Communications site block diagram.

trolled using a low-speed modem at 150 baud. The master equipment control processor controls the HF-80 equipment using an RS-232 line at 9600 baud.

In order to achieve maximum operator efficiency, it is important that the system respond rapidly to keyboard input and the CRT display reflect system status changes with minimum delay. Poor system response will also make it difficult to gain operator acceptance. For these reasons, the use of assembly language was chosen for most of the software, the exception being the use of IBM-compiled Basic for the data base programs. Response time of the logging function is typically less than 10 s. The equipment control functions typically respond in less than 1 s. The master equipment control processor is programmed to continuously interrogate the radio equipment and antenna matrix controller for status information. This information is immediately forwarded to all console processors, thus providing current status to the operators at all times. The console date and time are updated once each second. The master controller must also accept, translate, and excecute all equipment control commands from the consoles. To ensure the integrity of the data transfers to and from the console, each character received is checked for parity, framing, and overrun errors and a checksum is performed on each block of data. If an error is detected, the data is automatically resent. Interrupt processing is used extensively in the master control processor. This allows the servicing of the many I/O ports without delay. The console processor programs also use interrupt processing to streamline keyboard input and CRT display functions.

Radio communications stations offer many opportunities to utilize the power of the microcomputer, and the applications described here are by no means the limits of their exploitation.

Acknowledgment. The author wishes to acknowledge the assistance of the Manager of Radio Operations, Heinz H. Blankenhagen, who supplied the information for this section.

REFERENCES

1. *Aircraft Internal Time Division Command/Response Multiplex Data Bus,* U.S. Military Standard MIL-STD-1553B, U.S. Government Printing Office, Washington, DC, September 1978.
2. *Interface between Data Terminal Equipment and Data Communications Equipment Employing Serial Binary Data Interchange,* EIA Standard RS-232-C, Electronic Industries Association, Washington, DC, August 1969.
3. *Electrical Characteristics of Balanced Voltage Digital Interface Circuits,* EIA Standard RS-422-A, Electronic Industries Association, Washington, DC, December 1978.
4. *Digital Interface for Programmable Instrumentation,* IEEE STD 488-1775, IEEE, New York, Nov, 1978.
5. Donald Gibson, "Designer's Guide to Data Modems," *Electron. Des. News,* Vol. 25, Mar. 5, 1980, pp. 96–102.

Chapter 2

Solid-State Power Amplifiers

Roderick K. Blocksome

Recent advances in transistor technology have produced devices capable of considerable RF power in the HF range. These modern devices, unheard of a few years ago, form the heart of today's compact, yet powerful, RF power amplifiers.

This chapter will delve into the design of linear power amplifiers for the 1.6- to 30-MHz range at power levels up to 1000 W. Only linear operation will be covered, as it is commonly used in most SSB transmitters and forms the basis of the more sophisticated applications covered in Chap. 13. The normal HF range, usually considered to lie between 3.0 and 30 MHz, has been extended over recent years to the top of the AM broadcast band at 1600 kHz. This is a result of increased military and maritime usage, coupled with advances in solid-state wideband technology.

Transistors with ever increasing power dissipation capabilities have been developed, making practical high-power solid-state linear amplifiers. As few as eight output transistors are used in a Rockwell-Collins 1000-W (average) power amplifier. Such amplifiers have replaced tube-type amplifiers at lower power levels and seriously challenge them at the 1000-W (and above) level as component costs decrease, linearity improves, and higher-power devices become available.

12.1 A Typical HF Solid-State Power Amplifier

Figure 12.1 shows a block diagram of a typical solid-state HF power amplifier. A high-power system is shown to illustrate combining multiple-output

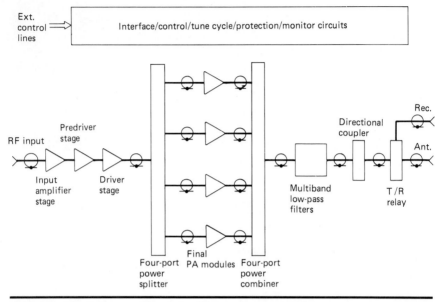

Figure 12.1   Block diagram of typical solid-state power amplifier.

modules and their attendant control systems. Multiple-output modules are presently required for output powers greater than 250 to 500 W, depending upon the types of devices used, the maximum ambient temperature, and the altitude of operation. There are several very important specifications which influence the output power obtainable from a single solid-state amplifier stage.

Output power

The factors determining maximum output power fall into two categories: device ratings and thermal considerations. The manufacturer's safe operating ratings of voltage breakdown and maximum current must not be exceeded under any circumstances. High-power RF transistors, unlike vacuum tubes, are very unforgiving of any transient condition which exceeds their electrical ratings. These ratings are usually adequately described in the device data sheet. Less well described are the subtleties of thermal limits.

Data sheet specifications are usually limited to specifying the *average* thermal resistance (θ_{jc}) of the junction-to-case and the maximum junction temperature of the device chip. Many devices specify 200°C as maximum rated junction temperature. However, 160°C maximum should be used for a reliable design.

θ_{jc} is a difficult number to obtain accurately since it is influenced by several variables inherent in the transistor manufacturing process [1]. The determination of θ_{jc} requires measuring the semiconductor junction and case temperatures during actual RF operation. Conventional thermocouples can be used to measure the case temperature but a scanning infrared microscope must be used to measure junction temperatures on the die. Each junction temperature on the die is recorded and the average obtained. Therein lies a potential problem for the design engineer. The transistor data sheets generally do not specify the maximum (or minimum) junction temperature, only the average. Yet the variation of junction temperatures across a single die is often considerable because of bonding voids under the die, effects of reactive loads (voltage standing wave ratio or VSWR), and variations in emitter ballasting. The hottest junction is stressed the most and therefore leads to an early failure of devices operated at or near the specified maximum limits. A conservative derating factor must be applied to the device thermal ratings to ensure a reliable design. The entire cooling system design must be an important and early task in designing solid-state power amplifiers.

Intermodulation distortion

IMD is a very important PA specification since it directly affects performance of the HF communication link and interference to adjacent HF channels. IMD products are formed when any device or component acts on the desired signal in a nonlinear fashion.

Generally, narrowband, tube-type HF amplifiers are capable of lower levels of IMD than current solid-state amplifiers. Many solid-state amplifiers on the market today exhibit relatively poor IMD because of a greater priority placed on RF output power at the expense of linearity. Aside from this, the better IMD performance of tube amplifiers can be attributed to the longer history of design improvements of RF power grid tubes for linear service and the relative ease of single- or multistage RF feedback circuits in tuned output tube circuits. Refer to Chap. 14 for a thorough discussion.

There are two ways to specify IMD performance: the two-tone and the noise loading test. The noise loading test more accurately simulates the conditions encountered in high-power fixed-station PAs transmitting multitone data. This technique and the mathematical derivation of IMD products for both methods are discussed in Chap. 14.

A really good test to closely simulate IMD performance of an SSB voice transmitter does not exist. The standard two-tone test is the one most readily made that provides reproducible results. This requires injection of two independent (not phase-related) equal-amplitude RF signals into the PA RF input. The frequency of the signals should be within the range of the typical SSB exciter baseband output, i.e., 300 to 2700 Hz. Typically, tones of 800 and 1800 Hz are used, giving a tone separation of 1000 Hz. The test is then performed at several RF frequencies throughout the operating range of the PA under test. The amplifier output is observed on a good-quality spectrum analyzer, the amplitudes of all spectra being noted in relationship to the two injected tones. The amplitude of each input tone must be adjusted to produce an output power exactly 6 dB down from the rated PEP of the PA.

This ensures that the combined two tones drive the PA exactly to the PEP power rating. The odd-order distortion products will lie on either side of the input tones, each spaced in frequency from each other (and the input tones) by the separation of the original input tones.

Herein lies an opportunity for playing the game of "specsmanship." Should the level of IMD products be specified in relation to PEP or the level of the two injected tones? If the former is used (as is nearly always the case in amateur products and many commercial amplifiers), a figure 6 dB larger results. However, a strong case may be made to reference the IMD level to one of the two equal desired tones. Since we are measuring IMD products in the frequency domain, they ought to be specified against a reference level also measured in the frequency domain. Figure 12.2 illustrates a typical PA output spectrum when driven by a two-tone test signal. The amplifier output in Fig. 12.2 exhibits IMD levels "not less than 30 dB below one of two equal tones." This is a typical specification for good-quality, commercial, high-power HF PAs. Typical amateur-grade solid-state PA specifications range from −30 dB to as poor as −20 dB below one of two equal tones. More expensive military solid-state PA specifications range from −26 to −40 dB.

How do these two-tone test results relate to the real-world problems of error-free data transmissions and minimum adjacent channel interference to other HF spectrum users? Consider a 1000-W PA producing third-order IMD levels of −24 dB. The unwanted distortion products are being trans-

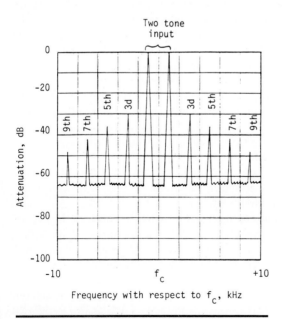

Figure 12.2 Typical spectral output of a power amplifier driven with two-tone test signal.

mitted in an adjacent channel at a power level of 1 W! This seems small until one considers the fickle characteristics of HF propagation which enable amateurs to communicate worldwide with a few tens of milliwatts!

Another, more effective, method of evaluating the effects of various IMD levels may be accomplished by operating an SSB voice transmitter for a long period of time while recording and storing the peak spectra of the output signal. The result is a power density display of in-band as well as out-of-band signals. This test was applied to three different grades of SSB equipment, each exhibiting markedly different IMD levels on the standard two-tone tests. Figure 12.3 shows the results for comparison. The power density curve of the in-band signal display is typical of a male voice into a particular type of microphone. The results shown in Fig. 12.3 graphically indicate the need for low-IMD designs in HF linear power amplifiers.

Frequency range

The frequency range of an HF wideband solid-state PA is usually 1.6 to 30 MHz, with some applications requiring only a 2.0-MHz lower limit. The frequency range specification affects the design primarily in the area of wideband RF transformers and decoupling networks on the dc line. A range of 1.6 to 30 MHz spans more than four octaves, requiring transformers and networks of more than casual design. Special ferrite cores have been developed to handle wide bandwidths and power levels of 1000 W or more. Transmission line transformers are preferred over conventional "wire-wound" transformers for their wide bandwidth and low insertion loss.

Harmonics

The harmonic levels specified for most HF SSB communications range from -46 to -80 dB below the fundamental. The radiation of unwanted harmonic signals and the interference which these signals cause are of primary concern. Only a class A amplifier can produce harmonic levels this low without output filters. However, it has very low efficiency—typically 25 down to 10 percent, depending upon allowable harmonic levels.

Class AB or B operation is commonly used for linear amplification. Typical collector/drain efficiencies are 40 to 55 percent but with significant harmonic output. In a push-pull stage, even-order (second, fourth, sixth, etc.) harmonics cancel to a degree (depending on circuit balance and device matching) while odd-order harmonics are significantly higher. The third harmonic is typically only 10 to 13 dB below the fundamental. A bandswitched low-pass filter can be used to improve the PA harmonic output levels.

Hum and noise

The hum and noise specification of modern SSB transmitters is usually 40 to 55 dB below the rated PEP output power. Hum on the signal refers to

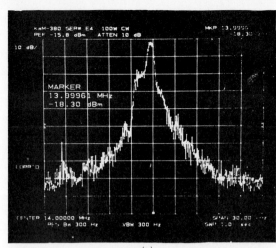

(a)

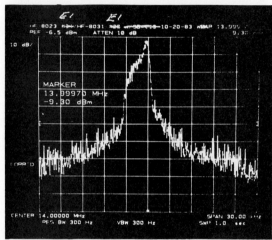

(b)

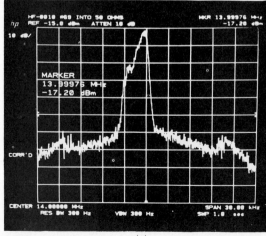

(c)

modulation of the signal by ripple products from the power supply rectifier and filter circuits. Noise can be caused by any other circuit such as voltage regulators that put a random low-level modulation on the PA output. Methods to suppress power supply ripple are covered in detail in Chap. 15. Solid-state power amplifiers offer only about 3 to 12 dB of ripple rejection, depending upon whether or not negative feedback is employed. The remaining ripple rejection must be accomplished in the power supply filter.

Applications

The solid-state linear power amplifier finds application in several broad categories which, due to prime power considerations, end up affecting the power level of the amplifier. Amateur radio applications often use 13.8 Vdc devices to allow operation directly from vehicular batteries. This low collector voltage limits the practical output power to around 150 W for a push-pull transistor pair. Higher power may be obtained by combining multiple modules; however, total current drain on the automotive battery becomes very high.

Amplifiers for military vehicular applications standardize on 28 Vdc. Correspondingly higher powers can be obtained from a single push-pull pair of RF transistors. RF power transistors for 28-Vdc operation are available in a wide range of power and frequency capabilities. As a result, these devices are often used for fixed-station or transportable applications. However, for higher power (up to 1 or 2 kW), higher-voltage devices are desirable for two reasons:

1. The higher collector voltage allows reasonable values (a few ohms or greater) of collector/drain load impedances. This allows efficient wide-band transformer design and implementation to couple the RF to a reasonable load impedance such as 50 ohms.

2. A minimum number of modules (push-pull transistor pairs) are required to be combined to achieve high power by operating each module at the highest practical output power.

Bi-polar transistors operating at 50 Vdc are available for designs which combine four modules to produce 1000 W of RF output power. Recently developed RF power FETs operate from 100-Vdc supplies; however, their thermal and current limitations so far have not allowed a significant increase in output power compared to 50-V bi-polar PA designs. Future high-voltage RF power FET development will provide higher power levels per module at wider bandwidths.

Figure 12.3 SSB signal comparisons (a) KWM-380 transceiver. IMD: − 24 dB below one of two tones; vertical: 10 dB/div; horizontal: 3 kHz/div; center: 14.0 MHz. (b) HF-8023/8031, 1-kW PA/PS. IMD: − 32 dB below one of two tones; vertical: 10 dB/div; horizontal: 3 kHz/div; center: 14.0 MHz. (c) HF-8010 exciter. IMD: − 50 dB below one of two tones; vertical: 10 dB/div; horizontal: 3 kHz/div; center: 14.0 MHz.

12.2   Design Considerations of an Amplifier Stage

Collector/drain load impedance matching
[2,3]

Solid-state PAs with large amounts of power gain often require several stages of amplification. The first stages must have a high degree of linearity in order to achieve low intermodulation distortion of the overall PA. Class A is often chosen for the driver stages for its high linearity. Since driver amplifiers are usually operated at comparatively low power, the low efficiency of class A can be tolerated. The class A amplifier may be either single-ended or push-pull. Wideband load impedance determination for the single-ended class A stage will be examined. The push-pull configuration is essentially the same as two single-ended stages operating 180° out of phase and combined in the output transformer.

A class A bi-polar junction transistor (BJT) amplifier is illustrated in Fig. 12.4. The bias is selected to achieve the desired quiescent collector current

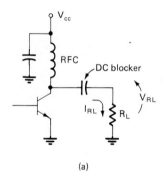

(a)

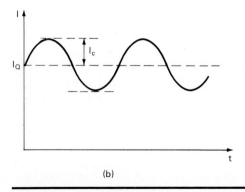

(b)

Figure 12.4 Class A BJT amplifier: (a) single-ended; (b) collector current.

within the device dissipation ratings and yet allow sufficient current "swing" to achieve the desired RF power output. The device will operate as a current source as long as the collector voltage does not swing into the saturation or cutoff regions of the transistor.

The amount of power that may be obtained from a class A stage may be found, starting with the fact that the current in the load (R_L) is: $I_{RL} = V_{RL}/R_L$. Since the voltage cannot swing into either saturation or cutoff, the peak RF voltage across the load resistor must be equal to or less than V_{CC}. This assumes that the transistor quiescent bias point has been selected such that RF collector voltage peaks are symmetrical with respect to saturation and cutoff voltages.

The RF output power is:

$$P_o = \frac{(V_{R,\text{peak}}/\sqrt{2})^2}{R_L} = \frac{V_{R,\text{peak}}^2}{2R_L} \tag{12.1}$$

but

$$V_{R,\text{peak}} \leq V_{CC}$$

Therefore $P_o \leq V_{CC}^2/(2R_L)$. In practice $V_{R,\text{peak}}$ cannot equal V_{CC} because of the saturation voltage $V_{CE,\text{sat}}$ of BJTs and the "on-resistance" of FETs.

The load resistance for maximum class A output power (for BJT) is then given by:

$$R_L \leq \frac{(V_{CC} - V_{CE,\text{sat}})^2}{2P_o} \tag{12.2}$$

The collector dissipation for class A is the difference between input dc power P_i and the RF output power P_o. The important point is that the device dissipation is at its maximum with *no* RF drive and at its minimum when maximum RF power is delivered to the load.

The basic design problem for a class A collector/drain circuit becomes:

1. A device must be chosen which has sufficient dissipation rating to deliver the required RF output power.

2. The device must have sufficiently high maximum current and voltage ratings.

3. Steps 1 and 2 must be reevaluated in the light of any required wideband impedance transformer requirements of the class A stage output and the actual RF load impedance.

Design consideration 3 has a large influence on the overall design. Transmission line wideband transformers offer superior performance in terms of bandwidth and low loss. However they only provide certain impedance transformation ratios such as 1:1, 1:4, 1:9, 1:16, and so on. To illustrate the

TABLE 12.1   Maximum Class A Power for Common Loads and Voltages

| Impedance ratio | 1:1 | 1:4 | 1:9 | 1:16 | | |
Load impedance	50	12.5	5.56	3.125	V_{CC}	$V_{CE,sat}$
RF output power	1.3 W	5 W	12 W	21 W	12.5 V	1.0 V
RF output power	1.6 W	6 W	14 W	25 W	13.5 V	1.0 V
RF output power	7.0 W	28 W	63 W	112 W	28.0 V	1.5 V
RF output power	23 W	90 W	203 W	361 W	50.0 V	2.5 V

design relationship between device ratings, class A power output, and transmission line wideband impedance transformers, Table 12.1 is offered. The example assumes the RF power is delivered to a 50-ohm load and a nominal value of $V_{CE,sat}$ is included.

Class B (or class AB) operation offers high-efficiency RF linear amplifi-

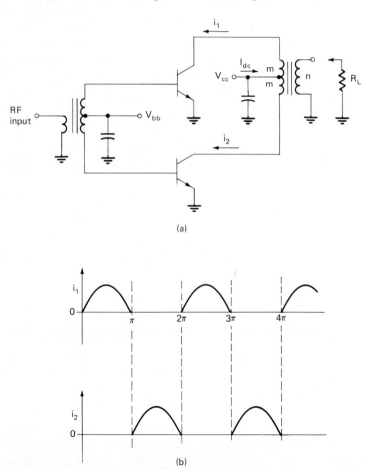

Figure 12.5 Class B amplifier: (*a*) push-pull; (*b*) collector current waveforms.

cation. It may be used single-ended with a tuned (narrowband) impedance matching network. More often it is found in a push-pull configuration with wideband impedance transformers on the input and output.

Figure 12.5 illustrates a push-pull class B circuit and the collector current waveform. Note that each device delivers current to the load only during half of the RF sine wave. The collector peak voltage cannot exceed the supply voltage V_{CC}. The maximum available RF output power is:

$$P_o \le \frac{(V_c/\sqrt{2})^2}{R} \tag{12.3}$$

where R is the collector-to-ground load resistance. Note that this is one-quarter of the collector-to-collector load impedance.

Considering $V_{c,\text{peak}} \le V_{CC}$ and collector-emitter saturation voltage $V_{CE,\text{sat}}$, we obtain:

$$P_o \le \frac{(V_{CC} - V_{CE,\text{sat}})^2}{2R} \tag{12.4}$$

The amplifier load impedance R_L is reflected to the collectors by the turns ratio squared of the output transformer, as shown in Fig. 12.6. Since

$$R = \left(\frac{2m}{n}\right)^2 R_L \tag{12.5}$$

then

$$P_o \le \frac{(V_{CC} - V_{CE,\text{sat}})^2}{8 \, (m/n)^2 \, R_L} \tag{12.6}$$

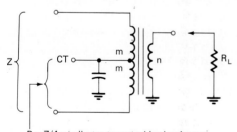

R = Z/4 = collector-to-ground load resistance

Turns ratio: $\dfrac{n}{2m}$

Impedance ratio: $\dfrac{n^2}{(2m)^2} = \dfrac{n^2}{4m^2}$

$$Z = \frac{R_L}{n^2/4m^2} = \frac{4m^2 R_L}{n^2}$$

Figure 12.6　Wideband impedance matching transformer.

TABLE 12.2   Transistor Load Impedances for Various Common Transformers

Turns ratio	Impedance ratio	Transformer model values	R_L, ohms	Coll.-coll. load impedance Z, ohms	Transistor coll. load impedance R, ohms
1:1	1:1	$n = 2, m = 1$	50	50	12.5
1:2	1:4	$n = 4, m = 1$	50	12.5	3.125
1:3	1:9	$n = 6, m = 1$	50	5.556	1.389
1:4	1:16	$n = 8, m = 1$	50	3.125	0.781

Table 12.2 shows the actual collector load impedance for various transformer ratios with a secondary load of 50 ohms.

There are two basic types of wideband impedance matching transformers used in modern solid-state power amplifiers [4,27]. They are commonly referred to as "wire-wound types" and "transmission line types." The term "wire-wound" refers to the common type of transformer in which the power is transferred from one winding to another by a magnetic flux linking the two windings. The transmission line type refers to transformers constructed of sections of transmission lines interconnected to give the desired imped-ance transformations. Magnetic core materials are also used, but their func-tion is to suppress "nontransmission line" currents.

The wire-wound transformer can provide a large number of impedance transformation ratios [5]. There are no inherent restrictions on the primary-secondary turns ratio that one may employ. The bandwidth that one obtains for a given turns ratio is another matter. In general it is not as great as a comparable transmission line transformer. The wire-wound transformer may also be a conventional auto-transformer.

The wire-wound transformer with separate primary and secondary wind-ings is easily connected to all combinations of source and load configurations. Table 12.3 lists all possible combinations of source and load configurations for a wideband transformer.

Figure 12.7 illustrates two common construction techniques for wire-wound wideband RF transformers. The "balun" core in Fig. 12.7a does not have to be a single block of ferrite (as shown); it may also be constructed of two separate ferrite tubes or sleeves. A number of toroidal cores can be

TABLE 12.3   Wideband Transformer Configurations

Source	Load
Balanced, floating	Balanced, floating
Balanced, center-tap-grounded	Balanced, floating
Unbalanced (single-ended)	Balanced, floating
Balanced, floating	Balanced, center-tap-grounded
Balanced, center-tap-grounded	Balanced, center-tap-grounded
Unbalanced (single-ended)	Balanced, center-tap grounded
Balanced, floating	Unbalanced (single-ended)
Balanced, center-tap-grounded	Unbalanced (single-ended)
Unbalanced (single-ended)	Unbalanced (single-ended)

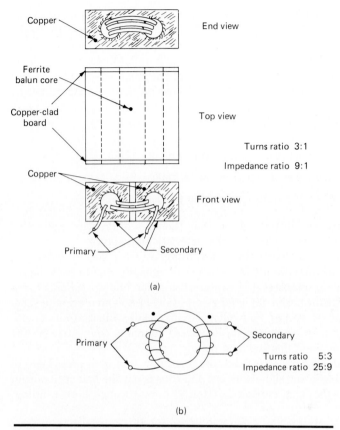

End view

Copper

Ferrite
balun core

Copper-clad
board

Top view

Turns ratio 3:1

Impedance ratio 9:1

Copper

Front view

Primary — Secondary

(a)

Primary

Secondary

Turns ratio 5:3
Impedance ratio 25:9

(b)

Figure 12.7 Two examples of wire-wound wideband RF transformers: (*a*) balun core construction; (*b*) toroidal core construction technique.

stacked to make a ferrite sleeve also. The type of construction shown in Fig.
12.7*a* has been proven in numerous designs and is especially useful for
matching to impedances as low as 1 ohm on the secondary and has the capability of a good symmetrical center tap on the secondary. Copper tubes are
inserted in the core to form the low-impedance secondary. Teflon-insulated
wire, wound through the copper tubes (and thus also the ferrite core) forms
the primary. Tin-plated copper braid may also be successfully used in lieu
of the copper tubes and copper-clad circuit board end pieces.

The toroidal core wire-wound transformer shown in Fig. 12.7*b* illustrates
another construction technique. Although the windings are shown physically
separate, the winding could also be wound bi-filar (two wires wound side by
side), tri-filar, quadri-filar, or even "multifilar." Various transformation
ratios are made by series connecting two or more of the windings. The "multifilar" winding technique provides close coupling between the windings and
improves the high-frequency performance of the transformer.

If a bi-filar winding is placed on a core, the source connected across the two ends at the start of the winding, and the load connected across the opposite end of the two wires, a transmission line balun transformer is formed. The term bi-filar implies that the two wires lie parallel to each other; however, the two wires may be twisted to achieve the same effect. The desired characteristic impedance (Z_0) of such transmission lines is determined by the following factors:

1. Wire gauge

2. Type and thickness of insulation on the wire

3. Distance between wires (for parallel or bi-filar)

4. Number of twists per length (for twisted pair)

Four or more wires may be twisted together, then half of the wires paralleled to achieve a lower transmission line characteristic impedance.

The 1:1 transmission line balun transformer is basic to understanding more complex transmission line transformer designs [6]. Figure 12.8a shows a typical balun using a twisted-pair wire transmission line wound on a toroidal core. The transformer is depicted as a physical implementation, a schematic representation, and an equivalent circuit to fully illustrate its operation. In this case a single-ended (unbalanced) source is connected via the balun to a balanced and floating load R_L.

The current which magnetizes the core must flow in a path that does not cause an imbalance in the signal current and thus upset the balanced output voltages. The magnetizing current i_m (Ref. 7) flows through both windings and the load

Figure 12.8b illustrates the same circuit except the balanced load has a grounded center. It is no longer floating, and the magnetizing current no longer flows equally in the windings and the load. The result is a current imbalance in the load. This situation can be corrected by adding a third or tertiary winding to the transformer as shown in Fig. 12.8c. The tertiary winding now provides a path for the magnetizing current around the load. This type of transformer is made by winding the core tri-filar or with three wires twisted. At first glance, the tertiary winding would indicate a wire-wound transformer. Only when the source and load are connected as in Fig. 12.8c can one identify it as a transmission line balun (with tertiary winding).

The twisted-pair or bi-filar transmission line winding may also be constructed of coaxial transmission line. Coaxial cables with characteristic impedances of 25, 50, 62, 75, and 95 ohms are readily available. Coaxial cables with other characteristic impedances can be obtained by special order and at premium prices. Lower-impedance lines may be obtained by paralleling two or more coax lines and winding them on a core. For example, two 50-ohm coaxial cables of equal length and connected in parallel will provide a 25-ohm line. Similarly, paralleling four 50-ohm lines results in an equivalent 12.5-ohm line.

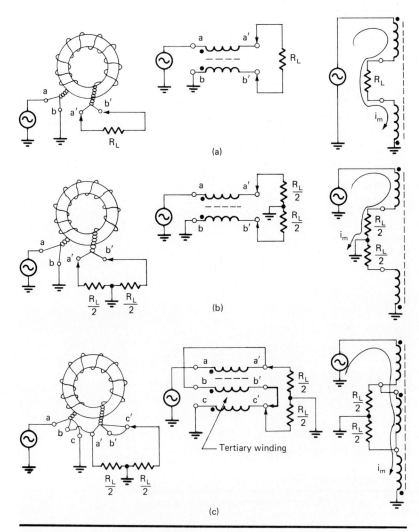

Figure 12.8 1:1 transmission line balun transformers with balanced load: (*a*) floating; (*b*) center-grounded; (*c*) center-grounded with tertiary winding.

The 4:1 transmission line transformer shown in Fig. 12.9 illustrates the practical details of interconnecting a ferrite-loaded transmission line to achieve unbalanced-to-unbalanced operation. Suppose the source must be loaded with 50 ohms. The transformer steps down the 200-ohm load impedance R_L by using a 100-ohm ferrite-loaded coaxial cable. The transformer may be used in reverse to step a 12.5-ohm load up to 50 ohms by using a ferrite-loaded 25-ohm coaxial cable. Other, more standard, coax cable impedances may be used if some degradation in bandwidth is acceptable.

The rule of thumb for selecting ferrite cores for transmission line trans-

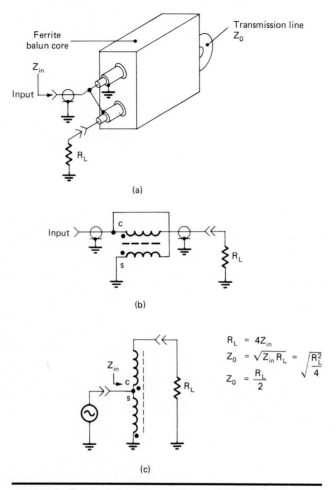

Figure 12.9 Transmission line transformer (4:1 unbalanced-to-unbalanced): (*a*) pictorial view; (*b*) schematic; (*c*) equivalent circuit.

formers is to use a sufficient combination of core size, permeability, and winding turns to achieve a winding reactance at the lowest frequency of operation equal to 5 times the transformer load impedance. Using more than a factor of 5 will do no harm except it will tend to make the winding go series-resonant at a lower frequency and thus limit the highest frequency for which the transformer is useful. In general, the best results involve using a high-permeability ferrite with low-loss, sufficiently high cross-sectional area, and as few winding turns as possible. Some examples of suitable core materials are Stackpole's 7D, Ceramic Magnetics' CMD 5005, Fair-Rite's No. 43, and Indiana General's H.

The high-frequency response also degrades when the length of coax in the Fig. 12.9 transformer becomes a significant fraction of a wavelength. As long as the line is electrically short, there is negligible phase difference between the signal at the line input and its output, where the output shield is connected to the input center conductor.

A subclass of transmission line transformer, called an "equal-delay transformer," eliminates the phase difference and extends the upper frequency limit. The equal-delay transformer was first investigated by W. A. Lewis [8] at Collins Radio in 1965, but the results were never widely published outside the company. Figure 12.10a illustrates the metamorphosis of an ordinary 4:1 transmission line transformer, Fig. 12.10b that of a "stretched-out" version, and Fig. 12.10c that of the equal-delay transformer. The interconnecting wire from shield to opposite end center conductor is replaced with a transmission line equal in length (and thus equal in phase delay) to the original transformer transmission line.

The equal-delay transformer's physical configuration lends itself nicely to good layout techniques since its input and output terminals are on opposite sides of the transformer. Additional impedance transformation ratios are possible by adding to the equal-delay transformer as shown in Fig. 12.11. An intuitive way to look at the equal-delay transformer is to recognize that the two transmission lines are connected in parallel at the load and in series at the input.

The "top" line must be ferrite-loaded to provide a high impedance to common-mode shield currents, in effect to isolate the input side of the shield from its grounded output side. In like manner three and four transmission lines may be connected to give impedance transformation ratios of 9:1 and 16:1, respectively. If the second line in a two-line (4:1) transformer requires one unit of ferrite for adequate isolation at the lowest frequency of opera-

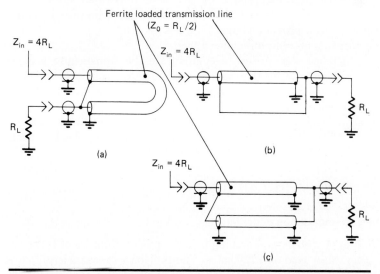

Figure 12.10 Derivation of the equal-delay transformer from the standard 4:1 transmission line transformer.

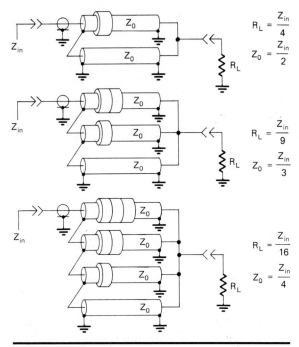

$$R_L = \frac{Z_{in}}{4}$$

$$Z_0 = \frac{Z_{in}}{2}$$

$$R_L = \frac{Z_{in}}{9}$$

$$Z_0 = \frac{Z_{in}}{3}$$

$$R_L = \frac{Z_{in}}{16}$$

$$Z_0 = \frac{Z_{in}}{4}$$

Figure 12.11 Equal-delay transformer configurations.

tion, the third line requires two units and the fourth line requires three units to provide adequate isolation to the higher voltages on the input shields.

Another very useful transformer is the 4:1 balun illustrated in Fig. 12.12. It may be constructed on either balun cores, as shown, or on toroidal cores. This transformer is a proven, compact method of coupling push-pull transistor collectors to a 50-ohm unbalanced load.

Shunt capacitance is required to compensate the transformer leakage reactance in order to obtain the maximum bandwidth from a given transformer design. The exact value often cannot be determined until the transformer is mounted to the final version of the printed circuit card. A clever method of evaluating transformer designs and leakage inductance compensation is to build two identical transformers and operate them back to back. Insertion loss and impedance data can then be taken with fairly accurate results. Construction of low-impedance loads for transformer testing usually gives poorer results the lower the impedance.

Base/gate load impedance matching

The techniques of wideband matching into the push-pull bases of BJTs are different from those used on FET gates. The BJT base presents a quite low impedance which must be transformed to 50 ohms at a reasonable VSWR over the frequency range of the amplifier. A low-input VSWR is desired to present a good load impedance for the driver stage. The RF power-FET input impedance is highly capacitive. It is possible to swamp this capacitance with a low value of resistance to obtain a good input VSWR and a flat frequency response from the FET amplifier.

Figure 12.13 is a typical BJT base circuit showing the circuit elements to consider in designing a wideband matching circuit. There is an element of "art" in designing such circuits because of the very low impedances involved and the uncertainty of the base input impedance changes under RF drive and various possible VSWR loads on the collectors. A recommended practical design technique is presented.

Start with a wire-wound transformer using a 1:16 impedance ratio. There should be no input compensation network, transformer leakage compensation capacitors, or base RLC networks connected at this point. Apply normal operating collector voltage and bias, and then sweep the frequency range. Obtain the input impedance data vs. frequency and plot on a Smith chart. Increase the base bias to several higher values, taking care not to exceed the transistor current or dissipation ratings. Record and plot the impedance data for each bias setting.

Next, apply RF at normal operating bias and drive the amplifier to full power. With a quality directional coupler in the RF input path, measure and

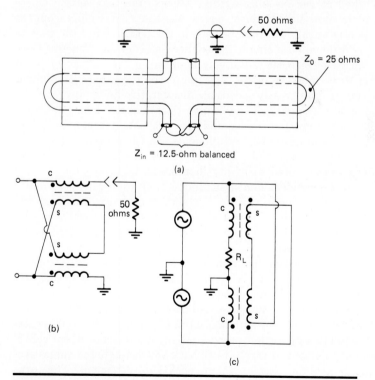

Figure 12.12　4:1 Transmission line balun transformer: (*a*) physical construction; (*b*) schematic; (*c*) equivalent circuit.

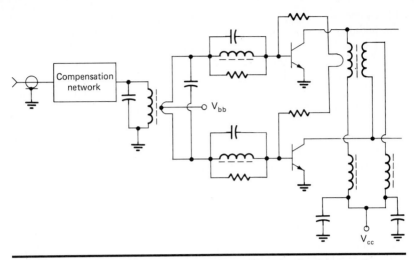

Figure 12.13 Typical BJT base impedance matching circuit with negative feedback.

record the VSWR vs. frequency. Compare this VSWR plot with the impedance plots taken at various bias settings. Choose the bias setting whose impedance plots show VSWRs most nearly like the VSWR plots from the RF test. This bias setting will then be used in the remainder of the tests to evaluate the additional base-circuit-impedance-determining elements. Once the circuit values have been tentatively assigned, a final check of input VSWR under drive must be made. The use of the impedance data under higher than normal bias greatly speeds up this iterative design process.

The series base RLC circuit should be investigated next. This circuit helps "swamp" the base input impedance and also prevents parametric oscillations. The type and value of these components can be first selected by considering the impedance data plots. The values are generally not critical, provided the parts are mounted with very short leads. Lap soldering of these components is recommended. The inductance is simply a ferrite bead on bus wire. If the inductor is not used, the bias should be fed to the bases via chokes rather than through the transformer center tap. Otherwise the series resistors will degrade the bias regulation and adversely affect intermodulation distortion performance.

Then look at compensating the input transformer leakage inductance by adding shunt capacitance on the secondary and/or the primary. This will have the largest effect on the high frequencies.

The next step is to add the negative feedback circuit, if one is to be used. This circuit affects not only the amplifier input impedance but amplifier stability, intermodulation distortion, gain variation, and to some extent collector efficiency. At this point it is wise to go back and evaluate the values previously selected to obtain further input VSWR improvement. The turns ratio of the transformer may have to be changed in this process.

The input compensation network may be required to achieve improved

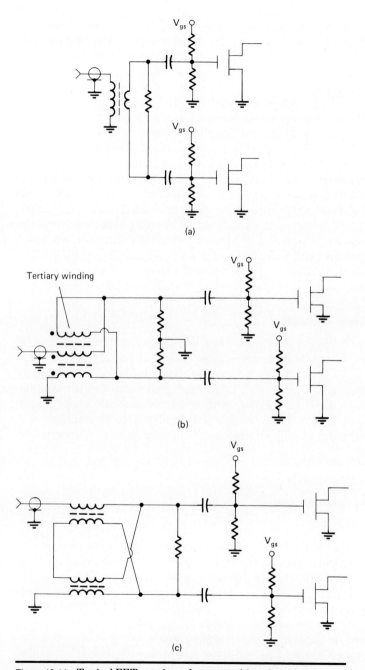

Figure 12.14 Typical FET gate impedance matching circuits: (*a*) wire-wound transformer; (*b*) transmission line 1:1 balun; (*c*) transmission line 4:1 balun.

input VSWR and also to flatten the gain variations encountered in high-power BJT amplifiers. A good computer-aided design (CAD) program will be useful in designing this network, but the cut-and-try method will work if one does not have access to CAD programs.

Once the circuit values have been refined, it is wise to go back and investigate the amplifier for any signs of instability. Keeping the networks as simple as possible and at low impedances will minimize the amount of frustration one must endure to stabilize an amplifier design.

Compared with the design of BJT amplifiers, that for an FET input wideband circuit is more straightforward. Figure 12.14 gives three examples of commonly used circuits. The FET input is mostly capacitive. Swamping this capacitance with a low-value resistor is an effective way to flatten the gain and to *choose* the secondary impedance for the wideband input transformer. Negative feedback, either coupled through dc blocking capacitors from the drain or transformer-coupled as illustrated on the BJT amplifier, will lower the input impedance and must be accounted for in the circuit design. The wide gain-bandwidth products of RF power FETs coupled with the swamping resistor give a very good input VSWR with comparatively simple circuits.

DC feed methods, decoupling

The method of feeding the collector/drain dc voltage and decoupling the RF for a particular design is determined after careful laboratory experimentation. Figure 12.15 illustrates four common circuit topologies. Each has its merits and demerits. Component values and choke/transformer windings and core materials are the variables with which the designer works to optimize the operation of a transistorized push-pull wideband amplifier. The amplifier parameters usually affected by the dc feed circuit design are:

1. Intermodulation distortion

2. Collector/drain efficiency

3. Even-order harmonic output

4. Amplifier stability

These parameters vary with frequency. A change in the dc feed circuit that improves a particular parameter at low frequencies will possibly either degrade it at high frequencies or degrade another parameter. It is important to evaluate all amplifier parameters over the operating frequency range when optimizing the topology and component values in the dc feed circuit.

We now present a few general remarks about each circuit topology. The center-tap feed on the wire-wound output transformer is useful for lower-powered (less than 100 W) PAs and those operating with collector-to-collector load impedances of a few ohms or less. The problem to watch for with this type of feed is dc saturation of the output transformer core, which will ruin the transformer action.

The split choke feed shown in Fig. 12.15*b* is used for medium-power levels and where the collector-to-collector impedances are more than a few ohms.

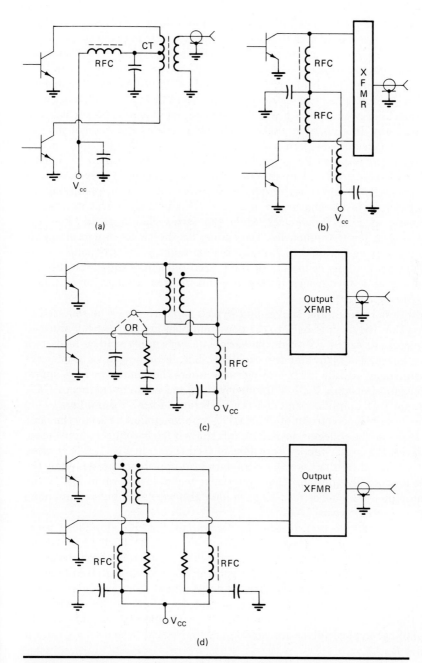

Figure 12.15 Collector dc voltage feed methods and RF coupling: (*a*) center top transformer; (*b*) split choke; (*c*) transformer, center-bypassed; (*d*) transformer, split center.

The chokes are constructed of wire, wound on a ferrite core, to give a low-frequency reactance at least 5 times the collector load impedance.

Another technique is shown in Fig. 12.15c and uses an RF transformer feed. This circuit, together with an output balun transformer, forms an 180° hybrid combiner. The bridging resistor could be connected from the dc feed point to ground. The bridging resistor, if used in this application, must have a dc blocking capacitor to prevent dissipating dc power. The resistor will dissipate any differences in phase (from 180°) and/or amplitude of the two transistor collector waveforms.

Simply providing an RF ground at the hybrid center with an RF bypass capacitor will provide adequate results in most designs. However, at high frequencies, IMD and collector efficiency can be improved by modifying the circuit to match that shown in Fig. 12.15d. This technique provides "light" bypassing at high frequencies while the series chokes allow "heavier" bypassing at lower frequencies. Depending on the choke design, damping resistors may be required to stabilize the amplifier at low frequencies. The RF current-handling capability of the bypass capacitors should be checked when a final dc feed design is chosen. Some designs use high-current, low-loss chip capacitors.

Additional decoupling chokes and bypass capacitors may be required to ensure that the dc lines back to the power supplies are free of RF. Failure to adequately filter the RF from the various power supply voltage feeds to a PA is the cause of many stability problems. The decoupling must be effective at frequencies outside the operating range where the transistors have appreciable gain. Decouple the low-frequency (LF) and medium-frequency (MF) range for BJT amplifiers and also the VHF range for FET amplifiers.

The base-bias feed techniques for BJT amplifiers follow basically the same topologies as the collector feeds. The transformer feed is not commonly used. However, the center-tapped transformer feed shown in Fig. 12.16a is often used with good results since the secondary load impedance presented by the bases is generally quite low. The split choke technique shown in Fig. 12.16b or individual RF chokes feeding each base also work well but require more parts and circuit board area.

Figure 12.16c is a typical gate bias feed circuit for FET amplifiers. Separate adjustable bias voltages are shown for each FET. This is usually required for FETs (but not in matched BJTs) in order to obtain balanced linear amplification. RF power FETs generally have quite high transconductances and simple low-current bias supplies allow individual bias adjustments. The gates draw only leakage current, so R_1 and R_2 are provided to load the bias supply. R_3 and R_4 are higher values and provide sufficient RF decoupling. Typical values are 10,000 ohms for R_3 and R_4 and 1000 ohms for R_1 and R_2.

Printed circuit design

Solid-state amplifier designs are usually implemented on a printed circuit (PC) board for ease of assembly and maintenance, reproducible phase and

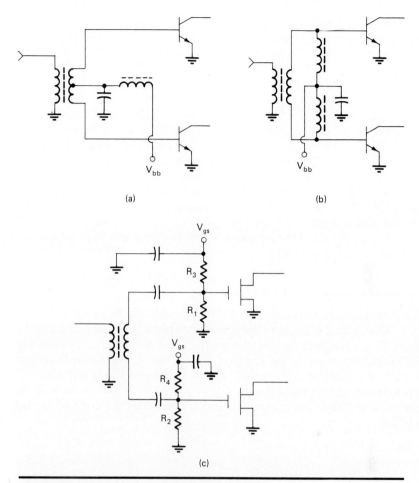

Figure 12.16 Base/gate bias feed methods: (*a*) center-stopped transformer; (*b*) split-choke bias feed; (*c*) separate bias feeds for FETs.

gain characteristics, and the ability to use low-impedance microstrip transmission line interconnects.

There are several layout techniques that the designer should consider to achieve top performance from a wideband solid-state PA. One of the most important is to use a symmetrical layout of the RF devices and the major components in the RF path. The interconnecting paths to or from each transistor in a push-pull amplifier must be equal in length. The circuit traces to each transistor should be symmetrical about a center line between the two push-pull transistors.

The bottom side of the PC card must be a solid ground plane with as few breaks as necessary for circuit traces and clearance around through-holes. The goal is to achieve a low-impedance ground plane with all points on the surface equipotential and as close to ground as possible when the high currents from the PA are returned to ground. This will help prevent unwanted intercircuit coupling through ground loops. This bottom ground plane must have a good electrical connection to the transistor heatsink for the same reason.

Figure 12.17 is an example of a 280-W PA module. The RF input and output are designed for 50 ohms to facilitate module testing and troubleshooting with standard RF test equipment. The PA module contains a pair of high-power bi-polar transistors of unique low-thermal-resistance design. Each transistor die is attached to a special cone slug which in turn is mounted in a high-efficiency heat sink. The transistors are operated push-pull class AB, into a 12.5-ohm balanced load line. A 4:1 (impedance ratio) transmission line balun transformer couples the collectors to the RF output 50-ohm load. The output module also contains a low-impedance bias regulator, RF gain compensation network, and current and temperature monitoring circuits. Simple, effective circuits were designed to reduce complexity and enhance overall reliability of the module.

RF grounding in low-impedance circuits

Ground areas on the top side of the PC board must also be connected to the bottom-side ground plane with low-impedance paths. Low impedance in the context here refers to inductive reactances in the milliohm range since the circuit impedances are as low as a few ohms. These low-impedance ground plane interconnections are especially critical in the area where high currents are returned to the ground. The emitter or source leads and grounds in the input or output impedance networks and transformers are areas of critical grounding.

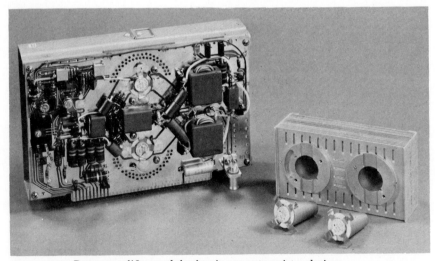

Figure 12.17 Power amplifier module showing cone transistor design.

Some practical techniques to accomplish low-impedance grounding are:

1. Solder a thin copper strap around the outside edges of the PC card, connecting top-layer ground areas to the bottom-side ground plane.

2. Solder a thin copper strap around the inside edges of the transistor cutout holes to connect the emitter/source lead grounds to the bottom ground plane.

3. Use several large [approximately 0.062- to 0.125-in (1.5- to 3.0-mm) diameter] plated through-holes in areas of high ground return currents to connect the top ground to the bottom ground plane. This technique can be used in lieu of steps 1 and 2 when working at frequencies below 30 MHz and results in adequate grounding at a low cost, whereas for optimum performance at VHF frequencies the more expensive techniques of steps 1 and 2 have to be employed. Examples of grounding holes may be seen near each emitter lead in Fig. 12.17.

4. In lieu of plated through-holes, eyelets or hollow brass rivets may be used to accomplish the same quality of grounding as in step 3. Do not rely on mechanical compression; solder the rivets or eyelets on both surfaces but do not fill the eyelet hole with solder.

Avoid circuit layouts that force a low-level or small-signal circuit ground return to share the same path as a high-current circuit ground [11]. This type of ground loop will upset the operation of the low-level circuit. Typical circuits that are susceptible include the bias control and regulation and the PA current analog types. The ground return for the collector/drain dc supply should attach to the PA module ground plane at a point that represents a nearly identical path shape and length to each emitter/source. Some deviation from this ideal is acceptable if there is a large ground area surrounding the emitter/source leads and the dc ground return connection.

Parasitic oscillation [12]

The elimination or suppression of parasitic oscillations (sometimes referred to as "spurious oscillations") is one of the toughest tasks which the solid-state PA designer faces. There are several modes that are peculiar to the solid-state PA because of the nature of the devices and the very low impedances at which power is coupled into and out of them. To further complicate things, a cure for one mode of parasitic oscillation may induce or aggravate another. The subject is quite involved, so only a cursory treatment will be given here. Experience and the scientific method in the laboratory are the most valuable tools a PA designer can apply to solving parasitic oscillation problems. The problem is compounded if the amplifier is to be built in production quantities since variations due to component tolerances must be considered.

Briefly, the basic test setup for searching out parasitic oscillations in a solid-state PA is to:

1. Terminate the RF output in a power attenuator (rather than a dummy load). Insert sufficient attenuation to reduce the level to that required for a spectrum analyzer. This will give a flat response over a very wide band of frequencies. The range of measurement must include frequencies from LF through VHF. The analyzer must be used with both wide- and narrowband frequency sweeps.

2. Monitor one or both collector/drain RF waveforms with a high-frequency oscilloscope. This will help spot transient or unusual spurious oscillations that may otherwise be overlooked with the spectrum analyzer.

There are three recommended steps or guidelines to follow in the search for spurious oscillations (assuming none has been found in earlier testing):

1. Operate the amplifier without the lowpass filter (if one is normally used) in series with the RF output. Drive the amplifier at various power levels and slowly sweep the signal generator through the frequency range of the amplifier. Look for abnormal or abrupt changes in the collector/drain waveforms and/or spurious spectra on the analyzer. Correct anything found before proceeding.

2. Install the low-pass filter and repeat step 1 for each filter band.

3. Operate the amplifier into various load impedances at several VSWRs and at many frequencies spaced throughout the high-frequency (HF) range. This task quickly becomes a very lengthy and tedious process. To do a thorough search, one should check four to eight impedances per VSWR circle, two to four VSWR circles, and all at four to eight frequencies. This works out to anywhere from 32 to 256 combinations of load impedance and frequency. More tests may be prudent depending on the types of parasitic oscillations found. This test may also be used to evaluate the dissipation protection circuit performance at the same time.

Generating the various load impedances can become a time-consuming problem in itself. Three methods of generating mismatched loads are:

1. Construct a tunable L network with a series inductor and shunt capacitor, both variable. Insert the network between the attenuator load and the PA. The input and output of the L network must be reversible to obtain impedances in all regions of the VSWR circle. With the aid of an impedance measuring instrument, the L network transforms the 50-ohm attenuator load to the desired load impedance. This method is very slow and time-consuming if a thorough search is to be conducted.

2. Similarly, "spot loads" may be constructed by shunting the 50-ohm attenuator load with capacitors or inductors. Various lengths of coaxial cable may be cut to move the spot loads around to other impedance points on

the VSWR circle. This method is somewhat faster than the one described in step 1, but still limited in flexibility.

3. A continuously variable length of transmission line is used at VHF and ultrahigh frequencies (UHF) to rotate an impedance around the VSWR circle. A similar device [13] may be constructed for VSWR testing of HF amplifiers by a system of coaxial relays that switch in or out a series connection of binarily related lengths of transmission line. Thus the VHF/UHF "trombone" line can be approximated by the binary step size of the shortest line section. Impedances of various VSWRs may be connected to one end of the binary stepped transmission line, and a large number of impedances around that particular VSWR circle [14] may be obtained by energizing the proper relays. Unterminated power attenuators and parallel combinations of 50-ohm loads are ideal for this application.

The most common parasitic oscillation problem encountered in BJT solid-state power amplifiers is at frequencies of 1 MHz and below. The BJT gain is quite high at these frequencies, and resonances in the collector dc feed decoupling network and/or the base-bias decoupling network often leads to this type of instability. The gain rolloff of HF power BJTs at VHF contributes to stability in this region. The RF power FET, however, has significant gain well into the VHF region. Therefore, it is likely to encounter VHF spurious oscillations. Common circuits involved are the input and output wideband matching transformers and the drain dc decoupling networks.

Three of the most common modes of parasitic oscillations are:

1. Feedback via unwanted coupling in the amplifier circuit and/or in conjunction with the device internal feedback capacitance.

2. Parametric oscillations caused by "pumping" a nonlinear reactance in the device by the drive signal.

3. Base-bias circuit instability.

Feedback oscillations may be readily identified with a spectrum analyzer. They may be either self-sustaining or driven oscillations. Some driven oscillations may require RF drive to get them started and then remain self-sustaining if the RF drive is removed. The cure for them is to locate the reactances involved and change values, add damping elements, add swamping elements, or try alternative circuit topologies.

Parametric oscillations are almost always driven oscillations, and are only present during RF drive. They are usually a subharmonic of the RF drive frequency. Resistive loading or swamping in the external circuit is usually an effective cure. This type of oscillation is more prevalent in BJT amplifiers operated on low collector voltages.

Base-bias instabilities are similar to parametric oscillations except they are not subharmonics. This type of oscillation is sometimes due to base-bias regulator circuit interaction with the envelope of the RF drive modulation. Do not use excessive gain bandwidth in the bias regulator circuit. Ferrite beads and resistive damping along with adequate decoupling from audio through VHF on the bias circuit are effective techniques. Pay particular attention to the diode temperature compensation circuit frequently used on the bias regulator. It must be thermally coupled to the RF devices and is therefore susceptible to RF coupling.

Distortion reduction

Several design considerations for low-distortion, class A, AB, or B, solid-state wideband amplifiers are briefly discussed. They are meant to be an aid to the amplifier designer in the quest for adequate linearity for the intended application. High-linearity requirements are addressed in Chap. 13.

The most obvious first approach to good linearity is a low-distortion device that is operating at optimum voltages and currents and is free from instabilities. Generally the high-performance BJT devices are no better or worse than comparable FET devices regarding IMD performance in a well-designed circuit. The FET outperforms the BJT in the levels of the higher-order IMD products [15]. The higher-order products decrease in level at a faster rate as one examines higher- and higher-order products in an RF FET rather than a BJT.

A well-regulated collector/drain dc supply is essential to obtaining good linearity. It allows optimizing the collector-to-collector (or drain) load resistance for good efficiency and controlled current swing without going into saturation. The collector-to-collector (or drain) load impedance must be maintained as close to resistive as possible. This in turn requires optimizing the output wideband transformer(s), combiner (if used), and low-pass filter passband VSWRs to as low values as possible.

The base/gate-bias regulator must be absolutely stable and free from RF or envelope modulation. The bias regulator for a BJT amplifier must be capable of supplying the peak current required from the lowest-gain devices anticipated in production and at the highest RF power level. Careful attention to the bias supply performance is necessary for the best linearity that the devices are capable of.

Noise figure

The congestion of the HF spectrum places ever increasing demands on the purity of the transmitted signals. This requirement is particularly severe when several transmitters and receivers must operate simultaneously in close proximity. The transmitted broadband noise from a solid-state PA is of particular concern since the gain bandwidth product is so large. Generally, the exciter synthesizer noise shelf will mask all but the noisiest PA. However, rapid improvements in synthesizer design and the use of automatically tuned postselectors between the exciter output and the PA input have placed more emphasis on low-noise-figure power amplifier designs.

Normally noise figure measurement equipment is used only on receiver front ends and preamplifiers. The high-power capability of the PA will easily damage an automatic noise figure instrument. Therefore, the PA broadband noise *output* level is measured with a spectrum analyzer at a convenient IF bandwidth and then converted dBW/Hz. Some analyzers may require a correction factor when converting to dBW/Hz (consult the instruction manual). The small-signal gain of the power amplifier must also be measured and the figure subtracted from the output noise level. This will give the noise level in dBW referenced to the amplifier input. A perfectly noiseless amplifier would be -204 dBW/Hz ($20 \log kTB$). The difference in the measured PA noise, referenced to its input, and -204 dBW/Hz is the noise figure of the power amplifier. This number can readily be used in system performance calculations for colocated receiver and transmitters.

A noise figure of 8 to 15 dB is not difficult to obtain with the RF power FETs available. The noise figure for cascade amplifier stages is given by:

$$\text{NF} = 10 \log \left(F_1 + \frac{F_2 - 1}{G_1} + \frac{F_3 - 1}{G_1 G_2} + \cdots + \frac{F_n - 1}{G_1 G_2 \cdots G_{n-1}} \right) \quad \text{dB} \quad (12.7)$$

where G = numerical gain
$\quad\quad F$ = noise factor
$\quad \text{NF}$ = noise figure
$\quad\quad n$ = amplifier stage designation (i.e., 1 = first stage)

The goal is to distribute the gain between the cascaded amplifier stages such that the first stage sets the overall amplifier noise figure. Extraordinary low-noise circuit design must only be done on one relatively low-power stage. A good "rule of thumb" is to make the gain of an earlier stage equal to the noise figure (in dB) of the succeeding stage plus 10 dB in order to make negligible the succeeding stage's contribution to the overall noise figure of the amplifier chain.

12.3 Miscellaneous PA Circuits and Functions

T/R relay

Simplex operation (transmitting and receiving on the same frequency) often requires the use of a single antenna for both transmit and receive. An antenna switching relay is usually used to perform this function. Often it is required to be a part of the power amplifier and is commonly called a "transmit/receive" or "T/R relay."

Several specifications affecting the T/R relay design will be discussed. The relay must be capable of withstanding the maximum RF voltage encountered. This voltage is the peak RF value calculated for the highest VSWR expected, with allowance for RF transient power levels likely to occur during the ALC attack time. These same factors must be used to find the maximum expected current through the T/R relay.

The amount of receiver isolation provided by the T/R relay is important in high-power transmitters to avoid damage to the receiver or preselector input circuits. Usually 36-dB or more isolation is required. This value subjects the receiver front end to 0.25 W from a 1-kW transmitter. The receiver isolation usually degrades as the frequency of operation increases. Achieving high receiver isolation in a practical design requires a second relay to switch the receiver input either to ground or to a 50-ohm termination or to an open circuit. The latter provides an additional interruption of the receiver input to the main T/R relay. The exact physical layout will determine which of the three techniques will ultimately provide the best isolation. Of course, extremely short direct interconnecting leads are required to optimize isolation and to maintain a low VSWR on the ports of the T/R relay.

The time required to switch the transmitter from transmit to receive to transmit is important in break-in CW and certain types of simplex error-correcting data communications systems. The T/R time requirements for these modes is 10 ms or less. The total T/R time includes relay contact bounce and any other transmitter (or receiver) delays from transmit command to RF output (or receive command to RF detection). Small, fast, vacuum relays can accomplish switching times in the low milliseconds, but the isolation is not as good as larger, slower relays since their contact spacing is very close. Over the life of the relay, the operation will slow down and contact bounce time may increase.

The ultimate expected life of the relay is critical when operation in the above modes is extensive. It is not unusual to find the expected lifetime is less than 6 months of continuous duty use in these modes. For this reason, a great deal of research has been conducted in finding a practical high-powered solid-state T/R switch. PIN diodes [16] have been successfully used at lower (100-W) power levels and higher frequencies. However, to date the tradeoff involves higher than desired insertion loss and large amounts of dc power to operate a PIN diode T/R switch at power levels of 1 kW and above *and* at frequencies down to 1.6 MHz. As better devices are developed with longer carrier lifetimes and lower "on-resistance," the solid-state T/R switch will replace the T/R relay.

In the past, vacuum tubes were used as electronic T/R switches with very fast switching times. But their circuit complexity and obsolescence and special voltages required have prevented them from becoming a practical solution.

Table 12.4 gives a comparison of the various T/R relay techniques.

TABLE 12.4   T/R Relay Techniques

	Open-frame relay	Coaxial relay	Vacuum relay	PIN diode	Electron tube
Cost	Low	Medium	High	High	Medium
Speed	Slowest	Slow	Medium	Fast	Fast
Complexity	Low	Low	Medium	High	High
Receiver isolation	Low	Medium	High	*	*
Transmitter loss	Low	Low	Low	Higher	Higher

* Depends upon complexity of specific design.

Directional couplers for wattmeter applications

There are basically three types of directional coupler circuits which find practical application as wideband (over four octaves) wattmeter circuits. The inductive loop coupler [17] is a common technique. It is used in BIRD Electronic Corporation products to measure forward and reflected power on a transmission line section. A second technique [18], developed by Warren Bruene of the Collins Radio Company in the 1950s, is a transformer-coupled bridge circuit. The third technique uses cross-coupled transformers and has the advantage of requiring no RF balancing adjustments. Each circuit will be discussed in detail.

The inductive loop coupler is shown in Fig. 12.18. It is simply a series resistor and a small loop inductively coupled to the center line of a coaxial line section by mutual inductance M and at the same time capacitively coupled by capacitance C. The current in the line and voltage across the line are represented by I and E, respectively, as shown in Fig. 12.18. The resistor and the capacitance of the loop to line form a voltage divider. The value of capacitive reactance (over the frequency range of interest) must be much larger

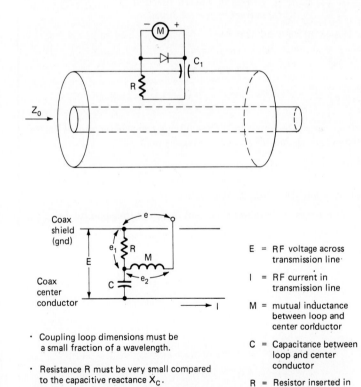

- Coupling loop dimensions must be a small fraction of a wavelength.

- Resistance R must be very small compared to the capacitive reactance X_C.

- $CR = M/Z_0$ required for good directivity.

E = RF voltage across transmission line

I = RF current in transmission line

M = mutual inductance between loop and center conductor

C = Capacitance between loop and center conductor

R = Resistor inserted in series with loop

Figure 12.18 Inductive loop directional coupler.

than the resistor value to minimize errors due to phase shift. The value of mutual inductance M is chosen to equal the product of the characteristic impedance of the line, Z_0 times C times R. The coupler output voltage e is the sum of two components: e_1 from the division of E by R and C and e_2 from induction of the current I, as shown in Fig. 12.19. Anywhere along the line the voltage E is the vector sum of the forward voltage E_f and the reflected voltage E_r. Likewise, the line current I is the vector sum of the forward current I_f and the reflected current I_r. The forward current is defined as a positive direction since it flows from the source to the load. If

$$e = e_1 + e_2$$

$$e_1 = \frac{RE}{X_C} \quad \text{for } R \ll X_C$$

$$e_2 = \pm I X_M$$

$$e = REj\omega C \pm Ij\omega M \quad \begin{cases} + \text{ for current in forward direction} \\ - \text{ for current in reverse direction} \end{cases}$$

$$CR = M/Z_0 \quad \text{chosen for directivity}$$

$$e = j\omega \left(\frac{EM}{Z_0} \pm IM \right)$$

$$e = j\omega M \left(\frac{E}{Z_0} \pm I \right)$$

The voltage across the transmission line (at any point) is the sum of the forward component E_f and the reflected component E_r.

$$E = E_f + E_r$$

The current in the transmission line (at any point) is the sum of the forward component I_f and the reflected component Ir.

$$I = I_f - I_r \quad (- \text{ because reflected current travels in the opposite direction})$$

$$I = \frac{E_f}{Z_0} - \frac{E_r}{Z_0}$$

$$e_f = j\omega M \left(\frac{E_f + E_r}{Z_0} + \frac{E_f - E_r}{Z_0} \right) \quad \text{forward direction}$$

$$e_r = j\omega M \left(\frac{E_f + E_r}{Z_0} - \frac{E_f - E_r}{Z_0} \right) \quad \text{reflected direction}$$

$$e_f = \frac{j\omega M}{Z_0} (2E_f) \quad \text{forward voltage}$$

$$e_r = \frac{j\omega M}{Z_0} (2E_r) \quad \text{reflected voltage}$$

Figure 12.19 Inductive loop directional coupler equations.

the load reflects energy, it causes a current to flow in the opposite direction and is given a negative sign.

By simply reversing the sense of the mutual coupling inductance, either the forward or the reflected current may be sampled. The output voltage e is directly proportional to frequency. If the output is terminated in a capacitor (C_1) of 500 to 2000 pF a wideband response is obtained. The output may then be rectified, filtered, and used to drive a sensitive microammeter calibrated to display power in watts.

The transformer-coupled wattmeter operates on the same principles as the inductive loop. A toroidal transformer is used to obtain a larger sample of the line current. Two voltage samples are taken via capacitive dividers. This allows displaying both forward and reflected power at the same time without the need to physically rotate the inductive loop coupling probe described previously. Figure 12.20 shows a schematic representative of this type of directional coupler wattmeter. Note that a Faraday shield is used to prevent unwanted capacitive coupling between the line and the toroidal windings. The basic difference between this circuit and the previous one centers on the inductive loop coupler's need for precision parts to control the mutual coupling and a precision series resistance. Typically, a very sensitive and expensive microammeter is required to display the power. The transformer-coupled wattmeter operates with larger current and voltage samples and therefore does not require a sensitive output meter. It is, however, a more complex circuit. Depending on the care taken in physical layout, the latter circuit is capable of very wide bandwidths. The low-frequency response is limited when the toroidal transformer winding reactance lowers to values comparable with those for the load resistance, resulting in signifi-

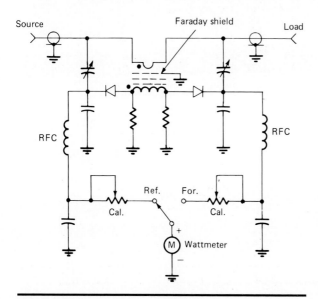

Figure 12.20 Transformer-coupled directional coupler.

cant phase-shift errors. The high-frequency response is limited by the series resonance of the winding and, additionally, by any inductive reactance in the load resistors.

The third type of directional coupler consists of two cross-coupled toroidal transformers and suitable RF detector circuits, as shown in Fig. 12.21. The amount of coupling and the input impedance depend upon the turns ratio of the transformers. A small turns ratio gives close coupling but introduces significant VSWR at the input port. It also increases the loss from input to output ports.

The input-to-output coupling (loss) is given by:

$$S_{oi} = -20 \log \left(1 + \frac{1}{2N^2} \right) \tag{12.8a}$$

The input-to-forward-port coupling is given by:

$$S_{fi} = -20 \log \left(\frac{1 + (1/2N^2)}{1/N} \right) \tag{12.8b}$$

The input return loss is given by:

$$S_{ii} = -20 \log \left(\frac{1}{2N^2 + 1} \right) \tag{12.8c}$$

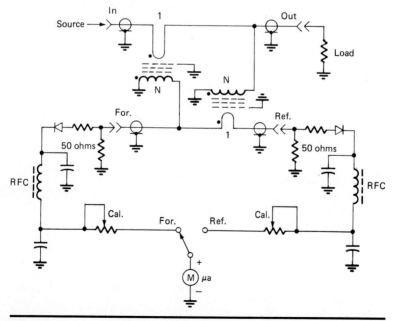

Figure 12.21 Cross-coupled transformer directional coupler.

Using these formulas, a directional coupler may be designed for any desired amount of coupling. The forward and reflected coupled ports are terminated in good low-reactance dummy loads of a value equal to the characteristic impedance of the system. In most cases this is 50 ohms. The rms RF voltage measured across the forward port, squared and divided by 50 ohms, will be equal to the forward RF power applied to the input port decreased by the amount of coupling. In like manner, the RF voltage at the reflected port is related to the RF power *entering* the output port, i.e., reflected from the load connected to the output port.

The RF voltage on the forward and reflected ports may be rectified and filtered to drive a dc meter with a power scale indicating forward and reflected power in watts. Figure 12.21 shows a typical design for a 1000-W solid-state power amplifier. If $N = 32$ turns (for a one-turn primary), the coupling is 30.11 dB. The power coupled to the forward port will be approximately 1 W. This gives a reasonable dissipation level for the terminations and good drive level to the wattmeter. The return loss calculates as -66.23 dB, and the insertion loss calculates as 0.004 dB.

Practical construction of this type of wattmeter circuit can result in very wideband responses. The interconnecting leads of the toroidal transformers should be very short and direct. A Faraday shield is recommended between the primary turn and the secondary windings of the transformers. A symmetrical layout will ensure accuracy at various power levels and VSWRs.

Teflon insulation on the core and/or the secondary wire is necessary to prevent corona or RF breakdown of the seondary winding through the core. The core material must be rated for the maximum anticipated flux density over the frequency range and load VSWRs. In general, it has been found that ferrite materials are superior to powdered iron at the 1-kW level in the HF band. Practical designs have been accomplished at the 1-kW power level over a bandwidth of 1 to 100 MHz.

Low-pass filters for solid-state PAs

Most solid-state power amplifiers require some type of RF output filtering to suppress harmonics. The filter could either be bandpass or low-pass. For a given level of harmonic attenuation, the low-pass configuration contains fewer elements and is thus less costly. Other considerations such as protection against unwanted RF coupled from colocated broadband transmitters or transmitter broadband noise attenuation may dictate bandpass filtering.

There is much excellent literature on RF filter design to which the reader is directed (see Refs. 19 through 22). The practical aspects and design considerations of implementing RF low-pass filtering on a solid-state PA will be discussed here.

The first step in filter design for a solid-state PA is to decide how many individual filters are required to cover the frequency range of the PA, given the required harmonic output suppression. Typical class AB or B push-pull PAs will generate a second harmonic that is at least 20 dB below the fundamental if the push-pull pair of transistors have somewhat matched characteristics. The third harmonic can be as high as 9 dB down. Higher-order odd and even harmonics will fall off in amplitude from these respective values. A typical PA output spectrum is shown in Fig. 12.22. Harmonics which fall in the transistor gain rolloff region and above will be at a considerably lower level. The designer can take advantage of this characteristic to reduce the complexity of the higher-band filters. This will also reduce the insertion loss and cost of the filter for these higher-frequency bands.

The next important practical consideration in choosing a low-pass filter design concerns the effect of load impedance on harmonic generation in the solid-state PA. The harmonic level before filtering determines how much stopband attenuation the output filter must have to suppress the harmonics below the design specification. A common design pitfall is to first operate the amplifier without a filter into a 50-ohm load and carefully measure the harmonic levels across the operating frequency range. A filter design is selected with a minimum stopband attenuation equal to the difference between the measured harmonics and the harmonic specification. The filter is then built, aligned, and tested with the amplifier. The resulting output harmonic levels are not what was predicted from the "filterless" data plus the filter's attenuation measured on a network analyzer. What went wrong?

The answer lies in the fact that most cataloged filter designs (for a 50-ohm load) are either for a 50-ohm source or a high-impedance source. The PAs source impedance is rarely close to either of these values. Thus the filter stopband response could vary as much as 6 dB from the predicted catalog value compared with its response when driven with the actual source imped-

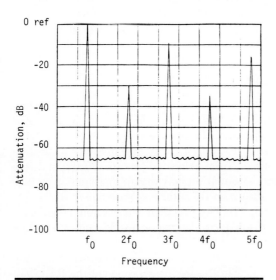

Figure 12.22 Typical unfiltered power amplifier harmonic spectrum.

ance of the PA. The RF waveform on the transistor collectors/drains depends upon whether the PA is terminated in a 50-ohm load or a harmonic filter. A dummy load on a "filterless" PA provides a 50-ohm load to all harmonics as well as the fundamental. Insert the low-pass filter and now only the fundamental is terminated in 50 ohms. The filter input impedance presents a highly reactive termination to the harmonic energy. The harmonics see a high VSWR at the filter input and are reflected back to the transistors, modifying the collector RF waveform. This phenomenon is also responsible for the different collector/drain efficiencies encountered in measurements made with and without RF output filters.

An iterative process is required to find the optimum number of filter bands and the lowest filter complexity. For example, given a certain harmonic output specification for the transmitter, is the lowest-cost design (for the low-pass filter bank) accomplished with numerous filter bands covering small segments of the frequency range or with few filter bands covering large segments? The first approach requires a simple filter design (few components) since the ratio of the lowest harmonic frequency to the highest operating frequency is relatively large. The second requires a more complex design but fewer bands. The limiting factor is that the filter operating frequency range cannot exceed (or even approach, in practical designs) one octave without allowing the second harmonic of the lowest operating frequency to fall in the passband.

The design tradeoff becomes a problem of the number of bands (filters) vs. filter complexity for lowest cost that provides adequate harmonic attenuation above the cutoff frequency. This allows a wider operating bandwidth for a particular filter. Figure 12.23 illustrates the problem.

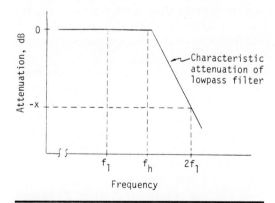

Figure 12.23 Low-pass filter bandwidth. x dB = minimum attenuation for adequate suppression of lowest second harmonic ($2f_l$); f_l = lowest operating frequency of filter band; f_h = highest operating frequency; $f_h - f_l$ = filter operating bandwidth.

The operating bandwidth ratio, if kept constant, will allow using the same normalized filter design for all bands. The band ratio may be found by:

$$\left(\frac{f_h}{f_l}\right)^{1/n} = \text{band ratio} \tag{12.9}$$

where n = number of desired bands
 f_h = upper frequency limit of the PA
 f_l = lower frequency limit of the PA

This band ratio, coupled with filter input harmonic levels, is then used in selecting a normalized elliptic filter design which provides sufficient attenuation at the harmonics of the lowest operating frequency. If a wide margin of attenuation is found to exist, the filter order (complexity) may be reduced, or the number of bands, n, may be reduced to better fit the filter to the requirements. Several iterations of this process will eventually reveal the most economical solution to this problem.

Typical filter designs have operating ranges of approximately one-half octave. The most cost-effective design solution is a careful weighing of the above factors to achieve the specified harmonic output level or better with the fewest number of capacitors and inductors in the bank of low-pass filters. The Cauer-Chebyshev or elliptic-function filters are commonly used since they have sharp rolloff characteristics. But they also have ripples in the stopband attenuation, which prevents increasing attenuation with frequency.

There are three main types of components in a filter bank for a solid-state PA: switches, capacitors, and inductors. The proper filter must be connected to the amplifier RF output and the external load or antenna. The switching arrangement must be capable of selecting the proper filter and maintaining the correct characteristic impedance, usually 50 ohms, through the system. Several approaches may be used. In general they involve rotary switches with either very short wire leads or coaxial leads, miniature relays and microstrip transmission lines [23], or a tree of coaxial relays and interconnecting coaxial cables.

The capacitors used in a low-pass filter must be rated for the maximum RF current expected in the design. Computer analysis of the proposed design is almost mandatory to determine the worst-case voltages and currents for each filter component. High-Q components are required to keep insertion loss low and to prevent excessive component heat. Attempts to parallel low-current, low-cost capacitors usually are not successful. It is very difficult to achieve a layout configuration that ensures equal sharing of the RF current, especially if more than two capacitors are paralleled.

The coils used in filters for 1 kW and above are usually air-wound, although successful filters have been made using toroidal core inductances at the 1-kW level. The coil Q is important for achieving as low insertion loss as possible. The length-to-diameter ratio is key to optimizing the Q for a given inductance. If the coils must be shielded, the dimensions of the shielding relative to the coil diameter are important considerations. Coupling between coils in different sections of the same filter or between adjacent filter bands will cause unwanted responses in the filter passband characteristics. This unwanted coupling can be minimized or eliminated by using a layout scheme that places the solenoid axis of any one coil orthogonal to any two adjacent coils within a filter band. Judicious interleaving of the locations of high-frequency-band filters and low-frequency-band filters can help eliminate the effects of coil coupling between adjacent filters. Shields between bands and/or between filter sections are the most effective but can have a detrimental effect on coil Q. Using silver-plated wire may have some slight advantage in reducing losses (in the higher-frequency bands) but will certainly increase the filter costs. Enameled copper wire or Teflon-insulated tin-plated bus wire is suitable for coils that must be close-wound, while tin- or silver-plated bus wire may be used for space-wound coils. Final alignment of the filters is accomplished by pushing or pulling the coil turns slightly while watching the filter characteristics (input impedance, passband, and stopband attenuation) on an automatic network analyzer. This process can become very tedious without the aid of the automatic network analyzer. If one uses close-tolerance parts and is not too fussy with the filter results, it is possible to dispense with the coil alignment and still achieve adequate results for many applications.

Many low-pass filter assemblies are constructed using printed circuit boards. The common fiberglass-epoxy (G-10) boards are adequate up to power levels of a few hundred watts. At higher power levels, a board with a lower dielectric loss is usually required. A Teflon-filled board is the usual choice. G-10 will overheat at high power levels wherever sufficient current flows in the capacitors formed from component pads and the ground plane on the bottom of the board. If the low-pass filter assembly is constructed on a single large board, some type of mechanical stiffening may be required for the Teflon boards, since they are considerably more flexible than G-10 and the component solder joints may deteriorate in time from mechanical stress if the Teflon board is allowed to flex.

The entire bank of low-pass filters can be assembled on one large circuit board to facilitate the switching method. However, a case may be made for mounting each filter band on an individual circuit board. It complicates the interconnect and switching arrangement but offers the advantage of a lower-cost replaceable subassembly in the event of a capacitor failure which can easily damage the circuit board.

The low-pass filter bank should be arranged for maximum physical separation between the input and the filter outputs. This is necessary to achieve the best stopband attenuation that the filter is capable of. This technique should also be considered in conjunction with controlling the filter currents (from shunt elements) that flow in the ground plane. The ground return current from the input RF should not intersect with the ground return current path for the output RF. Shielding of the input and output sections of the filter may also be necessary in some applications in order to achieve maximum stopband attenuation.

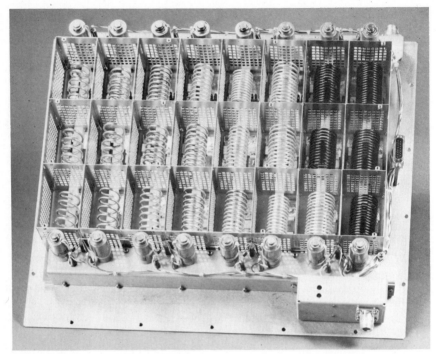

Figure 12.24   Low-pass filter assembly.

Figure 12.24 shows an example of a low-pass filter assembly for a 1-kW PA. It consists of eight individual filters to cover the 1.6- to 30-MHz frequency range. The filter band ranges are: 1.6 to 2.3, 2.3 to 3.4, 3.4 to 4.9, 4.9 to 7.0, 7.0 to 10.0, 10.0 to 14.5, 14.5 to 21.0, and 21.0 to 30.0 MHz. The proper filter is automatically selected and switched in series with the RF output. This particular design required a three-pole elliptic function low-pass filter to ensure harmonic suppression at least 55 dB below the fundamental. The elliptic function filter offers the advantages of a steep attenuation characteristic at cutoff and low attenuation ripple in the passband. The filter was constructed with high-Q porcelain capacitors and air-wound silver-plated coils for the high-frequency bands and close-wound enameled wire for the low-frequency bands. Each coil was carefully designed for maximum Q within the constraints of the necessary shielding requirements. The resulting filter has a measured maximum passband attenuation of 0.17 dB and suppresses harmonics to 60 dB or better below the fundamental.

The filters are switched in and out of the RF output line by a unique patented (U.S. Patent 4,349,799) transmission line switch. The filter is constructed on a large Teflon-glass printed circuit board. A solenoid-activated switch contact is located at the ends of each filter section. A 50-ohm printed microstrip transmission line runs along the filter inputs and outputs and carries the other half of the switch contacts. There is a transmission line stub in parallel with any selected filter except the one located at the far end of the line. The reactance of this stub is known and can be compensated by the values of the input and output filter elements. If the filters are arranged so that the longest stub is in parallel with the lowest-frequency filter, progressing to shorter stubs as the filter frequency increases, the stubs' effect on filter element values will be negligible. This technique of filter switching is fast and reliable.

12.4 Power-Combining Techniques

Multiple output modules

Multiple output modules may be combined to achieve higher-power levels than are possible from a push-pull pair of transistors. A push-pull pair is commonly termed a "module," but a module subassembly may in fact have two or even four pairs of transistors whose outputs are combined to a single 50-ohm output connector. Module subassembly outputs may be further combined to produce a single high-power output. High-level module combiners usually operate with 50-ohm impedance ports to facilitate testing and troubleshooting the equipment with common test equipment. However, the combining that takes place within a module of multiple pairs of transistors may be done at any impedance level. This impedance is often chosen in conjunction with other considerations such as matching to the collector/drain load impedance with easily achievable transformation ratios. These types of combiners will be discussed in detail in this section.

Power dividers and combiners [24, 25, 27]

A power divider will always be found on the input side of the modules where a combiner is used. In the discussion that follows, the combiners described can always be used in reverse to perform power dividing. It is imperative that the same type of divider be used on the input side of the amplifiers as the combiner used on the outputs. A 180° divider and an in-phase combiner will spell disaster.

A wideband power combiner must perform the following basic functions:

1. Provide isolation (minimum coupling) between the input ports

2. Provide low insertion loss over the required bandwidth

3. Provide a low VSWR load at the input ports over the required bandwidth

There are three basic types of combiners:

1. In-phase combiners (two or more ports)

2. Hybrid or 180° combiners (two ports)

3. Quadrature or 90° combiners (two ports)

The in-phase and 180° types will be described here, and practical implementation for HF applications will be presented. The quadrature hybrid is described in detail in Chap. 13. The following definitions apply:

R_L = output load resistance

R_B = bridging resistor

Z_0 = transmission line characteristic impedance

Z_{in} = input impedance (with output port terminated)

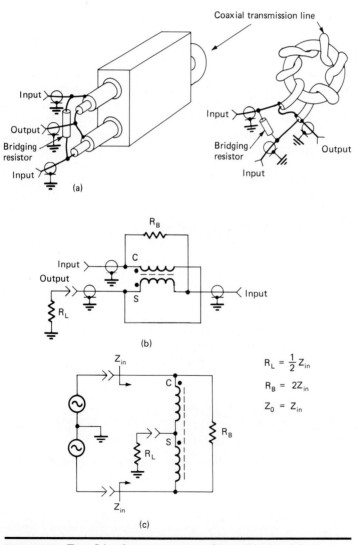

$$R_L = \frac{1}{2} Z_{in}$$

$$R_B = 2Z_{in}$$

$$Z_0 = Z_{in}$$

Figure 12.25 Type I in-phase two-port combiner: (*a*) pictorial view, balun and toroidal cores; (*b*) schematic; (*c*) equivalent circuit.

S = shield connection of coaxial cable

C = center connection of coaxial cable

In-phase combiners operate with two or more inputs of equal phase and amplitude to combine into a single output. There are two basic topologies for in-phase combiners, examples of which are shown in Figs. 12.25 and

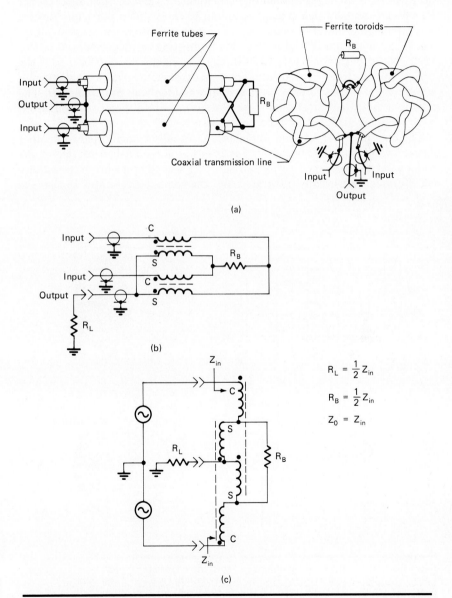

$$R_L = \frac{1}{2} Z_{in}$$

$$R_B = \frac{1}{2} Z_{in}$$

$$Z_0 = Z_{in}$$

Figure 12.26 Type II in-phase two-port combiner: (*a*) pictorial view, tubular and toroidal cores; (*b*) schematic; (*c*) equivalent circuit.

12.26. The differences are in the number and configurations of the ferrite cores which must be used and the value of the bridging resistor. The type I configuration uses a single balun core or toroidal core and a bridging resistor equal to 4 times the output load. The type II combiner must use two separate cores, which may be either straight tubular or toroidal. The bridging resistor is equal to the output load. Physical layout considerations as well as practical values of the transmission line impedance Z_0 and the bridging resistor R_B will determine which type of combiner to choose for a particular design. A comparison of input impedance and port-to-port isolation between a typical type I and type II combiner yields interesting results, as shown in Fig. 12.27. Note that an expanded Smith chart is used—the outside rim is the 1.67:1 VSWR circle. Both combiners were constructed with a single turn of 50-ohm coax in the cores. Core material was identical: Stackpole 7D. The test data indicates better port-to-port isolation with a type II combiner but better input VSWR with a type I combiner.

The combiner output load impedance is usually transformed to another desired value such as 50 ohms. This is easily accomplished by one of the wideband transformers described in Sec. 12.2. Usually the output impedance transformer is physically integrated into the combiner assembly so that the

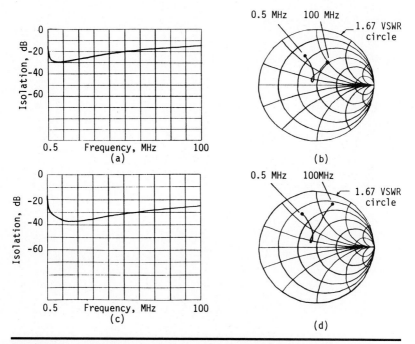

Figure 12.27 Comparison of isolation and input impedance for typical types I and II in-phase combiners. (*a*) Port-to-port isolation, type I in-phase combiner. (*b*) Input impedance, type I in-phase combiner. (*c*) Port-to-port isolation, type II in-phase combiner. (*d*) Input impedance, type II in-phase combiner.

odd impedance value can be handled easily. Strip-line techniques are often required to interconnect the wideband transformer and the combiner.

Theoretically any number of inputs may be combined with an in-phase combiner, but a practical limit is reached when the output impedance becomes too low to allow efficient wideband transformation back to the desired load impedance. An example of a type II four-port in-phase combiner is given in Fig. 12.28.

Four-port combiners may also be implemented by cascading two-port combiners. This technique is illustrated in Fig. 12.29 for both types of two-port combiners.

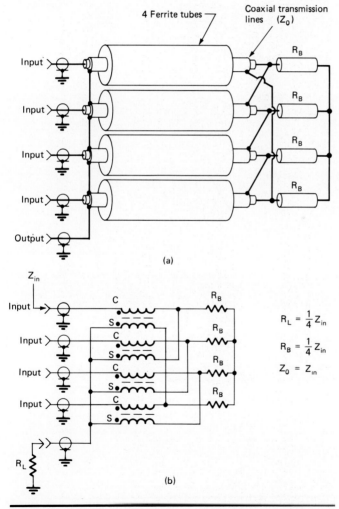

$$R_L = \frac{1}{4} Z_{in}$$

$$R_B = \frac{1}{4} Z_{in}$$

$$Z_0 = Z_{in}$$

Figure 12.28 Type II in-phase four-port combiner: (*a*) pictorial view; (*b*) schematic representation.

The in-phase combiners all use a floating bridging resistor. This may be difficult to implement, especially in combiners handling high power. A wideband balun transformer allows the use of a single-ended or unbalanced load. This balum can also transform the balanced impedance to 50 ohms. Standard coaxial dummy loads connected to the combiner with coax cable can then be used as bridging resistors.

If the roles of the bridging resistor and the load are interchanged, the result is a 180° hybrid combiner. The two input signals must be 180° out of phase and of equal amplitude. The output is balanced to ground unless the

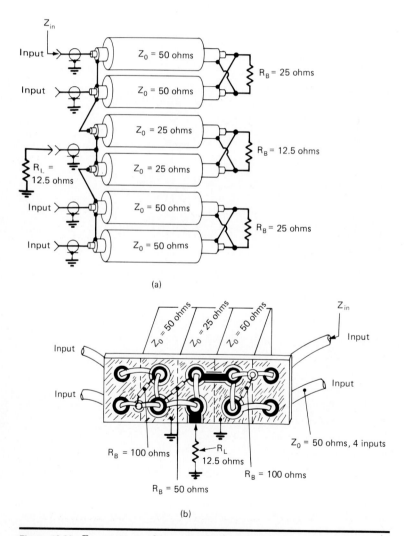

Figure 12.29 Four-port combiners implemented with two-port in-phase hybrids: (*a*) type II combiner; (*b*) type I combiner.

usual balun is used. Examples of type I and type II 180° hybrid combiners with output baluns are shown in Figs. 12.30 and 12.31.

Many unique combiner designs are possible by using various combinations of basic combiner types and balun transformers. Figures 12.32 and 12.33 are examples of a four-port combiner each using two type I in-phase combiners (cores A and F) and two parallel connected type II 180° hybrid combiners (cores D and C) with a 4:1 balun transformer (cores B and E) to couple the combined output to a 50-ohm load. Connecting two 180° hybrids in parallel avoids the need to use 25-ohm coax cable and provides the extra core material to handle the higher RF power.

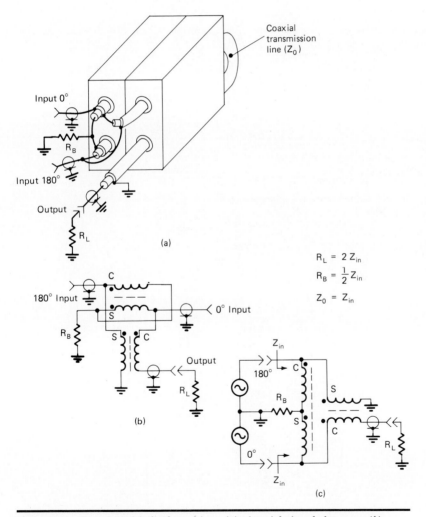

Figure 12.30 Type I 180° hybrid combiner: (*a*) pictorial view, balun core; (*b*) schematic; (*c*) equivalent circuit.

The third type of combiner is called a "quadrature combiner." It has two input ports, each of equal amplitude but one 90° out of phase relative to the other. Four-phase combining of four amplifier modules is feasible using two quadrature hybrids and an 180° combiner. The design and construction of quadrature hybrids is discussed in detail in Chap. 13.

Module gain-matching techniques

In order to effectively combine solid-state power amplifier modules, each PA module must have the same power gain and phase shift from input to output

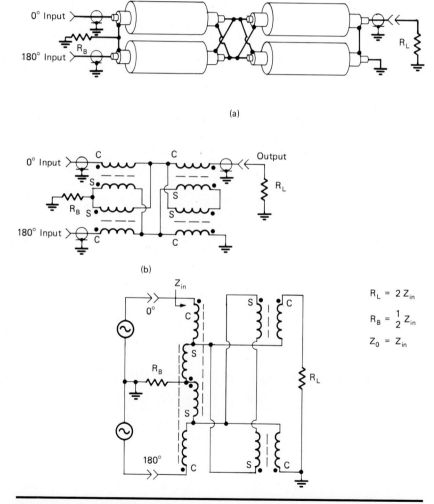

Figure 12.31 Type II 180° hybrid combiner: (*a*) pictorial view, tubular cores; (*b*) schematic; (*c*) equivalent circuit.

[26]. Otherwise some power will be dissipated in the bridging resistors of the power divider and combiner. Figure 12.34 can be used to determine the effect of power gain and/or phase-shift differences for various amounts of power lost in the bridging resistor power.

Phase-shift differences between identical modules are usually small for HF power amplifiers, provided the modules are constructed on a printed circuit board and use identical components (especially the wideband transformers). Another obvious precaution: Always use identical lengths of transmission line between the divider and the module RF inputs and between the module RF outputs and the power combiner.

Gain matching of the modules is usually required since the relative gain between matched pairs of transistors will vary considerably. Some type of "test-selected" attenuator normalizes the PA module gain to a given range. The attenuator is simply a "Tee" or "Pi" configuration resistive attenuator.

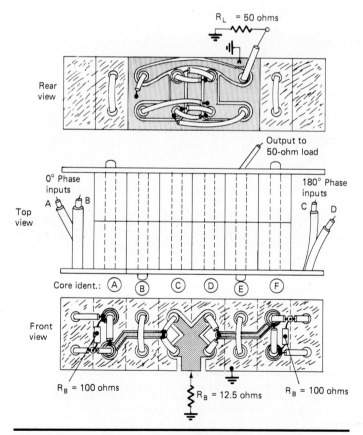

Figure 12.32 Four-port, two-stage combiner using types I and II hybrids, pictorial. *Note:* All transmission lines $Z_0 = 50$ ohms.

The value is chosen depending upon the measured module gain. Figures 12.35a and b give the topology for the two types of attenuators and the formulas to calculate the values for any given impedance and attenuation. The minimum-loss L pad shown in Fig. 12.35c is sometimes useful in conjunction with an attenuator. It provides impedance matching without the use of reactive elements but with additional loss. If the load impedance is greater than the desired source impedance, the network may simply be operated in reverse. An attenuator at the module input will improve the VSWR variation across the frequency range. The power dissipation and/or value required for each resistor element will influence the configuration selected.

The PA module gain variation over the frequency range should track from module to module; otherwise the gain matching will not be valid everywhere. Bi-polar transistor amplifiers are more likely to experience problems with this than FET amplifiers. Low-Q swamping networks are often used in the input circuitry to reduce the higher gain at low frequencies. A swamping network on the input also tends to narrow the gain differences between modules at low frequencies. Negative RF feedback around the PA stage will also flatten the gain response of BJT and FET amplifiers and narrow the gain differences between modules.

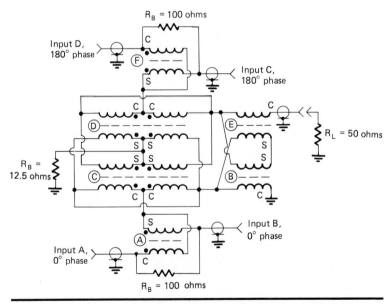

Figure 12.33 Four-port, two-stage combiner using types I and II hybrids, schematic. Inputs A and B combine in-phase, as do inputs C and D. The A/B output and the C/D output combine in two parallel connected 180° hybrids. Two in parallel avoids 25-ohm Z_0 coax cable. 180° combiner gives balanced 12.5-ohm load impedance; ideal for transformation with a 4:1 balun to 50 ohms. Circled letters A, B, C, etc., are the core identifications per Fig. 12.32.

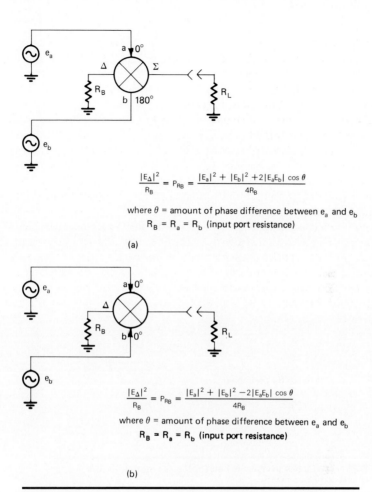

$$\frac{|E_\Delta|^2}{R_B} = P_{R_B} = \frac{|E_a|^2 + |E_b|^2 + 2|E_aE_b|\cos\theta}{4R_B}$$

where θ = amount of phase difference between e_a and e_b

$R_B = R_a = R_b$ (input port resistance)

(a)

$$\frac{|E_\Delta|^2}{R_B} = P_{R_B} = \frac{|E_a|^2 + |E_b|^2 - 2|E_aE_b|\cos\theta}{4R_B}$$

where θ = amount of phase difference between e_a and e_b

$R_B = R_a = R_b$ (input port resistance)

(b)

Figure 12.34 Calculations of combiner losses due to amplitude/phase imbalances: (*a*) 180° hybrid combiner; (*b*) in-phase combiner.

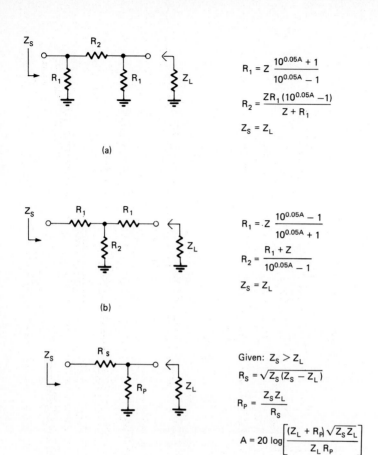

$$R_1 = Z \frac{10^{0.05A} + 1}{10^{0.05A} - 1}$$

$$R_2 = \frac{ZR_1(10^{0.05A} - 1)}{Z + R_1}$$

$$Z_S = Z_L$$

(a)

$$R_1 = Z \frac{10^{0.05A} - 1}{10^{0.05A} + 1}$$

$$R_2 = \frac{R_1 + Z}{10^{0.05A} - 1}$$

$$Z_S = Z_L$$

(b)

Given: $Z_S > Z_L$

$$R_S = \sqrt{Z_S(Z_S - Z_L)}$$

$$R_P = \frac{Z_S Z_L}{R_S}$$

$$A = 20 \log \left[\frac{(Z_L + R_P)\sqrt{Z_S Z_L}}{Z_L R_P} \right]$$

Figure 12.35 Attenuator designs: (*a*) pi; (*b*) tee; (*c*) minimum-loss L pad. *Note:* A = loss in dB.

REFERENCES

1. E. T. Rodriguez, "Model Semiconductor Thermal Designs Even with Scanty Vendor Data," *Electron. Des.*, vol. 27, Feb. 15, 1979, pp. 102–105.
2. H. L. Krauss, C. W. Bostian, and F. H. Raab, *Solid State Radio Engineering*, John Wiley & Sons, New York, 1980, Chap. 12.
3. J. Johnson, *Solid Circuits*, Communication Transistor Co., San Carlos, CA, 1973.
4. D. DeMaw, *Practical RF Design Manual*, Prentice-Hall, Englewood Cliffs, NJ, 1982.
5. A. J. Burwasser, "Wideband Monofilar Autotransformers," part 1, *RF Des.*, vol. 4, January/February 1981, pp. 38–44; part 2, *RF Des.*, vol. 4, March/April 1981, pp. 20–29.
6. G. Badger, "A New Class of Coaxial-Line Transformers," part 1, *Ham Radio*, vol. 13, February 1980, pp. 12–18; part 2, *Ham Radio*, vol. 13, March 1980, pp. 18–29.
7. J. J. Nagle, "Testing Baluns," *Ham Radio*, vol. 16, August 1983, pp. 30–39.
8. W. A. Lewis, "Low-Impedance Broadband Transformer Techniques in the HF and VHF Range," Collins Radio Co. Working Paper WP-8088, July 1, 1965.
9. H. O. Granberg, "Good RF Construction Practices and Techniques," *RF Des.*, vol. 3, September/October 1980, pp. 51–59.
10. G. R. Ek, *Grounding in Practical Circuit Design*, Collins Radio Co. Tech. Rep., 523-0756552-00181L, Nov. 1, 1963.
11. P. M. Rostek, "Avoid Wiring-Inductance Problems," *Electron. Des.*, vol. 22, Dec. 6, 1974, pp. 62–65.
12. N. O. Sokal, "Parasitic Oscillation in Solid-State RF Power Amplifiers," *RF Des.*, vol. 3, November/December 1980, pp. 32–36.
13. R. K. Blocksome, "A Binary Stepped Transmission Line," *RF Des.*, vol. 5, July/August 1982, pp. 22–29.
14. P. H. Smith, *Electronic Applications of the Smith Chart*, McGraw-Hill, New York, 1969.
15. H. O. Granberg, "Power MOS FETs Versus Bipolar Transistors," *RF Des.*, vol. 4, November/December 1981, pp. 11–15.
16. G. Hiller, "Design with PIN Diodes," part I *RF Des.*, vol. 2, March/April 1979, pp. 34–49; part II, *RF Des.*, vol. 2, May/June 1979, pp. 40–47.
17. *Watt's New from BIRD*, vol. 2, no. 2, March-April 1965 (published by Bird Electronic Corp., Cleveland, OH).
18. W. B. Bruene, "An Inside Picture of Directional Wattmeters," *QST*, vol. 43, April 1959, pp. 24–28.
19. W. H. Hayward, *Introduction to Radio Frequency Design*, Prentice-Hall, Englewood Cliffs, NJ, 1982.
20. P. R. Geffe, *Simplified Modern Filter Design*, J. F. Rider, New York, 1963.
21. R. Saal, *Der Entwurf von Filtern mit Hilfe des Kataloges Normierter Tiefpasse*, Telefunken GmbH, Backnang, West Germany, 1963.
22. A. I. Zverev, *Handbook of Filter Synthesis*, John Wiley & Sons, New York, 1967.
23. J. R. Fisk, "Microstrip Transmission Line," *Ham Radio*, vol. 11, January 1978, pp. 28–37.
24. H. O. Granberg, "Combine Power without Compromising Performance," *Electron. Des.*, vol. 28, July 19, 1980, pp. 181–187.
25. A. J. Burwasser, "Taking the Magic out of the Magic Tee," *RF Des.*, vol. 6, May/June 1983, pp. 44–60.
26. J. A. Benjamin, "Use Hybrid Junctions for More VHF Power," *Electron. Des.*, vol. 16, Aug. 1, 1968, pp. 54–59.
27. R. K. Blocksome, "Practical Wideband RF Power Transformers, Combiners, and Splitters," in *Proc. of RF Technology Exp. 86*, Anaheim, CA, Jan. 30–Feb. 1, 1986, pp. 207–227.

Chapter 13

Ultra-Low-Distortion Power Amplifiers

Edward G. Silagi

In applications where a high degree of linearity and low noise are required from the transmitter, external error correction may be added to improve performance. This chapter describes feedforward techniques for low transmitter noise and distortion.

13.1 Introduction

Linear power amplifier output

Linear power amplifier (LPA) performance may be characterized by the contents of the amplifier output spectrum. The output of the LPA generally includes the desired signal plus a number of undesired signals. The undesired signals take the form of noise and distortion. Noise transmitted by the LPA includes amplified exciter noise and internally generated noise. It may be described by the equivalent amount of power existing in a 1-Hz bandwidth (dBW/Hz).

The distortion existing at the LPA output is usually described in terms of harmonic and IMD content and also spurious responses. Harmonic frequencies exist at integer multiples of the desired transmit frequency. Harmonic amplitudes may be measured by injecting a CW signal at the input of the LPA and observing the output at the harmonic frequencies. IMD is created by the mixing of two or more different frequency tones in the LPA. The IMD products exist at sum and difference frequencies of the mixing tones and their harmonics. They may be measured by injecting two equal amplitude tones of different frequency at the input of the LPA while observing the output with a spectrum analyzer. Spurious responses, or oscillations, occur at random frequencies and can exist while the LPA is being driven or undriven. All three types of distortion may be described by the number of dB they are below the desired output (dBc—below either tone in the two-tone test case). A typical LPA output spectrum showing the desired transmit signal(s), noise, and distortion products is shown in Fig. 13.1.

Current LPAs may be divided into two categories, vacuum tube and solid-state designs. Each type has advantages and drawbacks. Vacuum tube LPAs generally exhibit a high degree of linearity (IMD = −40 dBc). Because of the high output impedance of the vacuum tube, the matching networks are narrowband designs. This provides for filtering of the noise, harmonics, and IMD far away from the desired signal frequency. It also reduces the mixing of colocated transmitter signals in the tube output circuit ("backdoor" IMD).

The narrow bandwidth of the vacuum tube LPA also proves to be disadvantageous for certain modern requirements. It does not allow for simultaneous transmission of a number of signal frequencies if the frequency separation is wider than the bandwidth. Also, to prevent the desired signal from being jammed by outside sources, frequency-hopping schemes have been developed. Because of the hop rates, the vacuum tube LPA servo-tuned output network does not have time between hops to retune to each new frequency.

Solid-state LPA designs are inherently broadband. This results in part from the broadband low-impedance matching transformers used in the transistor output networks. The instantaneous bandwidth of a solid-state LPA is generally limited only by the half-octave filters used in the output path to reduce harmonic level.

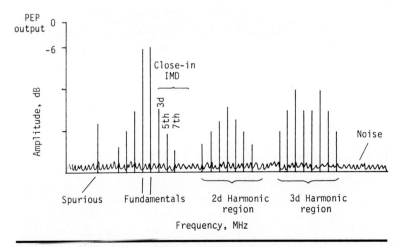

Figure 13.1 Typical power amplifier output spectrum.

The linearity provided by current solid-state LPA designs has not matched the vacuum tube designs described in Chap. 14. A push-pull transistor configuration may be used to reduce even-order harmonics, and quadrature hybrid combining may be used to reduce certain IMD products. Still existing are the close-in IMD products generated by the transistors. Typical IMD performance for a class AB solid-state LPA is −25 to −35 dBc. To increase the linearity beyond the limitations of the transistors of the solid-state LPA, external distortion reduction must be introduced.

Feedforward vs. feedback

The most familiar form of external error correction used in many types of amplifier design is negative feedback. This concept was developed by H. S. Black in the 1930s. Several years earlier, Black (see Ref. 1) patented another method of error correction known as "feedforward." Feedforward offers a number of advantages over feedback. The single fact that makes feedforward a more acceptable concept is that "it is not correcting for an error which has already occurred." That is, the correction is taking place in the same time frame that the error is occurring. Also, because there are no direct feedback paths, the correction concept is inherently stable over an infinite instantaneous bandwidth.

Early work by H. Seidel and others dealt with feedforward at VHF and microwave frequencies. The purpose of this chapter is to give the reader a working knowledge of feedforward as it applies to the high-frequency range of 2 through 30 MHz. For detailed derivations and additional information beyond the scope of this book, the reader is directed to a number of references listed at the end of this chapter.

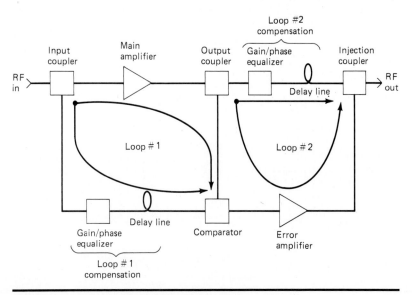

Figure 13.2 Feedforward amplifier block diagram.

13.2   Feedforward Error Correction

To gain an understanding of the feedforward concept, a number of terms pertaining to the basic operation will be defined. During the explanation, the reader is referred to Fig. 13.2.

The heart of the feedforward system is the main amplifier. Its purpose is to amplify the input signal to the desired output level. The output of the main amplifier contains the fundamental (desired) signal plus noise and distortion. As noted earlier, the noise and distortion are a combination of that already present on the input signal and of the products generated by the main amplifier. Feedforward will not correct for noise and distortion already existing on the input signal.

To accomplish the desired error correction, the process may be broken down into two "loops" (the term "loop" is used even though signal flow is not continuous in a single rotational direction). Loop #1 consists of the main amplifier, the input coupler, the output coupler, the loop #1 compensation, and the comparator. The purpose of the first loop is to obtain a sample of the distortion and noise added to the output signal by the main amplifier. This is accomplished by subtracting a sample of the "undistorted" input signal from a sample of the output signal. The input sample is obtained from the input coupler while the output sample is obtained from the output coupler. The subtraction takes place in the comparator. To make sure proper subtraction occurs, the input sample is adjusted in amplitude and phase by the loop #1 gain/phase equalizer and is delayed in time by the loop #1 delay line. The amount of delay is equal to the delay introduced by the main amplifier. The complexity of the gain/phase equalizer depends upon the characteristics of the main amplifier. The output from the comparator, in theory, consists only of a sample of the distortion and noise added by the main amplifier.

The distortion and noise output from the comparator is raised to a certain power level by the error amplifier. This amplified signal is then inverted and injected into the main output path such that it cancels the noise and distortion created by the main amplifier. The output signal is then an exact amplified replica of the input signal. To force proper time frame subtraction, the output signal is delayed by the loop #2 delay line. This delay is equal to the delay introduced by the error amplifier. The inversion of the correction signal may take place in either the error amplifier, the output coupler, or the injection coupler. This process of removing the noise and distortion from the main output is accomplished by loop #2. The second loop is therefore comprised of the output coupler, the loop #2 compensation, the injection coupler, the comparator, and the error amplifier.

13.3   System Component Requirements

Main amplifier

As stated previously, the primary purpose of the main amplifier is to raise the input signal to the desired output level. This output level may range from less than 1 W to a number of kilowatts, depending on the application. Regardless of the power level, the main amplifier of a feedforward system has a number of requirements unique to the application. These requirements are in the areas of gain, phase/delay response, IMD performance, and output impedance.

Gain. The gain requirement for the main amplifier is usually 5 to 10 dB greater than that needed by an equivalent amplifier in a nonfeedforward system. The increased gain is needed to make up for losses incurred in the input coupler, the output coupler, the loop #2 compensation, and the injection coupler. It is very desirable to have as flat a frequency response as possible to simplify the loop #1 compensation. The importance of flat response will become more apparent when loop null theory is discussed. As an example, a main amplifier with a gain of approximately +47 dB is required for a system with 100-mW input and 500-W output. This amplifier could be realized using three or four stages of solid-state devices.

Phase/delay response. The second area of consideration in designing the main amplifier portion of a feedforward system is the phase/delay response. It may be viewed from either a time-delay or a phase-shift perspective, where the two are related by the equation:

$$\text{Time delay} = \frac{\text{phase shift}}{360 \times \text{frequency}} \tag{13.1}$$

The unit for time delay is seconds and the unit for phase shift is degrees.

The phase characteristic of a solid-state amplifier is determined by:

- The transit delay of the solid-state devices
- The phase shift caused by the power splitters, combiners, and transformers used to interconnect the multiple-stage amplifier
- The phase shift resulting from dc coupling chokes and RF coupling capacitors

The desired phase response from the main amplifier is linear (constant time delay) with as small a delay as possible. As with the gain flatness, the phase flatness will determine the complexity of the loop #1 compensation network. An example of the phase response of a solid-state power amplifier is shown in Fig. 13.3. This response curve demonstrates the practical deviations from the ideal situation. On the phase response curve, the three areas of concern are the amount of delay, the phase linearity, and the zero-frequency phase intercept point.

The amount of delay is determined by the number and types of components existing in the signal path. The major contributors to the amplifier delay are the power transistors and the power-combining devices (splitters, combiners, and transformers). To obtain the required power output, either

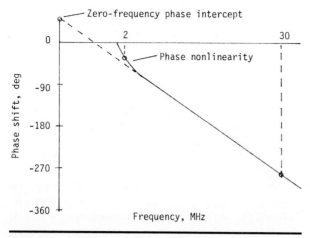

Figure 13.3 Solid-state power amplifier phase response.

BJT or metal-oxide semiconductor field-effect transistor (MOSFET) types of devices may be used. In the case of a feedforward amplifier, the MOSFET offers some distinct advantages over the BJT in terms of phase response. These advantages are:

1. *Gain.*   The power MOSFET generally exhibits more gain than its BJT counterpart; this allows amplifier realization with a minimum number of stages; the fewer the stages, the less delay there is.

2. *Delay.*   The power MOSFET transistor shows less transit delay than the power BJT; typical delay for a MOSFET is 5 ns; typical delay for a BJT is 10 ns.

3. *High input impedance.*   The relativity high input impedance of the MOSFET along with its high gain allows for resistive pad input matching instead of transformer matching; the elimination of transformers reduces delay (typically 2 ns/transformer) and also maximizes phase linearity.

   The phase linearity is defined by how well the phase response follows a straight-line path over frequency. This is determined by a number of factors. One is the phase linearity of the power transistor being used. RF power MOSFETs have an f_t which extends well above 100 MHz. This results in a linear phase response beyond the high end of the HF band. Some deviation, however, does occur in the 2- to 5-MHz region (as shown in Fig. 13.3).
   The low-frequency phase deviation is only partially due to the power transistor. A second cause of this deviation is passive component frequency response. The passive components include transformers, splitters, combiners, dc coupling chokes, and dc blocking capacitors. In the case of the inductive-type components, the deviation is due primarily to shunt induc-

tance to ground. This can be minimized by winding the components on a ferrite material. Care must be taken, however, to prevent overheating of the ferrite at low frequencies.

From Eq. (13.1), it can be deduced that the phase shift at zero frequency (dc) should be zero degrees. As shown in Fig. 13.3, if a straight-line plot of the phase response is extrapolated to zero frequency, zero phase shift is not obtained. The amount of this zero-frequency phase shift is referred to as the "zero-frequency phase intercept point." In solid-state amplifiers, this phase shift may be as great as 15 to 20°. The apparent nonzero phase intercept is caused by characteristics of both the power transistors and the passive components. If broadband operation of the feedforward system is required, the nonzero phase intercept and the phase nonlinearity of the main amplifier must be compensated. This can be done in the loop #1 compensation network. As with the gain flatness, the importance of the phase response will be seen in the discussion of null theory.

IMD performance and linearity.   The linearity of the main amplifier in a feedforward system must be inherently good before the error correction is added. This refers primarily to low levels of IMD and harmonic products within the passband of the power amplifier. Because filters limit the instantaneous bandwidth of the system, they can only be used for products outside the passband.

As stated earlier, typical IMD performance from a solid-state power amplifier is -25 to -35 dBc. This is true for push-pull transistors biased for class AB operation and transmitting a PEP output of 150 to 200 W. For a feedforward system it is desirable to have a main amplifier IMD performance of -40 dBc or better. The reasons for this will be seen in the discussions of the error amplifier and the number of correction loops required. There are a number of ways to obtain optimum linearity from a solid-state power amplifier before the feedforward is applied. These include:

- Reduction of power output
- Negative feedback
- Bias adjustment
- Using optimum circuit topology
- Choosing the proper transistors

Solid-state devices exhibit inherent linearity limitations which are a function of power output, bias level, and frequency. Both BJT and MOSFET devices show good linearity (-35- to -40-dBc IMD) at low frequencies in the 2- to 5-MHz range. For higher frequencies, the performance is degraded. For BJTs, the middle HF frequencies (5 to 20 MHz) show performance in the -25- to -35-dBc range, with some isolated frequencies showing poor IMD and/or efficiency. These "holes" are due in part to transformer resonances. Above 20 MHz (and up to 30 MHz), a phenomenon called "cancellation" may occur. With it, the third-order IMD actually decreases when power output is increased. The cancellation of the third-order products may be controlled somewhat by capacitive compensation of the output transformers and also by changing the bias level.

Power MOSFET devices show a more gradual IMD degradation with increasing frequency. This IMD degradation is also accompanied by decreased efficiency and decreased gain. The cancellation effect almost always seen with the BJT has been seen with some MOSFETs, but it occurs at a higher power level. The MOSFET does show some advantages over the BJT. New technology is pushing toward high drain-source breakdown voltages (greater than 100 V). This allows the use of increased supply voltages and higher-impedance output transformers (greater than the 2-ohm loading for low supply voltage, where series strays are difficult to overcome). The MOSFET also shows much lower-level high-order IMD (seventh order and greater) than the BJT.

Lowering the IMD levels to better than -40 dBc requires a reduction in output power and an increase in dc bias. For a pair of standard devices, the power output must be reduced from 150 W to the 30- to 70-W PEP range. Also, the dc bias level must be increased from low-current class AB (50 to 100 mA/device) to high-current class AB or class A mode (1 to 3 A/device). With the increased bias level, the efficiency of the power amplifier drops from about 40 to about 15 percent. Thermal performance now becomes a limiting factor, and the type of heat removal (forced air, water, etc.) is an integral part of the amplifier design.

Negative feedback applied by resistance from drain to gate and source to ground improves IMD performance on low- and medium-power amplifier stages (up to 30 W). The feedback also flattens gain and makes the input impedance of the transistors appear less reactive. This aids the impedance matching of the devices. For high-power stages, the feedback may help IMD at some frequencies and degrade it at others.

The methods described for reducing IMD also help to reduce harmonics generated by the power amplifier. If class AB bias is used for increased efficiency, the push-pull configuration should be used to reduce the even-order harmonics. Typical high-power performance produces third harmonics in the -10- to -20-dBc range and gradually decreasing higher odd-order harmonics. The even-order harmonics are usually in the -30- to -40-dBc range for a push-pull amplifier. This holds true as long as the two devices are closely matched in their gain characteristics.

PA output impedance.   Because of second-loop problems (to be discussed), it is desirable to have the output impedance of the main amplifier equal to the characteristic impedance of the system (normally 50 ohms). There are three methods which can be used to accomplish this:

1. Design the main amplifier for excess gain and power output capability and place an attenuator after the amplifier to dominate the output impedance.

2. Design the amplifier final stage to have an output impedance equal to the desired value.

3. Use a quadrature (90°) combiner at the output of the main amplifier.

The output attenuator method is a "brute force" way of obtaining a 50-ohm output impedance. With it, the main amplifier must be designed to overcome the loss of the attenuator. As an example, a 10-W system must have a 100-W main amplifier if a 10-dB attenuator is used. For this example, the attenuator would dissipate 90 W. Although inefficient, the attenuator method is simple in design as long as power requirements are low. It also provides a constant load to the main amplifier regardless of system load (VSWR condition).

The second method which can be used to set the main amplifier output impedance is to design the transistor stages for a specific output impedance. This may be done by using (for FETs) drain-gate feedback and source degeneration. The values of resistance may be approximated by using dc analysis if the g_m of the FET is known. From the design, the input impedance, output impedance, and gain of the transistor stage will be set.

As with the output attenuator method, the feedback method has practical limitations which become more apparent at power levels greater than 10 to 20 W. Because the FET characteristics are frequency-dependent, the dc approximation is less accurate as frequency increases. Some circuit tuning may be used as long as amplifier bandwidth is not substantially reduced. The FET characteristics are also dependent on the voltage and current applied to the device. In particular, g_m variation with drain current affects gain and matching of the device. This may be stabilized by using class A biasing for low- and medium-power applications (limited to 20 to 30 W because of the high power dissipation in the device). The source degeneration also limits maximum voltage swing at the output of the FET, which again limits maximum power output.

The third method which can be used to realize a 50-ohm output impedance is quadrature combining. This is used in most high-power applications because of the minimal additional requirements placed on the amplifier. It allows the main amplifier to be designed using standard modular techniques.

Quadrature hybrid combining. A quadrature hybrid is a four-port device with a unique relative phase relationship between the ports. When used as a splitter, a signal incident at the input is divided into two equal amplitude components which are different in phase by 90°. When used as a combiner, the two incoming signals must be equal in amplitude and 90° different in phase for the resultant to appear only at the output port. A power amplifier containing quadrature combining is shown in Fig. 13.4. This figure will also be used to describe why the quadrature combining results in an apparent 50-ohm output impedance. A wave traveling back to the power amplifier is split by the quadrature combiner into equal magnitude components which have a 90° relative phase difference. The two signals reach the power amplifier modules and are reflected back, fully or partially, depending on the output

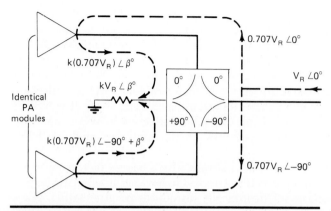

Figure 13.4 Quadrature hybrid combined-power amplifier.

impedance of the module. At this point, the one requirement for the modules becomes important. They must have identical output impedances so that the relative relationship of the signals does not change after reflection. The absolute impedance does not matter as long as the two are identical. This requirement should be easily satisfied since the output modules of a power amplifier are usually identical in construction.

The reflected signals returned to the quadrature hybrid remain equal in amplitude and quadrature (90° difference) in phase. The 90°-shifted signal is shifted another 90° by the quadrature hybrid. The new phase difference results in destructive combining at the output port and constructive combining at the dump port (the resistively terminated fourth port of the combiner). Since the recombined signal is dissipated in the dump port, there is no reflected power returning to the source. By definition, zero reflected power implies a matched impedance condition at the output port of the quadrature combiner.

Amplifier modules combined using a quadrature hybrid must have their input signals 90° out of phase to obtain maximum power output. This may be accomplished by using a second quadrature hybrid as the power splitter preceding the modules. The splitter should exhibit the same amplitude and phase characteristics as the combiner. It may be scaled down, however, since its power-handling requirement is much less.

Quadrature hybrid realization.   For operation in the HF band, the quadrature hybrid may be broken into two sections. The first is the power-combining network and the second the 90° phase difference network. The power-combining network requires two input ports, a summing port, and a difference port. It may be realized by standard HF power-combining techniques described in Chap. 12 as long as a resistive load is provided at the difference port.

The 90° phase difference network consists of two all-pass filters which maintain a 90° phase difference over the required frequency range. The ability of the filters to keep their 90° difference is critical to the operation of the hybrid. As described in the previous section, the apparent 50-ohm output impedance of the power amplifier depends upon the acquired phase difference of the signal which ultimately ends in the dump port. If, after passing through the phase-shift networks, the phase difference at the output port is not 180°, part of the signal travels back toward its source. This "reflected" portion of the signal may be characterized by calculating an effective VSWR at the amplifier output (see Table 13.1). The effective VSWR is now also dependent on the output impedances of the amplifier modules being combined.

The all-pass filter is a two-port network which has an increasing phase shift as a function of frequency. It is designed to have a characteristic impedance at all frequencies and theoretically introduces no attenuation. For a quadrature hybrid application, two all-pass networks which maintain a 90° phase difference over the given frequency band are required. The most common form of circuit topology for all-pass realization is the lattice network. The first-order lattice network along with its normalized phase response is illustrated in Fig. 13.5. As shown, the lattice network is a balanced circuit configuration. To change it to an unbalanced circuit, a balun must be added to one side. The other side may then be treated as an unbalanced port. The maximum phase shift which may be obtained from a first-order network is 180°. To obtain higher-order filters, first- and/or second-order networks of the same characteristic impedance may be cascaded.

The realization of two all-pass filters with 90° phase difference involves filter synthesis techniques. One method is to use a Chebyshev approximation of the phase difference (see Ref. 7). This approximation method will produce a phase difference ripple. That is, the phase difference between the two networks is 90° plus or minus a ripple magnitude. By specifying the ripple magnitude and the bandwidth, the order of the all-pass networks may be determined. All-pass filter order vs. ripple for a 2- to 30-MHz quadrature hybrid is shown in Table 13.2.

Figure 13.6 shows an example of a quadrature hybrid design for use from 2 to 30 MHz. It is designed for 50-ohm characteristic impedance and a phase ripple of $\pm 2°$. The combined filter order is four. This means that each all-

TABLE 13.1   Effective Output VSWR vs. Quadrature Hybrid Deviation from 90° Phase Difference for a Module Output VSWR = 10:1

Phase deviation, deg	VSWR
0	1.00:1
1	1.05:1
2	1.09:1
5	1.25:1
10	1.57:1

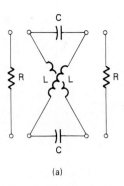

(a)

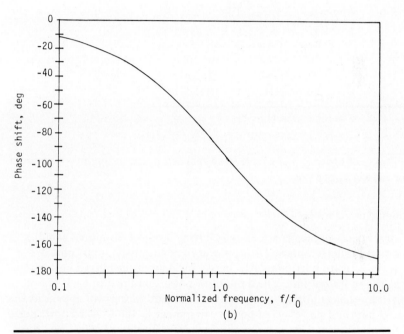

(b)

Figure 13.5 (a) First-order lattice all-pass network; (b) first-order all-pass filter phase response.

TABLE 13.2 All-Pass Filter Order vs. Phase Ripple for a 2- to 30-MHz Quadrature Hybrid

Ripple, deg	Combined filter order
0.5	6
1	5
2	4
10	3

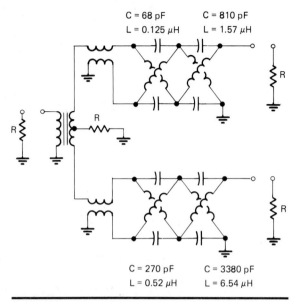

C = 68 pF   C = 810 pF
L = 0.125 μH   L = 1.57 μH

C = 270 pF   C = 3380 pF
L = 0.52 μH   L = 6.54 μH

Figure 13.6   2- to 30-MHz quadrature hybrid.

pass filter is of order 2. They have been realized by cascading two first-order lattice networks per side.

Directional couplers

The directional coupler is a four-port device used for obtaining samples of forward and reflected power. In it, power incident at the input port is sampled at the forward port. Similarly, power incident at the output port is sampled at the reflected port. The amount of power obtained in each sample is specified by the coupling ratio. Ideally, no forward power will appear at the reflected port and no reflected power will appear at the forward port. For a directional coupler, a measure of this isolation is referred to as the "directivity." Typical directivity in the HF band is 20 to 30 dB. The directivity is also a function of the terminating resistances at the four ports.

Figure 13.7 shows the schematic of a specific type of coupler called the "bidirectional coupler." It is bi-directional in that power may be fed into any of the four ports with a sample being obtained at the corresponding coupling port. It is not truly symmetrical because one set of coupling ports (in-forward or out-reflected) does not invert the sample while the other does (180° phase shift). This feature is utilized to obtain correct polarity in the feedforward loops.

The bi-directional coupler may also be used to inject power into signal paths. Such a case is the injection coupler of the feedforward system. There, the correction signal is injected into the main power path to cancel distortion. In a feedforward system, all the directional couplers may be con-

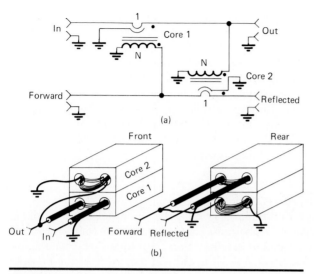

Figure 13.7 Bi-directional coupler. (*a*) Schematic; (*b*) pictorial.

structed using similar techniques. The differences will be in the amount of coupling required and the power-handling capability. A review of the couplers required for the system is shown in Table 13.3.

The construction of a bi-directional coupler at HF frequencies uses cross-coupled transformers (as shown in Fig. 13.7). The coupling ratio is determined by the turns ratio of the transformers. It may be approximately calculated using the following equation:

$$\text{Coupling ratio (dB)} = 20 \log (\text{turns ratio}) \tag{13.2}$$

The transformers are usually made with N:1 turns ratio where the one turn is the main signal path. This minimizes delay (typically 1 to 2 ns) and series stray inductances which limit frequency response. The one turn may be a piece of coaxial transmission line with one side of the shield terminated to ground. This aids the high-frequency response and also acts as a Faraday

TABLE 13.3   Directional Couplers Required in a Feedforward System

Coupler	Purpose	Typical coupling ratio, dB	Power handling in 500-W system, W
Input	Obtains input sample	3–10	<1 for 30-dB system gain
Output	Obtains distorted output sample	20–30	500
Comparator	Removes input sample from output sample-output distortion remains	3–10	<1
Injection	Removes distortion from main output	6–10	500

shield to protect against high-voltage arcing [electromagnetic pulse (EMP), lightning, etc.] to the surrounding circuits.

To minimize shunt inductive effects, the transformers are usually wound on some magnetic core material (ferrite or powdered iron). High-permeability ferrite offers the greatest improvement in the low-frequency response (coupling flatness and phase linearity). The use of ferrite, however, does introduce some problems. Besides getting hot, ferrites create distortion at low frequencies from 2 to around 5 MHz. This must be taken into consideration in the paths where the feedforward will not cancel the coupler-created distortion (i.e., in the injection coupler).

Error amplifier

The purpose of the error amplifier is to raise the amplitude of the error signal (main amplifier distortion and noise) obtained from the comparator. The amplified signal level is equal to the distortion amplitude at the main amplifier output raised by an amount equal to the coupling ratio of the injection coupler.

The error amplifier has a number of requirements:

1. *High linearity and low noise.*   The success of the feedforward operation depends on three areas: the first loop null, the second loop null (see Sec. 13.4), and the linearity of the error amplifier. Distortion products created by the error amplifier will be injected into the main output path along with the correction signal. Figure 13.8 shows this effect on the system performance. The error amplifier also controls the noise figure for the feedforward system, so it should be a low noise design.

2. *Power output lower than main amplifier.*   The power required from the error amplifier is determined by the distortion level of the main amplifier, the first loop null, and the coupling ratio of the injection coupler. It is typically 10 dB less than the main amplifier power output level.

3. *High-gain, flat-frequency response.*   The gain required is typically 30 to 50 dB. This is needed to make up for output coupler, comparator, and injection coupler losses. Flat gain vs. frequency is required to minimize loop #2 high-power amplitude compensation.

4. *Linear delay, short delay.*   Linear delay is required to minimize loop #2 high-power phase compensation. Short delay is required to minimize the length of the loop #2 delay line.

The error amplifier design includes a number of specialized circuit techniques to reduce noise, distortion, and delay. The first stage of the error amplifier may be a low-noise preamplifier utilizing transformer coupled lossless feedback for gain flattening and impedance matching. Low-power stages may include hybrid amplifier modules. These amplifiers exhibit 30 to 40 dB of gain with only 5 ns of delay. They are, however, limited in power output to less than 1 W for linear performance. A way of increasing power out of a

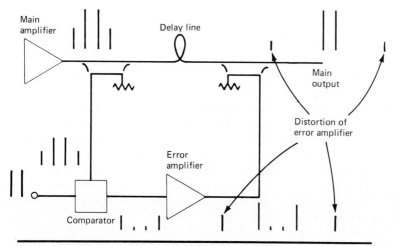

Figure 13.8 Error amplifier distortion at main output.

stage with minimum additional delay is to parallel power transistors. Power FETs may be paralleled as long as some resistive isolation is provided between the gates to ensure stable operation. By eliminating an input and output transformer, up to 4 ns of delay may be saved. In the extreme case where ultralinear operation is required, the error amplifier may in itself be a feedforward system. This does, however, increase both its complexity and delay.

The power output from the error amplifier is involved in a tradeoff with the main output power. This is because of the operation of the injection coupler. When using a bi-directional coupler for injection, the error amplifier is fed into a coupled port with respect to the main output. The majority of the power from the error amplifier is dissipated in the dump resistor. This configuration is necessary to provide proper combining of the main and error outputs for distortion cancellation. By making the coupling ratio of the injection coupler small, the error amplifier output power is minimized at the expense of main power loss. As an example, if the injection coupler is changed from 10-dB coupler to a 6-dB coupler, the error amplifier output and gain requirements are reduced by 4 dB. However, the in-out port loss (main output path through injection coupler) is increased from 0.5 to 1.23 dB. For a 500-W system, the main output loss would increase from 50 to 125 W.

Amplitude and phase/delay equalizing networks

Both loop #1 and loop #2 contain dual signal paths which must exhibit similar magnitude and phase characteristics. In each case, one side of the loop contains an amplifier which must be simulated in the opposite path. By choosing the proper coupling ratios for the directional couplers, the nominal amplitude of each path is equalized. The remaining deviations from nominal amplitude must still be corrected. Also, the delay and phase deviations must be compensated in the paths opposite the amplifiers. Therefore, the need exists for amplitude variation, delay, and phase equalizing networks to balance both loops.

Amplitude equalizers may be divided into two categories: frequency-independent and frequency-dependent. The frequency-independent amplitude equalizer has a fixed loss which exists for all frequencies. Because coupling ratios are limited by the integral values of turns in the transformers, only discrete values may be realized. The difference between the coupling ratio and the nominal amplifier gain can be eliminated by using a fixed-amplitude equalizer (Pi or Tee pad). If possible, the pad should be placed in a low-power path to minimize power dissipation.

Frequency-dependent (gain-sloping) networks are required if the gain of each amplifier is not flat over the frequency range of operation. In typical HF amplifiers, the gain has a tendency to decrease as frequency increases. To correct for this, a number of gain-sloping circuit configurations may be used (see Ref. 10). The phase response of these circuits is not linear, however. Therefore, only small amounts of rolloff can be corrected without disrupting the phase balance significantly.

The phase and delay characteristics of an amplifier are closely related. For the purpose of discussing equalizer networks, the delay is considered to be the linear portion of the phase response (slope of the phase-vs.-frequency plot). The phase error is then considered to be the deviation from constant delay.

As discussed in the earlier section, the phase deviation can be divided into two problems: the nonlinearity and the nonzero phase intercept. The nonlinear phase appears as a rolloff at the low-frequency end. The nonzero phase intercept may be characterized as a constant phase offset which is independent of frequency. Both problems can be corrected by using all-pass phase networks cascaded to form the complex phase function. These networks are best designed by using approximation methods (e.g., least-squares) with the aid of a computer. If desired, more empirical methods of realizing the phase equalization may be used. The phase rolloff at the low-frequency end can be simulated by placing an inductor shunted to ground in the path opposite the amplifier. If the value is not too large, the phase will be corrected without disrupting the amplitude balance.

The nonzero phase intercept may be corrected by one of two methods. The first utilizes a quadrature hybrid and three hybrid junctions to create a constant-phase-shift network. This method is described in Ref. 5. The second is to dynamically adjust the phase using a circuit such as the one in Fig. 13.9. This circuit uses a quadrature hybrid, one or two voltage-variable attenuators, and a combiner to form an active phase-shift network. In it, the input signal is split into quadrature (90° phase difference) components. The two components are then recombined, performing a vector summation. By adjusting the magnitude of one of the components with respect to the other, the phase of the resultant may be varied by as much as ±45°. The circuit

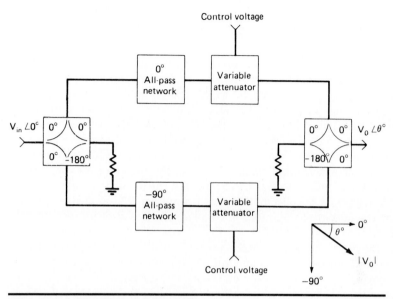

Figure 13.9 Active phase-shift network.

does, however, introduce a loss to the incoming signal. The minimum loss may vary from 3 to 6 dB, depending on the phase setting. This loss may be flattened in the circuit by adjusting both attenuators simultaneously. In many feedforward applications, only 5° to 10° of phase-shift range is necessary to balance the loop. The loss, then, is kept close to 3 dB. In high-power systems, the active phase-shift network would only be used in loop #1 because of the loss introduced.

Besides providing a way of adjusting the phase, placing the network in the path opposite the main amplifier also compensates for the phase shift due to one of the quadrature hybrids in the main amplifier. A second quadrature hybrid can be cascaded with the phase-shift network to compensate for the other quadrature hybrid in the main amplifier. Another advantage of the active network is that it can be used to obtain very accurate loop balance. It provides a means of maintaining balance over temperature and aging of the system. There are also some disadvantages in using the active network. The feedforward system is no longer instantaneous in its correction. Time must be allowed to adjust the balance. The control circuitry design now becomes a key factor to the success of the system. Finally, the loss introduced will degrade the noise performance of the system.

A delay line in each loop is required to compensate for the delays of the main amplifier and the error amplifier. In many applications, the delay line is realized by using a length of coaxial transmission line (coax). Coax has a very flat delay characteristic in the HF frequency range (approximately 1.44 ns/ft). The length required to simulate a high-power amplifier is 30 to 40 ft. In this case, the power lost in the coax can be substantial (0.7 dB).

13.4   Null Theory

Null depth

Feedforward operation depends upon the cancellation of signals at two points in the system. These two points are at the comparator and at the injection coupler. The degree to which this cancellation takes place is referred to as the "loop null." The amount of null is specified in dB and is referenced to the signal level present if no cancellation is occurring.

The first loop null is a measure of how well the input sample is removed from the sample of the main amplifier output spectrum. This "error signal" (output sample minus input sample) exists at the output of the comparator. The second loop null is a measure of how well the distortion and noise have been removed from the output of the main amplifier. This undistorted signal exists at the output of the injection coupler, which is also the output of the system.

Both the first and the second loop nulls utilize the same cancellation mechanism. They use the sum and difference properties of a directional coupler to perform a vector addition on the incoming signals. The canceled signal energy is not destroyed but rather diverted to the termination resistor on the remaining (fourth) port of the coupler, as shown in Fig. 13.10.

As stated throughout this chapter, the quality of the null depends upon the amount of amplitude and phase balance of the two opposing signals. Figure 13.11 shows the amount of null which can be expected as a function of both of these factors. As an example, for a 20-dB null, a 0.6-dB amplitude and a 4° phase balance would suffice. For a given null, amplitude and phase balance can be traded to a certain extent. However, as the null becomes deeper, the amount of available tradeoff diminishes. Typical broadband nulls in an HF feedforward system are on the order of 20 to 25 dB. If a deeper null (30 to 40 dB) is required, the active network must be used.

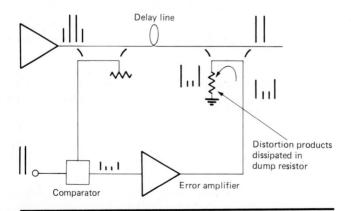

Figure 13.10   Distortion power dissipation.

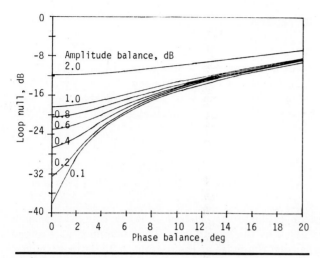

Figure 13.11 Loop null vs. amplitude and phase balance.

Null implications

The first loop null has a direct effect on the power capability of the error amplifier but only a secondary effect on the distortion reduction of the system. The PEP output from the error amplifier is determined by the number and magnitude of the signals at its input. The effect of the first loop null on this output varies, depending on the relative magnitude of the (nulled) fundamental signal with respect to the distortion product levels. If, after the first loop null, the fundamental signal level is still much greater than the distortion levels, the error amplifier output will be dominated by the fundamental power. If, on the other hand, the first loop null reduces the fundamental power to a level much less than the distortion, any additional improvement of the first loop null does not substantially reduce the error amplifier output.

The secondary effect of the first loop null on system linearity is a function only of error amplifier linearity. The fundamental power which is amplified by the error amplifier does not directly add distortion to the main ouput. However, distortion resulting from overdriving the error amplifier (because of an insufficient first loop null) will add directly to the main output at the injection coupler.

The second loop null is theoretically a measure of the distortion reduction from the main output. That is, a 20-dB second loop null implies that the distortion at the output has been reduced by 20 dB. The second loop null has only a secondary effect on fundamental power output. If significant fundamental power exists at the output of the error amplifier because of first loop null, part of it may add to or subtract from the main output at the injection coupler.

13.5 System Considerations

Noise figure

The noise figure of a feedforward system is determined by the noise figure of the error amplifier and the losses between the input to the system and the input to the error amplifier. With the assumption that both loop nulls are infinite, the noise figure may be calculated from the following equation:

$$\text{System noise figure (dB)} = \text{Error amplifier noise figure (dB)}$$
$$+ \text{ losses preceding error amplifier (dB)} \quad (13.3)$$

Perfect balance assumes that noise existing at the output of the main amplifier is totally canceled by the second loop. The remaining noise at the output of the system is then the noise at the output of the error amplifier, reduced by the amount of coupling in the injection coupler. Referring this back to the input, the noise figure expression is derived. The losses preceding the error amplifier include input coupler, loop #1 compensation, and comparator losses. For this reason, it is advantageous to configure the couplers such that the input signal experiences minimal loss before reaching the error amplifier input (see Fig. 13.12). This configuration, however, does increase the gain requirement for the main amplifier.

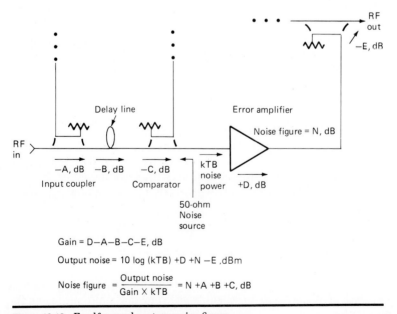

Figure 13.12 Feedforward system noise figure.

Effects of VSWR and colocation operation

Operating the feedforward system into a VSWR load (load not equal to the characteristic impedance of the system) or in close proximity to another transmitter has similar effects on the system. In both cases, a signal is incident at the main output. In the case of the VSWR load, the signal is a partially reflected portion of the output from the main amplifier. In the case of a colocated transmitter, the signal is totally independent of the fundamental output of the system. Each case will be investigated separately.

VSWR.   If the source impedance of the main amplifier is not matched to the characteristic impedance of the system (50 ohms), the returning signal from a VSWR load is rereflected by the main amplifier. A portion of this rereflected signal is coupled through the output coupler and comparator to the input of the error amplifier. The error amplifier can then be driven to the point of distortion (if not destruction). A second problem may be encountered even if the feedforward system is not being driven. If the VSWR load contains a reactive component, an oscillatory path may be established around loop #2. For these two problems, the solution is to design the main amplifier with a 50-ohm output impedance to prevent the rereflection of power (see Ref. 6 on quadrature hybrid combined amplifiers). A final problem resulting from the VSWR load exists because a portion of the rereflected power is coupled through the injection coupler to the output of the error

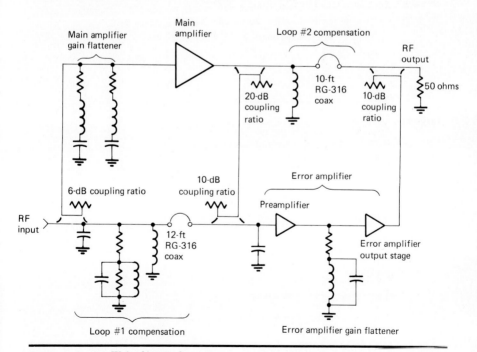

Figure 13.13   150-W feedforward system.

amplifier. In this case, the error amplifier must be designed to dissipate this power without creating distortion or overheating.

Colocation operation. An interfering signal resulting from a colocated transmitter creates two problems for the feedforward system. The first is from the actual signal being reflected by the main amplifier, similar to the case of the VSWR load. This is handled in the same manner as the VSWR load. The second problem results from the mixing of the interfering signal with the desired signal in the main amplifier and error amplifier outputs. In

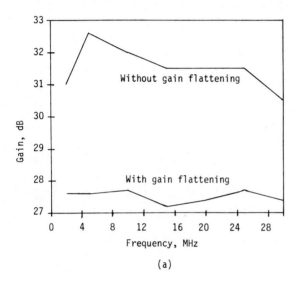

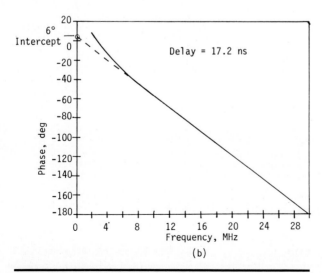

Figure 13.14 Main amplifier: (*a*) gain vs. frequency and (*b*) phase response vs. frequency.

the case of the main amplifier, the new IMD products will be reduced by feedforward as long as their frequencies fall within the correction bandwidth of the system. To eliminate products outside of the bandwidth, the system may be followed by a low-pass or bandpass filter. Feedforward will not correct for products generated in the error amplifier output. Again, the error amplifier must be designed to handle the reverse signal.

13.6 Working System Example

Figure 13.13 shows a schematic for a 150-W feedforward system. The main amplifier is a 165-W power MOSFET module with a nominal gain of +31 dB. By adding the gain-flattening networks, the gain variation was reduced from 2 to 0.5 dB (nominal gain reduced to +27 dB), as shown in Fig. 13.14a. The phase response of the main amplifier is shown in Fig. 13.14b. The delay of the main amplifier is 17.2 ns with a 6° zero-frequency phase intercept and an additional nonlinearity of 14° at 2 MHz. The length of coax used to compensate for the main amplifier delay was approximately 12 ft (3.7 m). To compensate for the nonlinearity, a 6-μH coil was placed in the path opposite the main amplifier. Also placed in the opposite path was a gain-flattening network for the 2- to 5-MHz region and a coax "length-tweaking" capacitor (<10 pF). The first loop null results are shown in Table 13.4.

The error amplifier consisted of a parallel device amplifier driven by a two-stage MOSFET preamplifier. The gain of the error amplifier was approximately 40 dB and the delay was approximately 13.3 ns. Because of the lack of transformers, the frequency response of the error amplifier was much flatter than the main amplifier (0.2 dB). The compensation required for the second loop was one gain flattener, a 10-μH coil (for the phase nonlinearity), and 10 ft (3.0 m) of coax for the delay line.

The overall system gain was +21 dB, with a worst-case third-order IMD improvement of 23 dB. Higher-order products (fifths and sevenths) were also reduced by at least 20 dB along with a minimum of 15-dB in-band harmonic reduction. A summary of the system operation is shown in Table 13.4.

TABLE 13.4 Performance of a 150-W 2- to 30-MHz Feedforward System

Frequency, MHz	First loop null, dB	System efficiency, %	Third-order IMD products	
			Without feedforward, dBc	With feedforward, dBc
2	30	11	41	65
5	28	12	41	77
10	23	12	38	83
15	26	12	35	66
20	24	12	35	58
25	22	12	35	61
30	23	12	35	65

REFERENCES

1. H. S. Black, Translating System, U.S. Patent 1,686,792, Oct. 9, 1928.
2. H. Seidel, Feed-Forward Amplifier, U.S. Patent 3,471,798, Oct. 7, 1969.
3. H. Seidel, H. R. Beurrier, and A. N. Friedman, "Error-Controlled High Power Linear Amplifiers at VHF," *Bell Syst. Tech. J.,* vol. 47, May–June 1968, pp. 651–722.
4. H. Seidel, "A Microwave Feed-Forward Experiment," *Bell Syst. Tech. J.,* vol. 50, November 1971, pp. 2879–2916.
5. T. A. Harrington, Feed Forward Wideband Amplifier, U.S. Patent 4,348,642, Sept. 7, 1982.
6. T. A. Harrington, Feed Forward Amplifier with Enhanced Stability into Loads with High VSWR, U.S. Patent 4,352,072, Sept. 28, 1982.
7. S. D. Bedrosian, "Normalized Design of 90 Degree Phase-Difference Networks," *IRE Trans. Circuit Theory,* vol. CT-9, June 1960, pp. 128–136.
8. H. J. Blinchikoff and A. I. Zverev, *Filtering in the Time and Frequency Domains,* John Wiley & Sons, New York, 1976, Chap. 5.
9. M. W. Heidt and E. G. Silagi, Phase Adjusted Feed-Forward Error Corrections, U.S. Patent 4,595,882, June 17, 1986.
10. Robert W. Landee, "Attenuators and Equalizers," Sec. 7 in L. Giocoletto (ed.), *Electronics Designers Handbook,* McGraw-Hill, New York, 1977.
11. J. T. Nemit and R. I. Wolfson, Low-Level Controllable Radio Frequency Phase Shifter, U.S. Patent 4,161,705, July 17, 1979.

High-Power Linear Amplifiers

Warren B. Bruene

This chapter describes transmitting tube circuits since tubes still provide the most practical and economical means of achieving the high performance necessary for multichannel (ISB) transmission at power levels above 1 kW (at present). The opening section provides a good discussion of IM distortion. This chapter will then show how to choose and compute tube-operating conditions. Tank circuit and coupling network requirements will be discussed, and neutralization and stabilization circuits will be shown. Finally, RF feedback circuits will be described as an effective means of improving IM distortion performance.

14.1 Intermodulation Distortion

High-power HF communication transmitters are typically designed to accommodate four 3-kHz voice channels in a 12-kHz band allocation. Each 3-kHz channel may carry voice or up to 16 RTTY or data tones. IM distortion can produce objectionable background "splatter" in voice channels in full-duplex operation. The IMD should be at least 40 dB below the voice signal level for a good-quality circuit. Lincompex (Chap. 6) can be employed to reduce the apparent background noise by about 15 dB. This would practically eliminate any problem with IMD. Lincompex achieves this advantage by compressing the SSB signal amplitude before transmission so that the weaker sounds are transmitted at a much higher level. The amount of compression used is transmitted to the receiver by the absolute frequency of a tone above the audio band. The receiver uses this compression information to change the receiver gain in an inverse manner to reduce the weak sound back to its original relative level. In so doing, it also reduces noise and interference (including IMD) by an equal amount. This greatly improves the apparent signal-to-noise ratio.

Low out-of-band emission is essential for achieving good spectrum utilization, or in other words, minimum interference to others occupying nearby channels. Figure 14.1 shows the out-of-band IM limits using the noise test signal specified in MIL-STD-188 for high-performance equipment.

IM distortion has been measured in the past by means of the two-tone test because it is the simplest signal that can be used to measure IM over an amplitude excursion of from zero to rated PEP.

The two-tone test does not accurately represent the degree of amplifier linearity when the SSB signal consists of many tones or of speech, however. For example, consider a signal consisting of 16 equal amplitude but randomly phased tones. Furthermore, transmit the same signal in two voice channels to achieve frequency diversity. Let us assume 62.5 W/tone, so the total average power is $62.5 \times 32 = 2000$ W. The PEP would be $62.5(32)^2 = 64,000$ W if all tones (at RF) were in phase at some instant. Actually a composite SSB signal consisting of 12 or more tones exceeds 5 times the average power only about 0.7 percent of the time. The amplitude distribution (as a percent of time which a given power is exceeded) is very close to that of a narrow band of white noise and therefore has a Rayleigh amplitude distribution. The curve is shown in Fig. 14.2.

Clipping peaks above 5 times average power creates IM distortion but the average IM level caused by this is over 40 dB below the signal. Power amplifiers which do not go into hard limiting until well above rated power will produce less peak clipping distortion than those with hard limiting just a little above rated peak power.

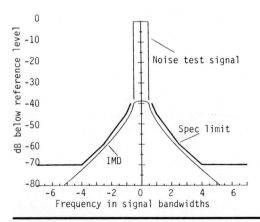

Figure 14.1 Power spectral density of IM products of a noise test signal and a representative specification limit.

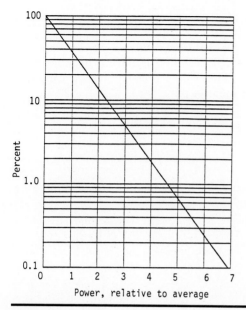

Figure 14.2 Amplitude distribution of a narow band of white noise.

A noise test signal will drive the amplifier up to its peak power limit. Therefore, a noise test signal will include IM produced by peak clipping as well as from nonlinearity below rated PEP.

Another deficiency of the two-tone test is that the "third-order" products observed on a spectrum analyzer are actually the sum of the third and all higher odd-order components. Typically, the fifth-order component is out of phase with the third, which tends to produce distortion cancellation. This leaves the false impression that the IM distortion is better than it really is.

For a two-tone test signal passing through an amplifier tube

$$e_g = a_1 \cos \omega_1 t + a_2 \cos \omega_2 t \tag{14.1}$$

$$i_b = I_{BO} + k_1 e_g + k_2 e_g^2 + k_3 e_g^3 + k_4 e_g^4 + k_5 e_g^5 \tag{14.2}$$

The "third-order" components of concern are:

$$(\tfrac{3}{4}k_3 a_1^2 a_2 + \tfrac{5}{4}k_5 a_1^4 a_2 + \tfrac{15}{8}k_5 a_1^2 a_2^3) \cos (2\omega_1 - \omega_2)t \tag{14.3}$$

Note that the first term in the coefficients is the part caused by third-order nonlinearity, while the other two terms are caused by fifth-order nonlinearity. Note also that the third-order terms vary as the cube of the two-tone signal level and that the fifth-order terms vary as the fifth power. This means that increasing the level of the two test tones by 1 dB each will cause the third-order components to increase by 3 dB and the fifth by 5 dB. The seventh and all higher odd-order nonlinearities also contribute to what is called the "third-order product." They may be either in phase or out of phase with each other.

Perhaps of even more importance is that each combination of three tones of a multitone signal produces other third-order products which are 6 dB higher than the $(2f_1 - f_2)$ products. These other products for one combination of three frequencies are on frequencies of:

$$f_1 + f_2 - f_3$$
$$f_1 - f_2 + f_3$$
$$-f_1 + f_2 + f_3$$

Other fifth-order products produced by each combination of five frequencies are on frequencies of:

$$f_1 + f_2 + f_3 - f_4 - f_5$$
$$f_1 + f_2 - f_3 - f_4 + f_5$$
$$f_1 - f_2 - f_3 + f_4 + f_5$$
$$-f_1 - f_2 + f_3 + f_4 + f_5$$

One can easily see that a group of 16 data tones will produce literally hundreds of distortion products.

The vowel sounds of voice signals consist of many frequency components which are mostly harmonics of the fundamental frequency (about 100 Hz for a male voice). Noise is a better representation of voice signals than two tones.

At the time of this writing there is a considerable amount of activity directed toward the use of SSB for HF broadcasting. Power levels probably will range from 50- to 2000-kW PEP. A good-quality broadcast signal requires a wide dynamic range and a lower background noise and interference level. IM from a strong signal in a nearby channel could create a serious interference problem; therefore, IM of HF SSB broadcast transmitters needs to be kept as low as practical.

Adjacent channel IM caused by peak limiting in the power amplifier can be greatly reduced by clipping the SSB signal envelope in the exciter and then filtering off the out-of-band IM before delivering it to the power amplifier (see Chap. 6). This technique allows the use of a higher average signal level and hence an improved signal-to-noise ratio at the receiver. This is done at the expense of increased in-band IMD, but it offers a very advantageous tradeoff when receiving S/N conditions are not the best.

High-power transmitters are generally required to have better IMD performance than low-power transmitters designed to carry a single voice signal. Therefore, simply adding a grounded-grid linear to a low-performance transmitter is not a satisfactory solution.

The voltage phasors of the distortion products generated in successive stages in a linear amplifier add in amplitude. Therefore, two "35-dB" cascaded amplifier stages might produce only a "29-dB" IMD amplifier. See Chap. 3 for a discussion of distortion in cascaded amplifiers.

Most high-power linear amplifiers are designed to be tunable over a wide frequency range. The number of tuned circuits can be minimized by achieving high gain per stage. This can be realized with tetrode-type transmitting tubes, which have become very popular.

Transmitting tube manufacturers have learned how to design the geometry of the elements within the tube to achieve IMD levels in the -35- to -40-dB region. RF feedback can be employed around the driver and final stages to achieve transmitter IMD performance considerably better than -40 dB, depending upon the tube and operating conditions chosen.

14.2 Nature of SSB Wave

An SSB wave may be considered (for amplifier design purposes) as a sine wave which changes relatively slowly in amplitude and in phase in a varying manner. Figure 14.3 illustrates an SSB wave. The envelope is determined by the audio signal components, while the number of cycles within the envelope is determined by the RF frequency. Typically, there are thousands of times as many RF cycles within an envelope as are illustrated.

Each cycle of the RF wave is slightly different from the preceding one, but the difference is very small. Other, more complex envelopes may be considered to have the same properties as far as the RF amplifier is concerned, even though the envelope may contain many frequency components.

RF amplifiers generally have tuned circuits in both their input and output circuits. One of the principal reasons for using tuned circuits is that they remove the shunting effect of the tube input and output capacitances as shown in Fig. 14.4. These tube and stray circuit capacitances are absorbed into the tuned circuits so that the circuits present substantially a resistive impedance at radio frequencies. The second principal reason for using tuned circuits is rejection of unwanted frequencies.

For purposes of discussing tube operating conditions, it will be assumed that the signal consists of RF sine waves. Any harmonics of the signal voltage that may exist in the input or are generated by the tube will be considered

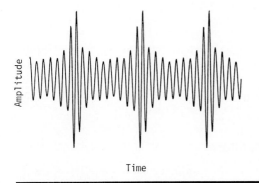

Figure 14.3 Representative SSB wave.

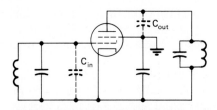

Figure 14.4 Tube and stray input and output capacitances are absorbed into tuned circuits to keep circuit impedances substantially resistive.

to be removed by the tuned circuits unless stated otherwise. The tank circuit requirements to perform this function are discussed in Sec. 14.7.

14.3   Classes of Operation

RF amplifiers are classified according to the angle of plate current flow, i.e., according to the approximate number of degrees during one cycle of the RF wave:

Class A   360° or continuous plate current flow

Class B   Approximately 180°

Class C   Less than 180°

Class AB   Between class A and class B

In addition, subscripts are used to indicate whether or not the tube is driven into the grid-current region. For example:

AB_1 signifies class AB operation with no grid current.

AB_2 signifies class AB operation with grid current.

Typically, class A operation is used in most small-signal applications such as receivers, exciters, and low-level stages of power amplifiers. Class A amplifiers are characterized by high gain, low distortion, and low efficiency.

Class AB operation is utilized in most linear amplifiers from a few watts upward. Gain is lower and distortion greater than for class A amplifiers, but the higher efficiency and smaller tube size and lower cost become determining factors at higher power levels. Either AB_1 or AB_2 may be used as determined by the choice of operating condition selected. Tubes designed for low distortion are usually designed for class AB_1 operation. This substantially eliminates nonlinear grid current as a cause of distortion.

14.4   The Ideal Tube Transfer Curve

The main sources of distortion are the nonlinear characteristics of the RF power amplifier tubes. One of the best ways to achieve low distortion is to avoid generating it in the first place. This is accomplished by the proper choice of tubes and their operating conditions.

Nonlinearity of plate current along the operating load line is the major source of distortion. Curves of plate current vs. grid voltage along selected load lines are shown on the right-hand side in Fig. 14.5.

An ideal zero-distortion plate current curve [1] for class AB_1 operation is illustrated in Fig. 14.6. The plate current follows a square-law curve between grid voltages of -300 to -100 V. From -100 to 0 V the plate current continues in a straight line with the same slope. The zero-signal operating point Q is located midway (horizontally) between the end points of the square-law portion of the curve (-200 V in this example).

Small signals whose peak RF voltage is less than 100 V operate on the pure second-order curve and generate no odd-order IM distortion. When the peak grid voltage exceeds 100 V, the positive and negative peaks enter linear regions at the same time. When the slope of the linear region is correct, there is no change in the gain of the fundamental component and no IM distortion is produced by these larger signals either.

The current at point Q determines the zero-signal value of plate current, and when multiplied by the dc plate voltage determines the zero-signal plate dissipation.

The actual value of bias voltage is unimportant but it must place the zero-signal plate current at the correct point Q on the curve. A sine wave grid voltage and the resulting plate current pulse are shown, as well as the dc and fundamental component of this pulse. The difference between the actual pulse and the fundamental component represents even-order harmonics of

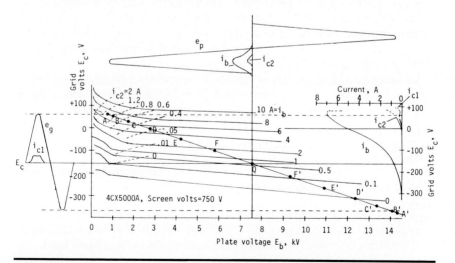

Figure 14.5 Load line (with 15° points marked) and associated relationships for 4CX5000A tetrode operating class AB_2 and delivering 12-kW RF power output. *(Basic tube curves courtesy Eimac Div. of Varian.)*

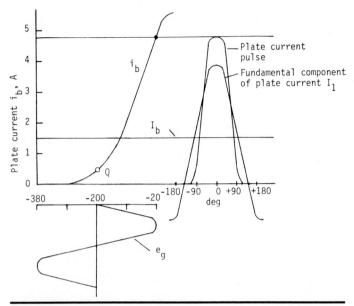

Figure 14.6 Ideal tube characteristic for class AB_1 operation suitable for 5-kW PEP output. i_b = 4.7-A peak plate current; I_b = 1.5-A dc plate current; E_b = 5000-Vdc plate voltage; e_p = 4500-V peak RF plate voltage; I_{b0} = 0.5-A zero-signal dc plate current; e_g = 180-V peak RF grid voltage; E_{c1} = −200-Vdc grid bias voltage; I_1 = 2.35-A peak fundamental component of plate current.

plate current which should be returned to the cathode through a low-impedance path and should not be coupled to the load.

The optimum value of zero-signal plate current for tetrodes and pentodes depends upon the value of screen voltage as well as the basic tube characteristics. The optimum value of plate current varies approximately as the three-halves power of the screen voltage. Lower screen voltages are desirable for this reason, but peak plate current is more limited. It is generally best to operate tubes at the screen voltage recommended by the tube manufacturer.

14.5 RF Power Output and IMD Ratings

The power output capability of SSB or ISB (independent sideband) transmitters has been specified in several different ways:

1. *Single tone.*   This continuous power rating is required if the transmitter is to be operated at full power with a single FSK TTY signal, for example. This rating is seldom applied to transmitters above the 10-kW level.

2. *Two tone.*   Continuous operation with a two-tone test signal at rated PEP is often specified. This permits a reduction in the dc current rating of the HV power supply.

3. *Noise power ratio (NPR).*   Noise loading will load the HV dc power supply the same as many data or TTY tones. The average dc plate current with voice modulation will be even less. This avoids power supply overdesign when the transmitter is not required to transmit a single-channel FSK signal (or equivalent).

Intermodulation distortion can also be specified in several ways. It is always associated with a power output rating such as, "at least 40-dB S/D at any power level up to 10-kW PEP using a two-tone test signal." (S/D is defined as "signal-to-distortion ratio.") This should be clarified to mean that the strongest IMD product as observed on a spectrum analyzer should always be at least 40 dB below the amplitude of either of the two equal-amplitude test tones. A specification of 40 dB at 10-kW PEP, for example, is not sufficient because the S/D may get worse when power is reduced if substantial distortion cancellation is present at rated power.

Sometimes one of the two third-order products of a two-tone test is larger than the other. This means that the power amplifier has phase nonlinearity (or AM to PM conversion) as well as amplitude nonlinearity. IMD components produced by amplitude and phase nonlinearities add on one side and subtract on the other.

The notched-noise test provides the best measure of power amplifier linearity for speech, multitone TTY, or data signals. Typically, the transmitter is driven to its noise power rating with a notched-noise test signal and the S/D measured. The noise IMD typically increases about 4 times as fast (in dB) as the noise power output (near rated power output) as the input signal is increased. Thus for a 10 percent increase in power output (about 0.5 dB), the IMD increases about 2 dB, leaving an S/D decrease of about 1.5 dB.

There is no fixed relationship between the two-tone S/D and the notched-noise S/D. It is different for each power amplifier design and operating condition. A transmitter with a 10-kW PEP rating and a two-tone S/D of 40 dB roughly corresponds to a 2.5-kW noise-power rating and an NPR measurement of 40 dB. There may be as many as a few dB difference, however, which points to the value of the notched-noise test which is more representative of actual operation.

14.6   Analytical Methods of Estimating Tube Operating Conditions

Choosing the load line

Constant-current curves of a tube characteristic as shown in Fig. 14.7 are used because the load line is a simple straight line. This assumes that the grid and the plate voltages are dc plus pure sine waves and are in the proper phase relationship. The use of properly tuned high-Q tank circuits produces a condition which approaches this ideal.

Figure 14.7 illustrates a load line for class AB_1 operation on a tetrode-tube characteristic curve for a 50-kW amplifier. The grid voltage to plate current

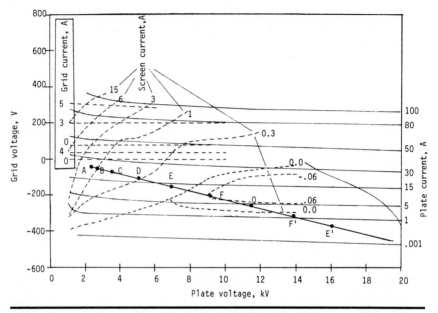

Figure 14.7 Load line (with 15° points marked) and associated waveforms for 4CW5000J operating class AB_1 with 60-kW PEP output. $E_b = 11.5$ kV, $E_{c2} = 1500$ V, $E_{c1} = -260$ V, $I_{b0} = 3.6$ A, $I_b = 8.5$ A, $e_p = 9100$ V, $i_p = 26$ A, E_f (filament voltage) = 12 V, screen voltage = 1500 V. ——— Plate current, A; ····· screen current, A; --- grid current, A. *(Basic tube characteristics courtesy Eimac Div. of Varian.)*

i_b transfer curve is also shown. The shape of the i_b-vs.-e_g curve determines the amplifier distortion characteristic, as discussed in the preceding sections.

The plate current at the zero-signal operating point is chosen for the best compromise between zero-signal plate dissipation and low distortion.

The plate current flows in pulses for class AB operation. For large-signal class A operation, plate current may be quite nonlinear, but it never goes to zero. One function of the plate tank circuit is to provide a resistive load to the fundamental component of the plate-current pulses and a very low impedance to all harmonic components. A loaded tank circuit Q of at least 5 is highly desirable.

The optimum load line for a desired amplifier operating condition is established by a trial-and-error process. A trial load line might be established as follows. The tube manufacturer's data is used to establish a value of dc plate voltage that should be suitable for the desired power output. A zero-signal plate current is then selected that will produce approximately two-thirds of rated plate dissipation. This establishes the trial zero-signal point Q on the load line. The formulas given below the next heading are used to assist in determining the coordinates of the load line end point A in Fig. 14.7. The voltage for point A may be located where the constant-current curves depart from their linear region. This establishes a trial value for e_p. A value of peak plate current is then computed by using the formula

$$i_b = \frac{4P_o}{e_p} \qquad (14.4)$$

where P_o is average power output. This establishes a trial value of i_b and locates point A on the tube characteristic curves. The approximate tube operating conditions for this load line are then computed using the formulas below. Additional trials will locate point A more precisely. Figure 14.8 illustrates the effect of moving points A and Q of the load line.

Formulas for estimating tube operating conditions [2]

Having selected a tentative load line, the following formulas can be used to estimate tube performance fairly accurately. The formulas are exact for a theoretical linear tube operating purely class B. Normal values of zero-signal plate current used for class AB operation have very little effect upon the accuracy of the following formulas at maximum signal conditions, however. The following formulas apply for a single-frequency signal:
DC plate current:

$$I_b = \frac{i_b}{\pi} \qquad (14.5)$$

Watts of plate input:

$$P_i = \frac{i_b E_b}{\pi} \qquad (14.6)$$

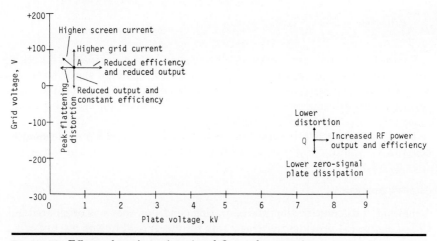

Figure 14.8 Effects of moving points A and Q on tube operation.

Watts of average RF output:

$$P_o = \frac{i_b e_p}{4} \tag{14.7}$$

Percent plate efficiency:

$$\text{Efficiency} = \frac{\pi e_p}{4 E_b} (100) \tag{14.8}$$

For a two-frequency SSB test signal the formulas are:
DC plate current:

$$I_b = \frac{2 i_b}{\pi^2} \tag{14.9}$$

Watts of plate input:

$$P_i = \frac{2 i_b E_b}{\pi^2} \tag{14.10}$$

Watts of average RF output:

$$P_o = \frac{i_b e_p}{8} \tag{14.11}$$

Watts of peak power output:

$$\text{PEP} = \frac{i_b e_p}{4} \tag{14.12}$$

Percent average plate efficiency:

$$\text{Efficiency} = \left(\frac{\pi}{4}\right)^2 \frac{e_p}{E_b} (100) \tag{14.13}$$

Figure 14.9 shows curves of plate efficiency and plate dissipation for both single-frequency and two-frequency signals as a function of signal level for a typical tube operating condition. It should be observed that plate efficiency is nearly a linear function of the ratio of maximum plate voltage swing to dc plate voltage.

The Chaffee analysis discussed in the following section will provide a more accurate computation of tube operating conditions.

Chaffee analysis

A method of calculating the tube operating condition that was originated by E. L. Chaffee [3] provides quite accurate results. A load line on a set of constant-current curves is selected as shown in Fig. 14.7. At points on this load line (*A, B, C*, etc.) corresponding to each 15° along the RF cycle, values of

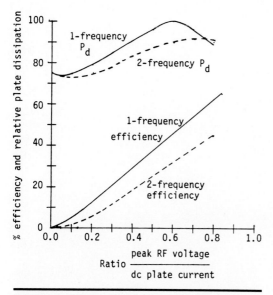

Figure 14.9 Efficiency and relative dissipation vs. peak RF plate voltage for typical class AB operation.

plate current, grid current, and screen current are read. Mechanical aids [4, 5] have been devised to simplify determination of these points. Each point is taken to represent the average value of current over each 15° range centered on that point.

Substituting into the following equations provides calculations of the average dc values of current and the fundamental and harmonic RF components:

$$I_{av} = \tfrac{1}{12}\left(\frac{A}{2} + B + C + D + E + F + Q + F' + E' + D' + C' + B' + \frac{A'}{2}\right)$$

$$(14.14)$$

$$I_1 = \tfrac{1}{12}[(A - A') + 1.93(B - B') + 1.73(C - C') + 1.41(D - D')$$
$$+ (E - E') + 0.52(F - F')] \qquad (14.15)$$

$$I_2 = \tfrac{1}{12}[(A + A' + C + C' - E - E') + 1.93(B + B' - F - F') - Q] \qquad (14.16)$$

The ac components calculated using the above equations are peak values, not rms values. The average (I_{av}) and fundamental (I_1) components should be calculated for plate current. The fundamental component of grid current needs to be calculated for AB$_2$ operation also. Calculation of harmonics is generally not necessary.

These values are used in the following equations to complete the calculation of the tube operating conditions for the selected load line:
DC plate current:

$$I_{av} = I_h \qquad (14.17)$$

Watts of input:

$$P_i = E_b I_{av,plate} \tag{14.18}$$

Watts of output:

$$P_o = \frac{I_{1,plate} e_p}{2} \tag{14.19}$$

Percent plate efficiency:

$$\text{Efficiency} = \frac{P_o}{P_i}(100) \tag{14.20}$$

Watts of plate dissipation:

$$P_p = P_i - P_o \tag{14.21}$$

DC control-grid current:

$$I_{av,grid} = I_{c1} \tag{14.22}$$

Watts of control-grid drive:

$$P_g = \frac{I_{1,grid} e_g}{2} \tag{14.23}$$

Drive consumed in bias supply

$$P_c = I_{c1} E_{c1} \tag{14.24}$$

Watts of control-grid dissipation

$$P_{g1} = P_g - P_c \tag{14.25}$$

DC screen-grid current:

$$I_{av,screen} = I_{c2} \tag{14.26}$$

Watts of screen-grid dissipation

$$P_{g2} = I_{c2} E_{c2} \tag{14.27}$$

RF plate load resistance

$$R_L = \frac{e_p}{I_{1,plate}} \tag{14.28}$$

The above equations can be programmed into a personal computer to greatly reduce the work of trying several different load lines.

It should be noted that all tubes do not have exactly the current shown in the tube data sheets. There are manufacturing tolerances and variations.

Also, allowances should be made for tube aging. The tube manufacturer should be consulted regarding a suitable safety factor for peak plate current. Small, high-g_m tubes may vary ± 20 percent, whereas large tubes may be well within ± 10 percent of published data.

Effect of screen voltage

The effect of changing screen voltage by small amounts, such as 10 to 20 percent, can be estimated by applying multiplying factors to the set of curves. If the screen voltage is 10 percent higher than that on the curves, multiply the grid- and plate-voltage coordinates by 1.10 and multiply the values of the current lines by $(1.10)^{3/2}$.

In general, it is desirable to use as low a value of screen voltage as will permit desired output plus some reserve for variation in tubes from published data. Typically, lower screen voltage results in a little lower distortion for a given zero-signal plate current.

Operation with RF feedback injection

An RF feedback voltage is generally applied to a tube element other than the one which receives the excitation signal. This is done to minimize the reaction of the feedback voltage upon the excitation signal. Figure 14.10 shows a cathode-driven stage with the RF feedback voltage applied to the control grid. The feedback voltage must be in phase with the cathode drive voltage. Figure 14.11 shows a circuit with the excitation applied to the control grid and the RF feedback applied to the cathode. The feedback voltage is in phase with the excitation but, of course, is a little lower depending upon the amount of feedback used. For example, if 12 dB of feedback is used, the RF cathode voltage is three-fourths the value of RF grid excitation voltage.

When the tubes in the circuits shown in Figs. 14.10 and 14.11 are operated class A with small signals, the operation is similar to that of a conventional class A amplifier with an applied signal equal to the difference between the excitation and the feedback voltage. There is an appreciable difference, however, when the RF voltage on the cathode is an appreciable fraction of the

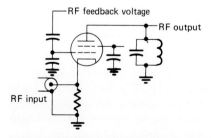

Figure 14.10 Cathode driven stage with RF feedback applied to the No. 1 grid.

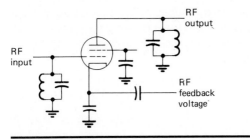

Figure 14.11 Grid-driven stage with RF feedback
applied to the cathode.

dc screen-grid voltage. In the circuit shown in Fig. 14.10, the RF voltage on
the cathode increases the cathode-to-screen-grid voltage when the plate current is maximum, while in the circuit shown in Fig. 14.11, it decreases it. In
Fig. 14.10, for example, a signal peak RF voltage of -40 V, a feedback peak
RF voltage of -30 V, and a dc screen-grid voltage of 250 V result in an
instantaneous cathode-to-screen voltage of 290 V when peak plate current
flows, as compared with 220 V in Fig. 14.11. For this reason the gain and
power-output capabilities of a given tube are quite different in the two circuits. The choice between the two circuits is usually determined by whether
or not a phase reversal of the RF signal is required.

14.7   Tank Circuits and Impedance-Matching Networks [6]

In contrast with solid-state amplifiers, high-power RF amplifiers generally
use tuned circuits in both their input and output circuits. Amplifier tubes
contain appreciable amounts of input and output capacitance, which presents an undesirable low-reactance shunting impedance. Tubes and transistors function best with a resistive load impedance at the signal frequency.

Tank-circuit functions

The following are the various functions that tank circuits are required to
perform:

1. Absorb undesired capacitance across the input and output circuits, as
   previously mentioned.

2. Provide a flywheel effect to maintain substantially sine wave voltages on
   the grids and plates of tubes operating class AB. The tank circuits absorb
   plate-current pulses and produce a nearly sine wave voltage and current
   output. When tubes are driven into control-grid current, the grid tank
   circuit supplies the pulses of control-grid current while maintaining a
   nearly sine wave voltage.

3. Provide a low-impedance return from both plate and control grid to cathode for the harmonics of plate and grid current. It is undesirable to allow significant amounts of harmonic voltage to appear superimposed upon the fundamental because loss of efficiency and increased harmonic output result. Requirements vary, but generally the harmonic voltage should not exceed 5 percent of the fundamental voltage. For class AB operation, the second-harmonic component of plate current is nearly one-half the value of the fundamental component, so to keep the second-harmonic voltage to 5 percent of the fundamental requires an impedance across the plate-to-cathode circuit at the second-harmonic frequency of one-tenth the value of the plate load impedance at fundamental frequency. The capacitors used for this purpose should provide a low impedance to harmonic currents. The Q of a tank circuit is often defined as the ratio of plate load resistance to the shunting capacitive reactance at fundamental frequency:

$$Q = \frac{R_L}{X_c} \qquad (14.29)$$

In the above example, the minimum Q required to prevent more than 5 percent second-harmonic voltage is 5. The value of R_L therefore places a limit on the maximum value of X_c.

4. Impedance matching is another function generally performed by tank circuits. The proper load resistances for most power amplifier tubes are on the order of 500 to 5,000 ohms. The final amplifier generally feeds a transmission line which couples the transmitter to the antenna. The transmission line input impedance may vary widely as a result of standing waves on the line. The transmission line characteristic impedance is usually 50 ohms unbalanced.

5. Harmonic attenuation is another important function. Licensing authorities typically require all harmonics of high-power transmitters to be 80 dB below the fundamental. The second-harmonic of a class AB power amplifier tube plate current is only about 6 dB below the fundamental to start with, so at least 74 dB must be provided by the tuned circuits and filters.

6. Tank circuits are also often required to satisfy the needs of the neutralizing circuit. Basically this involves a means of obtaining a 180° phase shift at signal frequency.

7. Another practical requirement is circuit simplicity for low cost, simple tuning, and frequency changing.

Typical circuits

Tetrode tubes behave substantially like constant-current sources for their output harmonics. Therefore, the harmonic attenuation of the output network should be computed assuming a current source.

Figure 14.12 shows a good circuit upon which to base an output network design [7]. It consists of three parallel resonant circuits with inductive coupling between them. Loaded circuit Q's of 12, 10, and 4 will theoretically provide 76 dB of second-harmonic attenuation. The passband response is monotonic on both sides of the resonant frequency. The three resonators are tuned so that the phase delay between them is 90°. Top coupling, bottom coupling, or mutual coupling may be used.

Sufficient harmonic attenuation can be achieved by omitting the third resonator and raising the Q of the first two resonators to 20 as illustrated in Fig. 14.13 [8]. Higher loaded Q's mean higher circuit loss but the simplicity sometimes is a good tradeoff. Coupled variable inductors have been designed so that the coupling betweeen them remains constant as the inductance is varied. It is possible to tune such a circuit with only three servos.

Methods of tuning

Tubes function best when their load impedance is resistive. When the circuit is not properly in tune, a reactive component appears in the load which causes an elliptical load line. An excessive amount of load reactance reduces efficiency and power output, increases dissipation, and changes the amplifier distortion characteristics. Generally, tank circuits should be tuned so that the phase angle of the tube load is within approximately $\pm 5°$ of being resistive.

Since a plate load with a phase angle of 0° is the desired objective, it is logical that a phase detector be used for the tuning indicator. Figure 14.14 shows a typical phase-detector circuit using a zero-center meter as the resonance indicator. Two balanced voltages e_1 and e_2 are developed across the resistors in series with the secondary of the toroid coil.

The values of these resistors are low (10 to 100 ohms) compared with the inductive reactance of the secondary. The voltages e_1 and e_2 are independent of frequency because the voltage induced in the secondary, and the secondary reactance, are both proportional to frequency so their effects cancel. Voltages e_1 and e_2 are, therefore, proportional to the current in the grid tank coil. The current in the tank coil, which passes through the ferrite or powdered-iron-core toroid to form a one-turn primary, lags the grid voltage e_g

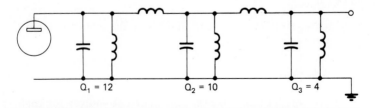

Figure 14.12 Output network with three inductively coupled resonators, which provides excellent harmonic attenuation and passband properties.

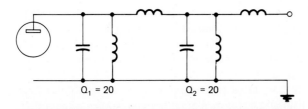

Figure 14.13 Output network with two inductively coupled resonators and combined L-network output coupling.

by 90°. e_1 and e_2 are, therefore, $\pm 90°$ from e_g. A sample e_3 of the RF plate voltage e_p is connected to the detector as shown. The output of one diode detector is proportional to the phasor sum of e_1 and e_3. The output of the other diode is proportional to the phasor sum of e_2 and e_3. When e_3 is phased 90° from e_1 and e_2, the detector outputs are equal and balanced, resulting in a zero meter reading. When the plate tank circuit is off resonance, e_p and hence e_3 have unequal phase angles with e_1 and e_2, so the unequal detector outputs cause a meter indication to one side of zero. Thus, it is only necessary to adjust the plate tuning for a zero meter reading to establish a resistive plate load for the tube. It should be noted that an off-resonance condition in the control-grid circuit does not create an error in the plate circuit resonance indication because the current in the control-grid tank coil lags e_g by 90° regardless of the resonance condition. The phase detector gives the proper indication regardless of the signal level, although it is less sensitive

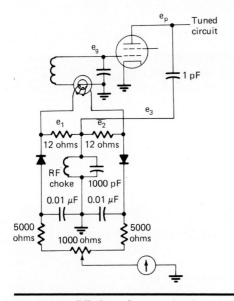

Figure 14.14 RF phase-detector circuit.

with smaller signals. Tuning does not require a constant-amplitude signal and can even be adjusted on a speech signal because the meter will kick to one side or the other if the circuit is slightly off resonance. In practice, it is found that more accurate tuning is easily accomplished with use of a phase detector than by other methods.

Automatically tuned transmitters use the phase-detector output to control a servomotor which positions the tuning elements to resonance when a signal is present.

Interstage coupling circuits

The coupling circuit between two small-signal amplifier tubes may be a simple parallel resonant circuit as shown in Fig. 14.15. The load placed on the tube plate, R_L, is sometimes just the QX of the circuit, but usually a parallel shunting resistance is added (shown dashed in series with a blocking capacitor) to lower R_L. This is often done to keep R_L fairly constant over a given RF range and reduce the effects of stray feedback and loading.

Figure 14.16 shows a driver tube coupled to a power amplifier tube. Impedance and voltage stepdown from plate to control grid is achieved by using a capacitive divider for the tank capacitance. A tuning range of two octaves can be covered in the HF range with a suitable variable inductor and fixed capacitors. A swamping resistance is placed across the circuit to stabilize the driver voltage gain.

In these two examples, the loading on the preceding stage is fixed by the transmitter design. This simplifies tuning, as no loading control is used. The trend in transmitter design is toward compact equipment designs with few controls and simple adjustments.

Power amplifier loading

Proper loading of a power amplifier tube means that the load resistance presented to the tube plate is the value desired. Most output networks have loading as well as tuning controls so that a range of load impedances can be

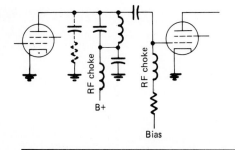

Figure 14.15 Capacitive coupling.

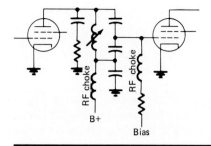

Figure   14.16 Impedance   stepdown   coupling
circuit.

matched to R_L. Some means of proper loading is then necessary. Proper
loading of linear amplifiers requires a specific relationship between two specific measurements. The only pair that has a linear relationship with varying
signal level is e_g and e_p.

A practical means of using this principle for loading is shown in Fig. 14.17.
RF voltage detectors are connected to the grid and plate of the tube to sample the respective RF voltages. The detector outputs are adjusted and combined to feed a zero-center meter. When the correct ratio of e_p/e_g exists, the
detector outputs are balanced and cause no meter deflection. This load indicator can indicate proper loading with nearly any signal of reasonable level.
Therefore, the loading can be adjusted during signal transmission. Automatically tuned transmitters use this type of load sensing to provide a signal
for the loading servomotor.

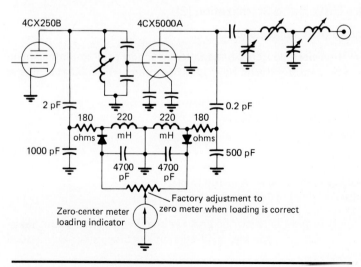

Figure 14.17 Loading-indicator circuit.

Low-frequency amplifiers

Linear amplifiers operating in the very-low-frequency to low-frequency (VLF/LF) (14- to 300-kHz) region need special consideration because tank circuit components become very large and bandwidth is a crucial consideration.

The harmonic attenuation requirements of the output network can be greatly reduced by operating a pair of tubes in a balanced (push-pull) circuit. An output transformer is employed with tight coupling between the two halves of the primary. Balanced operation theoretically neutralizes all even-order harmonic components of plate current. Balancing adjustments can reduce the second harmonic to -40 dB or better.

The tube odd-order nonlinearities which produce IMD are the same ones which produce the third and higher odd-order harmonics. Therefore, choosing an operating condition with good linearity will also minimize odd-order harmonic output.

RF feedback (either current or voltage feedback) can be employed to reduce harmonics still further. This makes it possible to greatly reduce the harmonic attenuation requirements of the transmitter output network. It is usually necessary to control the phase delay between the power amplifier tube plates and the antenna to achieve good passband symmetry. The phase delay from e_p to antenna current (in a series-resonated antenna) should be an integral multiple of 90° (including zero). The tube plate load variation is then minimum and symmetrical. A low-pass T-network is often used to increase the total phase delay of the entire power amplifier output network, transmission line, and antenna coupling circuit to some multiple of 90°. The low-pass network provides some harmonic attenuation also.

14.8   Neutralization and Stabilization [2]

Effects of grid-to-plate capacitance

The effects of undesired coupling impedances, such as grid-to-plate capacitance C_{gp}, can be greatly reduced by means of circuits which balance out or neutralize these effects.

In a conventional tuned RF amplifier using a tetrode tube, the input resistance caused by unneutralized C_{gp} is

$$R = \frac{1}{2\pi f C_{gp}(A \sin \theta)} \tag{14.30}$$

where A = voltage amplification from grid to plate
      θ = phase angle of plate load

This resistance is in parallel with the grid-tank-coil equivalent-shunt resistance, driving source impedance, grid-current loading, and any added swamping resistance.

This term can be either positive or negative, depending upon the phase angle or tuning of the tube plate circuit. When the plate circuit is tuned to the inductive (high-frequency) side of resonance, the term is negative. This means that energy is transferred from the plate to the grid circuit through C_{gp} resulting in positive feedback. When this negative resistance is lower than the equivalent positive resistance across the grid circuit, the amplifier will oscillate.

When the plate circuit is tuned to the capacitive (low-frequency) side of resonance, the term is positive and power is actually transferred from the grid to the plate circuit to produce added grid circuit loading.

This explains why grid current or RF grid voltage of an unneutralized amplifier swings considerably as the plate circuit is tuned through resonance. One important purpose of accurate neutralization, therefore, is to keep plate tuning from affecting the tube input resistance, which usually affects grid voltage and driver gain.

Unneutralized C_{gp} also causes a change in the effective grid-to-cathode capacitance by an amount $C_{gp}(1 + A \cos \theta)$. Tuning the plate circuit varies $\cos \theta$, and this reacts back on the grid-circuit resonance to some extent.

It should be noted that the effective values of input resistance and capacitance also depend upon amplifier gain A. In practice, the gain of linear amplifiers unavoidably varies a little with signal level. This causes slight variations in both input resistance and capacitance, which increases the amplifier distortion.

Accurate neutralization is, therefore, essential in nearly all high-gain linear amplifiers. Exceptions are those which have such a low impedance across the input circuit that input-impedance variations due to unneutralized C_{gp} are negligible.

Neutralizing circuits

Neutralization considerations have had a large influence on the evolution of RF power amplifier design. In modern linear RF amplifiers, triodes are nearly always used in cathode-driven circuits, thus avoiding the need for neutralization. The grid is at RF ground potential and acts as a screen between the input and output circuits, as shown in Fig. 14.18. As a result,

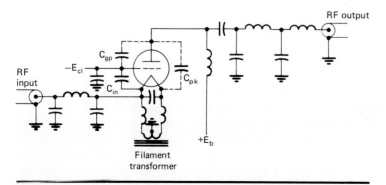

Figure 14.18 Cathode-driven amplifiers avoid need for neutralization.

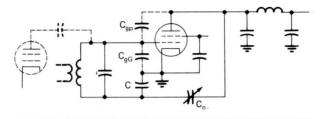

Figure 14.19 Bruene neutralizing circuit for single-ended tetrodes and pentodes.

the remaining plate-to-cathode capacitance $C_{\rm pk}$ is quite small. The tube-cathode input impedance is quite low, for example, 200 ohms or less, so the coupling from the plate to the input circuit through $C_{\rm pk}$ can generally be neglected.

Tetrode or pentode tubes are nearly always used in high-gain linear RF amplifier stages. The neutralizing circuit most widely used [9] is shown in Fig. 14.19. It is sufficiently broadband that when properly designed it holds neutralization over the entire HF range.

The relationship for neutralization is

$$\frac{C_n}{C} = \frac{C_{\rm gp}}{C_{\rm gG}} \tag{14.31}$$

where $C_{\rm gG}$ is the total capacitance from grid to ground and includes all stray grid-circuit capacitance and output capacitance of the driver stage if capacitive-coupled. The capacitor C may have on the order of 500- to 2000-pF capacitance and also serves to "bypass" the bottom end of the grid circuit to ground. Common values of C_n for this circuit are about 1 to 5 pF.

For broadband operation, it is essential that the common lead inductance in series with C be at an absolute minimum. Best results are achieved by using a feedthrough type of capacitor.

Parasitics

It is hardly necessary to state that all tendencies toward oscillation must be eliminated. Particular care must be used in the design of high-gain linear amplifiers to avoid these tendencies. Low-frequency parasitic circuits are usually caused by RF chokes and bypass and coupling capacitors in the dc feed circuits. UHF parasitic resonances almost always occur, and the designer must control them to avoid parasitic oscillation.

The principal UHF parasitic circuit is shown in Fig. 14.20. It is always present when a plate tank capacitor C_t is used. The grid-to-cathode impedance at this plate parasitic resonant frequency must be low enough so that oscillation cannot take place since neutralization is not effective at these parasitic frequencies. The tube-voltage gain can be very high since there is little

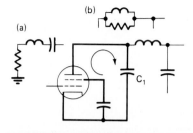

Figure 14.20 UHF parasitic resonant circuit and two types of suppressors. (*a*) Shunt type; (*b*) series type.

resistive loading in these parasitic circuits. If the grid-circuit impedance cannot be controlled well enough, the plate parasitic resonance can be lowered in frequency by adding some inductance in the lead from tube plate to the plate tank capacitor. This resonance must not fall on a second or third harmonic of the fundamental operating frequency, however. If it does, the harmonics of plate current will develop a substantial voltage across the resonant circuit and reduce efficiency, increase distortion, and possibly cause flashovers.

Resistance loading can sometimes be applied successfully to parasitic circuits. Two types of such parasitic suppression circuits are illustrated in Fig. 14.20. Figure 14.20*a* shows a series-resonant trap shunt-type circuit, and Fig. 14.20*b* shows resistance introduced in series with the circuit at the parasitic frequency. The resistance is removed at the operating frequency by the shunting effect of the low-value inductance across it. When the wattage rating of the resistor shown in Fig. 14.20*b* is selected, the dissipation due to harmonics of plate current must be considered.

Parasitic circuits appear in a great variety of unsuspected ways. The UHF resonance described can be quickly found with a grid dip meter. Others must be found by testing. A powerful method of finding oscillation tendencies is to measure tube gain across a wide range of frequencies such as from 100 kHz to 1000 MHz. Response peaks indicate parasitic resonances.

Swamping resistance

High-gain amplifiers can be made more stable by adding swamping resistance across their input or output circuits or both, as shown in Fig. 14.21. The gain of pentode or tetrode amplifiers is proportional to their load resistance, so added plate circuit swamping resistance reduces gain, but this gain reduction improves gain stability. The swamping resistance should be connected in the circuit so that it is effective at parasitic frequencies as well as at operating frequencies.

Swamping across the grid circuit is also effective in reducing the effects of

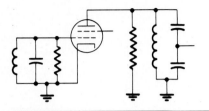

Figure 14.21 Grid- and plate-circuit swamping resistance.

imperfect neutralization. When the grid-to-plate coupling is low, such as in well-screened tubes, neutralization may not be necessary if swamping is sufficient. Grid circuit swamping also helps reduce the effects of reaction upon the input circuit due to impedance in series with the cathode.

Tank circuit losses sometimes vary considerably as the amplifier is tuned over a wide frequency range. The use of swamping resistance will reduce the total effective circuit-impedance variation. In fact, circuits may be added in series with the swamping resistor to equalize an interstage amplifier gain over its frequency range. This is particularly useful for maintaining uniform gain of amplifiers within a feedback loop.

Effects of series cathode impedance

A small amount of filament- (or cathode-) lead inductance will cause a resistive load to appear across the tube input. This inductance may be due to internal filament (or cathode) leads or external leads to ground through bypassing capacitors, as shown in Fig. 14.22. When two filament leads are involved, L_k is the equivalent parallel inductance of both of them. The magnitude of this added input resistance is:

$$R = \frac{e_g}{\omega^2 L_k C_{gk} I_{p1}} \tag{14.32}$$

For small-signal class A amplifiers, e_g/I_{p1} can be replaced with $1/g_m$. This source of positive input resistance can be better understood by realizing that

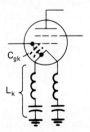

Figure 14.22 Total equivalent filament or cathode lead inductance.

it results from driving the cathode a small amount, as in a cathode-driven amplifier. RF grid voltage causes a current to flow through C_{gk} and L_k. The voltage developed across L_k by this current is the amount of cathode drive voltage. The cathode drive power fed through the tube is:

$$P_{ft} = \omega^2 L_k C_{gk} e_p I_{p1} \tag{14.33}$$

Note that the amount of grid loading due to this cause increases as the square of the frequency. It can be reduced by keeping L_k to an absolute minimum. Use of cavity-type circuits with ring-seal or coaxial-type tubes at VHF and higher is effective in minimizing input loading.

Very-low-impedance filament or cathode bypass capacitors are desirable. An appreciable amount of input loading can increase distortion. Any tube-plate-characteristic nonlinearity will cause a variation in this input loading signal level and thereby present a varying load to the driver, thus causing increased distortion in the drive voltage.

Effects of series screen impedance

Imperfect screen bypassing allows coupling from plate to grid in addition to that through C_{gp}. Figure 14.23 illustrates that current through C_{pg2} and Z_s, because of RF plate voltage, produces an RF voltage on the screen. This, in turn, is coupled to the control grid through the grid-to-screen capacitance C_{g1g2}. The resulting voltage on the grid from this coupling depends upon the impedance of the grid-to-cathode circuit. When the screen bypass impedance is capacitive, the coupling from screen to grid is in phase with the plate-to-grid capacitive coupling. It can be neutralized by increasing the neutralizing capacitance in the regular neutralizing circuit.

When the screen bypass impedance is inductive, because of tube leads or capacitor leads, the coupling is out of phase with that through C_{gp}. In fact, if Z_S is inductive by a certain value, the coupling from screen to grid will just neutralize the coupling through C_{gp}. With normal bypassing practice, this usually occurs somewhere in the VHF region. The self-neutralizing frequency is sometimes given on tube data sheets. Annular screen bypass capacitors built into the socket which surrounds the tube near the screen terminal are quite effective for small tubes like the 4CX250B. For tubes in the 10-kW category, the capacitor dimensions are so large that resonances within the capacitor become a problem.

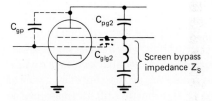

Figure 14.23 Screen bypass impedance permits coupling from plate to grid.

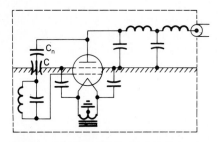

Figure 14.24   Grounded-screen circuit.

Nearly perfect screen "bypassing" can be achieved by using ring-seal tubes and grounding the screen terminal directly to the chassis deck all around the tube, as shown in Fig. 14.24. This eliminates all common screen lead impedance right up to the screen cage within the tube. It has been used very successfully in many power amplifiers with ratings from 1 to 250 kW to make neutralization more independent of frequency and to increase the stability of operation.

14.9   RF Feedback[10]

RF feedback has been found to be very effective for reducing both amplitude and phase distortion. The SSB wave may be looked upon as a single "sine wave" that varies in amplitude and phase. RF feedback will tend to restore any errors in amplitude or phase of the RF wave due to amplifier distortion.

It is generally advantageous to include as many stages as practical within the feedback loop. With current techniques it is necessary to limit this to two or three stages, however.

Two-stage feedback

One circuit that has been used a great deal is shown in Fig. 14-25. With two high-gain stages the gain is still very respectable even after a gain reduction of 12 to 15 dB by feedback. The feedback voltage is obtained from the power amplifier plate and applied to the cathode of the driver tube. The amount of feedback is determined by the ratio of the voltage from grid to ground and the voltage from grid to cathode.

There are several requirements that must be met to achieve satisfactory operation, however. The feedback-voltage-divider capacitance from driver cathode to ground must be high, i.e., on the order of 2000 to 5000 pF in the HF range. The feedback voltage drives the cathode, which takes some power. The load resistance that the cathode presents to the feedback voltage divider is on the order of 20 to 200 ohms. The reactance of the cathode capacitor must be much smaller than this to avoid a significant shift in phase of the voltage applied to the cathode. Also, RF amplifiers tend to be unstable when appreciable capacitive reactance appears in series with the cathode.

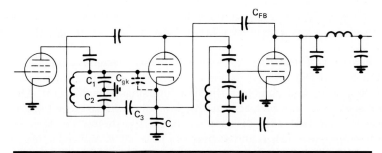

Figure 14.25 Two-stage feedback circuit, including neutralizing circuits.

Large values of C require fairly large values of C_{FB} to develop the necessary feedback voltage. This value of capacitance is across the output plate tank circuit and may raise the circuit capacitance more than desired, so a compromise must be made.

It is necessary to neutralize the cathode-to-grid capacitance to keep the feedback voltage on the cathode from coupling back into the grid tank circuit. The relationship

$$\frac{C_1}{C_2} = \frac{C_{gk}}{C_3} \tag{14.34}$$

must exist for this neutralization. The values of C_1 and C_2 need not be equal, and the capacitance C_2 is usually made about 5 times C_1. The grid-to-plate capacitance of both stages must also be accurately neutralized. These circuits are included in Fig. 14.25.

In medium- and high-power amplifiers, the effect of appreciable voltage on the driver cathode must be considered, as discussed in Sec. 14.6. All possible phase shift between the driver plate and the power amplifier grid is avoided by direct coupling between stages. A voltage or impedance stepdown may be used with tapped tank capacitance as shown. To avoid phase shift, any swamping resistance added to this circuit should be from driver plate to ground rather than from control grid to ground.

The input circuit is not within the feedback loop. It can be capacitively coupled to the plate of a high-output-impedance tube such as a tetrode.

When properly designed and neutralized, this two-stage amplifier is capable of quite high performance. A two-stage amplifier such as this can be made completely stable so it will not oscillate with any degree of mistuning or output loading. Some stray phase shifts always occur, but with careful design the normal losses in the output tank circuit will keep the gain from becoming too high, so stability can be maintained.

Three-stage feedback

Feedback around three stages with tuned coupling circuits between stages has been successfully used [10]. Since three tuned circuits contribute to the phase-gain characteristics of the feedback loop, it is not possible to use as much feedback for a given stability margin. Nevertheless, 10 to 12 dB can be used.

Larger transistors (both bi-polar and FET) have become available in recent years, so a better solution in many cases is to employ a broadband solid-state first stage and eliminate the first interstage tuned circuit. The transistor stage output can be loaded with a low value of resistance to minimize phase shift caused by the driver stage input capacitance. The transistors should be operated class A and as linear as possible. A reduced value of collector or drain dc voltage helps to keep dissipation within the device limits.

Details of the transistor amplifier circuit and the means of injecting the feedback signal at its input will be left to the ingenuity of the designer since larger and better devices are continually being introduced.

Adding the third stage for more gain within the feedback loop greatly reduces much of the complication of the two-stage feedback circuit. Also, this stage operates at a lower signal level (by the amount of feedback used) than if feedback were around just the last two stages. The capacitance of the feedback capacitor which shunts the output circuit is much less also.

Stability

The stability of linear amplifiers employing RF feedback is determined by the phase-gain characteristic of the feedback loop. This in turn is determined principally by the resonant coupling circuits. For this to be true, the screen, plate, and cathode RF bypass capacitors must have negligible reactance over the band of interest. Interstage connecting leads must also be kept short to prevent them from acting as transmission lines with resulting phase shift from the plate of one stage to the grid of the next.

The impedance of the output network, as seen from the final tube plate, is within the feedback loop. The input impedance of an output network which couples to the load resistance through one branch of the resonant circuit is not symmetrical about resonant frequency. Examples are low-Q Pi or Pi-L networks. It is better to use an output network with a more symmetrical passband such as previously illustrated in Fig. 14.12. The properties of the output network are modified in actual circuits by dc blocking capacitors and RF chokes. These must be chosen to have little effect within a few octaves from the operating frequency.

Phase-gain characteristics

The phase-gain characteristic around the feedback loop needs to be carefully controlled in the design and development testing of the RF amplifier. The greatest tendency to oscillate is when the phase shift is 180°. The gain must be down by more than the amount of feedback used where 180° of phase shift occurs, in order to avoid oscillation.

Initial testing of a power amplifier is done with the feedback loop opened. When all stages are functioning properly, the gain and phase shift around the feedback loop is measured. This is done by comparing the RF feedback voltage with the input voltage. Ideally, the feedback voltage is in phase with the input voltage. The amount of feedback that would be applied if the feedback loop were closed is:

$$\text{Feedback} = 20 \log \frac{e_{in}}{e_{in} - e_{fb}} \quad \text{dB} \tag{14.35}$$

For 12 dB of feedback, the feedback voltage e_{fb} would be three-quarters of the input voltage e_{in}.

The gain margin of stability can be found by raising the excitation frequency until the open-loop feedback voltage is 180° out of phase with the input voltage. The gain reduction caused by this frequency change, less the amount of feedback, is the gain margin on the high side of the operating frequency. This procedure is then repeated on the low side of resonance.

The phase margin can be found by raising the excitation frequency until the feedback voltage is down by the amount of feedback that is to be used. The phase angle between e_k and the feedback voltage is measured. This is the phase margin on the high side of resonance. The procedure is then repeated on the low side of resonance.

If the power amplifier employs automatic servo tuning, the servos should be allowed to tune the amplifier, then they should be disabled before shifting the input frequency for the above measurements.

The effect of a high-Q transmitter load impedance upon feedback amplifier stability is easily overlooked but it can create a serious instability problem. The high-Q load could be a tuned whip or resonant loop antenna, or it could be caused by a high-Q multiplexer or bandpass filter. The problem is that the high-Q load can unload the final amplifier on either side of resonance, causing a large increase in gain. Too much gain increase could cause spurious oscillation, which is indeed a very serious matter. Antenna systems above the 10-kW level seldom have high Q, but high-Q antennas or antenna coupling circuits are frequently encountered up to the 10-kW level.

The final stage phase-gain problem is worst when the load impedance variation is similar to that of a high-Q series-resonant circuit located at an even multiple of half-wavelengths of phase delay from the final amplifier plate.

The above words of caution are not intended to discourage the use of RF feedback but rather to stress the need for a thorough and careful design of the phase-gain properties of the feedback loop. Ideally, the amplifier should be stable with any load impedance and with any Q. Something less than unconditional stability can be accepted if the transmitter will always work into a low-Q antenna system such as log-periodic or other broadband antennas.

A computer is a very desirable aid in the design of linear amplifiers with feedback around more than two stages. The benefit of a stable amplifier with a substantial amount of RF feedback is superior IMD performance.

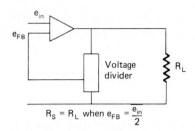

Figure 14.26 Diagram of a feedback circuit for producing a matched output source resistance.

Matched output source impedance

Occasionally there is a need for a linear amplifier with a matched output source impedance. In this case, a signal or reflected wave traveling toward the transmitter will be "absorbed" and not rereflected. One such need is in HF radar transmitters. Tetrode amplifiers have an effective output source impedance several times the magnitude of the plate load resistance. (This is related to the slope of the constant-plate-current curves.) About 5 dB of voltage feedback will make the effective plate resistance equal to the plate load resistance. Too much feedback will make the resistance too low. The amount of feedback would be 6 dB if the effective tube plate resistance without feedback were infinite. The relationship for this case is shown in Fig. 14.26.

One simple test is to make a large change in the output load impedance and see if the forward power in the output transmission line remains constant (with constant excitation voltage). Forward power is independent of load impedance if the output source is matched. The load change could be as drastic as an open or short circuit.

A linear amplifier with a matched output source impedance can tolerate a larger load impedance (or SWR) variation without exceeding the tube current or voltage limit. For example, a 10-kW amplifier with a matched output source impedance could deliver 5 kW anywhere around a 2:1 SWR circle without retuning. The forward power should be 5625 W and the reflected power 625 W. If the excitation level were left fixed and the load SWR reduced to 1:1, the real output power would rise to 5625 W since the forward power would remain constant while the reflected power went to zero.

REFERENCES

1. W. B. Bruene, "Linear Power Amplifier Design," *Proc. IRE,* vol. 48, December 1956, pp. 1754–1759.
2. E. W. Pappenfus, W. B. Bruene, and E. O. Schoenike, *Single Sideband Principles and Circuits,* McGraw-Hill, New York, 1964.
3. E. L. Chaffee, "Simplified Harmonic Analysis," *Rev. Sci. Instr.,* vol. 7, October 1936, p. 384.
4. Eimac Tube Performance Computer, Application Engineering Dept., Eimac Div., Varian, San Carlos, CA.

5. R. I. Sarbacher, "Graphical Determination of PA Performance," *Electron.*, vol. 15, December 1942, pp. 52–56.

6. W. B. Bruene, "How to Design R-F Coupling Circuits," *Electron.*, vol. 25, May 1952, pp. 134–140.

7. Thomas R. Cuthbert, *Circuit Design Using Personal Computers,* John Wiley & Sons, New York, 1983.

8. W. B. Bruene, Automatically Tuned Coupled Resonant Circuits, U.S. Patent 3,355,667, Nov. 28, 1967.

9. W. B. Bruene, "How to Neutralize Your Single Ended Final," *CQ,* vol. 6, August 1950, p. 11.

10. W. B. Bruene, "Distortion Reducing Means for SSB Transmitters," *Proc. IRE,* vol. 44, December 1956, pp. 1760–1765.

11. Laboratory staff at Varian-Eimac, *Care and Feeding of Power Grid Tubes,* 4th printing, Varian-Eimac, San Carlos, CA, 1982.

Power Supplies for SSB Equipment

Neil R. Coonrod
Wayne A. Kalinsky

The modern SSB radio can be divided into the following major sections: coupler (analog, digital), power amplifier (tube, solid state), receiver, exciter, post- and preselector, digital control (memory, synthesizer, speech processing), analog control (TGC, AGC, current sensing, RF sensing, speech processing). In this chapter each of these major sections will be considered as they affect the design approach used to create the power supply for SSB equipment.

15.1 Major Sections and Their Requirements within SSB Equipment

Coupler. A coupler may have some relatively severe operational conditions. Often it is exposed to the outside elements and therefore demands a sealed enclosure, not allowing outside cooling air and perhaps even being exposed to a sun load factor. This forces a highly efficient design which could include a switching regulator rather than a simpler linear regulator. High temperatures may be unavoidable and therefore require the use of high-temperature parts.

Power amplifier. Power amplifiers supply an output signal as pure as possible to the antenna. Designing a high-current, high-power-level supply in a small package and yet maintaining a clean output voltage is a challenge. A good ripple rejection, as low as 60 dB below the dc output, may be required. An SSB power amplifier needs a very low dynamic impedance from its power source. Often a large capacitor is needed at the amplifier's input bus to ensure this.

Receiver.   Receivers use very sensitive signal-path circuits and care must be taken to avoid hum and noise pickup. A linear regulator may use a power transformer that can couple 60-Hz hum into the receiver. A switching regulator has a good possibility of coupling its own switching frequency and switching harmonics into the receiver either by conduction or radiation.

Exciter.   Exciters are similar to receivers in their power supply requirements, although usually needing a much higher level of power. There is the same sensitivity to hum and noise on thier power supplies. Worst of all, the power amplifier usually follows the exciter, and any ripple on the exciter output will be amplified along with the desired signal.

Preselector.   Preselectors and postselectors for solid-state radios can be a mixture of power requirements from low voltage, high current to high voltage, low current. Some of the solid-state radios use back-biased diodes to isolate the antenna line. This method can require 200 to 500 Vdc for isolation.

Digital control.   The digital control section of the SSB equipment, which includes such circuits as memory, synthesizer, signal processing, and logic functions, is usually a high-speed 5-V transistor-transistor logic (TTL) or lower-speed 12-V logic. The former demands a large amount of quiescent current drain that results in more power supply losses because of the low efficiency at this voltage level. Digital circuits normally are insensitive to bias voltage variations or noise.

Analog control.   The analog control section of the SSB equipment, which includes such circuits as TGC and AGC, current-sensing, RF sensing, and general signal-processing circuits, usually operates from 12 V. Power supply fluctuations can modulate the analog signal and create errors in the processing of the signal.

15.2   Major Parameters of SSB Power Supply Design

Before a specific power supply design can proceed, some important circuit parameters must be defined. These parameters will influence the power supply regulation method selected. Very often a tradeoff will be necessary to compromise between two conflicting but desired parameters. For example, small size and low cost are somewhat contradictory.

The following are definitions of many of the common power supply characteristics that must be understood before proceeding with the actual design. The combination of these parameters in turn defines such matters as: Should a switching supply design or linear supply design be used in the application? Should a heavy heatsink be added? What are the working conditions, such as ambient temperature, space limitations, and regulation requirements? Along with the definitions of the parameters, references are listed that contain more in-depth analyses of their influence on power supply design.

Voltage regulation [1–4]. "Regulation" refers to the percent of change in a regulator's output voltage referenced to its nominal value. "Steady-state regulation" is an indication of the variations in output voltage that can be expected on a long-term basis. "Line regulation" is the change that occurs because of changes in the input line voltage. "Load regulation" is the change that occurs because of changes in the load current. Other parameters affecting regulation include component aging and changes in ambient temperature. "Dynamic regulation" is the regulator's ability to reduce the magnitude of variations resulting from changes that occur on the regulator's input voltage or output load.

Current capability [2, 4]. The current capability required from each power supply output has to be fully characterized. For example, it is not enough to list the required current as 2 A if the true condition is 4 A for half the time. This design requires a current capability of 4 A, but the average current capability of only 2 A. Current surges and duty cycles need to be specified. Often the specification of a load line is necessary.

Heatsinking[3, 5, 6]. The volume and weight of the power supply will be greatly influenced by the need of a heat exchanger for removal of heat dissipated by the power supply. If not enough space is available, or if increased weight is unacceptable, a more efficient design method, such as a switching regulator, may be required.

Temperature range. The most common commercial ambient temperature range is 0 to +50° C. A common extended temperature range is −20 to +55°C, whereas the military range is −55 to +71°C. The specified temperature range influences the selection of components. For example, the cold-temperature limit can dramatically increase capacitor equivalent series resistance, resulting in an increased size of capacitors. The high-temperature limit affects the maximum semiconductor junction temperature, which can influence such things as heatsink area, forced-airflow requirements, and the number of parallel transistors required. The actual working internal temperature rise must be considered when calculating maximum module component temperatures. Often the best way to cope with such thermal problems is to improve the efficiency.

Volume and weight. Specified power supply volume and weight restraints can dictate the design approach, e.g., off-line vs. conventional or low switching frequency vs. high. A measure of the volumetric efficiency of a power supply is given by its ratio of power output to volume in watts per cubic inch. Values up to 1.5 W/in^3 (90 mW/cm^3) for linear regulators and 2.5 W/in^3 (150 mW/cm^3) for switching regulators are considered low-risk goals. Switching regulators with conventional switching frequencies of 20 to 50 kHz can achieve 4 to 6 W/in^3 (240 to 360 mW/cm^3) with increased risk. High-frequency switching supplies having switching frequencies greater than 100 kHz can achieve greater than 6 W/in^3 (360 mW/cm^3).

Standby conditions (battery operation). Whenever battery operation is required, the conservation of power losses is very important. This is especially true if the battery is a primary source of power, i.e., if the battery is being used up and not recharged or is on a floating line. Even if it is floating on a power bus, when the power bus is lost the battery operation is needed for some defined time. If the power supply or the load is inefficient, a much larger battery system is required. If, perhaps, the load can be partially shut down for long periods of low use and if a very efficient power supply with very low quiescent power losses is used, the battery system requirement is greatly reduced.

Loop stability [3, 7].   Most regulated power supplies use control loops with negative feedback. Excessive loop phase shift with gain greater than or equal to unity can lead to instability. Phase margin of 45° or more and gain margin of 10 dB or more are desirable loop characteristics.

Transmit duty cycle.   For a transmitter, the transmit duty cycle is the ratio of transmit time to total operating time. This parameter has a strong influence on the thermal requirements of the power supply. A low transmit duty cycle allows less heatsink to be used and possibly requires fewer parallel devices. A continuous-transmit requirement can increase the required heatsink area substantially and possibly require forced-air cooling.

Current limiting.   A well-designed power supply can tolerate an overcurrent or short circuit condition on an output for an indefinite period of time. Current limiting can be in the form of fuses, circuit breakers, or active components. Active current limiters can utilize average current limiting or instantaneous current limiting and will automatically reset themselves. Fuses or breakers will require manual resetting. The type of current limiting depends on the protection and maintenance philosophy for a given system.

Voltage ripple [3, 6].   Voltage ripple is the ac component of the output voltage. This usually refers to the component that is at the line or switching frequency and its multiples. Spikes which often appear on a switching supply output voltage are usually classified as noise.

Transient response.   The transient response is the time required for an output voltage to return to its desired level and the magnitude of change that occurs after a step change in line voltage or load current.

Remote turn on/off.   It is often desirable to be able to turn the power supply on or off from a remote location using a logic command.

Grounding.   Care and planning must be exercised during the design and layout of a power supply to ensure a good grounding method both within the power supply and to the rest of the SSB circuits. The physical layout of the ground lines interconnecting the circuits is very critical and can cause many problems if not carefully planned. The ground currents must follow a definable path that the designer wants. For example, the charging currents in a rectifier system can travel along low-level signal paths, if not restricted to a defined route from rectifier to filter capacitor. This also holds true for dc power lines. The high currents of one voltage line may have to be isolated from chassis and grounded outside the power supply area at the user circuit so that the high currents get back to the power supply without finding parallel paths.

Line drops.   Line drops are the dc voltage losses between the power supply and the circuit using the specific output. A determination of how large a line drop can be tolerated must be made. Then a single adequate line or enough parallel lines must be used.

Output overvoltage protection.   When a dc output is going to circuits that are expensive or critical, an overvoltage protection circuit or device may be needed. This may be a zener diode, a silicon controlled rectifier (SCR) crowbar fired by a voltage level detector, or a spark gap device (for higher voltage levels).

Mechanical structure.   The specific application of a unit will dictate the mechanical structure needed. A unit built for portable field use must be more rugged than one built for an office environment. The level of vibration and shock must be determined so a guideline for structural strength can be made. Often, shielding requirements between sections can be combined with the strengthening of the overall mechanical structure. When heavy components such as power transformers and chokes make up a major part of a unit, the structural supports are built around these components. Reinforcement of the chassis with U-shaped channel iron can provide a light-weight yet very strong structure.

Electromagnetic interference.   Electromagnetic interference is the level of radiated field that can be measured around the unit and can be attributed to the unit. This field can cause interference to the rest of the radio or to external systems. There are commercial and military specifications that help define the acceptable level of radiation, such as MIL-STD-461.

Mobility.   Mobile SSB equipment is usually battery-operated and therefore requires a very-low-loss power supply. Care must be taken to ensure that such requirements as low power drain in a standby mode, high efficiency, light weight for portability, and small size are considered.

15.3   Major Power Source Parameters

Parameters

Of great influence on the design approach are the characteristics of the primary power source. The main parameters are, of course, line voltage and frequency. The total input voltage variation is very important. Equipment for foreign markets will most likely have to work with a more adverse power line than that built for the U.S. market. Critical applications may require uninterrupted operation, especially if loss of power could cause a shutdown of the system resulting from the loss of information such as tuning frequency or power level control. The voltage transients encountered on power lines have become much more critical to the modern SSB power supply. The regulators used, whether they are off the power line or isolated by a power transformer, are more sensitive to voltage transients than the older tube rectifier systems. Protection must be incorporated within the design, either across sensitive devices or as an overall protection across the power line.

The major standards define acceptable levels of conducted and radiated

EMI, which helps to ensure a compatibility between pieces of equipment operated from the same power line or the same location. The advent of the newer switching power supplies has created a whole new spectrum of noise. Care must be taken to ensure a low level of noise both inside and outside the radio. Characteristics of power sources are defined in such documents as *Electric Current Abroad* by the U.S. Department of Commerce for sources outside the United States and ITT's *Reference Data for Radio Engineers* for sources inside the United States [18]. Many government procurements will specify the MIL Standards for source definition (see the list below).

Specifications references

The following are sources for specifications references on various areas of interest:

1. The Federal Communications Commission (FCC) in Washington, DC, which can supply references on:
   - Transmitters
   - Receivers

2. The Superintendent of Documents, U.S. Government Printing Office, in Washington, DC, which can supply the FCC Part 15 Rules on:
   - Digital equipment
   - Switching power supplies

3. Verband Deutscher Electrotechniker (VDE) Verlag GmbH, in West Berlin, Germany, which can supply the following references:
   - Document 0875, *Regulations for Radio Frequency Interference Suppression*
   - Document 0871, *Radiated Emissions*
   - Document 0804, *Telecommunications and Processing Equipment*

4. Underwriters' Laboratories (UL), Inc., in Northbrook, IL, which can supply the following references:
   - Document UL478, *Electronic Data Processing Units and Systems*
   - Document UL1012, *Power Supplies*

5. U.S. Naval Publications and Forms, in Philadelphia, PA, which can supply the following references:
   - MIL-STD-461, *Electromagnetic Emission and Susceptibility Requirements*
   - MIL-STD-704, *Aircraft Electric Power Characteristics*

6. International Special Committee on Radio Interference, International Electrotechnical Committee (IEC), in Geneva, Switzerland, which can supply reference material on radio interference

7. Radio Technical Commission for Aeronautics, Washington, DC: RTCA DO-160B, *Environmental Conditions and Test Procedures for Airborne Equipment*, July 20, 1984

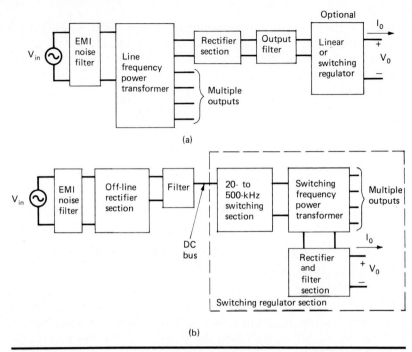

(a)

(b)

Figure 15.1   AC to dc power conversion: (*a*) conventional, and (*b*) off-line. AC source for both: 50-, 60-, or 400-Hz one- or three-phase.

15.4   Major Power Conversion Techniques

Power conversion in SSB equipment can generally be classified as ac to dc or dc to dc [8, 9]. The need for dc to ac or ac to ac conversion may occasionally exist, but these types cannot be treated adequately here.

The general block diagram for ac to dc power conversion will take one of the two forms shown in Fig. 15.1. The conventional ac to dc converter uses an EMI filter, a line-frequency transformer, a rectifier section, and an output filter to provide dc power to the load. A regulator is added when required, which can be either a linear or switching type. The off-line power converter

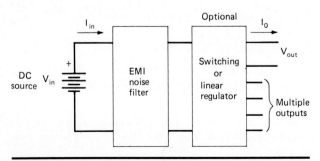

Figure 15.2   DC to dc power conversion.

uses an EMI filter, a rectifier section, and a capacitor input filter to provide dc power to a switching converter. Isolation of the load from the ac source is achieved in a high-frequency transformer.

The general block diagram for dc to dc conversion is shown in Fig. 15.2. It consists of an EMI filter and a switching or linear regulator. In some cases the dc source voltage can be applied directly to the load.

Conventional ac to dc power conversion

The purpose of the EMI filter is to provide attenuation of undesired frequency components produced by the regulator from getting back onto the power line. These result from the rectification and filtering process and are dependent on the current required by the load. The filter is also used to attenuate the spikes and transients from the power line to protect the following sections. The design of the EMI filter must consider the need for damping if the filter-resonant frequency is such that load or power line fluctuations can occur at its resonant frequency. In addition to picking the proper L and C values for the filter, the physical layout of not only the filter but the entire power supply is critical to the success of the EMI filter. Good layout practices include separating outputs from inputs and "canning up" the EMI filter at the input connector. Since the EMI filter can account for as much as 20 to 40 percent of the size and weight of the entire power supply, its design must be considered early in the design process.

The output filter will generally be either the capacitor or choke input type [6, 10]. The former employs a large capacitor to filter the rectified voltage waveform. A full-wave rectified capacitor input filter circuit is shown in Fig. 15.3 along with the filtered and unfiltered output voltage waveform.

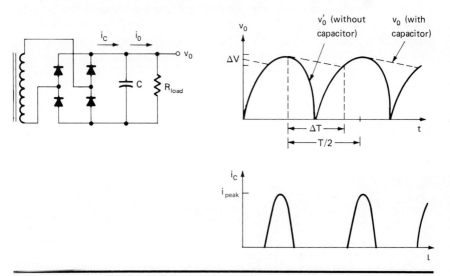

Figure 15.3 Capacitor input filter.

During the time V_0' is below v_0, the capacitor must source all the load current. A good approximation which can be used to determine the required amount of capacitance is:

$$C = I_0 \frac{\Delta T}{\Delta V} \tag{15.1}$$

where ΔV is the desired output voltage ripple. This relationship shows that the required capacitance increases proportionally with load current and inversely with desired voltage ripple. Also, as C is increased, the diode conduction time $T/2 - \Delta T$ decreases and the peak diode and capacitor currents increase. This effect should be considered when selecting diodes and capacitors. The increasing peak current will reflect to the primary and will affect the EMI filter design also.

The capacitor-input filter is a peak charging filter because its output voltage is essentially the peak of the rectified voltage waveform. The choke input filter shown in Fig. 15.4 is an averaging filter, and the output voltage will be the average of the rectified voltage v_r. For the single-phase full-wave rectified case $V_0 = 2V_{\text{peak}}/\pi$:

$$i_L = \frac{1}{L} \int (v_r - V_0)\, dt + I_0$$

The average inductor current is I_0 and will change with load; however, Δi_L is load-independent, assuming continuous inductor current. By selecting L to be large enough, continuous inductor current can be guaranteed. If the inductance selected is not large enough, at some point the inductor current will go to zero. When this occurs, the filter approaches a peak charging filter with an output approaching $V_{R,\text{peak}}$. The inductance which causes the inductor current to touch zero at only one point per period is called the "critical inductance." The critical inductance for a single-phase full-wave-rectified choke input filter is:

$$L_c = \frac{0.053 R_{\text{FL}}}{f} \tag{15.2}$$

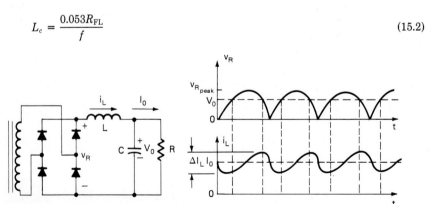

Figure 15.4 Choke input filter.

and for the three-phase line-to-line choke input filter is:

$$L_c = \frac{0.0015R_{FL}}{f} \tag{15.3}$$

where R_{FL} is the load resistance at full load and f is the line frequency in hertz. A good approach for designing the output filter is to find L_c and then select C based on the voltage attenuation required to achieve the desired output ripple. The values of L and C can be changed while keeping the same cutoff frequency until a combination is found which produces minimum overall filter size. The final value of L will generally be several times L_c. The larger value will decrease ripple current and also the voltage ripple caused by capacitor ESR (equivalent series resistance). The primary reflected current with a choke-input-type output filter has a square wave shape with a peak roughly equal to the reflected load current. Although the peak primary current is less than that in the capacitor input filter, the high-frequency spectral content is greater.

When a regulator follows the rectified (raw) direct current, the capacitor input filter has proven to be the most popular. The cost and size of the choke in a choke input filter makes it less desirable than the larger capacitor and slightly larger transformer of the capacitor input filter. Load regulation of an LC filter is good only as long as critical inductance loading is maintained.

When choosing the circuit for the regulator block shown in Fig. 15.1a, three approaches should be considered. They are: (1) unregulated, (2) linear-regulated, and (3) switching-regulated. The unregulated approach is least complex, least expensive, most efficient, and most reliable. Its major drawback, of course, is its lack of regulation. The output voltage is dependent on load and line variations. The unregulated supply is also susceptible to line ripple and transients. Even with these problems, it can be used for certain loads, such as relays. Another problem is that it may be too large. A regulator can be used to attenuate much of the ripple and take some of the filtering burden off the passive filter. A regulated supply can be smaller than its unregulated equivalent for a low ripple output. This is especially true when the power source is 60 Hz since the output filter is large, and significant decreases in size can be achieved with a regulator. However, when the source is three-phase, the unregulated approach is almost always the minimum size approach. This is because line-to-line rectified three-phase power requires little filtering. Even if regulation is not needed and size is not a problem, a regulator may be required to handle line transients and provide current-limiting protection.

There are two types of linear regulators used in SSB equipment. The shunt regulator shown in Fig. 15.5 is used primarily for loads requiring high voltage and low current [2, 3]. The shunt regulator works by sensing the output voltage and turning the shunt transistor on enough to cause the required voltage drop across R_s. If the output voltage begins to rise above the desired value, the error is sensed and base current to the transistor is increased, causing an increase in collector current. Increased collector cur-

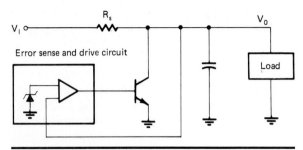

Figure 15.5 Shunt regulator.

rent causes an increased voltage drop across R_s which lowers V_0 to the desired value.

Notice that the shunt regulator is inherently protected against a load short-circuit condition. Another advantage of the shunt regulator is that the transistor drive circuit can consist of low-voltage components even with a high output voltage. A problem that usually prevents the shunt regulator from being used in high-power applications is its poor efficiency. For constant input and output voltages, the shunt regulator input current is constant. This means that if the load goes to a minimum-current condition, the shunt transistor must draw the excess current, which results in wasted power. The other type of linear regulator is the series regulator shown in Fig. 15.6 [4]. It is often used to provide output voltages from 5 to over 100 V at power levels of less than 1 to several hundred watts.

The series regulator maintains a constant output voltage by sensing it and comparing it with a reference in a negative-feedback control loop. The resulting error voltage determines the voltage drop across the series pass element Q_1. The control loop thus maintains an almost constant output voltage regardless of line and load changes.

The series regulator also provides active ripple filtering which reduces the passive filter size requirement and protects the load from potentially destructive line transients. A series regulator can include overcurrent protection which not only protects the series regulator, but protects the trans-

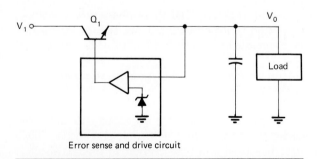

Figure 15.6 Series regulator.

former and rectifiers as well. At low power levels, series regulators are available in three-terminal TO-3 packages which require as few as two small external capacitors for noise rejection and stability. Some have external adjustments of the output voltage.

The major disadvantage of the series regulator is its high power dissipation. A typical design will require a minimum voltage drop of 3 V. The efficiency is approximately

$$\eta = \frac{P_{\text{out}}}{P_{\text{in}}} = \frac{V_0 I_0}{V_I I_I} \simeq \frac{V_0 I_0}{V_I I_0} \simeq \frac{V_0}{V_I} \tag{15.4}$$

Assuming the input voltage at the minimum ac line voltage condition is V_0 + 3 V, the efficiency will be $\eta = V_0/(V_0 + 3)$. The efficiency at the maximum ac line voltage condition is approximately

$$\eta = \frac{V_0}{(V_0 + 3)\,(V_{I,\text{max}}/V_{I,\text{min}})} \tag{15.5}$$

These equations show that the series regulator efficiency is better with higher output voltages and small variations in line voltage. For loads requiring relatively high output power, efficiency becomes critical in order to minimize internal system temperature.

Another type of series regulator which utilizes the active filtering benefit of the conventional series regulator, but maintains high efficiency, is the ripple regulator. It looks at V_I, the average or dc value of the regulator input voltage, and provides an output voltage which is a fixed drop from V_I, as shown in Fig. 15.7.

The ripple regulator is used primarily in high-power applications where very high efficiency, but not good regulation, is needed. It is often used in systems operating from a three-phase source. The output filter size and weight are minimized because of the excellent active filtering capability. Power dissipation is also minimized because of the low regulator voltage drop under all line voltage conditions. Heatsink size and weight are also

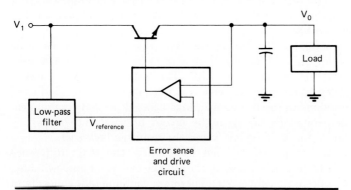

Figure 15.7 Ripple regulator.

reduced. In addition to the above benefits, the ripple regulator also provides: (1) protection of power supply from load overcurrent conditions, (2) fewer pass elements than the series regulator, (3) capability of removing the output voltage from the load, (4) load protection from input voltage transients.

In cases where high efficiency and good output voltage regulation are both required, a switching regulator is sometimes used in the converter illustrated in Fig. 15.1a. A disadvantage of the switching regulator is the EMI which is generated by the switching action; also, an increase in complexity and cost occurs. The improvement in efficiency allows less heatsink volume, thereby reducing overall power supply volume. If minimum size is the most critical requirement, however, the best approach is the off-line converter.

Off-line ac to dc converter

The off-line converter shown in Fig. 15.1b is an approach used when minimum power supply size and weight are crucial. Size and weight reduction are achieved primarily by eliminating the need for a line frequency power transformer. It has an EMI filter which is designed using the same considerations as in the conventional ac to dc converter. After passing through the EMI filter, the ac voltage is full-wave-rectified and filtered. The voltage at V_1 is dc (direct current) with superimposed line frequency ripple. The dc voltage is switched to provide the power transformer with an ac waveform v_p. Two of the more popular switching topologies are the half-bridge and the full bridge shown in Fig. 15.8. The most common switching frequencies have been 20 to 100 kHz. With high-voltage-power MOSFETs now readily available, switching frequencies up to 500 kHz are being used. By using a power transformer operating at over 20 kHz, transformer size and weight can be reduced to a small fraction of the size and weight required for a 60-Hz transformer [11]. The decrease when compared with that for a 400-Hz transformer is not as great, but is still quite significant. The output of the transformer is rectified and filtered. To achieve output regulation, the output voltage is sensed and an error signal is developed. Using pulse width modulation techniques (to be discussed in the next section), the switching transistors' "on" times are controlled in a manner that maintains constant output voltage. Methods other than pulse width modulation are possible, but will not be discussed here.

In addition to being smaller and lighter than the conventional ac to dc converter approach, the off-line converter is often more efficient. One disadvantage it has is that it can create EMI. The fast rise and fall times of switching frequency waveforms can cause a significant amount of conducted and radiated emissions in the frequency range utilized in SSB communications. Special care must be taken in the layout filtering and packaging. Another disadvantage is its complexity and the resulting high cost.

The requirement for source to load isolation is the main difference between the switching regulator used in the off-line converter and switching regulators used in dc to dc converters. Therefore fundamental concepts of

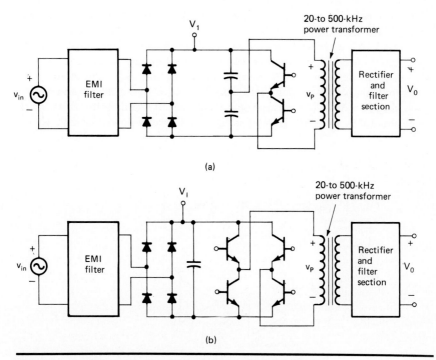

Figure 15.8 Off-line conversion: (*a*) half-bridge; (*b*) full bridge.

switching regulators discussed in the next section apply to off-line converters as well as to dc to dc converters.

DC to dc power conversion

DC to dc conversion is used in dc prime-power systems to provide an output that has the required ripple, regulation, and dc level. If the load can use the prime-power voltage level, but requires better ripple and transient characteristics, the conditioner can be as simple as a passive filter and a transient protection device. If the load requires a regulated voltage less than the source voltage, a linear regulator can be used. The use of linear regulators in dc to dc applications is limited to low-power applications because of its poor efficiency. An example would be a load requiring 5 Vdc at 10 A with a 29-Vdc power source, where the efficiency is only 18 percent. A switching regulator would provide an efficiency of 70 to 75 percent and a significant decrease in input power and heatsink area.

The basic idea behind any switching regulator is to convert the dc input power to ac and then level-shift, rectify, and filter to obtain the desired dc voltage [6, 12, 13]. Early types included the self-saturating transformer, the magnetic amplifier, and later the bang-bang controlled switching regulator.

The most popular technique in use today, however, is the fixed-frequency pulse-width-modulated switching regulator.

In order to understand the fundamental concepts involved in pulse-width-modulated switching regulators, the buck or stepdown converter shown in Fig. 15.9 will be examined. Voltage drops of the transistor and diode will be neglected in this discussion. The transistor Q_1 is switched on and off at a frequency $f_s = 1/T$. The ratio of on-time to period is called the "duty factor" α. While Q_1 is on, CR_1 is reverse-biased. Current flows through Q_1 and

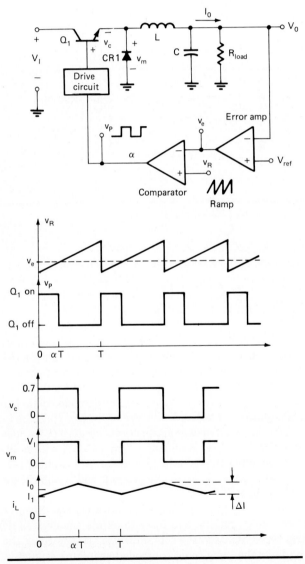

Figure 15.9 Stepdown converter.

through L to C and R_{load}. When Q_1 turns off, the voltage across L reverses and CR_1 becomes forward-biased, providing a path for inductor current. The relationships between duty factor, input voltage, and output voltage can be found by recalling that the average voltage across an inductor must be zero:

$$\frac{1}{T} \int_0^T V_L \, dt = 0$$

$$\frac{1}{T} \int_0^{\alpha T} (V_I - V_0) \, dt + \frac{1}{T} \int_{\alpha T}^T (-V_0) \, dt = 0 \tag{15.6}$$

$$(V_I - V_0)\alpha + (-V_0)(1 - \alpha) = 0$$

$$V_0 = \alpha V_I \tag{15.7}$$

This last equation shows that the stepdown converter produces an output voltage that is the input voltage times the duty factor. The preceding discussion assumes that i_L is always greater than zero, so that there are only two switch states. In practice, the circuit is designed so that i_L never reaches zero in normal operation by making L large enough. The i_L ramps up during transistor on-time and ramps down during off-time. The peak-to-peak amplitude of i_L is

$$\Delta I = \frac{1}{L} \int_0^{\alpha T} (V_I - V_0) \, dt = \frac{(V_I - V_0)\alpha T}{L} = \frac{(V_0/\alpha - V_0)\alpha}{Lf_s}$$

$$= \frac{V_0(1 - \alpha)}{Lf_s} \tag{15.8}$$

This equation shows that the peak-to-peak i_L does not depend on the I_0. If I_0 decreases, the average inductor current decreases but the peak-to-peak value remains constant. If I_0 continues to decrease, the value of I_1 will eventually become zero. Further decreases in I_0 will cause discontinuous inductor current. At the point where I_1 equals zero, the load current is

$$I_0 = \frac{1}{2} \Delta I$$

$$= \frac{V_0(1 - \alpha)}{2Lf_s} \tag{15.9}$$

Since V_0/I_0 is the load resistance,

$$L_c = \frac{R_{\text{load}}(1 - \alpha)}{2f_s} \tag{15.10}$$

where L_c is the critical inductance. This provides a minimum value for inductance. The capacitor is chosen so that the LC filter provides enough attenuation of the AC component of v_m to meet the output voltage ripple required.

Using the fact that the LC filter will provide 40 dB per decade of atten uation at frequencies above its resonant point, an LC filter resonant frequency of $1/\sqrt{L_c C}$ can be selected. The required C can then be chosen.

This approach will yield a filter whose volume is not minimum. The minimum-volume filter will have equal L and C volumes. By increasing L above L_c and decreasing C, while maintaining the desired resonant frequency, an optimum combination of L and C which produces a minimum-volume filter can be found. Using this approach, the value of L usually turns out to be more than 5 times the value of L_c.

The basic method by which the pulse-width-modulated control signal is generated is shown in Fig. 15.9. The regulator output voltage goes to the inverting input of an error amplifier stage and the noninverting input is given a reference voltage. The resulting error voltage V_e is compared to a sawtooth waveform operating at the switching frequency, f_s. The comparator output is high until the ramp voltage equals the reference voltage, at which time the comparator goes low. The logic and transistor drive circuits provide a transistor drive signal which turns the transistor on during the time the comparator output is high. If the output voltage begins to drop, the error voltage will increase because of the negative feedback. The increased error voltage will cause the duty factor from the comparator output to increase. Increased duty factor causes increased output voltage, resulting in the output voltage returning to its proper value.

The stability of the power supply is evaluated by calculating the open-loop transfer function around the loop. The circuit can be divided into three gain blocks $G_1(S)$, $G_2(S)$, and $G_3(S)$ corresponding to $V_0(S)/\alpha(S)$, $V_e(S)/V_0(S)$, and $\alpha(S)/V_e(S)$. The product $G_1(S)G_2(S)G_3(S)$ is the open-loop gain. $G_3(S)$ is the transfer function relating the duty factor to the error voltage, which is the ratio of the duty factor range to the corresponding error voltage range which is constant over frequency. That is, $G_3(S) = K_1$. $G_2(S)$ is the error amplifier gain. Normally a compensation circuit will be included in the error amplifier. The transfer function of the error amplifier and compensation circuit is $G_2(S)$. An analysis of the power circuit transfer function $G_1(S)$ is beyond the scope of this book. However, several good sources of information on this subject exist [22, 24]. For the stepdown converter shown in Fig. 15.9 the transfer function $V_0(S)/\alpha(S)$ is

$$G_1(S) = \frac{V_0(S)}{\alpha(S)} = \frac{V_I}{1 + 2(\delta_0/\omega_0)S + S^2/\omega_0^2} \tag{15.11}$$

where $\omega_0 = \dfrac{1}{\sqrt{LC}}$

$$\delta_0 = \frac{1}{2R_{\text{load}}} \sqrt{\frac{L}{C}}$$

Once the open-loop gain is known, Bode plots can be made and the proper compensation can be found.

There are two other basic voltage converters in addition to the stepdown, as shown in Table 15.1. That table indicates that the output voltage of the buck regulator is always less than the input voltage, the output voltage of the boost regulator is always greater than the input voltage, and the output voltage of the buck-boost has a polarity reversal and an amplitude which can

TABLE 15.1 Basic Voltage Converter Properties

Circuit	Topology name	Voltage transfer ratio	Critical inductance	$\dfrac{V_0(S)}{\alpha(S)}$
	Buck or stepdown	$\dfrac{V_0}{V_I} = \alpha$	$L_c = \dfrac{R_L(1-\alpha)}{2f_s}$	$\dfrac{V_0(S)}{\alpha(S)} = \dfrac{V_I}{1 + 2(\delta_0/\omega_0)S + S^2/\omega_0^2}$ $\delta_0 = \dfrac{1}{2R_L}\sqrt{\dfrac{L}{C}}$ $\omega_0 = \dfrac{1}{\sqrt{LC}}$
	Boost or step-up	$\dfrac{V_0}{V_I} = \dfrac{1}{1-\alpha}$	$L_c = \dfrac{\alpha(1-\alpha)^2 R_L}{2f_s}$	$\dfrac{V_0(S)}{\alpha(S)} = \dfrac{V_I(1 - S/z)}{(1-\alpha_0)^2\,[1 + 2(\delta_0/\omega_0)S + S^2/\omega_0^2]}$ $z = \dfrac{\omega_0}{2\delta_0}$ $\delta_0 = \dfrac{1}{(1-\alpha_0)2R_L}\sqrt{\dfrac{L}{C}}$ $\omega_0 = \dfrac{1-\alpha_0}{\sqrt{LC}}$
	Buck-boost or flyback	$\dfrac{V_0}{V_I} = \dfrac{\alpha}{1-\alpha}$	$L_c = \dfrac{R_L(1-\alpha)^2}{2f_s}$	$\dfrac{V_0(S)}{\alpha(S)} = \dfrac{V_I(1 - S/z)}{(1-\alpha_0)^2\,[1 + 2\,(\delta_0/\omega_0)S + S^2/\omega_0^2]}$ $z = \dfrac{\omega_0}{2\alpha_0\delta_0}$ $\delta_0 = \dfrac{1}{(1-\alpha_0)2R_L}\sqrt{\dfrac{L}{C}}$ $\omega_0 = \dfrac{1-\alpha_0}{\sqrt{LC}}$

NOTE: α_0 is the operating duty factor.

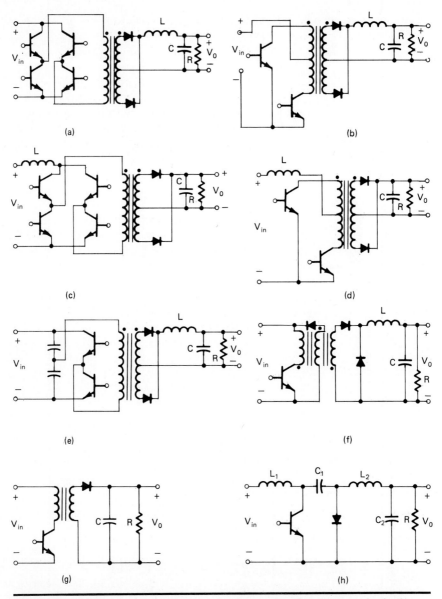

Figure 15.10 PWM converter topologies: (*a*) voltage-fed bridge reduces to buck; (*b*) voltage-fed center tap reduces to buck; (*c*) current-fed bridge reduces to boost; (*d*) current-fed center tap reduces to boost; (*e*) half-bridge reduces to buck; (*f*) forward reduces to buck; (*g*) flyback, transformer-coupled, reduces to flyback; (*h*) Cuk reduces to a current converter.

be greater than or less than the input. Also, from the table, the power stage transfer function for the boost and buck-boost topologies has a right-half-plane zero and the location of the zero is dependent on the dc operating point.

The fact that the right-half-plane zero can move with the operating point makes the boost and buck-boost topologies very difficult to compensate. The normal approach is to add a low-frequency pole so that the open-loop gain is -10 dB or less at the lowest resonant frequency, ω_0. This normally results in a low-unity-gain crossover frequency and can result in an insufficient line and load transient response and ripple rejection characteristics.

The discussion to this point has dealt with single-loop control only. One method of improving the boost and buck-boost bandwidth is to use a type of two-loop control called "current-injected control" in which the switch current information is fed back to the control circuit in addition to output voltage feedback [7, 14]. This type of circuit can be designed so that the right-half-plane zero is moved into the left half-plane. The boost and buck-boost converter can then be designed with bandwidths on the same order as the buck converter.

The three topologies shown in Table 15.1 are the basis for most of the converter topologies in use today. Figure 15.10 shows several different dc to dc converter topologies and gives the basic topology to which it reduces. One topology that is in use today and does not reduce to one of the three basic voltage converters is the Cuk converter. This is because the basic Cuk converter is a current converter rather than a voltage converter.

REFERENCES

1. Noel Malcolm Morris, *Industrial Electronics*, McGraw-Hill, New York, 1978.
2. Eugene R. Hnatek, *Design Solid State PS*, Van Nostrand Reinhold, New York, 1980.
3. L. Giocoletto (ed.), *Electronics Designers Handbook*, McGraw-Hill, New York, 1977.
4. Barry Davis, *Understanding DC Power Supplies*, Prentice-Hall, Englewood Cliffs, NJ, 1981.
5. *Standard Products Catalog*, EG and G Wakefield Engineering, Wakefield, MA, 1985.
6. Abraham Pressman, *Switching and Linear PS*, Hayden, Rochelle Park, NJ, 1977.
7. F. C. Lee and R. A. Carter, "Investigations of Stability and Dynamic Performances of Switching Regulators Employing Current-Injected Control," in *Proc. 1981 Power Electronics Specialists Conference*, Boulder, CO, June 29–July 3, 1981, pp. 3–16.
8. Jeffrey D. Shepard, *Power Supplies*, Reston Publishing, Reston, VA, 1984.
9. Samir K. Datta, *Power Electronics and Controls*, Reston Publishing, Reston, VA, 1985.
10. Reuben Lee, *Electronic Transformers and Circuits*, John Wiley & Sons, New York, 1975.
11. Nathan R. Grossner, *Transformers*, McGraw-Hill, New York, 1967.
12. Peter Wood, *Switching Power Converters*, Van Nostrand Reinhold, New York, 1981.
13. George Chryssis, *HF Switching PS*, McGraw-Hill, New York, 1984.
14. D. M. Mitchell, "An Analytical Investigation of Current Injected Control-Frequency Switching Regulators," in *Proc. 1985 Power Electronics Specialists Conference*, Toulouse, France, June 24–28, 1985.
15. George J. Angerbauer, *PS Modern Communication*, Prentice-Hall, Englewood Cliffs, NJ, 1974.
16. Walter H. Bucksbaum, *Handbook Practical Electrical Reference*, Prentice-Hall, Englewood Cliffs, NJ, 1978.
17. Colonel William McLyman, *Transformer and Inductor Design Handbook*, Marcel Dekker, New York, 1978.
18. ITT, *Reference Data for Radio Engineers*, Howard W. Sams, Indianapolis, 1975; U.S. Dept. of Commerce, *Electric Current Abroad*, U.S. Government Printing Office, Washington, D.C, 1975.

19. Johannes Schaefer, *Rectifier Circuits: Theory and Design,* John Wiley & Sons, New York, 1965.
20. A. C. Franklin, *J and P Transformer Book,* Butterworths, Stoneham, MA, 1983.
21. Irving M. Gottlieb, *Regulated Power Supplies,* 3d ed., Howard W. Sams, Indianapolis, 1981.
22. Kit Sum, *Switch Mode Power Conversion: Theory, Design,* Marcel Dekker, New York, 1984.
23. B. M. Bird and K. G. King, *An Introduction to Power Electronics,* John Wiley & Sons, New York, 1983.
24. R. D. Middlebrook and Slobodan Cuk, "General Unified Approach to Modelling Switching-Converter Power Stage," in *Proc. 1976 Power Electronics Specialists Conference,* Cleveland, June 8–10, 1976, pp. 18–31.
25. E. E. Von Zastrow, "Capacitor Input Filter Design," General Electric Appl. 200.30, General Electric, Syracuse, NY, 1963.
26. J. P. Stringham, "Go Graphic with Capacitor Input Filters," *Electron. Des.,* vol. 12, June 7, 1969, pp. 106–109.
27. D. M. Mitchell, "Choke-Input Filters for PS Ripple Reduction," Rockwell International Working Paper WP79-2039, February 20, 1979.

16

Antenna Matching Techniques

Richard C. Edwards *(Section 16.2)*
Glenn R. Snider *(Section 16.1)*

The role of the antenna coupler is to provide an impedance matching function in either of two ways: narrowband or broadband. With narrowband matching a near perfect impedance match is achieved at a single frequency. With broadband matching a less than perfect impedance match is achieved over a broad range of frequencies.

Section 16.1 will present the current techniques used for narrowband antenna couplers. Included is the basic approach to be followed, some of the pitfalls, and general engineering advice. It is assumed that the reader has a computer at his or her disposal. Section 16.2 considers broadband matching of antennas in applications where it is advantageous.

16.1 Narrowband Antenna Couplers

The discussion of narrowband couplers will be subdivided into three topics: R/X plane, two examples, and control techniques. The R/X plane is a very useful graphical representation of how individual RF elements affect the input impedance of a coupler. By visualizing the loci of points on a graph with axes of real and imaginary impedances, one can determine which RF network to choose, as well as how to automatically position the elements to the tune point. Two antenna coupler designs, shunt and whip, will demonstrate the practical application of the R/X plane graph and provide general information for the construction and specification of the RF elements. The last subdivision will deal with impedance measuring devices and the methods used to automatically control the RF tuning elements.

R/X plane

The first problem the engineer faces is, "What RF element configuration best suits the required specifications?" To make this decision, the antenna impedance can be plotted on the R/X plane. Then, by knowing how different types of RF elements, when combined with the antenna impedance, affect the resulting input impedance, logical decisions can be made. Smith has treated this in great detail (Ref. 1). The R/X plane is so important in the design of couplers that some of the basic concepts will be repeated here.

Consider the circuit shown in Fig. 16.1a, a series circuit consisting of C, L, and R. The input impedance is the vector sum of all the components. When one of the reactive elements is varied, the magnitude of input impedance always falls on a straight line passing through the real axis at R_s. Increasing the inductive component moves the input impedance upward in an inductive direction. Increasing the capacitive component moves the input impedance downward in a capacitive direction.

If the desired input were equal to R_s and the antenna impedance were equal to $R_s + j\omega L_s$, the antenna coupler would consist of a series capacitor of reactance $-j\omega L_s$. To summarize, impedance in series with an antenna translates the input impedance along a line of constant real value.

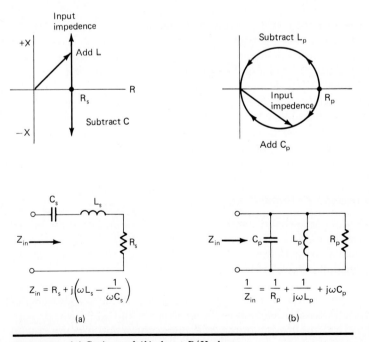

Figure 16.1   (a) Series and (b) shunt R/X plane.

Figure 16.1b shows the dual of Fig. 16.1a. The circuit consists of a parallel C, L, and R. Smith has shown that when one of the reactive elements is varied the magnitude of input impedance always falls on a circle of radius $R_p/2$ and center located on the real axis. Decreasing the inductive impedance moves the magnitude of input impedance in a counterclockwise direction. Decreasing the capacitive impedance moves the magnitude of input impedance in a clockwise direction. To illustrate, if the desired input impedance were R_p and the antenna impedance were $1/(1/R_p + j\omega C_p)$, the antenna coupler would consist of a shunt inductor of impedance $1/(-j\omega C_p)$.

Since antenna impedances are more complicated than the above examples, couplers rarely consist of a single element. It can be shown that with two RF tuning elements any complex impedance can be transformed to a desired resistive impedance. The series and shunt circuits shown in Fig. 16.1 can be combined to form a two-element network. Eight possible combinations of two elements are available, of which two will be discussed. The first consists of an input series C followed by an L in shunt with the antenna. The second consists of an input series C followed by a C in shunt with the antenna. These circuits will be developed on the R/X plane to show how each can be used to transform the antenna impedance to a desired resistive input value. In each case certain impedances cannot be transformed. These areas (no tune) must be avoided either by choosing a different network or by changing the antenna impedance.

Figure 16.2 is the R/X plane of a general-purpose antenna coupler. That

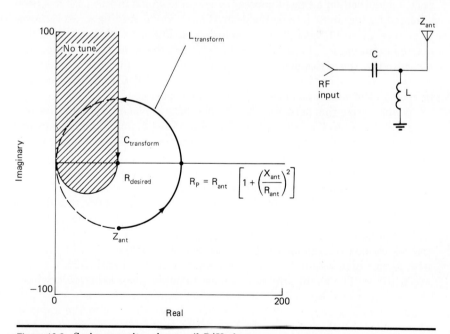

Figure 16.2 Series capacitor shunt coil R/X plane.

is, the circuit formed by the input C and shunt L can transform the maximum area on the R/X plane to the desired input impedance. The load is the antenna impedance, and the shunt L is closest to the load. Referring to Fig. 16.1b, the load impedance can then be modified by the L. If a very large L is present, the load will be modified very slightly in a circular counterclockwise direction. If the shunt L is near zero, the load impedance will be modified greatly in the same circular direction almost to the origin. The proper value of shunt L is one that places the modified load impedance at a value that has the desired real component and a highly inductive component. The reason for this will soon become apparent. From Fig. 16.1b, the diameter of the circle on which the transformation takes place is the parallel equivalent resistance of the load. The familiar equation $R_p = R_{ant} [1+(X_{ant}/R_{ant})^2]$ can be used to find this from the antenna impedance. Take note, the R_p of the antenna must be greater than the desired input impedance. If this is not the case, it is not possible to use this network for the antenna coupler. Because of the circular motion, a shunt element can only transform the real component of input impedance in the range of zero to R_p. Also note that if the antenna impedance is inductive, the antenna resistance must be greater than the desired transformed resistance. If this is not the case, rotation in a clockwise direction is required. This is not possible with a shunt inductor. These two conditions form the no-tune region on the R/X plane shown in Fig. 16.2.

The transformation by the shunt L has placed the modified load impedance at the desired real value. All that remains is to treat this modified load impedance as a new load for the series C. From Fig. 16.1a the load impedance is modified on a line of constant real value which in this case has been adjusted by the shunt L to be the desired input value. Adding series C causes the cancellation of the inductive component. The network is tuned to the desired input value. The shunt L could have left the transformed impedance presented to the series element at the desired real value with a capacitive reactive component. However, this requires a series L to reach the tune point, and the circuit has been equipped with a series C.

To summarize this network, the shunt L acts to "load" the input impedance and the series C acts to "phase" the input impedance. "Loading" means adjusting the real component of input impedance to the desired value. "Phasing" means adjusting the reactive component to zero.

The second circuit to be presented on the R/X plane consists of a series C and a C in shunt with the antenna. As can be seen from Fig. 16.3, this network transforms a very limited amount of load impedance to a desired real value. Since it is comprised of capacitors, the efficiency is very high for a given volume. Typically, antenna couplers use vacuum or ceramic capacitors which have quality factors Q in the range from 2000 to 5000. An inductor with Q this high requires such a large volume that is impractical for most applications. The shunt antenna coupler example given below will demonstrate the use of this circuit for a unique antenna type.

On the R/X plane, the shunt C is the nearest element to the antenna. From Fig. 16.1b, the load must be rotated clockwise on an R_p circle. As with

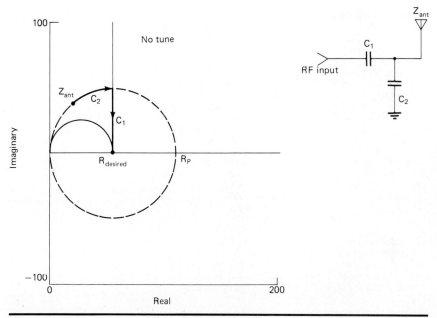

Figure 16.3 Series capacitor shunt capacitor R/X plane.

the first circuit, the clockwise rotation crosses the desired real line in two places. Since the phasing element is a series C, the correct transformation leaves the modified load impedance inductive. This determines one limit for the antenna impedance. The impedance to be tuned must be inductive and have a real value less than the desired input impedance. A second limit can be seen from Fig. 16.3. The parallel equivalent resistance R_p of the antenna must be greater than the desired input impedance. Once the antenna has been loaded, the series C can be used to adjust phase, completing the tune. To avoid some confusion, remember that regardless of which type of shunt element is used, the extent of rotation is limited to the origin. In this case, if the antenna impedance were greater than the desired value, the clockwise rotation would first cross the desired real value with a capacitive reactive component and stop at the origin. A second real value crossing is not possible. This circuit cannot tune antenna impedances which allow only one crossover point.

The previous discussion should allow one to analyze the remaining six possible combinations of two RF elements. For convenience all eight circuits are summarized in Fig. 16.4. The no-tune regions and element transformations on the R/X plane are shown there. This tabulation is a handy reference for the designer, since most antenna impedance-vs.-frequency characteristics require more than one network configuration. In addition, for all antenna impedances there are two possible RF configurations for tuning.

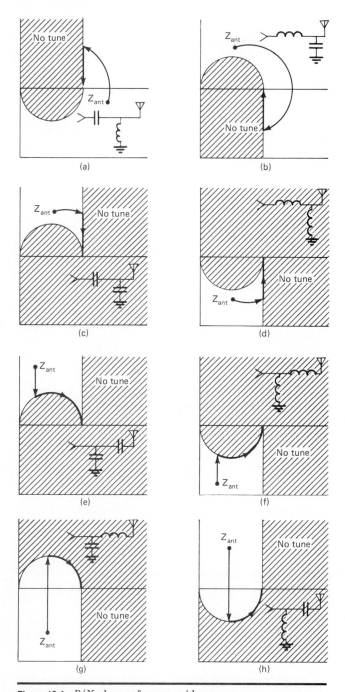

Figure 16.4 R/X plane reference guide.

Example shunt antenna coupler

Figure 16.5 is an R/X plot of an aircraft shunt antenna impedance. For this example the desired real input impedance is 50 ohms. By inspection of the graph the impedance covers all regions of the R/X plane with the exception of a circle with diameter of 50 ohms. The conclusion is drawn that to tune the antenna across the entire frequency range more than one RF network will be required. The configurations shown in Figs. 16.2 and 16.3 are chosen.

To make the proper choice for the network, more information is needed. The coupler is to be designed with the maximum possible RF efficiency in the low-frequency range. This is necessary since aircraft shunt antennas are poor radiators in that frequency range. Another fact that is extremely important for aircraft design is that the coupler be as small as possible. Usually, aircraft couplers are mounted at the antenna, which is located in the wing or vertical stabilizer where space is at a premium. Examination of vacuum capacitor specifications indicate that Qs of 3000 are readily attainable in compact volumes [100 in^3 (1639 cm^3)]. Inductor volume can be estimated with good accuracy using helical resonator techniques (Ref. 2). Calculate as follows:

$$Q = 60\ S\ \sqrt{F_{MHz}}$$

$$S = \frac{Q}{60\ \sqrt{F_{MHz}}}$$

$$V = 2S^3$$

for

$$Q = 3000 \quad \text{and} \quad F_{MHz} = 2$$
$$V = 88388\ \text{in}^3\ (1{,}448{,}419\ \text{cm}^3)$$

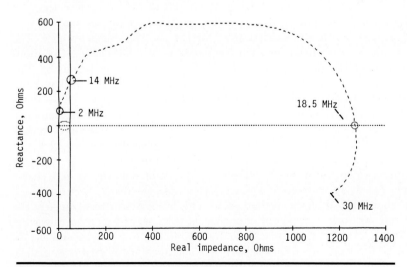

Figure 16.5 Aircraft shunt antenna impedance.

where Q = quality factor
$\quad\quad S$ = length of side of a square coil cavity, in
$\quad F_{\text{MHz}}$ = tune frequency, in MHz
$\quad\quad V$ = the required volume, in^3

From the calculation of inductor volume it is obvious that the coupler should consist entirely of vacuum capacitors for minimum size and maximum efficiency. The two all-capacitor networks shown in Fig. 16.4 will tune the 2- to 10-MHz range. Since the antenna impedance is very small, its current is very high. The design can be improved if the series capacitor is not placed directly in series with the antenna. If this were done, both of the capacitors would be required to carry high current. Placing the shunt capacitor directly at the antenna requires only the shunt capacitor to carry high current. The series capacitor then carries the smaller 50-ohm input current. The circuit of choice for the low-frequency range is shown in Fig. 16.3. Such a circuit has been computer-analyzed and with 1000 W of input power the shunt capacitor current is greater than 50 A. The series capacitor current is less than 10 A, and the circuit efficiency is greater than 80 percent.

Referring to Fig. 16.5 again, the antenna impedance in the 10- to 30-MHz range falls into the tune range of the circuit shown in Fig. 16.2. This has a series capacitor and an inductor in shunt with the antenna. The frequency range could be divided into two segments using two RF networks. However, to minimize size and complexity, this was not done. Since the low-band RF network has a series capacitor, it can be converted to the high-band network by replacing the shunt capacitor with a shunt coil. Fortunately the antenna in the high-frequency range has better radiation efficiency and, as a result, the antenna Q becomes smaller as frequency increases. This means that the Q of the shunt inductor can be lowered and still maintain reasonable efficiency as well as radiated power. A variable inductor with a Q greater than 100 can be constructed in a volume of 125 in^3 (2048 cm^3). Computer analysis indicates with this Q the efficiency will be greater than 60 percent.

Figure 16.6 shows the configuration for the shunt antenna coupler. The R/X plane is also shown for each frequency range. Notice that the shunt inductor is switched out of the circuit but the shunt capacitor is not. The reason for this can be found from the tuning algorithm. The low band requires the shunt inductor to be switched out of the circuit. The shunt capacitor is varied to cause impedance rotation in a clockwise direction until the 50-ohm line is reached. The series capacitor is varied to cause resonance. However, in the high band the shunt capacitor is placed at minimum capacity and left in the circuit. This results in minimum effect on the antenna impedance. The shunt coil is placed in the circuit and varied in a coarse manner to cause a counterclockwise rotation until the resulting real value of impedance is less than the desired value. This is within the tune range of the low-band network. The shunt capacitor is then servo-tuned to cause the reverse clockwise rotation to achieve the desired value of real impedance. To complete the tune, the series capacitor is again servo-tuned to resonance. The decision at which frequency to switch in the shunt coil has been ren-

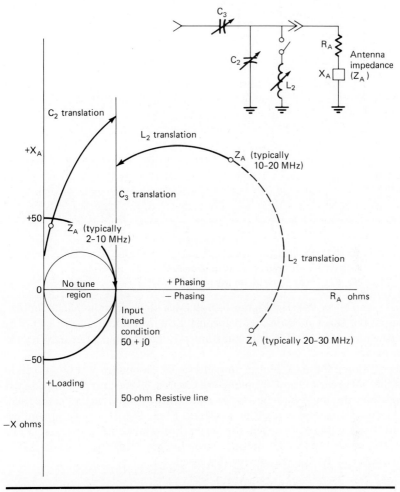

Figure 16.6 Shunt antenna coupler. *Note;* C_3 translates impedance on a resistive line (vertical). C_2 or L_2 translates impedance on a circle, as shown.

dered less critical. In fact, the control logic can make this, based on greater than 50-ohm real and inductive antenna impedance. This technique eliminates one servo system and one high-current switch from the coupler.

Example of a high-power whip coupler

To further illustrate the techniques used for couplers, assume that the antenna to be matched over the 2- to 30-MHz range is a 35-ft (10.67-m) whip. This impedance vs. frequency is shown in Fig. 16.7. The input power to the network is 20,000 W and the desired input impedance is 50 ohms. The network will be subdivided into three configurations covering 2 to 4 MHz, 4 to

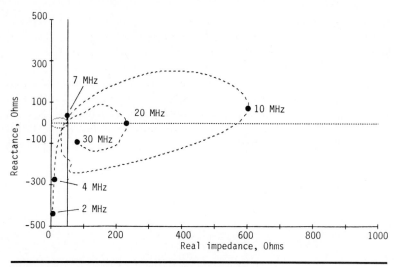

Figure 16.7   35-ft (10.67-m) whip antenna impedance.

20 MHz, and 20 to 30 MHz. Figure 16.8 shows a block diagram of the coupler. It consists of three modules: transformer, L network, and output coil. The factors which lead to this configuration are determined primarily by the input power.

Inspection of the R/X plot of impedance vs. frequency in Fig. 16.7 indicates that all areas of the R/X plane are covered by the antenna impedance. In addition, the low-frequency range contains a highly reactive component which requires special voltage precautions. From Fig. 16.4, several configurations are necessary to reach the desired 50-ohm tune point across the entire frequency range. The circuits shown in Figs. 16.4f and a are used. The three frequency bands will now be discussed.

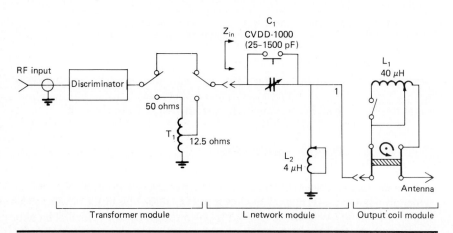

Figure 16.8   Block diagram, 35-ft (10.67-m) whip antenna coupler.

Three frequency bands

Band 1 (2 to 4 MHz). The antenna impedance in this range can be tuned by the circuits shown in Figs. 16.4a, d, f, and g. To help eliminate some of the possibilities, consider that with 20,000 W of RF power the antenna voltage will be extremely high when the reactive component is large. In this case antenna voltages up to 70,000 V are possible. This can be estimated by assuming that all the input power is dissipated in the antenna resistance. A current can then be found which flows into the antenna terminal. From this the antenna voltage can be calculated:

$$V_{peak} = \left| Z_{ant} \right| \sqrt{\frac{2P}{R_{ant}}}$$

$$= 400 \sqrt{\frac{2(20,000)}{1.31}} = 70,000 \text{ V}$$

Clearly the circuits shown in Figs. 16.4a and d can be eliminated since these have a common node at the antenna terminal which requires each of the elements to stand off most of the antenna voltage. The circuit shown in Fig. 16.4g may be the best choice if this is the only frequency range to be tuned. The use of a vacuum capacitor results in a more efficient design. However, to tune the remaining frequency ranges, the general-purpose network of circuit shown in Fig. 16.4a is required. This circuit has a shunt coil, and if the circuit shown in Fig. 16.4f is chosen for band 1, the shunt coil can be reused.

Tuning the chosen network is accomplished by translating the antenna impedance to a 50-ohm R_p circle using the series load coil and then phasing the remaining reactance using the shunt coil. As can be seen from the R/X plane, this network has a limited tuning region and is chosen to prevent extreme high voltage on more than one element. The lossless design equations are presented to aid in estimating coil sizes before a full-scale computer analysis is undertaken.

Shunt coil reactance:

$$X_2 = \sqrt{\frac{2500}{50 - R_{ant}}}$$

Series coil reactance:

$$X_1 = X_{ant} - \sqrt{-R_{ant}^2 + 50R_{ant}}$$

Band 2 (4 to 20 MHz). For 4 to 20 MHz, the series load coil used in band 1 is switched out. The shunt coil is now located at the antenna and becomes the loading element. To make the network tune all of the impedances, the general tuning circuit shown in Fig. 16.4a is chosen. The circuit shown in Fig. 16.4b would make an equally good network if it were not for the existing shunt coil availability from band 1.

Tuning is accomplished by matching the antenna to 12.5 ohms and then using a transformer to step up to 50 ohms. A capacitor in series with the antenna would make it possible to tune directly to 50 ohms. This capacitor can be positioned so that the no-tune areas can be avoided. The control logic required is complicated and to keep it simple a transformer which requires no tuning algorithm is used. The lossless ladder network design equations are as follows.

Shunt coil reactance:

$$X_2 = \frac{-X_{ant} - R_{ant} \sqrt{R_{ant}\left(\dfrac{Q_{ant}^2 + 1}{R_I}\right) - 1}}{1 - R_{ant}/R_I}$$

Series capacitor reactance:

$$X_{C1} = \sqrt{R_p R_I - R_I^2}$$

where $Q_{ant} = \dfrac{X_{ant}}{R_{ant}}$

R_p = parallel equivalent antenna resistance
R_I = desired input tune impedance

Band 3 (20 to 30 MHz).   The tuning network used for band 3 is the same as for band 2 except that the transformer is switched out of the circuit. The antenna will fall in the tune region of 50 ohms. The important design parameter is the minimum value of the series C. If the maximum parallel equivalent resistance of the antenna is less than 900 ohms at 30 MHz, the value calculated from the above equation is:

$$X_{C1} = \sqrt{(900)(50) - 2500} = 206$$
$$C_1 = 25.7 \text{ pF}$$

The reader may ask, "Why not tune to 12.5 ohms in band 3 as was done in band 2?" The answer lies in the required values of L and C. Tuning to 12.5 ohms requires a very small shunt L and a very large series C. By removing the transformer, the required range of inductance and capacitance is reduced. The exact reduction is of course determined by the frequency at which the transformer is switched out of the circuit.

Control techniques.   Once the RF network has been chosen which meets the requirements, the problem remains to automatically control the element values to achieve a match at all frequencies. This can be done either with digital or analog control circuitry. Both types require some way to know where, on the R/X plane, the transformed antenna impedance is located. The centerpiece of all control schemes is the impedance measuring device. This section will focus primarily on two types. The first is the low-cost conventional HF discriminator which has been used for many years. The second is a tracking impedance measuring system (TIMS) Ref. 3).

The HF discriminator is usually used as part of an analog tuning system. This consists of continuously variable RF elements, analog servo amplifiers, an HF discriminator, and logic to turn the servos on and off. The discriminator provides two variable-dc-voltage output error signals. The phasing output is proportional to the reactive component of impedance. A positive voltage indicates inductive and a negative voltage indicates capacitive. The loading output is a voltage proportional to the magnitude of impedance, and positive indicates an impedance magnitude greater than the desired input value and a negative voltage indicates less. When both outputs are zero, a tune condition exists.

The TIMS is usually used as part of digital tuning system. This system consists of digital variable RF elements, TIMS, and a computer. The TIMS provides an accurate digital representation of the impedance being measured. This allows complicated mathematical network computation to be done by the computer. Direct setting of the digital RF elements is possible without the time-consuming servo tuning associated with the HF discriminator.

Figure 16.9 is a simplified schematic diagram of a loading/phasing discriminator. The loading portion consists of a current sample (T_1) and a voltage sample (C_1, C_2). The current sample formed by T_1 coupling to the RF line produces a voltage across R_1 which is directly proportional to the line current. This voltage is peak-detected by CR_1 and capacitor C_3. The voltage

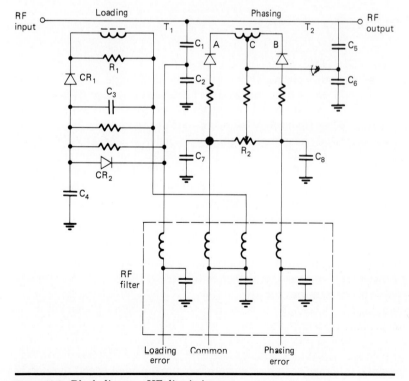

Figure 16.9 Block diagram, HF discriminator.

sample formed by C_1 and C_2 produces a voltage which is proportional to the line voltage. This voltage sample is peak-detected by CR_2 and C_4. Operation of the loading error detector is such that the output error voltage at the cathode of CR_2 is the sum of the two dc peak-detected sample voltages. The sample voltages are chosen to be exactly equal in magnitude and opposite in polarity when the impedance on the RF line is equal to the desired value. When the RF impedance is less than the desired value, the current-sample detected dc voltage increases and the voltage-sample detected dc voltage decreases. This produces a net potential difference on the loading error output. In the circuit shown a negative error signal is produced. When the impedance is greater than the desired value, the exact inverse occurs. Note that zero error signal occurs when the magnitude of the line impedance equals the magnitude of the desired value, not of the real component. This circuit is an impedance magnitude detector.

The phasing circuit is formed by current samples (T_2A, T_2B) and voltage samples (C_5, C_6). With respect to the center tap of T_2, two voltages are produced which are 180° out of phase with each other and 90° out of phase with the line current. The phase shift with the line current is a result of very light loading of the transformer. The transformer center tap is then connected to the voltage sample. This causes the RF voltage at points A and B to be the vector sum of the voltage sample and the respective current samples:

$$V_a = KI\underline{/+90 + \theta} + K_1 V\underline{/0}$$
$$V_b = KI\underline{/-90 + \theta} + K_1 V\underline{/0}$$

where K and K_1 are sample ratio constants, I is the line current, V is the line voltage, and θ is the phase angle between I and V.

When the impedance on the RF line is at zero phase angle, the line voltage and current are in phase (θ equals zero). This means the magnitudes of the sample circuit voltages are equal. When the phase angle of the line impedance is positive (θ less than zero), the magnitude of voltage V_b is greater than voltage V_a. When the phase angle of the line impedance is negative (θ greater than zero), the magnitude of V_a is greater than V_b. The circuit then compares the magnitudes of each of the voltage sums. This is done by peak detection using the respective diodes and capacitors. DC voltage comparison is accomplished by resistor R_2. The output phasing error signal is the voltage across R_2. A positive impedance phase angle results in a positive error signal and a negative angle in a negative error signal. Zero phase angle results in zero error.

The control circuitry which makes use of the loading and phasing discriminator consists of zero crossover detectors to convert the analog error signals to digital. This determines the area on the R/X plane where the impedance is located. Logical decisions can then be made as to which RF element must be changed. The discriminator can be used with either analog or digital elements. In the case of analog elements, the error voltages are fed to a servo motor which changes the variable capacitor or inductor. When used with digital elements, a binary search or some other type of high-speed method is used to position the elements to the correct values. When compared to the TIMS, the loading/phasing discriminator is best suited to analog applications. It does not accurately represent impedances at any other points than zero phasing or zero loading. It is not possible to take full advantage of the speed of digital RF technology without accurate magnitude and phase information.

The detailed design of the TIMS is not within the scope of this chapter; however, an overview will be given here. The TIMS is a true impedance measuring device providing very accurate measurement of the magnitude and phase angle of the voltage coefficient. These measurements are performed under normal operating RF power levels. Figure 16.10 shows the system in block diagram. The basic sensor is a dual directional coupler. The directional coupler has RF outputs proportional to the forward and reflected voltage at its location in the RF path. A shorting switch is provided to calibrate the system and establish the measurement point. Generally the directional coupler is located near the RF elements. A short coax connects the shorting relay to the directional coupler. Thus, precise location of the measuring point can be accomplished. The remainder of the circuitry determines the phase difference between forward and reflected wave fronts and determines the ratio of reflected to forward voltage. Recall from basic transmission line theory that the ratio of forward to reflected voltage is the magnitude of the reflection coefficient, and the phase difference is the phase angle of the reflection coefficient.

To accurately measure the reflection coefficient, the forward and reflected samples are mixed down to a standard IF frequency of 100 kHz. This is accomplished by using two matched receiver circuits with the IF injection frequency derived directly from the RF input. The downconverted samples are then fed into a phase detector and a ratio detector and converted to dc output samples. The dc outputs are then simultaneously stored in sample and hold devices to be processed by the digital circuitry. The digital circuits convert the analog samples to 12-bit information via the multiplexer, A/D converter, and latch. This scheme updates the digital information for magnitude of reflection coefficient and forward power and phase every 50 μs. This is a data rate which exceeds most of the currently available host microprocessor processing capabilities.

One of the greatest advantages of the TIMS is the lack of unwanted signals coupled back onto the RF line. When properly designed receiver circuits are used, the generated noise and spurious signals are well isolated from the RF line. The conventional discriminator couples a considerable amount of noise and spurious signals into the RF path. This may be a problem where multiple receivers and transmitters are located at the same site. The unwanted signals mask the low-level receive signals and interact with other local transmit signals to cause an increase in intermodulation products.

A second advantage of the TIMS can be seen from the application of the exact impedance information made available. When the control for the antenna coupler contains a microprocessor capable of numerical computation, direct calculation of the RF element values is possible. This is done in

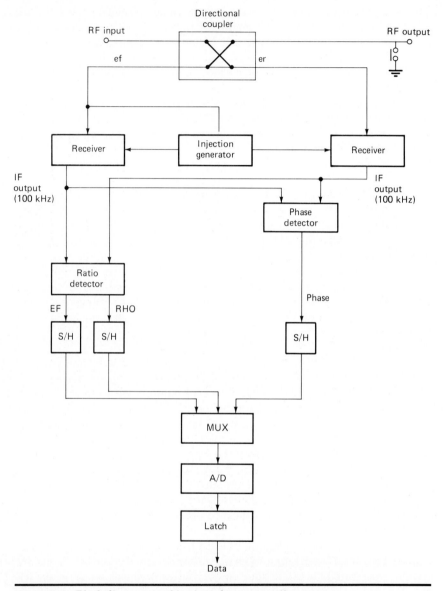

Figure 16.10   Block diagram, tracking impedance measuring system.

the same manner that network analysis is done on a mainframe computer. A model of the physical RF network including strays is included in the tune algorithm. The network is analyzed using model impedances and comparisons made with actual impedances measured with the TIMS. In this manner each element in the RF network is positioned. If the computer model is perfect, only one try is required for each element; however, the network strays cannot be measured with sufficient accuracy to achieve this. In practice two or three iterations (impedance measurements) are required. Typically, digital RF networks can be tuned with six iterations. This compares with several hundred required when the conventional discriminator and digital search methods are used. The TIMS dramatically improves the tuning time of a digital antenna coupler.

When the TIMS is used in an antenna coupler containing analog RF elements, the tune time is not greatly improved. This is a result of the nature of the RF elements themselves. Analog RF elements may require several seconds to change values over their entire range. The limiting factor is the speed at which the analog elements can change value. This is not meant to imply the TIMS should not be used in analog systems. Substantial improvement in tune accuracy and reliability are possible.

16.2 Broadband Matching of Antennas

Introduction

Matching nonresistive loads over a wide bandwidth is an old problem in electrical engineering. Because of parasitic components in electronic devices, even the earliest designers were aware that gain must be sacrificed to achieve wider bandwidths. Bode [4] was the first to find the theoretical limitations for matching to the simplest and yet very common matching load consisting of a resistor (R) in parallel with a capacitor (C). Using the basic premise that a passive network cannot have transmission poles in the right half-plane, he applied Cauchy's integral theorem to show that for a given bandwidth there is a maximum gain which can not be exceeded regardless of the complexity of the matching network—the limit equation is simply:

$$\text{Return-loss (Np)} \times \text{bandwidth (Hz)} = \text{constant} = \frac{1}{2RC}$$

Bode's elegant solution for this RC (low-pass) one-pole load was followed by Fano's classic work [5] which formulated the matching limits for a load of any complexity by a set of integral equations. Although the higher-order loads do not have known solutions, Fano did find the explicit limit solution for the two-pole load which consists of an L in series with Bode's parallel RC load. It should be emphasized that only the one-pole matching problem has a simple limit solution where the return-loss bandwidth product is constant. The two-pole problem requires the solution of a third-degree polynomial; and obviously the complexity of the return-loss bandwidth relationship becomes even more complex for higher-order solutions.

The most significant result of Fano's work applicable to antenna matching was his closed optimum solution for the one-pole load using the Chebyshev approximation function. Fano's technique assures that an explicit solution can be found which minimizes the mismatch VSWR for a given number of poles and bandwidths. Moreover, the synthesis can be completed by using simple recursion equations derived by Takahasi [6]. Levy [7] wrote an extremely useful paper that illustrates the use of these equations with Fano's algorithm.

Because of its simplicity, Fano's synthesis is undoubtedly the most widely used broadband matching algorithm. Cuthbert [8] has written an excellent book which not only summarizes Fano's technique, but also includes a program listing of his basic algorithm. In the brief treatment of broadband matching that follows here, it is assumed the reader is familiar with and has access to the Fano algorithm since it is central to the matching synthesis that is discussed in this chapter.

The main disadvantage of Fano's technique is that the matching problem definition requires the ideal load components shown in Fig. 16.11 rather than actual antenna impedance data. Furthermore, the typical antenna locus is not well described by these simple models. Because of this modeling problem, direct synthesis techniques are gaining in popularity. Carlins's synthesis [11] is the best current example and is also summarized by Cuthbert [8]. Regrettably, Carlin's synthesis requires a considerable amount of user interaction and expertise to get useful results.

What most designers want is an automatic program that requires only load data and very little user interaction. The expanded Fano algorithm developed in this chapter is surprisingly effective in achieving this goal and yet it is simple enough to be written by the nonspecialist. After combining the basic Fano algorithm with the new techniques described in this chapter, a very practical automatic algorithm results which can synthesize optimum matching networks directly from antenna data considerably more complex than the one-pole model.

For a design application of this expanded Fano algorithm, consider the two antenna loci A and B, shown in Fig. 16.12a. Our goal is to synthesize the optimum Fano matching networks, shown in Figs. 16.12b and c, that match the antenna loci to a 50-ohm source within a 3:1 VSWR from 10 to 20 MHz. It must be emphasized at the outset that these matching networks are nothing more than bandpass filters which are synthesized by absorbing unwanted load-reactive components into the filter topology. These reactive components are an integral part of the antenna and must be modeled in some suitable fashion before applying Fano's algorithm.

Before exploring the new expanded Fano algorithm that synthesizes matching networks such as those shown in Figs. 16.12a and b, let us consider an effective method for estimating the potential matching VSWR of the

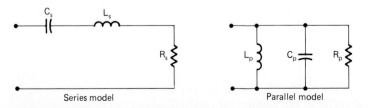

Figure 16.11 Schematics of ideal one-pole load models.

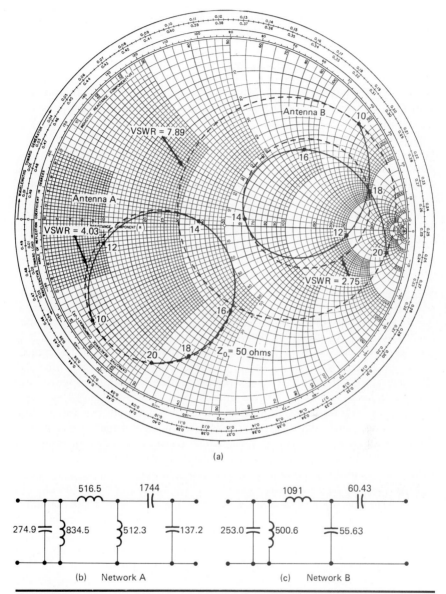

(a)

(b)   Network A   (c)   Network B

Figure 16.12 (*a*) Loci of antenna A and antenna B. (*b*) and (*c*) Matching networks which match antenna A and antenna B within a 3:1 VSWR from 10 to 20 MHz. *L*'s in nH; *C*'s in pF.

antenna loci in this figure. VSWR estimation techniques are especially useful in broadband antenna design because it is often desirable to estimate the matching VSWR without actually synthesizing the matching network. But these techniques can also be used to assure the designer that the networks synthesized by the new algorithm are approximately optimum. After discussing VSWR estimation techniques, we will explore the actual synthesis of the matching networks.

Estimating matching VSWR of a locus

A very useful theorem for estimating the matching potential of antenna loci is as follows: Given any positive real locus (i.e., a locus containing only real and positive R's, L's, and C's), the minimum theoretical matching VSWR can be shown to be less than or equal to the minimum VSWR circle that constrains this locus [13]. Furthermore, if the locus completes a circular loop approximately on the constraint VSWR circle, the minimum theoretical matching VSWR is approximately equal to this minimum-constraint VSWR.

To use this maximum VSWR theorem, it is necessary to find the smallest VSWR circle that constrains all the data points. A constraint-VSWR algorithm such as the one derived in Ref. 13 can be used, or the designer can find the minimum VSWR circle on a Smith chart as follows: Find the minimum (R_{min}) and maximum (R_{max}) constant resistance circles which are tangent to the smallest constraint-VSWR circle; the minimum circle VSWR $= \sqrt{R_{max}/R_{min}}$.

The smallest circle that constrains all the data points becomes the upper VSWR limit of the matching network. To find the lower VSWR limit, it is necessary to find the VSWR that constrains the data points of the largest loop. The matching VSWR is thereby bounded between these two limits. If the locus does not have any loops, the estimation technique supplies only the upper-limit VSWR; often this limit VSWR is several times the actual matching VSWR so it may not be an accurate estimation. But fortunately the expanded Fano algorithm synthesizes the optimum matching network directly and accurately for any locus which consists of only a portion of a loop. So for the simple locus case, the program algorithm can be used for obtaining not only an accurate VSWR estimate but also the actual synthesis.

Now let us try to estimate the matching VSWR of the two antenna loci in Fig. 16.12a. The locus of antenna A essentially coincides with the boundary of the minimum VSWR circle (shown by the dashed line); therefore, the upper-limit VSWR = 4.03 will also approximately equal the lower limit. Since this locus does not form a complete loop, the expanded Fano algorithm can be used with considerable confidence to find the matching VSWR directly. The matching network A in Fig. 16.12b was synthesized by the expanded Fano algorithm with a matching VSWR = 3.00. This is within 30 percent of the VSWR estimate, and as expected it is on the low side. The network for this particular example is the optimum Chebyshev synthesis for the given number of components.

For the antenna B locus, the constraining VSWR circle is much larger, resulting in an upper-limit VSWR = 7.89. Since the locus is primarily within rather than on the boundary of this circle, the matching VSWR can be improved considerably. By finding the minimum VSWR circle for the inner loop of this locus, a lower VSWR estimate is obtained; this dashed VSWR circle shown in Fig. 16.12a is equal to 2.75. The designer now knows that the matching VSWR must be between 2.75 and 7.89. Our estimate is verified by the network B synthesized by the expanded Fano algorithm shown in Fig. 16.12c with a matching VSWR = 3.00. It can be shown that network B is an optimum Chebyshev design for the given number of components.

When a locus loops many times, the matching VSWR is, for all practical purposes, limited by the largest VSWR loop, just as the limit of antenna B's locus in Fig. 16.12a is set by the single loop. One can infer an extremely important broadband matching concept from this simple approximation technique: When the matching VSWR must be reduced by using less band-width, the VSWR can not be improved appreciably until the largest VSWR loop is removed. But, unless this loop is close to the band edges, a drastic reduction in bandwidth may be required (this illustrates that the return-loss bandwidth product is certainly not constant for multiple-looped loci).

The designer can confidently use the expanded Fano algorithm, to be developed here, to directly find the matching VSWR of a locus that does not complete a loop; it is also accurate for most single-loop cases such as the antenna A locus shown in Fig. 16.12. But it certainly is not appropriate to use this algorithm for estimating the matching VSWR of complex loci such as are characteristic of most HF antennas operating over the entire HF band. The constraint-VSWR estimation technique discussed above provides the best VSWR estimate and often the best synthesis for such multiple-looped loci. Since the constraint VSWR for the largest loop often effectively con-strains the smaller loops, the best matching technique is to transform the desired source resistance to the center of the dominant constraint circle. The matching VSWR is equal to the largest constraint-VSWR circle centered around this optimum resistance value.

It is obvious from the above discussion that a designer should always avoid any components which might add a high VSWR loop. For example, a long transmission line can introduce a large VSWR loop in the antenna data, thereby causing an unnecessarily high matching VSWR. For this reason, it is better to place the matching network close to the antenna with the source resistance of the matching network equal to the Z_0 of the transmission line.

We now have a good VSWR estimate for the loci in Fig. 16.12a and can develop the expanded Fano algorithm for synthesizing the matching net-works. First, we consider various load approximation techniques for ideal one-pole and two-pole loads. Next, we integrate these techniques into the final algorithm and use it to synthesize networks A and B, shown in Fig. 16.12.

Approximating antenna impedance data with a one-pole load model

To use the Fano synthesis algorithm, the antenna data must first be approx-imated by one of the ideal one-pole load models shown in Fig. 16.11. We will only consider the case pertinent to RF problems—bandpass load modeling. Nevertheless, the designer should be aware that the low-pass prototype values are actually computed by the Fano algorithm and these values are then transformed to the bandpass case to complete the synthesis.

Depending on the choice of the error function minimized, there are many ways to approximate antenna impedance data by the bandpass models shown in Fig. 16.11. One obvious choice is a least squared sum of VSWRs, or reflection coefficient, between the component model and data points. Unfortunately, to minimize this error function an iterative solution is required which requires some experimentation with the starting values to reach convergence. The result is an algorithm that often converges with negative component values, or that may not converge at all. It should be noted that the Fano algorithm requires a positive R as well as at least one positive L or C before a network can be synthesized.

A better approximation method which always results in a positive resistance, and without convergence problems, is the least squared sum of the immittance (i.e., impedance or admittance) error. Using the equations in Table 16.1 results in the minimum least squared difference between the

TABLE 16.1   Solution for Ideal One-Pole Model

Solution for series model	Solution for parallel model
Input: $I_R(i) = R(i)$ $I_I(i) = X(i)$	Input: $I_R(i) = G(i)$ $I_I(i) = B(i)$
Output: $R_s = S$	Output: $R_p = \dfrac{1}{S}$
$L_s = T$ $C_s = U$	$C_p = T$ $L_p = U$

where the output components are identified in Fig. 16.11, and

$$S = \frac{\sum\limits_i I_R(i)}{N}$$

$$T = \frac{N \sum\limits_i [I_I(i)/W(i)] - \sum\limits_i [I_I(i) W(i)] \sum\limits_i 1/W(i)^2}{N^2 - \sum\limits_i W(i)^2 \sum\limits_i 1/W(i)^2}$$

$$U = \frac{\sum\limits_i 1/W(i)^2}{NT - \sum\limits_i [I_I(i)/W(i)]}$$

Variable definitions:

$B(i)$ = Array of load susceptance data, S (sometimes called mhos)
$G(i)$ = Array of load conductance data, S
$I_R(i)$ = Array of real immittance data
$I_I(i)$ = Array of imaginary immittance data
N = Number of data points
$R(i)$ = Array of load resistance data, ohms
$W(i)$ = Array of frequency data, radians/s
$X(i)$ = Array of load reactance data, ohms

immittance of the data and the LCR model summed for all data points. It must be remembered that either a series or shunt LCR model has a vertical straight-line locus (constant R or G lines) in the RX or GB planes, respectively. The line resulting from the equations of Table 16.1 is actually a regression line which minimizes the square of the immittance errors between the model and the discrete antenna data points.

Referring to the one-pole solution in Table 16.1, the reader should be aware that the parallel model solution is simply the dual of the series solution, and the component values can be obtained from the same algorithm by using $G + jB$ rather than the $R + jX$ data. R becomes G, L becomes C, and C becomes L for the parallel output variables. Using the dual concept, the designer can synthesize either circuit with the same algorithm.

The one-pole approximation method summarized in Table 16.1 can be used effectively until the change in antenna R or G over the bandwidth is approximately 30 percent. It then becomes obvious that a more complicated model is required such as the two-pole model shown in Fig. 16.13.

Approximating antenna impedance data with an ideal two-pole load model

Although direct regression equations are not available for the two-pole model, it can be readily approximated by several methods. Since we are utilizing the Fano technique, however, the inner pole (L_p and C_p for model 1 or C_s and L_s for model 2 in Fig. 16.13) must resonate at the geometric mean of the passband; consequently, a general fit of the inner pole is not necessary or even desirable. Note that the outer pole (C_s and L_s for model 1 or L_p and C_p for model 2 in Fig. 16.13) can be resonated by simply adding external components, whereas the inner pole cannot be resonated because its terminals are not accessible. To avoid this problem, we force the inner pole to resonate properly.

Although we have removed a degree of freedom in the model by choosing the resonant frequency of the inner pole, we can explicitly solve for the remaining four unknowns (C_s, L_s, B_p at W_0 and R_p, or L_p, C_p, X_s at W_0 and R_s) by using only two antenna data points. There are two equations for the real part of the data and two for the imaginary part of the data that must

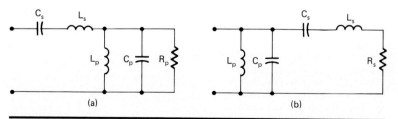

Figure 16.13 Schematics of ideal two-pole load models. (*a*) Model 1; (*b*) model 2.

TABLE 16.2   Solution for Ideal Two-Pole Model

Solution for model 1	Solution for model 2
Input:	Input:
$I_{R,1} = R_1$	$I_{R,1} = G_1$
$I_{I,1} = X_1$	$I_{I,1} = B_1$
$I_{R,2} = R_2$	$I_{R,2} = G_2$
$I_{I,2} = X_2$	$I_{I,2} = B_2$
Output:	Output:
$R_p = \dfrac{1}{S}$	$R_s = S$
$C_p = \dfrac{T}{W_0}$	$L_s = \dfrac{T}{W_0}$
$L_p = \dfrac{1}{TW_0}$	$C_s = \dfrac{1}{TW_0}$
$L_s = U$	$C_p = U$
$C_s = V$	$L_p = V$

where the output components are identified in Fig. 16.13, and

$$W_0 = \sqrt{W_{\text{low}} W_{\text{high}}}$$

$$F_1 = \frac{W_1}{W_0} - \frac{W_0}{W_1}$$

$$F_2 = \frac{W_2}{W_0} - \frac{W_0}{W_2}$$

$$S = \frac{F_1^2 I_{R,1} - F_2^2 I_{R,2}}{I_{R,1} I_{R,2}(F_1^2 - F_2^2)}$$

If $S < 0$ or $SI_{R,1} > 1$ or $SI_{R,2} > 1$, there is no solution:

$$T = \sqrt{\frac{(S - I_{R,1}S^2)}{I_{R,1}F_1^2}} \quad \text{or (if } F_1 = 0\text{)} \quad T = \sqrt{\frac{(S - I_{R,2}S^2)}{I_{R,2}F_2^2}}$$

$$K_1 = \frac{TF_1}{S^2 + (TF_1)^2} \qquad K_2 = \frac{TF_2}{S^2 + (TF_2)^2}$$

$$U = \frac{W_2(I_{I,2} + K_2) - W_1(I_{I,1} + K_1)}{W_2^2 - W_1^2}$$

$$V = \frac{1}{W_1[UW_1 - (I_{I,1} + K_1)]}$$

Variable definitions:

B_1 = Susceptance of first data point, S (sometimes called mhos)
B_2 = Susceptance of second data point, S
G_1 = Conductance of first data point, S
G_2 = Conductance of second data point, S
$I_{I,1}$ = Imaginary immittance of first data point
$I_{I,2}$ = Imaginary immittance of second data point
$I_{R,1}$ = Real immittance of first data point
$I_{R,2}$ = Real immittance of second data point
R_1 = Resistance of first data point, ohms
R_2 = Resistance of second data point, ohms
W_{low} = Lowest frequency in bandwidth, radians/s
W_{high} = Highest frequency in bandwidth, radians/s
W_0 = Geometric mean of W_{low} and W_{high}, radians/s
W_1 = Frequency of first data point, radians/s
W_2 = Frequency of second data point, radians/s
X_1 = Reactance of first data point, ohms
X_2 = Reactance of second data point, ohms

be satisfied simultaneously. The solution of these four equations results in the expressions for the model components shown in Table 16.2.

Any two antenna data points can be used to find the two-pole components except when the frequencies are the same ratio from the geometric mean frequency W_0 (note that the equations for F_1 and F_2 in Table 16.2 are defined by the ratio of the frequency of the data point to W_0). For this case the equation for S in Table 16.2 has a zero in the denominator (i.e., F_1^2 equals F_2^2) and there is no unique solution. To avoid this potential problem, use the points W_0 and W_{low}, or W_0 and W_{high}. Both sets should be tried because this model rarely fits the data and usually one set or the other results in a better synthesis.

Because of the forced resonance for the inner pole, the two-pole model is only effective for a narrow range of matching problems. Even so, this solution is very useful when combined with the pseudo-tuning technique, which we will now explore.

Approximating antenna impedance data with a pseudo-tuning model

We now consider a method of tuning the inner pole of the modified, two-pole model shown in Fig. 16.14. This model represents an intermediate case

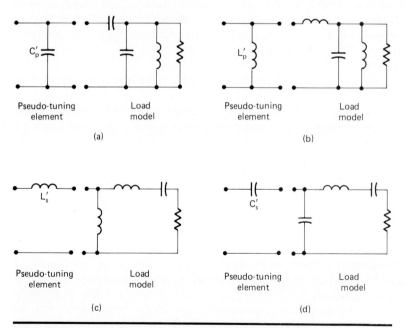

Figure 16.14 Schematics of pseudo-tuned, two-pole load models. The pseudo-tuning components C_p', L_p', L_s', and C_s' and their appropriate load models are shown in parts (a), (b), (c), and (d), respectively.

where only part of the second pole is present. They are, nevertheless, good models for a locus which does not form a complete loop. To resonate the inner pole of any one of these models, it is only necessary to add a pseudo-tuning component which forces both band-edge frequencies to have the same parallel or series resistance for the left or right models in Fig. 16.14, respectively. The pseudo-tuning components are readily found from the expressions in Table 16.3.

It can be shown that the composite model of the pseudo-tuning component and the load model shown in Fig. 16.14 now has an inner pole tuned at the geometric mean frequency as required for the two-pole model. Therefore, if the input immittance at the input of the pseudo-tuning component is now used as the input immittance for the two-pole solution given in Table 16.2, the resultant two-pole model now has a tuned inner pole as required for Fano's synthesis.

For example, assume the load model is as shown in Fig. 16.14a, with the inner pole not resonant at W_0. Now, if the pseudo-tuning component C_p' of Fig. 16.14a is calculated from the equations in Table 16.3, the composite of the load model and C_p' can be shown to be identical to the model 1 of Fig. 16.13 with L_s equal to zero. Moreover, L_p and C_p are now resonant at W_0 and the model is actually an exact representation of the load rather than the approximate model solution given by the equations in Table 16.2 without the use of the pseudo-tuning component C_p'.

The reader who is familiar with Norton transformers will note that this pseudo-tuning technique is really a manipulation of the transformation ratio. Although the same results can be achieved by manipulating Norton transformers, the solution given in Table 16.3 finds the proper transformation ratio implicitly without the necessity for finding the other components of the model shown in Fig. 16.14.

An interesting point about the pseudo-tuning technique is that it provides an exact synthesis for the case where the load is a two-pole high- or low-pass network. The network required to match either a high- or low-pass load is simply a low- or high-pass network, respectively. But since these loads are special cases of the models shown in Fig. 16.14, these ideal two-pole matching networks are synthesized by first using the pseudo-tuning solution followed by the ideal two-pole solution. The reader should be aware that this is only one of many ways that bandpass filters can be synthesized other than transforming a low-pass prototype to the bandpass topology. Fortunately, at reasonable bandwidths the Fano topology with the added pole/zero of the pseudo-tuning component is effective for modeling many variations of the bandpass load.

Even though the algorithm forces the proper tuning of the inner pole, the resultant second-pole matching components can be negative. Remember that Fano's synthesis provides complete absorption of the first pole (inner pole) only. Components must be added at the load interface such that the composite model of the second pole agrees with the value synthesized by the Fano algorithm. For example, if the value of L_s for model 1 in Fig. 16.13 is larger than the value required by the Fano synthesis, a negative inductor is

TABLE 16.3   Solution for Pseudo-tuning Model

Solution for C'_p	Solution for L'_s
Input:	Input:
$I_{R,1} = G_{\text{low}}$	$I_{R,1} = R_{\text{low}}$
$I_{I,1} = B_{\text{low}}$	$I_{I,1} = X_{\text{low}}$
$I_{R,2} = G_{\text{high}}$	$I_{R,2} = R_{\text{high}}$
$I_{I,2} = B_{\text{high}}$	$I_{I,2} = X_{\text{high}}$
$K = \dfrac{W_{\text{high}}}{W_{\text{low}}}$	$K = \dfrac{W_{\text{high}}}{W_{\text{low}}}$
Output:	Output:
$C'_p = \dfrac{S}{W_{\text{low}}}$	$L'_s = \dfrac{S}{W_{\text{low}}}$

Solution for L'_p	Solution for C'_s
Input:	Input:
$I_{R,1} = G_{\text{low}}$	$I_{R,1} = R_{\text{low}}$
$I_{I,1} = B_{\text{low}}$	$I_{I,1} = X_{\text{low}}$
$I_{R,2} = G_{\text{high}}$	$I_{R,2} = R_{\text{high}}$
$I_{I,2} = B_{\text{high}}$	$I_{I,2} = X_{\text{high}}$
$K = \dfrac{-W_{\text{low}}}{W_{\text{high}}}$	$K = \dfrac{-W_{\text{low}}}{W_{\text{high}}}$
Output:	Output:
$L'_p = \dfrac{1}{SW_{\text{low}}}$	$C'_s = \dfrac{1}{SW_{\text{low}}}$

where the output components are identified in Fig. 16.14, and

$$S^2(I_{R,\text{low}}K^2 - I_{R,\text{high}}) + S(KI_{R,\text{low}}I_{I,\text{high}} - \text{sgn}(K)I_{R,\text{high}}I_{I,\text{low}}) + I_{R,\text{low}}I_{I,\text{high}}^2$$
$$- I_{R,\text{high}}I_{I,\text{low}}^2 + I_{R,\text{low}}I_{R,\text{high}}^2 - I_{R,\text{high}}I_{R,\text{low}}^2 = 0$$

Notes:

1. If the quadratic radical, or both solutions for S are negative, there is no solution.

2. If both solutions for S are positive, use the smaller.

3. If $K > = 0$, sgn $(K) = 1$; if $K < 0$, sgn $(K) = -1$.

Variable definitions:

B_{low} =   Susceptance at low frequency, S (sometimes called mhos)
B_{high} =   Susceptance at high frequency, S
G_{low} =   Admittance at low frequency, S
G_{high} =   Admittance at high frequency, S
$I_{I,\text{low}}$ =   Imaginary immittance at low frequency
$I_{I,\text{high}}$ =   Imaginary immittance at high frequency
$I_{R,\text{low}}$ =   Real immittance at low frequency
$I_{R,\text{high}}$ =   Real immittance at high frequency
R_{low} =   Resistance at low frequency, ohms
R_{high} =   Resistance at high frequency, ohms
W_{low} =   Lowest frequency in bandwidth, radians/s
W_{high} =   Highest frequency in bandwidth, radians/s
X_{low} =   Reactance at low frequency, ohms
X_{high} =   Reactance at high frequency, ohms

required at the input to correct the inductance, whereas if L_s is smaller than the required value, the proper value is realized by simply adding a positive inductance at the load interface. The suggested procedure for eliminating this problem is to delete any negative components that occur at the load interface from the final matching network.

"Situation 2" synthesis for two-pole loads

When negative components do occur during the two-pole synthesis, a special synthesis procedure called "Situation 2" by Matthaei [9] is required. Chen [10] found a closed Chebyshev synthesis for this special case, but the resulting bandpass solution requires a Darlington "D" section (the low-pass solution requires a Darlington "C" section—see Ref. 9 for a description of Darlington sections). Since the Darlington "D" section requires two ideal transformers which are impossible to realize at RF frequencies, Chen's synthesis is not useful for synthesizing RF networks. However, his method can be used to find the optimum theoretical VSWR, which is useful for comparing the effectiveness of a given design with the ideal Chebyshev synthesis for Situation 2 loads.

Fortunately, there is still hope for solving Situation 2 problems without Darlington sections. Carlin [11, 12] has shown that a comparable performance can be achieved by his synthesis technique without Darlington sections. Moreover, the matching networks can have the standard bandpass topology with comparable or even less complexity, and yet surpass the performance of the ideal Situation 2 designs of Chen. This amazing result has also been demonstrated by this author [13] using an entirely different synthesis technique.

It should be mentioned that the optimum matching solutions which do not utilize Darlington sections are not necessarily Chebyshev; indeed, Carlin has shown this is not even necessary for the one-pole solution. It is easy to demonstrate this by optimizing a Fano two-pole synthesis, but the improvement in matching VSWR is typically less than 1 percent. However, it is much more difficult, if not impossible, to improve the performance of higher-order Fano solutions.

Parenthetically, it should be mentioned that the direct synthesis techniques, such as those described in Refs. 11 and 13, do not require load modeling. Although these techniques provide better solutions to more complex load loci, the program algorithms are also more complex than the Fano algorithm. However, by adding a "box approximation technique" (to be discussed below), in addition to the techniques described in Tables 16.1 to 16.3, an expanded Fano technique results that can provide excellent starting values for optimization of the more complex problems. Almost any synthesized broadband matching network can be improved by optimization, and solutions from this expanded Fano technique can find optimized solutions comparable with more complex methods.

Approximating complex antenna impedance data

The question might be asked, "Why not extend the approximation to more than a two-pole model?" The answer is that the higher-order load models do not fit Fano's one-pole synthesis (except for extremely unlikely, contrived, and trivial special problems where all the inner poles resonate at the geometric mean frequency and have the identical components to those synthesized by the one-pole algorithm). But, for certain types of complex loci, any of the solutions in Tables 16.1 to 16.3 can synthesize suitable matching networks. A very acceptable method for finding these networks is to try all combinations of these solutions and save the minimum VSWR solution for the output. There is certainly no guarantee of the success of this method; but if two more solutions, called "box 1" and "box 2," are added to the three already given, this trial-and-error method is very effective for matching loci of any complexity.

Approximating antenna impedance data constrained by a box. The box approximations are based on one-pole and two-pole synthesis models which are defined by coordinates of the minimum box which contains all the load data points in either the RX or GB planes. For example, the minimum boxes that contain the defining box loci shown in Figs. 16.15a and b result in a one-pole synthesis in Fig. 16.15a, called "box 1," and a two-pole synthesis in Fig. 16.15b, called "box 2." The syntheses for box 1 and box 2 are computed from the algorithm shown in Table 16.4 using the coordinates of the minimum box for the input rather than the actual load data points. The Fano matching networks synthesized for these ideal one-pole and two-pole models can provide a surprisingly good match for complex loci such as those shown in Fig. 16.15.

The box 1 solution forces the one-pole model locus to fit the left boundary of the minimum box constraining the data. This is illustrated by the synthesis locus with a 2:1 VSWR shown in Fig. 16.15a, which was computed by the box 1 algorithm given in Table 16.4. The rationale for selecting the left axis can be seen from the acceptable load area circles for a 3:1 VSWR shown by the dashed lines in Fig. 16.15a. These 3:1 circles show the acceptable region the load locus must be within at five geometrically spaced frequencies numbered 1 through 5 for the 2:1 VSWR Fano network that matches the left boundary locus. The general positions of these mapping circles are always the same relative to the position of the left boundary of the box.

Now, as long as a hypothetical load locus has data points within the corresponding area at each frequency, the Fano network that was actually synthesized to match the left boundary of the box will also match the hypothetical locus. The resultant matching VSWR at each frequency will be less than or equal to the VSWR of the mapping circle. This is illustrated by the defining box locus shown in Fig. 16.15a. Since at each of the five frequencies the locus is within the proper 3:1 VSWR circle, the matching VSWR will be

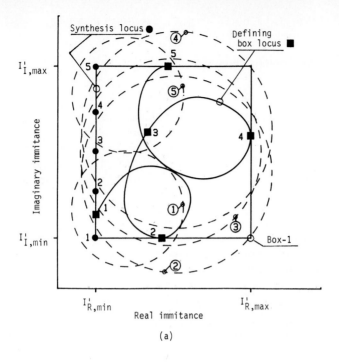

(a)

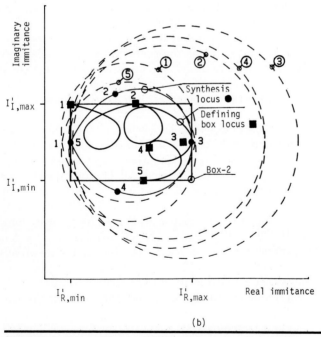

(b)

Figure 16.15 Acceptable 3:1 VSWR circle regions for the (*a*) box 1 and (*b*) box 2 solutions. The synthesis locus corresponds to a 2:1 VSWR Fano synthesis using a total number of network poles of three for the box 1 solution and four for the box 2 solution.

TABLE 16.4   Solution for Box 1 and Box 2 Models

Solution for series, box 1	Solution for parallel, box 1
Input:	Input:
$I_{R,\min} = R_{\min}$	$I_{R,\min} = G_{\min}$
$I_{I,\min} = X_{\min}$	$I_{I,\min} = B_{\min}$
$I_{I,\max} = X_{\max}$	$I_{I,\max} = B_{\max}$
Output:	Output:
$R_s = I_{R,\min}$	$R_p = \dfrac{1}{I_{R,\min}}$
$L_s = T$	$C_p = T$
$C_s = U$	$L_p = U$

where the output components are identified in Fig. 16.11, and

$$T = \frac{W_{\text{high}}I_{I,\max} - W_{\text{low}}I_{I,\min}}{W_{\text{high}}^2 - W_{\text{low}}^2}$$

$$U = \frac{1}{W_{\text{low}}(TW_{\text{low}} - I_{I,\min})}$$

Solution for model 1, box 2	Solution for model 2, box 2
Input:	Input:
$I_{R,\min} = R_{\min}$	$I_{R,\min} = G_{\min}$
$I_{R,\max} = R_{\max}$	$I_{R,\max} = G_{\max}$
$I_{I,\min} = \dfrac{X_{\min} + X_{\max}}{2}$	$I_{I,\min} = \dfrac{B_{\min} + B_{\max}}{2}$
$I_{I,\max} = I_{I,\min}$	$I_{I,\max} = I_{I,\min}$
Output:	Output:
$R_p = I_{R,\max}$	$R_s = \dfrac{1}{I_{R,\max}}$
$C_p = \dfrac{T}{W_0}$	$L_s = \dfrac{T}{W_0}$
$L_p = \dfrac{1}{TW_0}$	$C_s = \dfrac{1}{TW_0}$
$L_s = U$	$C_p = U$
$C_s = V$	$L_p = V$

where the output components are identified in Fig. 16.13, and

$$F = \frac{W_{\text{high}}}{W_0} - \frac{W_0}{W_{\text{high}}}$$

$$T = \frac{\sqrt{(I_{R,\max}/I_{R,\min} - 1)}}{FI_{R\max}}$$

TABLE 16.4   Solution for Box 1 and Box 2 Models (*Continued*)

$$K = \frac{FT(I_{R,\max})^2}{1 + (FTI_{R,\max})^2}$$

$$U = \frac{W_{\text{high}}(I_{I,\max} + K) - W_{\text{low}}(I_{I,\min} - K)}{W_{\text{high}}^2 - W_{\text{low}}^2}$$

$$V = \frac{1}{W_{\text{low}}(UW_{\text{low}} - I_{I,\min} + K)}$$

Variable definitions:

$B_{\min}$ =   Minimum susceptance of box, S (sometimes called mhos)
$B_{\max}$ =   Maximum susceptance of box, S
$G_{\min}$ =   Minimum conductance of box, S
$G_{\max}$ =   Maximum conductance of box, S
$I_{R,\min}$ =   Minimum real immittance of synthesis locus
$I_{R,\max}$ =   Maximum real immittance of synthesis locus
$I_{I,\min}$ =   Minimum imaginary immittance of synthesis locus
$I_{I,\max}$ =   Maximum imaginary immittance of synthesis locus
$R_{\min}$ =   Minimum resistance of box, ohms
$R_{\max}$ =   Maximum resistance of box, ohms
$X_{\min}$ =   Minimum reactance of box, ohms
$X_{\max}$ =   Maximum reactance of box, ohms

less than or equal to 3:1. The reader should note that if circles corresponding to a smaller VSWR than 3:1 were plotted, the locus would not be within the circles at all five frequencies.

The box 2 solution, also presented in Table 16.4, requires the limiting real coordinates rather than the limiting imaginary coordinates required for the box 1 solution (both methods require the minimum real coordinate). The box 2 solution is actually a special case of the ideal two-pole model solution with the required two data points at the band-edge frequencies. The real parts of the data points are now the minimum real box coordinates and the imaginary parts of the data points ($L_{I,\min}$, $L_{I,\max}$) are both equal to the center of the box (i.e., the average of the minimum and maximum imaginary coordinates). The synthesis model locus is, thereby, forced to cross at the center of the box on the left boundary at the band-edge frequencies; whereas, the locus touches the right boundary at W_0. As illustrated by the 2:1 locus shown in Fig. 16.15*b*, the synthesis locus for higher VSWRs can become an almost perfect circle for the box 2 approximation. The defining box locus shown in Fig. 16.15*b* is only one of an infinite number of possible load loci to match the network synthesized by the box 2 method for this example. Note that if $I'_{I,\min}$ is lowered the same amount that $I'_{I,\max}$ is raised, the synthesis is the same because only the average of these two numbers is used in the solution— the imaginary box dimensions are only used to center the solution. This is the reason that the synthesis locus is within not only the 3:1 but also the 2:1 VSWR circles and yet it is outside of the box shown in Fig. 16.15*b*.

It is easy to incorporate several variations of the box solutions by altering the immittance coordinates defining the box sizes by percentages. For example, the box 2 solution usually results in slightly lower VSWR if $I_{R,\max}$ is increased to utilize the circle area to its right in Fig. 16.15b. However, since the VSWR improvement is usually not significant for such changes in the box dimensions, the box 1 and 2 solutions as defined in Table 16.4 are the only box solutions used in the final algorithm.

The final algorithm.   The required solutions for the expanded Fano algorithm are now complete and a suggested solution sequence is shown in the steps listed below. Note that the pseudo-tuning components (steps 12 to 15) are used to alter the effective load data. This is the equivalent of using five different sets of load data (one unmodified set and a set for each of the four pseudo-tuning components). For each of the five equivalent sets of load data, there are five different model solutions as follows:

1:    ideal, one-pole

2:    ideal, two-pole

1:    box 1, one-pole

1:    box 2, two-pole

But, since each of these solutions has a normal and dual solution, the total number of model solutions is 10. Therefore, the total synthesis combinations of both the models with and without pseudo-tuning components are fifty. Usually less than half this number actually completes the entire synthesis because of negative values or imaginary solutions. Although this is a trial-and-error synthesis procedure, it is surprisingly fast and effective; the typical computation time on the IBM XT with an 8087 microprocessor is approximately 1 min.

The expanded Fano algorithm involves the following steps:

1. Input the antenna data and store. Compute and store the $R(i) + jX(i)$ and $G(i) + jB(i)$ arrays.

2. Select the number of poles for the Fano matching network (typically n is less than 5 unless extreme impedance transforming is necessary).

3. Input $R(i) + jI(i)$ data into the $I_R(i) + jI_I(i)$ immittance storage.

4. Compute and store the immittance coordinates of the minimum rectangular box which constrains the data.

5. Compute the one-pole model components in Table 16.1 corresponding to the proper immittance storage.

6. Complete the Fano synthesis and find the maximum matching VSWR for the synthesized network using the actual load data rather than the model. If it is less than the lowest previously computed VSWR, store this VSWR and the corresponding solution.

7. Compute the two-pole model components in Table 16.2 using W_{low} and W_0 data points corresponding to the proper immittance storage. Repeat step 6.

8. Compute the two-pole model components in Table 16.2 using W_{high} and W_0 data points corresponding to the proper immittance storage. Repeat step 6.

9. Compute the box 1 model components in Table 16.4 corresponding to the proper immittance storage. Repeat step 6.

10. Compute the box 2 model components in Table 16.4 corresponding to the proper immittance storage. Repeat step 6.

11. Input $G(i) + jB(i)$ data into the $I_R(i) + jI_I(i)$ immittance storage. Repeat steps 4 to 10.

12. Compute the L'_s pseudo-tuning component in Table 16.3. Compute and store the new $R(i) + jX(i)$ and $G(i) + jB(i)$ array data corresponding to L'_s cascaded with the actual load data. Repeat steps 3 to 11.

13. Compute the C'_s pseudo-tuning component in Table 16.3. Compute and store the new $R(i) + jX(i)$ and $G(i) + jB(i)$ array data corresponding to C'_s cascaded with the actual load data. Repeat steps 3 to 11.

14. Compute the C'_p pseudo-tuning component in Table 16.3. Compute and store the new $R(i) + jX(i)$ and $G(i) + jB(i)$ array data corresponding to C'_p cascaded with the actual load data. Repeat steps 3 to 11.

15. Compute the L'_p pseudo-tuning component in Table 16.3. Compute and store the new $R(i) + jX(i)$ and $G(i) + jB(i)$ array data corresponding to L'_p cascaded with the actual load data. Repeat steps 3 to 11.

16. Print the synthesis corresponding to the lowest VSWR.

It should be noted that the final topology for this expanded procedure can have an extra transmission pole or zero because of the pseudo-tuning component. This extra component in the topology is extremely important for finding solutions for more complex loci which are not reached even with optimization of the standard Fano topology.

Design example

We can now synthesize matching networks such as that shown in Fig. 16.12. The significant algorithm steps for synthesizing networks A and B are as follows (the numbers are the same as the algorithm step numbers given above):

		Solution of network A		Solution of network B	
1. Freq., MHz	$R(i)$, ohms	$X(i)$, ohms	1. $R(i)$, ohms	$X(i)$, ohms
10	3.249	-16.673	22.050	141.873
12	9.817	-4.303	246.750	-34.897
14	37.371	1.012	61.908	4.137
16	34.981	-41.044	64.266	81.833
18	12.255	-37.617	200.342	234.990
20	5.806	-30.517	336.865	-448.840

2. Let $n = 3$

  .
  .
  .

14. $C_p' = 137.2$ pF

  .
  .
  .

7. $R_p = 32.00$ ohms
 $C_p = 1715.$ pF
 $L_p = 73.84$ nH
 $L_s = 0.000$ nH
 $C_s = 686.1$ pF

6. VSWR $= 3.000$

  .
  .
  .

2. Let $n = 4$

  .
  .
  .

  .
  .
  .

7. $R_s = 61.47$ ohms
 $L_s = 3688$ nH
 $C_s = 34.34$ pF
 $C_p = 115.8$ pF
 $L_p = 874.9$ nH

6. VSWR $= 3.000$

  .
  .
  .

16. Minimum VSWR synthesis:

16. Minimum VSWR synthesis:

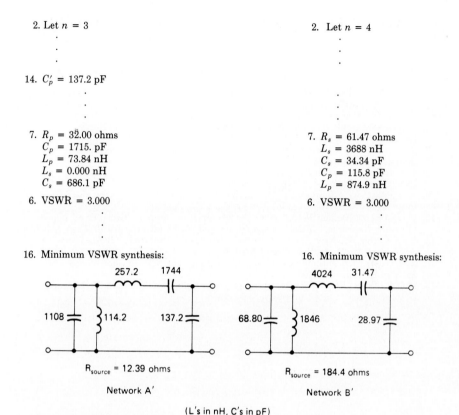

Network A'

R_source = 12.39 ohms

Network B'

R_source = 184.4 ohms

(L's in nH, C's in pF)

Note that network A' requires the pseudo-tuning component (C_p') to achieve the minimum VSWR. Although both networks A' and B' result in the same optimum VSWR of 3:1, the source resistances are not equal to 50 ohms (as noted in the schematics shown above). The theoretical synthesis is easily completed by simply adding an ideal transformer. So, it appears that the design effort must now include an approximation of an ideal transformer. Fortunately this is not necessary because the bandpass topology conveniently includes implicit transformers which are easily manipulated to achieve the desired source resistance. These transformers are called "Norton transformers" and are discussed in Refs. 7 and 8. After inserting the Norton transformers, networks A' and B' become networks A and B shown in Fig. 16.12.

REFERENCES

1. Phillip H. Smith, "Charts for L-Type Impedance-Transforming Circuits," in J. Markus and Vin Zeluff (eds.), *Electronics for Engineers*, McGraw-Hill, New York, 1945, pp. 272–278.

2. A. Zverev, *Handbook of Filter Synthesis,* John Wiley & Sons, New York, 1967, pp. 499–504.
3. H. L. Landt, Tracking Impedance Measuring System, U.S. Patent 4,506,209, Mar. 19, 1985 (assigned to Rockwell-Collins).
4. H. W. Bode, *Network Analysis and Feedback Amplifier Design,* Van Nostrand, New York, 1945, Chap. 16.
5. R. M. Fano, "Theoretical Limitations on the Broadband Matching of Arbitrary Impedances," *J. Franklin Inst.,* vol. 249, January 1950, pp. 57–83 (first part); *J. Franklin Inst.,* vol. 249, February 1950, pp. 139–155 (second part).
6. L. Weinberg and P. Slepian, "Takahasi's Results on Tchebycheff and Butterworth Ladder Networks," *IRE Trans.,* vol. 101, pt. IV, 1954, p. 192.
7. R. Levy, "Explicit Formulas for Chebyshev Impedance-Matching Networks, Filters, and Interstages," *Proc. IEE,* vol. 3, June 1964, pp. 1099–1106.
8. T. R. Cuthbert, *Circuit Design Using Personal Computers,* John Wiley & Sons, New York, 1983, Chap. 6.
9. G. L. Matthaei, "Synthesis of Tchebychev Impedance-Matching Networks, Filters, and Interstages," *IRE Trans. Circuit Theory,* vol. CT-3, September 1956, pp. 163–172.
10. W. K. Chen, "Explicit Formulas for the Synthesis of Optimum Broad-Band Impedance-Matching Networks," *IEEE Trans. Circuits Syst.,* vol. CAS-24, April 1977, pp. 157–169.
11. H. J. Carlin, "A New Approach to Gain-Bandwidth Problems," *IEEE Trans. Circuits Syst.,* vol. CAS-24, April 1977, pp. 170–175.
12. H. J. Carlin, "On Optimum Broad-Band Matching," *IEEE Trans. Circuits Syst.,* vol. CAS-28, May 1981, pp. 401–405.
13. R. C. Edwards, "Broadband Matching Synthesis Using New Computer Techniques," Master's thesis, Iowa State University, Ames, 1985.

Receiver Measurement Techniques

David H. Church

17.1 Measurements and Design

Performance measurements are an important and necessary part of the design and development of SSB receivers. Since theoretical predictions and analyses are often difficult to achieve, measurements ensure conformance to the design specifications. This chapter discusses many of the measurement techniques used in designing and testing SSB receivers.

17.2 Receiver Measurements

Many of the performance characteristics of receivers are related to two fundamental parameters. These are the internally generated noise and the nonlinearity of the transfer characteristics. Whereas past design emphasis has been on low-noise front ends for the reception of weak signals, today's spectral environment of large transmitter and jammer signals has focused attention on intermodulation products which may mask small desired signals.

Noise figure

To analyze the noise performance of a receiver (Refs. 1 and 7), the receiver may be thought of as a set of two-port networks (or "two-ports," for short) in cascade. These two-port networks are filters, amplifiers, mixers, and attenuators. In addition to its desired function of amplification or frequency translation, each two-port generates internal noise and distortion which contaminate the desired signal output.

A simple resistor is a one-port network which may be analyzed as a voltage source (thermal noise) in series with source resistance. The thermal noise source voltage, calculated from noise-power spectral density, is given by:

$$V_{noise}^2 = nB = 4kTBR \text{ [rms noise voltage}^2]$$ (17.1)

where n = noise power density, -174 dBm in a 1-Hz bandwidth
k = Boltzman's constant, 1.37×10^{-23} J/K
T = absolute temperature, K (293 K normal ambient)
B = bandwidth, Hz
R = source resistance, ohms

The two-port network includes noise sources associated with thermal resistances and junction noise found in diodes and transistors. To describe the effect of internal noise sources, the concept of "noise factor" has been developed. A model of a two-port network with the signal and noise sources is shown in Fig. 17-1.

Noise factor is defined as the ratio of the input signal-to-noise ratio to the output signal-to-noise ratio:

$$\begin{aligned} \text{Noise factor} &= \frac{S_{in}/N_{in}}{S_{out}/N_{out}} \\ &= \frac{(V_{in}^2/4R_{gen})/kTB}{(S_{out}/N_{out})} \\ &= \frac{V_{in}^2/4kTBR_{gen}}{S_{out}/N_{out}} \end{aligned}$$ (17.2)

Further:

$$\text{Noise figure} = 10 \log (\text{noise factor})$$ (17.3)

One method of measuring the noise factor of a receiver is derived from Eq. (17.2). If the effective noise bandwidth of the receiver is known, the noise factor may be calculated from the output signal-to-noise ratio resulting from a given input signal level (V_{in}). The effective noise bandwidth of a receiver

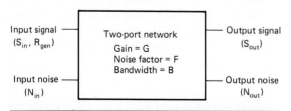

Figure 17.1 Signal and noise analysis of a two-port network.

is a single rectangular bandwidth which would pass as much white-noise power as the actual receiver bandwidth. As an approximation, the 3-dB bandwidth of the receiver may be used as the effective noise bandwidth. This approximation is good if the filter shape factor is small (less than 2 to 1), which is true of an SSB receiver.

Example Given a sensitivity measurement of 0.7 μV (open circuit from a 50-ohm generator) for a 10-dB signal-plus-noise-to-noise ratio (9.5 dB signal-to-noise ratio) in a 2750-Hz bandwidth:

Signal level	−116.1 dBm
Signal to noise	9.5 dB
Noise level in 2750-Hz bandwidth	−125.6 dBm
Correction factor for 1-Hz bandwidth	34.4 dB
Noise level in 1-Hz bandwidth	−160.0 dBm
Thermal noise in 1-Hz bandwidth, 50 ohms	−174.0 dBm
Noise figure of receiver	14.0 dB

A more exact method of determining the noise figure of a receiver uses a calibrated noise source. The noise source is a tube or diode which generates a shot-noise current equal to $2qI_B$, where q is electronic charge and I_B is direct current. The typical test setup is shown in Fig. 17.2.

The output noise power is measured with the noise source turned off. The noise source is then applied at a level to increase the output noise power by 3 dB. Alternatively, a 3-dB attenuator can be used after the receiver. This applied noise level is equal to the amount of noise generated by the receiver itself. The noise figure may be read directly from the noise source meter. An advantage of the calibrated noise source is that the receiver's noise bandwidth does not have to be measured.

Analysis of the input noise figure of a cascaded system shows the importance of a low noise figure in the first stages. Chapter 3 of this book and Ref. 1 provide a discussion of noise performance in a cascaded system.

Intermodulation

Two types of intermodulation performance are important in the operation of a receiver: in-band and out-of-band (Ref. 4).

In-band intermodulation performance is a measure of intermodulation products produced by two tones within the passband of the receiver. These tones may be desired signals, undesired signals, or a combination of both. In-band intermodulation products are produced by nonlinearities within the

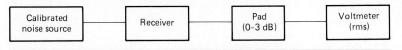

Figure 17.2 Test configuration for noise figure measurement.

amplifier stages and filters or by gain modulation from the automatic gain control.

The transfer characteristic shown in Fig. 17.3 illustrates the basic parameters used to describe nonlinearities in circuits. Intercept points (IPs) are the theoretical input levels (extrapolated from actual intermodulation data) at which the intermodulation products are of equal power with the input signals. The compression point describes the point at which the actual and theoretical transfer characteristics differ by 1 dB. Gain compression is often caused by the strong undesired signal affecting the amplifier's bias points and in turn reducing the overall gain. The points of intersection with the fundamental transfer curve are defined as the second-order intercept point and the third-order intercept point. A high intercept point means greater linearity in the transfer characteristic of the front end, resulting in less degradation of the receiver's strong signal performance.

To accurately measure intermodulation performance, a two-tone source must be available which does not generate its own intermodulation products. A typical setup is shown in Fig. 17.4. The attenuator is placed between the RF translator and the IF amplifier to prevent the intermodulation product from driving the IF into overload. The AGC is usually turned off. The narrowband filters reduce the harmonics of the source frequencies, eliminating their possible contributions to the intermodulation measurement. In addition, the filters isolate the two generators and thereby eliminate the "back door" phenomenon, by which intermodulation is generated in the output amplifier of each signal generator. Isolation between the two signal sources is improved by the pad networks and the isolation of the hybrid signal combiner. The combiner may be a hybrid transformer, a schematic of which is shown in Fig. 17.5a, or a simpler resistive combiner, shown in Fig. 17.5b.

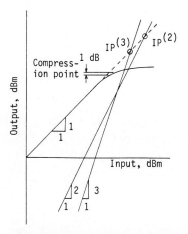

Figure 17.3 Characteristics of intermodulation distortion.

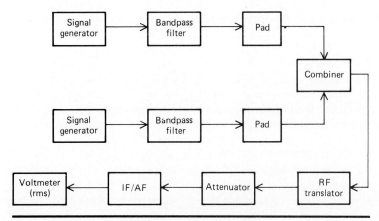

Figure 17.4   Test setup for intermodulation distortion.

Chapter 12 provides additional information on hybrid combiners. The transformer provides approximately 20 dB of additional isolation between the signal generators. The resistive combiner has 6 dB of isolation between any two ports and maintains a 50-ohm interface, as does the hybrid transformer.

For out-of-band intermodulation measurements, the frequencies F_1 and F_2 are outside the receiver's passband yet will produce intermodulation products which fall in band. As the two tones move further apart, IM improves because of selectivity which may be within the translator. It is always desirable to plot IM vs. frequency of separation.

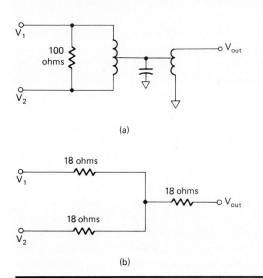

Figure 17.5 (a) and (b) RF signal combiner.

The intermodulation products are related to the out-of-band signals as follows:

Second-order products = $F_1 \pm F_2$ (17.4)

Third-order products = $2F_1 \pm F_2$ and $F_1 \pm 2F_2$ (17.5)

By determining the level of the intermodulation products in terms of equivalent input signal power, the out-of-band intercept points may be calculated:

$IP^{(2)}$ = second-order intercept point

= 2.0 (undesired signal) − 1.0 (equivalent product) (17.6)

$IP^{(3)}$ = third-order intercept point

= 1.5 (undesired signal) − 0.5 (equivalent product) (17.7)

The signal levels are given in terms of dBm (dB above a milliwatt).

Example Two out-of-band tones at −10 dBm/tone produce a third-order intermodulation product with an equivalent input level of −80 dBm. So we have

$IP^{(3)}$ = 1.5(−10 dBm) − 0.5(−80 dBm) = +25 dBm

Adjacent channel intermodulation is a special case of the out-of-band distortion measurement. The frequencies F_1 and F_2 are chosen such that one of the tones is 30 to 50 kHz from the tuned frequency of the receiver. Typically this intermodulation is produced in the first-mixer network and the first-IF filter. When measuring adjacent channel intermodulation, precautions must be taken to prevent the noise skirts of the signal generators from masking the true intermodulation performance. The effects of reciprocal mixing are discussed later in this chapter.

In-band intermodulation measurements will use frequencies F_1 and F_2 which are within the receiver's passband. The two desired in-band tones are typically chosen to produce audio tones of 900 and 1100 Hz. The intermodulation performance is easily measured with a spectrum analyzer or wave analyzer at the audio output. Intermodulation measured at the audio output is indicative of the total receiver's performance.

Cross modulation is a type of intermodulation distortion that is also caused by nonlinearities of the mixers, filters, and amplifiers. This distortion is a measure of the amount of modulation transferred from a strong, undesired, modulated carrier to a desired, weaker, unmodulated carrier at the tuned frequency when both signals are present at the antenna input.

The third-order curvature of an amplifier's transfer characteristic is the major factor in producing cross-modulation products and also third-order intermodulation products. Since third-order curvature is common to both, a relationship may be established between these two distortions such that predictions of cross-modulation performance can be made from intermodulation test results, or vice versa [2, 8].

If a strong undesired AM signal and a desired weaker, unmodulated carrier signal are present, a ratio between the transferred modulation appearing on the desired signal and the modulation of the undesired signal can be established. Similarly, a two-equal-tone signal results in a ratio of the intermodulation products to each of the two tones.

These undesired-to-desired ratios may be expressed as:

AM:

$$\frac{3U^2 A_3}{A_1}$$

Two tone:

$$\tfrac{3}{4}D^2 \frac{A_3}{A_1}$$

where U = amplitude of undesired signal
$\quad\quad D$ = amplitude of each fundamental tone
$\quad A_1, A_3$ = coefficients of transfer function polynomial

Since the coefficients of the transfer function are difficult to measure, they may be eliminated from the final ratio [Eq. (17.8)] if the peak signal in each test case is equal. This stipulation implies that amplitude D is equal to $0.65U$ when the undesired signal U is 30 percent modulated. That is, equal peak envelope signals ($2D = 1.3U$) are used to compare intermodulation and cross modulation. Figure 17.6 shows this relationship.

To compare cross modulation with two-tone intermodulation, the ratio of the AM and two-tone intermodulation may be calculated:

$$\frac{\text{AM cross-modulation ratio}}{\text{Two-tone intermodulation ratio}} = \frac{3U^2(A_3/A_1)}{\tfrac{3}{4}D^2(A_3/A_1)}$$

$$= 4\,\frac{U^2}{D^2} \tag{17.8}$$

$$= 9.47$$

where $D = 0.65U$ for 30 percent modulation.

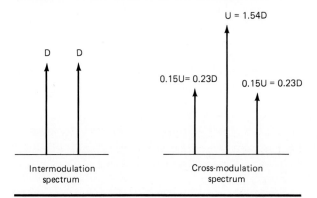

Figure 17.6 Comparison of two-tone and AM signals. The peak signals are equal. Modulation is 30 percent.

Since the original ratios were defined as undesired signal to desired signal, a larger ratio indicates poorer performance. The final ratio given above shows that for equal peak input signal levels, the AM cross-modulation ratio is 9.47 (19.5 dB) worse than the two-tone intermodulation test ratio. For example, if a two-tone intermodulation test yields intermodulation products 40 dB below the two tones, the cross-modulation test, with equal peak signals, will result in a −20-dB cross-modulation ratio.

Measurement of cross-modulation distortion uses a test procedure similar to that for out-of-band intermodulation. The difference is in the AM modulation of the undesired signal and the measurement of the relative difference between the desired and undesired carrier signals. A test setup is shown in Fig. 17.7.

A reference measurement is made by modulating the desired signal (1000 Hz at 30 percent modulation) and measuring the audio output level with the wave analyzer. The modulation of the desired carrier is then turned off. Modulation is then applied to the undesired carrier (1000 Hz, 30 percent modulation). The modulation frequency is monitored at the audio output with the wave analyzer. Test limits are the undesired carrier level required to produce the specified ratio of undesired to desired audio output. Cross modulation is usually specified as 10- or 20-dB cross modulation. That is, the audio due to the interfering signal is 10 to 20 dB below the modulation due to the desired modulated signal.

The gain control circuitry located at the front end may contribute to the intermodulation performance. If PIN diodes are used as attenuators, the intermodulation tests should be performed at different bias points of the PIN diodes. The most critical point is the turn-on threshold of the diodes.

Harmonic distortion (audio)

Harmonic distortion can be easily measured with a distortion analyzer (such as the Hewlett-Packard 331) or equivalent test equipment. A known good RF signal is applied to the receiver to produce the desired audio output. The

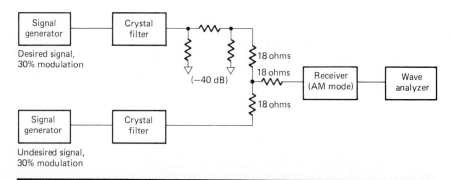

Figure 17.7   Measurement procedure for cross-modulation.

applied signal level must be strong enough to prevent the internal receiver noise from masking the distortion products.

The distortion analyzer uses an internal notch filter to remove the desired signal, allowing the distortion products, hum and noise, to be measured. Total harmonic distortion (THD) is defined as the ratio between the level of the desired signal and the rms level of all the distortion products.

The notch filter used in the distortion analyzer may affect the measurement of THD. In most applications the effect of the notch filter is ignored if the receiver bandwidth is greater than 2 kHz. If narrow bandwidths are used, the THD measurement must be corrected by calculating the distortion and noise level removed by the notch filter.

For applications where the audio signals are to be transmitted over a phone line (or its equivalent), a THD of less than 1 percent (40 dB) is desirable. Headphone and speaker outputs do not require the same high-quality reproduction, so that 3 to 5 percent THD performance is acceptable.

Ultimate signal-to-noise ratio

The ultimate signal-to-noise ratio is a measurement of the maximum achievable signal-to-noise ratio which may be obtained from a receiver. The sensitivity of a receiver is determined by the noise figure of the receiver and its noise bandwidth. At signal levels 40 dB and greater above the sensitivity level, the signal-to-noise level will be limited by the in-band phase noise of the oscillator injections to the RF mixers and by the internal noise of the detector and amplifier circuits.

The graph in Fig. 17.8 shows a typical response for output signal-to-noise ratio vs. the input signal level. As the close-in noise of the mixer injection begins to predominate, the curve no longer approximates a linear characteristic. Further increases in the input signal level will not increase the output signal-to-noise ratio. This is the ultimate signal-to-noise ratio. Figure 17.9

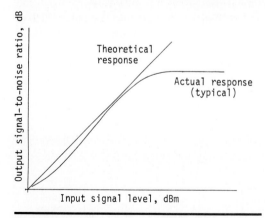

Figure 17.8 Characteristics of ultimate signal-to-noise ratio.

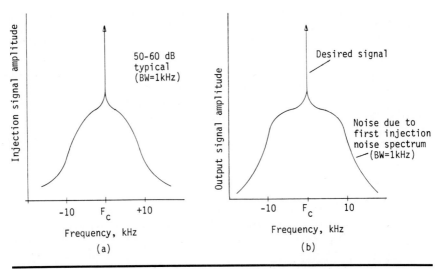

Figure 17.9 Spectral analysis of ultimate signal-to-noise ratio. (*a*) First injection synthesizer spectrum; (*b*) output signal spectrum.

shows the close-in noise of the first injection and the resultant receiver output spectrum.

The test setup shown in Fig. 17.10 may be used to measure the ultimate signal-to-noise ratio of an SSB receiver. For each CW signal level applied to the receiver, a reference level is set on the distortion analyzer. The internal notch filter is then tuned to remove the desired audio signal. The remaining "noise" is the in-band noise plus hum and distortion products. By measuring this in-band signal-to-noise ratio for various input signal levels, the graph shown in Fig. 17.8 may be obtained. If the "noise" contains hum and distortion products, these products may be measured using a wave analyzer and their effect subtracted from the measured signal-to-noise ratio.

Since the receiver SSB bandwidth is much greater than the bandwidth of the notch filter used in the distortion analyzer, the amount of in-band noise removed by the notch may be disregarded. The automatic gain control of the receiver is enabled for this test to prevent overload of the various amplifier circuits.

Image, IF rejection

Measurement of the image and IF rejection determines the relative strength of undesired signals at the image frequency and the intermediate frequencies

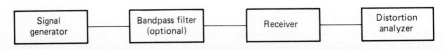

Figure 17.10 Measurement of ultimate signal-to-noise ratio.

required to produce a reference response at the audio output. A test setup similar to that shown in Fig. 17.10 may be used. A reference level is obtained by applying an on-channel signal to produce a 10-dB (S + N)/N ratio at the audio output. The signal generator is then tuned to the image and intermediate frequencies. The amount of signal increase required to obtain the equivalent reference output is the image and IF rejection. Typical rejection levels range from 80 to greater than 100 dB. The optional bandpass filter may be necessary to eliminate noise skirts and spurious responses of the signal generator.

A general discussion of image responses is provided in Chap. 3.

Reciprocal mixing

Performance of the receiver in the presence of strong adjacent channel signals is affected by the noise skirts of the injection signal to the first mixer. These noise skirts can mix with adjacent channel signals to produce noise signals at the intermediate frequency. This type of distortion is called "desensitization," "reciprocal mixing," or "noise modulation."

The mechanism of reciprocal mixing is illustrated in Fig. 17.11. An undesired signal located ΔF away from the desired tuned frequency will mix with the noise skirts of the injection signal to produce noise signals at the IF. In a signal environment containing strong undesired signals located adjacent to the desired signals, the injection noise mixed into the IF will reduce the signal-to-noise ratio of the desired signal, thus desensitizing the receiver to

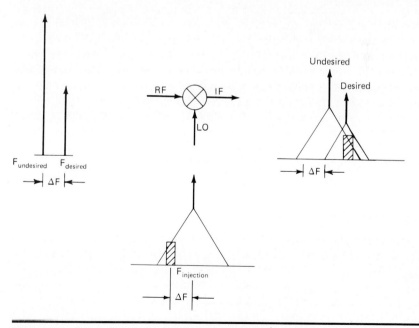

Figure 17.11 Spectral analysis of reciprocal mixing.

small signals. Refer to Chap. 2 for a discussion of colocated interference and to Chap. 3 for further discussion of reciprocal mixing.

The level of the noise signals mixed into the IF depends on the level of the noise skirts (phase noise) relative to the level of the injection signal. A plot of the undesired signal level (at ΔF from the tuned frequency) required to produce a 3-dB increase in receiver noise output characterizes the reciprocal mixing performance of the receiver. Figure 17.12 shows a typical reciprocal mixing response.

It is important to prevent the noise skirts of the undesired signal from affecting the measurements of reciprocal mixing. The test setup shown in Fig. 17.13 will produce accurate measurements. The crystal filter located after the signal generator removes the noise skirts of the signal generator. Since the signal generator and crystal filter are at fixed frequencies, the tuned frequency of the receiver is varied by ΔF from the applied signal. For a given tuned frequency, a reference level is measured for a 3-dB signal-to-noise ratio. This equivalent input signal is the noise floor of the receiver. The receiver is now tuned away from the generator frequency. By increasing the signal level until the noise output increases by 3 dB, a relative measurement of the noise skirts of the first injection signal is obtained. This data may be plotted to obtain the typical curve described above (Fig. 17.12).

The reciprocal mixing data may be used to determine the effect of adjacent undesired signals on the reception of a desired signal. The example below illustrates this concept.

Example Given:

1. A desired signal of -107 dBm produces a $+20$-dB signal-to-noise ratio.
2. An undesired signal of 0 dBm is located 200 kHz from the desired signal.
3. The reciprocal mixing level at 200 kHz is -7 dBm for 3-dB noise increase.

Since the undesired signal is 7 dB above the reciprocal mixing level at 200 kHz away, the undesired signal will produce a 10-dB increase in the noise level of the

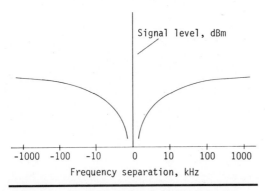

Figure 17.12 Typical reciprocal mixing characteristic. The signal level is that which will produce a 3-dB increase in receiver noise level.

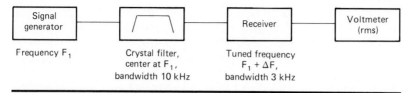

Figure 17.13   Test setup for reciprocal mixing.

receiver. This 10-dB noise increase will decrease the normal $+20$-dB signal-to-noise ratio to about 10 dB.

If the strong undesired signal is close to the weaker desired signal, the desired signal can be totally masked by the reciprocal mixing noise.

Spurious responses

Internally generated spurious responses, sometimes called "birdies" or "tweets," result from injection and other signals leaking between receiver sections to produce on-channel signals. The greater the isolation between the first and second mixers, the less likely that spurious will be generated by injection frequencies leaking between the mixer circuits. A second source of spurious responses is discrete signals at the IF or signal frequencies which are generated internal to the frequency synthesizer. These spurious are dependent upon the frequency generation scheme and the tuned frequency of the receiver.

One source of internal spurious signals previously mentioned is the harmonics or fundamentals of the first or second injections leaking into the second or first mixer, respectively. Two examples of these spurious are illustrated in Fig. 17.14. The isolation provided by electrical shielding around each mixer and the isolation provided by the IF filters will usually reduce and possibly eliminate spurious responses due to the injection frequencies.

Internal spurious can be characterized by an equivalent input signal. When a spurious response is detected, the audio output is measured as a reference. The receiver is then tuned off frequency by 10 kHz and an external signal applied to produce an output equal to the reference level. The

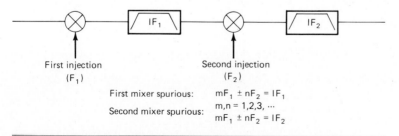

Figure 17.14   Internally generated spurious.

strength of the applied signal is the equivalent signal level of the internal spurious response. The AGC network is typically disabled when measuring the equivalent level of internal spurious. If the spurious is of a level to require AGC, the measured equivalent input must be corrected for the AGC attenuation applied.

Oscillator signals or digital clock signals which have frequencies within the operating frequency range of the receiver may also cause spurious responses. These frequencies must be checked during the design and test phases of any receiver development.

Spurious responses may also be the result of crossover points between the phase-locked loops used to generate the local oscillator injection. These crossover points are caused by signal leakage between the phase-locked loops generating discrete signals at or near the IF of the loop.

If these spurious responses fall in-band to the RF translator (i.e., first or second IF) they are classified as internal spurious. Those crossover frequencies which do not fall in-band to the translator may produce an in-band response when mixed with a strong out-of-band signal (external spurious response).

As an example of external spurious responses caused by undesired discrete signals superimposed on the local oscillator injection, see Fig. 17.15. These discrete signals are typically the synthesizer's loop reference signals appearing as sideband signals on the local oscillator injection. The levels of these discrete signals are measured by a test procedure similar to that used to characterize the spectral response of the local oscillator (see material on reciprocal mixing). External spurious responses are specified in terms of dB below an on-frequency reference signal.

Automatic gain control

An AGC network typically uses a peak detector to determine the strength of the received signal and thus the attenuation required to maintain a constant

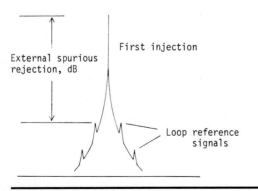

Figure 17.15 Source of externally generated responses.

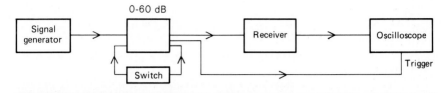

Figure 17.16 Measurement of AGC time constants.

peak output level. The attack and decay time constants determine how quickly a receiver reacts to changes in the input signal level. To prevent overload of the RF and IF amplifiers when a strong signal is applied, the attack time of the AGC circuit must be relatively fast. The decay time constants determine how fast the RF attenuation is removed when the input signal changes from large to small amplitude.

The test setup shown in Fig. 17.16 may be used to measure the attack and decay time constants of a receiver. To simulate the change in signal strength, a 60-dB attenuator is alternately applied to the signal path. Typically the time constants are defined as the time required to reach and stay within 3 dB of the final output level. These definitions are illustrated in Fig. 17.17.

Since the AGC circuit is a closed-loop control circuit, careful design must be maintained to prevent instabilities in the loop response. These instabilities can cause the attack characteristic to have an underdamped response. Filter networks within the AGC loop can cause instabilities at discrete frequencies because of differential delay distortion within the filter's passband, especially near the edges of the passband. When examining the characteristics of the AGC network, the stability of the loop should be measured at various frequencies within the passband.

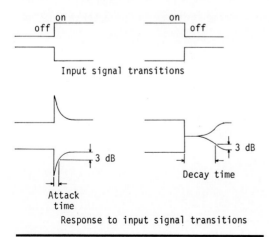

Figure 17.17 AGC time constants.

The control range of the AGC circuit and the AGC loop gain will determine the amount of rise allowed in the audio output for a given increase in the input signal. In an analog AGC circuit, a certain amount of rise is necessary because of tradeoffs between response characteristics and loop stability. In the newer digital receivers, the audio rise is minimized by the use of digital signal processing. Refer to Chap. 7 for further discussion of digital signal processing. The concept of audio rise is illustrated in Fig. 17.18.

Blocking

The effects of blocking are due to strong adjacent channel signals which may be present with the received signal. As the signal level of the undesired signal is increased, a level is reached where the input RF amplifiers and mixers become nonlinear. When this happens, the receiver's gain at the tuned frequency is reduced, i.e., the desired signal is blocked by the undesired signal.

When measuring the blocking characteristics, precautions must be taken to prevent reciprocal mixing from degrading the measurement (i.e., greater than 500-kHz separation). It may be necessary to use a bandpass filter for each local oscillator to remove the noise skirts of the oscillator signal. A typical measurement test setup is shown in Fig. 17.19. The filter located at the output of the "undesired" signal generator prevents the noise skirts of the generator from desensitizing the test procedure.

The frequency of the first signal generator provides an on-channel signal to the receiver. A desired signal level is chosen to provide a 10- to 20-dB (S + N)/N ratio at the output. Since the AGC is turned off during this test, a desired signal level is chosen such that the receiver's amplifiers are not overloaded by the desired signal. The level of the adjacent channel signal (greater than 500 kHz from the desired signal) is increased until the signal level of the audio output is decreased by 3 dB. This is known as "3-dB blocking." The signal levels, frequencies, and gain reductions mentioned here are typical of those used by the communications industry to characterize receiver performance.

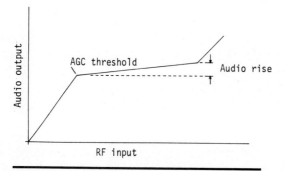

Figure 17.18 Definition of audio rise.

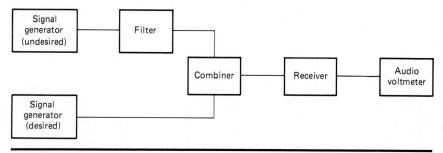

Figure 17.19 Test setup for measurement of blocking characteristics.

Selectivity

The selectivity of a network response is often measured by the 3-dB (half-power frequencies) and the 60-dB attenuation frequencies. The ratio of the 60-dB bandwidth to the 3-dB bandwidth is termed the "shape factor" of the filter.

A second characteristic of the passband is the response ripple. For most applications, the ripple will not exceed 3 dB. In special data transmission filters, the passband ripple will not be more than 1 dB.

Filter selectivity is measured using a test setup similar to that shown in Fig. 17.10. The filter under test is inside the receiver. A signal within the passband of the receiver is varied to obtain the maximum output response. Using this point as a reference, the frequency of the input signal or the receiver tune frequency is varied until the output response is 3 dB below the reference level. To measure the 60-dB attenuation frequencies, the input signal is increased by 60 dB. The input frequency or the receiver tuning is then varied to obtain the reference output level. For each attenuation point (3 dB, 60 dB) both the upper and lower response frequencies must be measured.

When measuring the selectivity, the applied signal level must not overload the input amplifiers. Automatic gain control is usually turned off to keep the gain control circuits from "correcting" the passband response. The signal generator must have a low noise level.

Phase-frequency distortion

An ideal receiver will produce a constant time delay for all frequency components with the desired signal. This constant time delay would be produced by a linear phase-frequency relationship. In reality, the phase-frequency response of a receiver is not linear, resulting in phase distortion or time-delay distortion.

Although voice communication can tolerate limited phase distortion of its signal, high-speed data signals rely on precise phase relationships to transfer information. Delay equalization may be added to crystal and mechanical filters to approximate a linear phase-frequency relationship. Developments in

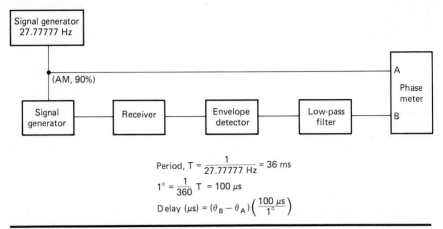

$$\text{Period, T} = \frac{1}{27.77777 \text{ Hz}} = 36 \text{ ms}$$

$$1° = \frac{1}{360} \text{ T} = 100 \text{ } \mu s$$

$$\text{Delay } (\mu s) = (\theta_B - \theta_A)\left(\frac{100 \text{ } \mu s}{1°}\right)$$

Figure 17.20   Measurement of envelope delay.

the application of digital signal processing for filtering have produced filters with nearly linear phase-frequency relationships.

The time-delay characteristics of a receiver are composed of differential delay and absolute delay. Differential delay measures the variation in delay with respect to a given frequency within the receiver's passband. The total time required for a signal to pass through the receiver is termed the "absolute delay."

If the phase-frequency response of the receiver is known, the delay may be calculated as the slope of the phase response at a given frequency. Since the phase-frequency response of a receiver is difficult to measure, the envelope delay can be calculated from the measurements of the delay encountered by a narrowband modulated signal applied to the receiver. The test

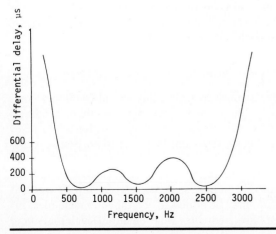

Figure 17.21   Envelope-delay response.

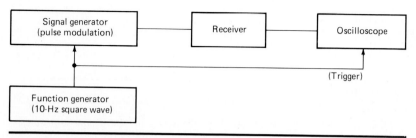

Figure 17.22   Absolute time-delay measurement.

setup shown in Fig. 17.20 is used to measure the envelope delay within the passband of a receiver.

The signal generator is offset from the receiver's tuned frequency to measure the phase difference at each point in the receiver's passband. Typically the offset frequencies range from 200 to 3000 Hz with an increment of 100 Hz. For the test setup shown in Fig. 17.20, a phase difference of 1° represents 100 μs of envelope time delay. This measurement is not the true absolute delay of the receiver because of the time delay introduced by the low-pass filter. Data from this measurement can be used to derive the differential delay measurement between adjacent frequencies or with reference to a given frequency in the passband. The response curve shown in Fig. 17.21 is typical of a single-sideband filter.

Measurement of the absolute time delay may be obtained using the test setup shown in Fig. 17.22. The time difference between the trigger signal initiating the RF pulse signals and the appearance of the output signal is the absolute delay of that frequency. Although various definitions are used to define this time difference, a typical definition is the time required for the signal to be within 3dB (70 percent) of its final amplitude. By varying the input signal across the passband of the receiver, the maximum delay time may be measured.

The delay characteristics of a receiver are specified in three parts:

1. Differential delay with respect to a reference frequency within the passband

2. Maximum change in differential delay for any 100-Hz increment

3. Maximum absolute delay within the passband

Each of these specifications may be measured using the test setups shown in Figs. 17.20 and 17.22.

REFERENCES

1. Fitchen and Motchenbacher, *Low-Noise Electronic Design,* John Wiley & Sons, New York, 1973.
2. Harold B. Goldberg, "Predict Intermodulation Distortion from Cross-Modulation Measurements," *Electron. Des.,* vol. 18, May 1970, pp. 76–78.

3. James Hardy, *High Frequency Circuit Design,* Reston Publishing, Reston, VA, 1979.
4. Wesley Hayward, "Defining and Measuring Receiver Dynamic Range," *QST,* vol. LXIX, July 1975.
5. H. Krauss, C. Bostian, and F. Raab, *Solid State Radio Engineering,* John Wiley & Sons, New York, 1980.
6. E. W. Pappenfus, W. B. Bruene, and E. O. Schoenike, *Single Sideband Principles and Circuits,* McGraw-Hill, New York, 1964.
7. William A. Rheinfelder, *Design of Low-Noise Transistor Input Circuits,* Hayden, New York, 1964.
8. K. A. Rigoni, *Relationship between AM Cross-Modulation and Third Order Intermodulation Distortion Products,* Collins Radio Co. Tech. Report, August 1961.

Appendix

Abbreviations and Acronyms

The following abbreviations are used in this book. They are defined on their first mention in text, but in cases where the same letters are used to abbreviate different terms, the meaning intended in any given instance will also usually be apparent from the context of the surrounding material.

ac	alternating current
ACP	automatic communications processor
ACS	automatic communications system
A/D	analog to digital
AF	audio frequency
AFC	automatic frequency control
AGC	automatic gain control
AI	articulation index
AJ	antijam
ALC	automatic level control
ALQA	advanced link quality analyzer
AM	amplitude modulation
AME	amplitude modulation equivalent
ARQ	automatic repeat request
ARRL	American Radio Relay League
ASCII	American Standard Code for Information Interchange
BCD	binary coded decimal
BER	(data) bit error rate
BFO	beat frequency oscillator
BITE	built-in test equipment
BJT	bi-polar junction transistor
BPF	bandpass filter
BW	bandwidth
CAD	computer-aided design
CATV	cable television
CCCS	Collins Control and Communications System
CCIR	International Radio Consultative Committee
CCITT	International Telephone and Telegraph Consultative Committee
CMOS/SOS	complementary metal-oxide semiconductor/silicon on sapphire

CPU	central processing unit
CR	carriage return
CRT	cathode ray tube
CW	continuous wave
D/A	digital to analog
DAV	data valid
dc	direct current
DCXO	digitally compensated crystal oscillator
DDS	direct digital synthesis
DPSK	differential phase-shift keying
DR	dynamic range
DSB	double sideband
DSBSC	double-sideband suppressed carrier
ECCM	electronic counter-counter-measure
ECM	electronic counter-measure
EDAC	error detection and correction
EIA	Electronic Industries Association
EMI	electromagnetic interference
EMP	electromagnetic pulse
EPROM	electronically programmable read-only memory
ESR	equivalent series resistance
FCC	Federal Communications Commission
FEC	forward error correction
FET	field-effect transistor
FIFO	first-in first-out
FIR	finite impulse response
FM	frequency modulation
FMR	frequency of maximum reliability
FMS	frequency management system
FOT	frequency of optimum transmission/traffic
FSK	frequency shift keying
GMT	Greenwich mean time
GPIB	general-purpose interface bus
HCMOS	high-level complementary metal-oxide semiconductor
HF	high frequency
HPF	high-pass filter
HV	high voltage
IC	integrated circuit
IF	intermediate frequency
IIR	infinite impulse response
IM	intermodulation
IMD	intermodulation distortion
I/O	input/output
IONCAP	Ionospheric Communications Analysis and Prediction Program User's Manual
IP	intercept point
ISB	independent sideband
ITU	International Telecommunications Union
JFET	junction field-effect transistor
K	× 1000
k	prefix for "kilo"

LCD	liquid crystal display
LF	line feed
LF	low frequency
Lincompex	Linked Compression and Expansion
LLSB	lower LSB
LMT	local mean time
LO	local oscillator
LOL	loss of lock
LPA	linear power amplifier
LPA	log periodic array
LPF	low-pass filter
LQA	link quality analysis
LSB	lower sideband
LSI	large-scale integration
MAD	multiply and add
MF	medium frequency
min-loss	minimum-loss
modem	*mo*dulator/*dem*odulator
MOSFET	metal-oxide semiconductor field-effect transistor
MSB	most significant bit
MSI	medium-scale integration
MUF	maximum usable frequency
NBFM	narrow-bandwidth FM
NDAC	not data accepted
NF	noise figure
NMT	not more than
NPR	noise power ratio
NRFD	not ready for data
NSR	noise-to-signal ratio
op-amp	operational amplifier
OW	order wire
PA	power amplifier
PC	personal computer
PC	printed circuit
PEP	peak envelope power
PIN	positive-intrinsic-negative
PLL	phase-locked loop
PM	phase modulation
PN	pseudo-noise
PROM	programmable read-only memory
PSK	phase-shift keying
PTO	permeability tuned oscillator
PWM	pulse width modulation
QMN	quasi-minimum noise
QSY	voice calls
RAM	random-access memory
RF	radio frequency
RFC	radio frequency choke
rms	root mean square
ROM	read-only memory

RTCE	real-time channel evaluation
RTTY	radio teletype
SAW	surface acoustic wave
S/D	signal to distortion ratio
SCR	silicon controlled rectifier
SIMOP	simultaneous operation
S/N	signal to noise
(S+N)/N	signal plus noise to noise
SSB	single sideband
SSN	sunspot number
SWR	standing wave ratio
TCXO	temperature-compensated crystal oscillator
TGC	transmitter gain control
THD	total harmonic distortion
TIMS	tracking impedance measuring system
TOD	time of day
T/R	transmit/receive
TRF	tuned radio frequency
TTL	transistor-transistor logic
TTY	teletype
UART	universal asynchronous receiver/transmitter
UHF	ultrahigh frequency
UL	Underwriters' Laboratories
URG	Universal Radio Group
USART	universal synchronous-asynchronous receiver/transmitter
USB	upper sideband
UT	Universal time
UUSB	upper USB
VCO	voltage-controlled oscillator
VFO	variable-frequency oscillator
VHF	very high frequency
VLF	very low frequency
VLSI	very-large-scale integration
VOX	voice-operated keying
VSWR	voltage standing wave ratio

Index